Nationalism and Policy Toward the Nationalities in the Soviet Union

Nationalism and Policy Toward the Nationalities in the Soviet Union

From Totalitarian Dictatorship to Post-Stalinist Society

Gerhard Simon

TRANSLATED BY
Karen Forster and Oswald Forster

Westview Press
BOULDER ■ SAN FRANCISCO ■ OXFORD

Westview Special Studies on the Soviet Union and Eastern Europe

This Westview softcover edition is printed on acid-free paper and bound in library-quality, coated covers that carry the highest rating of the National Association of State Textbook Administrators, in consultation with the Association of American Publishers and the Book Manufacturers' Institute.

All rights reserved. No part of this publication may be reproduced or transmitted in any form or by any means, electronic or mechanical, including photocopy, recording, or any information storage and retrieval system, without permission in writing from the publisher.

English-language edition copyright © 1991 by Westview Press, Inc. This translation has been revised and updated from the German original.

Published in 1991 in the United States of America by Westview Press, Inc., 5500 Central Avenue, Boulder, Colorado 80301, and in the United Kingdom by Westview Press, 36 Lonsdale Road, Summertown, Oxford OX2 7EW

First published in 1986 in the Federal Republic of Germany as *Nationalismus und Nationalitätenpolitik in der Sowjetunion* by Nomos Verlag

Library of Congress Cataloging-in-Publication Data
Simon, Gerhard
  [Nationalismus und Nationalitätenpolitik in der Sowjetunion. English]
  Nationalism and policy toward the nationalities in the Soviet Union : from totalitarian dictatorship to post-Stalinist society / Gerhard Simon ; translated by Karen Forster and Oswald Forster.
    p. cm.
  Translation of: Nationalismus und Nationalitätenpolitik in der Sowjetunion.
  ISBN 0-8133-7494-4
  1. Soviet Union—Ethnic relations. 2. Minorities—Soviet Union.
3. Nationalism—Soviet Union. I. Title.
DK33.S4213 1991
947'.004—dc20   91-6734
                                                                          CIP

Printed and bound in the United States of America

∞   The paper used in this publication meets the requirements
    of the American National Standard for Permanence of Paper
    for Printed Library Materials Z39.48-1984.

Contents

List of Tables   ix
Preface   xiii

I. Introduction   1

    1. Nationalities Policy, 1
    2. Nationalism, 5
    3. Comments on Methodological Problems, 9
       Notes, 16

II. Nation-Building   20

    1. From the Peoples' Right to Self-Determination to Korenizatsiia, 20
    2. The Workers, 25
    3. The Nationalization of Party and State Apparatuses, 30
    4. Language Policy and the Press, 42
    5. School Policy and Education, 48
    6. National Minorities, 58
       Notes, 62

III. "Great-Russian Chauvinism" and the Nationalism of the Other Peoples   71

    1. "The Battle on Two Fronts," 73
    2. Concentrating All Forces on One Front, 84
       Notes, 88

IV. Agricultural Collectivization and the Famine   93

    1. The Collectivization Campaign, 93
    2. The Crisis in 1932–1933 and the Famine, 99
    3. The East: Cotton Cultivation and Forced Settlement of the Nomads, 104
       Notes, 109

V. Industrialization and Migration — 114

1. Industrialization, 114
2. Migration and Urbanization, 118
3. The Nations' Social Structures, 125
   Notes, 131

VI. Stalin's "Solution" to the Nationalities Issue — 135

1. Ideological Illusions, 135
2. Abandonment of National Institutions and Centralization, 138
3. Soviet Patriotism and Russification, 148
4. The Great Purge, 155
   Notes, 166

VII. War — 173

1. Annexation of the Western Territories, 173
2. Mobilization of All Energies, 181
3. Collaboration and Deportation, 190
4. Demobilization, 203
5. Sovietization of the Conquered Western Territories, 209
   Notes, 218

VIII. De-Stalinization — 228

1. The Battle for Succession, 228
2. De-Stalinization, 233
3. Reaction, 245
   Notes, 258

IX. A New Nationalism — 265

1. The New Intelligentsia and the Participation Crisis, 265
2. National Consciousness and Its Manifestations, 278
3. Ethno-Social and Economic Imbalance, 290
4. Ideological Revision, 307
5. National Assimilation, Language, and Language Policy, 315
6. National Opposition, 333
   Notes, 350

Statistical Appendix 371
List of Abbreviations 421
Selected Bibliography 423
Index 457

Tables

Chapter II

Table 2.1:	Industrial Workers in the RSFSR's National Territories	26
Table 2.2:	Industrial Workers in the Union Republics	28
Table 2.3:	The *korenizatsiia* of the Party	32
Table 2.4:	Percentage of Jews in the Party	35
Table 2.5:	Members of Titular Nations in the Leading Soviet Apparatuses of the Union Republics (1929)	37
Table 2.6:	Members of the Titular Nation in the Central Government Apparatuses and Village Soviets in Their Respective Territories (some national territories in the European RSFSR)	39
Table 2.7:	Book and Newspaper Publication in the Ukrainian Language in the Ukraine	47
Table 2.8:	Literacy of the Population Aged 9 to 49 in the Union Republics (in percent)	49
Table 2.9:	Number of Children Who Attended General Education Schools Conducting Classes in the National Language of the Titular Nation (September 1938)	52
Table 2.10:	Languages of Instruction at Elementary and Middle School Classrooms in 1938/39 (selected Union Republics and ASSRs)	53

Chapter IV

Table 4.1:	The Rate of Collectivization in the National Territories	94
Table 4.2:	Grain Production and State Procurement (in millions of tons)	100
Table 4.3:	Livestock (in millions)	100
Table 4.4:	Demographic Development of the Nations That Particularly Suffered from the Famine and Forced Settlement of the Nomads (compared to the total population and to Russians)	101

Chapter V

Table 5.1:	Industrial Gross Production During the Second Five-Year-Plan (in billions of rubles)	116

Chapter VII

Table 7.1:	National Composition of More Than 200 Rifle Divisions (in percent)	187

Chapter IX

Table 9.1:	Seven-Year Education per 1,000 People	267
Table 9.2:	The Nations' Social Structures in 1970 and 1979 (in percent)	273
Table 9.3:	Distribution of Capital Investment According to Union Republics (in comparable prices)	299
Table 9.4:	Nominal Per Capita Income	301
Table 9.5:	Nominal Per Capita Income of Kolkhoz Peasants	302
Table 9.6:	Per Capita Retail Sales in State and Cooperative Trade (in current prices)	304
Table 9.7:	Per Capita Payments and Expenditures from Social Consumption Funds	306
Table 9.8:	Publications in Russian	329

Statistical Appendix

Table A.1:	Ethnic Composition of the USSR's Population (within the respective borders)	372
Table A.2:	National Composition of the Union Republics and Autonomous Republics (within the respective borders)	376
Table A.3:	Titular Nations and the Percentage Living in Their Own Republics	388
Table A.4:	Urbanization	390
Table A.5:	Differences in the Degree of Urbanization (USSR average = 100)	392
Table A.6:	The Union Republics' Social Structure (percent of people working in the economy)	393
Table A.7:	Structure of the Intelligentsia 1939, 1959 (per 10,000 people)	394
Table A.8:	Nations and Languages	395

Table A.9: Non-Russians Speaking Russian as a Second Language	397
Table A.10: Non-Russians and Their Native Languages	401
Table A.11: Non-Russians Speaking Russian as Their Native Language	402
Table A.12: National Composition of College Students	406
Table A.13: College-Graduate Specialists Working in the Economy	409
Table A.14: Specialists with Mid-Level Technical School Training Who Work in the Economy	413
Table A.15: National Composition of the Party (members and candidates)	415
Table A.16: National Composition of the Party's Leading Bodies (in percent)	418

Preface to the U.S. Edition

The Soviet Union is crumbling. When I wrote this monograph, the breakup of the multinational empire was only in its earliest stages and was hardly discernable. This book is a study of the causes of the fall of the Soviet empire. This study relates the story of Soviet nationalities policy from the 1920s to the mid-1980s and focuses on the strategies and instruments the Soviet leadership employed at various times to integrate the "Soviet" nations and to keep the empire together. At the same time, this monograph is concerned with the peoples' reactions to the policy from the center.

The end of the 1980s witnessed an enormous upsurge of national consciousness in all the nations within the Soviet Union's territory—from the largest, the Russian nation, to the tiny nations, the *narodnosti* (numbering only a few tens of thousands of people), in the Far East. Between November 1988 and October 1990, the Supreme Soviets of all the Union Republics adopted declarations of sovereignty, claiming the property rights to all soil and natural resources for the individual republics and, implicitly, confining the central government to the Kremlin in Moscow. The declarations of sovereignty also established the supremacy of republican legislation over all-Union legislation. It was by no means accidental that the movement for real sovereignty (as opposed to sovereignty on paper, which the Soviet constitution provides) started in the Baltic Republics and reached Central Asia last. This development bears out the predictions of Western experts, including this author, who have argued that the breakup of the Soviet Union would start in the west instead of in the Asian republics, as others had expected.

The next step the republics took was to formally declare their independence, with Lithuania being the pioneer in March 1990. After the Baltic states, Armenia, and Georgia, others are likely to follow suit. Even the Russian Federation threatened to leave the union in its declaration of sovereignty in June 1990.

The disintegration continues within the Union Republics, particularly in the Russian Federation, Moldavia, and Georgia. Several Autonomous Republics within the RSFSR have declared their sovereignty and have (without authorization) elevated themselves to the status of Union Republics. The Soviet system, which combines a supercentralized one-party state with certain concessions to the republics and non-Russian nations, no longer works. To be sure, declarations of sovereignty and independence are still a far cry from actual sovereignty and independence, but they indicate that the peoples are no longer content to live under conditions from the past and are prepared to fight for fundamental changes. A restoration of the status quo ante seems unlikely.

How could all this happen? This book examines the long-term causes of the disintegration. Under the surface, processes of decolonization have long been under way. The formation of new national elites, which started before World War II but developed on a large scale only in the 1960s and 1970s, has proved most important in this respect. In the long run, the non-Russian nations will no longer depend on Russian elites or the Russian language and culture to administer their own territories. In a slow but irreversible process, the new national elites (although educated in the Soviet fashion and, more often than not, in the Russian language) have started taking over their territories and begun to push aside immigrants.

In the 1980s, in an ironic reversal, precisely those strategies that the Soviets had earlier invented to keep the empire together now appeared to be working in reverse and threatened to tear the empire apart. For decades, Soviet federalism had proved quite successful in combining political hypercentralization with granting the republics certain rights in cultural and language affairs and granting many non-Russian nations their own autonomous territories named after the nations themselves. What had long been pseudofederalism became a basis for claims to real independence. The Soviet constitution has always kept an article reserving the right for the Union Republics to secede from the Union. What in Soviet political law had been the main "proof" for the "voluntary" alliance of nations now became a major argument for the right to leave the Union.

In many other areas, as well, Soviet strategies for integrating the empire are no longer applicable or, if applied, work against the empire's cohesion. Language policy, as it has developed since the 1930s, entered another aggressive phase in the late Brezhnev period, when the government attempted to make Russian the dominant language in public life. This policy was meant to securely and permanently cement the empire through the Russian language. Since the late 1980s, this strategy has had quite the opposite effect. Aggressive language policy from the center provoked first resistance and then countermeasures. In 1988 and 1989, the Union Republics adopted laws declaring the language of the respective titular nation the state language in the given republic, thus nullifying and reversing half a century of Soviet language policy.

Migration patterns since the late 1920s have brought hundreds of thousands of mostly Russian cadres into almost all national territories. They were natural agents of the central power at the periphery. Currently, this policy strategy is also backfiring. With the national revival gaining momentum and the new national elites working toward self-government, the Russian cadres and other immigrants are becoming a major target for national resentment and hatred. The remigration of Russians from the Transcaucasus started as early as the 1970s. Many more are now about to leave Central Asia and perhaps the Baltic states.

The Bolsheviks attempted to replace the Russian empire with a communist one. Marxist-Leninist internationalism in the form of Soviet patriotism was designated as a sort of supra-national imperial ideology. Marxism-Leninism, it was hoped, would once and for all replace nationalism and would not only guarantee the continuation of the multinational Soviet state but would make it the model for the "solution" to the national question all over the world. Ideological propaganda and agitation, which had a certain appeal during and after World War II, became countereffective when they became a hollow facade of sheer words, no longer to be taken seriously. The crisis of the ruling state ideology generated a huge spiritual vacuum, which was then filled by national consciousness. After the collapse of the revolutionary ideology and ethics, the nations turned back to their own heritage, traditions, and values. Nationalism became the natural alternative to a *weltanschauung* that had lost all legitimacy and strength. Because the Bolsheviks replaced the Russian empire with a communist one, the empire was doomed when communism collapsed.

Policy strategies that enabled the Soviet empire to outlive other European empires by many decades are no longer available. This includes not only Stalin's policy of all-out terror and the deportation of whole nations; a return to Lenin's nationalities policy also seems out of the question, for it rested on the assumption that the nations would be satisfied with cultural and language autonomy and, under socialism, would not strive for political sovereignty, let alone independence. Another precondition of Lenin's relatively liberal policy was that all nations accept the Communist Party as the ruling party. Only the strictly centralized (not federalized) Communist Party and its leadership were, in Lenin's mind, entitled to make political decisions. It is obvious that all these conditions no longer exist.

To sum up, Bolshevik strategies for running the empire are exhausted; new ones have not been developed, and it seems doubtful that they can be worked out within a political system dominated by the Communist Party. Therefore, it is no surprise that the Gorbachev leadership has proved unable to develop a new framework or new approaches to the old national question. Instead, the Gorbachev leadership has kept running behind events, unable to direct them and to devise a new policy concept.

The breakup of the Soviet empire is incomprehensible unless we realize that it coincides with the overall crisis in the political system. The Communist Party is no longer able to rule the country. For the first time since 1917, the question of power is finally on the agenda. Society is emancipating itself from one-party rule. The Communist Party has lost legitimacy because it was responsible for blood and terror in the past and for misery today. Fewer and fewer people give the Communist Party credit for developing prospects for a better future. Here the new post-communist national consciousness becomes an alternative. Nationalism is strong because the Communist Party is weak. Post-communist national consciousness has developed from an ideology of defense to one of attack. For decades, national consciousness defended nations and regions from encroachments from the center; at the end of the 1980s, it moved to attack and finally dismantle the center.

This comes as no surprise to students of comparative nationalism. Comparative research on nationalism has long since established the fact that, in modern times since the late eighteenth century, the old regime's crisis of legitimacy has invariably triggered nationalism. Modern nationalism developed as an emancipation movement that mobilized large parts of the society against traditional power structures. In nineteenth-century Europe, nationalism was closely tied to democratic and liberal movements. Today, these conditions again exist in the Soviet Union.

In addition to these historical factors, the late 1980s witnessed short-term causes that contributed to the dismantling of the empire. The nations interpreted *glasnost* as the call to finally speak out and voice their grievances and their hopes. They made the situation worse by publicly discussing problems that had existed for a long time. Many non-Russian nations abandoned historical taboos and filled in the blanks in their history. The Baltic nations declared that their incorporation into the Soviet Union was an act typical of Stalinism and insist that this situation must be amended and their political independence reestablished. In Transcaucasia and the Ukraine, writing and speaking publicly about that short period of independence after 1917, which the Red Army had quickly ended, is no longer politically unsafe. Although glasnost did not create the nationalities problem, glasnost allowed it to become a decisive political issue.

Glasnost also provided favorable conditions for the movement for environmental preservation to unfold and join forces with national consciousness. The writers, scholars, and politicians who were against the construction of new nuclear power plants and for cleaner water and air began to stand up for the preservation of national languages, national history, and the republics' true sovereignty. By the end of the 1980s, national consciousness had joined forces with de-Stalinization, de-Leninization, and the movement for environmental preservation. All these forces had become new and important coalition partners that had played only an insignificant role fifteen years earlier.

We are witnessing the second round of the dismantling of the Russian/Soviet empire. The main difference between events in 1917 and later ones seems to be the deep crisis in Russian national consciousness that is currently under way. Russian national consciousness is moving to become dissociated from the empire. In 1917, practically all Russian political groups, from the far right to the far left (including the Bolsheviks—their propaganda to the contrary not- withstanding), stood for the preservation of the empire. But since the end of the 1980s, ever growing parts of the Russian nation and a large number of political groups and movements are deliberately renouncing imperial aspirations and are speaking in favor of some sort of Russian isolation. Russia will only cope with its enormous internal problems (runs the argument) if it gets rid of the empire, which is perceived as a growing drain on Russia's strength. This change in Russian self-perception puts strong constraints on any government that might be willing to restore the empire as it existed under Brezhnev.

The Soviet empire is leaving the stage of history. But the prospects for the future are far from clear. Will the nations succeed in democracy-building after they succeed in nation-building? Or, on the contrary, will anarchy, national wars, and endless violent struggles of the national minorities be the order of the day? Nationalism is ambiguous. It can, as a movement for emancipation, join forces with democracy and liberal leanings, but it can also ally itself with racism and chauvinism. For the future, much will depend on whether the national movements succeed in combining the struggle for independence with efforts to achieve political pluralism and self-determination, not only for themselves but also for the national minorities in their territory. Much rests on the capability of post-communist national consciousness to fight integral nationalism, which could lead to a new totalitarian regime based on ethnocentrism.

I am grateful to Westview Press for accepting this book for publication. Oswald and Karen Forster took on the difficult task of translating the German text into English. Mrs. Dittmann and Mrs. LaVerne Hepburn helped with the proofreading and technical production of this book. My wife, Nadja, followed this book's genesis with much patience and encouragement.

Gerhard Simon
Cologne

I

Introduction

The Russian Empire still exists. War, revolution, a civil war, and yet another war dealt it some severe blows, but for the most part, the Empire's territorial confines have remained intact. Finland and Poland were the only territories the Soviets lost and could not reintegrate into the USSR. As if in compensation, however, the Empire managed to extend its reach westward into Galicia, Northern Bukovina, and the northern parts of East Prussia and into Khiva, Bukhara, Tannu-Tuva in Asia. Most of the non-Russian regions that had separated themselves from the USSR were reconquered within a few years or—as in the case of Poland—were integrated into the Soviet Union's sphere of influence. The persistence of this Russian multinational empire, which acquired many of its non-Russian territories in the late 1800s as a result of its cabinet's absolutist policy and its simultaneous colonial expeditions, is a remarkable phenomenon within the overall context of twentieth century history. The continuity of this multinational empire does not conform with the twentieth-century pattern of multinational and colonial empires disintegrating into their national or territorial constituents.

Nationalities Policy

This study asks how the Bolsheviks managed to prevent such disintegration. In the following, the introduction summarizes some main findings. Neither Russia's status as a land-based power—in contrast to naval empires—nor the unusually high percentage of Russian nationals among the empire's total population (in 1897, 44.4 percent of the population living within the USSR's present-day borders[1]) can explain why the "law" of decolonialization does not apply to the Russian Empire. Of course, there is no denying that both factors were influential. In particular, the numerical strength of the Russian elites made possible a mixture of direct and indirect rule over the national territories by Russian and coopted non-Russian functionaries after 1917. And this system's specific nature made such rule inconceivable in any other empire. Starting in the 1930s, Stalin purposefully employed this strategy to solidify Soviet power. He sent large numbers of Russian cadres into most non-Russian territories (except Armenia and Georgia), where these cadres had privileged opportunities for social advancement. In these non-Russian nations, the cadres remained the natural proxies of the central power that sustained them and left them dependent on its benevolence. So great was the potential of the Russians to populate non-Russian territories that large-scale migrations, which began in the late 1920s, shifted the national composition of nearly all non-Russian territories to the lasting disadvantage of indigenous peoples (see Appendix Table A.2). One consequence of this Russian migration—in which a limited number of Ukrainians and Belorussians participated—was that the Central Asian population structure lost its Muslim homogeneity, which had dominated until 1926. Since 1926, Asian and European subsocieties have coexisted—a situation that is probably irreversible and that has created fundamentally different conditions for political and social change from those prevailing in the homogenous Muslim societies in the states south of the USSR.

However, the crucial strategy that helped the Soviets prevent the disintegration of their multinational empire involved a specific balance between using force and granting concessions—a balance that is unprecedented and has proven surprisingly successful. In the course of Soviet history, the government has used force and concessions in various ways and in different proportions. In the 1920s, from 1941 to 1944, and in the late 1950s, accommodation prevailed. Ruthless use of power dominated during the civil war, in the 1930s, and from 1944–1952.

In this context, the term "use of force" does not refer only to military force, although military force was employed unscrupulously during the civil war to make a territory reverse its secession and during World War II to punish actual or alleged secessionist efforts. From the beginning, the police, the secret service, and the judiciary supported the army's efforts to suppress national movements and the organizations behind them. Once the overt anti-Bolshevik resistance had been defeated or its supporters forced to emigrate, Stalin's dictatorship focused its acts of repression primarily against "nationalist deviations" within the Soviet party and state. Although the terror waged against the national *nomenclatura* from 1936 to 1938 has never been repeated, even in the post-Stalin era, Party, state, and cultural institutions' leaders in the national territories are regularly shuffled around in a manner reminiscent of purges, under the pretext of "bourgeois nationalism." These personnel shuffles have seemed to occur in ten-year cycles (early 1960s, early 1970s, early 1980s). The 1960s also saw a return to police actions against oppositional national movements outside the Party.

The Soviets used another instrument of force to support their fight against resistance to the Party line from inside the Soviet apparatuses and from outside. This additional instrument, social "revolution from above," was used in this particular way for the first time to stabilize power in a multinational state. The Russian empire followed the tradition of multinational empires and left the social structures of conquered or annexed peoples and territories relatively intact. The Russian empire was content to subjugate them and extract their loyalty to coopt part of the indigenous elites as a means of establishing indirect rule, and to pursue these peoples' assimilation by means of long-term administrative adaptation and migration.

In complete contrast to this custom, over the comparatively short period of twenty years up to the late 1930s, the Soviets passionately and violently attacked the peoples' traditional social structures, undermined the economic foundations of the traditional societies in the Soviet East, and thus managed to make the peoples' social structures less and less distinct. This social assimilation constituted a stabilizing element that was an important prerequisite for maintaining Soviet power — all the more so, because this forceful social "revolution from above" affected the Russians as much as other peoples. However, Soviet collectivization had a more dramatic impact in the Ukraine, in the east, and particularly among the nomadic peoples, than on the Russian villages with their *mir* tradition. The destruction of the peoples' social orders focused on two objectives: the elimination of established elites — frequently this meant their physical destruction — and the collectivization of agriculture. In the late 1930s, the non-Russian leadership cadres that dated back to the civil war (national Communists in the Ukraine and the Transcaucasus and Jadidist politicians in the east) were finally eliminated. No other intervention can compare to this collectivization's long-term consequences or the number of its victims. Even if Stalin did not deliberately cause famine, he at least accepted it as a convenient means of breaking the non-Russian peoples' will to self-determination and of guaranteeing their long-term subjugation under his dictatorship. The main burden of suffering was borne by the Ukrainians and many nomadic peoples.

Of course, this social "revolution from above" did not completely homogenize the peoples' social orders; among the peoples of the east, vestiges of tribal loyalty and Islamic consciousness have survived. Industrialization, urbanization, and migration even generated new ethnosocial differentiations that had not existed previously. Nevertheless, the "revolution from above" diminished the differences in social orders and national consciousness. The new elites were much more aware of being part of a common state and power system than their predecessors.

In addition to using force and destruction to achieve their goals, the Soviets made concessions to the non-Russian peoples from the very beginning. In comparison to the cultural and administrative Russification the Czarist Empire had pursued during its final decades, these concessions seemed particularly positive. Essentially, these concessions came down to granting all citizens equality before the law, permitting linguistic autonomy, applying the constitutional structure of Soviet federalism, and working towards modernization. All rights to autonomy were subject to two provisions: the issue of the state's unity was not open to discussion, and the autonomous republics had to recognize the central Party leadership's monopoly on power which, from 1929 to 1953, was identical to Stalin's dictatorial will. Although these concessions did not imply political self determination, their impact on the nationalities policy should not be underestimated. For example, they allowed the development of written forms of many languages and, as a result, the establishment of non-Russian mass media as well as the rise of non-Russian-language literature. During periods such as the 1920s and the Khrushchev era, the non-Russian territories even enjoyed extensive rights of autonomy in the administration of their economies.

Soviet federalism, conceived as a temporary emergency measure, afforded the peoples prestigious state sovereignty. Although in many respects this sovereignty was no more than a legal fiction, the temptation to actually implement it politically has always existed, and many politicians such as Sultan-Galiev, Skrypnyk, Khrushchev, and Shelest, succumbed to this temptation and attempted to implement sovereignty. Soviet federalism has survived all efforts to replace it despite frequent (sometimes public) demands for its demise during and after the Stalin era. In the post-Stalin era, the system of federalism arranged in gradations guaranteed considerably more linguistic autonomy and, as a result, more national-language cultural activities to the Union Republics than to the Autonomous Republics and to the still lower national territorial units.

The Soviets started modernization in all national territories: modernizing transportation, establishing a public health system, mechanizing agriculture, and industrializing the economy. Since the mid-1950s, the rising standard of living in Russia has been paralleled in all areas of the union. Modernization was more advanced in the Soviet east than in the Islamic countries south of the borders; the same was true for the standard of living. In clear contrast, the economic development in the Baltic republics has lagged behind that in the Scandinavian countries. By the late 1970s, this development had created the paradoxical situation that the Baltic republics, which had been the most advanced in the USSR, compared poorly to the adjoining foreign countries, whereas the underdeveloped Asian republics came out ahead of their foreign neighbors.

The most important aspect of Soviet modernization was the development of an educational system among the non-Russian peoples that helped recruit new national elites. In the Ukraine and the Transcaucasus, the growth of large national intelligentsias began before 1941; in the Asian Union Republics, the development started after World War II. Such social change is the most significant change in the USSR's history dealt with in the framework of this study. The existence of broad national elites created fundamentally new starting positions for the Party's nationalities policy and for nationalism. In the 1920s, a somewhat broad secular intelligentsia had existed only among the Jews, Armenians, Georgians, and Tatars.

My findings, outlined on the previous pages, lead to the conclusion that processes of decolonialization did take place in the Soviet Union, too, although they were less obvious than with other empires and did not destroy the Soviet state. Derussification of the empire's national territories, which was actually the official Party line, was actively promoted until the early 1930s. During the following years, Stalin slowed this process and then reversed it. Modernization of the national territories and development of national intelligentsias slowed down. However, these processes could not be stopped completely and forever. Since the 1950s, an explosion of education among non-Russian peoples has fuelled these processes. Decolonialization did not destroy the Soviet state because its system of repression prevented the growth of separatist aspirations and because the new elites were socialized in a Soviet environment, that provided for a certain loyalty to the Soviet system.

Nationalism

How did the peoples—many of which became nations only during the twentieth century—respond to the objectives of the Party's nationalities policy and to the measures adopted to achieve them? What forms of nationalism developed among the non-Russian peoples? Following the civil war and the prohibition of all social revolutionary nationalist parties and organizations, some surviving members of these groups joined the Bolsheviks, thus reinforcing national Communist groups already among the Bolsheviks. Until the early 1930s, these national Communists determined the political course within many large non-Russian party organizations. These national communists did not form any organizations of their own, did not consider their ideas contradictory to Moscow let alone the Soviet system, but saw themselves as representatives of the global Party line. They enforced the policy of *korenizatsiia* (which means something like "taking root," from the Russian *koren,* "root"). They expected and promised economic and cultural progress in the underdeveloped national territories to catch up to the level of the Russian industrial centers. To the national Communists, the phrase "development of socialism" meant the consolidation of cultural and linguistic autonomy and of local powers in administering public and economic affairs. The gulf between the national Communists and Stalin's centralist dictatorship grew wider and wider.

In the early years of Soviet rule, nation-building was very successful and its effects are still felt. The small groups of national-Communist functionaries and "fellow travellers" (*poputchiki*) from their peoples' cultural and academic circles have proved that the phrase "Soviet system" can also denote derussification, preferential advancement of underdeveloped peoples, and economic and administrative decentralization. Some of the new national intellectual elites still carry the memory of the great opportunities nation-building represented in the 1920s. This memory has not become generally accepted because Soviet historiography and media take great pains to represent early national-Communist policy from a Stalinist perspective as a "deviation." However, until about 1933, the official Party line called for repression of the Russian language, Russian cadres, and Russian culture. The fact that the Soviets covered up the extent of pre-Stalinist nation-building and its anti-Russian thrust proves how politically volatile Party leaders considered the rediscovery of what the 1920s were really like.

Their fear is justified for the new national elites have become the representatives of national aspirations and expectations since the end of World War II. These elites are looking for a way to reconcile fundamental loyalty to the Soviet order with the advancement of national ambitions. The nation-building policy of the 1920s represents such a concept, which means that the new national intelligentsias have not become nationless representatives of Soviet values, behaviors, and of a denationalized Soviet patriotism. They have not allowed themselves to be blended into a "homogeneous Soviet society."

In this respect, ideological expectations did not materialize. Soviet ideology had assumed that the "socialist nations" that emerged after the revolution and modernization would exhibit behavior fundamentally different from that of "bourgeois" nations. No antagonistic conflicts would arise among socialist nations; they would pursue identical political interests, and would smoothly integrate themselves into the central state: In a word, they would follow a path to "rapprochement" and "merger." For this reason, from the beginning, Soviet ideology was convinced that by combining revolution and modernization, socialism—and only socialism—would solve the "nationalities issue." The Soviets were convinced that "the source from which bourgeois nationalism draws its strength dries up as economy and culture blossom and the socialist consciousness of the working masses . . . grows."[2] "The more intensive is the economic and social development of every national republic, the more graphic becomes the process of internationalization of our whole life."[3]

For a long time, Western scholars basically shared this assessment of the melting-pot effect of Soviet modernization. During the summer of 1931, Hans Kohn—one of the foremost scholars and theoreticians on the subject of nationalism—travelled extensively in the USSR and developed great admiration for the Soviets' attempt "to give new uniform content to the national cultures." His hope was that the Soviets might "perhaps" succeed in changing "nationalism from an all-commanding absolute into the servant of a supranational idea."[4] Even after World War II, leading scholars, who themselves were fundamentally opposed to the Soviet system, tended to conclude that the Soviets had overcome the nationalism prevalent among non-Russian peoples, and that Communism had taken on the "function of an ideology of integration." It appeared to these scholars that a society had emerged in the USSR "that, in terms of its uniting force, was similar to the nation-like religious community that occidental Christianity created during the Middle Ages."[5] Even as late as 1968, Aspaturian was convinced that "national distinctions within the Soviet elite ... will increasingly reflect national *origin* rather than national self-identification."[6] In their 1967 study, which appeared innovative at the time because the authors had employed methods adopted from economics, Nove and Newth came to the conclusion that national assimilation in Central Asia would probably progress to the level of that in the U.S.A. "in another half-century."[7] These pronouncements of the demise of (non-Russian) nationalism continue the tradition started with Karl Deutsch's theories, which not only link the process of modernization to the emergence of nations but also to transcending them in the sense of supranational social and political integration.[8]

The 1970s saw a radical change in the way both Soviet and Western scholars assessed the nationalism of non-Russian peoples. However, this "change of paradigms" was more pronounced in the West than in the USSR. Most Western scholars agreed that "the national polarization of the various Soviet peoples has advanced faster than their common consciousness of a new Soviet nationhood" and that the growing nationalism was "an outgrowth of the very policies of social mobilization that were intended to eliminate nationalism."[9] The consensus among Western scholars was that modernization was creating "the framework for a kind of nationalism that articulated itself more strongly and above all more consciously than its predecessors."[10] Today, Western scholars disagree with Soviet scholars who portray their country as one that has "solved the nationalities problem" by means of integration. Western scholars even contend that, on the contrary, "this issue in the Soviet Union is potentially the most devastating for the state in its long-range consequences and presents the deepest challenge to the legitimacy of the regime."[11] However, most Western experts assume that nationalism has not yet reached critical mass.

"Revolutionary optimism" has dissipated even in the Soviet Union. In the opinion of the socialist dissident Roi Medvedev, "nationality problems ... have intensified ... in recent years."[12] Secretary General Andropov openly declared "that the economic and cultural progress of all nations and peoples is accompanied by the growth of their national self-consciousness." He contended that this is "a principled, objective process" that cannot "be attributed exclusively to remnants from the past."[13] Soviet scholars and politicians from the Union Republics warn against "simplifying" and underestimating the "contradictions" of national relations within the socialist society.[14]

This change in the way scholars assess Soviet nationalism reflects the new nationalism that has emerged in post-Stalin society, albeit after the fact. This nationalism is new in the sense that such a great variety and number of proponents of nationalism — the national elites — has never existed before. This nationalism developed specific characteristics; many are adapted to the conditions of Soviet life, and others conflict with and oppose those same conditions. Characteristics adapted to Soviet conditions can be found particularly in two main areas:

1. Functionaries of the non-Russian republics do everything in their power — which varies from place to place — to push through their own demands in the areas of economy, culture, and personnel-policy against the interests of the central power and also against each other. In this context, it is not always possible to distinguish between national and regional interests. Any failure (for example, in the economic sector in Central Asia during the 1970s, or in the linguistic-cultural sector in the Ukraine after 1973) intensifies these conflicts. This means that on the level of Union Republics, the *nomenclatura* (to a limited extent) acts in the national interest. Because of this, the central government once again drastically cut its power in the mid-1960s, and by and large the Union Republics have remained excluded from leadership at the level of the central state.

2. Clinging to a native language, certain ways of life, and value systems — particularly within the framework of the (extended) family — are manifestations of national self-consciousness. In addition, national self-consciousness expresses itself in ways directly related to the process of modernization: literature, fine arts, or cinema. High literature has been important in the Asian nations' efforts to rediscover their cultural roots in Islamic culture. Literature reinforces Estonian and Latvian national identity because of these two nations' comparatively wide-ranging experimentation with literary form and because they have translated a great deal of Western literature into Estonian and Latvian; such activity supports awareness that Estonia and Latvia are part of "Western" Europe.

Some expressions of the new nationalism conflict with the Soviet system, which actively fights some of them: the national and ecclesiastical opposition in Lithuania, the Sufi in the northern Caucasus, or liberal civil rights groups. On the whole, the USSR's new national intelligentsia has conducted itself like its counterparts all over the world: Within a few decades, a national elite with a secular education had the opportunity for extraordinary social mobility. This elite is looking to the future for avenues of political self-determination and to the past for its national-cultural identity. The pluralism resulting from the great number of different nations has become an irrefutable political factor—as never before in Russian and Soviet history. The continued existence of the state and its social system depends largely on the loyalty of the new non-Russian elites. This fact does not necessarily imply that these new elites are disloyal. However, in their own interest, the Soviets must keep the ambitions of these social strata in mind and satisfy them to a certain extent. The political price for preserving the Empire is rising.

Comments on Methodological Problems

The outlined questions and answers, which form the topic of this book, make it necessary to focus on two time periods: the 1930s and the period from the early 1960s to 1985. The 1930s witnessed the gradual dismantling of the policy of nation building even though the Soviets never formally repealed that policy. Even the key Russian term describing this policy (korenizatsiia) has disappeared from the Russian vernacular. This turnabout was neither sudden, nor did it coincide with the advent of Stalinism. On the contrary, in many respects, the period of the first Five-Year Plan and collectivization coincided with the climax of the korenizatsiia policy. Never before had the percentage of non-Russian publications been as high, had as many non-Russians enrolled at universities, or had the percentage of non-Russian members of Party organizations been as high as in the early 1930s. These statistics show that during the crisis years of his revolution, Stalin managed not to establish another front against the non-Russian peoples. Although political and police actions against prominent national Communists had become more frequent since the late 1920s, the Party line on the national issue did not change until 1933—after the conclusion of forced collectivization and before the beginning of the "great purge."

Of course, this study might have included the formation of the Soviets' early nationalities policy during the first decade after the revolution, as the first period focused on. But this approach was not employed for practical reasons: On the one hand, I wanted to limit this study to a manageable length; on the other hand, comprehensive analyses of the civil war and the NEP period already exist.[15] In contrast, Western scholars have never dealt comprehensively with the Stalin era, particularly the 1930s. Previous studies deal only with World War II. Thus, my analysis starts, after briefly reviewing the origins of Lenin's nationalities policy, by discussing the political conditions in the late 1920s.

I chose the second period this study focuses on because I intend to show the far-reaching changes in Soviet society since the end of Stalinism. To document these changes, I contrast the comparative stability of Soviet rule (as exhibited in the relative continuity of the nationalities policy) with social change. I use the phrase *post-Stalinist society,* which indicates that de-

Stalinization has never been carried out in a consistent manner and that, as a result, Stalinism shaped the following era. However, the phrase also communicates the fact that the USSR has undergone profound changes, which prohibit us from referring to the USSR today as a totalitarian dictatorship.[16] As a social force from below, the new nationalism has found many ways of asserting itself that would have been unimaginable during the Stalin era. A typical sign of this self-assertion is that since the 1960s, the very peoples Stalin deported and tried to purge from history have become a hot spot of political trouble for the USSR. The seeds of violence are bearing fruit.

The theme of this study addresses not a marginal facet of the Soviet Union's internal development, but one of its central aspects. "Nationalities policy" does not govern the conditions of "national minorities" on the periphery; this policy affects half of the USSR's total population. In addition, the nationalities issue also includes the relationship between Russians and non-Russians, so all the USSR's society is involved. As a result, this subject can only be dealt with in the *context of internal development* as a whole because nationalities policy is an essential aspect of this development. Consequently, this presentation—as far as it is chronological—follows the turning points and periods of the Soviet Union's internal development. For this reason, I discuss nationalities policy and nationalism in connection with collectivization, industrialization, the war, and Khrushchev's reforms. Only within this framework does the subject of this study gain relevance and perspective. Thus, outlining this framework will be indispensable in certain instances (for example, in the context of the "great purge" or Khrushchev's struggle to become Stalin's successor).

This study is not limited to particular nations or regions, but tries to look at the "big picture." Without question, certain disadvantages go along with this approach: There is no room to discuss many peoples and ethnic groups whose numbers are small. The focus on "overall policy," has meant neglecting ethnological issues. Although I frequently refer to the extraordinary diversity of the particular national issues, my emphasis on Moscow's perspective on these issues may occasionally blur this diversity. This approach also prevents me from paying equal attention to all non-Russian peoples in all time periods analyzed and on all issues covered. I consider it more important to illustrate typical examples, the choice of which depends on practical aspects of research methodology—particularly the availability of data sources. In many cases, I present issues and courses of events based on data pertaining to the Ukraine and Central Asia. These areas are the most important national territories, and the conditions governing political actions differ considerably in both territories. In certain contexts, however, some peoples whose numbers are small, such as the Chechens and Ingushes, the Lithuanians, or the Germans are the center of my attention.

I have valid reasons for including, in principle, all non-Russian nations. The Party formulated and pursued its nationalities policy from the perspective of the Soviet state, with the goal of homogenizing the state and society. In contrast, the objective of nationalism is diversification. This study focuses on the relationship between these two opposing processes. The stage for the conflict between them is the Soviet state and society as a whole.

In addition, research methodology suggested a comparison of individual national issues whose impact on the Soviet state as a whole are not apparent when analyzed individually and independently. Western scholars have published numerous analyses of the post-Stalin era, focusing on particular national issues. Generally speaking, the authors of these studies do not discuss occurrences in neighboring territories or the Party's nationalities policy pursued within the framework of the Soviet state as a whole. This perspective frequently causes serious distortions in existing assessments of the situations described.

The present study aims to avoid such pitfalls. An assessment of the Jewish emigration movement changes when one is aware of the nationalist movement among the Crimean Tatars. The Sufi brotherhoods are assessed differently when contrasted with the nationalist Catholic protest movement in Lithuania. Up to now, few scholars have tried to synthesize the considerable number of Western studies on particular national issues. However, Western scholars have attained such a degree of specialization—at least as concerns events and developments in the early 1960s and later—that synthesizing these research results appeared necessary and feasible. H. Carrère d'Encausse's monograph pursues the same approach as I do in my study. However, she deals primarily with issues that emerged in the 1960s and 1970s and focuses her attention on Central Asia. I do not agree with her assessment that Islamization has the potential to "transform" the Soviet system "totally from within."[17]

The studies that take a historical perspective of the "big picture" over a long period treat independently the history and present of the individual nations.[18] In contrast, the present study focuses systematically on certain issues and periods, the presentation of which is based on data from selected nations or regions. In this context, I assume that phenomena typical of the nationalities issues are also representative of other nations or regions, and I accept the disadvantage of not being able to include many unique phenomena. My approach has only been employed in articles.[19]

For me to succeed in describing the events in question from various points of view, I had to move among various perspectives. I employed the methods and perspectives of social history side by side with those of the history of ideology and of "Kremlinology" (in discussing the struggle for Stalin's successor). No perspective in particular was used to the exclusion of another.

Any study covering events over a long period in a vast empire faces pressure to abstract from and leave out details. But "is there a 'correct' distance for a view of history, any more than for a view of a city—Paris from the level of those hopeful fishermen on the banks of the Seine, or of the *bouquinists* above them, or from the tower of Notre Dame, or the steps of the Sacré Coeur, or an overflying jet at 30,000 feet?"[20]

My study does not offer a new theory of nationalism. I use the term nationalism in a neutral sense. "Nationalism" does not denote a negative phenomenon; nor does "revolution" refer to something positive. In this respect, my use of these terms differs sharply from Soviet use, which gives the term nationalism clearly negative connotations when it is used for political conditions in the USSR after 1917. The Soviets use the term as equivalent to "national exclusiveness," "national chauvinism," or "integral nationalism." To refer to an awareness of ethnic identity, which means a cultural and political disassociation from "the others," modern Soviet language use employs the terms national self-consciousness and patriotism. Ideological discourses use the term "flourishing (*rastsvet*) of the nations."[21]

Western scholars in comparative research on nationalism disagree about certain individual manifestations of modern nationalism.[22] But they basically agree on the structural elements of nationalism.[23] My study proceeds on the basis of this consensus. Scholars agree that nationalism is about to become a worldwide phenomenon; that nationalism is functionally related to the disintegration of traditional societies; and that it is impossible to analyze nationalism independently of the processes of political, cultural, and technological modernization. The emergence of nationalism is an indication that the old social and political order is going through a crisis of legitimacy and is no longer accepted. A nationalist concept of political order assumes the principle of the peoples' sovereignty; a nationalist concept of social order assumes that the lower social classes must emancipate themselves.

Although nationalism is closely related to the modern world's emergence (which began in the late 1700s), no unilateral causality can be established to reduce nationalism to processes of modernization. On the contrary, nationalism is a chameleon that has a strong and independent life of its own and manages to join forces with the most diverse social groups and political ideologies. In this respect, nationalism can exist in the functional context of a society's democratization and liberalization, and nationalism can also serve to justify and propel dictatorship and conservative social ideologies. The most important vehicle of modern nationalism often proves to be the intellectual elites, which emerge from the obsolete upper and lower classes, and which, because of their origin, are particularly suited as a new element of integration.

In principle, nationalism works against the class structure of societies. Nationalism strives to overcome class antagonism for the sake of mutual national affiliations and to mobilize the different social strata to pursue a common national objective. Nationalism is particularly effective in situations where nationalist and social objectives merge, where social discontent and unrequited nationalism join forces, where social and national revolution are allies. On the other hand, building a class solidarity that goes beyond national borders can counter nationalism. Although this basic Marxist idea has failed on the international level, it has been implemented somewhat successfully within the closed society of the Soviet Union. The social "revolution from above" was intended to establish among the newly created social classes (kolkhoz farmers, workers, intelligentsia) solidarity that would go beyond national borders and to force nations into the role of secondary factors of integration. This approach has not been successful enough to resolve the Soviet nationalities issue, but it has certainly brought some temporary relief.

In this respect, too, the "revolution from above" is in irreconcilable conflict with the early Soviet policy of *nation-building*. The Soviets deliberately used this policy to promote non-Russian nationalism or, what is more, perhaps even create it. The predominant Soviet term for this policy in the 1920s and early 1930s was "korenizatsiia," but the phrase "natsionalnoe stroitelstvo," meaning nation-building, was also used. On the one hand, this term denoted the purposeful policy of Party and state, to consolidate or create nations. On the other hand, the term nation-building referred to the internal processes of change that convert an ethnic community into a nation.

Is the objective of establishing independent national states a constitutive element of nationalism and nation-building? National movements destroyed vast empires and led to the emergence of dozens of new national states. Nevertheless, we cannot conclude that one can only speak of nationalism and nation-building if a political movement strives to establish a sovereign national state. The early Soviet policy of nation-building was conceived with the expressed intention of preventing secessions. From the very beginning, the USSR considered the articulation of separatist demands as a political statutory offense — and soon after, as a criminal statutory offense. As a result, nationalism (unless it was involved in setting up secret organizations) had to find different ways to express itself. However, these were just as virulent as other forms of nationalism although the new expressions lacked the traditional objectives or at least did not subscribe to them publicly. On the other hand, the fact that the Soviets were able to continue criminalizing all separatist efforts is evidence of the strength of Soviet power and the efficiency of their tools of repression. The definition that says "the essence of all forms of nationalism" is "their character as a politically oriented movement towards autonomy"[24] must be modified and expanded in respect to the Soviet Union. In repressive systems, modern nationalism seeks its forms of expression in the forefield of political activity. Of course, as soon as the pressure decreases, these forms of expression can quickly turn into political demands. Repressive regimes enjoy the advantage of being able to repress any form of nationalism, but they have to live with the disadvantage that oppressed nationalism does not become obsolete; that it does not lose its function when confronted with reality; and that, as a political alternative, nationalism smolders under the surface.

I use the term *nation* as the Soviets define it and as a synonym for the term *people*. According to Stalin's 1913 definition of the term nation, which is still used today, nations must fulfill four criteria: all members share common economic conditions, a common language, the same territory, and a similar frame of mind (culture and national character). The minimum number of people necessary to constitute a nation is 80,000 to 100,000. Today, all ethnoses after which Union Republics and Autonomous Republics are named are considered nations. According to the Soviet definition, the nationalities (*narodnosti*) who lend their names to Autonomous Regions (*oblasti*) or Autonomous Territories (*okrugi*) or do not have any administrative-territorial unity of their own are generally at a lower developmental stage. In many cases, the Soviet scholars disagree about whether to call a people a nation or a nationality. Tsamerian, for example, lists forty-eight nations and thirty-nine nationalities by name; Kulichenko, on the other hand, names thirty-six nations and thirty-two nationalities.[25]

I use the term *intelligentsia* as the Soviets define it. This means the term does not refer to the social stratum called intelligentsia before the 1917 revolution; nor does the term refer to any one social group defined by Western sociologists. Soviet use of the term includes everybody who graduated from a technical school or institution of higher learning or who holds a position that generally requires such qualifications. As a result, the intelligentsia not only constitutes a very broad social layer, but it is also the stratum that has been growing the fastest within Soviet society since the early 1930s.

My sources and secondary literature come primarily from the following fields: Soviet journals, newspapers, and books; Soviet research, particularly since the 1960s; the Samizdat since the 1960s; and Western (i.e., primarily U.S.) research since the mid-1960s. I consider the question of the authenticity of Samizdat sources settled. The fact that the authors of many Samizdat sources have been in prison camps attests to the authenticity of these sources. Of course, Samizdat materials must be critically assessed in the same manner as any other historical source.

Soviet and Western scholars have concentrated on two particular periods: the years of the revolution and civil war, and the time after about 1960. My study is meant to contribute to closing the large gap between these two periods.

Introduction

No involved justification is necessary to explain why source availability makes it impossible to discuss the USSR's national problems in the same way as Irish or German nationalism. However, the source availability situation is probably not any worse than it is for many periods and problems of European history before the 18th century. The particular problem is not a lack of source material, but an abundance of material that contains very little usable information. And, in addition, the Soviets spread disinformation about themselves. It was difficult for me, on the other hand, not to take the suggestion arising from sources that consistently point in one direction and on the other hand, not succumb to the temptation to believe the opposite of what the sources say.[26]

The quality of available source materials differs considerably from period to period. Materials produced up to the mid-1930s proved surprisingly good. For this period, my study includes the first effort to systematically analyze the journal *Revoliutsiia i natsionalnosti (Revolution and Nationalities)*, which was published from 1930–1937. For the time up to the mid-1930s, comparatively abundant statistical material is available, which made it possible to document the policy of nation-building in the tables shown in Chapter II.[27] The limited amount of statistical data on the 1920s and 1930s preserved in Soviet statistical collections dating from the post-Stalin era often disagrees with the early Soviet publications and glosses over the facts. As a rule, I placed more trust in the authenticity of figures in early Soviet publications. In this context, one must not forget — at least in respect to nationalities statistics — that the figures must be seen as approximations. After 1929, many bureaucratic apparatuses were in chaos; this situation had a detrimental effect on data collection. However, there is no reason to suspect that the proponents of the korenizatsiia policy — as long as it existed — embellished their successes. Quite to the contrary, they were interested in using their data to show that this policy was necessary.

As expected, Soviet sources published between the mid-1930s and Stalin's death are the least informative. For good reason, hardly any Soviet scholar has dealt with these decades, even in the post-Stalin era. As a result, much of what went on during that time has remained obscure. Non-Russian sources on World War II are helpful with a number of problems, primarily with respect to the integration of the occupied western territories into the Soviet Union, German occupation policy, and collaboration with the Germans. Soviet information policy was comparatively generous during the years following Stalin's death until about 1961. Khrushchev was interested in denouncing Stalin's nationalities policy. Thus, the sources published during those years contribute to the illumination of what went on during the Stalin era.

These publications include Lenin's December 1922 notes on the nationalities issue, Khrushchev's revelations at the Twentieth Party Congress in February 1956, and speeches given by several leaders from the republics at the Twenty-Second Party Congress in October 1961.[28] For particular phases of de-Stalinization — for example, in the summer of 1953 — the central press organs are another important source of information on Stalin's nationalities policy. I refer to these in detail in the appropriate places.

In respect to events occurring after the mid-1960s, sources are strangely ambiguous. On the one hand, information provided by some official sources becomes increasingly sparse — culminating in the nearly complete concealment of the results of the 1979 census.[29] On the other hand, since the 1950s, some Soviet research has reached a level of professionalism and has also progressed in respect to data collection. I used the principal newspapers of the Union Republics to get information about particular events in individual Union Republics (for example, leadership shakeups, local Party congresses). In addition, Samizdat publications and the writings of emigrants were available to me.

This study is primarily based on Russian sources; some of the materials used were written in Ukrainian. Analysis of the issues raised in this study was made possible by the fact that not only are the central publications printed in Russian, but so are the majority of publications in the republics. I had no way of using information written in the non-Slavic languages in the USSR. Using information from Soviet archives was out of the question.

The transcription of non-Russian names generally follows Russian spelling, which was transliterated into the Latin alphabet. Because Ukrainian names of persons were transliterated from Ukrainian, they are exceptions to this practice. Ukrainian names of places always follow Russian spelling. For some names and terms like Tiflis, Volga, or Soviet, I used the traditional English spelling. The Select Bibliography at the end of the book provides complete bibliographical information on sources and literature referred to in an abbreviated form in the endnotes.

Notes

1. Lewis/Rowland/Clem, *Nationality and Population Change*, p. 216.

2. Khruschev in his "secret speech" at the Twentieth Party Congress (February 1956), in: *Chruschtschow erinnert sich*, p. 568.

3. Brezhnev, on the fifteenth anniversary of the USSR's founding in December 1972, in: *L.I. Brezhnev, Leninskim kursom*, vol. IV (Moscow, 1974), p. 59.

4. H. Kohn, *Der Nationalismus in der Sowjetunion* (Frankfurt a.M., 1932), pp. 94, 96.

5. E. Lemberg, *Nationalismus*, vol. I (Reinbek, 1964), pp. 232, 238.

6. V. Aspaturian, "The Non-Russian Nationalities," in: *Prospects for Soviet Society*, A. Kassof (ed.), (New York, 1968), p. 180.

7. A. Nove/J.A. Newth, *The Soviet Middle East* (London, 1967), p.132.

8. K. Deutsch, *Nationalism and Social Communication* (Cambridge, MA, 1953).
9. Rakowska-Harmstone, *Dialectics of Nationalism in the USSR*, pp. 1f.
10. Carrère d'Encausse, *L'Empire éclaté*, p. 272.
11. S. Bialer, *Stalin's Successors: Leadership, Stability, and Change in the Soviet Union* (Cambridge, 1980), p. 207.
12. R. Medwedjew, *Sowjetbürger in Opposition; Plädoyer für eine sozialistische Demokratie* (Düsseldorf, 1973), p. 95.
13. Andropov's speech of December 1982 on the sixtieth anniversary of the USSR's founding, in: *Neues Deutschland,* December 22, 1982.
14. G.T. Tavadov, "K kharakteristike sovremennogo etapa natsionalnykh otnoshenii v SSSR," in: *Nauchnyi kommunizm* 5/1984, pp. 33–39; T. Rakowska-Harmstone, "Minority Nationalism Today: An Overview," in: R. Conquest (ed.), *The Last Empire: Nationality and the Soviet Future* (Stanford, California, 1986), pp. 235–264.
15. R. Pipes, *The Formation of the Soviet Union: Communism and Nationalism; 1917–1923* (Cambridge, MA, 1957) (2nd ed.); F. Silnickii; *Natsionalnaia politika KPSS v period s 1917 po 1922 god* (Munich, 1981) (2nd ed.); H. Carrère d'Encausse, *Le grand défi: bolsheviks et nations 1917–1930* (Paris, 1987).
16. I have presented my thoughts on this subject in detail elsewhere: A.v. Borcke/G. Simon, *Neue Wege der Sowjetunion-Forschung* (Baden-Baden, 1980), pp. 54ff. The following readers and monographs summarize the way U.S. scholars assess the post-Stalinist USSR: P. Cocks/R.V. Daniels/N.W. Heer (eds.), *The Dynamics of Soviet Politics* (Cambridge, MA, 1976); J. Hough/M. Fainsod, *How the Soviet Union is Governed* (Cambridge, MA, 1979); J.G. Pankhurst/M.P. Sacks (eds.), *Contemporary Soviet Society* (New York, 1980); S. Bialer, *Stalin's Successors; Leadership, Stability and Change in the Soviet Union* (Cambridge, MA, 1980); R.F. Byrnes (ed.), *After Brezhnev* (Bloomington, Ind., 1983).
17. *L'Empire éclaté*, p. 253.
18. W. Kolarz, *Russia and Her Colonies* (New York, 1954); Z. Katz/R. Rogers/F. Harned (eds.), *Handbook of Major Soviet Nationalities* (London, 1975). A number of readers that represented the state of research at a given point in time also approached the issue in an additive manner: E. Goldhagen (ed.), *Ethnic Minorities in the Soviet Union* (New York, 1968); G.W. Simmonds (ed.), *Nationalism in the USSR and Eastern Europe in the Era of Brezhnev and Kosygin* (Detroit, 1977). The structure of the only Western bibliography available is also based on the additive principle: S.M. Horak (ed.), *Guide to the Study of Soviet Nationalities* (Littleton, CO, 1982). Hardly ever have Western scholars attempted to analyze the history of the Soviet nationalities policy by covering long periods and within the framework of the Soviet state as a whole: R. Conquest, *Soviet Nationalities Policy in Practice*

(New York, 1967); B. Lewytzkyj, *Die sowjetische Nationalitätenpolitik nach Stalins Tod, 1953-1970* (Munich, 1970); I. Maistrenko, *Natsionalnaia politika KPSS v ee istoricheskom razvitii* (Munich, 1978).

19. R. Pipes, "'Solving the Nationality Problem," in: *Problems of Communism XVI*, 5/1967, pp. 125-131; R. Szporluk, "Nationalities and the Russian Problem in the USSR: A Historical Outline," in: *Journal of International Affairs* XXVII, 1973, pp. 22-40. Also, a number of collections that deal with the present focus primarily on systematic-comparative problems: E. Allworth (ed.), *Soviet Nationality Problems* (New York, 1971); J.R. Azrael (ed.), *Soviet Nationality Policies and Practices* (New York, 1978). There are no new research findings in: R.L. Rockett, *Ethnic Nationalities in the Soviet Union. Sociological Perspectives on a Historical Problem* (New York, 1981).

20. Seton-Watson, *Nations and States*, p. XIV.

21. See the articles "Nationalism" in: *BSE*, vol. XVII, 1974 (3rd ed.) pp. 358f. and "Patriotism" in: *Sovetskaia Istoricheskaia Entsiklopediia*, vol. X, 1967, columns 926-929.

22. See, for example, W. Connor, "Nation-Building or Nation-Destroying?" in: *World Politics*, XXIV, 3/1972, pp. 319-355.

23. The elements of this consensus are apparent in a number of collections published in the 1970s; for example: E. Kamenka (ed.), *Nationalism: The Nature and Evolution of an Idea* (London, 1976); O. Dann (ed.), *Nationalismus und sozialer Wandel* (Hamburg, 1978); H.A. Winkler (ed.), *Nationalismus* (Königstein/Ts., 1978).

24. O. Dann, "Der moderne Nationalismus als Problem der historischen Entwicklungsforschung," in: *Nationalismus und sozialer Wandel*, p. 14.

25. See Stalin's *Werke*, vol. 2, p. 272; Tsamerian, *Teoreticheskie problemy*, pp. 160-162; M.I. Kulichenko, "60-letie Oktiabria i torzhestvo leninskoi natsionalnoi politiki v SSSR," in: *Istoriia SSSR* 5/1977, p. 63.

26. For more details, see G. Simon. "Zeitgeschichtliche Phänomene, die es gar nicht gibt. Methodische Überlegungen zum Nationalismus in der UdSSR," in: B. Bonwetsch (ed.), *Zeitgeschichte Osteuropas als Methoden- und Forschungsproblem* (Berlin, 1985), pp. 95-104.

27. Informative statistical material can primarily be found in: *Natsionalnaia politika VKP (b) v tsifrakh* (Moscow, 1930); S. Dimanshtein (ed.), *Itogi razresheniia natsionalnogo voprosa v SSSR* (Moscow, 1936); *Kulturnoe stroitelstvo SSSR* (Moscow, 1940).

28. Lenin's notes of December 1922, in: *Kommunist* 9/1956, pp. 15-26; Khrushchev at the Twentieth Party Congress in: *Chruschtschow erinnert sich*, pp. 529-586; Twenty-Second Party Congress: *XXII sezd Kommunisticheskoi partii Sovetskogo Soiuza. 17-31 oktiabria 1961 g. Stenograficheskii otchet*, 2 volumes (Moscow, 1962).

29. Five years after the census, the Soviets published a single volume containing its results: *Chislennost i sostav naseleniia SSSR. Po dannym*

Vsesoiuznoi perepisi naseleniia 1979 goda (Moscow, 1984). The results of the 1970 census were published in 7 volumes; the results of the 1959 census, in 16 volumes.

II

Nation-Building

From the Peoples' Right to Self-Determination to Korenizatsiia

It is doubtful that anybody anticipated how quickly and to what extent the 1917 revolution would cause the Russian Empire to crumble. At the height of the civil war, the Empire's territory had shrunk to a size barely larger than that of the Great Duchy of Moscow during the first half of the sixteenth century.[1] The end of the imperial and colonial phase of Russian history seemed at hand although not all seceding parts of the Empire immediately and formally declared their national independence and although some territories (Belorussia, Crimea, Bashkiria, Kazakhstan, Turkestan) strived to acquire a status that would grant them extensive political autonomy within a future Russian republic. The national movements of the non-Russian peoples were among the driving forces behind the fall of the Russian Empire although in many cases—particularly in the Islamic territories—these movements were still in the early stages and had not yet become mass movements. However, the simultaneous disintegration of the Austro-Hungarian and Ottoman Empires showed how quickly crises can transform diffuse national aspirations into successful political programs and threaten the existence of empires.

The disintegration of the Russian Empire put the Tsar's heirs—the Bolsheviks—into an embarrassing position, which was aggravated by the fact that—unlike other political groups—the Bolsheviks had chosen to focus their political agitation on the peoples' right to self-determination and even secession. The Bolsheviks correctly assumed that the only way they could convince the non-Russian peoples (most of which had no proletariat) to participate in the revolution was to promote the idea of national self-determination. However, from the start, the Bolsheviks had reservations about agitation to open the "peoples' prison" and to cast off the chains of "Russian colonialism." In 1913, Lenin wrote in a letter to S.G. Shaumian that he considered the right to self-determination an *exception* to the general Bolshevist premise of centralism and that he supported the *right* to secede although he was opposed to secession as such.[2] Whether the party would support or oppose a nation's secession was to be determined from case to case.[3] In Lenin's opinion, national demands were subordinate to the interests of the class struggle as far as the proletariat was concerned.[4] After Lenin, in addition to these restrictions on self-determination, the Bolsheviks always demanded unification of the workers of all the nations in a state into uniform proletarian organizations;[5] in other words, the national principle did not apply to the Party's organizational structure.

The most important and, in fact, the most significant objection to the right to self-determination was the assumption that, after a socialist revolution, the peoples would not be interested in secession but would, quite to the contrary, voluntarily join the socialist republic. In 1917, the Bolsheviks realized this assumption was an illusion, and this realization had far-reaching consequences for Bolshevik policy towards the nationalities. As late as April 1917, Stalin speculated that nine-tenths of the peoples would not want to secede[6] after the fall of tsarism. In fact, the disintegration of the Empire accelerated after the October Revolution. As a result, the Bolsheviks had to fight the civil war not only against the Menshevik armies and the intervention forces but also against the national movements of the non-Russian peoples, some of which were socialist (Transcaucasus). The Bolsheviks did not hesitate to use arms to enforce their erroneous assumption that a centralized state would evolve more or less spontaneously after the socialist revolution. Although Stalin agreed with Lenin that, as in any other nation, Russia's fringe regions had the inalienable right to secede from Russia, he also explicitly declared that *after* the socialist revolution and in the interests of the masses, he would consider the demand for secession of the fringe regions an altogether counter-revolutionary demand.[7]

Military measures alone, however, were not sufficient. One reason why the Bolsheviks won the civil war was because — apart from secession — they were willing to concede a great deal to the nationalities. In any case, the Bolsheviks were much more obliging than the White forces, whose uncompromising adherence to the idea of a "one and undivided" Russia made a permanent coalition with the non-Russian national movements impossible. At the declaration of autonomy in November 1920 by Daghestan, the People's Commissar of Nationality Affairs — Stalin held this position as long as it existed (October 1917–1924) — gave a good example of the limits of Soviet willingness to compromise. Stalin proclaimed that the Soviet government considered the *sharia* a traditional right that was as justified as the rights of all peoples living in Russia and that if Daghestan's people wished to preserve their laws and customs, they had to be preserved. He immediately added, however, that autonomy was not synonymous with independence.[8] Autonomy and the recognition of Islamic religious laws as public law were to counteract the anti-Soviet uprising under Uzun Haji, a leader of the Sufi brotherhoods of the Northern Caucasus (1919–1921).[9] Beginning in 1919, after their previous revolutionary excesses, the Soviets in a similar fashion considerably backed down in Turkestan, too, reinstituted the *sharia* courts, and returned mosques and religious schools to the Islamic clergy.[10] The Soviets had concluded that without such concessions, they could not win the fight against the Islamic guerrillas (Basmachi) — which nevertheless lasted until 1926.[11]

The nationalities policy the Bolsheviks pursued arose from the calamity that revolution and civil war brought. This policy differed fundamentally from Stalin's and Lenin's prerevolutionary programmatic statements. As they did in many other political areas, the Bolsheviks discarded their established doctrines after the October Revolution and developed concepts oriented toward the real task of establishing their dictatorship. As Stalin freely admitted in 1924,[12] the national movements proved "considerably more influential" than he had imagined before 1917. As a result, the Party had to develop new strategies. Although Lenin had unequivocally supported the idea of a revolutionary unitarian state before 1917, he became a pioneer of Soviet federalism. Stalin, however, intended to restrict non-Russian territories' right to autonomy from the beginning. He wanted to strengthen central power and looked on Soviet federalism as a facade behind which a unitarian state was to be built.[13] In late 1922, during the decisive conferences on the future constitutional structure of the USSR and on Soviet nationalities policy, Stalin and Lenin disagreed violently. The conflict ended in Lenin's decision to force Stalin's resignation from the position of the Party's General Secretary at the imminent Twenty-second Party Congress (April 1923). Lenin's illness made it impossible for him to carry out this plan.[14]

The goals of the nationalities policy did not spark the conflict. According to Marxist doctrine, these goals were based on the assumption that the peoples would merge into a Communist world society. The only controversy was about how to get to that point and how much the Soviets should concede to the unexpectedly strong national movements in the given political situation. Stalin followed a restrictive course and accused Lenin of promoting "national liberalism."[15] Because of his practical experience with the national problem in the Caucasus, Stalin probably was much more aware of the dangers the socialist state might face as a result of too lenient a policy towards the non-Russian peoples. Also, he probably did not share Lenin's optimism that the revolution had in principle ended nationalism and separatism or that the best way to neutralize these movements would be to make national concessions. In any case, there are many indications that Stalin considered nations historical constructs that could not be abolished.

When Lenin prevailed in the dispute over the constitutional structure of the USSR, he also secured the interests of Ukrainian and Georgian Communists. Contrary to Stalin's proposals, the constitution provided for gradual federal rights for the non-Russian territories—and not equal autonomy for all. Instead of joining the Russian Republic as Stalin had provided, the existing Soviet republics formed a federation in December 1922.[16]

But in the early 1920s, even the People's Commissar of Nationality Affairs was convinced that after the Bolsheviks had victoriously ended the civil war, they would have to make concessions to the non-Russian peoples if the Soviets were to win these peoples for the revolution—at least after the fact. Even after 1921, Soviet power was not at all established in many non-Russian territories; in some, like Central Asia and Kazakhstan, it barely existed. In the early 1920s, the Bolsheviks changed the prerevolutionary catchphrase of the peoples' right to self-determination, including secession (by that time, only peoples outside the USSR were allowed to claim this right), into the concept of a Soviet policy of nation-building. This program determined Soviet policy towards the nationalities during the 1920s and early 1930s.

This policy was directed at ethnic consolidation, not at the nation as a state.[17] Of course, the goal was not to allow the development of new national states within the "uniform federal state"[18] of the USSR. In his fundamental publication "Marxism and the National Question" (1913), Stalin did not mention statehood as a constitutive characteristic of a nation.[19] The socialist nations were to be joint representatives of the one and uniform Soviet state.

The Soviet variant of nation-building is marked by two particularities:

1. Support for non-Russian peoples occurred only on the condition and in the expectation of stabilizing or establishing the Party's rule. In this respect, nation-building was a tool of Sovietization.
2. The long-term goal of nation-building was not differentiation of nations but "merger" of nations. Soviet federalism was considered a "transitional stage on the way to a completely unified" state.[20] According to Bolshevik doctrine, nationalism and the national question were characteristics of bourgeois society and would lose all political significance under socialism. However, Lenin had repeatedly proclaimed that humankind could reach the inevitable merger of nations only by way of a transition period of complete liberation—that is the liberty of all suppressed nations to secede.[21] In the 1920s and early 1930s, no one in the USSR doubted that Soviet society was in a phase of "liberation" and "development" for the non-Russian peoples and not in the "merger" phase.

In October 1920, Stalin described Soviet nation-building policy in an article in Pravda. He explained that the Soviets could only be attractive to the masses in Russia's fringe regions if all Soviet organs in those regions—the courts, the administration, the economic organs, the direct organs of power (and also the Party) — were made up of as many locals as possible who were familiar with ways of life, customs, and languages of the local population. He was convinced that the local working masses had to be involved in all areas of the administration of their country, including military groups.[22] At the Tenth Party Congress in March 1921, the Party adopted this passage in its resolution on the nationalities question nearly verbatim. The resolution also stated that the Party's task was "to help the working masses of the non-Russian peoples catch up with the better-developed Central Russia and to help these peoples: . . . develop a local-language press, schools, theaters, clubs, and cultural and education facilities altogether; to establish and further a network of courses and schools for general and professional-technical education in local languages . . ."[23]

Two years later, the Twelfth Party Congress (April 1923) again dealt extensively with the problem of non-Russian peoples. It confirmed the programmatic statements of 1921 and declared that the nationalities problem would remain unsolved until, in addition to legally recognizing the equality of the peoples, which the October Revolution had established, the Soviets also made economic and cultural equality a reality.[24] At the Twelfth Party Congress, the Party publicly and vehemently argued about the nationalities problem for the last time.[25] In all essential points, Stalin's opinion prevailed over that of the Ukrainian and Georgian Communists, in particular. The latter demanded that the future federal constitution grant more political and economic rights to the federal republics. The criteria for evaluating the nationalities problem were by no means uniform within the Party. Both Stalin and the resolution on the nationalities problem, for example, promised "the underdeveloped peoples of the federation" that "the Russian proletariat would help" them overcome economic and cultural inequality. At the same time, the Georgian Mdivani demanded "reparations to the proletariat and working people of those nationalities that have been suppressed."[26] Because of the Russian chauvinism that dominated the Party and the political apparatuses, non-Russian communists repeatedly expressed their concerns that the attractive declarations and Party resolutions on the nationalities problem might prove nothing but "a useless scrap of paper."[27] Bukharin's request to the Russians at the Party Congress to "pretend" to be content with the role of the inferior to the non-Russian peoples, certainly followed Lenin's intentions towards the end of his political career. Stalin explicitly rejected this statement by Bukharin.[28] The fact that none of the speakers who contradicted Stalin in 1923 lived past 1938 is symptomatic of the events that were to take place in the Soviet Union during the following fifteen years.

The Workers

While the peoples' right to self-determination was degenerating into a fictional constitutional provision "guaranteeing" the right of the Union Republics to secede, the Soviets were implementing the nation-building program—if more slowly and less comprehensively than many of its supporters wanted. For ideological and practical reasons, the Bolsheviks had to be particularly interested in expanding their basis among the workers. Even in non-Russian territories such as the Ukraine and Turkestan, the Bolshevik revolution had received considerable support from Russian workers. Only among the Ukrainians, Azeri (Baku), Jews, and Tatars did a small non-Russian proletariat exist. This was another reason why the fringe territories saw Soviet power as Russian power. As a result, creating national proletariats was a high priority in programmatic statements of the Party.[29]

Although nearly everywhere in the national territories of the RSFSR the number of national industrial workers significantly increased (in both relative and absolute terms) with the beginning of industrialization in the late 1920s and early 1930s, hardly anywhere did it come close to matching the percentage of native peoples among the total population (Table 2.1). In addition, the number of industrial workers remained relatively low outside the Russian and Ukrainian industrial centers. In the three Transcaucasian Union Republics and Belorussia, Uzbekistan, Turkmenistan, and Tadzhikistan, the number of industrial workers increased from 115,000 in 1928 to 350,000 in 1932. During the same period, the number grew from 63,000 to 140,000 in sixteen autonomous territories of the RSFSR.[30] The ratios become more meaningful in light of the fact that the total number of industrial workers in the USSR jumped from 3.1 million in 1928 to 6 million in 1932.[31]

Korenizatsiia met with considerable resistance from the political machines. On August 25, 1931, a resolution by the Presidium of the Central Executive Committee's Council of nationalities declared that apart from Belorussia, Kazakhstan, the Tatar ASSR, and the ASSR of Volga Germans, "the percentage of the local population in industry in the national Republics and Regions is extremely small." The supreme economic authorities were instructed to design concrete directives that would help to develop local proletariats in the following years.[32] The available information indicates that this was not put into practice to the degree demanded. Factory management and subordinate authorities often justified the preferential employment of Russians with economic arguments: National workers were less qualified, their work morale bad, and the training necessary required additional funds. Contrary to the decisions of the organs of the Party and the Soviets, many enterprises did not keep records on the national origin of their employees to evade interference from above. Until the mid-1930s, such jus-

Table 2.1: Industrial Workers in the RSFSR's National Territories

	1926	1933
Kazakh ASSR		
Number of Industrial Workers (in thousands)	--	57
Natives of the Titular Nations (in percent)	--	45
Tatar ASSR	14	38
	25	37
Bashkir ASSR	13	26
	7	24
Crimean ASSR	10	29
	3	7
Karelian ASSR	6	15
	17	16
Chechen AR	--	13
	--	8
Daghestan ASSR	3	7
	19	23
Kirgiz ASSR	1	6
	10	27
Chuvash ASSR	1	6
	10	42
Buriat-Mongolian ASSR	1	6
	1	9
ASSR of Volga Germans	3	5
	66	65
Mordvinian ASSR	--	5
	12 (1930)	22
AR of Mari	3 (1928)	6 (1932)
	--	24 (1932)

Source: *Natsionalnaia politika VKP (b) v tsifrakh* (Moscow, 1930), pp. 126-128; *Itogi razresheniia natsionalnogo voprosa v SSSR* (Moscow, 1936), pp. 140f.; D. Selivanov/S. Krasnov, "Pobeda leninsko-stalinskoi politiki v Mariiskoi avtonomnoi oblasti za 15 let," in: *RN*, 7/1936, pp. 45f.; S. Bradeiev, "Novaia respublika," in: *RN*, 2/1935, p. 51. N. Nurmakov, "Avtonomii i natsionalnyie raiony RSFSR na sotsialisticheskom pod-eme," in: *RN*, 1/1935, p. 29. This table includes the national territories of the RSFSR that had more than 5,000 industrial workers in 1933.

tifications were considered unacceptable, and part of the Soviet press consistently denounced them as "concrete phenomena of superpower chauvinism."[33] However in 1932, of the 800,000 workers in the Middle Volga area (*krai*), only 13.4 percent were non-Russian—the percentage of non-Russians in the total population was 28.1 percent. In the Gorkii area, which included the ASSR of the Mari, Chuvashs, and Udmurts, the respective figures even indicate 3.6 percent in relation to 23.5 percent of the total population. In this area, there was a total of 161,000 workers.[34]

Essentially, the development of local proletariats made the same advances and met the same obstacles in the non-Russian Union Republics as it did in the RSFSR (see Table 2.2). However, in several republics (the Ukraine, Belorussia, Georgia, Kazakhstan), the percentage of local workers approached proportionate representation by the mid-1930s; in Armenia—which was an exception to the rule—there were proportionally more Armenians among workers than in the total population. The total number, however, remained insignificantly small (cf. Appendix, Table A.2 on the population percentage of the titular nations). The non-Russian workers were usually at the lower end of the scale of professional qualification.

Only in the 1920s were more or less comprehensive statistical data published, which provided the national breakdown of social structure. By the late 1930s, such data had completely disappeared. This was not only a consequence of Stalinism's notorious mystery mongering, but was also a consequence of the growing rift between political rhetorics and social reality.[35] However, the scattered isolated pieces of data available in Soviet publications provide enough information to substantiate this conclusion. Table 2.2 shows that the workers' korenizatsiia had come to a halt or had even regressed (Uzbekistan, Kazakhstan) by the late 1930s. One of the few modern Soviet studies on the social structure of the non-Russian peoples supports this statement (cf. Appendix, Table A.6). These figures document the claim that the number of workers continuously increased within the total population between 1939 and 1959. The figures show two more facts: First, in 1939, Russians were clearly over-represented among the workers. By 1959, this fact had changed only insignificantly—if at all. Second, although the number of non-Russian workers kept increasing at a quick pace after 1939, the proportionate under-representation of non-Russians among the workers did not decrease. Again, Armenia is the exception: In 1939, Armenians were better represented among workers than among the total population; twenty years later, Armenian representation was proportionate, and within their own republic, Armenians had reached the same level as had the Russians within the RSFSR. This means that in the late 1930s, korenizatsiia ceased; that is, the intensified effort to increase the number of non-Russian workers as opposed to Russian workers halted—this effort aimed

Table 2.2: Industrial Workers in the Union Republics[1]

	1926	1932/33[2]	late 1930s	
Ukraine	509,000	1,462,300		
Titular Nationals (in percent)	43	58		
Russians (in percent)	41	–	60	(1937, blue-collar and white-collar workers)
Belorussia	31,700	113,000		
	40	63	64	(1937, blue-collar and white-collar workers)
Jews	34			
Azerbaijan	47,400			
	24	28		
	36			
Armenia	5,000	85		
	75			
	1			
Georgia	12,000	59		
	–			
	–			
Uzbekistan	14,300	62,100	130,000	(1938)
Asians	46	50	28	
	39			
Tadzhikistan	100	5,700		
	72			
	–			

(continued)

Table 2.2 (continued)

	1926	1932/33[2]	late 1930s
Turkmenistan	2,800	12,200	
	11		
	54		
Kazakhstan	9,500	62,100	88,700 (1935, blue-collar and white-collar workers)
	23	45	41
	56		

Source: Natsionalnaia politika VKP (b) v tsifrakh (Moscow, 1930), pp. 126-128 (data from the 1926 census); S.I. Iakubovskaia, *Razvitiie SSSR kak soiuznogo gosudarstva, 1922-1936 gg.* (Moscow, 1972), p. 166; D. Lane, "Ethnic and Class Stratification in Soviet Kazakhstan; 1917-1939," in: *Comparative Studies in Society and History*, XVII, 1975, p. 181; *Formirovaniie sotsialisticheskikh natsii v SSSR* (Moscow, 1962), p. 205; L. Zinger, "Sotsialisticheskoie stroitelstvo soiuznykh respublik SSSR za 20 let," in: *RN*, 11/1937, pp. 79f.; N. Nurmakov, "Osnovnyie itogi leninskoi natsionalnoi politiki v RSFSR k XVII," in: *rn*, 2/1934, p. 31.

[1]Workers employed in the economy. Tadzhikistan became a Union Republic in 1929, Kazakhstan in 1936.
[2]The absolute figures refer to 1932. They include industrial employees. About 80 percent of all people employed are assumed to be blue-collar workers. The percentage figures refer to 1933 and to blue-collar workers exclusively.

to develop local proletariats with representation proportionate (at least) to the total population.

The Ukraine is particularly important: On the one hand, even before forced industrialization began, the Ukraine had a relatively large number of industrial workers. On the other hand, Ukrainian Party leadership placed great value on nation-building and considered it one of the most important goals of the Party's policy. In this context, Ukrainian Communists frequently quoted what Stalin had said at the Tenth Party Congress in 1921 when he had explicitly referred to the process of Ukrainization as a process of de-Russification. Stalin had said that although the majority of the population in Ukrainian cities was Russian, these cities would eventually and unavoidably be Ukrainized.[36] However, only the pauperization of Ukrainian villages after 1929 triggered a major migration from the country into the cities and the ensuing increase in the proportion of Ukrainians in the Ukraine's cities; this proportion increased from 47.2 percent in 1926 to 58.1 percent in 1939.[37] Ukrainian peasants received preferential treatment in integration into industry. Training and continued education in the Ukrainian language, Ukrainian factory newspapers, and the Ukrainian language at workplaces was to give Ukrainians the feeling that they had come to "their" city and not to a Russian city. Even in the south Ukrainian industrial center of Donbass, which traditionally was predominantly Russian, and where there were fewer locals among the skilled workers than among the unskilled workers (as in other national territories), the Ukrainian language and culture progressed rapidly. When the success of Ukrainization of the workers and the cities became apparent in the 1930s, the Soviets stopped this policy and changed it radically.

The Nationalization of Party and State Apparatuses

Before 1917, "two Belorussians, a dozen Turks Azeri, three Tatars, etc."[38] were among the Bolshevist partisans. But even in 1922 at the end of the civil war, 72 percent of the Party were still Russians. The remainder of Party members originated from several smaller nations, which, like Russian, were considerably over-represented as compared to their percentage in the population: Jews, Georgians, Armenians, Poles, and Latvians.[39] Jews, Georgians, and Armenians were even more overrepresented in leadership positions than in membership; during the following twenty years, this disproportionality increased even further. On the other hand, during the early 1920s, Ukrainians, Belorussians, and the Islamic peoples were hardly represented in the Party at all. The total number of Muslim communists in 1922 is estimated at 15,000; of these, 6,534 were Tatars and 4,964 Kazakhs. This means that for all practical purposes, the Central Asian peoples were not included in the Party.[40]

By the mid-1930s, a policy designed to recruit new Party members had considerably changed this situation. The percentage of locals within Party organizations in the national territories (Union Republics, ASSRs, Autonomous Regions, National *okrugs*) increased from its 1927 level of 46.6 percent (= 180,000 Communists) to a level of 53.8 percent (or 582,000) in 1932; by 1937, however, the representation of locals in their own Party organizations had once more decreased to 45 percent.[41] Analogously, the percentage of Russians in the entire Party had decreased from 72 percent in 1922 to 65 percent in 1927 and reached its lowest level in the mid-1930s. It is not possible, however, to quote exact statistics because the Soviet Union does not release pertinent data. By 1946, 67.8 percent of all Communists once again were Russians.[42]

Table 2.3 provides more details on the Party's korenizatsiia and its demise in the 1930s. In all territories, nationalization of Party organizations progressed rapidly until 1932. Initially, the collectivization and industrialization that had begun in 1929 did not lead to abandoning the policy meant to make all peoples equal and thus promoted the preferential advancement of non-Russians. In several republics, the nationalization of Party organizations gained momentum even during the First Five-Year-Plan period. Later, this policy was abandoned and the percentage of locals in the Party no longer increased, or even began to decrease. This happened — apart from some exceptions — although by the mid-1930s, non-Russians were by no means represented in the Party in proportion to their representation in the total population. Although the Party had never clearly committed itself in this matter, all its programmatic statements indicate that, at the very least, korenizatsiia was meant to bring about proportionate representation for non-Russians in all societal leadership groups. This implies the nationals were in a clear majority in their own territories. From this perspective, the goal of this policy had not at all been reached when it was abandoned.

The 1933–1934 purge, which was more comprehensive than any previous ones, and in the course of which a third of all Party members and candidates (1.2 million) were expelled from the Party, was a means to achieve the Party's re-Russification. The purge was concentrated in rural Party organizations — thus constituting retaliation for the resistance of these rural Party organizations in the face of agricultural collectivization. This meant that the non-Russian peoples, a larger-than-average percentage of whom were peasants, suffered the most severe consequences. In the national republics, there were 12 to 14 percent more Party expulsions than in industrial areas. Beginning in 1937 and after the end of the different waves of purges, the Party once more accepted new members. However, the Party preferred members of the technological intelligentsia, and again non-Russian peoples were disadvantaged because very few had such a social group.[43]

Table 2.3: The *korenizatsiia* of the Party

Party Organization	Percentage of Titular Nations in the Party Organization						Percentage of Titular Nations in the Total Population		
	1922	1927	1932 (4/1)	1937 (1/1)	1953	1959	1926	1939	1959
Ukraine	24	47	59	57		60 (1958)	80	73	77
Belorussia	21	47	60	53		67 (1962)	81	83	81
Georgia	62	55	66	67			67	61	64
Armenia	89	92	90	90			84	83	88
Azerbaijan	39	32	44	44			62	58	67
Kazakhstan	8 (1924)	38	53 (1933)	49	40 (1952)	36 (1960)	57	38	30
Uzbekistan	–	36	58	52	49	52	65	64	62
Turkmenistan	–	40	–	40			72	59	61
Kirgizistan	–	52	57	50	34	35	67	52	40
Tadzhikistan	–	49	53 (1933)	45			75	60	53
Tataria	20	32	42	42			45	49	47
Bashkiria	18	16	22	21			23	21	22
Chuvashia	61	58	62	61			75	72	70
Udmurtia	17	18	32	30			52	39	36
Kalmykia	31	65	73				76	49	35
Mari	38	38	41	37			51	47	43
Crimean Peninsula	2	5	14				25	–	–

(continued)

Table 2.3 (continued)

Party Organization	Percentage of Titular Nations in the Party Organization						Percentage of Titular Nations in the Total Population		
	1922	1927	1932 (4/1)	1937 (1/1)	1953	1959	1926	1939	1959
Republic of Volga Germans	67	27	48				66	–	–
Daghestan	20	26	66				64	76	69
Karelia	17	11	27				37	23	13
Komi	85	85	68	77			92	72	30

Sources: Itogi razresheniia natsionalnogo voprosa v SSSR (Moscow, 1936), p. 16; N.A. Barsukov/A.R. Shaidullin/I.N. Iudin, "KPSS—partiia internatsionalnaia," in: *VI KPSS*, 7/1966, p. 12; T.H. Rigby, *Communist Party Membership in the USSR, 1917-1967* (Princeton, N.J., 1968), pp. 371f, 380-382, 394-396; "The Communist Party of Ukraine: A Profile," *Radio Liberty Research*, 151/1978.

Calculations based on data on the origins of the delegates to the Party Congresses in 1939 and 1952 confirm that the overly high proportion of Russians among Party members continued to increase during the 1940s. During the "Great Motherland War," there was a clear bias towards preferential admittance of Russians into the Party. Similarly, Georgians and Armenians were able to bolster their already strong positions even more until the early 1950s. The difference between peoples which were represented in the Party in large proportions and those represented in small proportions increased during the last fifteen years of Stalin's dictatorship. This preference for Russians constituted a particular disadvantage for Ukrainians, Belorussians, and the Central Asian peoples, whose proportionate representation continued to decrease.[44]

The privileged position of the Georgians and Armenians in the Party was no accident. The following discussions will show that, during the Stalin era, the Transcaucasus, but particularly Georgia and Armenia, received preferential treatment in many ways. These are the only Union Republics that already had a higher percentage of locals among Party members in the early 1930s than in the total population (see Table 2.3).

It is typical that abandoning korenizatsiia did not reverse this development, either. The strong Georgian and Armenian position is in part explained by these peoples' socialist traditions, which had prevailed before the revolution. After the prohibition of the other socialist parties, a number of their supporters joined the Bolsheviks. The Kazakhs were the only Asian people represented in the Party in an above-average proportion. Table 2.3, which shows that the numbers had been declining since 1937, should not hide the fact that even before World War II, the Kazakhs were represented in the Party in greater numbers than they were among the total population of their republic. This situation has remained unchanged until today. Northern Kazakhstan was one of the few national territories that profited from the industrialization that began in the 1930s. This was one reason why the Kazakhs became integrated into Soviet society and the Party more rapidly than other peoples.

No other people supplied more Party members than the Jews. Even though the percentage of Jews decreased after 1940, and particularly after the distinctly anti-Semitic policy pursued between 1948–1953, the percentage of Jews in the Party was more than twice as high, even during the Khrushchev era, as in the total population. Several reasons explain this fact. As a people suffering discrimination, Jews supported the socialist movement in Tsarist Russia in disproportionately high numbers. Jews have by far been the most urbanized and educated ethnic group, and many members of the technical intelligentsia were Jews.[45] All these factors favored admittance into the Party, as did the fact that the Soviets actively pursued anti-Semitism in the 1920s and 1930s.

Table 2.4: Percentage of Jews in the Party

	1922	1927	1940	1961
Percentage Among the Party Members	5.2	4.3	4.3	2.8
Percentage in the CC			10.8 (1939)	0.3
Percentage in the Total Population		1.82 (1926)	1.78 (1939)	1.09 (1959)

Sources: Z. Katz, "The Jews in the Soviet Union," in: Z. Katz/R. Rogers/F. Harned (eds.), *Handbook of Major Soviet Nationalities* (N.Y./London, 1975), p. 368.

The national makeup of the Party leadership reflects even more clearly the respective overproportionate or underproportionate representation of individual peoples within Party membership. Between 1919 and 1935, the thirty-four members of the Politburo and the Secretariat included 65 percent Russians, 18 percent Jews, 6 percent Georgians, and 3 percent Armenians. The corresponding figures for the thirty-seven top leaders from 1939 to 1952 are 81 percent Russians, 5 percent Georgians, 3 percent Armenians, 3 percent Jews, and 5 percent Ukrainians.[46]

The nationalization of the Soviet organs, and of the village soviets, in particular, was probably the most successful effort of korenizatsiia.

In most national territories, the national makeup of the village soviets' Council of Deputies corresponded to the population's national makeup by the mid-1930s, that is, at the lowest level of the state apparatus, dominated non-Russians. The korenizatsiia of the Soviet organs was better institutionalized than the korenizatsiia of the Party or industry, for example. The Presidium of the Central Executive Committee's Council of Nationalities, which worked in many ways to further non-Russian peoples, was most effective within its own apparatus: the Soviet apparatus.

On the level of the Union Republics, the nationalities departments of the Presidia of the CEC corresponded to the Presidium of the Council of Nationalities on the level of the union. On the middle and lower administrative levels of the Russian territories, departments for minorities or plenipotentiaries for national minorities existed. In the 1920s, central and local commissions for the korenizatsiia of the state apparatus were established with the Presidia of the CECs and the mid-level Soviet organs in the national territories of the RSFSR and the other Union Republics. Although many of these commissions and plenipotentiaries existed only on paper, others emphatically supported advancement of locals. In the early 1930s, however, the gradual break-up of these institutions was beginning, first on the lower and middle levels. The Presidium of the Council of Nationalities existed until 1936. On the Party level, however, the CC's national sector and the national sections of the subordinate Party organs under it had already been dissolved in 1930.[47]

By the late 1920s, the integration of locals into their own territories' state bureaucracies had been achieved to varying degrees (Table 2.5).

As this table shows, korenizatsiia could be considered complete only in Armenia and Georgia. The table also shows that locals were clearly better integrated on the lower administrative levels than on the level of the Union Republics. In the Ukraine and Belorussia, at least the raions were staffed mainly with locals. But in Central Asia, the Russians determined the character of the government agencies, even on the local level. Very few locals progressed to the executive level of Central Asian Union Republics.

Table 2.5: Members of Titular Nations in the Leading Soviet Apparatuses of the Union Republics (1929)

	Apparatuses on the Republic Level	Apparatuses on the Raion Level	Percentage in the Republic's Total Population (1926)
Ukraine	36.2	75.9	80.0
Belorussia	49.5	72.7	80.6
Azerbaijan	35.8	69.1	62.1
Georgia	74.1	80.9	67.0
Armenia	93.5	94.6	84.1
Turkmenistan	8.4	24.1	71.9
Uzbekistan	11.5	41.6	65.9
Tadzhikistan	14.3	44.9	74.6

Source: *Natsionalnaia politika VKP (b) v tsifrakh* (Moscow, 1930), pp. 44-47, 199.

At that time, the Party was not willing to justify this situation by pointing to the fact that no native specialists were available and thus that having Russians carry out Soviet power was unavoidable. Quite to the contrary (probably in 1929), Uzbekistan's CC and CEC decided that by September 1, 1930, they would "Uzbekitize" all positions in the republic's highest administrative offices. The CC's Bureau for Central Asian Affairs in Moscow explicitly endorsed this plan. It remains a plan worth remembering although "Uzbekization" managed to fill only 22.6 percent of these offices[48] either with natives or with Russians or Europeans who could speak, read, and write the Uzbek language. Because of this, on November 28, 1929, Uzbekistan's Council of People's Commissars and its CEC decided that all members of the republic's central organs must learn the Uzbek language within six months.[49] The deadline was to be 1931. This resolution still has not been put into effect.

This resolution was as unrealistic as, for example, several resolutions the Party and Soviet organs passed in an attempt to make the native Mordvinian language the official language of Mordvinia when, out of a total population of 1.41 million in 1934, only 37.7 percent was Mordvinian.[50] The central apparatus of the Uzbek People's Commissar for Education adopted the Uzbek language as its official language in 1931. But this great success was an exception to the rule. The other People's Commissars' offices and Uzbekistan's railroad, postal, and telegraph services retained Russian as their official language — in clear violation of the Uzbek government's directions.[51]

Without question, a comparison of the individual republics shows Central Asia fared the worst when it came to establishing local languages as the official ones. A 1931 study conducted by the People's Commissar of Workers' and Peasants' Inspection in Moscow showed that, of 11,520 employees in 118 Soviet offices in Central Asia, only 10.5 percent were natives. Only 6.4 percent of the remaining non-nationals were competent speakers of the language "the apparatus is required to use." Even during the early 1930s, this situation was publicly denounced as "scandalous."[52] During the Stalin era, however, this situation did not change much because the great momentum of nationalization was already beginning to slow.

In the Ukraine, nationalization was more successful than in Central Asia because the population's higher level of education, beginning urbanization, and developed national identity provided a more favorable environment. In 1933 (the year korenizatsiia probably reached its climax), 87.6 percent of the deputies in the village soviets, 70 percent of the raions executive committees, and 58.4 percent of the city soviets (1925–1926 — 42.2 percent) were Ukrainians.[53] In nearly all local and many central Soviet organs, official correspondence was conducted in the Ukrainian language. The situation in Belorussia was similar.

Table 2.6 provides insights into the progress and the limitations of nationalization in the Russian republic where the participation of natives was essentially limited to the village soviets. The organs and authorities on the level of the ASSR and the Autonomous Regions were in the hands of Russians.

The percentage of non-Russian nationals in the total population is not the primary factor that determines the extent of non-Russian participation in government. Participation depends on how well a particular territory or people is integrated into Russian-Soviet society as a whole; the degree of integration, in its turn, directly corresponds with how long the territory or people has belonged to Russia. The Islamic peoples in the Volga region, who were already integrated into Russia during the sixteenth century, took over local Soviet power far more successfully than the Islamic peoples in the Northern Caucasus, which the Russians had only conquered in the nineteenth century. This study repeatedly demonstrates a correlation between national integration and assimilation on the one hand and the historical duration of coexistence within one state on the other hand. However, no "principle" without exceptions can be derived from the existence of this correlation.

Some general statements can be made about the progress of nationalization of the state apparatuses in the first half of the 1930s: First, the higher the administrative level, the lower the percentage of nationals in the govern-

Table 2.6: Members of the Titular Nation in the Central Government Apparatuses and Village Soviets in Their Respective Territories (Some National Territories in the European RSFSR)

	Percentage of Employees in the Central Administrative and Managing Apparatuses		Percentage of Elected Representatives in the Village Soviets		Percentage in the Total Population
	1930	1933	1927	1931	1926
Karelian ASSR	17.9	16.7	49.7	48.1	37.4
Chuvash ASSR	46.6	54.5	77.8	81.4	74.6
Bashkir ASSR	6.8	25.6	25.9	24.7	23.7
Tatar ASSR	30.7	38.5 (1936)	–	53.7	44.9
ASSR of Volga Germans	27.4	39.2	69.6	69.9	66.4
ASSR of Mari	28.0	35.4	52.5	54.1	54.1
Mordvinian ASSR	18.2	17.6	–	37.5	29.3
Crimean ASSR	10.6	14.8	37.4	37.5	25.7
Daghestan ASSR	23.2	15.0	89.2	82.5	62.5
Kabardino-Balkarian AR	14.2	17.5	84.5	78.9	76.3
North Ossetian AR	–	45.7	84.9	81.2	84.2

Sources: B. Rodnevich, "Korenizatsiia apparata v avtonomiiakh i raionakh natsmenshinstv RSFSR," in: *RN*, 1931, no. 12, pp. 12-15; N. Nurmakov, "Osnovnye itogi leninskoi natsionalnoi politiki v RSFSR," in: *RN*, 1934, n. 2, p. 28; *Itogi razresheniia natsionalnogo voprosa v SSSR* (Moscow, 1936), pp. 154-164.

ment agency. Second, the number of nationals who were leading personnel in agencies and institutions was significantly higher than the number of nationals among all personnel. This means that nationals were consciously favored to head government agencies and departments or to serve in other responsible and prestigious functions. Third, in all academic fields, very few specialists were nationals; in the Northern Caucasus and Central Asia, virtually none were nationals. The economic and planning agencies of the RSFSR's autonomous territories employed only a half to a third as many nationals as these territories' central apparatuses.[54] This lack of national specialists also explains why agencies and organizations employed considerably fewer locals than the respective councils of deputies of soviets (the elected organs). This situation existed on all administrative levels. In the 1930s, the Islamic peoples had produced hardly any agronomists, engineers, doctors, or accountants.

This situation lent an illusory quality to another goal of korenizatsiia: making a titular nation's language the official language. On December 25, 1930, the Presidium of the Council of Nationalities arrived at a resolution requiring the central organs of the Buriat-Mongolian ASSR to conduct their correspondence in both the Buriat and Russian languages. In the raions with a majority of Buriat nationals, the Buriat language was the only official language.[55] On May 10, 1931, the All-Russian CEC resolved that in general, a titular nation's mother tongue be introduced in all the national territories' government organs as the official language.[56] This resolution was for appearance only, like the Chuvash Party and soviet organs' "nearly annual resolutions" to introduce the Chuvash language as the official language of the ASSR's People's Commissariats.[57] Until the mid-1930s, the Party bureaus and Councils of People's Commissars in the national territories continuously passed resolutions reminiscent of korenizatsiia and harshly criticized delay and resistance to it—an additional indication that non-Russian nationals held a strong position in these bodies.[58]

Although resolutions advocating the adoption of non-Russian languages within the Soviet apparatus were frequently unrealistic, these resolutions had an impact in the RSFSR—particularly on the local level. By 1931, the national language was the official language of all the village soviets in the Crimean Tatar ASSR and of 90 percent of them in the Yakut ASSR. In other territories, however, the figures were considerably lower; for example, in the Mordvinian ASSR, only 25 percent of village soviets had adopted the national language as the official language and in the Kalmyk Autonomous Region, only 11 percent. Of the 12,766 village soviets in the national territories of the RSFSR in 1931, 55 percent were organized as soviets of the respective titular nations; not quite a third conducted correspondence in their respective national languages. On the level of the ASSR and the Autonomous Regions, the Russian language dominated as the official language in the early

Nation-Building

1930s. In some cases, officials corresponded simultaneously in the national language and in Russian. In nearly all instances, however, the nationals had the opportunity to make petitions and receive information in their mother tongues.[59]

The nationalization of judiciary organs had progressed surprisingly far. By the early 1930s, all organs of the prosecutors' offices, investigating commissions, and the courts in all twenty-eight Tatar raions of the Tatar ASSR and the seventeen Bashkir and eleven Tatar raions in the Bashkir ASSR were conducting correspondence in their respective mother tongues. In the ASSRs and the Autonomous Regions of the RSFSR, between 60 and 70 percent of judiciary personnel were non-Russian nationals. The five law schools in the RSFSR were required to enroll at least 30 percent of their students from the national territories; in Kazan, the prescribed quota was even 90 percent.[60]

The integration of non-Russian peoples in Soviet society's upper echelons, professions, and organizations helped the nations develop independent national identities. Examples of this process are the nationalization of the Komsomol, the unions, or the teaching profession.

Many factors indicate that the conscious and disproportionate promotion of nationals began to lose momentum in the mid-1930s and later even lost grounds. In 1935 and 1936, the press published more and more complaints about the failure and neglect of korenizatsiia. After 1937, this topic virtually vanished from the Soviet media; it had become taboo. A report from the Udmurt ASSR clearly exemplifies the crisis of korenizatsiia. This report claims that the successful introduction of Udmurt as the official language of the raions was lost in 1935 when the Russian language again became the official language. Also in 1935, the number of Udmurt chairmen of raion executive committees, chairmen of the village soviets, and members of the Presidium of the CEC of the ASSR diminished.[61]

The last public campaign to nationalize the Soviet organs occurred in 1936. On January 7, 1936, the Presidium of the CEC of the USSR passed a resolution, "On Violations of the Nationalities Policy in the Area (*krai*) of the Northern Caucasus," the style and content of which were extremely pointed.[62] According to the resolution, only seventeen of the 1,310 members of eighteen central governmental organs were Northern Caucasian nationals although these peoples constituted 65 percent of the area's total population; in the area's national territories, with few exceptions, Russian was the official language even on the village level—even in correspondence with the people, although most of them could not understand Russian. The area's executive committee was required to employ non-Russians in at least one-third of its positions over the course of two years, and the Russians remaining within the apparatus were required to learn the local languages. All village and raion soviets in the national territories were expected to complete the transition of making local languages official languages within two years. An additional stipulation was that at least half the industrial workers be nationals by January 1, 1937. Before that time, of Groznyi's oil industry employed virtually no nationals.

Although, as a result of this resolution, the plenum of the Northern Caucasus Area Executive Committee criticized itself and promised to execute the stipulated measures, in the summer of 1936, the Presidium of the Council of Nationalities had already become aware that the adjustments were not progressing as scheduled.[63] One may conclude that none of these measures was actually ever carried out.

Language Policy and the Press

Support for and development of non-Russian languages was one of the most visible signs of the policy of nation-building. In the 1920s and 1930s, publication of language projects, dictionaries, and spelling reference books flourished. Experts developed written languages for forty-eight nations and nationalities. This allowed these peoples to print their literatures for the first time in their histories. The Turkmen, Kirgiz, and Karakalpaks of Central Asia, and many small nationalities in the far north were among the peoples without written languages until then. This language policy's goal was to remove the Russian language from the national territories's public sectors (administration, the judiciary, education, the media).

The Ukrainian language had basically been a colloquial language and a language of belles-lettres, but not one that fit into the modern world. During this period, however, the Ukrainian cities, whose population and culture had been predominantly Russian, enthusiastically adopted Ukrainian for use in public life. In 1926, seven million people in the Ukraine were able to read and write Russian although only 2.7 million Russians lived there. They were balanced by 23.2 million Ukrainians, 6.3 million of whom could read and write Ukrainian.[64]

Not only did the majority of mass media, administrative, and judiciary organs adopt Ukrainian as their official language, but so did the whole educational system to a large extent. Thus, many institutions, from elementary schools to technical colleges, conducted classes in Ukrainian. A contemporary later characterized the situation around 1930 in the then-capital Charkov: "If a person did not speak Ukrainian in public, he was suspected of being an enemy of the revolution."[65] In 1926, only 38.3 percent (or 160,000) of Charkov's population were Ukrainian nationals; by 1933, this figure had risen to nearly 50 percent (or 330,000).[66] The Ukrainization of the cities was not only a consequence of migration from Ukrainian villages but also a result of the fact that many Ukrainian nationals who had spoken Russian as their primary language once again began using Ukrainian. After

1926, the number of Ukrainian nationals whose primary language was Russian declined in nearly all the Ukraine's conurbations.[67]

In some cases, establishing the national language required considerable administrative pressure and occurred against the will of those involved. This made nation-building seem somewhat artificial. For example, the Belorussian upper strata were mostly Russified or Polonized. The Belorussians' national identity was only marginal, but the new language policy vastly advanced it in the 1920s. As a result, some have called the Belorussian national consciousness a virtual "gift of the Soviet regime."[68] Many Belorussian teachers and peasants resisted the introduction of Belorussian as the teaching language for general education. Consequently, such people were publicly accused of being Russian chauvinists.[69] In the standardization of the Belorussian written language (which was by no means finished yet) and the creation of neologisms in economics and technology, the Belorussians explicitly borrowed from Western examples and thus contributed to increasing the distance between Belorussian and Russian. The rural population, who spoke a mixed dialect, were maligned as "Muscovites." Although the Belorussian SSR's language law of July 1924 had assigned equal status to the four languages spoken in the republic (Belorussian, Russian, Yiddish, Polish), Belorussian received priority in public life.[70]

Foreign policy considerations also influenced support for the Ukrainian and Belorussian languages and cultures. The Soviets never considered final the forced surrender of the western parts of the Ukraine and Belorussia to Poland in 1920–1921. Soviet linguistic and cultural autonomy stood in distinct contrast to the forced policy of Polonization in the western Ukraine and western Belorussia and was intended to make the Soviets look like the hope for a future national revival. This policy was successful in the 1920s.

Soviet policy in the west was directed at maintaining the unity and identity of the Ukrainian and Belorussian nations across international borders. In Central Asia and Bashkiria, on the other hand, the language policy's goal was to separate supranational communities and to create nations because the Soviets wanted to prevent the development of Pan-Islamic or Pan-Turkish movements. Not unlike Belorussia's, the Bashkir national identity was somewhat artificial because in Bashkiria, the educated strata were heavily Tatarized and had adopted the Tatar language as their written language. In the 1920s, the Bashkir dialect that was the least related to the Tatar language served as the basis for developing a Bashkir written language. With Russian, this dialect was declared the "state language." This legislation was unusual because Lenin is known to have repeatedly expressed fundamental objections to declaring an official state language and, to this very day, nowhere in the USSR is the Russian language called the official state language.[71] The Bashkir "state language's" purpose was to breathe life into a Bashkir national identity distinct from the Tatar national identity—to a certain extent, this strategy probably succeeded.[72] In 1926, 53.6 percent of Bashkirians listed the Bashkir language as their mother tongue; by 1959, this figure had increased to 61.8 percent.[73] In any case, the Soviets halted the Bashkirians' national assimilation process by fighting the theory and practice of "a uniform ethnic group of Tatars and Bashkirians."[74]

An important step was introducing the Latin alphabet, which allegedly created conditions conducive to achieving literacy rapidly in the Soviet East. This introduction affected first of all the sixteen Islamic peoples, who used Arabic script (the Azeri, Tatars, Uzbeks, Tadzhiks, Kazakhs, Chechens, Ingush, and other peoples of the Northern Caucasus). Their written languages were developed to varying degrees, and frequently, only the Islamic clergy used them. Over 90 percent of these nationals could neither read nor write. An extensive secular literature in Arabic script existed only in Azeri (Azeri-Turkic), Tatari, and Uzbeki. Besides Arabic script, the Latin alphabet also replaced the Uigur-Mongolian script that the Buriats and Kalmyks used. The revolutionary enthusiasm prevailing in the 1920s and early 1930s considered the Roman alphabet as the "only revolutionary" script and "the alphabet of the Communist world society."[75] As a result, in about 1930, the Udmurts, Komi, Ossets, and Yakuts, who previously had used the Cyrillic alphabet, not only adopted the Latin alphabet but some journalists and Party activists demanded serious and explicit efforts to change written Russian to the Latin alphabet, so all peoples would use the same alphabet after the allegedly imminent world revolution. On the other hand, the idea that non-Slavic peoples might adopt the Cyrillic alphabet was considered Russian colonialism and nationalism.[76] The Arabic alphabet disappeared from public life within a few years—much faster than originally planned—and a resolution by the USSR's CEC and the Council of People's Commissars, dated August 7, 1929, declared the Latin alphabet the official alphabet.[77] The "Central Committee for the New Turkic Alphabet," founded in Baku in 1927 and renamed the "All-Union Central Committee for the New Alphabet of the CEC of the USSR" in 1930, was relocated to Moscow and directed this law's actual enforcement and the development of the Latin alphabets. The committee worked in the national territories with numerous subcommittees until 1937 and considerably contributed to the development of the non-Russian written languages and orthographies. Under its aegis, scholars compiled dictionaries, wrote grammars, and expanded the vocabulary of languages so they could represent the concepts of the modern world. But, by the mid-1930s, the normative orthography and terminology even of languages like Uzbek were by no means considered complete. On the whole, seventy languages (among them Chinese, by the way) with more than 36 million speakers adopted the Latin alphabet.[78]

Particularly in the Tatar ASSR and Azerbaidzhan, this measure faced considerable resistance. On the one hand, the Islamic clergy and what was left of the old upper social strata were vehemently opposed to it; on the other hand, many national Communists joined this opposition because the Arabic alphabet symbolized for them the national singularity of the revolution in the Soviet East. In addition, after the revolution, a reformed Arabic alphabet had proven to be quite adequate. The Latinization "brought about such an acrimonious and embittered class struggle that it is hardly possible to compare any other social reform in the Soviet East with this one, in respect to the vehemence and extent of the ideological confrontations and discussions."[79] In the Tatar capital Kazan, publishers, newspaper editors, and the People's Commissariat for Education had originally expressed their opposition to Latinization. In 1927, eighty-two leading Tatar intellectuals approached the Party's Central Committee and demanded acknowledgement of the Arabic alphabet as the only official one in the Tatar ASSR.[80]

After the introduction of the Latin alphabet everywhere, a completely new development began to surface after 1937. This development negated all previous accomplishments although, even in February of 1937, Khatskevich, the Secretary of the CEC's Council of Nationalities, publicly cautioned against "jumping from one alphabet to the other."[81] During the next three years, the Soviets forced languages that had just adopted the Latin alphabet to change to the Cyrillic alphabet. A general change of the Party line in language policy accompanied this forced adoption of the Cyrillic alphabet. (This change is discussed in detail under the heading "School Policy and Education" later in this chapter.) Indications that moving closer to the Russian standard would be an essential feature of language development in the future had been discernible since the mid-1930s. Until then, there had been no question that the way to expand the vocabulary of the Turkic languages was to borrow from Arabic or Persian or to include historical Ukrainian words from the time of the Cossacks to enrich the contemporary Ukrainian language. Now, the Soviets denounced such efforts as "local nationalism" or even as "a nationalistic-counterrevolutionary principle" designed exclusively to keep national languages as far away as possible from Russian.[82]

"Constructing"[83] new written languages and expanding old ones was not the business only of institutes and commissions; the publication of books and newspapers in non-Russian languages also furthered the cause as it rapidly increased in the 1920s and 1930s. This increase was not only in total numbers but also in relation to publications in Russian. In 1913, only 7.5 percent of all individual copies of books published in the Russian Empire were written in non-Russian languages. By 1927, this percentage had increased to 14.5 percent and probably reached its climax at 26.6 percent in 1933. In 1938, only 21.2 percent of all copies printed were published in a non-Russian language; by 1956, this percentage had decreased to 17.2 percent and has kept decreasing ever since. During the same period, the total number of books printed increased from 86.7 million copies in 1913 to 462 million copies in

1940 and 1,107.5 million copies in 1956.[84] Newspapers experienced the same development. In 1928, only 10.5 percent of all newspapers (copies per single edition) were published in non-Russian languages. In the following years, this percentage increased considerably and climaxed at 37.5 percent in 1933. In 1938, only 23 percent of the newspapers were published in non-Russian languages, and by 1957 this percentage had decreased to 21.6 percent.[85] Table 2.7 clearly illustrates this development in the Ukraine.

Between 1876 and 1905, the Russian Empire prohibited printing Ukrainian books and periodicals, but even after this period, the supply of Ukrainian printed material was extremely limited. Only in the 1920s, did the distribution of literature in Ukrainian vastly increase. In 1913, only 3.2 percent of the book titles published in the Ukraine were in the Ukrainian language. By 1933, the percentage had increased to 70 percent but decreased to 52 percent in 1938. Similar data are available for newspapers. In 1933, 85.5 percent of the newspapers (titles) were published in Ukrainian. This percentage had decreased to 58.7 percent by 1938.[86]

For the first time in history, speakers of many languages got the opportunity to communicate in print. In 1913, books were published in forty languages; in 1928, in sixty-six languages; and in 1931, in eighty languages. These figures include languages of peoples that did not reside within the territory of the USSR.[87] In 1928, 205 non-Russian newspapers (titles) were printed in forty-seven languages; in 1931, 1620 newspapers in fifty-nine languages; and finally in 1938, 2188 newspapers in sixty-six languages.[88] The non-Russian periodicals developed much more slowly and involved fewer languages. In 1935, towards the end of the growth period for non-Russian publications, only 390 different periodicals (or 19 percent of all titles) were published in a language other than Russian.[89]

Of course, the majority of non-Russian publications — particularly in those languages that were just in the process of acquiring a written form — were elementary in nature. The publications were mainly primers for adults and children, elementary school books, and easy-to-read political propaganda. Even in the Ukraine, Russian still maintained its importance for scholarly publications. Non-political technical literature, including college textbooks, was not available in the new literary languages and only to a very limited extent in the old non-Russian literary languages. A high percentage of political propaganda and school books were translations from the Russian. In 1935, 57 percent of non-Russian titles were translations, the vast majority of them from the Russian.[90]

Despite all these shortcomings, the language policy's achievements in the 1920s and 1930s were praiseworthy. Three of the peoples that today have their own Union Republic (Kirgiz, Turkmen, Tadzhiks) received their written languages only then. The same is true for several titular peoples of Autonomous Republics (Bashkirs, Mordvinians, Buryats, Kalmyks, Ingush,

Nation-Building

Table 2.7: Book and Newspaper Publication in the Ukrainian Language in the Ukraine

	1913	1933	1938
Books			
Title	170	3,629	2,159
Copies (in thousands)	431	66,712	64,377
Newspapers			
Title	19	1,721	922
Daily Circulation (in thousands)	–	4,936	3,806

Source: *Kulturnoe stroitelstvo SSSR* (Moscow, 1940), pp. 205, 220; *Formirovanie sotsialisticheskikh natsii v SSSR* (Moscow, 1962), p. 110. More detailed data are in: Y. Bilinsky, *The Second Republic: The Ukraine After World War II* (New Brunswick, 1964), pp. 175, 178f.

Chechens, Karakalpaks). The introduction of written languages and of publications in national languages was an essential factor in the development of national identities. Communication among the members of individual peoples rose to a new level and simultaneously differentiated each nation from the other.

Although, from the start, the Soviets pushed the nations' presses to make their political messages conform to Soviet guidelines, these presses nevertheless developed a life of their own and by no means limited themselves to translating Pravda or Izvestiia. During the collectivization campaign, most local non-Russian presses (raion newspapers) practiced passive resistance by keeping quiet about this subject. The newspapers not only did not organize "the class struggle in the village" — as the central leadership had ordered them — but they even refused to acknowledge class antagonisms existed in national villages. Instead, they emphasized the national unity of non-Russian villages. The word was that only "about 15 percent" of the non-Russian local press followed the general political Party line.[91] In 1931, a third and fourth grade Tatar school book description of the new kolkhozes went: "Now the rural population is not able to eat meat on a daily basis. They also lack good tea with sugar and white bread."[92] Antireligious Tatar literature amounted to demonstrating that Islam was superior to Christianity.[93]

These examples clearly show that despite many translations, the national press — especially with the peoples with large populations — was by no means conforming nor uniform. Although restricted, the press expressed national interests. Fiction, poetry, and drama played an even more important role in developing national identity because the forms of these arts frequently deviated from Russian-European genres and because they used the historical tradition of the respective national folklore and depicted the national characteristics of countryside and people. In this manner, the creation of new written languages and the expansion of old non-Russian written languages contributed — contrary to this policy's intentions — to strengthening national identity.[94]

School Policy and Education

The development of a non-Russian school system was of utmost importance for the evolution of a modern society — particularly of an intelligentsia that generally embodies the national identity of young nations. Modern nations are not imaginable without a social stratum at their foundations that has enjoyed a more or less intensive formal education from a secular school system. During the 1920s and 1930s, the Soviet Union laid the foundation for such a system in a surprisingly short period by overcoming illiteracy and developing general school systems that used national languages. The introduction of compulsory education began with a CC resolution of July 25, 1930,[95] and the "cultural campaign" against illiteracy during the First Five-Year-Plan.

During the somewhat hysterical planning euphoria of those years, sights were set too high. It proved too much to demand that four years of compulsory elementary education be introduced even in remote rural national territories by the mid-1930s and that general intermediate education (grades 5–7) be established in all territories by 1937, as the Seventeenth Party Congress resolved in 1934. For the most part, the first goal was accomplished only in 1940; by 1958, the second goal had been reached for only 80 percent of the student population.[96]

Nevertheless, the successes in the struggle against illiteracy remain impressive (Table 2.8).

By the mid-1920s, the number of literate people had increased sharply in the Slavic republics and in Georgia and Armenia. In the Islamic republics, and particularly in Central Asia, the percentage of illiterates drastically decreased only in the 1930s. However, the figures convey an overly optimistic picture because they relate to territories and not to peoples. By 1939, the percentage of Russians had considerably increased in all Islamic republics, and the Slavic immigrants were better educated than the natives. The levelling of the peoples' literacy rates could not have progressed as far by 1939 as Table 2.8 might suggest. In 1935, 50 percent of the Kazakhs were still illiterate; the percentage of illiterates among the Uigurs and Dungans of Kazakhstan was even 90 percent.[97] Delayed partly by World War II and the

Nation-Building

Table 2.8: Literacy of the Population Aged 9 to 49 in the Union Republics (in percent)

	1897	1926	1939
RSFSR	29.6	60.9	89.7
Ukraine	27.9[1]	63.6	88.2[2]
Belorussia	32.0	59.7	80.8[2]
Azerbaijan	9.2	28.2	82.8
Georgia	23.6	53.0	89.3
Armenia	9.2	38.7	83.9
Turkmenistan	7.8	14.0	77.7
Uzbekistan	3.6	11.6	78.7
Tadzhikistan	2.3	3.8	82.8
Kazakhstan	8.1	25.2	83.6
Kirgizistan	3.1	16.5	79.8
Total USSR	28.4	56.6	87.4[3]

Source: *Itogi vsesoiuznoi peripisi naseleniia 1959 g. SSSR* (Moscow, 1962), pp. 88f. Data broken down according to nations have only been published based on the 1926 census. Generally, they are more differentiated than data of this table, broken down according to territories.

[1] Excluding Galicia and Northern Bucovina.
[2] Including Western Belorussia and the Western Ukraine, respectively.
[3] Within the borders established on September 17, 1939.

difficult post-war era, the eradication of illiteracy among all peoples was finished only in 1959.

The use of students' mother tongues in the classrooms and the employment of native non-Russian teachers was an important condition for the rapid development of national elementary school systems. Attempts to conduct in Russian the fight against illiteracy were denounced as "pure great-power chauvinism."[98] Already in 1927, most elementary schools in the Union Republics and in many Autonomous Republics were using native languages in the classroom. Before 1917, not a single public school conducted its classes in the Ukrainian or Belorussian language. By 1927, 93.7 percent of the Ukrainian children who attended school in the Ukraine and 90.2 percent of the Belorussian children who attended school in Belorussia attended elementary schools that conducted classes in their native national language. The corresponding percentage of children of the respective titular nation was 98.1 percent in Georgia, 95.5 percent in Azerbaidzhan, 88.3 percent in

Armenia, 96.9 percent in Uzbekistan, 93.5 percent in Turkmenistan, 89.1 percent Kazakhstan, 94.9 percent in Kirgizistan, and 95.7 percent in the Tatar ASSR.[99] On December 30, 1930, the RSFSR's Council of the People's Commissariat for Education passed a resolution requiring elementary schools (grades one through four) to use in the classroom exclusively the native language of the majority of students or the language of the respective titular nation by the school year of 1931–1932; analogous clauses in the resolution required the same results in intermediate schools by the school year of 1932–1933 and in colleges and universities by the school year of 1933–1934.[100] The other Union Republics passed similar resolutions. The elementary schools met their requirements nearly completely—however, no other educational level did. During the school year of 1933–1934, all children who were members of a titular nation attended classes in their native national language in the elementary schools of the Union Republics and Autonomous Republics of the RSFSR. Schools using the native language were available to a considerably smaller extent to the so-called national minorities residing outside their republics (for example, Ukrainians and Belorussians in the RSFSR).[101] In 1930, elementary schools conducted classes in seventy languages of instruction in the RSFSR; in 1935, in eighty languages. In 1932, for example, primers in the languages of several nationalities from the far north and the far east (Nenets, Chukchi, Nanai, Tungus, etc.) were published for the first time.[102] Jumping ahead to more recent developments, I should mention that during the 1970s, only forty-five languages of instruction were still used in the classroom in all the USSR. In Uzbekistan, for example, teachers used twenty-two languages of instruction in the classroom in the 1930s; in the 1960s, the number was only seven.[103]

Of course, this national school system, which appeared out of thin air, had considerable deficiencies that were even more striking than those of the Russian schools. Everywhere textbooks, class materials, and school buildings were lacking. In many instances, teachers conducted classes in farmhouses or buildings without furniture or heating. The main problem, however, was unqualified teachers. Tens of thousands of teachers began work without adequate training and with only several weeks or months of training in intensive courses. In many cases, the teachers at national elementary schools could barely read and write or had only acquired these skills the year before. They were underpaid, and material incentives to improve their qualifications remained minimal. In 1933, not a single teacher in Kabardino-Balkaria had finished at least seventh grade; in 1937, sixty percent of elementary school teachers in the RSFSR's sixteen Autonomous Republics had not graduated from an intermediate school.[104] In this respect, the situation in Central Asia remained particularly unsatisfactory for an even longer time. By 1939, the average percentage of teachers in schools for general education who had not graduated from an intermediate school had decreased to 23 percent within

Nation-Building

the Union; in Central Asia, this percentage still ranged from 55 percent (Kazakhstan) to 81 percent (Kirgizistan) at that time.[105] The consequences were drastic and graphic: A teacher in a Kirgiz aul, for example, wrote to the People's Commissariat for Education in Frunze: "In consideration of the fact that all the Roman letters you had sent have been learned, we request that you send new ones."[106]

This school and nationalities policy took this disadvantage in stride and has been able since the mid-1930s to claim as a great success the fact that the percentage of children attending national schools in the non-Russian Union Republics is almost the same as the percentage in the national population (Table 2.9).

This marked the achievement of an essential goal of korenizatsiia and a resultful investment in the future.

In the RSFSR's Autonomous Republics, the conditions were also considered satisfactory although, in some of these republics (Bashkiria, Kalmykia, Mari ASSR, Udmurt ASSR, and Chechen-Ingush ASSR), the percentage of children attending national schools still was clearly below the percentage of nationals among the total population.[107] On the other hand, the national schools had a distinctly nationalizing or de-Russifying effect in some republics. Table 2.9 shows that a considerable number of children of other nationalities attended Ukrainian or Belorussian schools in the Ukraine or Belorussia. The school system's Ukrainizing function in the Ukraine was particularly evident. In 1932–1933, 88.5 percent of the children in the Ukraine attended Ukrainian schools (as opposed to 4.8 percent attending Russian schools) although only 80 percent of the population were Ukrainians in 1926 (as opposed to 9.2 percent Russians).[108] The Ukraine considered this a great success for nationalization; Moscow, on the other hand, grew progressively suspicious of this development.

The elementary schools were nationalized within a few years. A thorough analysis of the data shows that the successes on the intermediate-school levels and even more so on the college level, were much more modest. Considering the starting conditions — for the most part, no educational system in languages other than Russian existed — it should not come as a surprise that the changing of secondary and college education into other languages took time. The decisive factor was, however, that the enthusiasm with which this policy was pursued abated in the late 1930s. Completely different priorities were at the basis of the new nationalities policy. As a result, attempts to nationalize college education stagnated at that time, or vocational training even went back to using Russian. The non-Russian secondary schools continued to expand only at a slow pace.

By the late 1930s, the national middle schools had developed to varying degrees depending on the respective starting conditions in the individual

Table 2.9: Number of Children Who Attended General Education Schools Conducting Classes in the National Language of the Titular Nation (September 1938)

	Percentage of Students from the Titular Nation	Percentage of the Titular Nation in the Republic's Total Population (1939)
Ukraine	78.2	73.5
Belorussia	93.3	82.9
Azerbaijan	59.8	58.4
Georgia	64.1	61.4
Armenia	77.7	82.8
Turkmenistan	61.5	59.2
Uzbekistan	65.1	64.4
Kazakhstan	32.4	38.2

Sources: *Kulturnoe stroitelstvo SSSR* (Moscow, 1940), pp. 73f.; V.I. Kozlov, *Natsionalnosti SSSR* (Moscow, 1975), pp. 108-112. No data were available for Tadzhikistan and Kirgizistan.

republics and the enthusiasm they invested in nationalizing their educational systems (Table 2.10).

The Slavic Union Republics, Georgia, and Armenia, had established many middle schools that used national languages in the classroom. In the Islamic territories of Central Asia and the Northern Caucasus (such as: Uzbekistan and Chechen-Ingushetia), on the other hand, the development of a system for post-elementary education was still in its initial stages. In the existing middle schools — particularly in grades 8–10 — Russian students were in the majority, and the language of instruction was Russian. The establishment of middle schools teaching in the vernacular in the Autonomous Republics in the Middle Volga Area had progressed surprisingly far. Although a considerable percentage of this region's population was Russian, the native languages were nearly as important in the middle schools as in the elementary schools. This means that in the post-elementary schools, the nationals received instruction in their national language, not in Russian. In the Tatar ASSR, for example, the educational opportunities available to Tatar children were as good as those available to Russian children. Of 113,000 students attending middle schools (grades 5–10 in 1935–1936), 54,000 were Tatar nationals; this number roughly corresponded with the percentage of Tatars in the total population. With but few exceptions, they attended middle schools with instruction in the vernacular. In Kirgizistan, the situation

Table 2.10: Languages of Instruction at Elementary and Middle Schools 1938/39 (selected[1] Union Republics and ASSRs)

	Number of Students	enrolled in grades		
		1-4	5-7	8-10
Ukraine	5,251,000	3,239,000	1,695,000	317,000
Language of Instruction				
Ukrainian (in percent)	78	79	77	76
Russian (in percent)	14[2]	14	14	15
Belorussia	1,021,000	684,000	287,000	51,000
Belorussian	93	94	94	88
Russian	7	6	6	12
Georgia	691,000	444,000	195,000	52,000
Georgian	64	62	67	69
Russian	9	9	9	10
Uzbekistan	1,004,000	811,000	178,000	15,000
Uzbek	65	67	53	25
Russian	10	8	17	51
Kazakhstan	979,000	708,000	242,000	28,000
Kazakh	32	35	27	20
Russian	52	50	56	71
ASSR of Volga Germans	114,000	84,000	27,000	3,000
German	62	64	56	42
Russian	30	27	36	45
Mordvinian ASSR	224,000	151,000	61,000	11,000
Mordvinian	34	35	34	34
Russian	61	61	61	64
Tatar ASSR	549,000	375,000	155,000	19,000
Tatar	47	47	47	36
Russian	44	44	44	53

(continued)

Table 2.10 (continued)

	Number of Students	enrolled in grades		
		1-4	5-7	8-10
Udmurt ASSR	209,000	146,000	57,000	6,000
Udmurt	19	23	11	14
Russian	57	57	54	74
Checheno-Ingush ASSR	118,000	94,000	22,000	3,000
Chechen	19	23	5	0.7
Russian	25	19	42	72

Source: *Kulturnoe stroitelstvo SSSR* (Moscow, 1940), pp. 73-77.

[1] By selecting these Union Republics and ASSRs, I wanted to document that the status quo of the respective educational systems was not uniform.
[2] The percentages do not add up to 100 percent because I did not include in this table schools that provide instruction in more than one language or in language other than the language of the titular nation and Russian.

was utterly different. Of the 48,000 students attending middle schools (grades 5–7 in 1935–1936), only 2 percent were Kirgiz nationals.[109] In Kirgizia, as in all Central Asia and the Northern Caucasus, comprehensive integration of non-Russian nationals into the middle schools succeeded only after World War II.

The ambitious plans of the 1920s had also envisioned the introduction of as many languages as possible into the classrooms of vocational schools and colleges – an essential prerequisite for developing a widespread non-Russian intelligentsia. Of course, nobody thought of giving lectures at universities in Chukchi, but the titular nations of the Union Republics and generally also the Autonomous Republics were to receive technical schools (*tekhnikumy*) and, in many cases, also colleges (*vuzy*) that were to teach in the vernacular. Initially, this plan failed because of lacking resources, and later, after the necessary resources were available, the political will to execute the plan had vanished. Nevertheless, in the twenty years following the 1917 revolution, the Soviets made considerable efforts under unfavorable conditions to integrate non-Russians into technical schools and colleges. Two sets of measures in particular were to serve this purpose: one was the partial or complete change in educational institutions to the students' native language and the other was preferential enrollment of nationals in Russian technical schools and colleges. Based on a quota system, educational facilities reserved a certain number of slots for non-Russian nationals in their own territories and in Russia. The standards for entrance examinations were lowered for such applicants. The territorial Soviet authorities, on the one hand, and the all-union authorities that gradually became responsible for the technical and industrial colleges after 1928 were in charge of determining the quotas. However, a quota plan for the whole USSR was never accomplished. Nevertheless, on the basis of these quotas tens of thousands of non-Russians were educated preferentially — particularly in the technical schools.

For the academic year 1930–1931, the Udmurt Regional Executive Committee, for example, determined that 60 percent of the freshmen at technical schools (*technikumy*) for engineering, 75 percent at *technikumy* for agriculture, and 85 percent at *technikumy* for the social sciences and cultural professions were Udmurts. Actually, the percentage was considerably lower, but without quotas, local nationals would have been excluded altogether.[110] For 1932, the colleges (*vusy*) belonging to the All-Union People's Commissariats had reserved 3,857 slots (or 4.9 percent) for freshmen from culturally backward peoples (for 1933, the figure was 4,962 or 11.7 percent).[111] Not all slots were filled — partly because of a shortage of suitable candidates, partly because the colleges refused to integrate ill-prepared students with an insufficient command of the Russian language. Anyway, in 1933, 10,700 Kazakhs, 10,200 Belorussians, 3,200 Kirgiz, more than 5,000 Armenians, and 1,300 Georgians were enrolled at the colleges and technical schools of the RSFSR.[112]

The Soviets suddenly abandoned the quota system in 1934 despite the CEC's Presidium resolution of March 1933. This resolution explicitly declared the quota system "necessary." The abandonment signalled a considerable change in political course.[113] The consequence was a decline in the percentage of national students — particularly in the Soviet East. In 1935, of 1,000 freshmen at the Tashkent Industrial Institute, only ninety-four were Asians. At the Central Asian State University of Tashkent (founded in 1920 and the leading eastern university), 6.7 percent of the students were natives in 1927, thirty-eight percent in 1935, and 32.5 percent in 1940. Similarly, the percentage of Tatar students at the colleges in the Tatar ASSR declined from 26.3 percent in 1934 to 17.2 percent in 1939.[114]

Even more important than reserving slots for underdeveloped peoples was the fact that technical and college education began conducting classes in native languages. Obviously, this change faced enormous difficulties, particularly in the East. Some of the Russian professors's lectures required interpretation into the native language. Only Armenia and Georgia managed to nationalize their technical schools and colleges nearly completely in the 1930s — both in respect to the language used in classes as well as in respect to the national origin of the student-body. In Armenia, the percentage of college, technical school, and workers' faculty students who were from the titular nation was ninety-five percent in 1928 and ninety-one percent in 1935; in Georgia, the corresponding figures were eighty-two percent and seventy-seven percent.[115] During this time, the Armenian and Georgian educational systems achieved a level of superiority that makes Armenians and Georgians the best-educated peoples after the Jews — and ahead of the Russians.[116] The reason was that besides having better starting conditions, at the heyday of korenizatsiia, Armenia and Georgia had introduced their national languages into every part of their educational systems.

The Ukraine was also very successful in this area. The percentage of college students taught in the Ukrainian language increased from 12.9 percent in 1925 to 27.4 percent in 1929. Analogously, the percentage of students with classes taught in Russian decreased from 28.1 percent to 8.4 percent. The majority of students, however, continued to attend classes conducted in either language.[117] Although no exact figures exist for later periods, it seems safe to assume that during the early 1930s, the Ukrainization of the colleges continued because during those years, vocational schools and factories conducted a considerable part of technical and industrial training in the Ukrainian language. The percentage of Ukrainian college students in their republic developed as follows: The percentage increased from 53 percent in 1928–1929 to 56 percent in 1932–1933 and decreased again to 54 percent in 1938 and 52 percent in 1946. In 1928–1929, 61 percent of technical-school students was Ukrainian; by 1932–1933, this figure had increased to 68 percent.[118] The introduction and later abandonment of the Ukrainian language in the classroom caused this fluctuation in the number of non-Russian nationals.

Among the Islamic peoples, the expansion of the Tatar intelligentsia progressed particularly far. However, among Russia's Islamic peoples, the Tatars had been the most modernized even before 1917. In 1911, 375 Tatar books (2.2 million copies) were published in Kazan. However, of the 4,000 students attending Kazan's colleges, only forty were Tatars in 1913; 2,200 students of 9,000 were Tatars in 1934.[119] The percentage of Tatars among college students in the Tatar republic increased from 14.6 percent in 1927–1928 to 26.3 percent in 1934–1935; at the technical schools, 42 percent of the students were already Tatars in 1934–1935 — which was nearly the percentage of Tatars among the total population.[120] The prime reason for this development is the fact that many technical schools adopted the Tatar language (at least to some extent) in the classroom. By the mid-1930s, Kazan's teacher college and the German teacher college in Engels were the only facilities of their kind that taught in a non-Russian language in the RSFSR.[121]

Efforts to nationalize vocational education were most successful in the training of teachers for elementary and intermediate schools at teacher-training schools (*pedtekhnikumy*). This claim is true for all non-Russian

Nation-Building 57

peoples and has determined the structure of the national intelligentsias until today. The introduction of compulsory education and the development of national elementary-school systems over a very short period produced an enormous demand for non-Russian teachers who could only be trained in their native languages because they were not proficient in Russian. A great number of teacher-training schools founded in the 1920s and early 1930s conducted classes in the students' native language from the beginning. As a result, the percentage of students of education among the non-Russian students was unproportionately high — and, less dramatically, has remained so until today. In the technical, agricultural, and economic fields, non-Russians remained vastly underrepresented. In 1939, 34.3 percent of all Soviet college students were training to be teachers. With the exception of the Ukraine (31.5 percent), this percentage was higher in all Union Republics and ranged between 40 percent (Azerbaidzhan) and 86 percent (Tadzhikistan). Similar data also applied to the students attending technical schools.[122]

Many teacher-training schools in the Union Republics and the Autonomous Republics of the Volga region taught in the national languages. Nationalization of agricultural education did not progress as quickly. The training of non-Russian agriculturists was particularly important because around 1930, with few exceptions (such as Jews and Armenians) about 90 percent of the non-Russian peoples did not live in cities (in 1926, 79 percent of the Russians lived in rural communities).[123] The Ukraine, Georgia, and Armenia successfully promoted both a native student population and national language in their technical schools and colleges of agriculture. Other peoples, however, were not so successful at making education part of their own culture. In 1935, only 20 percent of the students at colleges of agriculture in Samarkand and Tashkent were nationals; in Ashkhabad only 10 percent.[124] Of course, the reason was that all colleges of agriculture — except those in the Ukraine, Georgia, and Armenia — taught in Russian. On the technical-school level, some institutions adopted national languages in the classroom, but these schools could not train enough agricultural specialists for the national territories. As a result, Russians held more and more specialist positions. The introduction of non-Russian languages in technical schools and colleges (a process that once had been publicized with much aplomb) came to a halt in the late 1930s. Pertinent Party and Soviet resolutions were never published. One can conclude that educational facilities that had not adopted a national langauge by then continue today to adhere to Russian. The opposite direction moving from local national language to Russian — has been a very common course since the late 1950s.

The composition of the student-bodies is an indicator of the success of korenizatsiia: in 1927, 43.92 percent of college students were non-Russians; in 1935, 43.73 percent. Correlating these figures with the changes in the total population shows that the percentage of non-Russian students had increased. In 1926, 47.09 percent of the USSR's total population were non-Russians. By 1939, this percentage had decreased to 41.61 percent. In other words, the disproportionate number of Russians began to decline in the 1920s and 1930s. Later, the tendency reversed: Although in 1959 45.35 percent of the total population were non-Russians, only 38.23 percent of college students were non-Russians in 1960.[125] Clearly, non-Russian students were proportionately better represented in the Soviet student-body in 1930 than in 1960. Of course, the numbers of the various non-Russian nationals in colleges varied in the 1930s—as the previous discussions have shown.

Proportionately more Georgians, Armenians, and—most of all—Jews (in 1935, 13.27 percent of all college students were Jewish although only 1.78 percent of the total population was Jewish) attended college than Russians. At that time, the peoples of Central Asia were only beginning to attend colleges.

National Minorities

"National minorities" is an ambiguous term, and not only in the USSR. In the modern Russian vernacular, this term more or less means "non-Russians within the territory of the USSR." In the 1920s and 1930s, however, anyone who was not from a territory's titular nation was called a "national minority." For example, Russians in Kazakhstan or Belorussia were considered a national minority. After the "victory of socialism in the USSR" in the late 1930s, such a disrespectful classification of nationals of the imperial nation was no longer acceptable, and this classification actually had become too unrealistic.

In the twenty years after the 1917 revolution, the Soviets made considerable efforts (including monetary efforts) to protect and develop the linguistic and cultural rights of minorities living outside their own national territories and of those who did not have their own national republics or regions (for example, Jews, Poles, Finns). After all in 1926, nearly 8 million Ukrainians lived outside the Ukraine, and more than 700,000 Belorussians resided outside their own republic. The total number of national minorities who lived outside their territories and minorities without national republics or regions amounted to 20 million people.

The national raions and village soviets established in 1926 were to be the administrative tools to serve the administrative and educational needs of these minorities. By the mid-1930s, there were 250 national raions (about 10 percent of all raions) and 5,300 national village soviets; about half of these institutions were on the territory of the RSFSR. These raion and village soviets for nationals living in the diaspora existed in addition to the national raions and soviets of the titular nations within the territories and must not be confused with the latter.[126] In 1930, for example, there were twenty-eight national raions in the Ukraine (nine Russian, eight German, four Bulgarian, three Greek, three Jewish, one Polish). In 1934, ninety-three national village soviets existed in Belorussia (forty Polish, twenty-four Jewish, fifteen Russian, five Latvian, six Ukrainian, two German, one Lithuanian).[127] Protecting the Ukrainian minority in the Northern Caucasus (which had 3.1 million Ukrainian inhabitants in 1926, representing 60 percent of the population in some places) was the main issue of a resolution by the Council of Nationalities, endorsed by the Presidium of the USSR's CEC on February 12, 1930. The resolution declared that the area (*krai*) had not been sufficiently Ukrainized by that time. The Council of Nationalities Soviet resolved to establish Ukrainian cultural centers, theaters, and libraries. In addition, the classes that were taught in Ukrainian in the area's middle schools and colleges were to be encouraged. A few months earlier (in its resolution of December 8, 1929), the Council of Nationalities had made a similar decision in respect to the educational and cultural services to be provided for Ukrainians and Belorussians living in Western Siberia; nearly a million Ukrainians lived there.[128] These resolutions are memorable because only a short time later, the mostly rural Ukrainian population of these areas became the main target of national assimilation. In the Northern Caucasus, the number of people calling themselves Ukrainian decreased from 3.1 million in 1926 to 170,000 in 1959.[129] Although many Ukrainians were unsure of their national affiliation as early as the 1920s (42.9 percent of them considered Russian their native language in 1926), the important fact is that in its early years, Soviet nationalities policy's mandate was to stabilize the Ukrainian nationality in the Northern Caucasus and not to assimilate it.

Apparently, the national facilities for the Finno-Ugrian-speaking minorities in the Leningrad Region were particularly well established. In 1933, about 600,000 non-Russians (among them 130,000 Finns, 75,000 Estonians, 26,000 Veps), or 9 percent of the total population, lived in the Region. In the Leningrad Region, four national raions existed (two for Finns, one for Lapps and Izhoria, one for Veps). The two Finnish raions had adopted Finnish as the official language, the other raions had retained Russian. From a cultural and economic perspective, the Finns and Estonians in Ingermanland were superior to the Russians and had an adequate number of schools and a well developed literary tradition. In the Leningrad Region, a total of 284 Finnish, ninety Estonian, fifty-five Veps, twenty-three Izhoria, twenty-one Latvian, and seventeen German elementary schools existed. In the city of Leningrad, five pedagogical technical schools (Finnish, Estonian, Latvian, Polish, and German) trained elementary school teachers. Here, like everywhere else, even the kolkhozes were organized by nation. In January 1933, there were 434 Finnish, 129 Estonian, ninety-eight Veps, twenty-six Latvian, twenty-four Izhorian, twenty-two German, twenty Karelian, and even two Jewish kolkhozes.[130] Of course, these agricultural-production cooperatives were not completely homogenous from a national perspective, but members who were natives of the titular nationality were in the majority.

After Finnish peasants suffered heavy losses from collectivization, the Soviets deported about 27,000 from the villages along the Finnish and Estonian border in 1935 and 1936 — non-Russians were now considered an unreliable border population.[131] This deportation marks the profound change in the nationalities policy, as does the fact that the Soviets did not accommodate culturally and linguistically the large number of non-Russians (mostly Tatars, Bashkirs, and Belorussians) who migrated to Leningrad during the first two Five-Year-Plans. The old, mostly rural of the Finno-Ugrian minorities had been treated much better.

Not everywhere did the minorities achieve as high a level of national consolidation as did the Finnish villages in Ingermanland. During the mid-1930s, for example, the Kuibyshev Region (about 25 percent of this region's population consisted of non-Russians) contained fifteen national raions (seven Mordvinian, three Tatar, four Chuvash, and one German). But thirty-four (of 177) Mordvinian village soviets had Russian chairmen, and many Mordvinian schools taught classes in Russian.[132] Non-Russian languages as the official languages in these national village soviets were out of the question. Calling these village soviets national was often more name and claim than reality.

The Jews were the most important national minority — both in their numbers and in their presence in all Soviet elites.[133] During the two decades following the 1917 revolution, two developmental processes took place simultaneously. On the one hand, Jewish linguistic, cultural, and educational institutions flourished even though (as with all other nations) on condition that they follow the communist line; on the other hand, Jewish acculturation progressed rapidly. This linguistic and cultural Russification was one reason for the Jews' exceptionally fast upward mobility in society, which culminated during the 1930s. The Jews took advantage of the huge demand for specialists in all fields, which resulted from forced industrialization. They became the best educated people, and proportionately more Jews than any other people were among the elites. The Jews are maintaining this position in many areas even today although they have clearly been losing ground. In the 1930s, although Jews made up only 2 percent of the population, 16 percent of doctors and teachers, 14 percent of students, 13 percent of employees in scholarly institutes, and more than 4 percent of Party members were Jewish.[134] The upward mobility of the Jews within Soviet society corresponded with their migration eastward to the major Russian cities, primarily Moscow and Leningrad. The Jews were and have remained the most urbanized people in the USSR; the percentage of urban Jews increased from 53 percent in 1926 to 77 percent in 1959.[135]

Success of great efforts in the 1930s to settle Jews as peasants was limited. In the Ukraine, three national Jewish raions provided sufficient land for Jews willing to settle, and on the Crimean peninsula two raions served the same purpose. From 1924 until 1938, the "CEC's Committee for Rural Settlement of Working Jews" and its auxiliary organ the "Society for Rural Settlement of Working Jews," existed.[136] Settlement did not meet expectations. Probably, no more than 10,000 families settled in the five Jewish raions.[137] Also, the proclamation in 1934 of the Jewish Autonomous Region Birobidzhan, at the remote Amur River proved a failure. This region was meant to be a sort of Soviet Zion. While the Soviet press was denouncing British efforts "to create a bogus Jewish autonomy in Palestine" as "not lasting and artificial," the Soviets were not only proclaiming "Jewish statehood" within the USSR but were also declaring that the "national Jewish minority" had become a "nation."[138] However, this ideological flight of fancy (which contradicted Lenin's and Stalin's unambiguous statements that Russian Jews were not a nation) did not survive the purge of 1937–1938. Despite recruitment campaigns, the Jews remained a minority in Birobidzhan; in 1936, 19,000 of its 64,000 inhabitants were Jewish. After World War II, the Jewish portion of the population drastically declined both in proportion and in absolute numbers—in 1979 there were 10,000 Jews among 189,000 inhabitants.[139]

1937 marked a clear turning point in the policy towards national minorities. The Soviets dissolved most of the national raions, schools, courts, and village soviets between 1937 and 1939. In March 1939, for example, the seven German raions in the Ukraine were suspended.[140] Several dozen national raions for the peoples of the Far North with small populations survived and apparently existed until the early 1950s.[141] The dismantling of institutions within Soviet organs that served minorities in the diaspora had already begun in the early 1930s. In 1934, the "Sector for National Minorities" at Moscow's Regional Soviet and the "Commission for Working Among National Minorities" at the Moscow City Soviet were suspended.[142] This was not an isolated incident. National minorities were no longer considered as groups that needed protection and development because of their weakness. Instead from the point of view of the new Party line they became suitable objectives for national assimilation. This turn of events primarily affected the Ukrainians in the RSFSR, the Germans in the Ukraine, and the Finns in Ingermanland. But also many schools that taught in Yiddish closed in the late 1930s, and most of the Jewish newspapers and journals had to stop publishing. Few of the eighteen permanent Jewish theaters existing in 1934 survived into World War II.[143]

Notes

1. Cf. the map in: R.C. Tucker, *Stalin as Revolutionary: 1879-1929* (New York, 1973), p. 189.
2. Letter to S.G. Shaumian, November 23/December 6, 1913, in: Lenin, *Werke*, vol. 19, p. 496.
3. "Thesen zur nationalen Frage" (1913), in Lenin, *Werke*, vol. 19, p. 234.
4. "Über das Selbstbestimmungsrecht der Nationen" (1914), in: Lenin, *Werke*, vol. 20, p. 413.
5. "Resolution zur nationalen Frage" (1913), in: Lenin, *Werke*, vol. 19, p. 420.
6. Stalin, *Werke*, vol. 3, pp. 48f.
7. *Pravda*, October 10, 1920, in: Stalin, *Werke*, vol. 4, p. 311.
8. Ibid., p. 349.
9. A. Bennigsen, "Muslim Guerilla Warfare in the Caucasus: 1918-1928," in: *Central Asian Survey* II, 1/1983, p. 45-56.
10. A. Bennigsen/Ch. Lemercier-Quelquejay, *Islam in the Soviet Union* (New York/Washington, 1967), pp. 140, 146; H. Bräker, "Kommunismus und Weltreligionen Asiens," vol. I, 1, *Kommunismus und Islam* (Tübingen, 1969), pp. 95ff.
11. M. Broxup, "The Basmachi," in: *Central Asian Survey* II, 1/1983, pp. 57-81; R. Lorenz, "Die Basmatschen-Bewegung," in: A. Kappeler/G. Simon/G. Brunner (eds.) *Die Muslime in der Sowjetunion und in Yugoslawien* (Cologne, 1989), pp. 235-256.
12. Stalin, *Werke*, vol. 3, p. 28. Stalin explicitly emphasizes the fact that after the October Revolution, Lenin and he were split over the nationalities question. In contrast, Soviet historiography was, until the era of *perestroika*, interested in smoothing out these differences (cf. B. Meissner, "Entstehung, Fortentwicklung und ideologische Grundlagen des sowjetischen Bundesstaates," in: *Bundesstaat und Nationalitätenrecht in der Sowjetunion*, F.-Ch. Schroeder/B. Meissner (eds.) (Berlin, 1974), pp. 14-16, including detailed references to Soviet literature).
13. Stalin's letter of June 12, 1920 to Lenin, only in: V. I. Lenin, *Sochineniia*, 3rd edition, vol. XXV, 1931, p. 624.
14. Lenin's notes from December 1922 and January 1923 provide essential information on this conflict. They were first published in the journal *Kommunist*, 9/1956; also in: Lenin, *Werke*, vol. 36, pp. 577-596. Detailed presentation: Tucker, *Stalin as Revolutionary*, pp. 239-278. cf. Meissner, *Entstehung, Fortentwicklung und ideologische Grundlagen des sowjetischen Bundesstaates*, pp. 21-44; G. Stökl, "Die Entstehung der Sowjetunion und die nationale Frage," in: *Staatsgründungen und Nationalitätenprinzip*, Th. Schieder/P. Alter (eds.) (Munich, 1974), pp. 79-81.

15. Letter to Lenin and the members of the Politburo of September 27, 1922. This letter was first published in its entirety in: *Osteuropa*, XXII, 1972, pp. A 808–A 810.

16. J. Arnold, *Die nationalen Gebietseinheiten der Sowjetunion* (Cologne, 1973), pp. 15–35.

17. W. Connor ("Nation-building or Nation-Destroying?" in: *World Politics*, XXIV, 1972, pp. 319–355) is right in accusing the U.S. school of political development (Almond, Pye, etc.) of speaking of nation-building but meaning state-building. In connection with the USSR, the issue is clearly the ethnic factor.

18. Since the early 1920s, this self-contradictory term has been appearing in Party documents and Soviet publications when the USSR referred to itself. In 1977, this term was included in the constitution.

19. Stalin, *Werke*, vol. 2, p. 272.

20. The 1919 Party program, in: B. Meissner, *Das Parteiprogramm der KPdSU. 1903–1961* (Cologne, 1962), p. 128.

21. Lenin, *Werke*, vol. 22, p. 148.

22. *Pravda*, October 10, 1920, in: Stalin, *Werke*, vol. 4, p. 315. A similar formulation already appeared in an article Stalin had written for *Pravda* on April 9, 1918, in: ibid., p. 66.

23. *KPSS v rezoliutsiiakh i resheniiakh sezdov, konferentsii i plenumov CK*, vol. 2 (Moscow, 1970), p. 252.

24. Ibid., pp. 433–443.

25. *Dvenadtsatyi sezd RKP (b), 17–25 aprelia 1923 goda. Stenograficheskii otchet*, (Moscow, 1968), particularly pp. 201ff., 479ff., 567ff., 649ff.

26. Ibid., pp. 497, 694.

27. Lenin's notes from December 1922 on the right to secede, which is guaranteed in the constitution, express the same concern (Lenin, *Werke*, vol. 36, p. 591). Because Lenin's illness kept him from attending the Party Congress, these notes were read to the individual delegations of the Twelfth Party Congress in closed sessions. Publication was prevented until 1956.

28. *Dvenadtsatyi sezd*, pp. 613, 650.

29. For example, in the resolutions on the nationalities question at the Tenth and Twelfth Party Congresses (*KPSS v rezoliutsiiakh i resheniiakh*, vol. 2, pp. 253f., 437f.).

30. I. Ulianov, "Promyshlennoie razvitiie natsionalnykh respublik i oblastei," in: *RN*, 10–11/1932, pp. 69f.

31. *Dostizheniia sovetskoi vlasti za 40 let v tsifrakh*, (Moscow, 1957), p. 50; S.L. Seniavskii/V.B. Telpukhovskii, *Rabochii klass, 1938–1965 gg.*, (Moscow, 1971), p. 299.

32. *RN*, 10–11/1931, pp. 152f.

33. E. Popova, "Natsionalnyi proletariat Kryma," in: *RN* 8/1932, pp. 86f.

34. K. Trifonov, "Borba za sozdaniie rabochikh natsionalnikh kadrov na Srednei Volge," in: *RN*, 3/1933, pp. 92–94; A. Fedotova, "Sotsialisticheskoie stroitelstvo v natsavtonomiiakh, natsraionakh Gorkovskogo kraia," in: *RN*, 4/1933, p. 85.

35. Modern Soviet studies are also unsatisfactory: *Razvitiie rabochego klassa v natsionalnykh respublikakh SSSR*, (Moscow, 1962); *Formirovaniie i razvitiie mnogonatsionalnogo rabochego klassa SSSR v period stroitelstva sotsializma (1921–1937 gg.)*, (Tiflis, 1980).

36. Stalin, *Werke*, vol. 5, p. 42.

37. B. Kravshenko, "The Impact of Industrialization on the Social Structure of Ukraine," in: *Canadian Slavonic Papers*, XXII, 1980, pp. 340, 350.

38. *Itogi razresheniia natsionalnogo voprosa*, p. 13.

39. Rigby, *Communist Party Membership*, p. 366.

40. Bennigsen/Lemercier-Quelquejay, *Islam*, p. 136.

41. A. Bogdanov, "Chistka partii i zadachi partorganizatsii natsionalnykh respublik," in: *RN*, 2/1933, p. 28; N.A. Barsukov/A.R. Shaidullin/I.N. Iudin, "KPSS – partiia internatsionalnaia," in: *VI KPSS*, 7/1966, p. 13.

42. See Appendix Table A.15.

43. N. Dubrovskii, "Chistka eshche bolshe ukrepit partorganizatsii natsionalnykh raionov," in: *RN*, 10/1934, p. 4; Rigby, *Communist Party Membership*, pp. 204, 370.

44. Rigby, ibid., pp. 375f.; M. Fainsod, *Wie Ruland regiert wird* (Cologne/Berlin, 1965), p. 308.

45. Lewis/Rowland/Clem, *Nationality and Population Change in Russia*, p. 136.

46. S. Bialer, "Soviet Political Elite," Ph.D. Columbia University 1966, p. 217; cf. p. 188 on the CC's national makeup from 1939 to 1961.

47. S. Dimanshtein, "Rekonstruktivnyi period i rabota sredi natsionalnostei SSSR," in: *RN*, 1/1930, p. 12; Z. Ostrovskii, "K itogam raboty Otdela Natsionalnostei VCIK," in: *RN*, 5/1932, pp. 81–85; S. Abramov, "Organizatsionnye formy rukovodstva raboty sredi natsmen," in: *RN*, 6/1935, pp. 51–55.

48. P. Rysakov, "Praktika shovinizma i mestnogo natsionalizma," in: *RN*, 8–9/1930, p. 29. This is only one resolution among many similar resolutions that the leaders of the Uzbek Party and state made between 1928 and 1932; cf. also, Fierman, *Nationalism, Language Planning*, pp. 192–221.

49. S. Akopov, "K voprosu o uzbekizatsii apparata i sozdanii mestnykh rabochikh kadrov promyshlennosti Uzbekistana," in: *RN*, 12/1931, pp. 22f.

50. S. Baadrev, "Novaia respublika," in: *RN*, 2/1935, pp. 48, 53.

51. Akopov, ibid., pp. 23–27; Fierman, *Nationalism, Language Planning*, p. 227.

52. V. Velmin, "Komsomol v borbe za vospitanie natsionalnykh kadrov," in: *RN*, 3/1932, p. 22.

53. S. Kossior/P. Postyshev, *Der bolschewistische Sieg in der Ukraine* (Moscow/Leningrad, 1934), p. 29.
54. B. Rodnevich, "Korenizatsiia apparata v avtonomiiakh i raionakh natsmeshinstv RSFSR," in: *RN*, 12/1931, p. 15.
55. *RN*, 1/1931, p. 109.
56. *RN*, 2/1936, p. 73.
57. A. Matveev, "Sovetskoe stroitelstvo v Chuvashii," in: *RN*, 3/1930, p. 85.
58. No detailed statistical data on this issue are available. On the above-average degree of korenizatsiia among the executive members, cf. Rodnevich (footnote 54), p. 16.
59. Rodnevich (footnote 54), pp. 13–16.
60. E. Petrova, "Korenizatsiia organov iustitsii," in: *RN*, 3/1933, pp. 65–68.
61. F. Dombrovskii, "Korenizatsiia gosapparata v Udmurtskoi respublike," in: *RN*, 2/1936, pp. 35f.
62. *RN*, 2/1936, pp. 73f.
63. *RN*, 6/1936, pp. 39–43; 8/1936, pp. 75f.
64. G. Liber, "Language, Literacy, and Book Publishing in the Ukrainian SSR, 1923–1928," in: *Slavic Review*, 41 (1982), p. 685.
65. V.A. Kravchenko, *Ich wählte die Freiheit* (Zurich, 1947), p. 81.
66. Kossior/Postychev, *Der bolschewistische Sieg in der Ukraine*, p. 17.
67. J.A. Armstrong, "The Ethnic Scene in the Soviet Union," in: *Ethnic Minorities in the Soviet Union*, E. Goldhagen (ed.), (New York, 1968), pp. 17, 40.
68. V. Aspaturian, "The Non-Russian Nationalities," in: *Prospects for Soviet Society*, A. Kassof (ed.) (New York, 1968), p. 150.
69. P. Rysakov, "Praktika shovinizma i mestnogo natsionalizma," in: *RN*, 8/9/1930, p. 27; S. Dimanshtein, "Ideologicheskaia borba v natsionalnom voprose," in: *RN*, 3/1930, p. 8.
70. N.P. Vakar, *Belorussia: The Making of a Nation* (Cambridge, Mass., 1956), pp. 137–154; J.S. Lubachko, *Belorussia Under Soviet Rule 1917–1957* (Lexington, Ky., 1972), pp. 62–92.
71. Only in a few other republics was the titular language officially considered the state language for example in Georgia and Daghestan (Azeri-Turkish). Cf. A. Sheehy, "The National Languages and the New Constitutions of the Transcaucasian Republics," *Radio Liberty Research*, 97/78, May 3, 1978.
72. Sh. Tipeev/N. Emaletdinov, "Protiv izvrashchenii leninskoi natsionalnoi politiki v Bashkirii," in: *RN*, 8/31, pp. 20–28; A. Tagirov, "Voprosy korenizatsii v Bashkirii," in: *RN*, 5/1932, pp. 95–99.
73. Census data.
74. A. Kovalev, "Nekotorie svoeobraziia borby na dva fronta v Bashkirii," in: *RN*, 12/1933, p. 35.

75. L.M. Zak/M.I. Isaev, "Problemy pismennosti narodov SSSR v kulturnoi revoliutsii," in: *VI* 2/1966, p. 11. Cf. A. Lunacharskii, "Latinizatsiia russkoi pismennosti," in: *Kultura i pismennost vostoka*, 1930, pp. 20–26.

76. I. Chansuvarov, *Latinizatsiia — orudie leninskoi natsionalnoi politiki* (Moscow, 1932); cf. S. Dimanshtein's extensive review in: *RN*, 6/1934, pp. 96–103.

77. Reprinted in: *Bratskoe sodruzhestvo narodov SSSR: 1922–1936 gg. Sbornik dokumentov i materialov*, I.I. Groshev (ed.) (Moscow, 1964), pp. 383–385.

78. On Latinization: M.I. Isayev, *National Languages in the USSR: Problems and Solutions* (Moscow, 1977), pp. 236–254; M.I. Isaev, *Iazykovoe stroitelstvo v SSSR: Protsessy sozdaniia pismennostei narodov SSSR* (Moscow, 1979).

79. I. Aliev, "Pobeda latinizatsii — luchshaia pamiat o tov. Agamaly-ogly," in: *RN*, 7/1930, pp. 23f.

80. K. Chairov, "Pobednyi put latinizatsii v Tatarii," in: *RN*, 7/1933, pp. 66–70.

81. "VII plenum VTsKNA," in: *RN*, 3/1937, p. 65.

82. I. Trainin, "Voprosy natsionalnoi kultury," in: *RN*, 1/1934, pp. 39ff.; D. Korkmasov, "Ot alfavita k literaturnomu iazyku," in: *RN*, 9/1935, p. 38; S. Dimanshtein, "K 15-letiiu Kazakhstana," in: *RN*, 10/1935, p. 36.

83. In Russian: iazykovoe stroitelstvo.

84. *Kulturnoe stroitelstvo SSSR. Statisticheskii sbornik* (Moscow, 1940), pp. 206f.; *Pechat SSSR v 1956 i 1957 gg.* (Moscow, 1958), p. 50; K.S. Rychlevskii, "Natsionalnaia kniga v SSSR za 15 let," in: *RN*, 10/11/1932, p. 93; A.T., "Natsionalnaia pechat i poligrafiia," in: *RN*, 2/1935, p. 16.

85. Cf. previous note. *Itogi razresheniia natsionalnogo voprosa*, p. 215. I. Trainin, "Voprosy natsionalnoi kultury," in: *RN*, 1/1934, p. 42.

86. *Kulturnoe stroitelstvo* (1940), pp. 205, 220. For detailed information on book publishing in the 1920s, cf. G. Liber, "Language, Literacy, and Book Publishing in the Ukrainian SSR, 1923–1928," in: *Slavic Review* 41 (1982), pp. 673–685.

87. *Itogi razresheniia*, pp. 206–208; B. Rosal, "Itogi pervoi kulturnoi piatiletki v natsionalnykh respublikakh i nametki vtoroi," in: *RN*, 12/1932, p. 65.

88. *Itogi razresheniia*, pp. 214f.; *Kulturnoe stroitelstvo* (1940), p. 221.

89. B. Udintsev, "Natsionalnaia pechat SSSR," in: *RN*, 5/1937, p. 74.

90. B. Udintsev, "Natsionalnaia pechat SSSR," in: *RN*, 5/1936, p. 17.

91. "Litso nashikh natsionalnykh gazet," in: *RN*, 5/1931, pp. 99–101.

92. Quoted from: "Ozdorovit tatarskuiu literaturu," in: *RN*, 5/1931, p. 104.

93. Ibid., p. 105.

94. E. Allworth, "The Focus of Literature," in: *Central Asia. A Century of Russian Rule*, E. Allworth(ed.) (New York/London, 1967), pp. 397–433.

95. In German in: *Die sowjetische Bildungspolitik seit 1917: Dokumente und Texte*, O. Anderweiler/K. Meyer (eds.) (Heidelberg, 1961), pp. 173-176. For general information on the struggle against illiteracy: O. Anweiler, "Erziehungs-und Bildungspolitik," in: O. Anweiler/K.H. Ruffmann (eds.) *Kulturpolitik der Sowjetunion* (Stuttgart, 1973), pp. 39ff., 48ff.

96. J. Pennar/J.J. Bakalo/G.Z.F. Bereday, *Modernization and Diversity in Soviet Education* (New York, 1971), p. 288; Anweiler, *Erziehungs- und Bildungspolitik*, p. 52.

97. S. Dimanshtein, "K 15-letiiu Kasakhstana," in: *RN,* 10/1935, p. 34.

98. M. Velikovskii, "Zadachi natsionalnoi politiki v svete reshenii XVI sezda," in: *RN,* 4/5/1930, p. 19.

99. *Itogi razresheniia natsionalnogo voprosa,* pp. 182f.

100. A. Rakhimbaev, "Za tempy i kachestvo natsionalnogo kulturnogo stroitelstva," in: *RN,* 6/1932, pp. 42f. Cf. the resolution of the RSFSR's Council of People's Commissars of April 7, 1932 concerning the completion of the whole korenizatsiia of national elementary schools by the school year of 1932-1933 (*RN,* 6/1932, p. 103).

101. Cf. note 99.

102. "Natsionalnye shkoly na podeme," in: *RN,* 10/1936, p. 97; Gamalov, "Vseobshchee obuchenie natsmenshinstv," in: *RN,* 6/1930, p. 90.

103. Pennar/Bakalo/Bereday, p. 293.

104. V.V. Smirenin, "Pedkadry Kabardino-Balkarii na perepodgotovke," in: *RN,* 11/1933, p. 70; I. Karneev, "Natsionalnaia shkola k novomu uchebnomu godu," in: *RN,* 9, 10/1937, p.47.

105. Pennar/Bakalo/Bereday, p. 285.

106. Quoted in V. Zasukhin, "Kulturnoe stroitelstvo Kirgizii," in: *RN,* 5/1934, p. 75.

107. *Kulturnoe stroitelstvo,* (1940), pp. 75-77.

108. *Itogi razresheniia natsionalnogo voprosa,* p. 200.

109. "V presidiume Soveta Natsionalnostei CIK SSSR," in: *RN,* 10/1936, p. 93.

110. "Komplektovanie uchebnykh zavedenii-vazhneishii uchastok podgotovki kadrov," in: *RN,* 6/1931, p. 92.

111. A. Epshtein, "Vysshaia shkola i natsionalnye kadry," in: *RN,* 12/1933, p. 67; "Culturally backward peoples" was the term the Soviets officially employed. It denoted the peoples of Islamic extraction, the peoples of the Volga region, and the smaller nationalities of Siberia and the Caucasus. It did not pertain to Ukrainians, Georgians, Armenians, Jews, Germans, Poles, and members of the Baltic peoples.

112. *Bratskoe sodruzhestvo soiuznykh respublik v razvitii narodnogo khoziaistva SSSR 1917-1971* (Moscow, 1973), p. 218.

113. S. Akopov, "Podgotovka natsionalnykh kadrov," in: *RN,* 4/1934, pp. 58–60; T.I. Usubaliev, "Leninskaia teoriia nekapitalisticheskogo razvitiia i formirovanie natsionalnoi intelligentsii," in: *Voprosy filosofii,* 4/1980, p. 42.

114. "Prezidium Soveta Natsionalnostei CIK SSSR," in: *RN,* 3/1936, p. 89; W. Kolarz, *Die Nationalitätenpolitik der Sowjetunion* (Frankfurt/M., 1956), pp. 54, 331.

115. S. Trodiia, "Podgotovka natsionalnykh kadrov," in: *RN,* 1/1936, p. 65.

116. A. Nove/J.A. Newth, *The Soviet Middle East* (London, 1967), pp. 76–78.

117. Bilinsky, *The Second Soviet Republic,* pp. 170f.

118. S. Chugunov, "Sotsialisticheskoe stroitelstvo Ukrainy," in: *RN,* 4/1934, p. 68; R.S. Sullivant, *Soviet Politics and the Ukraine, 1917–1957* (New York/London, 1962), p. 392.

119. Cypin, "Respublika ordena Lenina," in: *RN,* 5/1934, p. 90.

120. M.A. Khasanov, "Kulturnoe stroitelstvo Tatarii," in: *RN,* 6/1935, p. 41.

121. *Itogi razresheniia natsionalnogo voprosa,* p. 187.

122. No data are available as to which subjects were most popular with students from the different nations—as opposed to territories; such data would show an even greater imbalance in favor of non-Russians studying education. *Kulturnoe stroitelstvo SSSR* (1940), p. 256. Corresponding figures from 1960 (Pennar/Bakalo/Bereday, *Modernization,* p. 300) show that this structure—the predominance of students of education in the non-Russian republics—has not changed over the years.

123. I.P. Tsamerian, *Teoreticheskie problemy obrazovaniia i razvitiia sovetskogo mnogonatsionalnogo gosudarstva* (Moscow, 1973), p. 167.

124. A. Bogdanov, "Podgotovka natsionalnykh kadrov," in: *RN,* 4/1936, pp. 48ff.

125. "O natsionalnykh kadrakh," in: *RN,* 10/1935, p. 53; Pennar/Bakalo/Bereday, *Modernization,* p. 353; G. Simon, "Russen und Nichtrussen in der UdSSR," *Berichte des BIOst* 11/1981, p. 37.

126. S.I. Iakubovskaia, *Razvitie SSSR kak soiuznogo gosudarstva,* p. 184; N. Nurmakov, "Avtonomii i natsionalnye raiony RSFSR na sotsialisticheskom podeme," in: *RN,* 1/1935, pp. 26–33. Soviet research still treats these diaspora raions and village soviets mostly as a taboo; although the pertinent handbook (*Istoriia natsionalno-gosudarstvenogo stroitelstva v SSSR: 1917–1978,* vol. 1 [Moscow, 1979], 3rd ed., p. 323) acknowledges their existence, it does not talk about their functions, effectiveness, or why and when they were dissolved later on. In this context as in others, Soviet research is forced to camouflage the great "liberality" of the early years.

127. I. Loginov, "Sovety Belorussii," in: *RN,* 4/1934, p. 42; M. Vasilenko, "Odin iz mnogikh. K 5-letnomu iubileiu Markhlevskogo polskogo raiona," in: *RN,* 4/5/1930, p. 40.

128. *RN*, 1/1930, pp. 109–111, 114–117.

129. V.I. Kozlov, *Natsionalnosti SSSR. Etnograficheskii obzor* (Moscow, 1975), p. 251.

130. P. Janson, "Rabota sredi natsmen v Leningradskoi oblasti," in: *RN*, 10/1933, pp. 48–53.

131. J.M. Matley, "The Dispersal of Ingrian Finns," in: *Slavic Review* 38, 1979, pp. 9f.

132. A. Bogdanov, "Vnimanie obsluzhivaniiu natsmenshinstv," in: *RN*, 1/1937, pp. 62f.

133. Of all the peoples, the Jews have been the most researched by Western scholars. Thus, their situation is not dealt with in detail here. Recent literature on this subject: Z.Y. Gitelman, *Jewish Nationality and Soviet Politics: The Jewish Sections of the CPSU, 1917–1930* (Princeton, 1972); B. Gurevitz, "National Communism in the Soviet Union, 1918–1928," Ph.D. University of Rochester, 1973; Z. Halevy, *Jewish Schools under Czarism and Communism* (New York, 1976); *The Jews in Soviet Russia Since 1917*, L. Kochan (ed.), (London, 3rd ed., 1978); The. E. Sawyer, *The Jewish Minority in the Soviet Union* (New York, 1979); B. Pinkus, *The Jews of the Soviet Union: The History of a National Minority* (Cambridge, 1989). A journal specializing in this topic, *Soviet Jewish Affairs,* is published in London.

134. Z. Katz, "The Jews in the Soviet Union," in: *Handbook of Major Soviet Nationalities*, pp. 358, 368.

135. Lewis/Rowland/Clem, p. 136.

136. *Komitet po zemelnomu ustroistvu trudiashchikhsia evreev pri CIK SSSR (Komzet)* and *Obshchestvo po zemelnomu ustroistvu trudiashchikhsia evreev (Ozet).* S. Dimanshtein, "Evreiskoe natsmenshinstvo SSSR na novom etape," in: *RN,* 5/1932, pp. 87–95; S. Dimanshtein, "Natsionalnaia politika sovetskoi vlasti i M.N. Kalinin," in: *RN,* 4/1934, pp. 18f.; Kolarz, *Nationalitätenpolitik der Sowjetunion,* pp. 200–203.

137. cf. A. Gitlianskii, "Leninskaia natsionalnaia politika v deistvii," in: *RN,* 9/1931, pp. 40f.; "Po sotsialisticheskomu puti," in: *RN,* 1/1934, p. 90.

138. S. Dimanshtein, "V otvet na vopros sostavliaiut li soboi evrei v nauchnom smysle natsiiu," in: *RN,* 10/1935, p. 77; S. Dimanshtein, in: *RN,* 2/1935, pp. 43f.

139. Kolarz, *Nationalitätenpolitik,* p. 209; *Vestnik statistiki,* 7/1980, p. 50.

140. The Soviet literature has not yet mentioned this fact; there is only circumstantial evidence. cf. M. Buchsweiler, "Deutsche Landkreise (Raions) und deutsche Kreiszeitungen in der UdSSR," in: *Osteuropa*, XXXII, 1982, pp. 671–682.

141. cf. *Bolshaia Sovetskaia Entsiklopediia,* 1st ed., vol. 41 (1939), column 380f.

142. A. i V. Elbaev, "O rabote sredi natsmen Moskovskoi oblasti," in: *RN*, 8/1936, pp. 16–21.
143. Katz, *Jews in the Soviet Union,* pp. 376f.

III

"Great-Russian Chauvinism" and the Nationalism of the Other Peoples

The Soviets intended nation-building as a means of carrying out social revolution and of stabilizing their new state. By no means was this policy meant to bring about separatism or to favor centrifugal development of individual peoples or regions. How the Soviets planned to accommodate these contradictory goals — building new nations and increasing state centralization — remains unclear. Until the mid-1930s, the Bolsheviks hid behind the illusion that no contradiction existed because the new nations would be "socialist," and as a result their class structure would not be "bourgeois." Socialist nations were expected to exhibit a positive attitude — not a separatist one — towards a state that was in the process of developing socialism.

Nevertheless, practical politics still faced the problem of finding the limits of nation-building, what areas it would not encompass, and how to regulate conflicts of interest between the central state and the individual regions. The Party never clearly defined the limits of its korenizatsiia policy. Numerous conflicts were the result because Georgian and Ukrainian comrades or the national Bolsheviks from the Tatar ASSR had different ideas of korenizatsiia than the central state. Consequently, between 1917 and 1937, continuous disputes raged concerning the "correct" course of the nationalities policy.[1] In this matter, the representatives of the non-Russian peoples (including those within the Party, in particular) fought for nation-building to be as comprehensive as possible, whereas the central state was willing to concede less and less as revolution and civil war became more and more a thing of the past. When Stalin had established his dictatorship in 1937, the central state emerged as the clear winner of this fight.

However, during the civil war, the Bolshevik leadership had already clarified its position in two important areas: the role of the Party and that of the military in the nation-building process; in both areas, nation-building was limited to recruiting non-Russians into the Party and the army. Any attempt at separation from the central organization, at raising national armed forces in addition to the Red Army, at founding autonomous or even independent national parties from the Bolsheviks was clearly going too far. When Stalin and Lenin developed the principles of Bolshevik nationalities policy, they were very aware of the disintegration of the Austro-Hungarian Empire's Social Democratic Party into its national elements before World War I. As a result, Stalin and Lenin were determined to prevent a similar development in Russia no matter what. In all national territories the Red Army conquered during the civil war, the Soviets forced all socialist parties that had emerged locally to dissolve; a number of their members and organizations merged with the Communist Party. Analogously, the Soviets either incorporated national armed forces into the Red Army or demobilized them.

In the 1920s, the national communists did not unanimously agree with the Party leadership's principles. The national communists reminded the leadership in Moscow that the peoples had a right to self-determination and attempted to attain for their regions comprehensive rights to self-administration and extensive political freedom to decide their own internal affairs. Such efforts not only produced the familiar conflicts with the Ukrainian and Georgian communists, the national communists in the Soviet east also resisted the centralist organization of Party and army. In 1920, top representatives of the Turkestan CP (lead by Turar Ryskulov, the Chairman of the Turkestan CEC) demanded the Central Committee in Moscow stop interfering with Turkestan's internal affairs. They demanded the withdrawal or disarmament of the Red Army units in Turkestan; Muslim units were to be raised and to take over the defense of the revolution. A "Turkic CP" was to be founded and given the political power. When Moscow's Central Committee rejected these demands, Ryskulov and his comrades-in-arms resigned their positions in protest; Moscow's Central Committee retaliated by dissolving the Party's Turkestan Area Committee (*kraikom*).[2]

Lenin was not willing to let the non-Russian peoples found national party organizations or raise military forces outside the Red Army. But he thought it necessary to make concessions on the issue of self-administration of state organs and the economy. Lenin meant these concessions to counteract national ambitions. The Party leadership perceived, however, Russian chauvinism as the greatest danger for the coexistence of the peoples and not separatist efforts of the non-Russian peoples. Lenin's last notes, written in December 1922, dealt with this issue. He condemned Stalin's, Dzerzhinskii's, and Ordzhonikidze's actions against Georgian Party leaders who had opposed the foundation of a Transcaucasian Federation.[3]

The Twelfth Party Congress in April, 1923 assessed the "fight against the remnants of Great Russian Chauvinism" as the Party's "most important task at present" in connection with the nationalities issue. The Congress repeated the statement of the Tenth Party Congress in March, 1921 about the "particularly dangerous and particularly damaging nature" of "behaving like a great power and colonialist." The Twelfth Party Congress' resolution explicitly stated a causal relationship between Great Russian chauvinism and the nationalism of the other peoples: "Insofar as the remnants of nationalism are a special way of defense against Great Russian chauvinism, the determined fight against Great Russian chauvinism is the surest way to overcome these remnants of nationalism." In other words, once Russian nationalism is defeated, the other forms of nationalism lose their reason for being and their base.[4]

Official Party statements in the 1920s unquestionably presented Great Russian chauvinism as a deviation from the Party line that was more dangerous than non-Russian forms of nationalism and consequently the primary foe to fight. In the main report to the Sixteenth Party Congress in June/July, 1930, Stalin also explicitly referred to the danger of Great Russian chauvinism as the Party's greatest danger in connection with the nationalities issue.[5]

"The Battle on Two Fronts"

Until the mid-1930s, the Party leadership described as a "battle on two fronts" its efforts to provide the process of nation-building with space to develop in, on the one hand, and to set tight limits on political autonomy, on the other. Nation-building met with considerable resistance from the political apparatuses (which were under Russian control) and from the Russian elites in the national territories. Usually, this resistance consisted of passive bureaucratic obstinacy. The responsible authorities did not carry out the resolutions and directions of superior organs or councils of deputies of the soviets. Sometimes the authorities pretended to do as they were told, and their reports of successes to their superiors were pure artifice. Factory directors did not hire the required number of non-Russian nationals; on the level of the Autonomous Republics, the People's Commissariats produced imposing plans for korenizatsiia, but nobody took care of their implementation. Resolutions to introduce non-Russian languages also often failed because of the bureaucracy's passive resistance. For example, in May 1931, the plenum of the Party's Bashkir Regional Committee ordered all employees of soviet and union organs (not of Party organs, however!) to learn the Bashkir language within two years. This well-meaning initiative, however, was as far as this activity would go, and like many similar resolutions never went beyond the planning stage.[6] One of the strategies lower and intermediate organs favored to avoid having to undertake concrete measures was declaring that, in their area, korenizatsiia had already been fully established and further efforts were superfluous.[7]

In the late 1920s and early 1930s, the Presidium of the All-Russian CEC issued many resolutions criticizing this unacceptable situation in the RSFSR's autonomous territories. These resolutions stated that the integration of indigenous nationals into the apparatuses had stagnated and that the progress in adopting non-Russian languages was unsatisfactory. The Presidium saw Great-Russian chauvinism as the main reason and assumed this chauvinism was supported by non-Russians who refused to use their own native tongues in government offices and factories because they were frequently unable to read and write their native languages competently.[8]

In many cases, the bureaucracy evaded its tasks in connection with nationalities policy by not collecting any pertinent data. For example, all People's Commissariats in the RSFSR had to include in their annual reports of activities an account of their efforts supporting nationalities policy. Most People's Commissariats did not comply with this requirement. In 1930, even the planning authorities in the RSFSR did not have "complete, systematic data to provide information on how the practical implementation of Lenin's nationalities policy had progressed and what results it had produced." According to the Soviet scholar, B. Rodnichev, great-power chauvinism was responsible for this lack of planning, as expressed in a 1930 statement by the Ural's Regional Economics Council. These functionaries believed "the policy of industrialization must be international, and they did not intend to let national considerations influence them in the processes of industrialization and job training."[9] The argument that nation-building was economically unprofitable came more and more to the fore during the 1930s and had certain effects during the first two Five-Year-Plans when only growth rates counted for anything.

Initially, however, in a joint resolution on February 10, 1931, the All-Russian CEC and the RSFSR's Council of People's Commissars criticized the fact that "the People's Commissariats and the local authorities" had planned and were managing the nationalities policy "in an unsatisfactory way and that their initiative was exceptionally inadequate and they lacked vigor in accomplishing the task." This resolution obliged the People's Commissariats and all Soviet organs (down to the regional level) to mention specifically in their plans measures to promote non-Russians economically and culturally.[10]

However, such resolutions could not eradicate deeply ingrained resistance to the costly process of integrating non-Russian nationals. The press particularly publicly deplored the insufficient consideration for national minorities living dispersed or in small groups. National minorities comprised 12 percent of the population in the Stalingrad Area, but the factories and sovkhozes usually did not keep national statistics. Nor did the factories undertake any particular measures to improve the vocational and cultural situation of local nationals. The few employees of the Area Executive

Committees' Nationalities Department were "systematically ignored" and were not even allowed to attend the meetings of the Presidium of the Executive Committee. Until 1935, these conditions were publicly denounced as "Great Russian Chauvinism".[11] Similar conditions prevailed in the Gorky Area, where no planned measures existed to develop a national proletariat and where, as a rule, the factories did not even bother to collect data on their employees' nationalities. A review showed that, in many cases, factories had never heard of an All-Russian CEC resolution of December 10, 1931, which said national workers were to be trained in large enterprises and then returned to their factories in their native national territories. Even eighteen months after this resolution was issued, not a single organization in the Gorky Area had initiated any concrete steps to execute it.[12]

However, not only did strong resistance to participation of nationals come from the bureaucracy, but this resistance was also deeply ingrained in society. Teachers balked at using non-Russian languages, the principals of technical schools refused to admit local nationals, and large-scale construction sites were often the scenes of animosities and physical altercations between Russian and non-Russian workers. Before his Buryat students, a Russian teacher said, "It would be nice if there were no Buryats in this world"; and in the Belorussian city of Bobruisk, another teacher barked at his students, "Speak Russian, I don't understand Belorussian."[13] In the city of Simferopol on the Crimean peninsula, a primary Party organization held that "at least 30 percent of the classes in the [Crimean]-Tatar schools should be in Russian."[14] In 1930, such ideas were considered Russian chauvinism. In view of political developments to follow, a point to note is that, this position reflects the official policy since the 1950s and is actually even a version of the official line that is relatively unthreatening to the nationalities.

Even in the early 1930s, school books appeared in Central Asia that were accused of being "permeated with the ideology of the colonizer." In Alatyr in the Chuvash ASSR, the local technical school for transport was publicly reprimanded because it resisted explicit Party directives to admit a larger number of indigenous Chuvashs and to teach its classes in the Chuvash language.[15]

The most basic form of conflicts among individuals of different nationalities arose from the discrimination non-Russian workers in multinational factories and at multinational construction sites faced. Frequently, it resulted in confrontations and brawls between Russian and non-Russian workers. In the city of Kazan, one factory sported graffiti saying, "Get the Jews" and "Kick out the Tatar yaps." The relationship was especially tense between Russian and Kazakh workers at the construction sites of the Turkestan-Siberian railroad.[16] Native workers were paid less for equal work and management justified this fact, arguing that others "must go over their work again." Frequent brawls took place at the construction sites.[17]

In the early 1930s, about 35 percent of the workers at the large-scale construction sites of Magnitogorsk were non-Russians. The material and cultural needs of these mostly unqualified workers were systematically ignored; they received neither bonuses nor working clothes, and their children had no schools.[18] The oil fields and sulfur mines in Shar-Su (Uzbekistan) were the scenes of "unbelievable displays of great-power swagger": 75 percent of the workers were Uzbeks, but only one among fifty managers was able to speak the Uzbek language. Factory-owned stores sold goods to the Russians first, and only then were the Uzbeks allowed on the sales floor. Russian workers also received apartment assignments before non-Russians.[19] The few Chechen workers in the oil industry in Groznyi experienced a similar type of discrimination; they received neither the jobs they qualified for nor lodging.[20]

These were not isolated incidents; rather they reflected the situation as it had existed since the beginning of forced industrialization in the late 1920s. The situation was tense in the national territories as well as in central Russia, where hundreds of thousands of national workers migrated during these years. National and social antagonisms intensified one another. As a rule, non-Russians were untrained workers, did not understand the language management spoke, received less money for equal labor, were excluded from shop-floor meetings because of their insufficient command of Russian, and were considered last—which frequently meant not at all—for social benefits (lodging, apportionment of food), which were often more important than wages.

However, until the mid-1930s, the press published these conflicts in a relatively straightforward way, and Russian workers and supervisors were called to account: At the electrotechnical factory in Bobriki near Moscow, where 1000 national workers were employed, "Blokhin, candidate member of the CPSU (B), systematically ridiculed the Armenian toolmaker Isakhanov, member of the Komsomol. The situation deteriorated to the point where Blokhin urinated on Isakhanov's head from the roof of a shed during working hours. The latter lost his temper and nearly brained Blokhin. Only after this outrageous derision of an Armenian worker did the local Party cell show an interest in the matter. Blokhin was expelled from the Party as a candidate member . . . that was all. He did not at all have to account for his actions before the law. Blokhin left Bobriki unscathed and is still free to this very day."[21]

But there were also more serious efforts to fight discrimination against non-Russian nationals; in a number of cases, courts convicted the culprits. In 1930, Goldman, the supervisor of the second construction sector of the Turksib, received a five-year jail term because he had systematically given preferential treatment to Russians and discriminated against Kazakh workers.[22] In 1931, at the large-scale construction site of Magnitogorsk, four trials dealt with discrimination against national workers; fifteen "chauvinists" lost their jobs.[23] In five regions or areas, for which data from 1932 are available, 197 individuals were tried on offenses relating to Russian chauvinism. One of the accused received a death sentence, sixty-four were given prison sentences, two were banned, 107 were sentenced to corrective labor, and thirty-two received fines. Nevertheless, the courts were relatively lenient and, as a rule, dealt with discrimination against non-Russians and defamation of them as "the usual hooliganism."[24] During the Party purges of 1929 and 1933, it was the rare exception when members were expelled for national hubris or discrimination against non-Russians.

In summary, even in public Russian nationalism was represented as a threat to the coexistence of the peoples until the mid-1930s. After that, concrete examples of "keep-your-trap-shut" nationalism disappeared forever from the Soviet media. Although the Soviets took measures against discrimination of the non-Russians by enforcing administrative and legal penalties during the twenty years following the 1917 revolution, they were not able to remedy the situation effectively. The battle against great-power chauvinism was limited to concrete individual cases and to the level of factories and local organizations. In contrast, the measures taken on the other "front," against "local nationalism" were directed at prominent functionaries in the non-Russian territories from the beginning. Because of this, the battle against non-Russian nationalism had a greater political impact.

In 1923, Sultan-Galiev, who was a member of the Tatar ASSR's CEC and who worked closely with Stalin in the People's Commissariat for Nationality Affairs, was the first prominent functionary expelled from the Party and arrested because of nationalism. Sultan-Galiev had been the highest ranking Muslim representative in the Party apparatus, publisher of the official magazine of the Narkomnats *The Life of the Nationalities* (*Zhizn natsionalnostei*), and leading theoretician of national communism. At no time, did the national communists from the various peoples constitute a united faction within the Party; most of these groups originated with prerevolutionary reformist or socialist groups that had been forced to disband after the civil war. They were united by the hope, however, that in the non-Russian territories, they would be able to combine social revolution with liberation from Russian colonialism. Like most non-Russian communists in the 1920s, Sultan-Galiev believed that the class struggle *within* the non-Russian peoples and the struggle against the national religions had to give ground to these primary objectives. In 1918, Sultan-Galiev said: "Because the colonialists have suppressed nearly every class in Muslim society, every class is entitled to the label proletarian."[25]

In the 1920s, national communist groups were most influential in the Ukraine, Georgia, and the Tatar ASSR. Their objectives for the future included de-Russifying the national territories as much as possible, expanding federalism, (that is, restricting central power), and developing true autonomy in culture, economy, and personnel policy. These groups' disputes with the Party leadership became most concrete in connection with the following objectives: to protect and develop national culture, independent of and in part in contrast to Russian tradition; to transfer leadership tasks to national intelligentsia, who generally were not of proletarian origin, whose background was not in the Bolshevik tradition of professional revolutionaries, and whom the Party leadership considered ideologically unreliable; to repulse Russian immigration; and, in addition, the Muslim national communists strove to maintain and develop the unity of Muslim peoples within the framework of the Soviet Union.[26]

As a result, Sultan-Galiev was accused of espousing pan-Turkism and pan-Islamism. Since the end of the 19th century, an integral part of any political activity of Russia's Islamic peoples had been the consciousness that they belonged together. The idea that the shared Islamic past and future in Russia were special shaped all reform efforts, including those of the liberal Jadidists (Renovationists) who hoped to combine Islamic tradition with Western European modernization, and those of Bolsheviks of Islamic origin. Thus, in the 1920s, the party leadership could not demand its Islamic members globally denounce their pan-Islamic loyalty. As a result, Stalin put his accusations against Sultan-Galiev into more concrete terms and claimed that loyalty to pan-Islamism was more important to Sultan-Galiev than loyalty to the CC and that he had developed conspiratory ties to the Islamic guerrillas (*basmachi*), who were still fighting the Soviets in Central Asia, and to the Bashkirian social revolutionary, Validov, who had fled abroad.[27]

In 1924, however, Sultan-Galiev went free without a trial, and he later became deeply involved in conspiratory political activities. Because of Sultan-Galiev's disappointment in the possibilities cooperation with the Russian Bolsheviks offered, he developed the idea of founding a sovereign socialist Republic of Turan, which would consist not only of Turkestan but also of the Tatar ASSR, Bashkiria, and possibly Azerbaidzhan and the Northern Caucasus. On the one hand, Sultan-Galiev envisioned a socialist Turan in the European mold, which would adopt modern technology and industry and a secularized system of education. On the other hand, however, he wanted Turan to become the seed of an anti-imperialist Fourth International of the colonial peoples because "only a dictatorship of the colonies and semi-colonies over the metropolises could create the material foundation for humanity's social reorganization."[28]

In contrast to the national communists in the 1920s (who had limited their demands to territorial autonomy and autonomy for their parties and armies), Sultan-Galiev explicitly articulated separatist goals. Such goals must also be seen as an expression of continuing resistance, both inside and outside the

Party, to Turkestan's "national delimitation" in 1924. To destroy all dreams of a Great-Turkic Soviet Republic, Moscow dissolved Turkestan (the possible center of such a republic) and Bukhara and Khiva and, along ethnic borders, created the Union Republics of Uzbekistan and Turkmenistan, the Autonomous Republic of Tadzhikistan, and the Karakirgiz (since 1925, Kirgiz) Autonomous Region. In 1929, Tadzhikistan was elevated to the rank of Union Republic, as was Kirgizistan in 1936, at the same time as Kazakhstan.[29]

The division of Turkestan clearly contradicted the political will of prominent local communists. In January 1920, the Third Muslim Conference of the RCP (B) had followed Ryskulov's suggestion and had objected to "efforts to divide the Turkish peoples into Tatars, Kirgiz, Bashkirs, Uzbeks, etc., and to create small separate republics but [proposed] to unite them ... in one Turkish Soviet Republic."[30] Resistance to the division of the Islamic peoples according to ethnic criteria continued after 1924. Several high-ranking Party leaders from the East maintained close relations with Sultan-Galiev's conspiratory organization. Among these leaders were Ryskulov (Vice Chairman of the RSFSR's Council of People's Commissars from 1926 to 1937, Veli Ibragimov (Chairman of the CEC of the Crimean ASSR until 1928), and possibly also Faizulla Khodzhaev (Chairman of Uzbekistan's Council of People's Commissars until 1937).[31]

By the late 1920s, the Party leadership felt strong enough to avoid political altercations with the Islamic national communists and let the police and the judicial system handle problems. Sultan-Galiev, who had not held any official position since 1924, received a ten-year prison sentence in 1928 and was sent to Solovki in the White Sea; after this time, no information about him exists.[32] An extensive purge of Party and state apparatuses in the Tatar ASSR began at the same time as Sultan-Galiev's trial; Mansurov (Chairman of the CEC) and Sabirov (First Secretary of the Regional Party Committee) fell victim to this purge. In addition, the purge focused primarily on Tatar educational facilities and the Tatar Union of Writers.[33]

Everywhere in the USSR, Veli Ibragimov's dismissal as Chairman of the Crimean CEC in the same year 1928, must have been understood as a signal that latitude in nationalities policy had shrunk. Ibragimov was the first prominent functionary arrested while still in office, and after a short closed trial, he received a death sentence for nationalism and was executed by a firing squad. The purge on the Crimean peninsula that followed Ibragimov's execution affected at least 3,500 Crimean Tatars, who were executed by firing squad, arrested, or deported from the Crimean peninsula.[34] The Crimean peninsula was among those territories where nation-building had been very successful, particularly in state administration and in education. Although they only made up 25 percent of the population in 1926, the Crimean Tatars had taken extensive control of their republic. Because the policy of korenizatsiia was continued even after 1928, this year cannot be considered the overall turning point in nationalities policy.[35] Stalin's leadership, however, had been clear in its unwillingness to tolerate the political consequences of nation-building—increasing autonomy—and in the fact that its lack of trust in the old leaders of the national revolution did not decrease but rather grew as revolution and civil war receded in time.

Articulating demands for national autonomy in public became increasingly difficult after the civil war, and this situation triggered not only the formation of Sultan-Galiev's group but also the formation of other conspiratory nationalist organizations. In the late 1920s, for example, the police uncovered the "counter-revolutionary nationalist organization," Milli-ittikhad (National Association), in Uzbekistan and its successor organization, Milli-istiklal (National Independence), in 1930. In both cases, the members were prominent functionaries, primarily from education, the judicial system, and literary circles. In 1928, Kasymov, the Chairman of the Supreme Court of Uzbekistan, was tried and sentenced for nationalism. The People's Commissariat for Education in Uzbekistan was the center of Milli-istiklal. In addition to People's Commissar Ramzi, seven of the nine members of the Council of the People's Commissariat were also members of this conspiratory organization. Consequently, their exposure triggered an extensive purge within the apparatus of the People's Commissariat, the schools of education, and among textbook authors.

Milli-istiklal was accused of following an educational policy according to principles of Jadidism and not those of Bolshevism. Also, the organization's cultural and educational policies were allegedly oriented towards Western modernism and Turkey, not towards Moscow and the international proletariat. Supposedly, the schools taught pan-Islamism and pan-Turkism, and allowed no anti-religious propaganda against Islam. The final political objective of the group was allegedly the establishment of a bourgeois state in Central Asia.[36]

In 1930, the police disbanded a group of Tatar writers that pursued similar objectives. The secret organization Dzhidigian (Great Bear) challenged the Party's right to determine the direction of literature and art and to adopt keeping to the Party line as a measure of literary quality. In addition, literary people refused to promote class struggle within the Tatar village because the class struggle only existed in the fantasy of the Moscow leadership.[37]

Scholarship knows these nationalist groups only as the Soviet process of "exposure" depicted them. Nevertheless, given the political situation in the late 1920s, the existence of these groups and their objectives appears quite plausible. Unlike in the late 1930s, in the late 1920s the NKWD (Narodnyi Kommissariat Vnutrennikh Del) was not yet inventing absurd organizations with fantastic objectives, to which "enemies of the people" were made to confess under torture. However, the line between fantasy and reality is blurred, and deciding where the programmatic statements of a political secret organization end and where the imagination of the OGPU (Obshchee Gosudarstvennoe Politicheskoe Upravlenie) begins is sometimes difficult — even for the 1920s. For example, during the 1920s, a nationalist organization was exposed in Turkmenistan that allegedly planned an armed uprising against the Soviet regime. Boriev and Orazov, Turkmenistan's People's Commissars for Education and for Supply, supposedly led this movement. The Turkmen nationalists not only supported pan-Turkic ideas and wanted to make Turkmen the only official language, but they also allegedly intended to found a Turkmen state under the protection of the British Empire.[38]

Disputes over Kazakhstan's nationalities policy became particularly heated because this policy would determine the fate of the Kazakh nomadic village, the *aul*. Among the colonial territories conquered in the 19th century, Kazakhstan was the only one to which a large number of Russian settlers had immigrated before 1914. At the beginning of World War I, more than one million Russian and Ukrainian settlers were already living in Kazakhstan. The government had generously allocated to these settlers farmland from which it had driven the Kazakh nomadic tribes. Kazakh communists, many of whom had started in the Kazakh autonomy movement, Alash-orda or were influenced by its program, considered nation-building reparation for colonial injustice. As a result, tens of thousands of Russian and Ukrainian peasants lost their settlements in the early 1920s; their land was allocated to Kazakhs. Kazakh national communists (led by S. Sadvokasov and S. Khodzhanov) also promoted "Kazakhstan to the Kazakhs" in other ways. They believed Kazakhs should lead not only the Party, but also the local Party committees and control commissions. As a result, in the 1920s, the Party recruited the few Kazakh intellectuals and assigned to them leading posts even if they were only loosely involved with the Bolshevik program.

In 1925, the Fifth Kazakh Party Conference decided to solve the land problem "in the interest of the Kazakh population" and practically outlawed for ten years immigration by settlers from other parts of the USSR — until the land allocation to Kazakhs was completed. Although in November 1927, after Moscow's CC applied great pressure and caused the Sixth Kazakh Party Conference to revoke its 1925 resolutions, in reality Kazakh applicants still received allocations on a preferential basis when land and pasture reforms were undertaken. In January and May 1928, the Moscow CC issued two more resolutions condemning Kazakh nationalists and sent a large group of functionaries to the republic to enforce the Party's general line. At the same time, the apparatus of the Kazakh People's Commissariat for Agriculture and the State Planning Committee were the subjects of another purge. The most prominent victim of this purge was Zh. Sultanbekov, the People's Commissar for Agriculture.[39]

The policy of nation-building was not discontinued in the late 1920s, but many of its non-Russian supporters were put in their places or were removed from their jobs. In contrast to events in 1936–38, the term "purge" usually did not yet mean physical destruction in the 1920s. The Party leadership had two reasons for these actions: First, in 1927, after Trotsky's fall from power, Stalin's leadership was stronger than ever. Second, the policy of nation-building was successful at promoting national autonomy, which was gaining more and more broad support in the non-Russian societies. Party leadership was determined to work against these "successes."

Events in the Ukraine also attest to this conclusion's validity. In April 1926, Stalin wrote a confidential letter to the Ukrainian Politburo and openly expressed his distrust of the fanatics promoting Ukrainization. Stalin considered A. Shumskyi, the People's Commissar for Education, the main proponent of such efforts towards Ukrainization. Stalin suggested that, to a certain degree, Ukrainization had become a battle against 'Moscow' and the Russians in general, against Russian culture, and its highest achievement—Leninism.[40] Shumskyi lost his office. However, a sign of the balance of power that existed between the center and the periphery and the intensity of Ukrainian national efforts is the fact that in 1927, M. Skrypnyk, who had vehemently opposed Stalin in many discussions about nationalities policy, became Shumskyi's successor. As a result, the policy of Ukrainization, particularly in the area of education, changed little for the time being.

Not only did the Ukraine fervently pursue nation-building, but the Ukraine's press gave the policy extensive theoretical justification and formulated objectives. For example, the economist M. Volobuev stated that "the Ukraine meets all requirements of an independent economic whole."[41] He accused Moscow of pursuing a colonialist economic policy and of exploiting the Ukraine economically. It was anti-communist to deprive the Ukrainian people of the right to control their own economic resources.[42] Like Volobuev in economics, the writer M. Khvylovyi was the champion of an independent Ukrainian course towards socialism in cultural policy, which he thought had to lead "away from Moscow." "The ideas of the proletariat are familiar to us without Moscow's art. On the contrary, as a young nation, we will feel these ideas more directly and pour them into the proper mold. Western European art, its style, its forms are our guidelines. . . . By now, Moscow has become the center of the all-union petite bourgeoisie."[43] Khvylovyi contended that Ukrainian culture would win the "fight of the two cultures" in the end and that the Ukrainian intelligentsia would take control of the Ukraine after "giving the Russian petite bourgeois," who held all the executive positions in the cultural institutions, "a knock on the head."[44]

Shumskyi, Volobuev, and Khvylovyi were forced to exercise self-criticism. Not until 1933, when a new phase began in the "battle against nationalism," did the police "discover a counter-revolutionary organization in the Ukraine," of which "the spy Shumskyi" was a member.[45] To avoid being arrested, Khvylovyi committed suicide in 1933. Volobuev was banished to Central Asia.[46]

The show trial against the "League for the Liberation of the Ukraine" (*Spilka Vyzvolennia Ukraiiny*) was meant to signal escalation of the conflict. In this trial, forty-five prominent representatives of the Ukrainian intelligentsia were in the dock and were sentenced to two to ten years of imprisonment in March 1930. According to the charges, the league's objective was not only secession of the Ukraine from the USSR and creation of an independent national state but also reinstitution of capitalism. To accomplish this, the accused allegedly had cooperated with the Ukrainian emigration abroad and with capitalist countries. The accused had been employees of several institutes of the Ukrainian Academy of Sciences, particularly the Division of History, the Institute for Ukrainian Scientific Terminology, and the Academy's Pedagogical Society; other intellectuals came from publishing houses, institutions of higher education, and the Ukrainian Writers' Union.

The trial's political purpose was obvious: to warn the Ukrainian philologists, historians, teachers, and writers away from understanding Ukrainization as increasing autonomy from Moscow. Deciding which charges were real and which existed only in the minds of the OGPU is difficult. It is highly unlikely that the accused had organized a political strike force determined to use extreme means. Many Ukrainian patriots, however, expected a national renaissance and either envisioned that in the future their country would be more oriented to the West or wished for an independent Ukrainian national state. Very probably, this was also true of the accused who had formed an informal political colloquium.[47]

In the same year, other shadowy organizations were "exposed." The prominent Marxist historian, M. Iavorskyi, and M. Hrushevskyi, the founder of a non-Bolshevik national Ukrainian historiography, supposedly belonged to the Ukrainian National Center. In 1924, Hrushevskyi (Chairman of the Ukrainian Rada, which had declared itself a state independent from Moscow, from 1917–18) returned to Kiev from exile and was appointed Chairman of the Division of History of the Ukrainian Academy of Sciences. Now in 1930 Ukrainian historians were accused of having a nationalist concept of history. Supposedly, they viewed Ukrainian history as part of Western European history and traced Ukrainian history back to the time of the Kievan Rus. In 1930, Hrushevskyi was forced to move to Moscow; he died in 1934.

At the same time, similar events occurred in Belorussia. Many prominent educators and scholars lost their jobs, and some of them even lost their freedom. Among them were A. Balickii and Z. Prishchepov, the People's Commissars for Education and Agriculture, and V. Ignatovskii, President of the Belorussian Academy of Sciences. They were disparagingly called "National Democrats," an underground political group that existed in the 1920s. It is very probable, however, that the OGPU exaggerated this group's significance considerably. The National Democrats were accused of working towards a bourgeois-democratic Belorussian state and of being culturally and politically oriented towards Poland. In 1930, the OGPU exposed a "League for the Liberation of Belorussia," which it probably had created, without so much as bothering to change the name of its Ukrainian counterpart. Many of the unseated functionaries were accused of being members of this "counter-revolutionary, bourgeois" organization or of sympathizing with it. However, there was no show trial against them.[48]

Concentrating All Forces on One Front

Although the number of retaliatory measures against non-Russian functionaries suspected of "local nationalism" increased considerably after 1927, Stalin repeated the familiar phrase that Great Russian chauvinism was the main threat in the Party with respect to the national question, at the Sixteenth Party Congress in June/July 1930.[49] In late 1933, this ideological rhetoric was also officially abandoned. In November 1933, the Ukrainian CC resolved that "from the perspective of the whole USSR and the whole CPSU (B) Russian great-power chauvinism is still the main threat. However, this does not contradict the fact that Ukrainian local nationalism, which is closely associated with imperialist interventionists, is currently the main threat in some republics of the Soviet Union, particularly in the Ukraine."[50] The Belorussian CC issued a similar resolution.[51] Of course, such an extensive revision of the Party's nationalities theory, which clearly contradicted Lenin's statements and previous Party resolutions, is only conceivable if one assumes Stalin ordered it. At the Seventeenth Party Congress in January 1934, Stalin declared that the dispute over the "main threat" was "formal" and "pointless."[52]

The new policy's practical consequence was that the media dealt with the threat Russian nationalism posed for socialist society less and less, but more and more often with "local nationalism," which by that time was usually referred to as "bourgeois nationalism." In December 1934, it was still possible to discuss in public the fact that living conditions were much worse for Uzbek students than for their Russian fellows at the Central Asian Combine for Irrigation Engineers and Technicians and that the European employees of the Tadshik-Gold Company earned five or six times as much as the local employees. But from 1936, the Soviet press avoided any reference to great-power chauvinism and discrimination against locals.[53] Of course, the issues did not disappear just because nobody talked about them anymore. On the contrary, the preferential treatment granted to Russians and the Russian language had become a policy. In this respect, the change in ideological rhetoric and topics of propaganda definitely reflects a change in political course.

It was no accident that the first indication of the Party line's ideological revision originated in the Ukrainian CC. In 1933, nowhere did the Party leadership strike out against nationalization and autonomy trends as hard as in the Ukraine. That year marks a decisive turning point in the history of the non-Russian republic that is by far most important. This turning point separates the period of increasing Ukrainization and de-Russification, which had begun at the end of the civil war, from an era of stagnation and gradual reversal of this trend. By late 1932, Ukrainian peasants' resistance to collectivization, the famine, the drastic decrease in industrial production, and the associated increase in anti-Russian sentiments and demands for national autonomy finally seem to have confirmed Stalin's distrust of the Ukraine. Until his death, he never overcame his doubts about the Ukraine's loyalty to the Soviet central state. The practical consequences were far-reaching.

In the spring of 1932, the Council of Nationalities of the ACEC praised korenizatsiia as conducted in the Ukraine as an exemplary campaign and demanded that the Ukrainian experiences with this policy be transferred to the republics of the RSFSR.[54] Only months later, the picture changed. In a joint resolution of December 14, 1932, the CC and the Council of People's Commissars sharply criticized this policy and demanded termination of the "mechanical execution" of Ukrainization.[55] In another resolution of January 24, 1933, the Moscow CC criticized the Ukraine's bad crop yield, agricultural policy, and the Party work in general. In three of the seven Ukrainian regions, Party leaderships were replaced. In addition, the CC removed from their positions three members of the Ukrainian Politburo and Secretariat. In their place, P.P. Postyshev, who had been a CC Secretary in Moscow and one of Stalin's most intimate confidants, received extensive powers and went to Kharkov to serve as the Second Secretary.[56] Thus, for the first time since the early 1920s, the center openly interfered with the affairs of Ukrainian Party leadership without waiting for the resolutions of the competent Ukrainian Party body as Party statutes prescribed. This move was followed by the most extensive wave of purges that any of the republics had experienced until then. The purges focused primarily on culture and education and agriculture.

In January 1933, Skrypnyk, the People's Commissar for Education and the driving force behind the Ukrainization, was demoted to Chairman of the Ukrainian Gosplan and Deputy Chairman of the Ukrainian Council of People's Commissars. Subsequently, the press attacked Skrypnyk and he became involved in great personal disputes with Postyshev. To evade arrest, Skrypnyk committed suicide on July 7, 1933. The campaign against him was not unlike personal revenge. The press emphasized that Skrypnyk had politically opposed Stalin since 1918; the press also alleged that Skrypnyk had lobbied against a "uniform union state and for a federation of individual independent states" in 1922 and that later, when he was People's Commissar for Education, he had forced Ukrainization on Russian and Jewish children.[57]

True, Skrypnyk had been one of the eminent national communists since 1918. One of his prominent characteristics was that he very much distrusted central power, which was continuously expanding its influence and threatening to politically undermine Soviet federalism. Skrypnyk believed the large number of linguistically and culturally Russified Ukrainians was a consequence of Russian colonial policy in the Ukraine, and he thought the Soviets were obliged to do away with this policy. At that time, propaganda not only slandered him and his followers as "agents of foreign secret services" but also, for the first time, called them ideologists of "Ukrainian Fascism" who allegedly helped "prepare the way for intervention by international Fascism."[58] Thus were born the Stalinist cliches in language and propaganda that sprouted more grotesque growths in the grand show trials of 1936–1938.

According to official reports, on the Ukrainian "cultural front" alone, "at least 1,200" executives were removed from their positions between January and November 1933. In 1934, Kaganovich informed the Seventeenth Party Congress that in the previous year, 5,581 functionaries from Russia had been sent to the Ukraine.[59] In addition to the People's Commissariat for Education and its subordinate organs, the purges particularly affected the Institute for Linguistics, the State Publishing House, the Institute for Philosophy, the Shevchenko Institute for Literature, and the Ukrainian Academy for Agriculture. Here too, public attacks consisted in part of absurd accusations. Allegedly, "a small group of counter-revolutionaries" had practiced their evil trade "for years" in the People's Commissariat for Agriculture. This group's supposed objective was "to grow sunflowers, particularly in those raions where sunflower disease was most prevalent."[60]

Officially, the policy of Ukrainization continued after 1933, after thousands of its most active proponents had lost their positions. In a Pravda article of March 1935, Postyshev, who was the primary agent in this purge, demanded that new cadres be recruited, primarily from among the Ukrainian intelligentsia and peasantry because easing up on the Ukrainization would play into the hands of the enemies of the Soviets.[61] In reality, nationalization in the Ukraine had come to a halt, as it had in the other republics, and, for the most part, the political will of its proponents had already been broken. "Nationalization" was increasingly stripped of its political goal of autonomy. "Nationalization" became an empty phrase that served an effective purpose for propaganda (like the "peoples' right to self-determination" and "Soviet federalism") but had no concrete political substance.

In 1933, the fight against "bourgeois nationalism" was not limited to the Ukraine. Not only were many Belorussian natives forced to give up their positions, but so were many Uzbeks and Tadzhiks. As they had in the Ukraine, the purges here affected education, cultural facilities, and the different levels of bureaucracy agriculture. The sweeping removals of native functionaries coincided with the extensive Party purge of 1933 and 1934, which often was used to strike native cadres.[62] One of this purge's explicit tasks was "to examine in a particularly thorough way" all former members of national communist and social revolutionary groups, such as those of Sultan-Galiev, the Azerbaidzhan Mussavatists, the Armenian Dashnaks, and the Kazakh Alash-orda party.[63]

In contrast to the events of 1937 and 1938, however, it seems that only in Tadzhikistan in 1933 was a republic's entire leadership replaced. In its resolution of December 3, 1933, the Moscow CC decided to remove Nusratula Maksum, Chairman of Tadzhikistan's CEC, and Abdurakhim Khodzhibaev, Chairman of the Council of People's Commissars, from their positions because they "pursued a bourgeois-nationalist course and violated Lenin's principle of internationalism." The resolution alleged that Maksum and Khodzhibaev had frequently talked about "Tadzhikistan's lack of kulaks, bais, poor peasants, or middle peasants; Tadzhikistan had only equal sons of the Tadzhik people."[64] From the Moscow leadership's perspective, one of the deadly sins non-Russians committed was then and continues to be their denial that the individual peoples experienced class struggles and that the nations' solidarity bridged their social and political differences. Turning the peoples' social classes against one another has always been a key instrument of the Party leadership in dealing with the nationalities issue.

An extensive purge of Tadzhikistan's state apparatus followed the removal of prominent leaders. In turn, this apparatus temporarily lost its ability to function. The following situation in one raion was considered as typical: "The first chairman of the soviet fled, the second was prosecuted for sabotage as a kulak, the third fled, the fourth was arrested, the fifth was arrested, the sixth was arrested, the seventh is still in office. This all occurred in the course of one year."[65] As a result, the Party's purge in Tadzhikistan was particularly radical; the number of Party members in Tadzhikistan decreased from 14,300 on January 1, 1933, to 4,800 on January 1, 1935.[66]

The fight against "bourgeois" (meaning non-Russian) nationalism also became apparent in the way the Soviets revised their general platform on literary policy. By founding the all-Soviet Union of Writers and holding the first writers' congress in 1934, they developed new tools for controlling writers and enforcing "socialist realism," which had become obligatory. Non-Russian writers were pressured to deal more with Soviet topics and encouraged to avoid national history and tradition. These latter topics were allowed only as background and only if the perspective clearly emphasized the class struggle. After the mid-1930s, almost any kind of national literature published before that date was considered a "national deviation."

For example, Uzbek literature was accused of "showing considerable evidence" of Jadidist influence (Jadidism was an Islamic social reformatory revival movement that began in the late 1800s). The writers "attempted to poison the working people of Uzbekistan with pan-Turkic and nationalist ideas and to alienate them from the USSR."[67] In 1934, the Turkmen writers Berdi Kerbabai-ogli and Garaia Burun-ogli, criticized their own works in Stalinist style and confessed that all their works had been inspired "by the perspective of counter-revolutionary nationalism," and they promised to change their ways in the future.[68]

While it was trying to repress national attitudes and political ambitions, the Stalin leadership was also creating a new slogan, which was developed into a full blown ideology of mobilization in the following years: Soviet patriotism. Patriotism had been considered "reactionary" and "bourgeois." In 1934, however, the mass media talked about the new formula of Soviet patriotism for the first time. The traditional national attitudes were to be replaced by new, all-Soviet values and attitudes.

In 1934, schools and mass media introduced a new view of history. In addition to teaching the previously dominant history of the socio-economic base, the schools returned to teaching the history of nations and states. The curricula also reintegrated the old heroes and great personalities of Russian history, whom Pokrovskii's Marxist school had reduced to products of socio-economic conditions. However, the patriotic rediscovery of Russian history did not inspire a parallel renaissance of other peoples' national histories. On the contrary, Russian history expanded to become the history of the Soviet Union's territory and the past of the non-Russian peoples appeared as the prehistory of integration into the Russian Empire and the Soviet Union. Behind the smoke screen of "friendship of the peoples of the Soviet Union"—a term first used by Stalin in a prominent place in one of his speeches in 1935[69]—Soviet patriotism and Soviet history became more and more Russian as far as concrete contents goes. This was meant to make it easier (at least for Russians) to identify with Soviet patriotism. Of course, this Stalinist Russian national consciousness of history was extremely eclectic and completely excluded vast domains of Russian history, such as the church, monasticism, anti-centralist regional traditions, or non-Bolshevik reform efforts.

Notes

1. I do not intend to give a detailed analysis of the 1920s. This period is the subject of: H. Carrère d'Encausse, *Le grand défi: bolcheviks et nations 1917–1930 (Paris, 1987).*

2. B. Hayit, *Turkestan zwischen Russland und China* (Amsterdam, 1971), pp. 286–289; I.I. Groshev, *Borba partii protiv natsionalizma* (Moscow, 1974), p. 82; I.I. Groshev, *Istoricheskii opyt KPSS po osushchestvleniiu leniniskoi natsionalnoi politiki* (Moscow, 1967), p. 183; *Revoliutsiia v Srednei Azii glazami musulmanskikh bolshevikov,* reprint (Oxford, 1985).

3. See Lenin's, *Werke,* vol. 36, pp. 591, 594 (notes of 12-30-1922 and 12-31-1922). Derzhimorda is a policeman in Gogol's "Examiner."

4. *KPSS v rezoliutsiiakh i resheniiakh,* vol. 2, p. 255 (Tenth Party Congress) pp. 438f. (Twelfth Party Congress).

5. See Stalin's, *Werke,* vol. 12, p. 324.

6. Sh. Tipeev/N. Emaletdinov, "Protiv izvrashchenii leninskoi natsionalnoi politiki v Bashkirii," in: *RN,* 8/1931, p. 28; A. Tagirov, "Voprosy korenizatsii v Bashkirii," in: *RN,* 5/1932, pp. 95f.

7. Tipeev/Emaletdinov, ibid., pp. 20–28.

8. B. Rodnichev, "Korenizatsiia apparata v avtonomiiakh i raionakh natsmenshinstv RSFSR," in: *RN,* 12/1931, pp. 17f.

9. B. Rodnichev, "Zadachi ucheta i planirovaniia v osushchestvlenii leninskoi natsionalnoi politiki," in: *RN,* 6/1931, pp. 22f.

10. Quoted from Rodnichev, ibid., p. 24; Z. Ostrovskii, "K itogam paboty Otdela Natsionalnostei VCIK," in: *RN,* 5/1932.

11. T. Anver, "Obsluzhivanie natsionalnostei v Stalingradskom krae," in: *RN,* 6/1935, pp. 69–72.

12. A. Fedotova, "Vnimanie rostu kadrov natsionalnogo proletariata," in: *RN,* 7/1933, pp. 49f.

13. S. Dimanshtein, "Ideologicheskaia borba v natsionalnom voprose," in: *RN,* 3/1930, pp. 7f.

14. P. Rysakov, "Praktika zhovinizma i mestnogo natsionalizma," in: *RN,* 8–9/1930, p. 27.

15. A. Safudri, "K nekotorym itogam politechnizatsii natsionalnykh shkol," in: *RN,* 7/1932, pp. 109f.

16. S. Dimanshtein, "Ideologicheskaia borba v natsionalnom voprose," in: *RN,* 3/1930, pp. 8–10.

17. P. Rysakov, "Praktika zhovinizma i mestnogo natsionalizma," in: *RN,* 8–9/1930, p. 28.

18. A. Nugaev, "Praktika natsionalnoi politiki na magnitostroe," in: *RN,* 8/1931, pp. 18f.

19. S. Dimanshtein, "Ocherednye zadachi natsionalnoi raboty," in: *RN,* 10–11/1931, p. 37.

20. V. Velmin, "Komsomol v borbe za vospitanie natsionalnykh kadrov," in: *RN,* 3/1932, p. 21.

21. A. Kachanov, "Kulturnoe obsluzhivanie rabochikh natsmen Moskovskoi oblasti," in: *RN,* 6/1932, p. 57.

22. F. Goloshchekin, "Zavoevanie oktiabrskoi revoliutsii. K desiatiletiiu sovetskogo Kazakhstana," in: *RN*, 6/1930, pp. 102f.
23. A. Nugaev, "Praktika natsionalnoi politiki na magnitostroe," in: *RN*, 8/1931, pp. 20f.
24. E. Petrova, "Korenizatsiia organov iustitsii," in: *RN*, 3/1933, p. 70; in several cases, the accused received several of these penalties at the same time.
25. "Znamia revoliutsii," Kazan 8. III. 1918, quoted from: Bennigsen/Lemercier-Quelquejay, *Islam*, p. 112.
26. cf. Bennigsen/Quelquejay, ibid., pp. 153f.
27. See Stalin's, *Werke*, vol. 5, pp. 264–273.
28. From a 1928 programmatic paper by Sultan-Galiev, quoted from: M. Arzhanov, "Burzhuaznyi natsionalizm—orudie podgotovki antisovetskikh interventsii," in: *RN*, 1/1934, p. 27.
29. J. Arnold, *Die nationalen Gebietseinheiten der Sowjetunion* (Cologne, 1973), pp. 50f.
30. Resolution of the conference quoted from: A. Ikramov, "O proekte Konstitutsii Uzbekskoi SSR," in: *RN*, 4/1937, p. 42.
31. Additional names of prominent communists from the East can be found in: A.A. Bennigsen/S.E. Wimbush, *Muslim National Communism in the Soviet Union* (Chicago, 1979), p. 87.
32. A. Bennigsen/Ch. Lemercier-Quelquejay, "Der Sultangalievismus und die nationalistischen Abweichungen in der Tatarischen Autonomen Sowjetrepublik," in: *Forschungen zur osteuropäischen Geschichte*, VIII, 1959, pp. 323–396; Bennigsen/Wimbush, *Muslim National Communism*, pp. 37ff. Soviet contribution: A.G. Titov, *Borba partii za leninskuiu chistotu natsionalnoi politiki v period stroitelstva sotsializma v SSSR* (Moscow, 1978), pp. 44–48.
33. Bennigsen/Lemercier-Quelquejay, *Islam*, pp. 158f.
34. A. Fisher, *The Crimean Tatars* (Stanford, California, 1978), pp. 140f.
35. A different point of view is held by: A. Bennigsen/Wimbush, *Muslim National Communism*, pp. 89ff.
36. S. Dimanshtein, "Sotsialisticheskoe stroitelstvo i natsionalnaia politika partii," in: *RN*, 6/1930, pp. 10f.; A.R. Rakhimbaev, "Natsionalno-kulturnoe stroitelstvo na sovremennom etape," in: *RN*, 8–9/1930, pp. 104f.; P. Rysakov, "Praktika shovinizma i mestnogo natsionalizma," in: *RN*, 8–9/1930, p. 31; E. Farid, "Formy klassovoi borby na sovetskom Vostoke v perekhodnyi period," in: *RN*, 7/1931, p. 25; M. Galin, "Kulturnoe stroitelstvo sredneaziatskikh sovetskikh respublik," in: *RN*, 5/1931, pp. 77–79; A.K. Valiev, *Formirovanie i razvitie sovetskoi natsionalnoi intelligentsii v Srednei Azii* (Tashkent, 1966), p. 102.
37. P. Rysakov, "Praktika shovinizma i mestnogo natsionalizma," in: *RN*, 8–9/1930, p. 32.

38. V. Vorshev, "Osnovnye etapy razvitiia partorganizatsii Turkmenistana," in: *RN,* 12/1934, pp. 73–79.

39. A.P. Kuchkin, "Zemelnaia reforma v Kazakhstane v 1925–27 godakh," in: *VI,* 9/1954. pp. 25–34 (The quote from the 1925 resolution is on p. 27.); Titov, *Borba partii,* pp. 50f.; Groshev, *Borba partii protiv natsionalizma,* pp. 97–99.

40. See Stalin's, *Werke,* vol. 8, p. 135. Excerpts from this letter were first published in: Stalin, *Marksizm i natsionalno-kolonialnyi vopros* (Moscow, 1934); the letter was first published in its entirety in volume 8 of Stalin's *Werke* in 1953.

41. *Bilshovyk Ukraiiny* 3/1928, p. 61.

42. On Volobuev: Mace, "Communism and the Dilemmas of National Liberation," Ph.D. (University of Michigan, 1981), pp. 231–273; I. Maistrenko, *Istoriia komunistychnoii partiii Ukraiiny,* 1979, pp. 131ff.

43. Quoted from: ibid., p. 121.

44. Quoted from: ibid., p. 120; on Khvylovyi: Mace, "Communism and the Dilemmas of National Liberation," Ph.D. (University of Michigan, 1981), pp. 169–230.

45. A.V., "Voprosy i otvety," in: *RN,* 4/1934, p. 95.

46. Maistrenko, *Istoriia,* p. 137. A more recent Soviet presentation: I.I. Kolomiichenko. "Borba Kompartii Ukrainy s mestnym natsionalisticheskim uklonom v nachalnyi period sotsialisticheskoi rekonstruktsii," in: *VI KPSS,* 8/1980, pp. 91–101.

47. Sullivant, *Soviet Politics and the Ukraine,* pp. 174–177; in memory of the trial conducted fifty years ago, see the articles by V. Gryshko in: *Suchastnist,* 9/1980, pp. 78–89; 10/1980, pp. 52–62; 12/1980, pp. 44–63.

48. Lubachko, *Belorussia Under Soviet Rule,* pp. 107–111; *Borba partii,* pp. 56f., 128.

49. See Stalin's, *Werke,* vol. 12, p. 324.

50. Kossior/Postyschew, *Der bolschewistische Sieg in der Ukraine,* p. 165.

51. Titov, *Borba partii,* p. 57.

52. See Stalin's, *Werke,* vol. 13, p. 321.

53. S. Dimanshtein, "Borba na ideologicheskom fronte v Srednei Azii," in: *RN,* 12/1934, p. 30; M. Tulepov "Velikaia druzhba narodov," in: *RN,* 10/1936, p. 38; M. Efendiev, "Stalinskaia konstitutsiia ordenonosnogo Azerbaidzhana," in: *RN,* 11/1936, p. 34.

54. A. Tadzhiev, "K 1 maia. O nekotorykh itogakh i perspektivakh," in: *RN,* 5/1932, p. 3.

55. Kossior/Postyschew, *Der bolschewistische Sieg in der Ukraine,* p. 122.

56. Sullivant, *Soviet Politics and the Ukraine,* p. 193; until 1934, Kharkov was the seat of the Ukrainian Party and state leadership and government; in the summer of 1934, Kiev once more became the capital of the Ukraine.

57. S.D., "Borbas natsionalizmom i uroki Ukrainy," in: *RN,* 1/1934, pp. 15–22, the quote is on pp. 19f.; Kossior/Postyschew, *Der bolschewistische Sieg,* pp. 61–66, 137, 146. On Skrypnyk's biography including an extensive bibliography: Y. Bilinsky, "Mykola Skrypnyk and Petro Shelest," in: *Soviet Nationality Policies and Practices,* J.R. Azrael (ed.) (New York, 1978), pp. 106ff. and Mace, "Communism and the Dilemma of National Liberation," Ph.D. (University of Michigan, 1981), pp. 274–334.

58. A.B., "Voprosy i otvety," in: *RN,* 4/1934, pp. 95f.; S.D., Borba, ibid., p. 16.

59. Kossior/Postyschew, *Der bolschewistische Sieg,* p. 134; Sullivant, *Soviet Politics and the Ukraine,* p. 369.

60. Postyschew/Kossior, *Der bolschewistische Sieg,* pp. 129f.; a description of the 1933 purge, containing much information: H. Kostiuk, *Stalinist Rule in the Ukraine* (Munich, 1960), pp. 22–78.

61. Sullivant, *Soviet Politics and the Ukraine,* pp. 214f.

62. A. Baltin, "Nekotorye itogi chistki KP (b) Belorussii," in: *RN,* 3/1934, p. 18.

63. A. Bogdanov, "Chistka partii i zadachi partorganizatsii natsionalnykh respublik," in: *RN,* 2/1933, p. 32; Rigby, *Communist Party Membership,* pp. 200–204.

64. The quotes from the CC resolution are in: P. Petukhov, "K rabote sovetov Tadzhikistana," in: *RN,* 8/1934, pp. 68f.

65. Ibid., p. 71.

66. T. Rakowska-Harmstone, *Russia and Nationalism in Central Asia: The Case of Tadzhikistan* (Baltimore, 1970), p. 40.

67. "Literatura Uzbekistana," in: *RN,* 11/1934, p. 75.

68. Quoted from: E. Allworth, "The Changing Intellectual and Literary Community," in: *Central Asia: A Century of Russian Rule,* p. 380.

69. Stalin, *Sochineniia,* vol. 1 (XIV), 1934–1940, pp. 114f. On Soviet patriotism: E. Oberländer, *Sowjetpatriotismus und Geschichte* (Cologne, 1967); on the "friendship of peoples": L. Tillett, *The Great Friendship: Soviet Historians on the Non-Russian Nationalities* (Chapel Hill, 1969).

IV

Agricultural Collectivization and the Famine

The Collectivization Campaign

The next two sections examine how social revolution since 1929 has influenced or even brought about the described changes in nationalities policy. Was the demise of the korenizatsiia policy an inevitable consequence of collectivization and forced industrialization? When Stalin conceived of his "revolution from above,"[1] did he also plan from the beginning to redefine the relationship between Russians and non-Russians by repressing national ambitions—which became increasingly dangerous to the Soviet Union's cohesiveness the longer they existed? Were Russians necessary to ensure the continued existence of a society that the "revolution from above" had shaken to its very foundations? And was that why Russians received preferential treatment?

During the First Five-Year-Plan, nationalities policy did not undergo any radical changes. On the contrary, it seems the leadership wanted to avoid establishing another front in the nationalities issue during this period of drastic social upheaval and dangerous conflicts. This does not mean, however, that collectivization and industrialization did not influence nationalities policy and nationalism.

The few data published in the Soviet Union up to this point, support the conclusion that in the "war against the nation" (Ulam), many non-Russian nations' sacrifices would have been greater than the Russians'. When the Stalin leadership introduced kolkhozes by force, Ukrainian peasants had more to lose than Russian peasants; in addition, the Ukraine lacked the prerevolutionary communal organization of land that had developed in Russia. In Central Asia, water reform and land distribution to individual peasants had not yet been completed when collectivization reversed these policies and caused a shock effect. Resistance to bringing revolution to the villages was stronger among a number of non-Russian peoples than in central Russia, and in many instances, this resistance developed a national, anti-Russian flavor.

Table 4.1: The Rate of Collectivization in the National Territories

	Percentage of Collectivized Farms		
	Spring 1928	Spring 1930	Spring 1932
USSR	1.7	23.6	61.5
RSFSR	1.6	20.3	60.3
Karelian ASSR	0.3	8.5	59.6
Udmurt AR	--	20.3 (1-1-1931)	56.9 (7-1-1932)
Bashkir ASSR	1.4	20.9	66.4
Tatar ASSR	0.5	8.8	62.6
ASSR of Volga Germans	--	65.0 (1-1-1931)	91.4 (7-1-1932)
Daghestan ASSR	1.0	6.0	22.8
Crimean ASSR	9.3	50.9	78.5
Kazakh ASSR	1.8	28.5	73.1
Karakalpak ASSR	1.8	28.5	67.0
Kirgiz ASSR	1.7	29.1	67.4
Buriat-Mongolian ASSR	1.2	22.6	49.3
Ukraine	2.5	38.2	69.0
Belorussia	0.7	11.5	47.8
Transcaucasian Republic	1.0	15.0	41.6
Uzbekistan	1.2	27.1	82.6
Turkmenistan	0.5	22.8	73.0
Tadzhikistan	--	13.3	41.9

Sources: *Itogi razrezheniia natsionalnogo voprosa v SSSR* (Moscow, 1936), p. 123; A. Bogdanov/G. Mulakov, "Selskoe khoziaistvo SSR k 15 oktiabriu," in: *RN*, 10-11/1932, p. 74.

As a rule, territories in which collectivization happened very quickly sacrificed the most victims. From 1929 to 1932, most victims fell prey to the so-called "liquidation of the kulaks as a class" (i.e., the expropriation and deportation of the better-off peasant families), and to the famine from 1932 to 1934. The national territories with an above-average share of collectives suffered most from the famine: the grain-growing regions in the Ukraine, the Middle Volga, and the principal cotton-growing regions in Uzbekistan and Turkmenistan. In 1932, Kazakhstan was also clearly more collectivized than the Union's average. In this case, dry statistical data hide the forced settlement of nomads, which became a national catastrophe for the Kazakh people.

In comparison, Daghestan and the Transcaucasion Union Republics were considerably less collectivized. In these regions, the number of deportation victims was smaller, and the Transcaucasus never experienced a famine. A large number of Azeri, Armenian, and Georgian peasants joined the kolkhozes only in 1936 and 1937. In July 1937, the Union's average of collectivized farms was 93 percent; at the same time, the percentages were only 86.5 percent in Azerbaidzhan, 88.7 percent in Armenia, and even only 76.5 percent in Georgia.[2] In Georgia, private agriculture has remained unusually important. Around 1970, private acreage produced around 40 percent of agricultural yield; this is one of the reasons why Georgia has a relatively high standard of living.[3]

Although the Soviet Union has only published bits and pieces of data about the victims and the extent of resistance to collectivization, the existing information clearly shows that the revolution in the countryside was carried out against the wishes of the great majority of the peasants — particularly in the national territories. In an effort to nip incipient resistance to collectivization in the bud, the Soviets began the collectivization process by expropriating the wealthier peasants first and deporting most of them to labor camps. Soviet publications have conceded that more than one million families, or five million people, were deported. Western experts estimate that the actual figures are considerably higher.[4] Many "dekulakized" peasants died during deportation or in detention camps; others starved.

By the end of 1930, according to official figures, in the Ukraine alone, 200,000 households had been expropriated and their owners driven away. Half the people affected were deported to labor camps in the north.[5] For Uzbekistan, between 1930 and 1933, official figures place the number of "dekulakized" peasant households at 40,000, or 5 percent of all peasant households.[6] At least 200,000 people were outcast just in Uzbekistan. There was no strong movement among the peasants, who owned little or no land, to "liquidate" the kulaks either in Russian or non-Russian villages. One reason was that the term "kulak" very quickly changed from a social term to a political one and no longer referred to the more-or-less wealthy peasant, but to opponents of collectivization. No rural person was safe from being labelled a kulak.

The "25,000 workers"[7] sent from the cities to rural villages organized angry locals against the village upper stratum and naturally managed to find followers among the poor by promising they would live better lives after property was redistributed in their favor. However, what propaganda celebrated as class struggle in the villages was often in reality a very arbitrary listing of peasants as "kulaks," "middle-class peasants," and "village paupers." The administration and the OGPU simulated the class struggle in the villages.

Resistance in non-Russian villages was influenced by national concerns. Soviet politicians and the press were quite aware that in non-Russian villages, protest against fomenting social revolution from above would take on a nationalist flavor and thus considered it particularly dangerous. "In their fight against the kolkhoz movement, the kulak and bai elements in the national republics use nationalism by claiming that the kolkhozes were 'imposed from Moscow,' that this movement went against 'the venerable spirit' of the nation, old traditions, the Koran, etc."[8] At the Eleventh Party Congress in the Ukraine in June 1930, Kosior, the first Party secretary of the Ukraine, had already declared: "Without question, the last years have seen a considerable increase in Ukrainian nationalism...."[9] Later, at the Ukrainian CP's November plenum in 1933, he made a direct connection between collectivization and nationalism: "There is a broader basis now for the growth of Ukrainian nationalism" because "the relics of the destroyed kulakdom are organizing the fight against collective farms...."[10]

Until today, the Soviet Union has been very careful not to talk about the dimensions of this "fight." Although only bits of information are available, one can conclude that, at particular times and in individual territories, peasant resistance was well organized and constituted a danger to the Soviets. However, a general peasants' rebellion never happened—there was no supraregional organization. But as a result of widespread peasant resistance, Stalin's famous *Pravda* article of March 2, 1930, "Dizzy with Success," temporarily halted collectivization and officially condemned "exaggerations" and "violence." According to Soviet data, between January and March 15, 1930, "1,678 armed incidents occurred, during which Party and Soviet functionaries as well as kolkhoz activists were murdered..."[11] all over the country (except in the Ukraine). In the Ukraine there were "more than 1,500 terrorist actions" that peasants committed between January and June 1930.[12] Resistance took a variety of forms: Peasants refused to work on the kolkhozes, butchered their animals, sold their agricultural inventory, set fire on buildings, and ran functionaries out of the villages or killed them. According to incomplete Soviet data, from January to August 1930, the authorities in Uzbekistan recorded about 200 "terrorist actions," including 113 murders.[13]

In the Northern Caucasus, where a considerable portion of the population was of Ukrainian origin, the Soviets apparently met with the most severe resistance. In the County of Salsk, 44 percent (1926) of whose population was Ukrainian, a virtual rebellion broke out in February 1930. It took Soviet cavalry and armored vehicles six days to subdue this rebellion.[14] But "the kulaks organized riots and anti-Soviet rebellions"[15] in Kabardino-Balkaria and Checheno-Ingushetia as well. Incomplete Soviet data give the impression that the peasants' loosely organized power of resistance had been broken by the summer of 1932.

When the Soviets collectivized, they granted an important concession to non-Russian peoples: Most collective farms were more or less homogeneous as far as the nationality of its members goes. For the beginning, nationally mixed kolkhozes remained the exception even for the national minorities that settled in various areas. Creating nationally homogeneous kolkhozes was in the spirit in which nationalities policy was conducted in the 1920s, and collectivization was not used to mix all the peoples because this would have made the situation even more explosive. In the Ukraine of 1931, 93.3 percent (=31,000) of all kolkhozes were Ukrainian, 2.3 percent were Russian, 1.6 percent were German, 1.2 percent were Moldavian, 0.8 percent were Jewish, and 0.5 percent were Polish. In Belorussia, 96 percent of the kolkhozes were Belorussian, 2 percent were Polish, 1.3 percent were Jewish, and 0.3 were Russian; in Azerbaidzhan, 83.7 percent were Turkic, 9.2 percent were Armenian, and 2.8 percent were Russian; in Armenia, 78.7 percent were Armenian, 10.8 percent were Turkic, and 9.4 percent were Russian.[16]

Within the RSFSR, representation of the titular nations in the collective farms was 89.1 percent in Chuvashia, 66.4 percent in Kazakhstan, 62.9 percent in the Republic of Volga Germans, 50.4 percent in the Tatar ASSR, 35.6 percent on the Crimean peninsula, and 28.7 percent in Karelia. In many cases, even the small national groups who were scattered over different areas received their own kolkhozes. In 1931, there were 700 (6.2 percent) Finnish and 300 (2.6 percent) Estonian collective farms in the Leningrad Region.[17] The figures show that most of the non-Russian rural population was organized in kolkhozes of their respective nationalities. In this context, it is worth mentioning that outside the confines of the RSFSR, special Russian collective farms were established to emphasize the fact that the Russians were a minority here. It seems a certain number of kolkhozes composed of people of different nationalities existed in some Autonomous Republics in the beginning—for example on the Crimean peninsula and with the Volga Germans. However, this phenomenon frequently produced altercations in the villages and caused the break-up of these kolkhozes. As a result, national kolkhozes had become the rule by 1932.[18]

Of course, the question remains, what does it mean to label a kolkhoz as Ukrainian or German except that the majority of the peasants were of the same nationality? Presumably, the Soviets had planned to introduce the national languages as the administrative and written languages in the kolkhozes, but it is safe to assume that—apart from the Ukraine and the Transcaucasus—in most cases, they did not succeed. One reason for this failure is the fact that the majority of higher agricultural administrators, without whose direct order not a single seed of grain went into the ground and not a single cotton ball was picked, were Russians.[19] At the same time, one must assume that national kolkhozes had a great deal of prestige. They were to give the rural population the feeling that collectivization did not prevent nation-building. In the late 1930s, the national designation of the kolkhozes was abolished; the Stalinist press did not even hint at this change.

In the Soviet East, collectivization pursued an additional objective: the disintegration or at least relaxation of clan and tribal loyalty, which played a much larger role in the way people thought and behaved in this area than did their affiliation to a nation. Ten years after the revolution, the Soviets had only superficially penetrated the Central Asian village. Family and tribal leaders, who also owned the land and the herds and thus combined economic and social power, were much more important than the village Soviets or the virtually non-existent local Party cells. The purpose of collectivization was to undermine the economic foundation of clan and tribal loyalty. However, such efforts met with great problems, and often the goal could not be achieved in one step because the "class struggle in the village" was even more fictitious in the Islamic territories than in the European Soviet Union. As a rule, clan ties proved much stronger than rural paupers' alleged class interest in stripping the bais of their power and running them off their land.

Because of this clan loyalty, the Soviets initially made concessions in Kazakhstan, Central Asia, Kalmykia and Buryat-Mongolia and permitted collective farms founded on clan affiliation; only in this way could they establish collectivization. Mainly, after 1932, the Soviets took the second step and began running the clan patriarchs off their land, calling them "kulaks." Clan kolkhozes were considered a necessary evil that "made the fight against the bais and the relics of clan structure more difficult,"[20] however, some of them continue to exist to this day.

Other considerations also forced the Soviets to give in somewhat to resistance to collectivization in the East and Far North at least for some time. In the Far North and in a large part of Soviet Asia (Kazakhstan, Tadzhikistan, Karakalpakia), the establishment of agricultural artels, which had been enforced in 1929–30 was cancelled, and a precursor to the kolkhoz, the cooperative for the communal tilling of the soil (TOZ = *Tovarishchestvo sovmestnoi obrabotki zemli*), was declared as the norm. Later, during the late 1930s, the Soviets gradually converted the cooperatives into artels and thus into full kolkhozes.

On June 22, 1932, for example, the CC resolved "not to allow full collectivization of farms in the Far North." In this area, "administration" had been "rough," and "the principle of free choice" had been violated. The resistance of the small nationalities of the Far North had practically eliminated reindeer breeding, so only "the initial stages of cooperation would be permissible" in the future.[21] At the end of 1933, in a similar resolution on the situation in Tadzhikistan, the CC determined that the standard form of collective farm at the time was the cooperative (TOZ). Following the pattern set by "Dizzy with Success," the CC blamed the republic's deposed leadership for the Stalin leadership's mistakes.[22] The former republic's leadership was accused of having left out the simple forms of collectivization and thus having perverted the Party line.[23]

The Crisis in 1932–1933 and the Famine

As far as is known, the rural population's active resistance was subdued by the summer of 1932. However, only then did the catastrophic consequences collectivization triggered begin to become apparent. From 1932 to 1934, at least 8 million people starved. Among the non-Russian peoples, the number of victims was considerably higher than among Russians because the famine was centered in the Ukraine, the Northern Caucasus, the Middle and Lower Volga River areas, and Kazakhstan. At least 4.5 million people died in the Ukraine alone. Although central Russia also had food shortages, there was no famine as such — as far as is publicly known. The famine affected primarily the rural population because the Soviets had forcibly requisitioned their harvests to feed the population in the cities and industrial centers.

One infamous aspect of this catastrophe is the fact that the Stalinist leadership consciously accepted this famine, or even purposely caused it, to subdue resistance to collectivization once and for all. In the summer of 1933, M.M. Khataevich, the second secretary of the Ukrainian CC said to a government functionary: "A merciless fight between the peasants and our government is in progress ... It took a famine to show them who is the boss. It took millions of lives, but the system of collectivization has prevailed. We won the war."[24] Stalin consciously used this "war" as an instrument to eliminate the Ukrainians as a political factor.[25]

The Soviets denied the existence of this famine in all their statements, and this topic was taboo in the USSR until 1988. To deceive the world public, the Soviet government even continued to export grain. During the last famine before the revolution in 1891–1892, the Tsarist government had at least decreed an embargo on grain exports. Since the late 1970s, the present Soviet government has been importing millions of tons annually to cover at least basic nutrition needs.

The figures in Table 4.2 illustrate that following a good harvest in 1930, production declined by 12 percent in the next three years. This in itself was not enough to cause a famine in the villages, but at the same time, the government's wholesale purchase increased by 44 percent because of forced requisitions, leaving the rural population with insufficient grain supplies. In 1932, net grain export amounted to 1.7 tons; in 1933, 1.8 million tons.

The first step the peasants took was to slaughter their livestock, which they were either unable to feed any longer or were unwilling to hand over to the kolkhozes. In the collectivization years, the amount of livestock decreased by about half.

Table 4.2: Grain Production and State Procurement (millions of tons)

	Production	State Procurement
Average 1927/28 to 1930/31	75.1	15.0
1931/32	66.1	22.8
1932/33	66.4	18.8
1933/34	70.1	23.3
Average 1934/35 to 1937/38	77.2	28.1

Source: D.G. Dalrymple, "The Soviet Famine of 1932-34," in: Soviet Studies, XV, 1963/64, p. 264.

Table 4.3: Livestock (in millions)

	1916	1929	1933
Horses	35.1	34.0	16.6
Cattle	58.9	68.1	38.6
Sheep and Goats	115.2	147.2	50.6
Pigs	20.3	20.9	12.2

Source: Stalin's report of accounts of the CC at the XVII Party Congress in January 1934, in: Works, vol. 13, p. 286.

Of course, to this very day, there are no official Soviet statistics on the number of people who starved, but the available statistics allow reasonable estimates. According to these figures, a total of 7.5 million people died prematurely or of unnatural causes between 1932 and 1938. Of these losses, 80 percent, or 6 million deaths, occurred before 1934. This figure, which only includes the adult population, must be increased by about 3 million children who were born during the famine years of 1932-34 and died of malnutrition during their infancy. Another Western estimate places the number of Ukrainians who starved—within and without the Ukraine—at 7.5 million.[26]

Table 4.4 illustrates which peoples suffered a particularly high death toll. Among the large nations, Ukrainians had the highest absolute number of fatalities; the Kazakh people suffered the highest percentage of dead. To counteract "the legend of the alleged famine" in Russia, the Soviets ran a propaganda campaign among the Volga Germans and had them collect money and food as donations for the unemployed in Germany.[27]

Agricultural Collectivization and the Famine

Table 4.4: Demographic Development of the Nations that Particularly Suffered from the Famine and Forced Settlement of the Nomads (compared to the total population and to Russians)

	1926	1939	Increase (in percent)
Total Population in the USSR (in thousands)	147,028	170,557	15.7
Russians	77,791	99,592	28.0
Ukrainians	31,195	28,111	-9.9
Kazakhs	3,968	3,101	-21.9
Turkmen	764	812	6.3
Kirgiz	763	885	16.0
Kalmyks	132	134	1.8
Buriats	238	225	-5.4
Yakuts	241	242	0.6
Evenk	33	30	-9.5
Khant	18	19	4.3
Chukchi	13	14	6.1

Source: V.I. Kozlov, *Natsionalnosti SSSR* (Moscow, 1975), pp. 249f.

In 1933, the worst year of the famine, the Soviet government not only declined all foreign relief measures (in contrast to 1921), but Stalin began new acts of retaliation against the rural population. These were intended as punitive measures in response to the peasants' active resistance in the preceding years and as a means of fighting the peasants' continuing passive resistance. This passive resistance consisted primarily of the rural population's miserable work or its refusal to work at all in the kolkhozes and sovkhozes, attempts to hide what harvest there was from the requisitioning commandos, and allowing the equipment of the kolkhozes and sovkhozes to fall into disrepair, particularly new tractors and other machines. In 1929–30, retaliatory measures had been directed at the kulaks; now the targets of punitive acts were the kolkhozes and sovkhozes and the people who managed them.

In his speech, "On Rural Work," at the CC's January plenum in 1933, Stalin announced this strategy very clearly when he spoke of "anti-Soviet elements" that had infiltrated collective farms' management. One should not look for kulaks outside the kolkhozes, because they were within the collective farm and held the positions of stockmen, managers, accountants, secretaries.[28]

The Party created a special instrument to "eradicate" these "wreckers," whose crime was that they not only considered the needs of socialist society but also their own advantage and that of their own kolkhozes: the polit-sections of the machine-tractor stations (MTS) and sovkhozes. Stalin personally conceived of these crisis institutions, which were in effect from January 1933 to November 1934. These institutions were directly subordinate to the CC, which staffed them with functionaries who were not native to the respective region. On the whole, a total of 3,368 polit-sections were established at the MTSs and 2,021 at the sovkhozes. In 1933, the CC sent 18,000 political functionaries, who were assigned to manage the kolkhozes, to these institutions.[29]

The polit-sections are institutions characteristic of the style of Stalin's dictatorship. As a rule, special plenipotentiaries sent by Moscow carried out important political measures — from collectivization to purges — without involving the regular apparatuses. Since the late 1920s, the villages had been swarming with emissaries with all kinds of extraordinary powers. In this way, Stalin suppressed any initiative and responsibility of the peasants. However, extraordinary commissions were also used on the middle and high level — for example, to overcome difficulties at large-scale construction sites or to arrest Ukrainian Party leaders.

The functionaries of the polit-sections did not "manage" the kolkhozes by taking over the everyday responsibilities of a kolkhoz chairman but essentially by conducting witch hunts for "kulaks" in the collective farms. By this time, the term "kulak" had permanently metamorphosed from a social term into a political one. This also became apparent in the fact that propaganda used other terms synonymously for "kulaks": "former kulaks," "kulak helpers," "former popes and their sons," "anti-Soviet elements from the bourgeois-nationalist intelligentsia," "kulak agents."[30]

The repressive measures against the kolkhozes followed the same pattern everywhere: Whenever a kolkhoz did not meet the fixed delivery to the state in effect since January 1933, "wreckers," "enemies," or "former bais" and "beks" were "exposed" in management, the village soviet, and in the other rural apparatuses. Punishment ranged from removal from office to court-issued death sentences. The events that took place in the Udmurt raion, Balezino, are typical. There, the flax harvest was only 52 percent of what was planned. Kulaks were "exposed" all over the raion. The raion's leaders were said to have also "become allies of the class enemy and submitted to their influence." The whole rural Soviet and Party apparatus was "renovated." "Many were sentenced to death by firing squad."[31] The same sequence of events was repeated in dozens of variations: unsatisfactory fulfillment of the plan or delivery to the state, exposure of kulaks, and their punishment.

It is even possible to prove the Party did not consider kulak to refer to social origin but to those whose production was low, as the following reversal shows: A kulak who produces in abundance is no "kulak." In the Belorussian raion, Mogilev, the villagers informed on the chairman of the kolkhoz "Bolshevik" during the 1933 Party purge, saying he was a "former deacon." The purge commission determined that this kolkhoz was one of the best in this raion; the chairman had achieved excellent harvest. "In this way, *the investigation did not confirm the truth of accusations against him.*"[32] Equating "anti-Soviet elements" with unsatisfactory production seems typical of the early and mid-1930s. Stalin explicitly distanced himself from this position at the beginning of the 1937 wave of terror.[33] By 1937–39, not even economic successes offered protection from reprisals any more. Until then, however, a statement from a speech that Kalinin, then head of state, had delivered in 1925 in Uzbekistan described the political situation fairly accurately: "If a project starts with a prayer to Allah and ends in great success — excellent. However, if it starts with the 'International' and ends as a failure, then this project is a crime."[34]

The 1933 reprisals against the rural population especially affected the non-Russian peasants and functionaries. Although no extensive material is available on this matter either, the sparse data speak in no uncertain terms. In the raion Apostovsk in the Tatar ASSR, for example, members of ten village soviets and members of twelve kolkhoz leaderships (a total of fifty-two people) were tried during spring sowing in 1933.[35] In 1933–34, forty-six (of a total of seventy-five) polit-sections in Uzbekistan drove about 8,000 peasants from the kolkhozes.[36] In late 1932 and early 1933, 3,953 "kulaks" (among them 158 chairmen or secretaries of kolkhozes) were removed from the kolkhozes in Turkmenistan, which had a total of 1,340 collective farms.[37] In Georgia, about 7,000 "kulaks, kulak elements, . . . and lazy persons" fell victim to the purges even though only about half of the peasant households were collectivized there.[38] In 1933, 5,870 members of village soviets were removed from their positions in the Region Kiev alone.[39]

After the 1933 witch hunt, the rural areas experienced a distinct relaxation following the summer of 1934. The mass deportations stopped. Although the delivery obligations to the state continued to be extremely high and often could not be met, the rural population no longer starved. In May 1934, the CEC issued a resolution "On the Procedure for Reestablishing the Civil Rights of Former Kulaks." In November, the polit-sections were dissolved. In July 1935, those kolkhozniki who had received sentences of up to five years in labor camps and also rural functionaries who were in forced labor camps for sabotaging the grain requisitions were granted amnesty.[40] Stalin had won on this front.

I have repeatedly shown that, particularly during the years after the end of collectivization, the new course in nationalities policy became increasingly distinct: The domestic political front had abandoned the fight against the "kulaks" and had turned to the destruction of "bourgeois nationalism." The year 1933 is key in the sense that terror was simultaneously directed at both adversaries, which were frequently considered identical.

The East: Cotton Cultivation and Forced Settlement of the Nomads

In Soviet Asia, the "revolution from above" had specific characteristics, some of which are discussed above: It helped integrate the East into the Soviet state's political and economic structure. The Sovietization of Central Asia and Kazakhstan lagged about ten years behind the same process in the European USSR. Guerrilla groups (Basmachi) offered military resistance until 1926. In 1925, the structure of land ownership and, as a result, the social structures of the non-Russian peoples south and east of the Ural Mountains had hardly changed since 1917. Until then, land expropriated in the east had nearly exclusively affected Russian and Ukrainian settlers. Land and water reforms intended to expropriate the local "feudal lords" began in Uzbekistan in 1925, in Kazakhstan in 1927, and in Buryat-Mongolia only in 1930. Before collectivization, 66,000 peasants who did not have land of their own had been allotted plots of land, which shows how limited this reform was. In Kazakhstan, only 4 percent of livestock changed owners.[41]

How far Asia actually lagged behind in the Sovietization process is also apparent in the fact that the first soviet in Kirgizistan in a nomad territory was established in 1927. Only after this were soviets created in the Kazakh nomad territories, and a CC resolution of May 3, 1928, demanded "actual realization of the Sovietization in the [Kazakh] auls, establishment and stabilization of soviets, and strengthening of the leadership role of the Party cells."[42] Asia's Sovietization frequently was only a formality: Traditional Islamic and tribal institutions received Soviet labels. The plenum of the Turkmen CC stated in May 1928: "In the vast majority of cases, the Party cells in the auls of the raion Merv are groups of aksakals."[43] The 1931 inventory of Central Asia says: "In most cases, . . . the secretaries of the village soviets were the sons of bais, traders, and clergymen."[44]

Because Asian villages had resisted the 1917 revolution, the leaders wanted collectivization to revolutionize them and make them socially homogeneous by adapting them to a general Soviet "standard." Forced cotton growing in irrigated areas and the settlement of nomads in the steppe illustrate these efforts. Both measures were carried out not only despite resistance from those affected but also against the wishes of the republican Party leadership.

The official objective after 1929 of very quickly (and, as became evident immediately very ineffectively), expanding the acreage devoted to cotton growing was to make the USSR independent of cotton imports.[45] The Stalin

Agricultural Collectivization and the Famine 105

leadership was at least equally interested in integrating the cotton growing areas (primarily Uzbekistan) into the Soviet economy and in suppressing efforts to gain economic autonomy. Because Uzbekistan had to reduce the amount of grain it grew to plant cotton, the area became dependent on grain imports from the north. The expansion of cotton cultivation did not trigger development of a corresponding cotton-processing industry. As a result, the economy of Central Asia still exhibits colonial characteristics. Agricultural goods produced there — aside from cotton and raw silk — are exported primarily to the RSFSR and processed there.

Between 1925 and 1930, the acreage devoted to cotton cultivation in the USSR tripled from 1.46 million acres to 3.71 million acres. In Central Asia, cotton was grown on 1.58 million acres in 1913; by 1931, this acreage had increased to 3.53 million acres. The amount of raw cotton harvested, however, remained nearly the same; in 1915, 1.13 million tons of cotton were harvested; in 1931, 1.07 million tons.[46] This means productivity had dropped to less than 50 percent of pre-1917 production. This drop in productivity was a direct consequence of collectivization. The following figures prove this fact: In the Soviet Union's cotton sovkhozes, the yield per acre dropped from 2.07 tons of raw cotton in 1928 to 0.92 tons in 1932.[47] The merciless speed at which collectivization was instituted took a high toll. By the spring of 1932, 82.6 percent of peasant households in Uzbekistan were organized in kolkhozes. This put the cotton republic far above the Union's average and even clearly above the Ukraine (cf. Table 4.1).

There was general resistance to cotton in Central Asia. This resistance increased when grain deliveries from the north drastically declined after 1931 and the Soviets prohibited the local peasants from growing a sufficient amount of grain. "You can't eat cotton,"[48] the peasants told functionaries. Like everywhere else, resistance became national in form here, too: "Using the excuse that they are defending national interests, the kulaks and bais depict cotton as a culture the chauvinist Russian nation is forcing on them, and they attempt to boycott the increase in cotton-growing acreage. . . ."[49]

In reality, it was not of "kulaks and bais" at all, but in 1930 such people as the chairman of the Uzbek State Planning Committee, Shur, who publicly declared that expanding the cotton-growing acreage any further was "almost out of the question."[50] Faizulla Khodzhaev, chairman of the Uzbek Council of People's Commissars, was very assertive and made fulfilling the cotton plan dependent on whether Moscow would first meet Uzbekistan's "demands" — as he phrased it: sufficient delivery of grain, funds for construction of an irrigation system, and expansion of the Central Asian transport system.[51] Khodzhaev was strictly opposed to one-sided development in Central Asia on the basis of a monocultural agriculture. In vain, he frequently demanded establishment of a cotton-processing industry in Uzbekistan.[52] Later, in March 1938, Khodzhaev was tried in the last Moscow show trial (the Bukharin trial) and faced a firing squad. The "confessions," forced by means of torture, are very unreliable. For example, during the trial, Khodzhaev confessed he had collaborated with Ikramov, the first secretary of the Uzbek CC—who was also accused and executed—and worked for Uzbekistan's secession, hoping to turn it into a "British protectorate." During the trial, however, Khodzhaev also accused himself of infractions in line with his earlier public statements. He confessed, for example, that he had purposely lowered cotton production in favor of other agricultural products and had promoted industrial development in Uzbekistan "in such a way as to be more economically independent than ever of the Soviet Union, at the end of the First Five-Year Plan."[53]

Not until the great retribution in 1937–38 did Uzbek leaders pay with their lives for their objections to Stalin's policy in Central Asia; many second-level functionaries had already lost their positions in 1931. According to Stalinist propaganda "wreckers had won executive positions" in all Central Asian leading organs responsible for cotton growing, particularly in Uzbekistan's State Planning Committee (Uzgosplan) and in the central board for cotton cultivation (Glavkhlopkom) in Tashkent.[54] These denunciations only cover up the fact that the experts conceded the economic ineffectiveness and political harmfulness of Stalin's policy in Central Asia.

The most radical form of resistance was the revival of the Basmachi movement in Tadzhikistan and Turkmenistan. In March 1931, guerilla leader Ibragim Bek returned from Afghanistan and took control of parts of rural Tadzhikistan for a short time. In Turkmenistan, the revolt was the most successful; there, from the spring to the fall of 1931, rebels controlled the raions Krasnovodsk and Kazandzhik on the eastern shores of the Caspian Sea and nearly all of the Karakum desert, including its oases. In September 1931, after the Soviet armed forces had completed their primary attack, the Soviets announced they had killed, injured or taken prisoner 3,300 fighters. Individual rebel groups were operative until 1933.[55]

Military resistance had only managed to gain a foothold because much of the population sympathized with Islamic anti-Bolshevik fighters. The expulsion of the bais and clergymen from the villages and the forced relocation and persecution of the nomads were considerable sources of recruits for the guerrillas. The Soviet leaders had ordered forced relocation of tens of thousands of families to gain the work force necessary for forced cotton cultivation. In Tadzhikistan, for example, during the First Five-Year-Plan, 45,000 families from remote mountain villages of the Pamir were relocated into the valleys and oases and forced to grow cotton there. They were not familiar with cotton cultivation and could feed neither themselves nor their livestock with cotton. Only one third of these families stayed in the plains; many fled to Afghanistan, and others joined the Basmachi.[56]

The forced settlement of the nomads was among the worst outrages during the "construction of socialism." The Kazakh people were hit particularly hard by this policy, which resulted in genocide. Although the Stalin leadership maintained its official stance that the settled peasants had voluntarily joined the kolkhozes, the press did not cover up the fact that the nomads had been settled by force.

The nomad regions were the least Sovieticized, and even the land reform of the late 1920s had only partially dissolved the nomads' economic and social structure, which was based on the clans' use of land and ownership of herds. As a result, when the Soviets attempted to settle the nomads, the purpose was not only increasing grain production but also revolutionizing the nomads' social order "because clinging to the nomadic economy requires maintaining the vitality of the remnants of half-feudal and clanlike interests...."[57]

In addition to affecting the Kazakhs, by far the largest nomadic people (4 million), settlement particularly affected the Kirgiz, Karakalpaks, Kalmyks, and Buryats as well as the smaller nationalities of the Far North. Like collectivization, in 1930, large-scale settlement began without preparation, without long-term plans, and without sufficient funds. The first draft of the First Five-Year Plan, which the Kazakh People's Commissariat for Agriculture prepared, had still envisioned "maximum development of the nomad economy."[58] Now nomad clans were often forced to move to very distant parts of the country and to settle in locations that provided neither a sufficient water supply nor enough feed for their livestock. The houses promised them were not finished, and no construction materials were available. The pastures available at the settlement locations were too small, and the livestock died of starvation because the herds could not migrate. Among the individual authorities, utter confusion prevailed as to who was in charge, and soon the executive functionaries were only interested in covering up chaos and failure.[59] "Settlement was carried out in a terrible and at times criminal fashion: In a number of cases, houses were so unsuitable for human habitation that the nomads preferred to live in their yurts and kept their livestock in the houses."[60]

When the catastrophic consequences of this misguided policy forced Stalinist leaders to take counter measures, they returned to their proven strategies: A CC delegation lead by Kaganovich arrived in Kazakhstan and removed the Party leaders headed by F.I. Goloshchekin, the first secretary of the Kazakh Area Committee (Kazkraikom), from their positions. A resolution the Moscow CC issued on September 17, 1932, sharply criticized the "exaggerations" committed in Kazakhstan, determined that the basis of the kolkhoz be cooperative land use (TOZ) — an early form of the artel, and promised to amend the mistakes made during the overhasty settlement of the nomads.[61]

Although Stalin must undoubtedly have ordered the settlement campaign, he told the new Party head in Alma-Ata, the Armenian L.I. Mirzoian, that "those comrades are wrong, who think that a nomadic economy could not support keeping livestock and thus should be completely eradicated."[62] Again, the Soviets used their "Dizzy with Success" trick: Stalin punished the province's leading functionaries for mistakes he had made.

However, the consequences of two and a half years of persecution of the nomads were irreversible. The effects can be felt today. A comparison of the 1926 and 1939 census figures, documented in Table 4.4 (cf. above p. 101), shows the great losses of human lives the nomadic peoples of Central Asia and the Far North suffered. The Union's total population increased by 15.7 percent; the population of the Kazakh people declined by 20 percent. Many died of starvation or when they were deported during collectivization; many others fled to Sinkiang with their livestock or joined the Basmachi. According to Soviet figures, 15 to 20 percent of the Kazakh population left its republic in 1930-31. Modern Soviet regional historiography also states that the number of Kazakh households declined from 1.2 million in 1929 to 565,000 in 1936. According to these figures, the losses of human lives were even higher than census results indicated.[63] In 1926, the Kazakhs were the largest Turkic-Tatar people in the territory of the Soviet Union, numbering 60,000 more people than the Uzbeks. In principle, the great losses the Kazakhs suffered during the early 1930s account for the fact that today there are only half as many Kazakhs as Uzbeks (6.6 million as opposed to 12.5 million; cf. Table A.1 in the Appendix).

It is unclear how many nomads were actually settled. Soviet figures always obscure the losses; as a result, these data are extremely inconsistent. One publication states that "over one million" nomadic or semi-nomadic households existed in Kazakhstan during the mid-1920s.[64] Another publication quotes the number at 544,000 for 1930.[65] In 1935, the USSR's People's Commissariat for Agriculture estimated that 198,000 households had been settled in the RSFSR, and 263,000 nomadic economies were still in existence.[66] This relatively low number of settled nomads confirms other data, which show that only one-third of all officially settled Kazakhs actually stayed in the villages assigned to them.[67] According to modern Soviet data, 400,000 nomad households were settled in Kazakhstan by 1936; 150,000 of them continued to live nomadic or semi-nomadic lives.[68] Relating these data to the losses of human lives indicates that about one million Kazakh nomad households existed in the late 1920s. The number of 544,000 households mentioned above is apparently the result of doctored data. Although the majority of Kazakhs had to settle in grain-growing areas, some were settled in northern Kazakhstan, where industrial urban centers began to develop. During the mid-1930s, for example, part of the population of Karaganda lived a semi-nomadic life. Locations for setting up yurts were established in the city.[69] As a result, a relatively high percentage (40 percent) of the industrial workers in Kazakhstan were Kazakhs (cf. Tables 2.1 and 2.2, Chapter II).

In Kazakhstan, livestock declined from 36.3 million animals in 1929 to fewer than one-tenth this number (3.3 million) in 1933. Only in the mid-1960s, did the amount of livestock again reach the level of 1929.[70] On the whole, the devastation the "war against the nation" caused was worse in the Kazakh nomad territories than anywhere else in the USSR. But particularly here, collectivization confirmed Stalin's political doctrine: No means is as effective as violence. Since the holocaust, the Kazakhs have been the Asian people best integrated into Soviet society. They are represented among the Soviet elites at a disproportionately high number — in the Party, among executive functionaries, and among industrial workers. In some categories (such as students), Kazakhs are proportionately more numerous in present-day Soviet society than Ukrainians (for example). These observations cannot be explained just by the fact that the Kazakh Republic has been shaped by the great numbers of Russians who have been immigrating to it since the 1930s. The terror of collectivization broke the Kazakhs' resistance and increased their willingness to live under the existing conditions and to use them to their own advantage.

Termination of the nationalities policy of the 1920s and promotion of Russians within Soviet society were not necessarily the tacit goals of collectivization from the start. However, the intent of collectivization was to promote the spreading homogenization of society and to integrate agriculture into an all-Soviet economic cooperative that assigned particular production tasks (grain, cotton) to individual regions. The objective was to continue centralizing the economy and state administration as a counter measure to regionalization and personal initiative in the peripheries. In this respect, the objectives of collectivization contradicted the policy of nation-building from the very beginning. Collectivization contributed greatly to undermining the foundations of nation-building.

Notes

1. Stalin himself referred to collectivization as a "revolution carried out from above, on the government's initiative and whose impact equalled the October 1917 revolution" (*Geschichte der Kommunistischen Partei der Sowjetunion [Bolschewiki]. Kurzer Lehrgang* Berlin, 1946, p. 369).

2. A.V. Likholat, Sodruzhestvo narodov SSSR v borbe za postroenie sotsializma. 1917–1937 (Moscow, 1976), pp. 315–317.

3. *Handbook of Major Soviet Nationalities,* p. 162.

4. M. Lewin, *Russian Peasants and Soviet Power: A Study of Collectivization,* (London, 1968), pp. 507–509.

5. *Ocherki istorii kollektivizatsii selskogo khoziaistva v soiuznykh respublikakh*, (ed.) V.P. Danilov (Moscow, 1963), p. 183.
6. Ibid., p. 252.
7. Resolution of the CC plenum of November 1929 (*KPSS v resoliutsiiakh i resheniiakh*, vol. 4, 1970, p. 350).
8. S. Dimanshtein, "Bolshevistskii otpor natsionalizmu," in: *RN*, 4/1933, p. 5.
9. Quoted from: *RN*, 3/1930, p. 13.
10. Kossior/Postyschew, *Der bolschewistische Sieg*, p. 71.
11. B.A. Abramov/T.K. Kocharli, "Ob oshibkakh v odnoi knige. Pismo v redaktsiiu," in: *VI, KPSS* 5/1975, p. 137; quoted from: Davies, *The Industrialization of Soviet Russia*, vol. I, p. 258.
12. Malanchuk, *Istoricheskii opyt KPSS*, p. 152.
13. O.B. Dzhamalov, "Iz istorii kollektivizatsii selskogo khoziaistva v Uzbekistane," in: *VI*, 11/1958, p. 56.
14. Davies, *The Industrialization of Soviet Russia*, vol. 1, pp. 258f.; *Vsesoiuznaia perepis naseleniia 17 dekabria 1926 g.*, vol. 4 (Moscow, 1928), p. 75.
15. Likholat, *Sodruzhestvo narodov SSSR*, p. 269.
16. G. Mulakov, "Rukovodstvo kolkhozami v novoi obstanovke," in: *RN*, 1/1932, p. 70.
17. Ibid., p. 71.
18. S. Dimanshtein, "Zadachi kulturno-massovoi raboty sredi natsionalnostei," in: *RN*, 9/1931, p. 74.
19. A. Bogdanov, "Kolkhoznoe stroitelstvo v natsionalnykh respublikakh i oblastiakh," in: *RN*, 1/1931, p. 56.
20. S. Dimanshtein, "Istoricheskie resheniia XVII partkonferentsii," in: *RN*, 3/1932, p. 11; Bogdanov, Ibid., p. 55.
21. E. Kantor, "Sever zovet," in: *RN*, 10–11/1932, p. 135; this is where the quotes from the CC resolution are printed.
22. See pp. 96, above.
23. A. Andreev, "Zhivotnovodstvo—pervoocherednaia zadacha," in: *RN*, 8/1934, p. 31. On Kazakhstan: M.B. Olcott, "The Collectivization Drive in Kazakhstan," in: *Russian Review*, XL, 1981, pp. 122ff.
24. V.A. Kravchenko, *Ich wählte die Freiheit* (Zurich, 1947), p. 164.
25. D.G. Dalrymple, "The Soviet Famine of 1932–34," in: *Soviet Studies*, 1963/64, vol. XV, pp. 250–284; this is the basis for: "The Great Ukrainian Famine of 1932–33 as an Instrument of Russian Nationalities Policy," in: *Ukrainian Review*, 4/1978, pp. 11–23; 1/1979, pp. 31–59.
26. Maksudov, "Pertes subies par la population de l'URSS: 1918–1958," in: *Cahiers du monde russe et soviétique*, XVIII, 1977, pp. 234f.; J.E. Mace, "Famine and Nationalism in Soviet Ukraine," in: *Problems of Communism*, XXXIII, 3/1984, p. 39 (7.5 million Ukrainians starved), cf. W. Kosyk, "Der

Hungergenozid in der Ukraine 1932–1933," in: *Jahrbuch der Ukrainekunde,* 1983, pp. 89–126.

27. "15 let Respubliki Nemcev Povolzhia," in: *RN,* 11/1933, pp. 48f.
28. See Stalin, *Werke,* vol. 13, p. 205.
29. A. Bakulov, "O zadachakh politotdelov MTS i sovkhozov," in: *RN,* 4/1933, pp. 13–18; P. Zaitsev, "O resheniiakh noiabrskogo (1934 g.) plenuma CK VKP (b)," in: *RN,* 1/1935, pp. 10, 13; Likholat, *Sodruzhestvo narodov SSSR,* p. 308.
30. U. Turat, "Nizovaia natsionalnaia pechat i rabota s rabselkorami," in: *RN,* 5/1932, pp. 30f.; "Celi i zadachi politicheskikh otdelov MTS i sovkhozov," in: *RN,* 1/1933, pp. 21f.
31. G. Ponomarev, "Uroki Balezinskogo raiona," in: *RN,* 8–9/1933, pp. 42f.
32. A. Baltin, "Nekotorye itogi chistki KP (b) Belorussi," in: *RN,* 3/1934, pp. 16f.
33. A.B. Ulam, *Stalin: The Man and His Era* (New York, 1973), p. 430.
34. Quoted from S. Dimanshtein in: idem., "Natsionalnaia politika sovetskoi vlasti i M.N. Kalinin," in: *RN,* 4/1934, p. 12.
35. S. Nosov/A. Bogdanov, "Perestroiku partiinoi raboty podchinit zadacham dnia," in: *RN,* 11/1934, p. 22.
36. O.B. Dzhamalov, "Iz istorii kollektivizatsii selskogo khoziaistva v Uzbekistane," in: *VI,* 11/1958, p. 59.
37. V. Vorshev, "Osnovnye etapy razvitiia partorganizatsii Turkmenistana," in: *RN,* 12/1934, p. 79.
38. I. Babintsev, "Sotsialisticheskoe stroitelstvo Gruzii," in: *RN,* 4/1934, p. 76.
39. M. Galiev, "Ukreplenie nizovogo sovetskogo apparata v 1933 g.," in: *RN,* 12/1933, p. 11.
40. Iakubovskaia, *Razvitie SSSR kak soiuznogo gosudarstva,* p. 196.
41. Dzhamalov, loc. cit., pp. 46–49; M.B. Olcott, "The Collectivization Drive in Kazakhstan," in: *Russian Review,* XL, 1981, p. 124.
42. Iakubovskaia, *Razvitie SSSR kak soiuznogo gosudarstva,* pp. 88f.; Uraz Isaev, "15 let borby i pobed," in: *RN,* 11/1935, p. 47 (quote from the CC resolution of May 3, 1928).
43. V. Vorshev, "Osnovnye etapy razvitiia partorganizatsii Turkmenistana," in: *RN,* 12/1934, p. 73. "Aksakal" (Turkish), literally white beard, is the term for (family, clan) elders.
44. E. Tarid, "Formy klassovoi borby na sovetskom vostoke v perekhodnyi period," in: *RN,* 7/1931, p. 29.
45. CC resolution of July 18, 1929, "On the Development of Cotton Growing" (A. Ananev, "Khlopkovyi plan 1932 goda," in: *RN,* 2/1932, p. 34).
46. A. Bogdanov/G. Mulakov, "Selskoe khoziaistvo SSSR k 15 oktiabria," in: *RN,* 10–11/1932, p. 72; G. Podvarkov/V. Kryklov, "Nekotorye itogi pervoi piatiletki Srednei Azii," in: *RN,* 10–11/1932, p. 112.

47. A. Ananev, "Zadachi politotdelov khlopkovykh sovkhozov," in: *RN*, 4/1933, p. 20.
48. A. Bakulov, "Nekotorye itogi seva pervoi vesny piatiletki," in: *RN*, 7/1933, p. 21.
49. P. Petukhov, "Na podstupakh k polnoi likvidatsii natsionalnoi otstalosti," in: *RN*, 2/1934, p. 39.
50. N. Shur, "K kontrolnym tsifram Uzbekistana na 1930/31 god," in: *RN*, 6/1930, p. 43.
51. Faizulla Khodzhaev, "Khlopok," in: *RN*, 6/1930, pp. 27–32.
52. Idem, "Nekotorye voprosy vtoroi piatiletki v Uzbekistane," in: *RN*, 5/1932, p. 12.
53. Conquest, *Great Terror*, pp. 384f. (ibid., the quotes from Khodzhaev's confessions).
54. P. Rysakov, "Otgoloski vreditelstva v natsionalnykh raionakh," in: *RN*, 7/1931, p. 52.
55. M.B. Olcott, "The Basmachi or Freeman's Revolt in Turkestan 1918–1924," in: *Soviet Studies*, XXXIII, 1981, pp. 361f.; Soviet perspective: Iu.A. Poliakov/A.I. Chugunov, *Konets basmachestva* (Moscow, 1976), pp. 133–165; A.I. Zevelev/Iu.A. Poliakov/A.I. Chugunov, *Basmachestvo: vozniknovenie, sushchnost, krakh* (Moscow, 1981), pp. 156–181.
56. P. Petukhov, "K rabote soveto: Tadzhikistana," in: *RN*, 8/1934, p. 69; I. Kolychev, "Bolnye momenty pereseleniia v Tadzhikistane," in: *RN*, 6/1930, pp. 62–68.
57. Kosakov, "Ob osedanii kochevogo i polukochevogo naseleniia sovetskogo vostoka," in: *RN*, 5/1932, p. 50.
58. P. Rysakov, "Otgoloski vreditelstva v natsionalnykh raionakh," in: *RN*, 7/1931, p. 47.
59. A. Mukhardzhi/N. Nazarevskii, "Osedanie kochevnikov Kirgizii," in: *RN*, 12/1933, pp. 16–25.
60. "Soveshchanie po voprosam osedaniia kochevykh khoziaistv i zemleustroistva kolkhozov natsionalnykh respublik i oblastei," in: *RN*, 10/1935, p. 84.
61. I.D. Kulumbetov, "Reshenie CK VKP (b) i SNK SSSR o Kasakhstane," in: *RN*, 5/1935, pp. 18f.
62. Gorshechnikov, "Osnovnye momenty razvitiia natsrespublik vo 2-i piatiletke," in: *RN*, 4/1935, p. 31
63. Olcott, *Collectivization Drive in Kazakhstan*, pp. 128, 136.
64. A.P. Kuchkin, "Zemelnaia reforma v Kazakhstane v 1925–1927 godakh," in: *VI*, 9/1954, p. 27.
65. Likholat, *Sodruzhestvo narodov SSSR*, p. 271.
66. "Soveshchanie po voprosam osedaniia kochevykh khoziaistv . . .," in: *RN*, 10/1935, p. 83.
67. Olcott, ibid., p. 133.

68. Ibid., pp. 138f.
69. S. Abramov, "Kommunalnoe stroitelstvo v natsionalnykh respublikakh," in: *RN*, 1/1935, p. 60.
70. Olcott, ibid., p. 123.

V

Industrialization and Migration

Industrialization

In the late 1920s, enthused by their belief in progress and ignoring economic reason, the Soviets stepped up industrialization. The purpose of forced industrialization was to catch the Soviet Union up technologically and economically with developed capitalist countries "in not more than ten years."[1] The objective in the domestic realm was—as Stalin had already stated at the Tenth Party Congress in 1921—to make "the government, culture, and economy" of underdeveloped nations "catch up with Central Russia."[2] Because of this, the Fifteenth Party Congress in December 1927 issued directives for the First Five-Year-Plan, determining "faster economic and cultural development" in "underdeveloped peripheral national areas."[3]

The Soviet Union could neither compete with capitalism, nor could it accomplish more or less balanced regional economic development. The Soviets seriously pursued the first objective, however—at least in some key areas of heavy industry and munitions. The second goal remained a propaganda slogan. For planning, the actual priorities were completely different. The first priority was to increase production in heavy industry and means of production. As a result, Soviet capital investment was primarily directed to old industrial areas: Moscow, Leningrad, and the Donets Basin.

The two goals of Soviet economic policy (maximum growth in production at minimum cost, and economic leveling to benefit underdeveloped areas) are, in principle, mutually contradictory. In reality, the Stalin leadership decided to concentrate on the first alternative. In propaganda, however, it maintained the illusion that the two objectives were virtually identical. The economic criterion of maximum production under the cheapest possible conditions, however, stood in opposition to the development of new heavy industry in the east. The Soviets put together the ore deposits in the Ural Mountains and the coal and mineral resources of Western Siberia and Northern Kazakhstan to form a new center for heavy industry in the east (the Ural-Kuznetsk Combine). As in Northern Kazakhstan, the population in these eastern areas of the RSFSR was primarily Russian. This meant the

Industrialization and Migration

"underdeveloped peoples" did not profit from industrialization. Economic development of the eastern RSFSR was essentially a political decision, which military considerations heavily influenced.

In the 1930s, aside from Kazakhstan, one-sided development of centers for heavy industry only benefitted the Bashkir ASSR, where extensive mineral-oil deposits were discovered in the early 1930s. The other Autonomous Republics in the Volga area, Central Asia, and Belorussia experienced a modest increase in consumer-goods production, which was generally neglected.[4] During the First Five-Year-Plan, the growth of industrial production in the industrial areas of the RSFSR was far above the Union's average. The autonomous territories within the RSFSR obtained only 1 to 2 percent of the capital investment allocation the Russian Union Republic received.[5]

An isolated example shows the direction economic centralism took. In 1934, a total of 834 million rubles was available for municipal buildings and public housing in the RSFSR. Of that total, the Soviets planned to spend only 72 million rubles in the twelve ASSR's, but allotted 350 million rubles for the construction of Moscow's subway.[6]

Nevertheless, industrial growth was considerable in the non-Russian periphery.

Table 5.1 shows that industrial production during the Second Five-Year-Plan increased a little faster in the underdeveloped republics than in the RSFSR. However, this growth was essentially the result of the Asian republics' very low initial level of industrialization. Even in 1937, Belorussia, with an economy based on agriculture, still produced more industrial goods than Uzbekistan. In 1939, Belorussia had a population of 5.6 million, Uzbekistan 6.3 million. The difference in industrial production between these two republics diminished only marginally during the 1930s.

The national territories could not even keep up with Russia in efforts to mechanize agriculture although propaganda continued to enlist that, in the non-Russian republics, agricultural development had priority over industry. From 1930 to 1933, the number of tractors in the machine-tractor-stations grew from 7,102 to 73,160, or by 1,030 percent. In all the national Union Republics and ten Autonomous Republics together, the combined increase amounted only to 926 percent (from 3,708 to 34,327 tractors).[7] In summary, although Stalin's industrialization campaign (which began in the late 1920s) was instrumental in creating the foundation for industrial development in the national republics, this catch-up industrialization was not a high priority in concrete economic planning and ranked far below economic growth, military security, and promotion of industrial centers with Russian populations.

Table 5.1: Industrial Gross Production During the Second Five-Year-Plan (in Billions of Rubles)

	1932	1937	Increase (in percent)
RSFSR	31.4	69.2	120
Ukraine	7.79	17.39	120
Belorussia	1.02	1.93	90
Georgia	0.503	1.047	110
Armenia	0.111	0.255	130
Turkmenistan	0.129	0.293	130
Uzbekistan	0.684	1.666	140
Tadzhikistan	0.051	0.187	270
Kazakhstan	0.406	0.982	140

Source: *Itogi vypolneniia vtorogo piatiletnego plana razvitiia narodnogo khoziaistva SSR* (Moscow, 1939), pp. 42-55. No data were available on Azerbaijan and Kirgizistan.

As a result, some important indicators showed increased distance between Russia's industrialization level and that of the national territories; one such indicator is the per capita production of industrial goods. In 1913, the territories of the future non-Russian Union Republics generated 44 percent of the per capita production among the territories that later comprised the RSFSR. By 1940, this figure had declined to 33 percent. The corresponding ruble value, however, increased nearly sixfold during the same period.[8] The difference was not quite as large in per capita capital investment in government enterprises and cooperatives; on the average, the non-Russian Union Republics received 63 percent of per capita investment in the RSFSR from 1933 to 1940.[9] From 1928 to 1932, the non-Russian Union Republics received 32.2 percent of all capital investment in the USSR. Although the non-Russian territories and their populations had considerably increased in size because of the 1939-1940 annexations, this percentage declined to 30.3 percent between 1938 and 1941.[10]

An examination of the way the Soviets distributed available investment among the national Union Republics, shows that Kazakhstan and the three Transcaucasian republics received more than the average amount. The Soviets neglected Belorussia and particularly the Ukraine. After Stalin's death, this pattern reversed: The percentage of investment available to the Transcaucasian republics declined and the percentage for the Ukraine increased. During the decade following Stalin's death, however, financial support for Kazakhstan (the virgin land campaign) even increase.

In many cases, local Party leaders opposed Moscow as it set out to establish planning priorities and to concentrate efforts at industrialization on the European (Moscow, Leningrad) and non-European (Ural, Western Siberia) areas settled by Russians. In the 1920s, some of these disputes took place in public. In later years, the "fight against nationalism," which was primarily directed at signs of interest in economic autonomy, prevented such public replay.

The most famous efforts were by Ukrainian politicians and economists, who wanted to prevent the development of a basis for heavy industry in the eastern RSFSR (Ural-Kuznetsk Combine) and to divert investment to the Ukrainian industrial district instead. Disputes between "Ukrainians" and "Uralians" took place at the 1925 and 1929 Party Conferences, at the level of the economic bureaucracy's central authorities (Gosplan, Supreme Economic Council), and at the Fifteenth Party Congress in 1927. In the press, Ia.V. Dimanshtein, a member of the Ukraine's Gosplan, stood out by publishing a series of articles in 1928. In these articles, he demanded that, for reasons of economic efficiency, investment in the Ukraine be given priority. He claimed that the establishment of new industrial centers would slow down growth in the old ones, particularly in the Donets Basin. In addition, all major industrial centers had depended on coal. Transporting coal to the ore centers (from the Kuznetsk Basin to the Ural Mountains) was not profitable.

The Uralians and Siberians reversed the argument: Developing heavy industry is the first step in a region's comprehensive economic development. Consequently, considerations of short-term profitability had to yield to the long-term perspective. The decision to build the Ural-Kuznetsk Combine was made in the fall of 1928.[11]

The national territories' attempts to catch-up in industrialization did not go far. However, the Party and propaganda continued to produce boastful directives. The gap between reality and illusion grew. The promises that had been made during the initial phase of industrialization had aroused great expectations among all Soviet peoples. The ensuing disappointment must have been even greater because the expectations of some Party members and young people resulted from true enthusiasm. In the 1930s, aware that they could move from underdevelopment and create a socialist society, thus putting themselves at the forefront of historical progress, many intellectuals and Party workers viewed misery and injustice as the justifiable price for a shining future.

The directives issued at the Seventeenth Party Congress in early 1932 for the Second Five-Year-Plan, served their intended purpose and mobilized powers. By 1937, "the classless socialist society" would evolve in the Soviet

Union. The rapid growth of socialist economy "helps the national republics and regions overcome the nationalities' economic and cultural underdevelopment."[12] V.V. Kuibyshev, the chairman of Gosplan, declared at the Party Congress that in respect to "per capita consumption of the most important products for personal needs" by 1937, "the Soviet Union will be the leading country on earth and will demonstrate to every worker what the working class, which builds socialism, is able to accomplish."[13]

From such statements, Party leaders in the national territories derived concrete expectations: In the course of the Second Five-Year-Plan, "Central Asia must be elevated to the same level as the most advanced districts of the Soviet Union."[14] The underlying assumption was that industrialization would basically be achieved by local non-Russian workers and that "Great-Russian chauvinism" was the greatest obstacle to be overcome on the way to training native specialists.[15] S. Dimanshtein, the leading publicist of nationalities issues, sharply polemicized against proposals suggesting there was no need to construct textile mills in cotton-growing areas because it was less expensive to process mill cotton in the RSFSR. Dimanshtein referred to this position as "counterrevolutionary" and called it "Great-Power chauvinism."[16]

None of the expectations the Party raised came true. Neither did the "classless society" come into being, nor were textile mills constructed in Uzbekistan in numbers worth mentioning. However, these disappointed expectations had not only a psychological side to them but also a political one, and Stalin realized this. The liquidation of leadership groups from 1936 to 1938, which took place in a particularly radical fashion in the national territories, must be viewed in this context. This was Stalin's way of dealing with the pressures that had developed within a decade from the Party's and society's expectations.

Migration and Urbanization

In terms of population policy, the most significant consequences of collectivization and industrialization were sharp increases in migration and urbanization. Two primary migratory routes are discernable: migration from the country to the cities and migration eastward. With a few exceptions, the involvement of non-Russian peoples in the process of urbanization was below average; apart from the Jews and Tatars, they hardly participated at all in eastward migration. The findings of analysis of industrialization's social consequences are the same as the description of the process itself: Although the non-Russian peoples were involved in the modernization processes and their traditional social structures were disintegrating, as a rule, compared to that of the Russians, their modernization was in no way accelerated; only such accelerated modernization could have assured the often-invoked catch-up.

The Russians proved to be the Soviet Union's "true nomads."[17] It is possible to view the new wave of migrations to the east and those into the Northern Caucasus, which began with industrialization and collectivization, as continuing a centuries-old tradition in Russian history. In contrast to agricultural colonization before 1917, this was essentially industrial colonization. Whatever industrialization and mechanization of agriculture was accomplished in the national territories was to a large degree the result of Russian specialists' efforts.

Thus the 1931 demands that the new qualified work forces in the national industrial factories "must essentially come from among the native, local population"[18] could not be met. Even heavy industry in Kazakhstan was to be developed by Kazakh workers and engineers.[19] As is well known, there were no Kazakh workers or engineers, and the chaos of the upheavals in the 1930s made all previous plans for korenizatsiia illusory.

Maybe, it was not one of the Stalinist leadership's objectives when they planned forced industrialization to intentionally undermine the nationalities policy that had been in effect in the 1920s. But undermining the nationalities policy now became quite a desirable and welcome side effect of industrialization. Stalin interpreted the increasing number of Russians in the national territories as a factor contributing to political stability. A newly arrived Russian upper class secured Soviet dominance. This new upper class had the violent social upheavals of the 1930s to thank for its position and this class contributed to suppressing the unfulfillable aspirations and illusions of the non-Russian elites.

From the perspective of the nationalities, the decades between the censuses of 1897 and 1926 did not witness any significant redistribution of the population.[20] After 1926, the mix of individual nationalities in the population changed decisively. From 1926 to 1939, the number of Russians outside the RSFSR (within the 1939 borders) grew from 5.1 million to 9.3 million people.[21] In 1897, 8.4 percent of the population outside the RSFSR's present borders was Russian; in 1926, this percentage was 8.6 percent. By 1939, the percentage had jumped to 14.9 percent and culminated at 17.8 percent in 1959.[22] Between 1926 and 1939, 1.7 million people migrated to Kazakhstan and Central Asia alone. From 1864 to 1913, 1.3 million people migrated. In both instances, the overwhelming majority of migrants was Russian.[23]

But even within the RSFSR, a large part of the Russian population moved east. In 1926, 76.9 percent of all Russians lived in the traditional Russian settlement areas in European Russia (excluding the Northern Caucasus); by 1959, this percentage had declined to 62.3 percent (for 1939, no corresponding figures are available). In comparison, the percentage of Russians living in the Asian part of the RSFSR increased from 10.3 percent in 1926 to 15.6 percent in 1959.[24]

Table A.2 in the Appendix documents typical effects of Russian migration on the national composition of the population in the Union and Autonomous Republics: the percentage of Russians increased and the percentage of natives of the respective titular nation decreased. Within the RSFSR, the increased number of Russians in the population is particularly apparent in the Autonomous Republics of the northern Caucasus (except in Daghestan) and in the Kalmyk ASSR. In part, this shift resulted from development of the oil industry in the Northern Caucasus. The locals' participation in this process was very limited. Most likely, however, Russification of many of the Ukrainians living in the Northern Caucasus also contributed to the precipitous increase in the number of Russians among the population.[25]

Few Russians migrated to the Autonomous Republics of the Middle Volga region; Tataria and Mordvinia actually experienced a slight decline in the percentage of Russians in the population. However, even before the revolution, many Russians lived in these republics, and by the late 1920s, the percentage was more than 40 percent nearly everywhere (except the Chuvash ASSR). Since the mid-1500s, the peoples of the Middle Volga region had lived with Russians under one government. In this region, integration was very advanced. It was not necessary for the Soviets to establish the influence of the Russians and the Russian language on society and culture. In these republics, the basic requirements for launching separatist political movements did not exist.

Unlike in the Middle Volga region, in the five Asian Union Republics, Russian migration decisively changed the demographic situation. From 1926 to 1939, the percentage of the titular nation in the overall population decreased by about 15 percent in Kirgizia, Tadzhikistan, and Turkmenistan; in Kazakhstan this decrease was even 20 percent. In 1939 the number of Kazakhs amounted only to a little more than a third of their republic's population. Only about half the population in Kirgizia was Kirgiz. However, the decline in the percentage of Kazakhs in the population also resulted from the high losses the Kazakhs suffered because of forced settlement of the nomads. Only in Uzbekistan, did more than 60 percent of the population consist of natives of the titular nation in the late 1930s.

From a demographic perspective, the number of Russians who migrated to the Ukraine and Belorussia during the 1930s was insignificant. In Belorussia, the percentage of Russians even declined, and the slight increase experienced by the Ukraine was basically the result of the famine in the Ukrainian villages; the percentage of Ukrainians among the republic's population declined because of the famine.

In anticipation of future developments, I want to point out that in the late 1950s, the percentage of Russians in the population reached a high in the

Industrialization and Migration

eastern and southern national territories and then began to decline in a dramatic reversal of previous demographic development. Eastward migration slowed or came to a complete halt. At the same time, the Islamic peoples' birth rates increased and surpassed that of the Russians. The percentage of Russians in the USSR's total population within its contemporary borders consistently increased from 44.4 percent in 1897 to 54.6 percent in 1959; since then it has been decreasing.[26]

In the 1960s, ever fewer Russians migrated eastward; after World War II, westward migration began and continues today. Russians moved into all national territories — except Lithuania.

Only the Tatars and Jews migrated as much as the Russians, and like the Russians, these peoples also migrated primarily eastward. The Tatars either migrated into the neighboring Bashkir ASSR, which had always had a large Tatar population, or into the neighboring industrial region of the southern Ural Mountains (Magnitogorsk). In addition, the Kazan Tatars migrated to distant Central Asia. In 1926, only 39,000 Kazan Tatars lived in Central Asia; calculations for 1959 place the number at 388,000.[27] The fact that in 1926, 40 percent of the Tatars lived in the Tatar ASSR, (as opposed to 33 percent in 1939 and 27 percent in 1959 — see Table A.3 of the Appendix) show how widely dispersed the Tatars were. No other nation with its own republic (except Mordvinians) has a diaspora as large as the Tatars. This holds true even when one considers that in 1926, about 460,000 Tatars (and, in 1939, 780,000) lived in neighboring Bashkiria, which has a culture much like Tataria's. One has to keep in mind, however, that Soviet statistics include Crimean Tatars (of whom there were 179,000 in 1926, and circa 202,000 in 1936) among the Kazan Tatars. This inclusion makes the diaspora figures too high.

In the Tsarist Empire, the areas where Jews were allowed to settle were strictly limited, and they generally were only allowed to settle in the west Russian provinces that roughly correspond to the territory of the modern Ukraine, Moldavia, Belorussia, and Lithuania. When industrialization began, many Jews left their ghetto-like "Shtetl" in the west and moved to the Russian cities (primarily to Moscow and Leningrad) and to the Ukrainian industrial district on the Donets River. In 1926, 17.3 percent of the Soviet Union's Jewish population (within the present borders) lived in the three economic areas (according to 1961 zoning) northwest, center, and Donets-Dnieper. By 1959, the percentage had doubled to 35.5 percent.[28] However, the reliability of these figures is limited because they document not only eastward migration but also indirectly reflect the extermination of Jews during German occupation in the west.

Between the two censuses of 1926 and 1939, the number of Jews in the Ukraine declined from 1,574,000 to 1,532,000; and in Belorussia, from 407,000 to 375,000. In the same period, however, the number of Jews in the RSFSR increased from 566,000 to 969,000.[29] Many Jews settled in Moscow and

Leningrad. In 1959, 239,000 Jews lived in Moscow and 169,000 in Leningrad. Second to the Russians only, the Jews were by far the largest national minority in both cities.[30]

Two other social processes interacted with Jewish migration: the Jews' linguistic-national Russian acculturation and their social rise within the developing Soviet industrial society. Jews who left their traditional, relatively concise, settlement areas and moved to a linguistic-cultural environment where Russian culture was dominant could rise into the social strata of the medical, cultural, or technical intelligentsia if they became linguistically assimilated. (This was also true for the Ukrainian industrial district on the Donets River.) One sign of their great willingness to assimilate is the fact that, in the 1930s, more than a third of all Jewish marriages were mixed marriages.[31]

The Jews met all the requirements for geographic, social, and ethnic mobility: Among the peoples of the Soviet Union, the Jews were the most urbanized, they had a well-developed elementary school system, and their literacy rate had been the highest among all the peoples since the nineteenth century.[32] In addition, the Jewish minority had suffered discrimination before 1917 and their participation in the revolutionary movement had been significant. As a result, the Bolshevik nationalities policy of the 1920s furthered the Jews and fought against the popular anti-Semitism.

For the Jews, not unlike for the Russians, mobility meant rising into the elites. As a rule, this was not the case with other non-Russians who migrated to the cities and new industrial centers after the late 1920s. They lacked the elementary prerequisites: education and proficiency in the Russian language.

In 1931 alone, 40,000 workers in the Tatar ASSR were recruited to work in the Donets basin, bringing the number of Tatar workers to 50,000 to 60,000 in 1932; however, "there was not a single Tatar engineer or technician in the whole Donbass."[33] In subsequent years, this situation changed only a little. The Soviet Union was no longer willing to create expensive educational facilities for national minorities living in the diaspora as in the 1920s but — without actually saying so — preferred to rely on national assimilation. The fact that in April 1932, the "All-Ukrainian Conference of Tatar Union Functionaries" decided to organize Tatar colliery plants in the Donbass "to consist of only Tatar workers and with a Tatar administrative and economic apparatus,"[34] is indicative of the assertiveness of Tatar workers in the Donbass. At the same time, this decision is reminiscent of the early Soviet days. Even during the prime of korenizatsiia, the Party would hardly have accepted such a resolution. Demands for nationally homogeneous industrial plants, just like the organization of nationally uniform Party structures — which the Tatar workers also demanded in the Donets basin — were considered a clear transgression against nation-building in the Party's sense.

The industrial cities in the Ural Mountains were another center to which national workers migrated. In 1929–1930, only 50,000 non-Russian industrial and construction workers were employed there; by 1932, their number had increased to 100,000. These mostly Tatar and Bashkir workers made up 16.5 percent of all workers in the industrial and construction fields. On the large-scale industrial construction sites in Magnitogorsk, up to 50 percent of the workers were non-Russian. Among the engineering and technical personnel, there were virtually no nationals; 80 to 95 percent of the nationals were unskilled laborers. The economic administrations in the Urals neither organized continued professional education for the nationals nor provided adequate cultural services in the respective national languages. Local newspapers were printed exclusively in Russian. Production meetings and other mass activities also excluded local nationals for linguistic reasons. As in the other industrial centers, the only national measure carried out in the Urals was assembling national work brigades. These brigades served to integrate non-Russians into the work process and were supposed to increase production.[35]

Production figures, output targets, and short-term criteria of economic efficiency became the exclusive measure of policy. Just as socialist realism was perceived as a means to an end within cultural policy, nationalities policy was viewed from the perspective of how useful it was for increasing production. Whenever a conflict arose, it was decided in favor of production. In the 1920s, some of the old, established national diaspora groups had been able to develop a surprising cultural economy.[36] The often considerably larger groups of national immigrants to the industrial centers had no such support system available during the "construction of socialism."

By 1936, the number of non-Russian workers in the city and region (oblast) of Moscow had grown to 150,000. Among them, the Tatars were the most numerous; in addition, there were many Chuvashs and Mordvinians. The plants only put together national work brigades. The only local Tatar newspaper had been shut down, and the fifty Tatar one-room schools merely existed without a sufficient number of buildings, teachers, and educational resources. Many children did not attend school at all. Some non-Russian Stakhanov-workers were even illiterate; nobody cared.

Reports describe the living conditions among Tatar workers in Moscow as "terrible." "At number 30 2nd Izvoznaia Street, sixty-nine Tatar metro workers live in a basement.... They exist under disgusting conditions: They have no blankets or sheets; their mattresses are dirty and infested with vermin. This dormitory does not even provide hot water for tea."[37]

Like the Russians, many of the national workers came to the industrial districts because rural authorities had signed recruitment contracts with the industrial economic organs. Some came voluntarily, others were forced by their kolkhozes to migrate to the cities; as when the Tatar population offered considerable resistance to the recruitment of Tatar workers for the Donets basin in the Tatar ASSR in 1931.[38]

Many recruits remained seasonal workers and regularly returned to their kolkhozes to work on the agricultural farm. Under such conditions, the fluctuation in the number of workers was tremendous and a great obstacle to economic efficiency.

The recruitment system introduced in 1931 required industrial plants to recruit only in specific rural areas. This system failed to control the chaos. The scale of this social revolution, which the leadership had triggered from above, becomes apparent when one remembers that in 1931 alone, 2.66 million people (from all nations) were supposed to be integrated from the kolkhozes into the industry and the sovkhozes. This plan, it is true, was only partially fulfilled.[39] Altogether, the number of workers and employees involved in production (including the sovkhozes) increased from 8.5 million in 1928 to 18.7 million in 1932.[40]

Correspondingly, the populations of the cities increased equally dramatically, and living conditions in the cities deteriorated at the same rate. The population of Moscow increased from 2 million in 1926 to 3.7 million in 1933; over the same period, the population of Leningrad grew from 1.6 million to 2.8 million.[41] Even Tashkent's population of 323,000 people in 1927 had already grown to 500,000 people by January 1, 1933.[42]

If we relate the rate of population growth in Tashkent to the data in Appendix Table A.4 (which indicate that in the same period, the Uzbek urban population of Uzbekistan did not increase), we see that the population increase resulted solely from Russian immigration. Tashkent is probably a representative example of the capitals of the five Asian Union Republics. The Russian immigrants who moved eastward relocated primarily in the cities. This caused the Russian percentage of the urban populations in non-Russian territories to increase faster than it did in respect to the total population. Already by 1926, the percentage of Russians among the urban population in the national territories was much larger than among the rural population. Migration, which began in 1930, made this trend even more pronounced. For example in 1926, 3.6 percent of the population of Georgia were Russians; among the urban population, 11.8 percent; in 1959, 10.1 percent of the total population was Russian. In the cities, however, the figure was 18.8 percent. In 1926 in Uzbekistan, 5.4 percent of the population was Russian, in the cities 19.2 percent. By 1959, these figures had increased to 13.5 percent and 33.4 percent, respectively. In Kirgizia, the corresponding figures for 1926 were 11.7 percent and 37.2 percent, and for 1959, 30.2 percent and 51.8 percent.[43]

Dramatic differences in the national composition of the populations of the cities on the one hand and rural areas on the other developed in the five Asian Union Republics and the Autonomous Republics in the RSFSR. Russians and their language and culture influenced the character of the cities — particularly the capitals; the rural areas to a large extent remained nationally homogeneous. These demographic conditions necessarily influenced all processes of modernization, which have their driving forces in the cities.

Appendix Table A.4 demonstrates the unchallenged superior position Russians enjoyed during the USSR's urbanization. Except for the Jews and Armenians, the Russians were by far the most urbanized people in 1926 as well as in 1939. Already in the nineteenth century, the Armenians had taken residence as enterprising citizens in many cities of the Empire. Only about half the Armenians lived in the Armenian SSR (cf. Appendix Table A.3). All non-Russian Union Republics had and have a higher percentage of urbanites than the respective titular nations; for the reasons mentioned, the Armenians again are an exception. The ratio is reversed among the Russians: As a nation they were and are more urbanized than the RSFSR.

In the 1930s, urbanization among Russians, which had started at a higher level than urbanization in the titular nations, increased at a rate near the country's average. Later, the rate of urbanization among Russians even rose above the average, making Russians the nation with the highest increase in urbanization of all nations between 1926 and the 1970s. "Indeed, very few, if any, peoples in human history have urbanized as rapidly as the Russians in the Soviet era."[44] Thus, catch-up urbanization of the non-Russians was out of the question.

In the 1930s, demographic development in Ukrainian cities deviated from the general pattern: The percentage of Ukrainians among the urban population increased from 47.2 percent in 1926 to 58.1 percent in 1939.[45] There are two reasons for this: the zeal with which the local party leaders pursued the policy of Ukrainization and the lack of massive Russian migration into the cities. As a result, the difference between the Russian and Ukrainian urbanization levels decreased considerably by 1939; later, this difference again began to increase (cf. Appendix Table A.5).

The Nations' Social Structures

The nations' social structures are among the central aspects of the nationalities issue. Although all nations in the USSR have experienced decisive social changes during the last fifty years, Soviet scholars have not yet managed to describe these processes in a satisfactory way. The censuses collected data on the social structures of the nations, but this information has been published only in part or not at all. It is likely that these data do not agree with Soviet ideological doctrine and Party slogans that claim the nations' social structures are continuously becoming more and more homogeneous and that the fundamental differences among the peoples had been overcome by the 1930s.[46]

Findings so far give rise to the expectation that industrialization and Russian migration during the 1930s slowed rather than accelerated modernization of non-Russian peoples' social structures. What data are available support this expectation. Members of only a few nations (in addition to the Russians, Jews, Armenians, and Georgians) were over-proportionally recruited into skilled positions, the number of which had mushroomed in the industrial and technical sector, in the bureaucracies, in the Party, and in academia. These few nations must be considered the winners of the social mobilization Stalinism triggered.

In the national territories, Russian cadres, which were delegated for this task by the central government and Party apparatus, were the primary agents in the development of the new bureaucracies for agriculture and economic planning as well as development of Soviet administration and industrial plants. A few examples will clarify this: In the mid-1930s, 700 specialists from European Russia arrived in Tashkent to develop the local textile combine.[47] From 1937 to 1940, 600 teachers, all university graduates, and more than 500 industrial and agricultural specialists were "dispatched" to Kirgizia.[48] Specialists for Kirgizia were primarily recruited in the regions Tambov and Penza.[49]

From 1931 to 1937, 1,200 qualified miners and technicians from the Donets basin (in addition to 450 from the Kuznetsk basin and 800 from other industrial centers of the RSFSR) were relocated to the budding coal-mining district of Karaganda (Kazakhstan).[50] In 1937 alone, 1,299 specialists, graduates of universities or technical middle schools, immigrated to Tadzhikistan.[51]

The list of examples can be continued, but no Soviet data are available that would make generalizations possible. The range of specialists sent to the east is large and includes every academic profession as well as industrial workers. In October 1935, for example, the CEC ordered 170 fully trained medical doctors to relocate to Kazakhstan "for permanent residency." In a similar fashion, in December 1935, the Presidium of the Council of Nationalities ordered 100 medical doctors and 190 teachers sent to Buriat-Mongolia.[52] But a great number of Russian workers also went to the east. 3,062 workers from central Russia in 1933, 3,500 workers in 1934, and 3,000 workers in 1935 were sent to the industrial construction sites in Uzbekistan alone. As a result, by the late 1930s, the percentage of Russians in the working-strata was higher in all Union Republics (except in the Ukraine) than it had been at the end of the 1920s;[53] the trend of the 1920s had been reversed.

In addition to the people's commissariats and the CEC, the CC also ordered many top executives from Russia to move to the national territories. Between 1930 and 1933, the CC dispatched a total of 45,000 functionaries to serve a great variety of management functions (from 1928 to 1930, the corresponding number had only been 10,000); the CC sent 5,581 functionaries to the Ukraine, 3,197 to the Northern Caucasus, 2,140 into the Lower Volga region, 1,625 into the Middle Volga region, 1,927 to Central Asia, and 2,261 to Kazakhstan. It is remarkable that Kaganovich explicitly stated at the Seventeenth Party Congress in January/February 1934 that only a few cadres had been sent to the Transcaucasus because a sufficient number of local top executives was available in that area.[54] This is another example of how Stalin treated the Transcaucasus preferentially. A number of the above mentioned functionaries were employed in the development of the previously mentioned political departments of the MTS and the sovkhozes.

In 1932, only 10 percent of the MTS top executives — not including the polit-departments — in Kazakhstan and Turkmenistan were natives. In comparison, 83 percent of the top executives in Belorussia were natives, 67 percent in the Ukraine, and 60 percent in the Transcaucasus. In Tataria, an average of 34 percent of top executives were natives.[55]

No one knows how many people left Russia voluntarily and how many left against their will. Probably, many people who had originally been "dispatched" against their will later began to appreciate their new living conditions in the east. For, in general, migration was synonymous with a rise in social status and membership in social groups with a considerably higher standing than those of the majority of natives. In addition, the Soviets created favorable starting conditions for Russian immigrants. Even in the most remote industrial settlements and administrative centers, the Soviets opened Russian schools and cultural facilities, which let the Russians feel at home everywhere. In comparison, the cultural and linguistic autonomy of all the other national diaspora groups were drastically diminished in the mid and late 1930s. The abandonment of the original plan to modernize the Soviet Union in a hundred languages made it possible for Russians everywhere in the national territories to speak their mother tongue in their work places.

To explain Russian "nomadism," it is necessary to consider these exclusively Russian privileges, which began with industrialization. For people from other nations, this opportunity for vertical social mobility connected with geographical mobility was available only if they were prepared to become acculturated to Russian.

In vocational schools and universities, efforts to teach in languages other than Russian slowed; after the mid-1930s, other languages in the classrooms even decreased again. This made admission more difficult for people from underdeveloped nations. The hopeful start at cultivating modern national elites in the 1920s withered. Only 11.6 percent of the 31,000 university-educated specialists who worked in Central Asia's economy on January 1, 1941, were local nationals: 2,900 Uzbeks, about 300 Tadzhiks, about 200

Turkmen, and about 100 Kirgiz.[56] In 1936, only 160 Uzbek, 120 Kazakh, and thirty-five Tadzhik medical doctors were practicing in all the USSR.[57]

During the Stalin era, many people who had risen through the ranks, from accountants and brigadiers to the regional Party secretary, held prominent positions. These people were called *vydvizhentsy*. Party and Komsomol members as well as workers either were sent to professional—primarily technical—training courses or, even more frequently, promoted directly to responsible positions in their plants and organizations although they had no appropriate qualifications. The estimated total number of students mobilized and practicians promoted between 1928 and 1933—the height of this movement—is "at least 1.5 million."[58] The *vydvizhenie* was an important tool of controlled social mobility.

After the 1936–1938 purge, opportunities for students and professional climbers, whom the Party had mobilized during the First Five-Year-Plan, to rise into leadership positions were extremely good. In 1952, more than a third of the CC's full members and about half the ministers and their deputies on the union level were *vydvizhentsy* who had been delegated as adults to enter colleges during the First Five-Year-Plan. This group has been referred to as the Brezhnev generation.[59]

Most of the non-Russian peoples—with the probable exception of the Ukrainians, Georgians, Armenians, and Jews—were hardly at all able to take advantage of this means of upward social mobility. The preferential treatment of the "practicianers" in the factories had the same consequences as sending management personnel from the center to the periphery: It slowed down the development of local national elites. Among the groups that were advanced (Party members, workers), few were non-Russians, who often did not have the linguistic and educational prerequisites to fill the technical and industrial positions that went to the people who worked up through the ranks. As a result, complaints were endless about the "extreme lack of *vydvizhenie*" of the nationals.[60] The fact that the Soviets had treated preferentially masses of workers who climbed through the ranks since the First Five-Year-Plan did not help homogenize the people's social structures; on the contrary, this preferential treatment was advantageous only for Russians and a few other nationals.

Tables A.6 and A.7 in the Appendix give a rough outline of the nations' social structures. In 1939, more Russians than the average were in the two relatively privileged social groups of blue-collar workers and employees—most of the intelligentsia belonged to the latter group—and clearly fewer Russians than the average were in the underprivileged class of kolkhoz peasants. The opposite was true of all other nations. The only exception was Armenia; more Armenians were blue-collar workers and employees than the average for the total population; a disproportionately high number of Armenians were in those groups. In 1939, the fact that fewer Armenians were kolkhozniks than could have been expected from the number of Armenians in the total population of their republic corroborates this observation. The data in Appendix Table A.6 refer to the Union Republics. A comparison of this information and (unpublished) data for the entire union would show even more clearly the distance between Russians and Armenians, on the one hand, and all the other nations on the other: Outside the RSFSR, the percentage of blue-collar and white-collar Russian workers was considerably higher than in the RSFSR. Russian kolkhoz peasants, on the other hand, were of no statistical significance outside their own republic.

This Russian dominance was particularly pronounced among blue-collar workers and employees in the Islamic republics; even Azerbaidzhan, which had already possessed a highly developed oil industry before the revolution, was no exception. Oil production and refining was and remained in Russian hands. In 1939, the percentage of Uzbek blue-collar workers and employees was about a third of the union average.

In 1939, most non-Russian peoples had remained kolkhoz peasants. In Central Asia, 80 percent of the natives belonged to this social group; in Azerbaidzhan, 70 percent; and even in Kazakhstan, Georgia, and Belorussia 60 percent. In comparison, fewer than 40 percent of the Russians in the RSFSR (this percentage is even lower on the scale of the whole Union) lived in kolkhozes. Already in 1939, about as many Russians were workers as were kolkhoz peasants (generally the sovkhoz workers were counted as workers). Even by 1959, the non-Russian peoples — except the Armenians and Kazakhs — were far from achieving an even balance of workers and kolkhozniks. In addition, only a small percentage of the Kazakh workers were industrial workers; in 1959, the majority of Kazakh workers were sovkhozniks.

A survey of the late Stalin era from 1939 to 1959 shows that the global picture did not change profoundly. Even after twenty years, the percentage of Russians among the mobilized classes of blue-collar and white-collar workers was far above the average; non-Russian peoples primarily constituted the rural kolkhoz population. Only the annexed Estonian nation enjoyed a much more favorable social structure similar to the Russian social structure within the RSFSR in 1959. In addition to Estonians, only Georgians and Armenians had about as many white-collar workers (which is to say members of the intelligentsia) at the end of the Stalin era as did the Russians. Obviously, these two Transcaucasian republics' exceptional level of support for education played a role in creating this situation.

As expected, over twenty years, the social structure shifted on the whole to favor blue-collar workers and employees. The number of Russians in these social groups remained above average without changing much. Nevertheless, the Islamic peoples experienced trends that moved them closer to the average. In comparison, the percentages of Ukrainians and Belorussians continued to fall below the average. As a result, in 1959 their overrepresentation in the underprivileged group of kolkhozniki was considerably higher than it had been twenty years earlier. This fact can only in part be traced to the consequences of the war. It also shows the lack of concern for the development of the Ukraine and Belorussia in the late Stalin era. Another reason why these people's social structure did not develop in a positive way is because many mobilized and urbanized nationals were assimilated into Russian society. In relation to the Union average, Ukrainians and Belorussians were more rural in 1959 than they had been in 1939.

Appendix Table A.7 provides information about how the intelligentsia was structured and how it developed towards the end of the Stalin era. Although the absolute numbers grew considerably, the total picture of the relationships among the nations remained essentially the same for twenty years: With the exceptions of Georgians, Armenians, Estonians, and Jews, the number of Russian intellectuals was considerably higher than that of non-Russians (the Jews are not included in Appendix Table A.7). Surprisingly, the growth rates of the much less developed Islamic peoples—with the exception of the Kazakhs—was barely higher than that of the Russians, and the growth rates of the Belorussians and Ukrainians were even significantly lower. This means that homogenization, which was supposed to bring the peoples closer together, did not take place. A comparison of the individual groups of intelligentsia shows that the distances between the nations were comparatively small in the areas of art and education and that Russian dominance was by far most pronounced in the sphere of material production. This situation had not changed even by the late 1950s. Only the scholarly intelligentsia of the other peoples was able to significantly narrow the gap between them and their Russian counterparts; in this area, the Central Asian nations began to catch up with the Russians. To a smaller extent, this is also true of the intellectuals involved with production. On the other hand, the distance between the Russians and the Ukrainians and Belorussians in the area of science and production increased.

During the Stalin era, the Soviets invested a great deal of propaganda into publicizing their efforts to reduce the number of specialists working in the administration. It remains unclear how much the Soviets wanted this "fight against bureaucracy" to obscure reality and whether they were waging it more on the level of statistical records than on the level of reality. In any case, they did not use this reduction of administrative personnel to balance the number of local nationals in administration. Basically, the proportion of nationals has remained the same; however, the difference was never as dramatic as in the areas of production and science.

In summary, although modernization after the 1930s considerably increased the number of mobile social groups, it basically served only the Russians and a few other nations, the Jews, Armenians, and Georgians. Although the Central Asian nations started from an extremely low level, they were able to reduce the distance between themselves and the Russians only to a very limited degree; in many instances, the gap between the Russians and the Ukrainians and Belorussians even increased. By the late 1950s, Russian dominance in the leading strata of Soviet society had not been broken. Efforts to nationalize Soviet power were suspended after the mid-1930s. The constraints arising from the "revolution from above" and the leadership's political decisions had complemented each other: The Soviets were unable to force partial industrialization in a hundred languages; it rather depended on Russian specialists. Collectivization, sovietization, and the famine had challenged the loyalties of the non-Russian peoples in many territories. According to Stalin's wishes, a comparatively privileged upper class was to maintain Soviet rule and to counteract illusions of continuously growing national autonomy raised in the 1920s.

Notes

1. Stalin, in a speech presented to industrial functionaries in February 1931, in: *Werke,* vol. XIII, p. 37. In this speech, Stalin returned to the motto of "catching up with and passing capitalism," which Lenin had already used in September 1917. (On the motto, "catching up with and passing" cf. A. Buchholz, "Wissenschaftlich-technische Revolution und Wettbewerb der Systeme," in: *Osteuropa,* XXII, 1972, pp. 332–337).

2. See Stalin, *Werke,* vol. V, p. 34.

3. E. Kogan, "Vypolnenie piatiletnego plana po natsionalnym respublikam," in: *RN,* 6/1931, p.47.

4. *Postroenie fundamenta sotsialisticheskoi ekonomiki v SSSR* (Moscow, 1960), pp. 176, 189.

5. Iakubovskaia, *Razvitie SSSR kak soyuznogo gosudarstva,* pp. 158f.

6. L. Svedov, "Plan khoziaistvennogo i kulturnogo stroitelstva RSFSR v 1934 godu," in: *RN,* 1/1934, p. 71.

7. B. Roshal, "Stroitelstvo MTS v natsionalnykh respublikakh," in: *RN,* 12/1933, p. 57.

8. V. Holubnykhy, "Some Economic Aspects of Relations among the Soviet Republics," in: *Ethnic Minorities in the Soviet Union,* p. 73.

9. Ibid., p. 77.

10. Ibid., p. 82.

11. T. Kirstein, *Sowjetische Industrialisierung—geplanter oder spontaner Proze? Eine Strukturanalyse des wirtschaftspolitischen Entscheidungsprozesses beim Aufbau des Ural-Kuzneck-Kombinats 1918–1930* (Baden-Baden, 1979) pp. 161, 165f., 188f. (Gosplan, Supreme Economic Council), 114, 236–239 (1925 and 1929 Party Congress), 226–234 (Fifteenth Party Congress), 194f. (Dimanshtein).

12. Quotes from the resolution issued at the Seventeenth Party Congress in: I. Karneev, "Nekotorye tsifry po podgotovke inzhenerno-tekhnicheskikh kadrov iz korennykh natsionalnostei," in: *RN*, 3/1933, p. 86.
13. Quotes from Kuibyshev's speech in: I. Ulianov, "Ko vtoroi piatiletke legkoi promyshlennosti," in: *RN*, 9/1932, p. 37.
14. D. Rozit, "Promyshlennoe razvitie Srednei Azii vo vtoroi piatiletke," in: *RN*, 1/1932, p. 44.
15. S. Akopov, "K voprosu ob uzbekizatsii apparata i sozdanii mestnykh rabochikh kadrov promyshlennosti Uzbekistana," in: *RN*, 12/1931, pp. 22–28.
16. S. Dimanshtein, "K IX sezdu profsoiuzov," in: *RN*, 4/1932, p. 4.
17. Carrére d'Encausse, *L'Empire clat*, p. 72.
18. S. Dimanshtein, "Rech vozhdia—boevoe rukovodstvo k deistviiu," in: *RN*, 8/1931, p. 6.
19. A. Balgaev, "Mesto Kazakhstana v Uralo-kuznetskom kombinate," in: *RN*, 8/1931, p. 71.
20. R.A. Lewis, "The Mixing of Russians and Soviet Nationalities and Its Demographic Impact," in: *Soviet Nationality Problems*, E. Allworth (ed.), p. 134.
21. Calculated from: Kozlov, *Natsionalnosti SSSR*, pp. 108ff., 249f.
22. R.A. Lewis "The Mixing of Russian and Soviet Nationalities," p. 141.
23. T.F. Kravchenko, "Istochniki i formy popolneniia rabochego klassa Kirgizskoi SSR v gody dovennykh piatiletok," in: *Voprosy istorii*, 3/1982, p. 10.
24. Lewis/Rowland/Clem, *Nationality and Population Change*, p. 206, Tables 6,4 and 6,5.
25. For 1939, no corresponding figures are available. Kozlov, *Natsionalnosti SSSR*, p. 251.
26. Lewis/Rowland/Clem, *Nationality and Population Change*, p. 216.
27. Ibid., pp. 230f.
28. Ibid., pp. 403f., cf. pp. 238–247.
29. Kolarz, *Die Nationalitätenpolitik der Sowjetunion*, p. 202.
30. *Itogi Vsesoiuznoi perepisi naseleniia 1959 goda: RSFSR* (Moscow, 1963), pp. 312, 316. For 1939, no corresponding figures are available.
31. *Handbook of Major Soviet Nationalities*, p. 380.
32. In 1926, 72 percent of Jews could read and write, as opposed to only 45 percent of Russians. (*Natsionalnaia politika VKP (b) v tsifrakh*, p. 271).
33. N. Alfadeev/N. Safarov, "Kulturno-politicheskaia rabota sredi rabochikh-tatar v Donbasse," in: *RN*, 4/1932, pp. 50–55.
34. N. Safarov, "Protiv iz rashcheniia natspolitiki," in: *RN*, 4/1933, p. 75 (ibid., the quote from the resolution).
35. N. Iushunev, "Natsionalnyi proletariat Urala," in: *RN*, 6/1932, pp. 91–95; S. Dimanshtein, "K IX sezdu profsoiuzov," in: *RN*, 4/1932, pp. 8f.

36. Cf. above II/6. *National Minorities*.

37. A. Bogdanov, "Usilit rabotu sredi natsmen," in: *RN*, 2/1935, p. 82; A. i V. Elbaev, "O rabote sredi natsmen Moskovskoi oblasti, in: *RN*, 8/1936, pp. 16–21.

38. O. Mirov, "Dostizheniia Tatarii na khoziaistvennom fronte," in: *RN*, 3/1932, p. 65.

39. G. Mulakov, "Organizatsiia otkhodnichestva v natsionalnykh kolkhozakh," in: *RN*, 10–11/1931, p. 93.

40. Lorenz, *Sozialgeschichte*, vol. I, p. 238.

41. P. Zaitsev, "O resheniiakh noiabrskogo (1934 g.) plenuma ZK VKP (b)," in: *RN*, 1/1935, p. 11.

42. P. Petukhov, "Nemedlenno perestroit rabotu Tashkentskogo gorsoveta," in: *RN*, 4/1934, p. 33.

43. Kozlov, *Natsionalnosti SSSR*, pp. 86, 88. For 1939, no figures are available.

44. Lewis/Rowland/Clem, *Nationality and Population Change*, p. 131.

45. Krawchenko, *The Impact of Industrialization on the Social Structure of Ukraine*, pp. 340, 350.

46. Even modern Soviet publications are unsatisfactory. In describing the changes the social structures of the nations experienced, they either resort to isolated data of questionable reliability, or they analyze data that apply to the Union Republics, i.e., to territories instead of nations. This research strategy more obscures than illuminates the social changes the nations experienced. For example, the publications deal with the workers in Uzbekistan or the intelligentsia in Tataria but not with the Uzbek working class or the Tatar intelligentsia. Cf. P.T. Timofeev, *Formirovanie natsionalnykh kadrov rabochego klassa SSSR* (Moscow, 1982); *Izmenenie sotsialnoi struktury narodov SSSR*, V.M. Selunskaia, ed. (Moscow, 1982).

47. Groshev, *Istoricheskii opyt KPSS*, pp. 230f.

48. T.U. Usubaliev, "Leninskaia teoriia nekapitalisticheskogo razvitiia i formirovanie natsionalnoi intelligentsii," in: *Voprosy filosofii*, 4/1980, p. 41.

49. T.F. Kravchenko, "Istochniki i formy popolneniia rabochego klassa Kirgizskoi SSR v gody dovoennykh piatiletok," in: *VI*, 3/1982, p. 9.

50. Likholat, *Sodruzhestvo narodov SSSR*, p. 297.

51. Valiev, *Sovetskaia natsionalnaia intelligentsiia*, p. 36.

52. *RN*, 1/1936, p. 85–88.

53. *Izmenenie sotsialnoi struktury*, pp. 25, 27.

54. Kaganovich's report on issues of organization, in: *XVII sezd VKP (b). Stenograficheskii otchet* (Moscow, 1934), pp. 530f.

55. A. Bogdanov, "Za organizatsionno-khoziaistvennoe ukreplenie kolkhozov," in: *RN*, 4/1932, pp. 62f.

56. Valiev, *Formirovanie i razvitie sovetskoi natsionalnoi intelligentsii v Srednei Azii*, pp. 121–123.

57. Resolution of the Presidium of the Council of Nationalities the CEC of the USSR "On the State and Further Measures to Educate National Medical Cadres" Early 1937, in: *RN*, 5/1937, p. 93.

58. S. Fitzpatrick, "Stalin and the Making of a New Elite, 1928–1939," in: *Slavic Review*, 38, 1979, p. 387.

59. Ibid., p. 400.

60. E. Mostovaia, "Zhenshchinu-natsionalku — v proizvodstvo," in: *RN*, 10–11/1931, p. 105.

VI

Stalin's "Solution" to the Nationalities Issue

Ideological Illusions

The cornerstone of Bolshevik doctrine on the nationalities issue consists of two contradictory principles:

First, socialism makes nationalism obsolete. The victorious socialist revolution ends nations' existence as politically influential historical powers. As soon as antagonistic classes disappear, nationalism loses its foundation in society. The separatist fervor inherent in national ideology — one of the deadly menaces to capitalism — is no threat to socialism because nationalism results from class struggles within a nation and a state. In this context, the nationalities issue is of secondary importance after a victorious socialist revolution. The "merging" of the peoples marks the end of the trail — the victory of the revolution on a worldwide scale.

Second, the Russian revolution opened the Tsarist "peoples' prison," abolished national oppression, declared all nations equal, and offered to the previously oppressed nations and nationalities extensive opportunities to develop and express themselves. As a result, not only do the nations continue to exist after the victorious socialist revolution, but they increase in numbers and flourish. This principle led the Soviets to grant the Union Republics the constitutional right to secede from the Union.[1]

These mutually exclusive principles have had invaluable advantages for the Party's policy. They let the Soviets justify and legitimize a broad spectrum of political measures from korenizatsiia to breaking up national elites — when the need arises, the Soviets accuse these elites of maintaining the consciousness and political behavior of a long-gone, bourgeois-capitalist epoch; they accuse them of conducting a counterrevolution. On the other hand, it is obvious that Soviet ideologists have always found it difficult to present and explain contradictory concepts as if they were complementary parts of a single theory. Within the Party and among Soviet experts, these theoretical contradictions also raised false expectations about the nations and how their elites would behave and, on the whole, obscured the nature of the national issues facing the Soviets.

In March 1929, Stalin addressed "The National Issue and Leninism" and associated problems in a long expos and suggested the solution lay in clarifying the term "socialist nation."[2] He explained that the internal structure and, in particular, the political behavior of the socialist nation differed fundamentally from those of the bourgeois nation. Not only had the revolution "established equal rights for all the nations in our country," but it had also "brought about . . . the national rebirth of previously suppressed nations . . ." This is followed by a quote from a speech Stalin had delivered at the Communist University of Workers of the East in 1925. In this speech, he had elaborated that, previously, the socialist revolution had not reduced but increased the number of languages because, by stirring man's deepest reaches and introducing them to the political arena, the revolution had revived a number of new nations that had previously been completely unknown or not very well known.

Stalin described in clear terms the policy the Soviets pursued (in this study, I refer to it as the policy of nation-building). He claimed that the period of socialism's victory in *one* country would not create the conditions that are necessary to merge nations and their national languages. In his opinion, the opposite was more likely to happen: This period created favorable conditions for nations that Tsarist imperialism had suppressed before and that the Soviet Revolution had liberated from their national yoke to experience a renaissance and to blossom.

Of course, Stalin continued to pursue the objective of "merging the nations" but postponed it to the "second phase of the period of proletarian world dictatorship," or into a period long after the victory of the worldwide revolution. The phase of "socialist nations," is to bridge the gap between "blossoming" and "merging"—assuming that socialist nations do not seek separation but an internationalist coalition, which, in Stalin's opinion, was to strengthen the friendly international ties among the country's peoples. Stalin emphasized that socialist nations that had developed after the revolution were much more tightly knit than any bourgeois nation in existence. In Stalin's opinion, socialist nations were not subject to the irreconcilable class antagonisms that devour bourgeois nations and they represented the whole of a people to a much higher degree than did any bourgeois nation.[3]

Stalin claimed that socialist nations are "more tightly bound together" and are fundamentally different from bourgeois nations. They do not develop antagonisms towards one another and allow themselves to be integrated into a socialist central state with ease. This concept of socialist nations was based on the illusion that this "new" type of Soviet nation would be satisfied with whatever degree of autonomy the central state was willing to grant and would not demand more. Most importantly, socialist nations would never demand separation from Moscow. It is conceivable that for some time Stalin believed the concessions the policy of korenizatsiia provided would succeed in satisfying national ambitions and silence them. Even by 1929, he still perceived these concessions as the best means to overcome nationalism and national hostility.[4]

Political reality did not meet these expectations. Nation-building created social forces with demands that did not diminish in time but increased. Stalin possibly began to question his own ideological concepts—this study was only published posthumously in his *Works* in 1954. Anticipating later developments, note that the term "socialist nation" has only received a broader meaning within Soviet ideology since the 1960s and then became a central concept to nationalities doctrine. Publicly however, Soviet literature never refers to Stalin as one of the proponents of this doctrine. With the introduction of the term "socialist nation" theory left the firm ground of nineteenth century Marxist tradition. In respect to the nationalities, Stalin's position began increasingly to resemble Austro-Marxism, a philosophy he had vehemently opposed in 1913.[5]

At the Sixteenth Party Congress in June 1930, Stalin's report repeated some of his 1929 statements in watered-down form. The stance that the period of socialist construction in the USSR was a period of decay and elimination of national cultures, Stalin explicitly termed "Great Russian chauvinism." He explained that the Party line demanded the opposite: Stalin thought it necessary to provide the national cultures with the opportunity to develop and grow. He saw this as a prerequisite for the nations' merger into one common culture with a common language by the time socialism had been victorious all over the world.[6] Stalin himself referred to this stance as "paradoxical" and "contradictory." For him, however, exactly these characteristics constitute its "dialectics." Anyone who "does not understand this is lost to Marxism."[7] One of these lost souls is this author.

Two points are important: First, "flourishing" refers to culture, language, and lifestyles; it does not suggest political or economic autonomy, and separation by no means. Second, "flourishing" and "merging" are two subsequent developmental phases of the Party's nationalities policy that are clearly distinguished from another.

During the First Five-Year-Plan, the Party officially stuck to its 1920s stance that the Soviet Union was at present in the "flourishing" phase. In Stalin's era, the Soviets never changed or revoked this ideological phraseology. After the mid-1930s, it simply disappeared from the press. Only since about 1960 has a fundamental revision in the ideology of nationalities policy taken place: The Soviets no longer perceive "flourishing" and "drawing-together" of socialist nations as consecutive processes but as simultaneous and parallel events. Since the 1970s, ideologists have referred to "drawing-together" as the "predominant tendency." This mental tight-rope act, however, has not made ideology any more compelling or understandable.

An incoherent doctrine does not prevent a coherent policy from evolving. Presumably, during the decisive years of the "revolution from above," Stalin concluded the korenizatsiia policy was based on several false assumptions and that the time for revision was high. After all, ten years before, Stalin had disagreed with Lenin about nationalities policy and had supported a more restrictive approach than Lenin. By 1935, S.M. Dimanshtein, one of the leading ideologists, still claimed that "for our epoch, Comrade Stalin has clearly determined that the underlying tendency is not towards assimilation but towards an increase in the number of nationalities and languages."[8] By that time, however, such a statement was already an anachronism, for which the author had to pay with his life; since 1938, no word has been heard from Dimanshtein.[9]

In the mid-1930s, Stalin began to enforce a nationalities policy that assumed the USSR had entered the phase of national assimilation, of the "merger of nations." The unexpected consequences of nation-building, the nation's increasing efforts to attain autonomy (which remained not at all limited to the area of language and culture), and the resistance the nations had offered to the "revolution from above" convinced Stalin that the Russians and Russification were a more reliable means of ferment for establishing the central dictatorship than the national elites, which necessarily develop centrifugal forces.

Abandonment of National Institutions and Centralization

On October 26/November 8, 1917, when the Bolsheviks proclaimed that the Council of People's Commissars had seized power, a "People's Commissar for Nationalities Issues" (*Narkomnats*) was among the fourteen members of the government (Lenin was chairman and there were thirteen People's Commissars).[10] This showed that the nationalities issue in Russia was very important to the new masters and that winning the non-Russian peoples for the revolution was a high priority. Until 1920, Stalin's tenure as the People's Commissar for Nationalities Issues was marked by the civil war. His objective was either to align non-Russian national movements with Bolshevik policies or, when this proved impossible, to defeat them with military force.

After the establishment of the USSR in December 1922, the Soviets did not convert the People's Commissariat for Nationalities of the RSFSR into an All-Union Commissariat, but the federative reorganization triggered by the union constitution of 1923–1924 did away with it altogether. Why? When Stalin expanded the base of his power, the People's Commissariat had only been of limited significance. Since he had become the Secretary General of the CC in the spring of 1922, he no longer needed this government office to assure his rise to power. However, there were also objective reasons for supporting the dissolution of the People's Commissariat for Nationalities Issues. The Soviets had won the civil war, they had reversed the disintegration of the empire for the most part. The most pressing and threatening aspect of the national question appeared to be solved: Apart from several Western nations, the Soviets had defeated political separatism. They intended to abolish all nationalities issues by creating Soviet federalism.

Originally, the Bolsheviks underestimated the power of the national movements. The response was to create Soviet federalism, which excellently served two tasks simultaneously: In reality, it created a central state governed by a strong executive government, and, at the same time, constitutional law took all peoples into consideration in organizing the Union's administrative-territorial structure. Naming territorial units after the peoples living in them not only increased those peoples' prestige tremendously, but korenizatsiia also instilled life into national consciousness. With this, the Bolshevik leadership made very clear that it would not tolerate political separatism and that the nationalities issues were not only subordinated to the class struggle but also to the maintenance of the Soviet Union's integrity. We must interpret the dissolution of the Narkomnats as a symptom of the demotion of nationalities issues.

In addition, the Soviets wanted to make it clear to the national communist forces that they were in no position to demand privileges and that they would not have a lobby on the level of the central government. Unlike other Soviet leaders, in November 1922, Stalin was declaring publicly that the People's Commissariat for Nationalities had to be eradicated from the structure of the Soviet system.[11] Stalin became the chairman of the Politburo's constitutional commission and played a major role in discussions about the constitution the following spring. In the course of these discussions, Stalin began to support the suggestion that the Union's CEC should be expanded and that a second chamber, which was to represent the nations, should be added. This would create the opportunity to listen carefully to the peoples' needs and provide them with the help they needed at the right time.[12]

This expression of a parliamentary chamber's tasks reveals the true Bolshevik understanding of parliamentarism. Simultaneously, Stalin made it clear that, from his perspective, the second chamber was only the continuation of the Nationalities Soviet, which had existed within the People's Commissariat for Nationalities since 1920. It was a committee consisting of the representatives of different non-Russian nationalities. This committee, which the People's Commissar appointed and chaired, had only advisory function. One could say that the first constitution of 1923–1924 only preserved the board of the People's Commissariat in the guise of a second chamber of the Union's CEC. This was equivalent to the non-Russian peoples losing actual representation of their interests on the federal level.

In the discussions about the constitution, the representatives of the Ukrainian CP attempted to compensate for this lack of representation by suggesting the second chamber should have its own presidium with legislative powers. In addition, the Ukrainians proposed that only the Union Republics — not all national territories — be represented in the new Nationalities Soviet. This body was to provide the large non-Russian nations, which had a strongly developed national self-consciousness, with visible representation. In respect to the makeup of the Council of Nationalities, the Ukrainians did not get their way, and on the issue of the presidium, they only partially prevailed against Stalin's stands, which were decidedly contrary to theirs. According to the constitution, every Union Republic and Autonomous Republic sent five delegates to the Council of Nationalities, the Autonomous Republics of Adzharia and of Abkhazia and the Autonomous Regions were represented by one delegate apiece.[13]

Stalin had repeatedly expressed his determined opposition to the idea that a Presidium of the Council of Nationalities should have legislative powers. He asked if anyone really thought it was an accident that the Ukrainians' counter proposal suggested dividing the CEC's power between each of its two chambers' presidia, thus stripping the CEC's presidium of all power.[14] Actually, a compromise settled this issue. Although the constitution called only the Presidium of the CEC the "highest organ of power" between sessions of the CEC, each of the two chambers received its own presidium. The members of these presidia were *ex officio* also members of the overall presidium of the CEC.[15]

The Presidium of the Council of Nationalities remained a constitutional organ until 1936. It fought for the interests of non-Russians in many specific individual cases, and, even in the 1930s, its resolutions continued to reflect its engagement for the realization of korenizatsiia. The presidium was particularly interested in standing up for the economic interests of non-Russian peoples to the Supreme Economic Council, the People's Commissariats, and to Gosplan. The presidium's resolutions contained lists of priority investments, reminded the authorities of industrial development measures, or demanded surveys of particular mineral resources. The issues the presidium dealt with ranged from a list of priorities for the Second Five-Year-Plan to the construction of a particular telephone line in Buryat-Mongolia.[16]

The compromise the Ukrainians reached with Stalin in organizing the presidium of the CEC cannot hide the fact that in determining the wording of the constitution, Stalin got his way against more extensive demands for autonomy on many other controversial issues. For example, the Ukrainian draft of the constitution suggested establishing the People's Commissariats for Foreign Affairs and for Foreign Trade as Union and Union Republic organs and not — as the CC intended — as purely organs of the Union. The Ukrainian communists wanted the Union Republics to be involved in foreign relations. This suggestion made Stalin launch polemic attacks against them in June 1923. He responded in a similar fashion to the Ukrainians' wish to strike from the constitution the phrase that the republics would "unite to form a federal state." Stalin accused the Ukrainians of not striving towards a "uniform federal state" but towards a "confederation."[17]

The extraordinary importance of nationalities issues during the civil war became apparent not only in the organization of a specific people's commissariat but also in the fact that, in 1918, within the Party apparatus, specific national sections under the CC's national sector were established. The tasks of the national sections, which were organized down to the level of raions, consisted of drawing non-Russians into the Party, of serving as a catch basin for the forces from the dissolved left-wing national parties that were more or less loyal to the Bolsheviks, and finally of propagating the political goals of the revolution among the vast masses of non-Russian peoples. The national sections contributed greatly to carrying out korenizatsiia. Particularly, the Jewish sections (*evsektsii*) functioned as a substitute for the nonexistent Jewish territory and promoted Jewish linguistic, cultural, and media policy interests.[18]

Although in the early 1920s, the Party attempted to prove its great interest in the nationalities issue by widely propagandizing for the national sections, they disappeared unnoticed from the Party's structure in 1930. In January 1930, the CC decided to dissolve its national sector and the national sections within the CC apparatuses of the Union Republics and subordinate Party organizations. Soviet organs were to take over the functions of these institutions.[19] Like the dissolution of the People's Commissariat for the Nationalities, this step must be regarded as another example of the Soviets playing down the nationalities issue after the Bolshevik dictatorship was consolidated. After 1930, the Party apparatus no longer included special institutions exclusively concerned with nationalities issues. Initially, however, this situation did not bring about any changes in the general political line.

On the other hand, politicians all over the country generally perceived the dissolution of national Party sections and the transfer of their tasks to lower-ranking Soviet organs as a signal to assign reduced priority to the national interests of non-Russian peoples. In the early 1930s, however, the overall state of domestic affairs still permitted advocacy of korenizatsiia on a large scale, and proponents of this policy publicly bemoaned the neglect it had received.[20]

After 1930, the most important institutional sponsors of the policy of nation-building were the Soviet organs, with the previously mentioned Council of Nationalities and its presidium at the forefront. The two-chamber system that represented the nationalities separately on the Union level did not extend to the subordinate levels. In the Union Republics, the section for the nationalities (*otdel natsionalnostei*) or the national commission (*natskomissiia*) of the presidium of the republican CEC were responsible for nationalities policy.

To handle local concerns, a resolution of the ACEC of April 29, 1929, decreed that, for issues concerning national minorities, plenipotentiaries be appointed in the executive committees of the areas, ASSRs, regions, towns, and raions of the RSFSR. These plenipotentiaries were to coordinate and watch over the work of the executive committees and other organizations. They were to merge the various currents of national endeavors.[21] Similar provisions followed in the other Union Republics. Apparently, however, these directives were not enforced at all or were interpreted differently. As a result, on March 20, 1932, the ACEC presidium resolved that permanent sections for the national minorities be established within the presidia of the executive committees on the level of areas, regions, and ASSRs. On the one hand, these sections were subordinate to the presidia of the respective executive committees; on the other hand, they executed the directives of the nationalities section of the ACEC presidium.[22]

It seems that from among all parts of this administrative machinery, which was extensive on paper, only the ACEC presidium and its nationalities section protected the interests of the nationalities in a relatively efficient manner. The organs in the provinces remained inactive in most cases. In the 1930s, the ACEC presidium issued many resolutions intended to promote the interests of the non-Russian peoples in the RSFSR. Among them were the construction of individual factories, railroad lines, and housing as well as the publication of newspapers and books in non-Russian languages.[23]

The power of the ACEC presidium, however, remained limited because, in many cases, the administrative foundation was a fiction. "In most cases, the plenipotentiaries for the national work exist only on paper."[24] Even the ACEC's 1932 resolution was not carried out in many cases. "The majority ... of the area and regional executive committees and the town soviets assign nobody to supervise national work."[25]

The situation was not any better outside the RSFSR. "The national commission of Belorussia's CEC ... is a dead committee — in light of the survey of the work actually performed.... The national commissions exist only on paper in the town soviets and raions."[26]

The mid-1930s witnessed "great confusion in the way the supervision ... of national minorities' work was organized." The needs of the individual locales by no means determined the various forms of organization, but they were the result of accidents, arbitrariness, and carelessness.[27] This in itself was not at all atypical for the Soviet bureaucracy of the time. More important is the fact that this bureaucratic inefficiency reflected political intentions. After the mid-1930s, Stalin's leadership not only was willing to accept the fact that the bureaucratic machinery was increasingly ignoring nationalities policy but even dismantled institutions meant to further this policy.

The subordinate organs were the first to be affected by this approach. In 1934, the executive committees of several areas, Autonomous Republics, and regions dissolved their sections, commissions, or respective institutions designed to serve the interests of national minorities. Even in the city and region of Moscow, these organs ceased to exist in 1934. The following years witnessed the closing of sections for national minorities in the CECs of several Union Republics.[28]

The key year seems to be 1934, because after that time, the dismantling of institutions that had previously represented the interests of non-Russian peoples began to speed up. Triggered by Stalin's initiative, the CC and the Council of People's Commissars decided in October to dissolve the CC's Central Asian Bureau and the Central Asian Economic Council (*Sredneaziatskoe ekonomicheskoe soveshchanie*). These institutions were of a singular nature and served the purpose of Sovietization, but they were also intended to support the modernization efforts of the underdeveloped Central Asian republics. Already by 1924, the ACEC's Turkestan commission, which had been created after the revolution, closed down as a result of Central Asia's administrative reorganization.[29]

The elimination of national institutions also included facilities of less political importance than the CC's Central Asian Bureau. In 1924, the ACEC presidium's Committee for the North was established. In July 1935, the Soviets eliminated it. Apparently, this directive took the functionaries affected by it completely by surprise. During the decade of its existence, the Committee for the North made extensive efforts to protect the interests of the small populations of the peoples in the far north. The committee initiated the development of writing systems for the languages of the peoples in the far north, established elementary schools, and advanced Sovietization by founding local soviets and nine National Territories. In 1925, the Institute for the Northern Peoples was founded in Leningrad — an institution that was one of a kind and prepared functionaries and experts for their work in the far north.[30]

With the elimination of national institutions came centralization, which continued the process of whittling away the periphery's rights to autonomy, which were limited as it was. This was primarily true in economic administration. In this area, "the Union Republics' range of responsibilities ... progressed further in the 1920s than during any other previous era in Soviet history."[31] On the one hand, by establishing the economic councils, the Union Republics were extensively involved in the administration of factories in their territories. On the other hand, because

Moscow only set the total amounts budgeted for the Union Republics' revenues and spending, these republics enjoyed considerable budgetary independence, which permitted them to allocate funds according to their own needs and to raise revenues according to their own resources. The budgetary law ratified on May 25, 1927, had also determined what percentages of which taxes were available for republics' budgets.[32]

As a result of the First Five-Year-Plan and the related tampering with economic and financial policy after 1929, centralization of the financial system and the economic administration increased dramatically. On December 5, 1929, the CC decided "to reorganize industrial management." The main administrations (*glavki*) within the system of the Supreme Economic Council were dissolved and replaced with "factory combines."[33] In reality, this resolution meant that the key industries were joined to form factory combines on the All-Union level, thus preventing the republican and local state organs from exercising any influence over them. During the First Five-Year-Plan, the Soviets created thirty-three combines on the Union level, for example, the "Steel Combine" and "Coal Combine." In 1932, these combines were reorganized and reduced in size, creating seventy-eight such combines.[34] The central government determined whether a factory was important to the whole Union and, consequently, whether the republican and local authorities had a say in its administration. On August 28, 1929, the CEC and the Council of People's Commissars had determined that the CEC's presidium was to have the final decision should a Union Republic refuse to recognize a factory in its territory as a production facility important for the whole Union.[35]

A 1930 bank reform centralized the credit system; the All-Russian and All-Ukrainian cooperative banks were eliminated. The USSR's State Bank was the only financial institution permitted to grant loans to industry.[36]

The increase in the Union's share of the USSR's total budget reflected the fact that Union organs were the main administrators of the financial system. During the 1920s, 55 to 60 percent of budget spending came from the Union's budget. In 1930, this percentage jumped to 74.5 percent and culminated at nearly 80 percent in the early 1950s. After 1930, the Union Republics' share of the total spendings of the state budget amounted to 5 to 8 percent, the share of the other territorial authorities never exceeded 14 to 18 percent during the Stalin era.[37]

In January 1932, the Soviets eliminated the USSR's Supreme Economic Council and all its subordinate authorities on all territorial levels and replaced it with the Union People's Commissariat for Heavy Industry, the Union People's Commissariat for Wood Industry, and the Union and Republic People's Commissariat for Consumer Goods Industry.[38] In a long sequence of regulatory acts, this was the decisive step in replacing the previous territorial economic administration with a branch-oriented economic administration. The branches that were very important to industrial progress, particularly to heavy industry, were assigned to pure Union People's Commissariats. The Union Republics and other territorial authorities were no longer involved in the planning and management of these economic branches. The January 1932 resolution left only the consumer goods industry under the responsibility of a multi-leveled, "unified" people's commissariat, whose apparatus extended to the levels of the Union Republics and lower territorial units. As a result, the Union Republics' Supreme Economic Councils were reorganized to form People's Commissariats for Consumer Goods Industries.

Until 1934, factories and branches that were only locally important and did not fit into any of the industrial people's commissariats were administrated in a complex system subordinating them to the people's commissariats and the republics' other state organs. A CEC resolution of August 10, 1934, created People's Commissariats for Local Industry in the Union and Autonomous Republics and corresponding management authorities for local industry in the areas and regions.[39] Management responsibilities for locally important factories were redistributed. Some remained with the industrial people's commissariats, which had been founded in 1932, the others were subordinated directly to the newly founded People's Commissariats for Local Industry.

Because, within the Union and Republic ("unified") people's commissariats, power was increasingly concentrated at the top (i.e., on the Union level), the periphery could only effectively participate in industrial administration in the People's Commissariats for Local Industry. These commissariats included such branches as clothing, book printing, sheet music, drugstore goods, and breweries.[40] These sectors were very important for supplying the population, but they received the lowest priority in Stalin's economic plans.

During the first onslaught of collectivization in December 1929, direct management of agriculture "became concentrated in the central government." A newly created People's Commissariat for Agriculture in the USSR, which was organized as a Union-Republic people's commissariat, took over "unified management." This caused the authorities, which previously had been organized purely as Republics' People's Commissariats for Agriculture, to lose their relative autonomy in the Union Republics, and they were integrated into the new people's commissariat as subordinate authorities.[41]

The move towards unification, concentration of management, and, consequently, reduction of autonomy also characterized education policy in the 1930s. Before that time, some Union Republics, primarily the Ukraine, had pursued special policies in the way they organized their schools and universities. The constitutional basis for this autonomy was the fact that the peoples commissariats for education were purely Republic authorities and thus were not subordinate to central management on the Union level. In contrast to those of industry and agriculture, this administrative structure was preserved, but the Party found other ways to intervene in educational administration.

The Council of People's Commissars and the CC issued several joint resolutions sharply criticizing the People's Commissariats for Education and prescribed a uniform school system for the whole country. The decree of May 16, 1934, allowed only three types of schools on the primary and secondary level: elementary school with four grades, middle school with seven grades, and middle school with ten grades.[42] A decree, "Organization of Instruction and Internal Order," issued by the same authorities on September 3, 1935, determined in great detail and for the whole country the structure of Stalin's new school system. This system, based on rote learning and achievement, replaced an educational philosophy that delighted in experimentation and focused on the child. This system not only standardized class and vacation schedules, but the CC even determined the number and duration of recesses between classes.[43] The CC's education department, which enforced these regulations, filled in as a peoples' commissariat, which did not exist on the Union level.

In 1928, administrative centralization of the institutions of higher learning began when one institution of higher learning after another was removed from the jurisdiction of the Union Republics' People's Commissariats for Education and eventually put under the aegis of the Supreme Economic Council of the USSR or the People's Commissariats for Industry and Agriculture created in the following years. In addition, in July 1928, the CC decided to standardize the USSR's technical training system to eliminate special policies in the Ukraine and Belorussia.[44]

In November 1933, an All-Union Committee for Advanced Technical Training with the USSR's CEC was established; in May 1936, this committee received the rank of an All-Union Committee for Institutions of Higher Learning with the Council of People's Commissars of the USSR.[45] The committee's chairman was of "cabinet rank;" he was a member of the Council of People's Commissars.[46] Although direct management of institutions of higher learning remained under the jurisdiction of the competent people's commissariats, the All-Union Committee for Institutions of Higher Learning made the important decisions in many areas (spanning from personnel policy to prescribing compulsory textbooks), and guaranteed uniform internal structure in the institutions of higher learning. In 1946, its status grew further when it became the Ministry for Higher Learning of the USSR.

There was one area where the reduction in the number of national institutions and the increasing shift of responsibilities from the peripheries to the center did not seem to apply. This exception was Soviet federalism, which prospered. Not only were no national territories eliminated, but the number and status continued to increase until 1936. The Autonomous Jewish Region of Birobidzhan was the last to be newly established in 1934. When the first constitution was adopted in January 1924, the USSR consisted of four Union Republics, sixteen Autonomous Republics, and seventeen Autonomous Regions. However, in December 1936, at the time of Stalin's constitution, the national-territorial structure consisted of eleven Union Republics, twenty-two Autonomous Republics, nine Autonomous Regions and nine National Territories. The 1936 constitution elevated many territories' status: Georgia, Armenia, and Azerbaidzhan became Union Republics when the Transcaucasian Socialist Federative Soviet Republic was dissolved. Kazakhstan and Kirgizistan moved from the rank of Autonomous Republic to the rank of Union Republic. Five Autonomous Regions were awarded the rank of Autonomous Republic (Kabardino-Balkaria, Komi, Mari, Northern Ossetia, Checheno-Ingushetia). Generous promotions within the system of Soviet federalism had also occurred before 1936. For example, the Autonomous Regions of Karakalpakia (in March 1932), Mordvinia and Udmurtia (in December 1934), and Kalmykia (in November 1935) became Autonomous Republics. In December 1930, National Territories for the small peoples of the far north and the far east were created.[47]

After 1936, the Soviets founded new national-territorial units or increased the rank of existing ones only if this process directly involved annexing of foreign territories. This policy also was meant to show that the establishment of socialism had "solved" the national issue *within* the USSR.

The development of Soviet federalism in the 1930s only seemed auspicious. Although, superficially, the constitutional status of the national territories was improved, in reality, the territories were continuously deprived of more and more responsibilities. Stalin created a "constitutional myth" (cf. Fainsod), and extended it in the formulation of the 1936 constitution. He granted the Council of Nationalities, which was the second chamber of the Supreme Soviet, rights equal to those of the Soviet of the Union. He considerably increased the number of delegates (to twenty-five from every Union Republic, eleven from every Autonomous Republic, five from every Autonomous Region, and one from every National Territory) and determined that they be directly elected.[48] Stalin wanted to create the impression that non-Russian nationalities were better represented and more involved in the political decision-making process than before. The appropriate alteration of the original draft of the constitution, which Stalin personally introduced, originated with a suggestion by F. Khodzhaev, the Chairman of the Uzbek Council of People's Commissars.[49] Incidentally, Khodzhaev was executed by a firing squad as a "traitor to the people" in 1937.

Actually, the Supreme Soviet was inconsequential within the political power system. As a result, increasing the constitutional status of the Council of Nationalities in no way restricted the centralist dictatorship. The Presidium of the Council of Nationalities, which had actually attempted to establish a way to represent the interests of non-Russian peoples, did not return in the 1936 constitution. Even in 1923, its inclusion in the constitution had been contrary to Stalin's wishes.

A comparison of the constitutions of 1923–1924 and 1936 shows that centralism increased and the responsibilities of the periphery decreased. In this respect, the new constitution partially reflected reality. In December 1936, four of the six purely Republican people's commissariats were converted to Union and Republic People's Commissariats (for internal affairs, law, public health, agriculture). Of the people's commissariats existing in 1923–1924, the Union Republics retained exclusive administrative powers over only the People's Commissariats for Education and Social Welfare. The People's Commissariats for Local Industry and Communal Economy were added.[50]

Article 14 of the 1936 constitution, which listed the rights of the central government organs, also illustrates the increase in competencies at the top. For example, the Union usurped exclusive management of state security organs, banks, and those factories that were important to the whole country. From a constitutional perspective, the competencies of the Union Republics were always less extensive than those of the states in the U.S. or the Federal Republic of Germany. The 1936 constitution only emphasized this fact. Not everyone will be inclined to agree with the maxim, which was typical for the time, by Makarenko who at the time was one of the leading Soviet educators. "The history of mankind is divided into two periods: before the Stalin constitution and after the Stalin constitution."[51]

Soviet Patriotism and Russification

"In our times, patriotism's role is that of an extremely reactionary ideology, whose task is to justify imperialist robbery and to lull the proletariat's class consciousness to sleep . . ."[52] "Soviet patriotism—the burning sensation of boundless love, unreserved devotion towards the homeland, deep responsibility for its fate and defense—bubbles from the depths of our people like a mighty spring."[53] Only a few years separate these two definitions of patriotism. They reflect an ideology's genesis, which began with Stalin's doctrine of "socialism in one country" (1924) and led to the rehabilitation of "homeland" and "mother country" and finally to "Soviet patriotism."[54]

The progress of the dictatorship shows in the fact that a state of consciousness, allegedly rooted in the "depths of the people," was proclaimed as the new mobilization ideology at a precisely identifiable time—the summer of 1934. This "new, higher" patriotism was to bind the nationalism of all the USSR's peoples in a kind of "imperial idea." The homeland addressed here was "socialist," its tradition "revolutionary." At a time when revolutionary enthusiasm within the Party had vanished, when collectivization and famine had destroyed all revolutionary illusions even in the villages, Stalin had Soviet patriotism created as surrogate, so to speak, for a revolutionary idealism that no longer existed. In addition to love for the homeland and pride in "progressive" traditions, this patriotism was informed by the danger of imminent war posed by "capitalist encirclement." Very soon, starting in about 1936, Stalin's personality cult became another integral part of Soviet patriotism.[55]

Although Soviet patriotism was artificial and manipulative, it gradually became a reality. Two factors are responsible: first, Russian patriotism gave substance to Soviet patriotism; and second, the Soviets defeated Germany in World War II. The war made it necessary to defend the homeland and Russian nationalism facilitated at least Russians' identification with Soviet patriotism.

In the early years, Soviet patriotism promoted the "internationalist motherland" and love for the all-Soviet homeland; elements of Russian nationalism were completely lacking. Without question, the Leninist tradition of fighting "Great-Russian nationalism" was an obstacle. Only after 1937 did propagandist language use convert the Great-Russian people into the "great Russian people," "first among equals," whom "all the Union's peoples" treat with a "holy" "feeling of friendship, love, and gratitude."[56] Before World War II, Russian-national slogans were quite moderate, continuing what Stalin himself—long before 1937—had considered the content of his "revolutionary national pride." Already in 1926, in a letter to the Ukrainian Politburo, he had called Leninism the "greatest achievement" of "Russian culture,"[57] and in December 1930, in a threatening letter to Demian Bednyi, he spoke of the "Russian workers' class" as "the vanguard of Soviet workers," which "the revolutionary workers unanimously applaud as their accepted leader."[58]

After 1937, the "Russian people's help" for the USSR's "underdeveloped nations" in building socialism became a topos in agitation and propaganda—and it has remained one to this day.[59] But also the Ukrainian people's freedom and independence were now seen as "bought with streams of the blood of the best sons of the Russian people."[60] The "workers and peasants of Russia" or the "Russian workers' class" was replaced with the "great Russian people," who helped "altruistically" and "continuously" and whom, for example, the "Uzbek people treated with boundless love."[61] Agitation and propaganda assigned the attribute "great" (*velikii*)—which expresses in Russian not something countable, but a semantic quality—only to the Russian people. As a result, the language of propaganda had equipped this multinational state with a central, state-supporting people, surrounded by the other peoples, who were in need of help. The term "friendship among the peoples" had been used to describe the relationship among the peoples ever since Stalin had conspicuously used this term in a speech in December 1935.[62] This friendship was not only "strong," but was also described as "indestructible" and "eternal;"[63] this description was to keep separatists from even dreaming of a future.

Before World War II, Russian nationalism was used only to a limited extent to substantiate Soviet patriotism. Nevertheless, all-Soviet chauvinism grew to phenomenal dimensions even then. The Soviet Union not only appeared "as the grandest and only example of how to resolve the nationalities issue in the proper way,"[64] but it also "was the first state in the whole world to show all humankind the way towards a wonderful life."[65] Twenty years after the October Revolution, the language of chauvinism and centralism had fully developed. On November 7, 1937, Molotov said in his speech, "a moral and political unity, pervaded by deep internationalism, had developed" in the Soviet Union. This unity would "weld the USSR's peoples and nationalities into a whole. The peoples of other countries will see in this a model of their own future."[66] At times, the new "whole" was referred to as "Soviet people" and immediately declared "immortal."[67] Only in the 1960s, however, did the Soviets apply this term to its full ideological potential in the whole country. For the time being, "friendship among the peoples" was the ideological term that described national relationships within the USSR.

The new doctrine and the political measures that complemented it suggest that Stalin thought that at the end of the 1930s, the Soviet Union had entered the phase of the peoples' "merger." Nevertheless, a revision of the ideology did not occur as Lenin had often stated that "merger" was only possible after socialism was victorious worldwide and as Stalin had explicitly emphasized, even by the early 1930s, that no one could realistically expect "merger" in the near future. As a result, the ideology only partially expressed the realignment of nationalities policy towards Russification and assimilation.

However, Stalin's language policy was clear. On March 13, 1938, the CC and the Council of People's Commissars resolved to introduce compulsory Russian classes in all non-Russian schools in the Union Republics and Autonomous Republics. They considered Russian proficiency necessary to guarantee contacts and relationships among the peoples, to develop national cadres in science and technology, and to prepare youngsters for military service.[68] The reasoning behind this legislation expresses the changes in the political line more than the legislation itself, for, in their reasoning, the Soviets expressly abandoned the objective of teaching science and technology to non-Russian peoples in their respective indigenous languages. In addition, the Red Army was to use only one language; previously, the Soviets had been particularly proud of the linguistic pluralism of their armed forces.

In principle, Russian was already a compulsory subject in all of the RSFSR's non-Russian schools.[69] The Ukrainian language law of July 1927 had also declared Russian a compulsory subject in all non-Russian schools in the Ukraine.[70] However, these laws had not been enforced. Not only were the educational prerequisites, particularly teachers, unavailable, but the political desire to teach Russian often did not exist. Before 1937, schools that had incorporated Russian classes into their curricula were "a rarity" in the villages of Daghestan, Kazakhstan, Kirgizistan, Kara-Kalpakia, or Checheno-Ingushetia.[71] In 1937–1938, 2,159 of a total of 3,481 non-Russian elementary schools in Uzbekistan did not teach Russian. In most schools that taught Russian, the classes were badly planned, and the courses had little success.[72]

After 1938, the law prescribed that four hours a week of Russian be included in class schedules of most grades, beginning in second grade for non-Russian elementary schools (and third grade for middle schools). In the schools providing general education, this subject usurped a primary position in the curriculum. It is doubtful, however, that all schools implemented these regulations during the Stalin era. Even in schools that followed the rules formally, the quality of Russian instruction left much to be desired. This is evident in the fact that, until the 1960s, the Soviet education system did not offer specific training for teachers of Russian working in non-Russian schools. Only brief supplementary courses prepared these teachers for their task. In reality, Russian teachers who were either not at all or only barely proficient in their students' indigenous languages conducted these classes. Only after World War II, did Russian-language programs for schools appear that were tailored to the respective indigenous language; before that, only one general program existed, which was to help teach children Russian irrespective of whether their native language was Finnish, Turkish, or Mongolian.[73]

Nevertheless, the 1938 school laws had far-reaching consequences. For the first time, Russian became compulsory in all schools providing general education. Equally important were the unpublished parts of the resolution of March 13, 1938 (cf. endnote 68), and other similar unpublished legislation. Such legislation regulated two aspects of the language issue: the tertiary educational sector and the "national minorities" — the members of a nation who live outside their territories.

The great efforts to introduce non-Russian languages as communicative media in vocational schools and universities did not continue. Except in the Transcaucasian republics, classes in the tertiary educational sector were taught primarily in Russian. This put strong pressure on non-Russian middle schools to teach Russian intensively or to teach the upper grades in Russian, as did schools in some parts of the RSFSR. Even more important was another consequence: Because classes in the tertiary educational sector were taught in Russian, Russian children received preferential treatment in the Union Republics and helped these children climb the social ladder quickly; in other words, the development of non-Russian elites stagnated.

Beginning in 1938, nearly all the national minority schools, the establishment of which had cost much money and effort, disappeared from the Russian education system. This was true for the Ukrainian schools in the Northern Caucasus and Siberia, the Yiddish schools in the Ukraine and Belorussia, and the German schools in the Ukraine. This measure probably affected hundreds of thousands of children, most of whom attended Russian schools from that point on. Stalin had always supported the territorial principle in nationalities policy but put it into practice inconsistently in the USSR; now it was emphatically enforced.[74]

Not without cause did the term "Leninist-Stalinist nationalities policy" emerge for the first time in the context of these language-policy measures; previously this policy had been identified with Lenin's name only.[75] Without being referred to by name, korenizatsiia was now defamed as the policy of the "enemies of the people." In June 1938, a resolution of the Fourteenth Ukrainian Party Congress said, "The bourgeois nationalists, Trotzkyites, and Bukharinites shyed away from no hatefulness and rottenness to chase the great Russian language from our schools and universities. The efforts of the Trotzkyites, Bukharinites, and bourgeois nationalists were directed at separating the Ukrainian people from the brotherly friendship of the great Russian people, at separating the Soviet Ukraine from the USSR, and at the reestablishment of capitalist enslavement."[76] Thus, Khrushchev, the new head of the Ukrainian Party not only turned historical truth upside down, but above all he indicated he would be an uncompromising defender of the new Party line.

In spite of the education system's Russification, some of the groundwork laid in the 1920s remained essentially unaffected: Indigenous languages continued to be the media for teaching classes in the elementary schools and a large number of the middle schools. In 1957, for example, all peoples in the RSFSR whose languages had written forms disposed of elementary schools that taught in their native languages; twelve nations in the RSFSR taught in their native languages in schools with seven grades; and six nations even had schools with ten grades that were taught in native languages.[77] Only the language policy of the 1960s began to dismantle these accomplishments.

One of the arguments the leadership used to justify the necessity of learning Russian was universal compulsory military service, the completion of which depended on a sufficient proficiency in Russian. This argument was not convincing and met with a great deal of cynicism because, only in their joint resolution of March 7, 1938, had the Council of People's Commissars and the CC eliminated the national military units, thus making Russian the Red Army's only language.[78]

National units, most of which had originated during the civil ar, existed in all Union Republics and many Autonomous Republics in the RSFSR. In the Union Republics, their strength was at least that of a division. In the Ukraine and Georgia, several national divisions existed. In these units, most of the non-commissioned officers, those in the middle ranks, and nearly all polit-officers were natives. At no time, however, did all or even the majority of non-Russian soldiers serve in the national units. These units probably never numbered significantly more than 10 percent of the Red Army's effective strength.

The national units made it possible to draft recruits, who spoke no Russian, from Central Asia, where universal compulsory military service was introduced only in 1931. The national units also allowed the growth of a class of non-Russian career officers and non-commissioned officers. The army created several special training facilities in the military and political sector for these officers. The resolution mentioned above also eliminated these non-Russian military schools. Of course, the officers in the national units had to be very proficient in Russian. Within the units, however, and particularly for the purposes of political indoctrination the army used the national languages, a practice "which had not been allowed in the Tsarist armed forces because these languages were considered inferior," as someone proudly wrote as late as in 1935.[79]

After 1938, all soldiers served in regular, nationally mixed units. Thus, non-Russian soldiers were purposefully exposed to Russian, "internationalist" socialization. The percentage of non-Russian officers declined because the non-Russian cadets were disadvantaged at the Russian training facilities. In the military sector, Stalin pursued the same objective as in other areas of society: He preferred to give leadership positions to Russians.

The transition from the Latin to the Cyrillic alphabet must have had an even greater effect than the measures in the educational system and the armed forces. All peoples who, only a few years previously and sometimes resistantly, had been forced to adopt the Latin alphabet now had to switch to the Cyrillic alphabet between 1937 and 1940. Ten years before, this measure had been termed a "regression to the old Tsarist Russification policy" and "great power chauvinism." Now, it was "in the interest of economic and political practicality" and "facilitated and accelerated acquisition of and proficiency in Russian."[80] This legitimization does not mention this dictatorial measure's high costs. Typewriters, printing presses, and many other machines and instruments, which had been acquired only a short time earlier, became trash or required expensive rebuilding. Millions of editions of schoolbooks and other teaching materials became waste paper. Other consequences were even more significant: Children and adults who had just learned how to read and write again became illiterate. Parents were no longer able to read their children's letters. The percentage of illiterates among the total population increased again, the school systems of the affected peoples experienced regressions that could only be compensated for after World War II. Most affected were the Islamic peoples, who had been trying for ten years to learn to read and write in the Latin alphabet. The renewed change of alphabet appeared particularly arbitrary and grotesque in the cases of the peoples, whom the Russian Orthodox missionaries had already acquainted with Cyrillic before 1917. In the late 1920s, they had been forced to adopt "the alphabet of the communist world society."[81] Now they were forced to return to Cyrillic. Among them were the Finnish peoples of the Volga area and the north of the European Soviet Union, Udmurts and Komi, the Ossets in the Northern Caucasus, and the Yakuts in Eastern Siberia. The Russian church had sent missionaries to all of these peoples and had laid the foundation for a Cyrillic writing system. During the storm of the "cultural revolution," the Mordvinians, Mari, and Chuvashs had been allowed to stay with Cyrillic.

Eliminating the Latin alphabet was by no means the result of careful long-term planning. Circumstances suggest that Stalin arbitrarily decided on this measure in the spring of 1937. In its session on March 7, 1937, the CEC's Presidium had approved two improved Latin alphabets for Buryat-Mongolian (consisting of twenty-nine letters) and Turkmenian (consisting of thirty letters) and put them into force.[82] During the same session, however, the Presidium had also ratified thirteen Cyrillic alphabets for the peoples of the far north because attempts to introduce Latin allegedly had not proven successful.[83] This indicates that the experts and responsible Soviet organs considered the writing issue primarily a pragmatic problem that did not allow any doctrinarian decisions.

The transition to Cyrillic affected a total of forty million people. As had happened ten years previously, no attempts were made to replace the Georgian, Armenian, and Yiddish scripts.[84]

What did the Soviets accomplish by establishing the Russian alphabet? Learning Russian certainly became easier. In addition, the Russian letters contributed to isolating the Soviet Union's peoples from the outside world. The borders in Asia and particularly with the Islamic world became tighter. Ultimately, Stalin's dictatorship was founded on isolation, separation from the outside, and prevention of all uncontrolled contacts. The Cyrillic alphabet separated many peoples from their compatriots living outside the Soviet borders: from the Uigurs and Kazakhs in Singkiang, the Tadzhiks and Uzbeks in Afghanistan, from the Azeri-Turks in Iran. It also separated the so-called Moldavians and the Moldavian SSR (founded in 1940) from Romania.

The Great Purge

For two years, from autumn 1936 to autumn 1938, the most extensive and bloodiest purge ever shook the country. The revolution did not devour its own children, but the dictatorship, which by now had unlimited power, destroyed its own elites: particularly the political elite of Bolshevik fellow revolutionaries and leaders who were appointed after the revolution, but also many of the artistic intelligentsia. The purges in the national territories were complete in that they destroyed the leadership cores nearly everywhere — whereas, in Moscow, the center, Stalin's immediate entourage stayed alive.

The statistics are unique in history: In January 1934, the Seventeenth Party Congress had appointed 140 members to the CC; by the fall of 1937, only fifteen of them had not been arrested. Only eight of the twelve Politburo members stayed in office. In May 1937, an army purge began claiming three of five marshals, thirteen of fifteen army generals, sixty-two of eighty-five corps commanders, 110 of 195 division commanders, and 220 of 406 brigade commanders. About 1,500 of the 6,000 higher ranking officers were executed by firing squads.[85]

In 1939, when the witch hunt ended, more than 850,000 members had been expelled from the Party, which is more than one-third of the total membership in 1937. Most of those expelled were arrested and disappeared in labor camps. Several hundred thousand people died in these camps or were immediately executed by firing squads. The persecution was primarily directed at the Party. Non-members were primarily arrested because they were family members, friends, or colleagues of "repressed" communists.[86] In spite of the high loss of human life, the number of victims was smaller than in the early 1930s, during the *dekulakization* and the famine. Then, the peasants had died; now, members of the Soviet elites perished.

Stalin clarified the differences in his speech of March 3, 1937, to the CC plenum, when he announced the elimination of the CC and the Party apparatus in no uncertain terms: The "wreckers," "saboteurs," and "spies" were now active within the Party. He repeated his theory, which had appeared during the campaign against Bukharin and the NEP in 1928–1930 for the first time: The closer the final victory of communism, the more extreme the class struggle. Stalin reversed one particular principle, which had represented the Party's morality during the "development of socialism": A good worker cannot be a "wrecker." Now, Stalin said, "On the contrary, a real wrecker occasionally must demonstrate the success of his work because this is the only way for him ... to continue his subversive actions." The most dangerous wreckers fulfill the plans and wait for the war. Even the Stakhanov-workers were no longer immune to persecution.[87]

It is interesting that the Ezhovshchina—named after N.I. Ezhov, the NKWD's People's Commissar from 1936 to 1938—was not a purge in the formal sense of the Party statutes as had been the ones of 1929 and of 1933 to 1936. Stalin's dictatorship destroyed all the rules and continuously developed new instruments of power, which he employed without warning, when nobody expected them, and purposefully. What were the motives behind the great purge, and what did Stalin want to accomplish when he eliminated the leadership's elites? The people involved, contemporaries, and historians have tried to discover the motives for the official Stalinist explanations convinced no one—except a few diplomats and some left-wing Western intellectuals. The propaganda claimed that "Trotskyite-Zinovievite fascist terrorists and counter-revolutionary nationalist gangsters"[88] had infiltrated Party and Soviet power and were threatening their existence. On all levels of the hierarchy, ranging from kolkhoz chairmen to the chairman of the Council of People's Commissars, the NKWD "discovered" and "exposed" "spies," "saboteurs," "wreckers," "fascists," and "enemies of the people." "Because the bourgeois nationalists are now too weak to attack the Soviet power directly, they have joined the Trotskyite-Bukharinite spies, saboteurs, and wreckers and adopted double-facedness and deception as their means of camouflage in their vicious subversive work."[89]

This is not only monstrous language, but randomly lumping political groups together and the verbal abuse indicate that the authors of these bloody denunciations, which they had written to save their own hides, were conscious of the fact that their talk was nonsense. Consequently, it is also very unlikely that Stalin "who inspired the trials came to believe in the *essential* veracity of the fantastic tales of treason and sabotage woven by his servants and confessed to by his former rivals and opponents."[90] On the contrary, Stalin consciously used denunciation, lies, and confessions (extracted through torture) to crimes never committed, to maintain the appearance of legitimacy and to hide his true motives.

So far, researchers have not at all been able to agree on Stalin's motives. Many of them see his insatiable hunger for power and the consolidation of unrestricted dictatorship as his prime motives.[91] The fact that, by 1936, Stalin had already acquired unrestricted power refutes these arguments; his power was not the result, but the prerequisite for the great purge.[92] But even Ulam's interpretation, which says Stalin was convinced imminent war was unavoidable and thus wanted to eliminate all possible traitors, is not convincing.[93]

Other motives researchers attribute to Stalin definitely came into play: Purge and terror were excuses for the failure of boastful visions for the future that had marked the start of the "revolution from above." The dictator needed scapegoats to blame for his unrealistic, failed, inhumane policy. Terror and the fear of sudden arrest were to put the elites and the whole society into a state of paralysis, submission, and discipline.[94] Stalin's experiences in the early 1930s had taught him that the only way to govern an industrial society in the process of modernization was by means of ruthless violence and physical extermination of complete social strata — even that such means were the only way to secure personal dictatorship over the long term.

The elimination of the elites increased the upward mobility of the next generation and let its members move quickly into the top positions of all bureaucracies. In 1941, about 90 percent of all college students who graduated during the First Five-Year-Plan held executive positions; as did more than 70 percent of the students who graduated during the Second Five-Year-Plan. In 1979, this "Brezhnev generation" made up 50 percent of voting Politburo members. Some Western researchers assume that Stalin used the purge quite consciously as part of a long-term plan to replace old comrades (who owed their positions to the revolution but not to Stalin's policy) with new executive elites that depended on him and were loyal to him.[95] Undoubtedly, the Stalinists' quick rise in the Party, economic bureaucracy, and armed forces was a welcome result of the 1936–1938 purge. By assuming, however, that Stalin had planned this step since 1928 would be to overestimate his political vision and to believe in planning magic.

So far, researchers have only marginally hinted at the idea that eliminating the elites was the final step in the process of establishing a new general line. Stalin had justifiable doubts that the old executive elites would be willing to establish the new line.[96] This is the decisive aspect. No matter how arbitrary its individual steps, the 1936–1938 purge was a planned political action executed with unbelievable brutality, and it sealed the establishment of Stalin's dictatorship. Without the purge, the totalitarian dictatorship probably would not have existed very long.

None of the great promises made during the enthusiastic period of the First Five-Year-Plan were kept: "development of socialism," "elimination of the classes," "solution of the nationalities issues," "surpassing capitalism." The rift between illusion and reality had become insurmountable. Stalin's violent solution consisted of replacing reality with illusion; not of developing socialism but of declaring it developed. Stalin was right when he doubted his old comrades would support this new policy. This is why he exterminated those who had promoted the illusion and had insisted on its realization. Propaganda declared that all nations had already developed to the same level. Anyone who held to this developmental equality as a political objective for the future was considered an "enemy of the people" and a "spy."

The nationalities policy demonstrates this causal relationship between the new general line and the purge in a particularly impressive manner. Previous sections of this book have shown that the nationalities policy changed after 1933. Initially, demonstrative actions were largely restricted to the Ukraine, and lip service was paid to the old objectives. The strategies changed after 1936, when elements of Russian nationalism were incorporated into Soviet patriotism; non-Russian nations were forced to adopt the Cyrillic alphabet; and the development of educational systems using indigenous languages was changed to provision of compulsory, intensive Russian lessons for all. Non-Russian executive elites must have considered this last step a provocation and the final proof that the policy of nation-building was dead. Stalin knew he could not expect Bolshevik executive groups to eliminate a policy they had supported for fifteen years and to offer no resistance. Stalin reasoned that he could replace this policy only if he eliminated its supporters.

The "revolution from above" had aggravated the situation by raising unrealistic expectation in nationalities policy: industrialization of the East, equal economic and cultural development for all national territories, and development of modern elites in educational systems using indigenous languages on all levels. By the late 1930s, the divergence between these expectations and the reality Stalin's dictatorship created had become a crucial factor contributing to instability in the system. Supporters of these illusions either had to be replaced with Russian functionaries sent from Moscow or with native functionaries who loyally supported the new centralist course and accepted the fact that no longer did one hundred different peoples live in the Soviet Union, but rather one people and ninety-nine others.

The purge in the national territories began systematically in the fall of 1936. It started at the bottom and, initially, did not touch many of the Union Republican Party leaderships. Apparently, no national territory was spared. The number of victims was particularly high in many small territories that had no significance for the central state. Of course, all enemies were now "bourgeois" non-Russian nationalists; the Soviets did not "discover" any Great Russian chauvinists anywhere. In an August 1936 Pravda article, Beriia, first secretary of the CP's Transcaucasian Area Committee and secretary of the Georgian CC, set the tone that would dominate the media for the following two years. "Quite consciously, individual Trotskyite-Zinovievite counter-revolutionary elements pretend to support the national hopes of the working peoples of the Transcaucasian republics as a way to hide their wrecking and terror activities."[97] Now was the time for a decisive effort to finish the fight against these "enemies." In the media, Beriia had not only signaled the start of the purge in the republics but by shooting and killing the secretary of the Armenian CC Khandzhian, in his Tiflis office on July 9, 1936, he had literally fired the starter's gun.[98] Of course, such an action required Stalin's personal approval.

Initially, the elimination of the executive level focused on the lower and middle executive levels and the empire's geographic periphery. The Union

Republics' top leaders took over this bloody work, apparently hoping this would prove their unreserved loyalty to the dictator and deflect his distrust from them. Stalin personally called on the populace, "non-Party members" and "workers," to denounce the authorities under whom they suffered daily—factory directors, school principals, Soviet functionaries—and thus to work out their disappointment and anger over their miserable living conditions. Thus, the dictator not only diverted political responsibility from himself, but he also punished the "guilty."

In the fall of 1936, fifty "Trotskyites" were removed from the city Party organization of Stalinabad (Dushanbe) alone. In Kazakhstan, "Trotskyites" were "exposed" in the telephone and postal service of the capital Alma-Ata and at the construction site of the road from Karaganda to Balkhash. In the remote Jewish Autonomous Region of Birobidzhan, "Liberberg, the chairman of the executive committee, proved to be a Trotskyite-nationalist in disguise."[99] Nor did Liberberg's successors have much luck. Kattel and Geller, the two chairmen of the executive committee who succeeded Liberberg, were also purged, along with four Party secretaries of the Regional Committee, for being "Trotskyites" and "Japanese spies."[100] This illustrates another characteristic typical of the purges in the national territories: Frequently, leadership positions were filled two or three times before the witch hunts ended in 1939.

Two other examples may show that even remote territories were not spared and that accusations grew into grotesques of Gogol-style dimensions. In fall 1936, a "counter-revolutionary nationalist group" was exposed in the Oirot Autonomous Region (Altai Mountains Autonomous Region), which Eiche, the first secretary of the Party's Western Siberian Area Committee and candidate member of the Politburo, eliminated. Before he was arrested in April 1938 and subsequently shot by a firing squad in February 1940, Eiche earned his reputation by demonstrating particular brutality in persecuting "enemies of the people."[101]

In December 1936, Beriia had Lakoba, the chairman of the Central Executive Committee of the Abkhaz Autonomous Republic, poisoned. This remained a secret, and Lakoba was buried as a "firm Bolshevik and revolutionary and an excellent organizer of socialist development in Abkhazia, Georgia, and the Transcaucasus." In October 1937, however, a "counter-revolutionary, terrorist-rebellious spy organization that conducted sabotage and wrecking activities," was sentenced, and the dead Lakoba was identified as the leader of these "counter-revolutionary bourgeois nationalists." The alleged objectives of this organization had been "armed rebellion and terrorist actions" "to accomplish the defeat of the Soviet power in Abkhazia, to separate Akhazia from the USSR . . . and to create an 'independent' Abkhaz state under the protection of a foreign state."[102]

Of course, there are no exact figures on the number of people purged, not to mention their national origin. Nevertheless, scattered individual figures permit conclusions. In the Chechen and Ingush ASSR, the great wave of arrests began on July 31, 1937. A total of about 14,000 people, or 2 percent of the population, were arrested.[103] Considering that the arrests included mostly individuals in prominent functions and their relatives, it becomes obvious that these arrests amounted to decapitating of the Soviet society. Shortly after the Tenth Party Congress in Georgia (May 1937), 425 of the 644 delegates (about two thirds) were arrested, deported, or shot. In 1937–1938, 4,238 new individuals were appointed to executive positions in Georgia's Party, state, or economy.[104]

Most of the Union Republican leadership groups met their fate in September 1937. At a plenum of the Armenian CC, Mikoian and Malenkov, who had travelled there on Stalin's order, held the Armenian Party leaders responsible for the death of Khandzhian whom Beriia had shot and killed. In his letter to the Armenian CC of September 8, 1937, Stalin harshly criticized the republic's agriculture and economic and cultural development, thus supporting this action. Among other things, Stalin's letter said: "It is intolerable to permit enemies of the Armenian people to roam Armenia as they please."[105] Nearly the whole CC and the Council of Armenian People's Commissars were arrested. By late September of 1937, none of the sixteen voting members and candidates of the CC Bureau appointed in June 1935 was still in office. By 1940, only two of those functionaries who formed the new Bureau were still in office. "More than 3,500 responsible members of the Party, soviets, economy, armed forces, and komsomol ... were arrested during a few months in 1937 [in Armenia]. Many of them were shot by firing squads without trials and the necessary investigations."[106]

The elimination of the leadership groups in the other republics followed a pattern similar to that observed in Armenia. In the fall of 1937, a special commission sent by the Moscow CC arrested the republican Party leaders who themselves had sent special commissions into the provinces only several months earlier. In Kazakhstan, nearly all the CC's members fell victim to the purge; for months, no CC at all existed in Turkmenistan.[107] Although the purge had not started in the Autonomous Republics of the RSFSR previously, the storm also hit them in the fall of 1937. The complete Council of People's Commissars of the Tatar ASSR was under arrest in the summer of 1937. In the fall, "outrageous facts about distortions of the Party's nationalities policy" were "exposed" in the Buryat-Mongolian ASSR. Among others, M.N. Erbanov, the first secretary of the Regional Party Committee, and the "spy" Dampilov, chairman of the Central Executive Committee, suffered for these exposures. Bashkiria was allegedly ruled by a "band of bourgeois nationalists." Among these were the "enemy of the people" and "spy" Tagirov, chairman of the Central Executive Committee; Bulashov, chairman of the Council of People's Commissars, "who issued directives damaging to the people and destructive to agriculture;" Abyzbaev, People's Commissar for Education, and Bykin, first secretary of the Regional Party Committee. In the Autonomous Region of the Karachai, the chairman of the Regional Executive Committee Kurdzhiev also "proved" to be a "traitor and nationalist."[108]

In the last Moscow show trial in March 1938, two prominent national leaders were tried and then shot: Faizulla Khodzhaev, who had been chairman of the Uzbek Council of People's Commissars since 1925, and Akmal Ikramov, who had been first secretary of the Uzbek CC since 1925. Both were among the longest serving top functionaries of the Union Republics and were the most prominent representatives of the Islamic peoples in the Soviet leadership. In June 1937, Khodzhaev was arrested; on September 8, 1937, Pravda denounced him and seven other leading Uzbek communists, including four members of the CC Bureau, as "enemies of the people." At the same time, Stalin and Molotov sent a letter to the Uzbek CC accusing Ikramov of having ignored the bourgeois nationalists lead by Khodzhaev. On September 27, Pravda reported Ikramov had been "exposed" and arrested.[109]

During the trial of the "bloc of right-wingers and Trotskyites," in which Bukharin was the most prominent defendant, Khodzhaev and Ikramov—like the other defendants—confessed global crimes, which the NKWD had invented: They had worked towards the "re-establishment of capitalism" in Uzbekistan, prepared an "armed rebellion," and intended to place Turkestan under "British protection."[110] In addition, under torture, they played the role of scapegoat by accepting the responsibility for the disastrous collectivization in Uzbekistan and the catastrophic consequences it triggered. Thus, Stalin's leadership, which was solely responsible, appeared pure and innocent. The Uzbek leaders admitted purposely causing the "reduction in cotton production" as a "provocation" and "wrecking." By establishing forced cotton monoculture, they had triggered the peasants' "mass actions against collectivization" to heat up anti-Soviet sentiments.[111]

This pattern was followed throughout the great purge: Stalin's policy of "building socialism," was condemned, while at the same time, the results of that policy were established as the incarnation of historical progress, and Stalin was permanently enthroned as the "father of the motherland." National communism and many hopes that national leaders had placed in Lenin's nationalities policy were also put on trial. Khodzhaev declared the "nationalists" intended to make the Central Asian Republics "economically . . . more independent from Soviet Russia than ever before . . . after the completion of the First Five-Year-Plan," "so we do not depend on imported Russian grain."[112]

In previous years, Khodzhaev had often made similar public statements. He was an outspoken opponent of cotton monoculture and had high hopes in the fascinating perspective held out by the "building of socialism." "The industry of processing agricultural raw materials... the construction, paper, and chemical industries Uzbekistan will grow at tremendous rates." In 1932, he wrote that by 1937, Uzbek industrial workers would live in at least ten to twelve square meters of living space per person (instead of the present four to four-and-a-half square meters) and the rest of the urban population in Uzbekistan would have seven to eight square meters per person.[113] His expectations and demands were half a century ahead of reality.

The elimination of the Ukrainian leadership elites demands particular attention, for it was in the Ukraine that the Soviets had developed the policy of nation-building. The Ukraine was the only national territory represented in the Politburo: First secretary S.V. Kosior had been a voting member of the Politburo since 1930; G.I. Petrovskii, Chairman of the Supreme Soviet, had been a Politburo candidate since 1926; and second secretary P.P. Postyshev since 1934. The Ukrainian purge promoted N.S. Krushchev into the innermost circle of leaders surrounding Stalin; in January 1938, Khrushchev replaced Kosior. The manner in which Khrushchev was relocated to Kiev from the position of the first secretary of the Moscow city and regional committee shows that Stalin had eliminated the Politburo's political decision-making authority. "In early 1938, Stalin offered me the position of first secretary of the Ukrainian CP's CC... I travelled to Kiev and relieved Kosior of his duties," Khrushchev wrote in his memoirs. Stalin angrily dismissed Khrushchev's objection that it was "not very clever to send me, a Russian, to the Ukraine."[114] We can assume that Stalin considered only a Russian suited to enforce the new nationalities policy in the Ukraine.

The purge essentially followed the same pattern in the Ukraine as in the other territories. In the spring of 1937, it started on the local and regional levels. In the process, about 20 percent of the Party members were expelled. About 66 percent of the executive functionaries on the regional level and 33 percent on the local level lost their positions.[115] Stalin sent Postyshev to the Ukraine in 1933 to eliminate Skrypnyk and his followers, and in 1937, Postyshev excelled by denouncing hundreds of "enemies of the people." Nevertheless, when he attended the CC plenum in Moscow in February/March 1937, Postyshev expressed some doubts about the legitimacy of several cases in which high functionaries had been arrested. As punishment, Stalin transferred him to Kuibyshev, where he continued the brutal purges until he himself was arrested in the spring of 1938 "for the extermination of cadres." Postyshev was then shot by a firing squad in December 1940.[116]

In July 1937, Shelekhes, the first member of the Ukrainian Politburo, was arrested. In August — several weeks before the republican leadership groups in Central Asia and the Transcaucasus were eliminated — Stalin sent a Politburo delegation including Molotov, Ezhov, and Khrushchev, to Kiev to demand the Ukrainian CC relieve Kosior, Petrovskii, and P. Liubchenko, the Chairman of the Council of People's Commissars, of their duties.

In a demonstration of the Ukrainian leadership's self-confidence, the Ukrainian CC's plenum made a rare attempt to resist Stalin and refused to carry out Moscow's directives. This made Molotov demand the Ukrainian Politburo come to Moscow. Once there, several members were arrested immediately, and others returned to Kiev and disappeared later. Liubchenko committed suicide on August 30, 1937.

Between August 1937 and the summer of 1938, the entire Ukrainian Politburo, Orgburo, and the CC Secretariat and all seventeen people's commissars were arrested. Only three of the 102 members and candidate members of the Ukraine's CC survived. All regional secretaries lost their positions, and most also lost their lives. A single Ukrainian top functionary remained free, although he lost all his political offices: Petrovskii survived and became the deputy director of the Museum of the Revolution in Moscow. Before the revolution, he had been a Bolshevik Duma delegate. Perhaps Stalin gave in to a rare feeling of sentimentality; in any case, none of the former Bolshevik Duma delegates was arrested.[117]

Kosior, the head of the Ukrainian Party and a voting member of the Politburo, was nominally assigned to the position of Deputy Chairman of the Council of People's Commissars of the USSR in January 1938. In April 1938, he was arrested, and without the Politburo ever discussing the case, he was shot by a firing squad in February 1939.[118]

Supported by a dozen top functionaries, whom he brought along from the Moscow CC apparatus, Khrushchev continued the purge.[119] In May and June 1938, he again relieved the entire Ukrainian Council of People's Commissars of its duties. Between February and June all twelve recently appointed first secretaries of the regions and most of the second secretaries met with the same fate. The elimination of the Party apparatus was complete; in 1938, 1,600 new secretaries on the raion and municipal levels were appointed. Among those rising from the Party's fragments were Brezhnev and Kirilenko.[120]

The purge did not restrict itself to the Party and state bureaucracy. In addition, it affected the educational system and the writers' union — both systems had been important promoters of national expectations in the Ukraine and in the other republics. In 1930, 259 Ukrainian authors had their writings published; by 1938, the work of only thirty-six writers managed to remain in print.[121]

As is well known, the great purge found many victims among the Bolsheviks who had held leading positions in the 1920s but were drastically demoted later on. In the area of nationalities policy, Stalin eliminated those who had opposed him during the USSR's founding phase and who had attempted—while Lenin was still alive—to make the federative principle politically more prominent in the state and the Party than Stalin was willing to tolerate. Stalin's vindictiveness joined his determination to eliminate men who represented the intentions and far-reaching expectations of early Soviet nationalities policy.

To name a few examples, among the victims were Ryskulov, Mdivani, and Rakovskii. Turar Ryskulov was Stalin's deputy as People's Commissar of Nationality Affairs from 1921 to 1922 and chairman of the Turkestan Council of People's Commissars from 1922 to 1924. Making him Deputy Chairman of the Council of People's Commissars of the RSFSR from 1926 to 1937 was equivalent to a demotion and essentially excluded him from decisions about nationalities policy.[122] Budu Mdivani was among the prominent personalities in Georgia's CC when the CC protested the policy Ordzhonikidze and Stalin pursued in the Transcaucasus and collectively resigned in October 1922. At the Twelfth Party Congress in April 1923, Mdivani also criticized Stalin's nationalities policy. After he was expelled from the Party for being a Trotskyite (1928–1931), he again rose to Georgia's First Deputy Chairman of the Council of People's Commissars by 1936. In July 1937, he was tried in Tiflis behind closed doors. The court sentenced him to death, and he was shot by a firing squad. During Bukharin's Moscow show trial in March 1938, it was even claimed that Mdivani had been a British agent.[123]

Ch.G. Rakovskii was chairman of the Ukrainian Council of People's Commissars from 1919 to 1923. Although he was a Bulgarian, the discussions about the Soviet Union's federative structure and the first federal constitution found him clearly on the side of the Ukrainian communists who wanted to reserve considerably more political competences for the Union Republics than the 1923–1924 constitution granted them in the end. In 1923, Rakovskii was taken out of the picture when he was appointed Soviet chargé d'affaires in London and later in Paris. He was expelled from the Party from 1927 to 1934 because he was a Trotsky supporter; afterward he was assigned a position with the Soviet Red Cross. In late 1936, Rakovskii was arrested and, in the Bukharin trial, sentenced as a "British and Japanese spy" to a twenty-year prison term. In 1941, he perished in the Gulag.[124]

Who was appointed to the tens of thousands of leadership positions that became vacant in the national territories alone in 1936 to 1938? The Soviets preferentially assigned functionaries from the Moscow CC apparatus or the capital's other central bureaucracies to the top positions in the Union Republics. In this process, the few natives working in these central apparatuses were given their chances. Primarily, however, Russians were sent to national republics to fill the vacant positions of Party secretaries and people's commissars.[125] The republics' leaderships were not intended to stand up to the center for the territories' interests, but were supposed to execute the center's will in the republics. Russian dominance in the top offices is apparent in the national make-up of the CC in Moscow. Of the CC's 139 members and candidates appointed at the Eighteenth Party Congress in March 1939, 66.2 percent were Russian. By 1952 (the Nineteenth Party Congress), the percentage had increased to 71.5 percent of the 235 members and candidates; later this percentage decreased considerably. In 1939, Kazakhs, Kirgiz, Turkmen, and Tadzhiks were not at all represented in the CC although these nations were titular nations of Union Republics. By 1952, at least one member of each of these nations was a member in the CC.[126]

Of course, many positions on the middle and lower levels had to be filled with local functionaries, but even then, Russian immigrants were preferred. The national make-up of the republican Party organizations demonstrates that the privileged position the Russians held among the elites improved. In 1933, the percentages of Party members from the titular nations peaked in Uzbekistan, Kirgizia, and Tadzhikistan at 61 percent, 59 percent, and 53 percent, respectively, and then continuously fell, reaching its lowest level after World War II. After Stalin's death, the numbers again began to increase considerably. In 1949, 45 percent of the members of the Uzbek Party were Uzbek. In 1953, 34 percent of the Kirgiz Party organization were Kirgiz. In 1940, the Tadzhik Party organization included only 45 percent native members. Correspondingly, the percentages of Russians increased — in Uzbekistan, for example, from 20 percent in 1933 to 27 percent in 1949.[127] Although no concrete figures are available, we can assume that the role the Russians played among the elites of the Autonomous Republics increased to a comparable extent. Georgia and Armenia were the exceptions to this rule; the data do not support any proportionate decrease in the number of native Party members and elites.

In late 1938, the mass terror ended. In December 1938, when Beriia replaced Ezhov as head of the NKWD, the great purge entered its last phase: elimination of the eliminators. At the Eighteenth Party Congress in March 1939, Stalin declared, "We cannot say the purge was executed without grave mistakes. Unfortunately, more mistakes were made than anticipated. Without question, we will no longer use the method of mass purge."[128] These statements reflect a level of cynicism that is difficult to achieve; they also demonstrate, however, that — in spite of the arbitrariness and unpredictability of the individual cases — the terror was the result of a calculating political mind and not a sick dictator's paranoid hysteria. In respect to nationalities policy, the elimination of the elites was the consistent conclusion of the enforcement of a new general line.

Until Gorbachev's glasnost, the claim that the USSR's nationalities issue was resolved was continuously repeated in the Soviet Union. Generally, the late 1930s were given as the date of this resolution. "The victory of socialism in the USSR accomplished during the Second Five-Year-Plan fundamentally changed national relationships. This issue was resolved in the USSR, for the first time in the history of mankind...."[129] The 1930s were referred to as the "concluding stage in the development of the socialist nations,"[130] during which "the factual equality of the nations was essentially" accomplished.[131] In his report to the Twenty-fourth Party Congress in 1971, Brezhnev stated that in the 1930s, "a new historical community of people — the Soviet people — developed in our country."[132]

These ideological statements confirm that, also from the Soviet perspective, the essential structures of the Soviet system were created in the 1930s. The general line of nationalities policy that Stalin determined was essentially valid until the late 1980s — although the conditions under which it can be enforced, and thus the reality of national relations, changed fundamentally.

Notes

1. Article 4 of the first constitution of the USSR, January 31, 1924. This provision has remained unchanged and is also included in the presently valid 1977 constitution (Article 72). Describing the USSR as a "uniform, multinational federal state" (Article 70 of the 1977 constitution) incorporates the first principle of the nationalities doctrine into the constitution. Although this term does not appear in earlier versions of the constitution, many Soviet publications have referred to the Union as "uniform" (edinyi) and to its parts as "inseparable" (neotemlemaia chast) since the 1930s.

2. See Stalin, *Werke,* vol. 11, pp. 298–317.

3. Quotes ibid., pp. 315, 307, 308, 311, 315, 305.

4. Ibid., p. 315.

5. See Stalin, *Werke,* vol. 2, p. 297. Justifiably, G.W. Strobel points out that Soviet nationalities theory integrated a number of theorems from Austro-Marxism — in spite of all the polemical statements the Soviets made against it ("Ethnie-Nationalität und der Führungsanspruch der Sowjetunion," in: *Deutsche Studien,* 17, 1979, pp. 21–37).

6. See Stalin, *Werke,* vol. 12, p. 322.

7. Ibid., p. 323.

8. Dimanshtein, "Otnoshenie marksizma-leninizma k voprosu ob assimiliatsii natsionalnostei," in: *RN,* 7/1935, p. 62.

9. On Dimanshtein's biography, cf. *Bolshaia Sovetskaia Entsiklopediia,* 1st edition, vol. 22, 1935, column 416; also: Z.Y. Gitelman, *Jewish Nationality and Soviet Politics* (Princeton, N.J., 1972), pp. 518–521; Dimanshtein was probably shot in 1938.

10. *Istoriia sovetskoi konstitutsii (v dokumentakh): 1917–1956* (Moscow, 1957), pp. 43f.

11. *Pravda,* November 18, 1922, in: Stalin, *Werke,* vol. 5., pp. 126f.

12. *Pravda,* March 24, 1923, in: Stalin, *Werke,* vol. 5, p. 167.

13. Article 15 of the 1923/24 constitution (Istoriia sovetskoi konstitutsii dokumentakh, p. 463).
14. See Stalin, *Werke*, vol. 5, p. 293, cf. p. 259.
15. Articles 25 and 26 of the 1923/24 constitution.
16. *RN*, 10–11/1931, pp. 151–154.
17. See Stalin, *Werke*, vol. 5, p. 293; B. Meissner, "Entstehung, Fortentwicklung und ideologische Grundlagen des sowjetischen Bundesstaates," in: *Bundesstaat und Nationalitätenrecht in der Sowjetunion*, pp. 39–41.
18. I. Sharapov, *Natsionalnye sektsii RKP (b)* (Kazan, 1967); Z.Y. Gitelman, *Jewish Nationality and Soviet Politics: The Jewish Sections of the CPSU, 1917–1930* (Princeton, N.J., 1972).
19. S. Dimanshtein, "Ideologicheskaia borba v natsionalnom voprose," in: *RN*, 3/1930, p. 7. Dimanshtein was the last head of the national sector of the CC.
20. "Soveshchanie redaktorov natsgazet," in: *RN*, 8–9/1930, pp. 143–147.
21. S. Abramov, "Organizatsionnye formy rukovodstva rabotoi sredi natsmen," in: *RN*, 6/1935, p. 51.
22. Z. Ostrovskii, "K itogam raboty Otdela Natsionalnostei VZIK," in: *RN*, 5/1932, p. 83.
23. Ibid., pp. 84f.
24. N. Iushunev, "Natsionalnyi proletariat Urala," in: *RN*, 6/1932, p. 95.
25. Abramov, ibid., p. 54.
26. I. Loginov, "Sovety Belorussii," in: *RN*, 4/1934, p. 44.
27. Abramov, ibid., p. 51.
28. A. & V. Elbaev, "O rabote sredi natsmen Moskovskoi oblasti," in: *RN*, 8/1936, p. 18; "O sostoianii raboty v Armianskoi SSR," in: *RN*, 12/1936, p. 86.
29. S. Dimanshtein, "Natsionalnosti Soiuza SSR k XVII godovshchine Oktiabria," in: *RN*, 11/1934, pp. 4f.
30. A. Skachko, "Desiat let raboty na Severe," in: *RN*, 7/1934, pp. 38–41; ibid., "Narody Severa na novem etape," in: *RN*, 9/1935, pp. 31–33.
31. A. Bilinsky, "Die Zuständigkeit der Union und der Unionsrepubliken auf dem Gebiet der Wirtschaftsverwaltung von 1922–1972," in: *Bundesstaat und Nationalitätenrecht in der Sowjetunion*, p. 139.
32. *Loc. cit.*, pp. 136f.
33. *Direktivy KPSS i Sovetskogo pravitelstva po khoziaistvennym voprosam*, vol. 2, pp. 126–133.
34. Iakubovskaia, *Razvitie SSSR kak soiuznogo gosudarstva*, p. 157.
35. SZ SSSR, 1929, no. 56, Article 521 "O poriadke peredachi v venedie organov SSSR predpriiatii, imeiushchikh obshchesoiuznoe znachenie."
36. Iakubovskaia, *loc. cit.*
37. Penkaitis, *Der Finanzausgleich in der Sowjetunion*, pp. 110f.

38. "Postanovlenie CIK i CNK SSSR, 5.I. 1932," in: *Direktivy KPSS i Sovetskogo pravitelstva po khoziaistvennym voprosam*, vol. 2, p. 333.

39. "Postanovlenie CIK SSSR 10. August 1934," in: *loc. cit.*, pp. 425–426; E. Zaleski, *Stalinist Planning for Economic Growth, 1933–1952* (London, 1980), pp. 22–27.

40. D. Shapiro, "Zadachi narkomatov mestnoi promyshlennosti," in: *RN*, 10/1934, p. 20.

41. "Postanovlenie CIK SSSR 'Ob obrazovanii Narodnogo kommissariata zemledeleniia SSSR'," (of December 7, 1929), in: *Istoriia sovetskoi konstitutsii (v dokumentakh)*, pp. 612–614 (quotes p. 613).

42. *Die sowjetische Bildungspolitik seit 1917. Dokumente und Texte*. O. Anweiler/K. Meyer (eds.), (Heidelberg, 1961), p. 203.

43. *Loc. cit.*, pp. 210–214.

44. *Loc. cit.*, p. 163; Pennar/Bakalo/Bereday, *Modernization and Diversity in Soviet Education*, pp. 59f.

45. *Die Sowjetische Bildungspolitik seit 1917*, pp. 220 f; Pennar/Bakalo/Bereday, pp. 172, 217f. For a general survey of the educational policy in the 1930s, see: O. Anweiler, "Erziehungs- und *Bildungspolitik,"* in: *Kulturpolitik der Sowjetunion*, pp. 53–66.

46. Article 70 of the 1936 constitution.

47. Iakubovskaia, *Razvitie SSSR kak soiuznogo gosudarstva*, pp. 129 f, 131 f, 203.

48. Stalin, *Sochineniia*, vol. 1 (14), p. 186.

49. Iakubovskaia, *Razvitie*, p. 199.

50. Article 67 and Article 37 of the 1923–1924 constitution; Article 83 and Article 70, 77 of the 1936 constitution (*Istoriia sovetskoi konstitutsii (v dokumentakh)*).

51. Quoted from Barghoorn, *Soviet Russian Nationalism*, p. 181.

52. "Patriotizm," in: *Entsiklopediia gosudarstva i prava*, vol. 3 (Moscow, 1927), p. 252; quoted from: Oberländer, *Sowjetpatriotismus und Geschichte*, p. 56.

53. *Pravda*, March 19, 1935; quoted from: Oberländer, *Op. cit.*, p. 62.

54. A. Martiny, "Nationalismus und Nationalitätenfrage in sowjetischer Sicht," in: *Nationalismus*, H.A. Winkler (ed.), p. 105.

55. Oberländer, *Sowjetpatriotismus und Geschichte*, particularly pp. 20–28.

56. *Pravda*, January 15, 1937, quoted from: Oberländer, *Op. cit.*, pp. 68f.

57. See Stalin, *Werke*, vol. 8, p. 135.

58. See Stalin, *Werke*, vol. 13, p. 22. The term "revolutionary national pride" appears there.

59. A. Kiselev, "Pod znamenem Stalinskoi konstitutsii," in: *RN*, 2/1937, p. 19.

60. P.P. Liubchenko, "O proekte konstitutsii USSR," in: *RN*, 3/1937, p. 33.

61. A. Ikramov, "O proekte konstitutsii Uzbekskoi SSR," in: *RN*, 4/1937, p. 47.
62. Stalin, *Sochineniia*, vol. 1 (14), pp. 114f.
63. "Natsionalnosti k XIX godovshchine velikoi proletarskoi revoliutsii," in: *RN*, 11/1936, p. 6.
64. *Loc. cit.*, p. 3.
65. M. Arzhanov, "Konstitutsiia proletarskogo internationalizma," in: *RN*, 10/1936, p. 23.
66. V.M. Molotov, "K 20-letiiu Oktiabrskoi revoliutsii," in: *RN*, 12/1937, p. 26.
67. "Velikaia druzhba narodov SSSR," in: *Bolshevik*, 13/1938, p. 7; quoted from Oberländer, *Sowjetpatriotismus*, p. 70.
68. T.I. Baranova/N.S. Rozyeva, "Iz istorii prepodovaniia russkogo iazyka v nerusskikh shkolakh SSSR (1938–1966)," in: *Sovetskaia pedagogika*, 12/1977, p. 116. This resolution of March 13, 1938, is still unpublished. The regulations of implementation, however, were published in the Union Republics, for example, the resolution of the Ukrainian Council of People's Commissars of April 20, 1938, "On Compulsory Russian Classes at Non-Russian schools in the Ukraine," in: *Kulturne budivnytstvo v Ukraiinskii RSR*, vol. I (Kiev, 1960), pp. 740–744.
69. F. Sovetkin, "Rodnoi i russkii iazyk v nerusskoi shkole," in: *RN*, 1/1937, p. 84.
70. Sullivant, *Soviet Politics and the Ukraine*, p. 232.
71. Sovetkin, *loc. cit.*, p. 84.
72. Barghoorn, *Soviet Russian Nationalism*, pp. 98f.
73. Baranova/Rozyeva, *Iz istorii*, pp. 119–121.
74. The most important indication of these measures is the fact that, after 1938, the institutions mentioned no longer appear in the Soviet media.
75. *Kulturne budivnytstvo v Ukraiinskii RSR*, vol. 1 (Kiev, 1960), p. 740.
76. *Op. cit.*, p. 751.
77. I. Kreindler, *The Changing Status of Russian in the Soviet Union*, p. 12.
78. *KPSS o vooruzhennykh silakh Sovetskogo Soiuza* (Moscow, 1969), p. 294.
79. S. Kurbanbaev, "Vernyi strazh sotsialisticheskoi rodiny," in: *RN*, 3/1935, p. 36. On the situation of the non-Russians in the Red Army in the 1920s and 1930s cf.: E. Jones, "Minorities in the Soviet Armed Forces," in: *Comparative Strategy* III, 1982, pp. 288f., 304–306; S.L. Curran/D. Ponomareff, *Managing the Ethnic Factor in the Russian and Soviet Armed Forces* (Rand Corporation, July 1982), pp. 20–25.
80. M.I. Isaev, *O iazykakh narodov SSSR* (Moscow, 1978), p. 15; A.K. Valiev, *Sovetskaia natsionalnaia intelligentsiia i ee sotsialnaia rol* (Tashkent, 1969), p. 133.

81. This is the term the "Committee for the New Alphabet of the Peoples of the Far North," coined for the Latin alphabet. This committee was founded in May 1932 (Isayev, *National Languages in the USSR*, p. 249).
82. *RN*, 4/1937, pp. 104f.
83. *Loc. cit.*, pp. 103f.
84. On the transition to Cyrillic, see the books by M.I. Isaev, *O iazykakh narodov SSSR* (Moscow, 1978) and idem., *Iazykovoe stroitelstvo v SSSR* (Moscow, 1979).
85. G. v. Rauch, *Geschichte der Sowjetunion* (Stuttgart, 1969), 5th ed., pp. 280, 287.
86. R.A. Medvedev, "New Pages from the Political Biography of Stalin," in: *Stalinism*. Tucker (ed.), p. 214.
87. Stalin's speech of March 3, 1937, in: *Sochineniia*, vol. XIV, pp. 189–224. The quote is on p. 214.
88. T. Enchinov, "Borba s kontrrevoliutsionnym natsionalizmom v Oirotii," in: *RN*, 10/1936, p. 17.
89. "Iskorenit do kontsa kontrrevoliutsionnykh natsionalistov," in: *RN*, 9–10/1937, p. 15.
90. cf. Ulam, *Stalin*, p. 412.
91. For example, cf. Conquest, *Great Terror*, pp. 66, 81; Medvedev, "New Pages from the Political Biography of Stalin," in: *Stalinism* Tucker (ed.), p. 220.
92. Ulam, *Stalin*, p. 399.
93. Ibid.
94. R. Lorenz, "Historische und politische Voraussetzungen der 'Moskauer Prozesse' (1936–1938)," in: *Kritische Justiz*, XII, 1979, pp. 364–375.
95. Sh. Fitzpatrick, "Stalin and the Making of a New Elite. 1928–1939," in: *Slavic Review*, 38, 1979, pp. 398–401.
96. R. Tucker, "Stalinism as Revolution from Above," in: *Stalinism*, Tucker (ed.), pp. 88, 91.
97. *Pravda*, August 19, 1936.
98. Medwedew, *Die Wahrheit ist unsere Stärke*, p. 230.
99. "Trotskistsko-zinovevskie banditi-restavratory kapitalizma," in: *RN*, 10/1936, pp. 6–8.
100. Kolarz, *Nationalitätenpolitik*, p. 209.
101. T. Enchinov, "Borba s kontrrevoliutsionnym natsionalizmom v Oirotii," in: *RN*, 10/1936, p. 16; Conquest, *Great Terror*, pp. 450, 474.
102. These are typical examples of the linguistic style of that period. S. Dimanshtein, "Vysshe bolshevistskuiu bditelnost," in: *RN*, 12/1937, pp. 58f.; *RN*, 1/1937, pp. 72f. Medwedew, *Die Wahrheit ist unsere Stärke*, p. 299.
103. Conquest, *Great Terror*, p. 287; not three percent, as Conquest writes.
104. Medwedew, *Die Wahrheit ist unsere Stärke*, p. 229; Conquest, *Great Terror*, p. 250.

105. Medwedew, *Die Wahrheit ist unsere Stärke,* p.326.
106. *Kommunist* (Erivan) November 15, 1961, quoted from Conquest, *Great Terror,* p. 250.
107. The details of what events are known, are presented in: Conquest, *Great Terror* and Medwedew, *Die Wahrheit ist unsere Stärke.* I will not reiterate them here.
108. "Iskorenit do kontsa kontrrevoliutsionnykh natsionalistov," in: *RN,* 9–10/1937, pp. 22f.
109. *Pravda,* September 8, 1937; Medwedew, *Die Wahrheit ist unsere Stärke,* p. 337.
110. *Prozebericht über die Strafsache des antisowjetischen "Blocks der Rechten und Trotzkisten"* . . . *Vollständiger Stenographischer Bericht* (Moscow, 1938), pp. 250, 379.
111. Ibid., pp. 245, 376.
112. Ibid., p. 244.
113. F. Khodzhaev, "Nekotorye voprosy vtoroi piatiletki v Uzbekistane," in: *RN,* 5/1932, pp. 9–11. Ikramov was rehabilitated in 1957, Khodzhaev in 1966. None of the defendants in the Moscow show trials was honored as much after their rehabilitation as the two Uzbek leaders, who were remembered in the 1970s in extensive biographies and three volumes of "selected works" each (D.S. Carlisle, "K istorii destalinizatsii v Uzbekistane," in: *Obozrenie,* no. 2, December 1982, pp. 32–34).
114. *Chruschtschow erinnert sich* (Reinbek, 1971), pp. 106, 120.
115. Conquest, *Great Terror,* pp. 252, 255.
116. Medwedew, *Die Wahrheit ist unsere Stärke,* p. 450.
117. Conquest, *Great Terror,* pp. 255f., 469f.
118. Ibid., pp. 273, 450, 468.
119. *Chruschtschow erinnert sich,* p. 122.
120. Conquest, *Great Terror,* pp. 258f.
121. A. Bolubash, "The Great Ukrainian Famine of 1932–1933 as an Instrument of Russian Nationalities Policy," in: *Ukrainian Review,* 1/1979, p. 42.
122. Ryskulov's biographies disagree considerably from one another in many details: Valiev, *Formirovanie i razvitie,* pp. 91f.; Bennigsen/Wimbush, *Muslim National Communism,* pp. 205f. Essentially, I follow Valiev's data. cf. *Revoliutsiia v Srednei Azii glazami musulmanskikh bolshevikov,* reprint (Oxford, 1985).
123. *Who Was Who in the USSR* (Metuchen, NJ, 1972), p. 377.
124. Ibid., p. 471.
125. *Chruschtschow erinnert sich,* pp. 122f.
126. S. Bialer, *Soviet Political Elite,* Ph.D. (Columbia University, 1966), p. 188.

127. Rigby, *Communist Party Membership,* pp. 372, 394f.; cf. Chapter II, Table 2.3.
128. Stalin, *Sochineniia,* vol. XIV, pp. 373f.
129. Titov, *Borba partii,* p. 58.
130. Sh.B. Batyrov, *Formirovanie i razvitie sotsialisticheskikh natsii v SSSR* (Moscow, 1962), p. 111.
131. A.K. Azizian, *Leninskaia natsionalnaia politika v razvitii i deistvii* (Moscow, 1972), p. 277.
132. *Material XXIV sezda KPSS* (Moscow, 1971), p. 76.

VII

War

The territories of non-Russian peoples in the USSR made up a large part of the German-Soviet war theater. More than two-thirds of the territory German troops occupied belonged to non-Russian Union Republics or Autonomous Republics. Only in non-Russian areas did German civil administration exist. German military administration controlled whatever purely Russian territory of the RSFSR the Wehrmacht occupied. Non-Russian nationals were subjected to the rule of German occupational forces for a longer time. They were the main target of Hitler's policy of exploiting the *Untermensch*. But they also had more opportunities to collaborate with the Nazis than did the Russians. After the Soviets won the war, they retaliated against the non-Russian nations for their alleged or actual collaboration with the Nazis. In some instances, this retaliation was more severe than the rule of German occupation forces. As a result, many of the USSR's western and southern border nations became the objects and victims of the German-Soviet war.

However, the war also focused on the western USSR in another sense. When the Nazis and Soviets signed the German-Soviet treaties in the fall of 1939, Stalin managed to demarcate the two countries' mutual spheres of interest in Eastern Europe and thus guaranteed the USSR its most important spoils of war before a single shot had been fired. Stalin was so convinced he was a diplomatic genius that — at least for a short while after the treaty — he no longer anticipated a German-Soviet war. Actually, the Soviets had to go to battle in the bloodiest war in history to keep the 1939 and 1940 annexations that seemed so easy to acquire.

Annexation of the Western Territories

The Soviet Union's most significant territorial expansion ever was the result of a diplomatic coup that has remained unmatched in recent history: the German-Soviet agreement of August 1939. On the basis of their nonaggression pact of August 23, 1939, their "German-Soviet Frontier and

Friendship Treaty" of September 28, 1939, and particularly the secret supplementary protocols included therein, Germany and the Soviet Union determined the "demarcation of their mutual spheres of interest in Eastern Europe."[1] These treaties guaranteed the Soviet Union a free hand in reintegrating those territories that had been a part of the Russian Empire before 1917: Finland, Estonia, Latvia, Lithuania, Western Belorussia, and Bessarabia. In addition, the USSR received Eastern Galicia (that is the Western Ukraine including Lvov), and in June 1940 after additional diplomatic conferences, northern Bukovina—territories that had never been part of the state of Moscow.[2]

Nazi Germany and the Soviet Union agreed that Poland, Finland, Estonia, Latvia, and Lithuania should no longer exist as sovereign states and that Romania should be forced to give Bessarabia and northern Bukovina to the USSR. Apart from the elimination of Finland, all plans included in these treaties were carried out. Because Finland offered unexpectedly determined military resistance during the 1939–1940 winter war and because the Western powers threatened to join the Finnish defense efforts, Finland managed to maintain its sovereignty by ceding territory to the USSR. For fifty years, until 1989, the Soviet Union officially denied the existence of the secret protocols, which contain the substance of the treaties.

The territories the Soviet Union gained by moving its state borders westward were exclusively non-Russian ones in which Russians constituted a marginal minority among the populace. The annexations between September 1939 (the Red Army's invasion of Poland) and August 1940 (the incorporation of the three Baltic states into the USSR) increased the USSR's population by more than twenty-three million people: 8.7 million lived in the Western Ukraine, 4.6 million in Western Belorussia (that is, 13.4 million in the former Polish territories), 3.2 million in Bessarabia, 0.5 million in northern Bukovina, 1.1 million in Estonia, 2.0 million in Latvia, and 3.0 million in Lithuania.[3]

The Soviet power used historical and national reasons to justify these annexations. They referred to "reunification," thus emphasizing the USSR's historical identity with the Russian Empire once more. In addition, the Soviets justified incorporating the territories of the Western Ukraine (including Lvov) and northern Bukovina (both had previously been a part of the Austro-Hungarian Empire) and annexing the Carpatho-Ukraine in 1945 by claiming it was necessary to unify the whole Ukrainian people in one "state," namely the Ukrainian SSR. In 1940, Molotov justified the USSR's belated demand for Bukovina to the German ambassador von der Schulenburg by declaring that this was "the last missing part of the Ukraine, which belongs together."[4] The Soviets could take credit for uniting all Ukrainian territories for the first time. In a similar manner, they intended to satisfy Lithuanian national pride and create a pro-Soviet attitude in Lithuania during the reorganization of the Soviet west by returning Vilnius to Lithuania in October 1939—that is, before Lithuania became incorporated into the Soviet Union.

The Soviets had never really accepted their loss of western territories after the revolution and civil war despite the internationally binding treaties they had signed to that effect.[5] In 1924, the Fifth Comintern Congress made the communist parties of Poland, Czechoslovakia, and Romania accept the Soviet demand of "separating Ukrainian territories from Poland, Czechoslovakia, and Romania and uniting them with the Soviet Ukraine and thus with the USSR."[6] The Soviet Union demonstrated its irredentist attitude in particularly clear terms in the case of Romania. The Moldavian Autonomous Republic, which had been founded on the left bank of the Dniester river in 1924, was to keep alive the demand for the "reunification" of all "Moldavians," to support demands for the return of Bessarabia. Only 30 percent of the ASSR's populace was "Moldavian," and thus the Moldavian ASSR was not only an artificial construct but was located largely in Ukrainian territory. In August 1940, after the USSR had actually regained Bessarabia and founded the Moldavian Union Republic, the Soviet Union admitted to this when it transferred to the Ukraine 1,900 square miles of a total of 3,200 which had comprised the former Moldavian Autonomous Republic.[7]

In its dealings with Finland in the north, the Soviet Union also pretended it had only national reunification in mind: The Soviets disguised the military aggression against Finland in November 1939 by claiming they were fulfilling "the Finnish people's national hopes of being reunited with the Karelian people."[8] In the process of integrating the Karelian Isthmus (including Vyborg, which Finland had surrendered) and additional Karelian territories along the border, the Karelian ASSR in March 1940 was reorganized to form the Karelo-Finnish Union Republic. This elevation in status survived only until July 1956. Probably the Soviets had intended for the Karelo-Finnish Union Republic to be only the first step in the planned Sovietization of all Finland.[9] In any case, the fact that the events here parallel developments in the Moldavian Republic seems quite obvious.

The Soviets still hold to the justifications that define the 1939 and 1940 annexations as territorial and national "reunification." In his radio address of September 17, 1939, Molotov not only announced the Red Army's invasion of eastern Poland, but he also declared it impossible for the Soviet government "to remain oblivious to the fate of its own blood brothers, the Ukrainians and Belorussians living in Poland."[10]

The political conditions under which Sovietization occurred varied from case to case: On the one hand, the Soviet Union annexed the formerly independent states of Estonia, Latvia, and Lithuania, and on the other hand, territories surrendered by Romania or acquired in the division of Poland.

Most of the population of the previously Finnish territories in Karelia left their homeland and moved to Finland, leaving mostly depopulated territory to the USSR. In spite of the varying conditions, the annexations and the first steps of Sovietization followed a similar pattern everywhere:

1. Occupation by the Red Army; in the Baltic states, this step was preceded by a phase of forced establishment of Red Army military bases.
2. Installation of provisional "people's governments" or provisional Soviet organs.
3. Prohibition of all political parties, organizations, and labor unions; establishment of the CP and Soviet mass organizations in the acquired territory.
4. Organization of elections based on single lists. These assemblies voted "unanimously" for incorporation of the respective territory into the USSR. Formally, this integration was decreed by the Supreme Soviet in Moscow.
5. Nationalization of the industrial, trade, and banking systems; dispossession of the owners without indemnification and integration of the new territories into the system of the central administrative economy.
6. Assignment of thousands of leadership positions in all areas to specialists from the Soviet Union; many of these specialists were local nationals, and many were Russians.
7. Land reform, expropriation of land from its owners if it surpassed a predetermined acreage, and distribution of this land among peasants who had little or no land.
8. Mass deportations. Even before the incorporation of these territories into the USSR, leading politicians and individuals who had actively resisted Sovietization were deported. Several months after the incorporation, the NKVD staged mass deportations, the victims of which were large sections of the elites, inter alia staff members of all non-communist parties and organizations, businessmen, writers, clergymen.
9. First steps toward collectivization of agriculture, which included the deportation of "kulaks."

Although there was not much time, most of these measures were completed before the German-Soviet war began. A faster pace was pursued in Belorussia, the Ukraine, and Moldavia than in the three Baltic states. When the Red Army invaded a particular territory, the Soviets only spent a few weeks building a democratic facade—elections, convening of an assembly, adoption into the USSR: In the Western Ukraine and Western Belorussia the process lasted from September 17, 1939, to November 1–2, 1939; in Lithuania, Latvia, and Estonia, from June 15–17, 1940, to August 3–6, 1940. There was no time, however, to undertake massive collectivization campaigns before the—unexpected—outbreak of the German-Soviet war. In

June 1941, only 13 percent of the Western Ukraine's farms and 3.7 percent of those in the newly acquired Moldavian territories had been organized into kolkhozes.[11] In the Baltic republics, virtually no collective farms existed at all.

In one respect, Sovietization in the Western territories of the Ukraine and Belorussia exhibited a special characteristic: Here, the Soviets carried out a few elements of the korenizatsiia policy to win the population for Soviet objectives. This approach must have been all the more effective as the opening of Ukrainian theaters and schools and the expansion of Ukrainian-language mass media stood in sharp contrast to the previous rude policy of Polonization and Romanization (in northern Bukovina). Lvov University was Ukrainized and the Ukrainian Shevchenko theater was opened in Lvov in October 1939. These measures were introduced immediately after the Red Army's invasion and thus fed into the widespread and justified anti-Polish sentiments in the Ukrainian and Belorussian territories.[12]

Bessarabia shall serve as an example to explain some of the techniques and instruments used in the annexations. Western researchers have paid comparatively little attention to the annexation of the Romanian territories.[13] Northern Bukovina was added to the Ukraine as the Chernovtsy region. The southern part of Bessarabia was also added to the Ukraine and became the Izmail region, which remained an autonomous administrative unit until 1954 when it became part of the Odessa region. Because an intensive policy of Romanization had been pursued since 1918, it is safe to assume that the Ukrainians who made up the majority of the population in both regions and — as in Galicia and Volhynia — most of whom were peasants did not reject annexation to the USSR in principle.

On August 2, 1940, Bessarabia's six counties of Beltsy, Bendery, Kagul, Kishinev, Orgeev, and Soroki were united with the six raions of the Moldavian ASSR, located on the left bank of the Dniester and with a primarily Moldavian population, to form the Moldavian SSR. An assessment of the sentiments of the Romanian (Moldavian in Soviet terminology) majority in most of Bessarabia reveals an attitude different from that of the Ukrainian population in Bessarabia and northern Berkovina. Bessarabia's 1918 annexation to Romania was a voluntary act and expressed the will of the politically active forces in the Romanian population.

In Bessarabia, contrary to their practices in all the other newly acquired territories, the Soviet authorities did not consider it necessary to maintain even the appearance of democracy, or they thought they could do so only with great difficulty. They did not hold any elections. During the weeks following the Red Army's invasion on June 28, 1940, only a "delegation" was formed consisting of representatives of the Party and Soviet organs of the Moldavian ASSR and "Bessarabian workers and peasants." In early August 1940, this delegation presented the "Moldavian people's request" for integration into the Union to the Supreme Soviet in Moscow. The Chairman of the Council of People's Commissars of the Moldavian ASSR (with the very un-Moldavian name T.A. Konstantinov) headed the delegation.[14]

Immediately after the troops had marched into Bessarabia, the army's political Administration established provisional Soviet organs in the villages. The Soviet authorities of the Ukraine and the Moldavian ASSR "appointed" executive committees for the counties (*uezdy*), districts (*volosti*), and towns. "The competencies of the Tiraspol regional Party committee (Moldavian ASSR), of the Supreme Soviet, and of the Council of People's Commissars of the Moldavian ASSR were "temporarily" extended to include Bessarabia. This extension of state and Party power remained in force until the elections to the soviets on January 12, 1941 and long after Bessarabia's formal integration into the USSR.[15]

As early as July 1940, all political parties, organizations, and societies were proscribed. A resolution of the All-Union Central Trade Union Council broke up the Bessarabian trade unions and formed new Soviet trade union committees.[16] On August 15, 1940, the Presidium of the USSR's Supreme Soviet decreed the "nationalization of banks, industrial and trade businesses, and railroad, shipping, and telecommunication systems in Bessarabia," thus sanctioning a development which had already nearly been completed.[17] All factories with more than ten employees and all printing plants were expropriated. All hospitals, pharmacies, schools, theaters, larger hotels, and apartment buildings also became nationalized property.

By November 1940, the land reform program had been completed in principle. It resulted in the complete expropriation of land owned by landed gentry and by monasteries and — depending on the individual counties — a restriction of the acreage peasants were allowed to own to ten to twenty hectares. The Soviet authorities distributed a total of 230,000 hectares of land among 184,700 peasant families, or about 40 percent of all peasant families living in Moldavia.[18] As in all other territories, the "revolution from above" in the villages was consciously postponed to a later phase of Sovietization. Initially, sovkhozes and kolkhozes only developed on former state and private estates and in the former German colonial villages. As they did in all acquired territories, the Soviets honored a German-Soviet agreement and granted ethnic Germans living in Bessarabia the right to return "home to the Reich." In October and November 1940, 80,000 Germans left Bessarabia.[19]

In one area, integration of the Moldavian territories surpassed that of the other regions. In February 1941, Moldavia abandoned the Latin alphabet and adopted Cyrillic. On the one hand, this reestablished the conditions existing before 1917 because, in contrast to neighboring Romania, the Latin alphabet had never prevailed in Russian Bessarabia. On the other hand, this measure was to prove the Soviets' claim that the Moldavian language was different from Romanian, the aim was to establish an additional border between the Moldavian ASSR and Romania, and counteract Romanian irredentism.[20] The rapid expansion of the system of elementary schools was among the positive Soviet accomplishments that supported land reform in winning the rural Moldavian population. By the spring of 1941, twice as many children attended school as in previous years. In the late 1930s, about 70 percent of Bessarabia's population was still illiterate.[21]

Integration into socialism started massive migrations everywhere. In accordance with German-Soviet agreements, about 390,000 Germans between Tallinn and Izmail migrated westward.[22] A harder fate awaited those hundreds of thousands whom the Soviets deported to Siberia, the far north, or Central Asia for having belonged to the social and political elites in the annexed territories. These mass deportations were an integral part of the spreading "revolution from above" and were meant to help establish a lasting dictatorship. Immediately after the invasion of the Baltic states, only individuals who had been prominent when the Baltic states were still independent were arrested. Just before the "parliamentary" elections, however, during the night of July 11, 1940, about 2,000 people in Lithuania alone were arrested and deported. In late 1940, the NKVD began to prepare the mass deportations of all members of certain elites in the Baltic states. According to a directive from the Lithuanian NKVD of November 28, 1940, which later arrived in the West, these groups included all members of former political parties and organizations, former ministerial officials, officers, policemen, clergymen, former nobility, owners of landed estates, merchants, owners of hotels and restaurants, but also citizens of foreign states, individuals who had contacts abroad, and "Esperantists and philatelists."

The deportations began during the night of June 13, 1941. By June 19 — three days before the German attack on the USSR, about 11,000 individuals from Estonia, about 16,000 from Latvia, and about 21,000 from Lithuania had been deported.[23] Total losses suffered due to deportation, executions by firing squads, and the Red Army draft are estimated at 60,000 in Estonia — where the Red Army drafted a comparatively large number of men — 35,000 in Latvia, and 34,000 in Lithuania.[24]

Elimination of the political and social elites in the previously Polish territories of the Ukraine and Belorussia followed a similar pattern. In addition, however, the "revolution from above" acquired a national aspect here because the deportations affected primarily Poles and Jews. Probably, only 20 percent of the deportees were Ukrainian or Belorussian. This reflects the social structure of the territories of former eastern Poland, where most of the rural and peasant population was Ukrainian and Belorussian; Poles and Jews were in the majority in the cities, among the bourgeoisie, the intelligentsia, and the gentleman farmers with large holdings. Khrushchev, the head of the Ukrainian Party, arrived in the Western Ukraine immediately after the Red Army to direct the integration. He realized that the majority of Lvov's population was Polish and that "most Poles living in Soviet-occupied territory were against the Soviet system."[25] In 1939, 13.4 million people in eastern Poland became Soviet citizens; according to Polish data, 5 million of them were Poles. The Soviet annexation turned the Poles, who previously had been the state-nation and the leadership elite in a part of the country primarily inhabited by foreigners, into a "counter-revolutionary" national minority.

Thousands of politicians, publicists, officers, and government employees were arrested immediately after the Red Army's invasion. In four surges (in February/March 1940, April 1940, and two waves in May/June 1941, the NKVD deported hundreds of thousands to the inner USSR — besides members of former parties and organizations, judges, prosecutors, businessmen, intellectuals, well-to-do farmers, Polish colonists, railroad workers, and anyone who had tried to resist Sovietization. In addition, skilled workers — particularly those from engineering and technical professions — were recruited to do forced labor in the Donets Basin.[26]

At least 250,000 deportees were refugees who had sought protection from the German occupational forces in the Soviet Union. The vast majority were Jews who hoped to escape Nazi persecution, and, like most Jews in eastern Poland, were sympathetic to the Soviets. Their hopes were disappointed though, because rather than integrate them they were deported into the inner USSR and thus (in a twist of historical fate?) were saved from the holocaust after June 1941.[27]

Estimates of the total number of people arrested and deported in the former Polish territories vary from 450,000 to 1.5 million.[28] Over half were Polish nationals, and probably about a quarter were Jews. Because a dramatic decline in the standard of living and in supplies accompanied the Sovietizations, the people in Belorussia and the Ukraine became hateful and bitter towards the Soviet power. But the deportations did not disrupt Belorussian and Ukrainian social structures as much as in the Baltic nations. In Bessarabia, too, former "owners of landed estates," "capitalists," "politicians of bourgeois parties," and "individuals not working in production" were "eliminated" as a "class." During and after the Red Army's invasion, many managed to escape to Romania. A Soviet scholar tallies the number of people enlisted in the first year after the annexation to work in the USSR's industrial centers at "about 100,000."[29]

Thousands of Party and Soviet functionaries, business managers, and journalists who were either members of the same nation or Russians sent to the new territories to take over executive functions replaced deported elites. In the Western Ukraine, Khrushchev directed the development of the Party; "regional committees were established, with members primarily from the Soviet Ukraine; the district committees were consisted mostly of local Party activists."[30] In December 1939 alone, the Ukrainian CC relocated 760 functionaries from the Eastern Ukraine into the region of Lvov and 942 into the region of Stanislav (Ivano-Frankovsk).[31] In Bessarabia, too, the RSFSR, the Ukraine, and particularly the Moldavian ASSR "helped" and "sent leading cadres and specialists from various branches of the economy into the liberated raions of Moldavia."[32]

What had the Soviets accomplished before the Wehrmacht started its attack on June 22, 1941, and overran the annexed Western territories within a few weeks? Even in areas where much of the populace had welcomed integration into the USSR — as in Belorussia — or accepted it with hopes — as in the Ukraine — eighteen months of Stalin's rule had sufficed to create anti-Soviet sentiments and prepare ideal conditions for collaboration with the German aggressors. In Estonia and Latvia, the Soviets succeeded in replacing distrust of everything German, which had developed over generations, with a hatred for everything Russian-Soviet. Forced Sovietization laid the foundation for the guerrilla fight which the Lithuanians and Ukrainians in Galicia in particular fought in Galicia after Soviet troops reconquered their territories after 1944. Eighteen months of Stalin's Soviet rule were enough to stir up people's desire for resistance, but not enough to destroy it.

Mobilization of All Energies

The Soviet Union's military and political preparation for the German attack on June 22, 1941, was poor. However, Soviet patriotism and the fact that it had gradually been pumped up with Russian-national values had ideologically already opened up the opportunity to fall back on Russian patriotism, which dominated propaganda during the war and post-war era. On November 7, 1941, in his speech for the Day of the Revolution, Stalin created the famous list of heroes, whose "manly appearance" was to "inspire" the defenders of the homeland: Aleksandr Nevskii, Dmitrii Donskoi, Kuzma Minin, Dmitrii Pozharskii, Aleksandr Suvorov, and Mikhail Kutuzov.[33] It is impossible to overlook the fact that the members of this gallery are all Russian; there was no room for the heroes of the other peoples.

Stalin wanted to be seen as perpetuating the line of Russian autocrats and as similar to Ivan IV. Groznyi or Peter the Great. Russia and the Soviet Union became indistinguishable entities. Personally, Stalin metamorphosed amazingly from revolutionary to leader of an imperial power. During the Russo-Japanese war of 1904–1905, he wrote in a Bolshevik pamphlet: "Let us hope that this war will become a still even greater disaster for the tsarist regime than was the Crimean war."[34] In his radio address on the occasion of the Russian victory over Japan on September 2, 1945, he identified with this vilified tsarist Russia, "The defeat of the Russian army in 1904 . . . left hard memories in the people's memories . . . Our people believed and waited for the day to come when Japan was crushed and the disgrace expunged.

For forty years, we people of the older generation have been waiting for this day. Now, the day has arrived."[35]

During World War II, the Soviet Union defended "the Russian culture," "the Russian people," "old Russian cathedrals and churches" against the "fascist barbarians."[36] "Fascist" and "German" became synonymous. "Today, there is only one thought: Kill the Germans ... otherwise they will desecrate all of Russia ...," Erenburg wrote in August 1942, after the Wehrmacht had reached its eastern-most position.[37] But even in 1945 — the Red Army had already reached Pommerania — the hate propaganda climaxed once more, "The hour of revenge has come!" "Germany is a witch. ... We are in Germany. The German cities are burning, and I am happy about it. ... The Germans have been punished but not enough."[38] For a few — decisive — years, the Soviets forgot their class perspective and international solidarity among the "working masses." The Bolsheviks saw themselves "continuing the best patriotic tradition of the Russian people."[39] "The Russians" were defending themselves against "the Germans." Soviet patriotism degenerated and at the same time experienced an immense boom as "the natural continuation of Russian patriotism."[40]

Following the banner of "friendship among the peoples" and "unity," the non-Russian peoples gathered around the "great Russian people," "the older brother," the "first among equals," who carried "the main burden in the fight against the German invaders."[41] The Soviets called on the heroic epochs of Russian history and its heroes to mobilize armed forces and the home front to fight with all their might, whereas recourse to the history of the other peoples remained strangely pale and abstract.

This becomes evident in the "anti-fascist demonstrations of the peoples' representatives," which Soviet propaganda took great pains to organize between November 1941 and September 1942.[42] In the face of the immediate threat the Wehrmacht presented in late summer of 1942, the "meetings" of the peoples of the Caucasus beseeched their compatriots not to surrender "an inch of Caucasian soil" to the "barbarians." They appealed to the "freedom-loving peoples" of the Caucasus, the "Stalinist family of the peoples in the USSR," and their "unity" and "friendship;"[43] the peoples of the Caucasus would "never be slaves."[44] But even this patriotic toughening up shortly before German troops occupied the Northern Caucasus made it very clear that the "great Russian people" was "our older brother," whose example everybody must follow. There is no concrete recourse anywhere on the living traditions of freedom fighting among the Caucasian peoples, because these traditions had developed in the defensive struggles against the Russian conquerors.

In general, traditions of a common military effort against an aggressor from outside were rare among the peoples. Most of the heroes the peoples remembered had fought for freedom from Russia, not for Russia's freedom.

The Cossack hetman Bohdan Khmelnytski, who had placed the Ukraine under the protection of the Russian Tsar in the mid-17th century, was one of the few non-Russian historical personalities popularized all over the country. In October 1943, on the occasion of the Ukraine's liberation, a Bohdan-Khmelnytskyi-medal was created. In the Ukraine, the red partisans led by Kovpak claimed to be the descendants of the Zaporogian Cossacks and competed with the nationalist Ukrainian partisans of the UPA (Ukraiinska Povstanska Armiia) for the right to claim the Cossacks' traditions of liberty. Soviet propaganda drew a direct line from Khmelnytskyi to Kovpak and the Ukraine's other red partisan leaders.[45]

Outside mass propaganda, the Soviets could not limit patriotic awareness and patriotic publications to either the myth of "friendship among the peoples of the USSR" or to political and military cooperation with Russia and the Russians. Quite the contrary, the Russian nationalism officially propagated provoked reactions from the non-Russian peoples. During the war years, for example, outlines of the histories of several non-Russian peoples were published, and they were not compatible with the official Russo-centric view of history in crucial aspects.

A history of Kazakhstan is particularly interesting. The Kazakh Party leadership backed its unorthodox perspective and many other republics imitated it.[46] This history depicted Russia's conquest of Kazakhstan as an act of the Tsar's colonial policy. The national rebellions, on the other hand, were shown as fights for national independence and thus "without question as a progressive factor,"[47] even if these fights had been against Russia (such as the rebellion Sultan Kenesary Kasymov led from 1836 to 1847) and had been led by "feudal lords." With this strategy, the authors went against the dogma of the "lesser evil," which had been decreed in 1937. It stated that integrating non-Russian territories into Russia was a lesser evil than subjecting them to foreign rule or letting them disappear into historical oblivion. In part, the "history of Kazakhstan" returned to early Soviet assessments of tsarist Russia that interpreted the Empire as a "prison for peoples," in which the peoples' struggles against their colonial masters was termed "revolutionary."

The non-Russian peoples' patriotism acquired a life of its own that was contrary to the general line of Stalin's nationalities policy, and only the fact that the Soviets mobilized all energies during the war years can explain its resurrection. Even before the end of the war, countermeasures began. In its resolution of August 9, 1944, the CC reprimanded Tataria's Party organization for "neglecting agitation and propaganda" and criticized the "serious nationalist shortcomings and mistakes of the way Tataria's history was presented." The resolution claimed that the presentation idealized the Golden Horde and the Mongolian Khan Ögädäi and exaggerated its popularization.[48] It is obvious that the heroic epoch of Tatar history was not very well suited to motivate the peoples of the Volga area to join the Russians in their defensive struggle against the Germans.

The Soviet power and Stalin identified with the Russian side of the 200-year medieval struggle instead with the Tatar side. In 1943, an article in the Russian-national magazine *Leningrad,* on Dmitrii Donskoi and his victory at the Kulikovo Field in 1380 said, "The Russian Prince . . . and the Russian people uniting around Moscow, threw off the Tatar joke, and organized that tremendous Russian force, which now rules a sixth of the earth, and is the most advanced and democratic principle in the world, and the guiding principle of world history."[49]

Although the first war years did not end the political terror and did not produce domestic liberalization, Soviet power was threatened in its existence. Hoping it would keep the society from falling apart, concessions were granted to specific social groups and vague rumors were spread of a real domestic new beginning and a thaw after the war. One of the concessions granted to the nations was the reintroduction of the national military units, which had been eliminated only a few years previously. In August 1941, the first national unit, a Latvian infantry division was activated. In December 1941, preparations began for the activation of Estonian and Lithuanian rifle divisions. In November 1941, this had been preceded by the decision of the State Defense Committee—the supreme political supervisory authority during the war—to activate non-Russian units.[50] Part of their personnel consisted of what was left of the retreating territorial defensive units that had been activated in the Baltic republics in 1940. The other part was made up of the communist emigrants in the USSR. The Baltic units were very much Sovieticized, and they were not only given a military mission but a political one as well. It was planned to use the national units as the core of the Soviet system to be reestablished after the reconquest of the Baltic republics. Indeed, after the war, members of these divisions "directed important sectors of the economic and cultural upbuilding of their republics."[51] Because of this intention, great efforts were made not to let the percentage of the titular nationals drop too much in these divisions after losses suffered during front-line service. In 1943, 81 percent of the Seventh Estonian Rifle Division, for example, were Estonians. Of the 149th Estonian Rifle Division, 63 percent were Estonians. Of the 43rd Latvian Guard Division, 38.8 percent were Latvians. And of the 16th Lithuanian Rifle Division, 36.5 percent were Lithuanians.[52]

Soviet data are contradictory on the number of national divisions, regiments, and smaller units.[53] The numbers varied during the course of the war, and after 1943, they probably declined. As a result, the following data on the number of divisions must be considered a minimum: Two Latvian, two Estonian, two Lithuanian, three Azeri, four Armenian, and four Georgian infantry divisions and five Uzbek, one Tadzhik, three Kirgiz, two

Turkmen, and three Kazakh cavalry divisions were mustered. But, national divisions were formed in the Autonomous Republics, too. For example, there were two Bashkir, one Kalmyk, one Chechen-Ingush, and one Kabardino-Balkarian cavalry divisions. In addition, there was a considerable number of smaller military units, reserve and support troops.

The national units were drafted as an addition to the Red Army's regular plan of mobilization. The national territories financed the mobilization and basic training.[54] This opportunity to raise additional funds for the war effort may have made it easier for the State Defense Committee to agree to the activation of national units. Most non-commissioned and mid-level officers were natives of the titular nations; generally, however, the commanders were Russian. The percentage of local nationals among the divisions' enlisted personnel varied considerably. The number surpassed 80 percent only in rare instances, and it decreased dramatically in the course of the units' front-line deployment for most losses were replaced with regular troops. At the beginning of the war, for example, 40 to 70 percent of the personnel of the eight Transcaucasian divisions were locals. By 1943–44, the percentage had declined to 1 to 15 percent.[55]

National languages were in use primarily for political agitation and, of course, for interpersonal communication. In August 1943, fifty-five front-line newspapers were published in non-Russian languages.[56] Soviet data are contradictory in respect to the command language. Some authors say Russian was the only command language even in the national units. Others claim that "all military operative work" was conducted in the respective nation's language.[57] Probably, the situation varied among the divisions, and language use depended on the percentage of local officers in the units and on the degree of homogeneity of personnel structure. The training facilities for non-Russian non-commissioned officers and officers that had existed before 1938 were not put back into use. This clearly indicates that the national units were the result of temporary concessions born of necessity and not a return to the korenizatsiia policy.

It is striking that no Ukrainian and Belorussian national units were mustered. The rapid advance of the Wehrmacht and the fact that it was impossible to mobilize such units on location do not offer sufficient explanation for this oversight. The Baltic divisions were organized far behind Russian lines. Probably, the Red Army did not activate any Ukrainian and Belorussian units for many different reasons. Because the Belorussians did not develop enough national self-awareness to distinguish themselves substantially from the Russians, Moscow may have felt it unnecessary to activate special Belorussian formations to mobilize the Belorussian will to defend the USSR. The Belorussians were the only non-Russian nation whose members joined the fight of the red partisans in great numbers. Four-fifths of all

Soviet partisans were Russians or Belorussians.[58] The partisans' most important theaters of operations were in Belorussia.

Because of Ukrainian particularist tendencies, Stalin had always distrusted them. His doubts in the loyalty of the Ukrainians probably grew even more intense during the first period of the war when those divisions, which had been manned primarily from local reserves in the Ukraine, exhibited bad fighting morale and the population, particularly in the Western Ukraine, welcomed German troops. It seems plausible to surmise that Stalin refused to activate national Ukrainian units because he assumed they would become a melting pot of Ukrainian nationalism—Soviet in appearance, Ukrainian in nature.

Probably at no time did more than 10 percent of the non-Russians drafted into the Red Army serve in the national units.[59] This means the overwhelming majority of non-Russians drafted served in the mixed-national units. To date, the USSR has not yet published comprehensive data on the Red Army's national composition during the war or on the national origins of its officers and non-commissioned officers. However, the published data show that this information exists in the archives of the Ministry of Defense. Similarly, the USSR has not yet allowed publication of a breakdown according to nationalities of the 25 million lives lost in the war.

Data on the national composition of more than 200 rifle divisions with over one million soldiers during four different periods between January 1, 1943, and January 1, 1944, nevertheless allow several general conclusions (see Table 7.1). Apparently, during the war's middle phase (after the Red Army had retreated from the Western USSR), Russians were considerably over-represented in the armed forces, and Ukrainians were under-represented. After 1943 (when the Red Army had reconquered the Ukraine), the proportions began to reverse. In July 1944, 33.9 percent of the soldiers in the 100 rifle divisions Artemev analyzed were Ukrainian. Beginning in late 1943, along with the Russians other nations' representation in the Red Army also began to decrease; the explanation is that Ukrainians were mobilized in large numbers. Apart from this, on the whole, the non-Russian nations were proportionately represented in the Red Army. In any case, they supplied considerably more soldiers than they did members of Soviet society's elites.

We must assume that the proportion of non-Russian officers was considerably lower than that of enlisted men. In many cases, their chances for promotion were objectively worse because of their insufficient knowledge of Russian, worse educational background, and the small number of national units. The national origin of the officers is indirectly reflected in the practice pursued in recruiting new Party members. During the war, primarily armed forces personnel was admitted into the Party; the great majority of officers were Party members. Statistical data indicate that the existing Russian over-representation among Party members increased in the 1940s. The

Table 7.1: National Composition of more than 200 Rifle Divisions (in percent)

	1-1-1943	4-1-1943	7-1-1943	1-1-1944	7-1-1944[1]	Percentage in the Total Population According to the 1939 Census
Russians	64.60	65.62	63.84	58.32	51.78	58.41
Ukrainians	11.80	12.37	11.62	22.27	33.93	16.56
Belorussians	1.90	1.68	1.35	2.66	2.04	3.11
Armenians	1.49	1.77	1.40	1.36	0.81	1.27
Georgians	1.82	1.48	1.17	1.52	0.50	1.33
Azeri	1.75	1.40	1.57	1.48	0.81	1.34
Uzbeks	2.42	2.62	4.44	2.02	1.25	2.86
Tadzhiks	0.25	0.33	0.87	0.46	0.32	0.72
Kazakhs	3.05	2.22	2.77	1.57	1.12	1.83
Turkmen	0.30	0.33	0.84	0.40	0.23	0.48
Kirgiz	0.52	0.57	0.84	0.36	0.22	0.52
Karelians	0.12	0.09	0.08	0.06		0.15
Finns	0.04	0.02	0.01			
Jews	1.50	1.56	1.35	1.28	1.14	1.78
Chechens and Ingush	0.04	0.04	0.04	0.03		0.29
Kabardins and Balkars	0.07	0.06	0.06	0.05		0.13
Ossetians	0.19	0.16	0.15	0.14		0.21
Peoples of Daghestan	0.26	0.14	0.17	0.15		0.50

(continued)

Table 7.1 (continued)

	1-1-1943	4-1-1943	7-1-1943	1-1-1944	7-1-1944[1]	Percentage in the Total Population According to the 1939 Census
Tatars	2.69	2.34	2.58	1.83	1.70	2.54
Chuvash	0.90	0.73	0.79	0.58	0.52	0.81
Mordvinians	0.95	0.75	0.82	0.62	0.56	0.86
Bashkirs	0.60	0.49	0.57	0.35	0.31	0.50
Kalmyks	0.08	0.08	0.11	0.06		0.08
Udmurts	0.30	0.25	0.28	0.20		0.36
Mari	0.31	0.27	0.28	0.19		0.28
Komi	0.20	0.13	0.16	0.13		0.24
Buriats	0.14	0.16	0.14	0.09		
Moldavians	0.03	0.04	0.04	0.04		
Latvians and Latgalians	0.22	0.18	0.19	0.29		
Estonians	0.86	1.35	0.92	1.01	0.92	
Lithuanians		0.27	0.11	0.14		
Poles	0.05	0.04	0.03	0.09		
Others	0.55	0.46	0.41	0.25	1.84	
Total	100.00	100.00	100.00	100.00	100.00	100.00

Source: A.P. Artemev, "Iz istorii sodruzhestva narodov SSSR v Velikoi Otechestvennoi voine," in: M.P. Kim et al. (eds.), *Bratskoe sotrudnichestvo sovetskikh respublik v khoziaistvennom i kulturnom stroitelstve* (Moscow, 1971), pp. 85, 87.

[1] The data pertaining to July 1, 1944 result from the analysis of 100 rifle divisions.

same is true for Armenians and Georgians; the number of Ukrainians and Belorussians continued to decrease.[60] Probably, only a few of the many Ukrainians drafted after 1943 rose through the ranks to become officers. The seniority of comrades and the lively Soviet distrust of anything Ukrainian worked against them.

The fact that many nations served shoulder to shoulder in the armed forces and that the civilian population suffered destitution and privation made national antagonisms less prominent. To a degree, Soviet patriotism became a reality. The fight for survival, the defense against the German aggressor, and the euphoria of victory made the USSR's peoples closer. The mobilization of millions of non-Russians in the Red Army's nationally mixed units promoted the spread of the Russian language. Also, when great masses of people were evacuated early in the war, this promoted the mixing of the peoples.

Since the summer of 1941, the Soviets evacuated many industrial factories from the endangered Western territories and central Russia eastward. Personnel not drafted into the armed forces moved with them to the Urals, the Volga region, Kazakhstan, Siberia, and Central Asia. During the first month of the war alone, 1.4 million people were evacuated from Moscow and 400,000 from Leningrad. They were joined by refugees from the territories the Germans occupied. 1.5 million people left Belorussia, and 3.5 million left the Ukraine; they were temporarily relocated to the eastern territories. During the war, a total of about 25 million people were evacuated, 17 million of them between June and December 1941.[61] Almost all refugees were Slavs who reinforced the Russian-Slavic element in the national territories and thus had an effect similar to that of the Russian migration, which had started in the early 1930s. Some of these evacuees returned west after the war, others remained in their new homes.

During the war, Soviet authorities also conscripted workers from Central Asia and Kazakhstan to work in the Urals and Siberia. For example, factories in the Sverdlovsk region employed 36,000 workers from the five Asian republics, and in the Cheliabinsk region, 18 percent of the workers were Uzbek, Turkmen, Tadzhik, Kazakh, or Kirgiz.[62] After 1945, all of them probably returned to their homelands.

At first sight, the surprising constitutional amendments of February 1, 1944, are the most important compromises granted to the "republics' national interests" and the "republics' intrinsic needs concerning their state organizations."[63]

The Union Republics were granted the right "to activate their own troops" and "to take up direct relations with foreign states, to make mutual agreements, and to exchange diplomatic missions and consulates with them."[64] The People's Commissariats for Defense and Foreign Affairs no longer were Union agencies but became Union and Republic agencies. Thus, according to the amendment of the constitution, every Union Republic was entitled to establish its own People's Commissariats for Defense and Foreign Affairs, which they had never had since the USSR was founded in 1922. The reason for this was that the Bolsheviks had insisted on these two sectors being under the exclusive authority of the central government. These constitutional amendments of February 1, 1944, were the most spectacular expansion of the Union Republics' authority ever to take place in the history of the USSR. Compelled by the pressures of war, Stalin seemed to follow the course to a politically alive federalism.

What triggered this step, which was surprising even to the Soviet public, and what were its consequences? Foreign affairs alone triggered it, and its consequences were minimal. The amendments did not substantially increase the competencies of the Union Republics. Stalin considered these constitutional amendments prerequisite to claiming a seat and a vote in the United Nations for each of the sixteen Union Republics in the imminent negotiations about the foundation of this new world organization. Strong American resistance to this plan caused the Soviet Union to reduce the demands at the Yalta Conference in February 1945 and ask only for three votes: In addition to the Union, the Ukraine and Belorussia were to be represented.

Indeed, during the post-war era, both Union Republics were very active in the United Nations and many of its subordinate organizations and signed many multilateral acts bound to international law. Their bilateral activities in respect to international law, however, have remained singular and insignificant exceptions. The Union Republics never exchanged diplomatic missions with foreign states. The Ukraine and Belorussia have missions only with the United Nations. The other Union Republics' Ministries for Foreign Affairs consist only of a few employees, and their primary function is to take care of visiting foreign diplomats.[65]

The constitutionally provided opportunity for the Union Republics to activate their own troops had even fewer consequences. The Union Republics neither increased the number of national units, nor did they establish People's Commissariats for Defense. Although the Ukraine appointed V.P. Geradymenko People's Commissar for Defense, no People's Commissariat for Defense existed. "Minister" Geradymenko did not have a successor in this position when he was transferred from the Ukraine in 1947.[66] In 1977, article 18b (the constitutional provision pertaining to the activation of Republic units) was quietly deleted from the new constitution.

Collaboration and Deportation

Stalinism created conditions that practically invited the USSR's population to collaborate with the enemy. Large social strata, many elites, whole nations or large parts of them waited and hoped for liberation from Stalin's dictatorship. The populations of many national territories, such as the Western Ukraine, the Baltic republics, and the Northern Caucasus, welcomed the German troops. Hopes for a better and freer life, however, were replaced by disappointment and bitterness in only a few weeks.

From the very beginning, the Soviet leadership were aware of the danger that the Nazis might use the nations' antagonism towards the Soviets to bring about the quick collapse of the Soviet state.[67] Their preoccupation with ideology nearly blinded the Germans completely to the possibilities of collaboration. They half-heartedly began to encourage collaboration with the non-Russian peoples only after the USSR's victory had become inevitable. In this respect, Stalin's fears were unwarranted. Despite Soviet claims to the contrary, the Germans never had a military or even a political plan to take advantage of the peoples' willingness to collaborate with them. The occupational force was only interested in defeating the USSR on the battle field and exploiting the conquered territories economically as much as possible. The Nazis classified the peoples as *Untermenschen* of varying degrees.

In light of these conditions, it is amazing how much collaboration occurred. In spite of their racial mania, Wehrmacht, SS, and German civil authorities realized quickly that they could not govern the conquered territories unless they cooperated with the defeated population somewhat. The limited availability of German reserves made the enlistment in particular of non-Russians for auxiliary services in the Wehrmacht unavoidable. Essentially, the defeated peoples collaborated with the Germans for two reasons: For most of them, collaborating with the occupational force was a way to survive. The prisoners of war in the camps and the population in the cities hoped that this was a way not to starve to death or be executed by a firing squad. Indigenous collaborators attached to German military units (Hilfswillige), the local police departments, or the guard formations (Schutzmannschaften) were not politically motivated, and by no means did they support Nazism's political ideology. The second reason why the defeated peoples collaborated with the Germans was because it was the only way for them to pursue their own political goals, which seemed unattainable without German help. Nationalist groups among the non-Russian peoples hoped to gain or regain political independence by collaborating with the victorious Nazis. Contrary to Stalin's fears, the Germans were not prepared to pay this price. When they decided to make compromises a few months before the collapse of the German war effort, collaboration had already acquired the eeriness of political irreality.[68]

The most significant group of politically motivated collaborators were the Ukrainian nationalists, who wanted to win their independence as a nation-state with German help. By the late 1930s, the Organization of Ukrainian Nationalists (*Organizatsiia Ukrainskykh Natsionalistiv,* OUN), founded in

1929, had become the by far strongest political force in the Western Ukraine. This conspiratory underground organization supported an integral nationalism â la Maurras and was one of the fascist movements in Eastern Europe. The determined suppression of Ukrainians in Poland between the two World Wars was one reason why the great majority of the Ukrainian population in the Western Ukraine actively championed the idea of a Ukrainian nation-state and why many politically active adolescents supported the extreme nationalism of the OUN.[69]

Although the OUN was decimated by two years of NKVD persecution, the existing network of conspiratory organizations (particularly in Galicia) survived. The combat effectiveness of the Ukrainian nationalists would have been even greater if the OUN had not split into two factions in 1940: into the comparatively moderate faction of Melnyk's followers (OUN-M), who espoused political struggle, and into the radical faction of Bandera's followers (OUN-B), who advocated political terrorism and military action.

The OUN had already been collaborating with the Germans since before the war. The most important result of this collaboration was the activation of two Ukrainian military units under the auspices of German military intelligence. "Nightingale" and "Roland" consisted of only several hundred men each and were *de facto* under the command of the OUN-B, although they were formally commanded by German officers. The OUN dreamed that these two units would become the core of the Ukrainian national armed forces, which would be activated after the Germans conquered the Ukraine.[70] On June 30, 1941, "Nightingale" reached Lvov with the first Wehrmacht troops. Without coordinating their actions with the Germans, the OUN held a meeting the same day, began to call itself "national assembly," and proclaimed a "sovereign All-Ukrainian state" in the name of the OUN-B. Iaroslav Stetsko acted as president of the congress and future prime minister. In a pastoral letter, Metropolitan Andrei Sheptytskyi, the head of the Ukrainian Greek Catholic Church of Slavic rites, which was united with Rome, recognized the Stetsko government and wrote: "We greet the victorious German army as deliverer from the enemy."[71]

The Lvov act went beyond the Germans' tolerance limit. After a few days, the SS task force in Lvov prohibited any "government" activity; in September 1941, the Germans arrested Stetsko, Bandera, and other prominent members of the OUN-B. Nevertheless, the Ukrainian nationalists, for whom conspiratory work had a long tradition, continued to use the opportunities open under the protection of the German occupational forces. Their most important objective was to expand their influence into the Eastern Ukraine. They wanted to gain as many followers as possible to meet their goal of establishing a Ukrainian nation-state. Although they failed to establish a base in the eastern Ukrainian society as solid as that in Galicia and Volhynia, they nevertheless succeeded in mobilizing some followers. In spite of the extreme conditions war and occupation created, some representatives of the Ukrainian intelligentsia were nevertheless willing to commit themselves to militant anti-Russian and anti-Bolshevik Ukrainism. In several cities, primarily in Zhitomir and Kiev, in the fall and winter of 1941, Melnyk's followers, who had expanded their ranks by recruiting former lower- and mid-level Soviet functionaries, succeeded in gaining control of key functions in the municipal administrations, which the Germans had established. The nationalists founded newspapers, opened theaters, and literary clubs. In Kiev, a Ukrainian national council formed, but due to German resistance, it had to go underground after a short time.[72]

In February 1942, the SS security police smashed most national Ukrainian facilities in the Reich Commissariat Ukraine. In Kiev, German firing squads executed about forty Ukrainian nationalists, among them, Mayor Bahazii. In 1942, the nationalist Ukrainian partisan movement began to develop; in the spring of 1943, this movement called itself the Ukrainian Insurgent Army (*Ukraiinska Povstanska Armiia,* UPA). The OUN-B leadership (*Provid*) installed Roman Shukhevych, who had raised the special unit "Nightingale" for German military intelligence, as military commander. The ranks of the nationalist partisans quickly expanded because many members of the police forces, which the Germans had established and which OUN partisans had infiltrated, deserted and joined the partisans. The greatest responsibility for the increase of the partisan movement, however, lies with German occupation policy. In 1944, the Germans forced 1.5 million Ukrainians to enlist as Eastern workers (Ostarbeiter), requisitioned harvests in the villages, and executed hostages by firing squad, thus showing the *Untermensch* the way to the partisans. This benefitted the red partisans and the UPA, which continued to see the Soviets and their Red Army as the prime enemy, in spite of their bitterness towards the Germans.

By the fall of 1943, the UPA controlled the rural areas of Volhynia where the German occupational forces were only present in the cities. The UPA could count on support from the great majority of the population and began to organize an independent administrative system that included schools, hospitals, and barracks. In late 1943, German authorities estimated the number of UPA members at 40,000.[73]

The extent of anti-Soviet sentiments in the USSR's Western territories and the nations' determination to prevent a return of Soviet power became apparent when, in late 1942 and against its ideology, the SS began to raise native armed units that were to defend their homelands. In May 1943, the anti-Soviet Ukrainian Central Committee, which was led by Kubiiovych and which collaborated with the Germans, appealed to young Ukrainians to report to the SS division "Galicia." Galicia's leading political and social groups, among them the OUN-M, the Greek Catholic Church, and the Ukrainian Autocephalus Orthodox Church (*Ukraiinska Avtokefalna Pravoslav-*

na Tserkva, UAPTs), which had been revived during the war, supported this appeal. The appeal was answered by 100,000 volunteers, and nearly 30,000 of them passed muster. In July 1944, the Germans deployed this division at Brody in Galicia; the Red Army nearly annihilated it.[74]

What reason did the Ukrainian nationalists in the war's final stages have for putting on German uniforms and fighting under German command? It was not because they expected the Germans to win the war, but because they—erroneously—calculated that the Soviets and Germans would annihilate one another and that, during the subsequent reorganization of Eastern Europe, the Ukrainians would be able to establish their own sovereign national state.

The fight against the Soviet system and the mirage of political self-determination in a Europe after Hitler and Stalin also motivated the Vlasov movement, which on November 14, 1944 founded the Committee for the Liberation of Russia's Peoples (*Komitet osvobozhdeniia narodov Rossii*). In January 1945, 35 to 40 percent of the Vlasov army's 300,000 men were Ukrainian. Because the Vlasov committee did not support Ukrainian independence, Ukrainian nationalists in Germany vehemently fought them to the very last day. Nevertheless, many Soviet Ukrainian prisoners of war joined the Vlasov movement.[75] Opposition to Stalin found more general support than did the Ukrainian nationalists, for whom any political goal was secondary to the establishment of a nation-state.

As in the Ukraine, the Germans found a spontaneous readiness to collaborate in the Baltic states in 1941. Willingness was motivated by anti-Sovietism and nationalism and rested on the hope that the pre-1940 sovereign Baltic states would be reestablished. When the war broke out, anti-Soviet revolts occurred in all three Baltic republics. A large part of the Red Army units, which consisted primarily of Baltic natives, surrendered to the Germans without fighting. The anti-Soviet resistance organization, the Lithuanian Activist Front (*Lietuviu Aktyvistu Frontas,* LAF), which had been founded in 1940, declared Lithuania's independence and formed a provisional government. This government was willing to collaborate with the Germans but not to let them issue all the orders. Consequently, the Germans did what they had already done in Lvov and dismissed this provisional government in early August 1941.[76]

On the whole, the occupation regime was less brutal in Estonia, Latvia, and Lithuania than in the Reich Commissariat Ukraine. Also, the number of Eastern workers the Germans forced to enlist remained lower, particularly in Estonia and Latvia. In the Ukraine, the German civil administration employed natives only on the lowest level, as mayors in villages and towns and as heads of raions; in the Baltic states, German authorities created administrative organs on the republic level that had to collaborate to function. Each republic had between five and twelve top administrators (land directors in Estonia, general directors in Latvia, and general counselors in Lithuania) who, in essence, were executive organs of the German occupation force. Because of them, however, collaboration occurred on a higher administrative level than in most other occupied territories in the USSR. Many Baltic volunteers served in Wehrmacht units and after the fall of 1942, in the "Waffen-SS." In most cases though, they did not enlist on an entirely voluntary basis because at the beginning of the war, their alternative was to become prisoners of war (for former soldiers of the Red Army) or forced laborers after 1943.

In the Baltic states, the Wehrmacht raised the first national units and deployed some of them — contrary to direct order from the Führer — even on the front in the winter of 1941–1942. In the fall of 1941, twenty Lithuanian guard battalions (Schutzmannschafts-Bataillone) totalling 8,400 men were in existence; 15,000 men served in Latvian guard battalions, and 10,000 men in thirteen Estonian battalions. The Germans used them primarily for guard and security duties behind the frontlines and to fight partisans. However, these so-called indigenous security units (Landeseigene Sicherungsverbände) were also involved in guarding Jewish ghettos.

In the fall of 1942, the SS began recruiting local natives into the "Waffen-SS." After 1943, two Latvian and one Estonian SS divisions existed; the Estonian unit totalled 11,000 men. In Lithuania, SS efforts to recruit soldiers failed. The majority of the volunteers originally recruited to serve under national command and to defend their Lithuanian homeland deserted and hid in the forests when they realized their units were to come under SS command. In Estonia and Latvia, however, mobilizations climaxed in 1944. Prominent political figures, such as the last Estonian pre-war prime minister Uluots, supported these efforts because they shared the Western Ukrainians' opinion that it was necessary to place as many men under arms as possible to defend their own independence until the Western allies were able to assist the Baltic peoples in their freedom fight. By mid-1944, about 60,000 Latvians and 50 to 60,000 Estonians fought on the German side against the Red Army.[77] The fact that in late 1943 the SS began to exhibit more understanding for Baltic demands for national autonomy than it had previously made it easier for Estonian and Latvian politicians and officers to collaborate with the Germans.[78]

In Belorussia, the political collaborators, who saw collaboration as a good opportunity to realize their own political objectives, were by no means as strong as in the Ukraine and the Baltic states. In Belorussia, separatism did not have a strong basis of support in society. Nevertheless, in 1942, political underground groups disappointed with the initial results of collaboration with the occupation forces developed in Minsk. Now, these groups wanted "neither Russians nor Germans!" Like in the Ukraine, these Belorussian groups were led by political forces from the former Polish territories of Belorussia. A Catholic priest, Godlevskii (Hadlevskii), led the "Belorussian People's Front," which had risen from the remains of the Christian Democrats. The "Belorussian Independence Party" (Nezalezhnickaja) expressed its platform in its name. In the summer of 1942, the German intelligence service (SD) broke up these nationalist groups; some of their leaders, including Godlevskii, were executed by firing squads.[79]

Other Belorussian collaborators, who offered their services to the Germans unconditionally, apparently had little influence in the republic although the German civil administration had granted them certain political rights after December 1943 when the partisan movement had become increasingly powerful. The Commissar General appointed a Beloruthenian Central Council (*Belaruskaia Centralnaia Rada,* BCR) that was to support the administration and the fight against partisans. Actually, the rada decreed compulsory enlistment in the armed forces and organized about sixty battalions to form the Beloruthenian Defensive Corps (*Belaruskaia Kraevaia Abarona,* BKA). These units were of little military use for the Germans, however. In the face of an advancing Red Army and due to the brutalities the occupation forces committed, by 1944 it was too late for the Germans to turn Belorussian battalions against the Soviets.

As a result, the "Second Belorussian Congress," which took place in Minsk on June 27, 1944, while Soviet artillery bombarded the city, was uncanny. In the tradition of the first congress of December 1917, the speakers declared Belorussia's independence and expressed their gratitude to the Nazis before more than one thousand "delegates."[80]

In contrast to the approach they took in the Slavic territories and the Baltic republics, the Germans made concessions to the national aspirations of the peoples of the Northern Caucasus, on the Crimean peninsula, and in the Kalmyk steppe. These concessions were facilitated by the fact that these peoples were small in number and that they ranked higher in the Nazi racial theory than the Slavs. The fact that these territories remained under Wehrmacht administration also worked in their favor. When the Germans offered these peoples the opportunity to collaborate, the offer was to a considerable degree accepted.

The Crimean peninsula remained under the rule of German occupation forces for thirty months; in the Western Kalmyk steppe and the Northern Caucasus, German rule only survived for two to five months. On the Crimean peninsula, the Tatars experienced definite preferential treatment in comparison to the Russian-Ukrainian population. The Germans let them reopen about fifty mosques and establish culturally and socially active so-called Muhammadan committees. However, the Germans undermined the Tatars' efforts to represent their political interests. Soon after their arrival they began to draft military units. In January 1942, eight Tatar self-defense companies existed; by November, they had grown to a total of eight guard battalions. The Germans successfully deployed them on the Crimean peninsula against the red partisans.[81]

The Kalmyk cavalry corps, which the Germans raised and built up to 3,000 men by 1943, made it easier to maintain control in the Western Kalmyk ASSR. Unlike most of the national units the Germans raised, the Kalmyk soldiers were not former prisoners of war and in this respect were actual volunteers. The cavalry corps and the Crimean-Tatar battalions joined the Wehrmacht in its westward retreat.[82]

In the Northern Caucasus, the Wehrmacht also managed to convince some non-Russian peoples to cooperate. The Karachai began an anti-Soviet revolt even before the German troops had arrived. The Wehrmacht appointed a Karachai national committee that actually had self-administrative functions. Similar events occurred in the Kabardino-Balkar ASSR, where the Muslim Balkars, who are closely related to the Karachai, were more willing to cooperate with the Germans than the Kabardins. The mountain nationalities were won over particularly because the Germans not only promised the future elimination of kolkhozes — as they had in the other occupied territories — but that they actually kept their promise, particularly to the cattle breeders in the mountains. In contrast to nearly all other occupied territories, the Northern Caucasian peoples' friendliness with the Germans did not turn to animosity. There was hardly any partisan activity.[83]

The Cossacks played a special role in the way the Nazis mythologized history. At times, the Germans saw them as an autonomous nation; in any case, they did not assign them "Untermensch" status. In 1941, the Germans had already raised the first units for fighting the partisans. After its advance in the Northern Caucasus, the Wehrmacht established a Cossack raion in the north of the lower Kuban in October 1942. About 160,000 people lived in this territory. The Germans granted the raion extensive freedom in its self-administration. When the Germans retreated from the Northern Caucasus, many Cossacks joined them. In late 1943, about 20,000 Cossacks (or people claiming to be Cossack) fought in the units the Germans had raised.[84]

The short-lived success of collaboration in the southern USSR, which was restricted to a limited geographical area, demonstrates that national resistance and the rejection of the Soviet system not only continued in the recently annexed Western territories, but also that the promise of political autonomy remained a dangerous political explosive, which "friendship among the peoples" could not withstand. However, the Nazis usually were not willing to promise the peoples future national self-determination. They were interested in collaboration without granting political concessions.

This concept also was the organizing principle behind raising the so-called "eastern legions" — a project the Germans pursued with some emphasis starting in early 1942. In their war prison camps, the Germans enlisted Turkestanis, Northern Caucasians (primarily Daghestanis), Georgians, Armenians, Azeri, and Volga-Tatars in national legions. German officers commanded all units above the company level. Most of the few local officers had to content themselves with the duties of a sergeant. These national units never grew beyond battalion strength (about 1,000 men), and the Germans did not deploy them jointly in the same missions. In Poland, the Wehrmacht organized fifty-three field battalions (fourteen Turkestan, eight Azeri, seven Northern Caucasian, eight Georgian, nine Armenian, and seven Volga-Tatar). In the Ukraine, another German staff had raised an additional twenty-five field battalions and a number of construction and reserve units by May 1943. In these units too, soldiers from the Islamic peoples were in the majority. Most soldiers were not motivated. They had volunteered because they thought it would help them survive. Many battalions proved unreliable when they saw action on the front lines; in response, the Germans moved 70 to 80 percent of them to Western Europe, where these soldiers had no political incentive at all anymore to risk their lives in battle.[85]

The ethnic Germans in Russia had a special function in the cooperation with the occupation forces. Nazi race ideology had chosen them for a key function as one of the promoters and outposts of Germanism in the future rule over the "Eastern Territory." After the Wehrmacht had conquered the Ukraine, 320,000 Germans were under Nazi occupation's rule. Soviet authorities had moved about 100,000 ethnic Germans from the Ukraine and deported them eastward before the Wehrmacht reached the German villages.[86] The German authorities treated the Ukraine and Black Sea Germans in the Reich Commissariat of the Ukraine and so-called Transnistria (the area between Dniester and Bug north of Odessa), which was governed by a Romanian civil administration, considerably better than the populations of any of the other conquered territories. They were provided special I.D.s to protect them and their possessions; they were supplied with food, housing, and clothing before all others; they were paid more wages for equal work; and they had to pay fewer taxes.[87] The German authorities used many ethnic Germans as translators and employees in the Wehrmacht, the SS, and the civil and economic administration. They appointed them village mayors, kolkhoz chairmen, heads of local auxiliary police departments, and administrators of industrial units. In the opinion of Reich Commissar Erich Koch and his assistants, however, the ethnic Germans neither subscribed to the appropriate *weltanschauung,* nor were they sufficiently qualified for leadership positions in the hierarchy of the German occupation.[88] Nevertheless, they were the only ethnic group that benefitted from the occupation's rule in the Ukraine without ever having strived for it or subscribed to Nazi ideology.

However, Soviet power, collectivization, and the persecution of the Church had eroded ethnic Germans' loyalty to the Soviet Union. Remembering the terror they had suffered in the 1930s, many hoped the German conquerors would blaze their trail "back to the homeland." It is not surprising that they used the opportunities to collaborate that the occupational authorities offered them. Using the strategy they used with other non-Russian nations, the SS began to raise German self-defense units in Transnistria in late 1941. The intended purpose of these units was primarily to fight the partisans and to protect the privileged German population. The total German population in Transnistria amounted to 130,000 people; the SS drafted about 8,000 men for their protection. At the latest, by December 1941, members of the self-defense units were also involved in executing Jews in the area north of Odessa. In this area, SS firing squads executed tens of thousands of Jews, some of whom they had deported from Odessa, and some of whom they had driven from Romania eastward across the Dniester.[89]

In the summer of 1943, ethnic Germans in the occupied territory began to leave the Soviet Union in organized treks and moved towards the Warthegau (the Pozman area), where the Nazis wanted them to settle. Here, the Red Army overran them and deported them to Siberia and Central Asia. Ever since, ethnic Germans from the Ukraine have shared the fate of their fellow Germans, whom the NKVD had already deported at the beginning of the war and sent to compulsory settlements (*spetsposeleniia*).

Stalin had no false hopes about the results his policy might produce and was always aware that it was very probable the non-Russian peoples would collaborate with the Nazis. Assuming war was imminent, he had ethnic nationals of the potential enemy states (Germans, Poles, and Finns) deported from territories adjoining the border as early as 1935 and 1936. In April 1935, 2,000 Finnish peasants and their families (about 7,000 people) were forced to leave their villages in Ingermanland near the Finnish and Estonian border and were deported to Central Asia and the Urals. In May and June 1936, another 20,000 people from northern Ingermanland were deported eastward into the Leningrad region.[90] Similarly, in 1935, the German and Polish population were required to leave their villages in a one-hundred-kilometer strip along the border to Poland. The Soviets eliminated the Polish national raion of Markhlevsk and the German raion of Pulin (both in the Zhitomir region). They deported the Germans to the Murmansk region.[91] In 1937, the NKVD also arrested thousands of people, considered unreliable in the event of war, in the Ukrainian border areas and had firing squads execute them. In 1943, while they had occupied this territory, the Germans discovered mass graves in Vinnitsa. A German commission investigating this discovery counted 9,432 bodies. The actual number of victims of this measure, which the Soviets had taken in preparation for the expected war, must have been considerably higher, for mass executions also occurred in other Ukrainian cities.[92]

At the same time, potential collaborators from the Far East were deported: Several tens of thousands of Koreans were forcibly evacuated to Kazakhstan. All these measures were top secret. No one abroad knew of them.[93]

After the mid-30s, the Soviets apparently had plans for the forced relocation of the entire German population if a war broke out. The measures began in July 1941, a few weeks after the war began. In many instances, the first phase consisted of mobilizing all men from sixteen to sixty into the labor army (*trudarmiia*). They were employed primarily in mines under prison-like conditions. Only in the territory between the Dniester and the Bug (which later was to become Transnistria), did the Soviets fail to mobilize the men because the Germans advanced too fast. As a result, the SS later managed to raise military formations. The actual deportation of women, children, and old people began without warning. Within a few hours, the NKVD loaded them into cattle cars. Many died during the week-long journey to Kazakhstan or western Siberia. Once they reached their destinations, they were assigned to "special settlements," which were located on utterly unprepared, bare soil. More lives were lost to famine, diseases, and sub-zero temperatures in the dug-outs the people dug.

In the Volga republic, refugees from the Western territories arrived in the houses and villages left by the Germans and frequently found half-eaten meals on set tables and screaming farm animals that had not been taken care of in hours or days. On August 28, 1941—long after the deportations had begun—the Supreme Soviet's Presidium resolved to "relocate" the German population because "thousands and tens of thousands of them were diversants and spies," who were only waiting "for a sign from Germany" to sabotage the Soviet Union's efforts.[94] The NKVD did not shy away from outright provocations: In August 1941, paratroopers wearing German uniforms appeared in the German villages in the Volga republic. Firing squads shot all who took them into their homes.[95]

From July to October 1941, a total of 650,000 to 700,000 Germans (400,000 of them from the Volga republic) were deported and separated from their families, and lost their possessions and homeland. Their new legal status was very similar to that of prisoners. The Supreme Soviet's resolution on September 7, 1941, eliminated the Volga Germans' autonomous republic. After they had driven away the people, the Soviets destroyed every trace of the Germans: They changed all German names of towns and villages and destroyed architectural monuments and cemeteries. The press no longer mentioned the Germans, and any reference to them from encyclopedias and even from statistics was removed. The Germans had become a taboo. The deportation of all ethnic Germans, whose fate was to be shared by other peoples shortly thereafter, makes very clear how serious Stalin and his leaders were about the "friendship of the peoples" and "Soviet internationalism." These strong-arm measures excluded neither Party members, nor Soviet functionaries, nor Stakhanov workers. On the contrary, even before the deportation, Germans who held positions of responsibility in Soviet society were arrested and executed in most cases. Enlisted men and officers of German origin were discharged from the Red Army and transferred to the work army.

These deportations were preventative measures. After the Red Army reconquered the territories the Wehrmacht had occupied, whole peoples were punished for their alleged collaboration with the enemy and deported to Siberia and Central Asia. The NKVD did not care who was guilty of the charges and who was not, who was communist and who was not. Collaborators and Red partisans alike were deported, those who had suffered under German occupation and those who had survived by collaborating. They were "guilty" because they belonged to a people, some of whose members had been collaborators. Similarly, during the revolution's early phases, belonging to the bourgeoisie or the kulaks had constituted sufficient reason for the Soviets to eliminate a person.

The following peoples were deported: the Karachai in November 1943, the Kalmyks in December 1943, the Chechen and Ingush in March 1944, the Balkars in April 1944, and the Crimean Tatars in May 1944.[96] Hundreds of thousands of people disappeared in compulsory settlements in the Asian USSR without the Soviet public learning about it. Only in July 1946, did the *Izvestiia* give the first (and only, for a long time) clue to what had happened. The newspaper published a resolution of the Presidium of the RSFSR's Supreme Soviet concerning the dissolution of the Chechen and Ingush ASSR and the conversion of the Crimean ASSR into the Crimean region. The article said that "many Chechen and Crimean Tatars" had joined "the volunteer units the Germans had organized" and fought against the Red Army.[97]

The Soviets still keep quiet about the number of people deported. On October 14, 1944, the first secretary of the Crimean regional Party committee reported (this report has not been published in the USSR) to the Moscow CC that 194,111 Crimean Tatars had been deported in May 1944.[98] In respect to the other peoples, Western scholars must rely on data from the 1939 census in order to estimate the number of deported people. That census counted 408,000 Chechen, 134,000 Kalmyks, 92,000 Ingush, 75,000 Karachai, and 43,000 Balkars. Apparently, Stalin did not decide in one day which peoples were to be punished. His decision was based on the reports local Party organizations and partisan units issued during and immediately following the Wehrmacht's retreat. Some local functionaries exaggerated the level to which people had collaborated with the Germans to camouflage their own weaknesses.[99]

A few weeks after the Red Army had reconquered the Crimean peninsula in April 1944, the Crimean Tatars were deported under particularly brutal circumstances. During the early morning of May 17, people were roused from their sleep so that many of them had no opportunity to pack their belongings. At gunpoint, people were loaded onto trucks and transported to the nearest train stations. The cattle cars they had to board travelled for several weeks. Most Crimean Tatars were forced to settle in Uzbekistan. Any attempt to resist deportation resulted in the resistor's immediate execution. From July 1944 to December 31, 1945, about 20 percent of the Crimean Tatars who had reached Uzbekistan died. Among children, the death rate was even higher. Over half the individuals deported were children under sixteen—this is true for all deported peoples; only 20 percent were—mostly elderly—men.[100]

The Balkars were deported only fourteen months after the Germans had retreated. On January 4, 1944, the Kabardino-Balkar ASSR celebrated with great pageantry the first anniversary of the banishing of fascists. There was no indication of any planned punitive actions. On March 8, 1944, NKVD troops moved into the Balkar villages, forced the people to climb onto trucks, and loaded them into cattle cars. Also, many Kabardins were forced to join the Balkars and leave their homeland, although in their case, the Soviets did not deport the whole people.[101]

The situation of the Chechens (who were the most numerous of the deported Caucasian peoples) and the Ingush (who are closely related to them) was different from that of the other deported peoples. Aside from a narrow strip of land around Malgobek, the Wehrmacht never set foot in the Chechen and Ingush ASSR. In their case, deportation was not to avenge collaboration but to break this mountainous region's long-lasting anti-Soviet and national resistance, which had triggered several armed rebellions.

Already in the nineteenth century, the legendary Imam Shamil had led the Caucasian tribes in the Chechen mountains in a guerilla war against the Russian conquerors for decades. Hardly any other people resisted Sovietization as consistently as the Chechen, whose clan loyalty was still intact and who were controlled by militant Sufi brotherhoods. Soviet authorities were unable to establish collectivization in the mountains, and in the plains, the people also managed to circumvent it to a large extent. Many clans succeeded in keeping their land in their possession although the Soviets labelled it as kolkhoz. Even after 1937, the "revolution from above" continued here. "Kulaks" were driven out and "mullahs" and "nationalists" excluded from the village soviets and the Party. Supported by their clans, the purged went into the mountains.[102]

There in early 1940, Khasan Israilov proclaimed the "war of liberation" and appointed a "temporary revolutionary people's government of Chechenia and Ingushetia." The rebels, who fought for a "free Caucasus," controlled several raions in the mountains and managed to hold their positions until 1942. Israilov saw the approaching German front as his chance and issued proclamations declaring his willingness to collaborate with the Germans. Many soldiers in the Chechen and Ingush units raised by the Soviets began to desert. The Soviet position became so unstable that in March 1942, the Soviets temporarily stopped drafting Chechen and Ingush into the Red Army. They wanted to avoid arming anti-Soviet rebels.[103] In the fall of 1942, the Soviet air force helped subdue the rebellion.

After the deportation of the Chechen and Ingush, the names of towns, village lands, and raions were changed, as had been the case in the territories of the other deported peoples. The Chechen and Ingush ASSR was now called Groznyi region, and villages and houses were assigned to tens of thousands of Russians, Avars, Darginians, and Ossets. The problems caused by disloyal peoples seemed "resolved" once and for all.

Demobilization

The soldiers at the front and the people in the country expected and hoped that better times follow after war, death and misery. War propaganda and rumors, which the leadership purposefully spread, led the people to believe that victory over Nazi Germany would improve the standard of living, end the terror, and open the USSR to the West. The government wanted partisans to believe "they fought for a new Russia, not for the old one whose terror and dictatorship . . . had betrayed them." In the Ukraine, even Red partisans promoted "illusions of true autonomy . . . once the enemy was driven away."[104] After the war, the internal affairs policy of Stalin's leadership focused primarily on destroying these expectations and revoking concessions granted during the war.

Special units of the NKVD followed the victorious Red Army into all liberated territories. Primarily, the NKVD started hunting for real or alleged collaborators, "thousands of whom were shot by firing squads, hundreds of thousands of whom were banished."[105] As a nation, the Ukrainians evaded deportation only "because there are too many of them, and there is no space to deport them to."[106] In their efforts to reconstruct the apparatuses, the Soviets used many leadership cadres from unoccupied territories. In April 1944 alone, nearly 3,000 functionaries were relocated from the RSFSR's eastern regions to the Ukraine. In the Vinnitsa region, by 1946, 800 Russians from the RSFSR had been assigned to leadership positions.[107] In 1945 and 1946, about half the positions in the Ukraine's Party and state apparatus were filled with new personnel. For example, on the raion level, 38 percent new Party secretaries and 64 percent new chairmen of the raion soviets were appointed.[108]

The need for reeducation in the previously occupied territories swelled the ranks in the propaganda apparatus. "Ideological work with the masses" and Party education had a high priority because for a long time, people in the occupied territories had been cut off from "reliable Soviet information" and had been exposed to "fascist propaganda's lies."[109]

Now the modest concessions to non-Russian peoples' patriotism were called "bourgeois nationalism" and the historiographic and cultural emphasis on individual national traditions during the war was labelled "idealization of the past." In a conversation with film director Eizenshtein in 1947, Stalin declared: We must "overcome the revival of nationalism we are experiencing with all the peoples."[110] Only Russian nationalism was excluded. The already limited forms in which non-Russian nationalisms had been able to express themselves during the war were eliminated; Russian national pride, on the other hand — as Stalin conceived of it — could express itself after the war as never before or since in Soviet history.

In the summer of 1946, following Stalin's orders, Leningrad's Party chief A.A. Zhdanov staged a pogrom against the cultural and intellectual life. In the non-Russian republics this was waged as a crusade against "bourgeois nationalism" that destroyed all hopes for the development of cultural national self-consciousness. At a plenum of the Ukrainian CC in August 1946, Khrushchev criticized the *Survey of the History of Ukrainian Literature,* which had just appeared, because it entertained "bourgeois-nationalist ideas about the history of the Ukrainian people and its culture," and the first volume of the *History of the Ukraine* (published in 1943) because it contained "serious nationalist errors." In the Ukraine, there were "attempts to revive the bourgeois-nationalist concepts of historian Hrushevskyi and his 'school.'"[111]

A few days later, K. Litvin, the secretary of the Ukrainian CC responsible for ideology, again heavily attacked the writers at a meeting of Ukrainian writers. He claimed the authors of the *Survey of the History of Ukrainian Literature* had "left out the relationship between Russian and Ukrainian literature and had exaggerated the influence of Western European literature." Many recently published novels and short stories "nationalistically distort[ed] the past of the Ukrainian people and Soviet reality." Litvin's critique devastated the Ukrainian Union of Writers and the publishers of the three most prominent literary magazines: *Vitchyzna (Homeland), Dnipro (Dnieper),* and *Radianskyi Lviv (Soviet Lvov),* which "had forgotten our Party's most basic ideological demands in literature."[112] All three magazines received new publishing staffs and the prominent personalities in the Ukrainian Union of Writers, including chairman Rylskyi, lost their positions.

From August to November 1946, the Ukrainian CC issued six resolutions to eradicate "bourgeois-nationalist deviations" in Ukrainian culture.[113] The following year, the Soviets once more reprimanded Ukrainian historians separately. Litvin accused them of being influenced by Hrushevskyi's "bourgeois-nationalist" historiography. He also claimed that Hrushevskyi had falsified historical facts to prove "that the Ukraine had never had anything in common with Russia, that the Ukraine was the dividing line between Asia and Europe.... Any progressive developments originating in Russia—culture, science, the traditions of the democratic movement and of the revolutionary fight—Hrushevskyi rejected and considered harmful." According to his interpretation, "the historical development of both peoples was not determined by mutual friendly relations and influences but consistent and continual antagonism." This kind of historiography claims the Kiev Rus exclusively as part of the history of the Ukrainian nation. Litvin associated Hrushevskyi's historio-political concept—and indirectly the Ukrainian historians—with the goals of the OUN, which had joined the Nazi occupational forces "in the hope they could poison the consciousness of the Ukrainian people with bourgeois nationalism. . . ."[114] This must have been a very potent poison because Hrushevskyi's historical school had already been damned in 1930.

In a resolution "On the Political Errors and Deficiencies in the Work of the Institute of History at the Academy of Sciences of the Ukrainian SSR" on August 29, 1947, the CC of the Ukrainian CP (B) demanded that the historians exhaustively criticize the opinions of Hrushevskyi and other Ukrainian historians, show that the Kiev Rus was the cradle of all three Eastern Slavic peoples, and, on the whole, focus more attention than before on the fact that the Russian people led the Slavs' fight for unity.[115]

The purges in Ukrainian culture and science occurred during another famine. An extreme drought during the summer of 1946, the war destructions, and exaggerated levies placed on the kolkhozes triggered another famine in the villages of the Ukraine, the Lower Volga region, and Central Russia in the winter of 1946–1947. Hundreds of thousands perished. Due to the exaggeratedly high agricultural production quota, Khrushchev had anticipated a famine in the Ukraine. He warned Stalin and demanded government aid for the areas affected by the famine. When Khrushchev told Stalin that cannibalism was occurring in the villages around Odessa, Stalin answered, "You're a sissy, they're lying through their teeth to appeal to get your sympathy!"[116] In 1947, Khrushchev was suspended for ten months from his office as Ukrainian Party chief, but he remained Chairman of the Council of Ministers of the Ukrainian SSR.[117]

The *zhdanovshchina* pertained to all national republics and attempted everywhere to fix historical and political consciousness on all-Soviet values, reduce independent cultural and scientific national traditions, fight against Western (but also Arabic and Persian) cultural influences, emphasize the close relations between the individual nations and the Russians since the beginning of time, present Russian culture as the superior, leading world civilization, to which all other nations look for a standard.

In September 1947, the plenum of Armenia's CC criticized "books about Armenia's literature and history" that had appeared "in the last few years" because they "idealized the past." "Armenia's old times were declared a 'golden era' in the history of the Armenian people," but historians and writers "avoid topical problems of the present." Not only the philological institutes of the Armenian Academy of Sciences and the Armenian Union of Writers were publicly attacked for "nationalist and reactionary opinions;" the CC's responsible secretary for ideology, Grigorian was assailed in the same way.[118]

Now "bourgeois-nationalist distortions" were discovered even in remote Buriat-Mongolia. Historians "contrasted the Buriat and Russian peoples and thus attempted to disrupt the strong friendship that had grown between them and their joint efforts in the socialist development." These historians had completely underrated the cultural influence the Russians had exerted on the Buryats.[119]

Denunciation and prohibition of the Islamic peoples' century-old epics were among the most extensive efforts to destroy the nations' cultural heritage and to impose an official Party and Soviet culture. These epics (*dastans*), which originated from the oral traditions of the Inner-Asian nomads, were a central part of the culture of the Caucasian and Central Asian Islamic peoples. Even in 1949, the Azeri epic *Dede-Korkut* was still considered an "outstanding literary and cultural monument," which sings of "loyalty, justice, love for the homeland."[120] Two years later, A.A. Bagirov, the Azeri Party chief, discovered that this epic contained "the poison of nationalism." "Its publication was a gross political mistake committed by the republic Academy of Sciences."[121] Similarly, the Turkmenian epic *Korkut-Ata*, which is related to Azeri-Turkic, was anathematized as a "blood-thirsty chronicle of Oghuz feudals, a poem of religious fanaticism and of brutish hatred of non-Muslims."[122]

The pressure from anti-national Stalinist cultural policy turned the Uzbek heroic epic *Alpamysh* from a "folktale about valor, courage, and hatred of the enemy"[123] into a remnant of the past "impregnated with the poison of feudalism and reaction, breathing Muslim fanaticism and preaching hatred towards foreigners."[124] Due to the atmosphere of fear and terror, most Islamic writers and intellectuals bowed to Moscow's new commandments.

As a result, it is surprising that there was open and public resistance in the small Union Republic of Kirgizia. From February to June 1952, Kirgiz and Russian newspapers vehemently polemicized about how to interpret the national epic *Manas*. The new Stalinist line declared that it "endangered the upbringing of the Kirgiz youth in the spirit of proletarian internationalism, Stalinist friendship among the peoples, and Soviet patriotism."[125] The defenders of national culture maintained that *Manas* was "one of the world's most beautiful heroic epics" and "its Islamic character [was] no more shocking than the Christian character of the Russian bylinas, the *Tale of the Host of Igor*, or the Georgian *The Hero in the Leopard's Skin*."[126] Of course,

Moscow's new cultural policy, which was directed at eradicating the memory of battles against infidels, Russians, Georgians, and Buddhists along with the heroic epics, won this uneven fight.

We can only assess this policy of destroying national cultures if we consider the hitherto unimagined development of Russian chauvinism. Stalin's often quoted toast to the Russian people at the reception for the Red Army commanders on May 24, 1945, gave the signal: "I drink . . . to the health of the Russian people because it is the most outstanding of all the Soviet Union's nations . . . the Soviet Union's leading power . . . because it has a clear mind, a firm character, and patience." The protocol notes "roaring, unending applause."[127]

During the following years, this narcissism of everything Russian became grotesque at times. Soviet scientists were obliged to demonstrate the superiority of everything Russian in all areas. For example, historians received the assignment of establishing the influence of the Kiev Rus on Western Europe, of refuting the "harmful" Norman theory once and for all, and of presenting Medieval Russia as Europe's savior from the Tatars. The USSR's history was a "single organic process," which gives meaning to the histories of all nations only in their relationship to the history of the Russian people.[128] "The homeless cosmopolitans denounce the great Russian people by spreading lies about its centuries-old backwardness, the Russian culture's foreign origin, and the Russian people's lack of national traditions."[129]

All significant technological inventions were credited to Russian scientists. "The Russian people's achievements for humanity are indelible." "Russian literature and Russian art . . . have . . . won the first rank in the world . . ."[130] Russian opera is "the world's best opera."[131] Now, not only do the Soviet Union's peoples see "the Russian people as their paragon," but also the Eastern European peoples "look to the Russian people as their older brother."[132] In 1949, even the 150th anniversary of Pushkin's birthday was used to demonstrate Russian messianism and the superiority of Russian culture. Like no one before him, Pushkin had understood the "soul" of the Russian people, "whom history has assigned the great mission of liberating humanity."[133]

The other side of celebrating everything Russian was a campaign against "servility and obsequiousness to the West and its capitalist culture."[134] The denunciation of the "decadent, decayed culture of the present bourgeois West" and the battle against "a reduction in the value and independent significance of Russian culture"[135] was necessary to justify within the USSR the lowering of what Churchill called the "iron curtain" in Eastern Europe.

This urgent need to stabilize the Soviet system by closing it off also motivated the anti-national cultural policy's turn against the Jews and Jewish culture in the USSR. Relatively late—at the end of 1948—*zhdanovshchina* became clearly anti-Semitic. Initially, the Soviet Union watched the birth of the state of Israel with a wait-and-see benevolence and recognized Israel in May 1948 immediately after its declaration of statehood. Since September 1948, the USSR distanced itself from the state of Israel; at the same time, a domestic propaganda campaign against "Zionism" started. More and more Jews joined the ranks of the "rootless cosmopolitans," and soon this group consisted nearly exclusively of Jews, who were accused of "national nihilism," "denunciation of national traditions," "servility to the West," and soon even "sabotage" and "espionage."[136]

The press appealed to the population's widespread anti-Semitism and thus contributed to the destruction of Soviet-Jewish culture in 1948–1949. The Soviets had already eliminated many Jewish cultural facilities in the late 1930s when they assimilated "national minorities" living outside their national territories. During the war and shortly after, however, the Soviets revived or created several Jewish institutions. In particular, in April 1942, a Jewish Antifascist Committee was founded that included many famous Jewish writers, artists, and scientists. This committee was to mobilize Jews for the Soviet war effort and to exert a pro-Soviet influence on Western Jews. Because of its activities in the press and culture, this committee became the main source for a national Jewish identity in the Soviet Union.[137]

In November 1948, the Jewish Antifascist Committee and its newspaper *Ainikeit*, had to shut down. During the following weeks, all other Yiddish newspapers and the Jewish publishing house Emes (Truth) in Moscow were closed. Only the small local paper *Birobidzhaner Shtern*, published at the remote Amur river, survived the elimination of Yiddish culture. In the summer of 1949, the last Yiddish schools in Vilna, Kovno, and Birobidzhan closed. The seven remaining Jewish theaters, including the renowned Jewish State Theater in Moscow, shared the same fate. In late 1948 and early 1949, prominent Jewish writers and intellectuals in Moscow (Itsik Feffer, Perets Markish, David Bergelson, Leib Kvitko, etc.), Kiev (Eliagu Spivak), Minsk, Bessarabia, and elsewhere were arrested; hundreds of others were to meet the same fate. All members of the Jewish Antifascist Committee (apart from Ilia Erenburg, who wrote in Russian) lost their freedom.

Firing squads executed several arrested Jewish intellectuals and Party functionaries; others died of torture or in the camps. Others survived imprisonment, and were rehabilitated after Stalin's death. In July 1952, a secret trial in Moscow sentenced twenty-five well-known Jewish writers and had them executed by firing squads. In the style of the 1930s, they were charged with planning a Jewish state on the Crimean peninsula and secession from the Soviet Union. In contrast to terror in the 1930s, however, this time the trial was kept secret from the public so that to this day it is impossible to establish a complete list of the accused. Like the deportation of whole peoples a few years earlier, the elimination of Soviet-Jewish culture occurred very quietly. Soviet authorities denied to foreign countries that they repressed Jews in any way.

In late 1952 and early 1953, Zionists were "discovered" at universities, factories, and in Soviet organs; a campaign was waged against these "wreckers" and "imperialist spies." A public desire for a pogrom was stirred up. Jews had to expect passers-by to abuse them verbally in the streets, their neighbors to maltreat them in communal apartments, or to lose their jobs. On January 13, 1953, *Pravda* reported that a "terrorist group of doctors" had "been discovered," who had already murdered several Soviet leaders by giving them the wrong medical treatment and who planned further assassinations. Seven of the nine doctors named were Jewish. This so-called doctors' plot not only signalled an imminent new great wave of purges, but must also be seen as a preview of the mass deportation of Jews, which Soviet authorities had already planned concretely and in detail. Stalin's death saved the Jews from meeting the same fate as Soviet Germans, Crimean Tatars, and the other deported peoples.[138]

Sovietization of the Conquered Western Territories

The Soviets were conscious that the Western territories they had annexed in 1939–1940 would not automatically rejoin the USSR after the German occupation forces were driven out. After the destruction of the political system and brutal deportation of many people before the German-Soviet war, the great majority of the Baltic and Western Ukrainian population did not want to be reintegrated into the USSR. After reconquering those territories, the Soviets had to face three facts: First, the majority of the population was hostile. Second, the Baltic states and the Western Ukraine prepared for national military resistance. Third, before June 1941, the Western territories had not yet been completely sovieticized.

To counteract the hostility, Soviet authorities started an intensive propaganda and indoctrination campaign immediately after reconquering these territories. In the Western Ukraine, the Party appealed to Ukrainian national pride. "Only the Soviet government, the Bolshevik Party, and the great Stalin enabled the Ukrainian people to unite all its lands in a single Soviet Ukrainian State."[139] In his speech in March 1944, Khrushchev repeatedly referred to the "free" Ukraine and the "free" Ukrainian people who would gain the victory for "the liberation of its homeland, the Ukraine, for its national independence and liberty." Khrushchev even called the Ukrainian people "great" — an epithet typically reserved for the Russian people.[140] By acknowledging Ukrainian hopes for liberation, Soviet propaganda attempted to steal Ukrainian nationalists' thunder and to take advantage of the mood in the Western Ukraine. The UPA was denounced as "bootlickers of the Hitlerists," "Ukrainian-German nationalists," "quislings," and "enemies of the Ukrainian people."

The Soviets were justified in claiming they were the first to unite into a "state" nearly all Ukrainian territories and thus to have accomplished goals the Ukrainian nationalists only talked about. After the Red Army conquered the Carpathian Ukraine, Soviet authorities immediately set out to integrate into the Soviet Ukraine the last province, which they had not been able to acquire before World War II. The Red Army's arrival triggered the creation of "people's committees" dominated by communists and led by local functionaries trained in the USSR. On November 26, 1944, the "First Congress of the People's Committees of the Carpathian Ukraine" decided in the proven pre-World War II manner to pursue "reunification" with "the great mother, the Soviet Ukraine." In addition to a Hungarian minority, about half a million Ukrainians lived in the Carpathian Ukraine. In a treaty of June 29, 1945, Czechoslovakia formally relinquished the area to the USSR. In its decree of January 24, 1946, the Presidium of the Ukrainian SSR's Supreme Soviet transferred the Soviet Ukraine's whole legal system to the Subcarpathian territory. Apparently, there was no organized resistance to the victor's annexation.[141]

Nevertheless, in general, the Soviets assumed that the population of the Western territories did not support them. Even in Belorussia and in the aftermath of three years of ruthless German exploitation, a CC resolution on August 9, 1944, demanded that people "overcome the mentality the occupation planted, which was directed at private property, against the kolkhoz, and against the government."[142]

Military conquest was followed by non-military conquest. The thousands of leadership cadres transferred into the Western territories played a central role in propaganda, education, economy, and the Party. They were partly local nationals and partly Russians, a tactic successfully used before in other non-Russian territories. In September 1944, the CC gave orders "to permanently transfer the necessary number of politically reliable and qualified scientific and cultural employees from the Ukrainian SSR's eastern regions to educational facilities and cultural institutions in the Ukrainian SSR's Western regions... to assure successful performance of ideological-political work."[143] After the war, leadership positions on the regional level in the Western Ukraine were nearly exclusively filled with non-natives. In Lvov, it was possible "to count on one's fingers the number of local comrades who have been advanced to leading posts."[144] According to Soviet data, in 1946, local nationals held only 11.5 percent of the nomenklatura positions of Lvov's regional Party committee; however, they held 58.3 percent of the nomenklatura positions on the city and raion level in the Lvov region. The corresponding figures for the Stanislav region (Ivano-Frankovsk) were 23 percent and 73 percent, for Volhynia 14.8 percent and 65 percent, and for

Drogobych (which was integrated into the Lvov region in 1959) 16.6 percent and 59.5 percent, respectively.[145]

Sovietization had particular problems because of the new border established between the Soviet Union and Poland. Pressured by the Western powers, Stalin had essentially agreed to accept the Curzon Line as the USSR's Western border. This meant that he moved the border back eastward a considerable distance in relation to the German-Soviet demarcation line of the fall of 1939, which followed the Bug in the north and the San in Galicia for long stretches. In particular, the million people living in the city of Bialystok, its surroundings, and some areas east of the San river in Galicia became Polish citizens. Several areas in Western Galicia and the Carpathian mountains that had a large share of rural Ukrainian population were now part of Poland (Liubachuv, Iaroslav, Pshemysl, Sanok, Baligorod). Retracting the border[146] and the surrendering of territory inhabited by Ukrainians to the new Poland triggered considerable resistance in the Ukrainian CP. In his memoirs, Khrushchev accused Stalin of having "failed to take into account the national interests of both the Ukrainians and Belorussians. The Ukrainians were particularly unhappy [about the new border]."[147]

To reduce minority problems on both sides of the border, Ukrainians, Belorussians, and Lithuanians living west of the Curzon Line were granted the right to move to their respective national Soviet republics; Poles and Jews living east of the Curzon Line were granted the privilege of moving to Poland. On September 9, 1944, the Ukrainian SSR, the Belorussian SSR, and the Polish Committee for National Liberation ratified the treaties in Lublin; on September 22, the Lithuanian SSR accepted an analogous agreement.[148] Excluding United Nations acts, these evacuation treaties are among the Union Republics' very few acts of international law. They let about 520,000 Ukrainians leave Poland. By December 1946, about 1.5 million Poles had left the USSR. In 1950, census figures indicated that 2.136 million people living in Poland originated from the territories integrated into the USSR.[149]

Although the treaties explicitly provided for voluntary evacuation, the actual resettlement of Ukrainians from Polish national territory became compulsory. After 1944, many Ukrainian peasants living in the Zakerzonnia (the land west of the Curzon Line), who chose not to move into the USSR, were the UPA's staunchest supporters. The Ukrainian partisans undertook their greatest military actions on Polish national territory, or logistically supported them on Polish national territory.

The UPA and OUN were determined to continue their resistance even after the German retreat. Of course, because of the imbalance in military strength, they were not thinking of open military confrontation with the victorious Red Army. While still under German occupation the Ukrainian nationalists themselves had broken conspiracies in Volhynia in 1943, the

NKVD easily managed to break Ukrainian resistance there. Consequently, the UPA was restricted to its area of operation in Galicia, where it had traditionally enjoyed its greatest support because of the network of OUN conspiratory organizations and the population's political attitudes, and in the Ukrainian districts west of the Curzon Line. In addition, the forested territory of southern Galicia and the Carpathian mountains offered the geographical conditions necessary for guerilla warfare, which depended on a relatively safe territory to withdraw to.[150]

Until 1948, about 6,000 Ukrainian partisans operated on Polish national territory and, at least periodically, controlled public life in the Ukrainian border districts. According to Polish information, practically no Polish administration existed, for example, in the province of Rzeszow in 1945. The UPA, who saw protecting Ukrainian villages from Polish transgressions and deportation as their direct task, collected taxes and assumed police duties.[151] In 1947, the Polish Army deployed five infantry divisions and air support to fight Ukrainian partisans. On Polish territory and near the border, the UPA organized relatively large military missions and not only controlled the villages but temporarily even invaded small towns.

In contrast, the UPA's partisan warfare on Soviet territory was restricted to surprise attacks, assassinations, and shoot-outs with NKVD units. For security reasons, the UPA split its units into small groups, most of which numbered less than twenty men and operated in relative autonomy. In many parts of the regions of Lvov, Stanislav (Ivano-Frankovsk), and Ternopol, Soviet power was not solidly established until the late 1940s, and Soviet representatives could move only in convoys and under military protection. According to Khrushchev, the USSR lost "thousands of people" in its fight against the Ukrainian nationalists.[152]

In addition to their military actions, the UPA and OUN also worked politically with the Ukrainian population, whose support made these groups' existence possible. Underground printing facilities produced and distributed magazines, fliers, and pamphlets. After 1943, the Ukrainian nationalists' program moved away from totalitarian Fascism and shifted towards a more democratic and socialist nationalism. In August 1943, the Third Congress of the OUN-B presented a political program for nationalizing large factories and banks and for establishing workers' self-administration. A future Ukrainian state would also guarantee free public health services, education, and retirement pensions. Clearly, these programmatic statements reflect the influence of Ukrainians from the Eastern Ukraine, who had gradually reinforced the OUN's ranks. The Ukrainian nationalists could not afford for the Soviets to offer better social services.

In July 1944, the OUN created as its supreme political organ the Supreme Ukrainian Council for Liberation (*Ukraiinska Holovna Vyzvolna Rada*, UHVR), which was to be open to all political movements for an independent

Ukrainian state. Although the UHVR's "ideological-programmatic principles" continued to treat national unity as the "first and supreme goal of every healthy national organism," social and personal rights became more important to them. The Council restricted the principle of a single strong leader but did not abandon the idea altogether.[153] The UPA and OUN formally made themselves answerable to the Supreme Council; however, because of the real balance of power and personal union in the Council, the OUN-B possessed the leading political power.

Ukrainian national politicians' hopes that the war coalition would break quickly and that Great Britain in particular would support their efforts to establish a Ukrainian national state were soon disappointed. As a result, the military and political fight of the UPA and OUN increasingly became a consciously chosen path to defeat in the name of Ukrainian national principles. The nationalists' defense of their ideas was more a token than a real effort and more expressed their hopes for the future than their actual expectations for the present. The Soviets used every available means to fight the partisans and the OUN. These methods included infiltrating rebel ranks with Soviet supporters and provocation. For example, Ukrainian peasants were forced to enlist in a kind of people's militia to fight the partisans (*istrebitelnye batalony*) or to become MVD agents. Many UPA units did not see through this trick, annihilated this people's militia or these "agents," and thus lost their support in the villages.

The instrument that ultimately assured the success of Sovietization in the Western Ukrainian villages was forced collectivization of agriculture, which the Soviets successfully implemented from 1948 to 1950. By staging assassinations and surprise attacks, the partisans tried to prevent collectivization, which gradually robbed them of their bases for supplies and replenishments. On Polish territory, the measures employed to break the social basis of Ukrainian resistance were even more radical: The Polish government deported most Ukrainian peasants from the Zakerzonnia and resettled them in the former German provinces. In March 1950, Shukhevich, the UPA commander and UHVR secretary general, was shot and killed in the vicinity of Lvov in a skirmish with the MVD. In essence, this ended the Ukrainian nationalists' military resistance, although occasional terror acts continued during the following years.

The Soviets not only eliminated the Ukrainian nationalists' military and political resistance, but immediately after the war, they also destroyed the strongest spiritual and institutional pillar of Ukrainian nationalism: the Greek Catholic Church of Slavic Rite in Galicia.[154] Since the start of the Ukrainian national movement in the nineteenth century, the Uniate Metropolitan Church had maintained close ties to the new Ukrainianism. Count Andrei Sheptytskyi (1865–1944) was the leader of the Uniate Church. He consciously strengthened the Church's Ukrainian and Orthodox traditions, remained somewhat reserved towards Latinism, and revived the Union's original hope that one day all Ukrainians would be united under the Greek Catholic Church. Despite the ties to Ukrainianism, the Soviets wrongly accused Sheptytskyi and the Uniate Church of subscribing to the OUN-B's political program let alone the methods of political terror.

After the failure of the initial efforts to destroy the Union in 1940–1941 right after the reconquest by the Red Army, a massive press and slander campaign started against the Uniate Church and accused it of "treason," "collaboration with the enemy," and "bourgeois nationalism." The atheist state demanded that priests and believers "reunite" with the Moscow Patriarchate's Russian Orthodox Church. Because the Uniate Church did not give in to the administrative pressure, Soviet authorities applied a combination of previously proven measures: physical violence against leaders and establishing of a democratic facade that provided the legitimation needed to accomplish the pre-planned political goals.

In April 1945, Metropolitan Slipyi, Sheptytskyi's successor, and all bishops were arrested and sentenced to long prison terms for collaborating with the Germans. In May, the NKVD actively participated in the efforts of a few Uniate priests to form a "Group of Initiators for the Unification of the Greek Catholic Church and the Russian Orthodox Church." On the one hand, these priests saw the Church's only chance for survival in giving in to Soviet pressure. On the other hand, they were willing to let opportunism and egotistical ambition make them tools of Soviet policy. Soviet authorities recognized this Group of Initiators as the Uniate Church's only legitimate representative. In March 1946, this group held a council in Lvov, which 214 priests and nineteen laymen attended. This church assembly decided to end the Church's 350-year-old union with Rome and to unite with the Moscow Patriarchate.

Even after this decision, only about half the 2,000 Uniate priests were willing to be affiliated with the Orthodox Church. Those who refused were arrested and deported; others joined the underground. Many congregations and priests only formally subjugated themselves to the jurisdiction of the Moscow Patriarchate, but continued to consider themselves part of the Catholic Church. The Ukrainian Uniate Church, which had more than four million believers and had maintained a very active religious community, ceased to exist as a legal institution in the USSR. In the Subcarpathian Ukraine, a similar "re-unification" was staged in August 1949.

In addition to destroying old political and social structures, the Soviets also strived to advance the Western Ukraine's political and economic assimilation by extending the education and training systems and establishing industry. By 1947, industrial production had grown back to its pre-war level; by 1950, it had surpassed this level by 2.3 times.[155] Industrial investments were concentrated in Lvov, where the number of industrial workers increased to 148,000 in 1959, from its 1945 level of 43,000. Industrialization and extension of the education system had a double effect on the Western Ukraine's social structure. On the one hand, these measures increased the influx of Russian and Eastern Ukrainian skilled workers. Soviet authorities were interested in this development because it stabilized their rule. This meant a development occurred in the Western Ukraine that had started in the other non-Russian territories already in 1930. From 1944 to 1949, 16,000 Russian skilled workers, technicians, and engineers moved to Lvov alone. Collectivization brought 9,500 Russian experts to the Western Ukraine.

On the other hand, there was not enough immigration to replace all the evacuated Poles and the Jews who had perished in the holocaust. As a result, the percentage of Ukrainians among the Western Ukraine's population increased considerably. In the Lvov region, for example, the percentage increased from 59.3 percent in 1931 to 86.3 percent in 1959.[156] This Ukrainization particularly changed the national composition of towns that had been primarily Polish and Jewish before the war. Sovietization produced a stratum of Ukrainian workers and a broad intelligentsia of Ukrainian nationals. Because of these intellectuals, the Western Ukraine's political and economic assimilation did not result in Ukrainianism's self-destruction, but new Ukrainian autonomy movements have developed since the 1960s.

After 1944, the Soviets encountered the same problems in the Baltic countries as they had in the Western Ukraine, and for the most part, they used the same political measures. In the Baltic states, resistance was more determined because what was at stake was the eradication of state sovereignty, and not prevention of its inception as it was in the Ukraine. Of all nations, Lithuanians resisted integration most stubbornly and longest. The Lithuanian partisans' military resistance also surpassed UPA activities.[157]

Establishing Soviet power in the Baltic states with the few local forces available there was out of the question. Therefore, immediately after the Red Army arrived, several hundred executive functionaries came to the Baltic states—after the war, several tens of thousands followed them. These were officers and soldiers of the Red Army's Baltic units. The majority, however, were Estonians and Latvians, some from families that had lived in Russia since the nineteenth century. Now they were to Sovieticize the Baltic states. Virtually no exiled Lithuanians lived in Russia, so the Soviets had to use many Russian cadres—a circumstance that increased Lithuanian willingness to resist both actively and passively. The executive functionaries ordered to the Baltic states held positions on all levels, from the Republic's first Party secretary, to administrative positions in the education system, to the local police chief. The make-up of the Party in the three republics indirectly reveals the great number of "imported" executive functionaries.

Even in 1949, only one third of Party members were natives; in Estonia and Latvia, half were Russians; in Lithuania, the number was probably close to two thirds; the rest consisted of formerly exiled nationals. The peoples' passive resistance also shows in the fact that during the first five years of Soviet rule, only 0.3 percent of local Lithuanians and 0.7 percent of local Latvians and Estonians joined the Party. This means the percentages were five to ten times below the Soviet average at that time.[158]

Of all Soviet measures, deportations before the outbreak of the German-Soviet war most embittered the population. After the reconquest from the Germans, Stalin's regime again used this method of Sovietization and contributed to the enormous growth of partisan ranks. The first wave of deportations in late 1944 and early 1945 affected former members of the Wehrmacht in particular: At least 30,000 Estonians and 38,000 Latvians were deported. From the summer of 1945 to the spring of 1946, 100,000 Lithuanian men, women, and children and 60,000 Latvians followed them.

After 1944, partisan units that called themselves "Forest Brothers" developed in the three republics, but only Lithuania succeeded in organizing a central resistance organization, the "United Democratic Resistance Movement" (*Bendras Demokratinio Pasipriešinimo Sajudis*, BDPS), from 1946 to 1951. The military units were called freedom fighters. The United Democratic Resistance Movement and its soldiers saw themselves as the legitimate representatives of the Lithuanian state. They hoped the anticipated war between the USSR and the Western allies, who had never acknowledged Soviet annexation of the Baltic states, would result in the reinstitution of their state.

At the height of the partisan movement from 1945 to 1948, about 30,000 Lithuanians, 10,000 to 15,000 Latvians, and 10,000 Estonians fought the Soviets. Because the partisans suffered great losses and many alternated between partisan war and civilian life, we must assume that about 100,000 Lithuanians joined the "Forest Brothers" to fight against the Soviets for varying periods. Some rural areas were outside the control of the Soviet administration, and for some time, the partisans frustrated Soviet attempts to establish local soviets. The "Forest Brothers" carried out the state's administrative and control functions themselves. They avoided major military conflicts and never initiated attacks on Red Army units. Most of their military actions were surprise attacks on MVD troops and efforts to intimidate and kill collaborators. In the case of Lithuania, data about the number of victims killed by the partisans between 1945 and 1952 vary from 4,000 to 13,000.

Because the partisans considered all Soviet measures illegal in principle, they also resisted land reform, which the Soviets resumed in 1945 and which preceded collectivization in all territories. The purpose of the land reform was to win over the peasants with little or no land by assigning them land of their own to cultivate. In Lithuania, about 700,000 hectares were distributed among 96,000 families by 1948. The partisans committed terror acts against these new settlers alienating part of the population.

As it had in the Ukraine, Soviet collectivization and the accompanying deportations in 1949 struck the decisive blow against the partisan movement. The Soviets relied on the strategy that had proven successful in the 1920s and prepared collectivization by levying ruinous taxes on "kulaks," who saw no chance to continue working their farms successfully after 1948. Resistance to collectivization was broken by deporting considerably more people than in the previous years. By late 1947, the Soviets had deported 70,000 Lithuanians. Another 70,000 were to follow on May 22, 1948. After March 20, 1949, MVD units deported 60,000 Estonians, 50,000 Latvians, and 40,000 Lithuanians within a few days by using prepared proscription lists. Another 40,000 people had to leave Lithuania in the summer of 1949. As usual, people were loaded onto cattle cars during the night; many died during the trip to Western Siberia or northern Kazakhstan. Families were separated: Able-bodied men were put to work in labor camps, and women and children on kolkhozes where they fought for survival. By late 1949, 93 percent of Latvian, 80 percent of Estonian, and 62 percent of Lithuanian farm households were collectivized. The slower pace in Lithuania probably resulted from partisan resistance that was still too strong.

For a short time, deportations and compulsory collectivization created new Lithuanian partisans. In the long run, however, the elimination of peasants deprived them of their source of supply and refuges to retreat to. The peasants had previously provided supplies for the partisans voluntarily and because they shared their political convictions; now, partisans broke into and looted kolkhozes and government stores, which they considered illegal Soviet property. This partisan strategy deprived the population of goods that were barely sufficient for survival and undermined the people's trust, which was the basis for the partisans' existence. By late 1949, the "Forest Brothers" were no longer able to paralyze the local soviets. In Estonia and Latvia, they had already lost that ability in late 1946. By 1950, the number of armed freedom fighters decreased to 5,000; by late 1952, to 700.

Immediately after the war, the Soviets began extensive industrialization in Estonia and Latvia. This development dramatically changed economic and social structures and was designed to integrate the two republics into the Soviet Union. Both republics provided favorable conditions for capital investments: Because of the much-higher-than average level of education and training, Estonia and Latvia had a large reservoir of qualified workers. Their well-developed infra-structure was damaged comparatively little in the war. In addition, the creation of new jobs made many Russians immigrate. These Russians changed the population's national make-up, and they were highly welcomed because they stabilized Soviet rule.

The Latvian center of industrial development was Riga, where the machine-building and metal-working industries in particular expanded on the basis of existing industrial capacities. In north-eastern Estonia, the focus was primarily on mining and refining oil shale. In the second half of the 1940s, per capita capital investment in these two republics was twice the Soviet average; in contrast, capital investment in Lithuania, which preserved its primarily agrarian character until the 1960s, remained below this average.

In contrast to the Western Ukraine, industrialization in the Baltic states did not mean reinforcing native social elements but weakening them. At the height of the immigration wave from 1945 to 1947, 180,000 foreigners immigrated to Estonia. From 1945 to 1959, about 400,000 Russians and an additional 100,000 natives of other nations immigrated to Latvia (most of them arrived before 1953). This massed and directed immigration and the simultaneous deportation and flight of local natives westward decreased the percentage of Latvians in Latvia from 83 percent in 1945 to 60 percent in 1953. In 1945, 94 percent of the population of Estonia were Estonian; by 1953, this proportion had decreased to 72 percent.[159] Lithuania never—neither immediately after the war nor later—experienced a comparable wave of industrialization and immigration. Because of this, the population's national composition remained considerably more homogeneous in Lithuania. This was also an indirect result of the lasting partisan resistance.

In spite of the revolutionary interferences in the Baltic states' political, economic, and national structure, the three peoples continued to exist as national cultures. Vernacular cultural life began to flourish again in the decades after Stalin's death despite censorship and Soviet reprisals. In the 1950s, a new elite began to develop, which gradually replenished the losses suffered by the Baltic peoples during the war and post-war era. The fact that—in contrast to the Soviet East—the educational and professional qualifications of Russian and Slavic immigrants was not superior, but often inferior to the natives', facilitated development of a new national elite in the Baltics. Most immigrants were unskilled industrial workers. The resurgence of vernacular cultural life, which was not restricted to copying the generic Soviet-Russian culture, was accompanied by a considerable change of consciousness among the Baltic peoples. The active and passive resistance of the post-war years was replaced by the Baltic peoples' conviction that they should make the best possible use of the leeway left to them and should not block avenues to their national cultures' self-preservation by remaining fixated on the—for the time being unreachable—political sovereignty.

Notes

1. "Geheimes Zusatzprotokoll vom 23. August 1939," in: *Das national-sozialistische Deutschland und die Sowjetunion 1939–1941, Akten aus dem*

Archiv des Deutschen Auswärtigen Amts, (1948), p. 86. The treaties of August 23, 1939, ibid., pp. 84–86 and of September 28, 1939, pp. 116–119.

2. Cf. the German-Soviet arguments and agreements of June 1940 concerning northern Bukovina in: ibid., pp. 174–184.

3. Vakar, *Belorussia,* pp. 159, 259; Lazarev, *Vossoedinenie,* p. 27; D. Kvitkovsky/T. Brindzan/A. Zhukovsky (eds.), *Bukovina* (Paris, 1956), pp. 429ff.; Misiunas/Taagepera, *Baltic States,* p. 274.

4. Von der Schulenburg's letter of June 25, 1939, to Foreign Minister of the German Reich von Ribbentrop, in: *Das nationalsozialistische Deutschland und die Sowjetunion,* p. 179.

5. Molotov's speech of August 1, 1940, delivered to the Supreme Soviet, in: *Soviet Documents on Foreign Policy,* J. Degras (ed.), vol. III (London, 1953), pp.461–469, particularly pp. 464–466.

6. Resolution passed by the Fifth Comintern Congress quoted by Bilinsky, *Second Soviet Republic,* p. 7.

7. *Handbook of Major Soviet Nationalities,* pp. 417f.

8. Mutual assistance and friendship pact between the USSR and the Democratic Republic of Finland (the Soviet puppet regime under Kuusinen) of December 2, 1939, in: *Soviet Documents on Foreign Policy,* J. Degras (ed.), vol. III (London, 1953), p. 407.

9. A.F. Upton, *Finland 1939–1940* (London, 1974), pp. 149ff.; cf., however, S. Myllyniemi, *Die baltische Krise, 1938–1941,* (Stuttgart, 1979), p. 154.

10. *Mirovoe khoziaistvo i mirovaia politika,* 9/1939, p. 13.

11. Bilinsky, *Second Soviet Republic,* p. 336; Lazarev, *Vossoedinenie,* p. 148.

12. The chronology of these annexations and the Soviets' first measures are common knowledge — in respect to the Baltic states — and need not be repeated in detail here. Recent studies of the Baltic states include: Misiunas/Taagepera, *Baltic States,* pp. 15–43; Myllyniemi, *Die baltische Krise.* An older study is B. Meissner, *Die Sowjetunion, die baltischen Staaten und das Völkerrecht,* (Cologne, 1956). On the Ukraine: Bilinsky, *Second Soviet Republic,* pp. 84–110; on Belorussia: Vakar, *Belorussia,* pp. 155–169.

13. Dima, *Bessarabia and Bukovina,* pp. 43–59; C. Cioranesco, et al., *Aspects des relations russo-roumaines* (Paris, 1967), pp. 133ff. deals with the annexation exclusively from the perspective of foreign affairs.

14. Lazarev, *Vossoedinenie,* pp. 61ff.

15. Ibid., pp. 37f.

16. Ibid., pp. 38f.

17. Ibid., pp. 43f. In the other annexed territories, the locally elected assemblies executed the respective regulations. In Bessarabia, the Soviets never established such an assembly.

18. Ibid., pp. 51–53.

19. Ibid., pp. 68, 139, 146–148.

20. On the Soviet-Romanian polemics concerning the identity of or difference between the Moldavian and Romanian nations and languages and the ensuing irredentist fears and demands that developed after the war, cf. D. Ghermani, *Die nationale Souveränitätspolitik der SR Rumänien* (Munich, 1981), pp. 178–188; N. Dima, *Bessarabia and Bukovina: The Soviet-Romanian Territorial Dispute* (Boulder, Colo., 1982). From a linguistic perspective, Moldavian and Romanian are the same language, distinguished only by local accents (N. Dima, "Moldavians or Romanians?" in: *The Soviet West*, pp. 30–45).

21. Lazarev, *Vossoedinenie*, pp. 171–176.

22. Maksudov, *Pertes subies par la population de l'URSS*, p. 237.

23. Myllyniemi, *Die baltische Krise*, pp. 143f.

24. Misiunas/Taagepera, *Baltic States*, p. 41.

25. *Chruschtschow erinnert sich*, pp. 151, 154.

26. I. Blum, "Polacy w Zwiazku Radzietckim," in: *Wojiskowy przeglad historyczny* 1/1967, p. 147.

27. B.C. Pinchuk, "The Sovietization of the Jewish Community of Eastern Poland 1939–1941," in: *Slavonic and East European Review*, 56, No. 3, 1978, pp. 387–410.

28. B.C. Pinchuk, "Elimination as the 'Highest Stage' of Sovietization," in: *Ukrainian Quarterly*, 33, No. 3, 1977, pp. 281–285; Blum, *Polacy*, pp. 150, 154; L. Rêvêcz, *Volk aus 100 Nationalitäten*, pp. 207–211.

29. Lazarev, *Vossoedinenie*, p. 47.

30. *Chruschtschow erinnert sich*, p. 155.

31. J.A. Armstrong, *The Soviet Bureaucratic Elite. A Case Study of the Ukrainian Apparatus* (N.Y., 1959), p. 112; cf. Sullivant, *Soviet Politics and the Ukraine*, p. 237.

32. Lazarev, *Vossoedinenie*, p. 41.

33. Stalin, *Sochineniia*, vol. XV, p. 35.

34. Quoted from: H. Kohn, "Soviet Communism and Nationalism," in: *Soviet Nationality Problems*, p. 60. This passage is not included in Stalin's "Werke."

35. Stalin, *Sochineniia*, vol XV, p. 214.

36. Pravda editorial of December 21, 1941, quoted from: Oberländer, *Sowjetpatriotismus*, p. 73.

37. *Kraznaia zvezda*, August 13, 1942, quoted from: Werth, *Ruland im Krieg*, p. 297.

38. Excerpts from newspaper articles by Ilia Erenburg (early 1945), quoted from ibid., pp. 644–646.

39. According to the headline of a Pravda article by E. Iaroslavskii of December 27, 1941.

40. Erenburg in: *Pravda* June 14, 1942.

41. "Doklad tov. A.S. Shcherbakova 21 ianvaria 1942 g. na torzhestvennotraurnom zasedanii, posviashchennom XVIII godovshchine so dnia smerti V.I. Lenina," in: *Bolshevik*, 2/1942, p. 10. For additional evidence of the frequent use of these terms, cf. Tillett, *Great Friendship*, pp. 60ff.

42. "Anti-fascist demonstration" of the Ukrainian people in November 1941, of the Belorussian people in January 1942, of the Latvian, Estonian, and Moldavian peoples in March 1942, of the Lithuanian people in April 1942, of the peoples of the Northern Caucasus in August 1942, and of the peoples of the Transcaucasus in September 1942 (Tillett, *Great Friendship*, pp. 64f.).

43. "Antifashistskii miting predstavitelei narodov Severnogo Kavkaza," in: *Bolshevik*, 15/1942, pp. 38–42; "Antifashistskii miting predstavitelei narodov Zakavkazia," in: *Bolshevik*, 15/1942, pp. 43–48.

44. A. Azizian, "Narody Kavkaza nikogda ne budut rabami," in: *Bolshevik*, 15/1942, pp 28–37.

45. Tillett, *Great Friendship*, pp. 75f.; Armstrong, *Ukrainian nationalism*, p. 138.

46. *Istoriia Kazakhskoi SSR. S drevneishikh vremen do nashikh dnei*, M. Abdykalykov/A. Pankratova (eds.) (Alma-Ata, 1943); Tillett, *Great Friendship*, pp. 70–83.

47. A.M. Pankratova at a conference: "Obsuzhdenie v redaktsii 'Istoricheskogo zhurnala' knigi 'Istoriia Kazakhskoi SSR," in: *Istoricheskii zhurnal*, 11–12/1943, pp. 85–90; quoted from: Tillett, *Great Friendship*, p. 73.

48. "O sostoianii i merakh uluchsheniia massovo-politicheskoi i ideologicheskoi raboty v Tatarskoi partiinoi organizatsii," in: *KPSS v resoliutsiiakh i resheniiakh*, vol. VI, pp. 113–120 (the quotes are on pp. 115, 119).

49. *Leningrad*, 12–13/1943, quoted from: Barghoorn, *Soviet Russian Nationalism*, p. 241.

50. Curran/Ponomareff, *Managing the Ethnic Factor in the Russian and Soviet Armed Forces*, pp. 27, 30f.

51. Artemev, *Iz istorii*, p.72.

52. Ibid., p. 82.

53. A.P. Artemev, *Bratskii boevoi soiuz narodov SSSR v Velikoi Otechestvennoi voine* (Moscow, 1975); N.A. Kirsanov, *Partiinaia mobilizatsiia na front v gody Velikoi Otechestvennoi voiny* (Moscow, 1972); Curran/Ponomareff, *Managing the Ethnic Factor*.

54. Gurvich, *K voprosu o vliianii Velikoi Otechestvennoi voiny*, pp. 43f.

55. Artemev, *Iz istorii*, p. 80.

56. Gurvich, *K voprosu o vliianii*, p. 44.

57. Gurvich, *ibid.*; Malanchuk, *Istoricheskii opyt KPSS*, p. 194 (quote).

58. *Soviet Partisans in World War II*, J.A. Armstrong (ed.) (Madison WI, 1964), p. 150.

59. Gurvich, *K voprosu o vliianii*, p. 44.
60. Rigby, *Communist Party Membership*, p. 376.
61. Gurvich, *K voprosu o vliianii*, pp. 40, 42.
62. Ibid., p. 42.
63. "O sozdanii voiskovykh formirovanii soiuznykh respublik . . ." and "O predostavlenii soyuznym respublikam polnomochii v oblasti vneshnikh snoshenii . . .," in: *Istoriia sovetskoi konstitutsii (v dokumentakh)*, pp. 823f. The quotes are from the speech Molotov delivered to the Supreme Soviet on February 1, 1944, on the occasion of the ratification of these laws, in: *Bolshevik*, 2/1944, pp. 11, 13.
64. *Istoriia sovetskoi konstitutsii (v dokumentakh)*, pp. 823f.
65. Arnold, *Die nationalen Gebietseinheiten*, pp. 137–147, 157–162; H.-J. Uibopuu, *Die Völkerrechtssubjektivität der Unionsrepubliken der UdSSR* (Vienna/New York, 1975).
66. Sullivant, *Soviet Politics and the Ukraine*, p. 261.
67. A.S. Shcherbakov, "Speech Delivered on January 21, 1942, on the Occasion of the Eighteenth Anniversary of Lenin's Death," in: *Bolshevik*, 2/1942, p. 10; I.V. Stalin, "Speech of November 6, 1943," in: *Sochineniia*, XV, p. 118; V.M. Molotov, "Speech of February 1, 1944," in: *Bolshevik*, 2/1944, p. 8.
68. There are no satisfactory treatments of collaboration in the USSR. The best effort still is: Dallin, *Deutsche Herrschaft in Ruland* (1958). A. Alexiev, *Soviet Nationalities in German Wartime Strategy: 1941–1945* (1982) only offers an outline and leaves many questions unanswered. Western researchers widely disagree as to the extent of collaboration and in their assessments. For example, v.z. Mühlen emphasizes the collaboration's small military use and the national units' preparedness to desert (*Zwischen Hakenkreuz und Sowjetstern*, pp. 63ff.); Alexiev concludes that "great parts" of the non-Russian peoples saw the Germans as "the lesser evil" (*op. cit.*, p. 34).
69. Standard reference: Armstrong, *Ukrainian Nationalism*. On the beginnings of the OUN: A.J. Motyl, *The Turn to the Right: The Ideological Origins and the Development of the Ukrainian Nationalism. 1919–1929* (New York, 1980).
70. J.S. Reshetar, Jr., in: *Ukrainians in World War II*, pp. 25f.
71. Armstrong, *Ukrainian Nationalism*, pp. 77–82, the quote is on p. 81.
72. Armstrong, ibid., pp. 91–93 (Zhitomir), pp. 101–117 (Kiev).
73. Ibid., p. 156; Y. Tys-Krokhmaliuk, *UPA Warfare in Ukraine* (New York, 1972); O. Martovych, "The Ukrainian Insurgent Army," in: *Ukrainian Review*, XXX, 1982, No. 2, pp. 3–26; No. 3, pp. 3–28.
74. Dallin, *Deutsche Herrschaft in Ruland*, pp. 612f.; Armstrong, *Ukrainian Nationalism*, pp. 170–175.

75. Dallin, *Deutsche Herrschaft in Russland*, pp. 636f.; Armstrong, *Ukrainian Nationalism*, pp. 181–185.
76. Misiunas/Taagepera, *The Baltic States*, pp. 44–73; S. Myllyniemi, *Die Neuordnung der baltischen Länder: 1941–1944* (Helsinki, 1973); Z. Ivinskis, "Lithuania During the War," in: *Lithuania Under the Soviets*, pp. 61–84.
77. Misiunas/Taagepera, *Baltic States*, pp. 57f.
78. Dallin, *Deutsche Herrschaft in Ruland*, p. 612.
79. Vakar, *Belorussia*, pp. 189f.
80. Ibid., pp. 202–206; Dallin, *Deutsche Herrschaft in Ruland*, pp. 225–237.
81. v.z. Mühlen, *Zwischen Hakenkreuz und Sowjetstern*, pp. 183–186; Hoffmann, *Ostlegionen*, p. 47.
82. J. Hoffmann, *Deutsche und Kalmyken 1942 bis 1945* (Freiburg, 1974).
83. Dallin, *Deutsche Herrschaft in Rußland*, pp. 256–264.
84. S.J. Newland, "Cossacks in Field Grey: A History of the Recruitment of the Cossacks into the German Army, 1941–1945," Ph.D. (University of Kansas, 1982).
85. Hoffmann, *Ostlegionen*; v.z. Mühlen, *Zwischen Hakenkreuz und Sowjetstern*, pp. 61–68.
86. Buchsweiler, *Ethnic Germans in the Ukraine*, p. XXVII.
87. A survey of the treatment of the ethnic Germans: Fleischhauer, *Das Dritte Reich und die Deutschen in der Sowjetunion*.
88. Ibid., pp. 162ff.
89. Ibid., pp. 138–144; Buchsweiler, *Ethnic Germans in the Ukraine*, pp. XXII–XXV.
90. J.M. Matley, "The Dispersal of the Ingrian Finns," in: *Slavic Review*, 38, 1979, p. 9.
91. I. Fleischhauer, "'Unternehmen Barbarossa' und die Zwangsumsiedlung der Deutschen in der UdSSR," in: *Vierteljahrshefte für Zeitgeschichte*, 30, 1982, p. 304; B. Pinkus, "Die Deutschen in der Sowjetunion beim Ausbruch des Zweiten Weltkrieges," in: *Heimatbuch der Deutschen aus Ruland, 1973–1981*, pp. 9–19.
92. *Ukrainian Quarterly*, V, 3/1949, pp. 238–248. Professor Yaroslav Bilinsky gave me this information.
93. A. Solshenizyn, *Der Archipel Gulag*, last volume, (Bern, 1976) pp. 388f. *Koreans in the Soviet Union*, Dae-Sook Suh (ed.), Honolulu, Hawaii 1987.
94. Fleischhauer, "Unternehmen Barbarossa," pp. 310ff. The quotes were taken from the resolution of the Supreme Soviet's Presidium, pp. 312f.
95. Ibid., pp. 311f.
96. A.M. Nekrich, *The Punished Peoples* (New York, 1978); R. Conquest, *The Nation Killers* (London, 1970).
97. *Izvestiia*, June 26, 1946.
98. Nekrich, ibid., p. 112.
99. Ibid., pp. 31, 81f., 96.

100. Ibid., pp. 114f.
101. Ibid., pp. 63, 92.
102. Ibid., pp. 46–51.
103. A. Uralov (A. Aftorkhanov), *Narodoubiistvo v SSSR. Ubiistvo chechenskogo naroda* (Munich, 1952), pp. 59–64.
104. V.A. Kravchenko, *Ich wählte die Freiheit* (Zurich, 1947), pp. 453–455.
105. Kravchenko, op. cit., p. 525.
106. Khrushchev in his "secret speech" at the Twentieth Party Congress in 1956, in: *Chruschtschow erinnert sich,* p. 565.
107. Armstrong, *Soviet Bureaucratic Elite,* p. 17.
108. *Pravda,* August 23, 1946.
109. Resolution of the CC of the CPSU (B) on August 9, 1944, "On the Next Tasks of Belorussia's Party Organizations of the CP (B) Concerning Political Work with the Masses and Cultural Education of the Population," in: *KPSS v rezoliutsiakh i resheniiakh,* vol. 6, p. 107.
110. L.Z. Kopelev, *Khranit vechno* (Ann Arbor, 1975), p. 533.
111. *Pravda,* August 23, 1946; *Narys istoriii ukraiinskoii literatury* (Moscow, 1945); *Istoriia Ukrainy,* vol. 1 (Ufa, 1943).
112. *Pravda,* September 2, 1946.
113. "On the Distortions and Errors in the Interpretation of the History of Ukrainian Literature," in: *Survey of the History of Ukrainian Literature* (August 24, 1946); "On the Satirical Magazine *Perets (Pepper);* "On the Magazine *Vitchizna (Homeland);*" "On the Repertory of Amateur Theater Groups;" "On the Repertory of Dramatic and Opera Theaters in the Ukrainian SSR and Measures to Improve Them" (October 12, 1946); "On Measures to Continue Improvement of Schools in the Ukrainian SSR" (November 13, 1946); bibliography in: Bilinsky, *Second Soviet Republic,* pp. 394f.
114. K. Litvin, "Ob istorii ukrainskogo naroda," in: *Bolshevik,* 7/1947, pp. 41–56; the quotes are on pp. 44, 48.
115. *Radianska Ukraiina,* October 3, 1947; Tillett, *Great Friendship,* p. 93.
116. *Chruschtschow erinnert sich,* pp. 233–239; the quote is on p. 239.
117. Lewytzkyj, *Die Sowjetukraine,* pp. 61–64.
118. *Pravda,* September 26, 1947.
119. V. Shunkov, "O razrabotke istorii Buriat-Mongolii," in: *VI,* 5/1949, pp 87–89; the quote is on p. 87.
120. *BSE,* vol. I, 1949 (2nd ed.), p. 467.
121. *Bakinskii rabochii,* May 26, 1951. Quoted from: A.A. Bennigsen, "The Crisis of the Turkic National Epics, 1951–1952: Local Nationalism or Internationalism?" in: *Canadian Slavonic Papers,* XVII, 2–3/1975, pp. 463–474. This is the fundamental study on the prohibition of the Islamic epics.
122. *Turkmenskaia iskra,* August 14, 1951; quoted from: Bennigsen, op. cit., p. 466.

123. *BSE*, vol. II, 1950 (2nd ed.), p. 135.
124. *Literaturnaia gazeta*, September 14, 1952; quoted from: Bennigsen, op. cit., p. 468.
125. *Sovetskaia Kirgiziia*, February 2, 1952.
126. *Sovetskaia Kirgiziia* and *Kyzyl Kyrgyzstan*, March, 19, 1952. This and other bibliographical information can be found in Bennigsen, op. cit., pp. 469–472.
127. The document is in: Oberländer, *Sowjetpatriotismus*, p. 80.
128. G. Aleksandrov, "O nekotorykh zadachakh obshchestvennykh nauk v sovremennykh usloviiakh," in: *Bolshevik*, 14/1945, pp. 12–29.
129. "O zadachakh sovetskikh istorikov v borbe s proiavleniiami burzhuaznoi ideologii," in: *VI*, 2/1949, pp. 3–13; excerpts of this in German are in: Oberländer, *Sowjetpatriotismus*, pp. 167–173, the quote is on p. 167.
130. "Velikii russkii narod," in: *Literaturnaia gazeta*, May 4, 1950; in German in: Oberländer, op. cit., pp. 81–83.
131. The decree about music by the CPSU's CC of February 10, 1948: "Ob opere 'Velikaia druzhba' V. Muradeli," in: *Pravda*, February 11, 1948.
132. See note 130.
133. *Pravda*, June 6, 1949.
134. V.M. Molotov, *Tridcatiletie Velikoi Oktiabrskoi sotsialisticheskoi revoliutsii* (Moscow, 1947), p. 29.
135. "Protiv burzhuaznoi ideologii kosmopolitizma," in: *Voprosy filosofii* 2/1948, pp. 14–29; German excerpts are in: Oberländer, op. cit., pp. 93–97.
136. Gilboa, *Black Years of Soviet Jewry*, pp. 146–186.
137. S. Redlich, *Propaganda and Nationalism in Wartime Russia: The Jewish Antifascist Committee in the USSR 1941–1948* (New York, 1982).
138. Gilboa, *Black Years of Soviet Jewry*, pp. 187–335; *Jews in Soviet Russia Since 1917*, pp. 121–131, 316–323. An insider reports concrete examples illustrating the methods and means used to persecute Jews: A. Nekritsch, "Der Feldzug gegen die 'Kosmopoliten' an der Moskauer Staats-Universität," in: *Kontinent*, 19, VIIth year, October 1981, pp. 47–68. The popular anti-Semitism of the early 1950s and the banishing of the writer Perets Markish and his family is described in his son David Markish's autobiographical novel: *Priskazka* (Tel Aviv, 1978).
139. Soviet pamphlet "To the Members of the So-Called UPA and UNRA (*Ukraiinska Narodna Revoliutsiina Armiia*)," February 12, 1944, quoted from: Bilinsky, *Second Soviet Republic*, p. 128.
140. Khrushchev's speech in: *Bolshevik*, 6/1944, pp. 7–35.
141. V. Markus, *L'incorporation de l'Ukraine Subcarpathique a l'Ukraine sovietique, 1944–1945* (Louvain, 1956); (pp. 114ff. contain a facsimile of the "Manifesto of the First Congress of the People's Committees of the Carpathian Ukraine for the Reunification of the Carpathian Ukraine with the Soviet Ukraine," on November 26, 1944; this is the source of the passages

quoted); F. Nemec/V. Moudry, *The Soviet Seizure of Subcarpathian Ruthenia* (1955), (reprint Westport, Conn., 1981); Magosci, *Shaping of a National Identity*, pp. 252ff.

142. Resolution of the CC of the CPSU (B) on August 9, 1944, "On the Next Tasks of Belorussia's Party Organizations Concerning Political Work with the Masses and the Cultural Education of the Population," in: *KPSS v rezoliutsiakh i resheniiakh,* vol. 6, p. 108.

143. Resolution of the CPSU (B)'s CC "On the Shortcomings of Political Work Among the Population of the Ukrainian SSR's Western Regions," September 27, 1944, in: *KPSS v resoliutsiiakh i resheniiakh,* vol. 6, p. 128.

144. *Radianska Ukraiina,* August 14, 1946, quoted from: Bilinsky, *Second Soviet Republic,* p. 91.

145. Armstrong, *Soviet Bureaucratic Elite,* p. 121; the data are from an unpublished Soviet dissertation.

146. In their treaty of August 16, 1945, the USSR and the Republic of Poland determined the border on the basis of international law (*Dokumenty i materialy po istorii sovetsko-polskikh otnoshenii,* vol. 7 [Moscow, 1974], pp. 451f.).

147. *Khrushchev Remembers. The Last Testament,* p. 158.

148. *Dokumenty i materialy po istorii sovetsko-polskikh otnoshenii,* vol. 7 (Moscow, 1974), pp. 213–219, cf. pp. 467–472.

149. Maksudov, *Pertes subies par la population,* p. 237; Bilinsky, *Second Soviet Republic,* p. 51.

150. On the UPA: Bilinsky, *Second Soviet Republic,* pp. 111–140; Armstrong, *Ukrainian Nationalism,* pp. 290ff.; Tys-Krokhmaliuk, *UPA Warfare in Ukraine.*

151. I. Blum, "Udzial wojska polskiego w walce o utrwalenie wladzy ludowej: Walki z bandami UPA," in: *Wojskowy przeglad historyczny,* 1/1959, p. 12.

152. *Chruschtschow erinnert sich,* p. 152.

153. Armstrong, *Ukrainian Nationalism,* pp. 163–165; Litopys, *Ukraiinskoii Povstanskoii Armiii, vol. VIII. Ukraiinska Holovna Vyzvolna Rada,* book 1, 1944–1945, Ie. Shtendera/P. Potichnyi (ed.) (Toronto, 1980), pp. 36–38.

154. B. Bociurkiw, "The Uniate Church in the Soviet Union: A Case Study in Soviet Church Policy," in: *Canadian Slavonic Papers,* VII, 1965, pp. 83–113; Bilinsky, *Second Soviet Republic,* pp. 95–110.

155. These and the following data are in: Lewytzkyj, *Sowjetukraine,* pp. 42–44.

156. The table detailing the national composition of all Ukrainian territories from 1926 to 1959 in: Bilinsky, *Second Soviet Republic,* p. 57.

157. An excellent summary is: Misiunas/Taagepera, *Baltic States,* pp. 68–125; on Lithuania: *Lithuania Under the Soviets,* pp. 85ff.
158. Misiunas/Taagepera, *Baltic States,* pp. 77f.
159. Ibid., p. 108.

VIII

De-Stalinization

The Battle for Succession

The nationalities issue and the republics' non-Russian leadership groups were important in the battle to determine the dead dictator's successor. A few weeks after Stalin's death, it had already become apparent to the outside world and the Soviet public that the dictator had not solved the nationalities problem, only suppressed it for a while. Unfulfilled nationalism and the national elites, whom Stalin had neglected in favor of Russians, represented a political potential that the claimants attempted to mobilize for themselves. No one could succeed Stalin without wide support or at least benevolent neutrality on the peripheries. Concessions were the only way to gain non-Russian nations' support. Stalin's nationalities policy would have to be revised at least partially and non-Russian elites would have to be more involved in ruling and society to make them assets in the succession battle. Two rivals followed this course: Beriia unsuccessfully and Khrushchev successfully.

In early June 1953, Beriia presented several memos to the CC's Presidium. In essence, these memos condemned Stalin's nationalities policy since the late 1930s and advocated a return to the policy of the 1920s. Beriia correctly assumed the Party leadership would not contradict him and that his stand would make him out to be the champion of non-Russian peoples. Not even his most determined opponent Khrushchev could counter this strategy. Beriia "preached that Russian dominance in the leadership of the non-Russian republics had to end. Everybody knew this was true..."[1]

To that effect, on June 12, 1953, the CC's Presidium passed a resolution: "1. All Party and state organs shall radically improve conditions in the national republics and end the distortions in Soviet nationalities policy. 2. They shall organize the education, advancement, and promotion of as many local nationals as possible to leadership positions. The replaced Nomenklatura functionaries, who do not speak the local language, are to be recalled to the disposal of the CPSU's CC. 3. In the national republics, correspondence is to be conducted in the local vernacular."[2] In the same resolution, Party leaders probably also determined "that, in all republics, a man native to the republic and not a Russian sent from Moscow should be first Party secretary."[3]

The CC's Presidium followed this principle. First they relieved the head of the Ukrainian Party, L.G. Melnikov, and appointed as his successor A.I. Kirichenko, a Ukrainian and the former second secretary. The appointment of A.E. Korneichuk also strengthened the Ukrainian presence in the Bureau of the Ukrainian CC. The Ukrainian CC's plenum formally made these personnel changes and reproached the old Ukrainian Party leadership for "allowing distortions in our Party's Leninist-Stalinist nationalities policy. These came to light in the ruinous practice of preferential promotion to Party and Soviet leadership in the Ukraine's western territories of functionaries from other territories in the Ukrainian SSR and adopting Russian as the teaching language at western Ukrainian universities."[4] What had been the Party's official policy, was now considered a "distortion" of the Party's nationalities policy.

Shake-ups occurred in favor of natives in the Party and state apparatuses in many other republics as well, particularly in the Baltic republics. The Lithuanian CC's plenum complained about "inadequate advancement and promotion of Lithuanian cadres for top positions in the Party, soviets, and economy."[5] In late June 1953 — shortly before Beriia's fall and arrest, the Latvian CC used nearly identical words to condemn the policy that had been the Party's official policy and pledged "comprehensive promotion of Latvian cadres to executive positions in Party, soviet, and economic organs."[6] In the summer of 1953, all three Baltic republics replaced their Russian second secretaries with natives. Nationalization of such crucial functions — the second secretary is responsible for personnel policy — did not last long. In Lithuania, this function was again taken over by a Russian in 1955; in Latvia, in 1956; in Estonia, in 1971.[7] Nevertheless, in the summer of 1953 (and at a slower rate, in the following years), the Soviets reshuffled thousands of top and mid-level executive positions in the Union Republics and gave them natives. This trend was particularly evident in the western republics; in Central Asia, this development was less pronounced. In Georgia and Armenia, Slavs did not control the apparatuses, even in the Stalin era.

The summer of 1953 witnessed indications that the Party would initiate a full-scale return to the korenizatsiia policy. *Communist,* the CC's theoretical organ, celebrated the "flourishing" and the "continuous development of the spiritual body and the national character of all the USSR's socialist nations." There was no mention of "merger" or even of "drawing together." These prospects were reminiscent of programmatic statements in the early 1920s: "Our task is to continue diligently to advance and promote local cadres, who know their peoples' languages, life styles, and traditions; to develop schools and theaters . . . to raise the material and cultural standard of the broad working masses in all republics and territories."[8] The Soviets "abolished" Great-Russian chauvinism in the mid-1930s by outlawing reference to it in the press because it endangered coexistence among the peoples. A few weeks after Stalin's death, *Literaturnaia gazeta* mentioned that "being diverted to Russian nationalism" was as despicable as being diverted to "local nationalism."[9] At the Nineteenth Party Congress in October 1952, twenty-three speakers condemned "bourgeois nationalism." No one mentioned Great-Russian chauvinism.[10] Attacks in the press on great-power chauvinism and the ensuing demands for cadre policy to consider non-Russians peaked in June 1953. Beriia's fall changed linguistic prescriptivism, and the media returned to presenting the Russians as the USSR's "leading nation."[11]

In the dramatic session of the CC's Presidium—probably on June 26, 1953—during which Beriia was relieved of his duties and arrested, Khrushchev's main accusation against him was "interfering with Party organizations in the Ukraine, Belorussia, and the Baltic republics." Beriia had relied on "national antagonisms" "to undermine Soviet unity."[12] In December 1953, a special court sentenced him to death because, among other infractions, he had taken measures to "activate the remnants of bourgeois-nationalist elements in the Union Republics, to spread animosity and dissent among the USSR's peoples, and particularly to undermine the friendship of the USSR's peoples with the great Russian people."[13]

After he had eliminated Beriia, Khrushchev adopted Beriia's policy in an attempt to expand his own power in the non-Russian republics and to strengthen his position in the battle for succession. Ukrainian and non-Ukrainian functionaries from the Ukraine gained the most advantage from this policy. Khrushchev supported these groups for two reasons that reinforced one another: The Ukrainians, whom Stalin had distrusted for two decades, appeared to be the natural allies of a new, anti-Stalinist policy, and, from 1938 to 1949, Khrushchev had been the head of the Ukrainian Party, so the most important foundation of his power was there; the Ukrainian Party apparatus were his constituents who supported his climb to power and shared in it.

In 1952, sixteen CC members were Ukrainian. By 1956, this number had increased to thirty-nine; by 1961, to fifty-nine. In other words, the number of Ukrainian members and candidates jumped from 6.8 percent in 1952 to 15.5 percent in 1956 and 18.5 percent in 1961. This meant Ukrainians, who were underrepresented among the CC members in the Stalin era, now had more representation than average. (In 1959, the percentage of Ukrainians in the total population was 17.7 percent.) This "Ukrainization" worked to the disadvantage of Russians, Georgians, and Armenians—of those nations particularly supported during the Stalin era. In 1952, the percentage of Russians in the CC was 71.5 percent. By 1956, this number had decreased to

67.1 percent; by 1961 to 62.7 percent. In 1952, 5.6 percent of the CC's members and candidate members were Georgians and Armenians. By 1956, this number had dropped to 2.8 percent; by 1961, to 2.4 percent.[14]

In the Ukraine, the percentage of Ukrainian Party members and of Ukrainian representatives in the apparatus in responsible positions increased. In 1940 (data from the Stalin era's later years are not available), Ukrainians constituted 63.1 percent of the republic's Party organization. By 1956, this percentage had climbed to 74.2 percent. By the late 1970s, it had decreased to 66 percent. In 1940, only 40 percent of the executive Party functionaries in the Ukraine were Ukrainian. In 1956, statistics showed a considerable increase to 67.8 percent. In the same year, 76 percent of the deputies to the Ukraine's Supreme Soviet were Ukrainian. At the same time, 84 percent of the deputies of all soviets were Ukrainian and thus there was a greater percentage of Ukrainians in the local soviets than in the total population.[15] In comparison, during the Khrushchev era, the Soviets did not succeed in permanently changing the national composition of the professional elites in favor of Ukrainians. In 1957, 56.8 percent of all college graduates employed in Ukrainian economics were Ukrainian; in 1964, this figure was still 58.1 percent; during the same period, the percentage of Russians increased from 25 percent to 28.1 percent.[16]

The rise of Ukrainians into the highest leadership positions was particularly apparent in Moscow. Never in the USSR's history, have as many Ukrainians held top positions in the CC's Presidium, the Ministry of Defense, and other central apparatuses as in the years of Khrushchev's one-man rule after 1957. These promotions resulted from the successful successor's gratitude for support received during his struggle with his rivals. R.K. Malinovskii, who was appointed Minister of Defense in October 1957, and his successor, A.A. Grechko, were Ukrainian. The Ukrainian general K.S. Moskalenko was particularly close to Khrushchev. In June 1953, he played a prominent role in the coup against Beriia. In March 1955, Khrushchev promoted him to marshal and, in 1960, to Assistant Minister of Defense and commander of missile troops. In November 1961, another Ukrainian, V.E. Semichastnyi, was appointed head of the KGB.

In late 1964 – after Khrushchev's fall – three of the eleven full members of the CC's Presidium were Ukrainian (N.V. Podgornyi, D.S. Polianskii, and P.E. Shelest). In addition, Western literature often classifies as Ukrainian A.P. Kirilenko – he was co-opted as a full member of the Presidium in April 1962 – because he was born in the Ukraine and pursued his career in the Party apparatus there until 1955. Officially, however, in the Soviet Union his nationality is given as Russian. After November 1962, the Ukrainian V.N. Titov was a CC secretary and strengthened Ukrainian representation in the Party headquarters. Traditionally, the Ukraine had a de facto claim to representation in the Politburo and the CC's Presidium only in the form of the first secretary although the heads of the Ukrainian Party had all been non-Ukrainians before 1953. The first Ukrainian in this capacity, Kirichenko, had an unusual career. He was accepted into the CC's Presidium as a candidate in May 1953 and as a full member in July 1955. In December 1957, he was also appointed CC secretary for cadre policy; this promotion possibly made him something like Khrushchev's proxy. In December 1957, Podgornyi succeeded him as head of the Ukrainian Party. In May 1960, however, Khrushchev brought down Kirichenko, who lost all his functions in Moscow and altogether disappeared from political life a few months later.

Although the Soviet Union has never given any reasons for Kirichenko's downfall, apparently he initially was the driving force behind the new nationalities policy in Kiev and Moscow and its beneficiary. Later, when Khrushchev was solidly established as Party chief and state leader and began to thoroughly revise this policy in the late 1950s, it seems that he made Kirichenko the scapegoat for the policy's failure.[17] Kirichenko almost certainly represented Ukrainian interests and supported non-Russian cadres on an all-Soviet scale. Of course, this does not answer the question of whether the unusually large number of Ukrainians in the Party's leadership actually represented or even attempted to represent Ukrainian interests in the Khrushchev era. Haven't all non-Russians who have reached top leadership positions always been "homines sovietici" and without national ties? The available Soviet sources do not provide a direct answer. Indirect clues, however, suggest that the top leadership's national composition was not at all irrelevant and had political consequences, even if no Ukrainian or other national "faction" existed, which it definitely did not. After Khrushchev's downfall, the number of Ukrainians in the CC, in the CC's Secretariat, and later also in the Politburo, decreased gradually even though Brezhnev was also from the Ukraine and recruited his supporters—though they were primarily Russians—from the Ukraine to fill leadership positions in Moscow. Other indirect evidence that the great number of Ukrainians in the leadership was relevant in the Ukraine and Moscow seems even more significant: In the Ukraine after the mid-1950s, a rather quiet Ukrainization of language, culture, education, and personnel policy began, in which P.E. Shelest, who was first secretary from 1963 to 1972 and who survived Khrushchev's downfall by several years, played a role.

The victorious successor supported not only Ukrainians but also non-Ukrainian—mostly Russian—functionaries from the Ukraine. Many were appointed Party chiefs in important territories of the RSFSR or other Union Republics; several continued their careers in Moscow, including M.M. Stakhurskii, Z.T. Serdiuk, A.I. Struev, I.D. Iakovlev, and V.P. Mzhavanadze. Brezhnev became the most prominent member of this group. In 1954, Khrushchev sent him to Kazakhstan as his representative to head the virgin land campaign, which the Soviets had started there, accompanied by great propaganda efforts. Also, Khrushchev's rise to one-man rule was very much the result of this campaign's success.

The Ukraine's special role also became apparent in propaganda and official ideology when the 300th anniversary of the "Reunification of the Ukraine and Russia" was celebrated in 1954 with pomp and splendor that was unusual even for the Soviet Union's standards. For months, the "friendship of the Ukrainian and Russian peoples" dominated the media, which praised this friendship's unsurpassed merits for the "Russian empire" and the USSR. The "Soviet Union's other peoples" faded into the background, which conveyed the idea of a special partnership, which was meant to flatter Ukrainian self-esteem and make the Ukrainian Party apparatus indebted to the person responsible for this campaign: Khrushchev. The ideological catchphrase of the "great Russian people – the leading nation" remained in circulation, but close on the great nation's heels came its "blood brother," the Ukrainian people, "the first to follow the Russian people on the glorious path to socialism."[18] No one had a chance against the "indestructible friendship of the Ukrainian and Russian peoples" – this was the message Soviet ideology and propaganda efforts sent to increase the value of the Ukrainians as junior partners. In honor of the anniversary, the RSFSR made a bombastic gesture and "presented" the Crimean peninsula to the Ukrainian SSR even though Ukrainians were a minority in the Crimean region: Only 22.3 percent of the population were Ukrainian and 71.4 percent were Russian (1959 figures).[19]

De-Stalinization

In the battle for succession, the Ukraine played a special role. In addition, Khrushchev's extensive measures to promote decentralization from 1954 to 1958 significantly increased the political importance of all non-Russian nations and territories. The prevalence of the motto "Back to Lenin" made it seem for a few years as if the Soviet Union were on the way to a politically lively federalism. The Soviets granted the non-Russian territories and their increasingly non-Russian leadership competencies, some of which went beyond those they had in the 1920s and were intended to give the multi-national state new impulses. This goal became even more important as the contrast to totalitarian dictatorship became more and more pronounced with every initiative the new leadership took.

Initially, the new policy showed in an abundance of administrative reforms that were to become typical for the Khrushchev decade. From 1954 to 1956, many all-Union ministries were converted into Union-Republic ministries or dissolved altogether. Their competencies were transferred to Republic ministries. On April 19, 1954, the Soviets divided the all-Union Ministry of Coal Mining into a Union-Republic ministry. At the same time, they established a new Ministry of Coal Mining of the Ukrainian SSR in Kiev.[20] On May 18, 1954, the corresponding transformation of the Ministry of Oil Industry occurred; on December 28, 1954, the Presidium of the USSR's Supreme Soviet decreed the decentralization of the Ministry of Communications and, on December 29, 1954, of the Ministry of Higher Education. Two-part Union-Republic agencies replaced all central all-Union ministries.[21] On August 10, 1955, the corresponding transformation of the Ministry of Paper and Wood Processing Industries followed. Again, this transformation met the interests of the Ukraine, in particular because the Soviets established a Ministry of Paper and Wood Processing Industries of the Ukrainian SSR in Kiev at the same time.[22]

In 1956, the Soviets continued to shift economic-administration competencies to the individual republics. They converted these all-Union ministries into Union-Republic ministries: the Ministry for Geology on January 12, 1956; the Ministry for Site Construction of the Metallurgical and Chemical Industry on January 12, 1956; the Ministry for Site Construction of the Coal Mining Industry on April 9, 1956; and the Ministry for Grain Production on May 31, 1956. On May 30, 1956, the USSR's CC and Council of Ministers decided to encourage decentralization of state administration by initiating "additional measures to continue strengthening the Union Republics' role in economic administration." The Soviets had Union Republics operate many factories from all areas of the economy, expecting "this to contribute to the improved use of available resources and increase production and better satisfy economic needs." The administration of factories and organizations from the following economic areas was transferred to republican organs: the food, fishing, grain production, consumer goods, meat and milk, textile, construction-materials, paper and wood processing, automobile transportation and road construction, inland navigation, public health, and retail trade and gastronomy industries.[23]

On May 31, 1956, the Presidium of the USSR's Supreme Soviet decreed the dissolution of the all-Union Ministry for Inland Navigation, the Union-Republic Ministry for Automobile Transport and Road Construction, and the Union-Republic Ministry of Justice.[24] The functions of the Ministry for Inland Navigation were taken over by a republic ministry in the RSFSR by the same name and the corresponding administrative organs for inland navigation in the other Union Republics' Councils of Ministers. The Soviets also transferred most of the competencies of the Ministry for Automobile Transport and Road Construction to the Union Republics' Councils of Ministers. The Council of Ministers of the USSR's newly created Head Office for Road Construction retained the competencies the central government had not transferred.[25]

In their joint resolution on May 30, 1956, the USSR's CC and Council of Ministers explicitly justified the dissolution of the Ministry of Justice by claiming it would "eliminate unnecessary centralization" and "strengthen the Union Republics' role" "in the management of the functions of the courts and (other) judiciary organs."[26] The Soviets transferred judiciary administration to the competence of the individual republics and reorganized the local ministries of justice into exclusive republic organs. This reinstituted the conditions in effect under the USSR's first constitution in 1923–1924.[27] However, these conditions did not prevail for long because decentralization was carried yet another step further. In 1957 and 1958, the Soviets dissolved the Autonomous Republics' ministries of justice and, from 1957 to 1963, those of the Union Republics. The respective territories' Supreme Courts took over some of their competencies, and the newly created Judicial Commissions in the Republics' Councils of Ministers took others.[28]

Ideological pronouncements at the Twentieth Party Congress in February 1956, which were reminiscent of programmatic statements in the 1920s, also expressed the new Party line. The resolution that followed the CC's accountability report said the Party assumed "that socialism does not at all eliminate national differences and particularities but, to the contrary, guarantees that the economy and culture of all nations and nationalities develop and flourish. The Party must consider these particularities carefully and seriously in all its practical activities now and in the future."[29]

The reorganization of the economic administration from 1954 to 1956 considerably increased the competencies of the Union Republics' Councils of Ministers and their subordinate authorities. In 1950, factories managed by republic or local organs had produced only 33 percent of industrial goods; by 1956, this percentage had increased to 55 percent. This meant the factories that central organs managed produced less than half of all industrial goods.[30] In the Ukraine, this general shift in the economic administration from the center to the periphery was particularly pronounced. In 1953, republic authorities managed 36 percent of the Ukraine's industrial production; by 1956, this percentage had increased to 76 percent.[31]

Revisions in planning and financial administration accompanied the reforms in economic administration. On May 5, 1955, the USSR's Council of Ministers decided to change the planning and financing of the Union Republics' economy.[32] All the measures were designed to give the Republics' Councils of Ministers and ministries considerably more room for decisionmaking than they previously had and to reduce the central state's planning injunctions and fund allocations to generally less detailed instructions. The central government provided only the framework and expected the republic's authorities to assume the responsibilities for filling in the details. "The Union Republics' Councils of Ministers confirm the plans for producing and distributing all industrial goods the republic ministries' factories, respective authorities, and trade cooperatives produce." The

USSR's State Plan prescribed only the factories' gross production for the individual Republics as a whole. Differentiating these plans and distributing the quota among the individual factories was the responsibility of the Republics' Councils of Ministers.

The Councils of Ministers also independently administrated and carried out investment and reinvestment in the factories the republics managed. Projects involving the union-republic ministries required a vote in the respective ministries in Moscow. The USSR's State Plan only prescribed general data to the Union Republics for raising productivity of industry and construction, determining the number of blue-collar and white-collar workers, and overseeing the payroll funds for the factories the republic ministries and authorities managed. Within the framework of general data, the Councils of Ministers also made the final decisions about the structure and staffing schedule of the republic ministries and authorities.

The Soviets also made changes in their budgeting procedures. In respect to the Union Republics' spending and revenue, the USSR's integrated budget no longer distinguished between republic and local budgets. This differentiation was now the responsibility of the Union Republics' Councils of Ministers. The USSR's state budget allotted funds globally to the Union Republics, which they were to use to finance their economies, social and cultural programs, and to maintain state authorities. Here, the Councils of Ministers were also responsible for local distribution and limitation of these funds. A few years later, the Soviets included in the law of October 30, 1959, governing the USSR's and the Union Republics' budgetary rights this restriction of the USSR's state budget to providing only global sums for spending and revenue for the Union Republics' budgets.[33]

The Union Republics extended to lower administrative levels the decentralization of planning and finances introduced in May 1955. For example, on July 19, 1955, the RSFSR's Council of Ministers and, on November 12, 1956, Uzbekistan's government decreed that the Union Republics would allot funds to subordinate administrative-territorial units (Autonomous Republics, area (krai) executive committees, regional executive committees, and municipal executive committees) by specifying only three essential uses (as was the situation in the Union Republics themselves). Local authorities were responsible for distributing the funds for individual purposes. Local authorities also ratified the plans of the local factories and trade cooperatives they managed.[34]

These measures considerably increased the power of functionaries and economic managers in the Union Republics and naturally in Russia. On the periphery, Khrushchev had created a solid base that made its presence known in the conflicts surrounding his claim to power in June 1957. Before events culminated in the decisive trial of strength, however, a new batch of decentralization measures took effect in February 1957, which brought the

Union Republics and other territorial units a greater degree of domestic participation than ever before.

On February 11, 1957, the Economic Commission of the USSR's Council of Nationalities was created and explicitly assigned the task of "considering all aspects of the Union Republics' needs." The commission was to guarantee "that the issues of the republics' economic and socio-cultural development were decided more [than previously] based on their economic, national, and other particularities." The commission consisted of one chairman and thirty members, two from each Union Republic. The Council of Nationalities' deputies from the Autonomous Republics, Autonomous Regions, and national territories (okrug) had the right to participate in the commission's work on issues that concerned their territories. The new institution was to prepare autonomous proposals on "the Union Republics' economic and socio-cultural development" and monitor whether economic plans considered "the tasks of the Union Republics' economic and cultural development."[35] Before 1936, the Presidium of the Council of Nationalities, which Stalin's constitution had abolished, had fulfilled the functions of this commission, which existed until 1966.

The Supreme Soviet's constitutional amendment on February 11, 1957, gave the Union Republics exclusive and final power over how to organize administration of their territories into regions and districts. Previously, any administrative organization in the Union Republics required the approval of the USSR's Supreme Soviet. Now, such approval was only required when a new Autonomous Republic or Autonomous Region was founded.[36] Although this innovation had little practical significance, it satisfied the Union Republics' need for prestige.

In contrast, continuing decentralization of the court system and extension of the Union Republics' legislative competencies were practically relevant. On February 11, 1957, the Supreme Soviet passed a law that gave the Union Republics the power to pass their own judiciary and procedural legislation and to determine their own codes of civil and criminal law. In all sectors, however, the Union reserved the right to pass skeleton laws (*osnovy*).[37] This law reinstituted pre-1936 constitutional conditions. In 1958, the Union passed a skeleton law covering criminal law; in 1961, a skeleton law covering civil law. The Union Republics followed these leads and passed their own codes of civil and criminal law. However, the differences among the Union Republics' civil law codes remained marginal. In contrast to and with the exception of crimes against the state, the individual Union Republics' criminal law codes were quite different from one another. The individual codes of criminal law differed considerably in the definition of crimes and the punishment, particularly in areas in which the Union's skeleton law did not provide binding guidelines.[38]

On February 12, 1957, the Supreme Soviet passed a law making all presiding judges of the Union Republics' Supreme Courts official members of the USSR's Supreme Court.[39] This increased the Union Republics' involvement in their own affairs and re-established a situation that had existed from 1923 to 1938.[40] In addition, the new statute governing the USSR's Supreme Courts[41] awarded the Union Republics' Supreme Courts "considerably expanded" rights. Before the new statute was in effect, only the USSR's Supreme Court had the power to revoke a resolution by a college of a Union Republic's Supreme Court; now, the Presidium of a Union Republic's Supreme Court had the same power. In the Stalin era, the USSR's Supreme Court had the privilege to become involved in and re-evaluate at will any civil and criminal matter pending in any Union Republic court. The statute restricted this privilege to cases in which Union Republic courts' resolutions and rulings infringed on the interests of other Union Republics or conflicted with Union laws. The increased independence of the Union Republics' courts quickly produced "great positive results." Previously, for example, the USSR's Supreme Court had dealt with hundreds of cases each year from Uzbekistan alone; in 1958, the court handled only a dozen criminal and civil matters from the Uzbek SSR. In 1957 and 1958, the USSR's Supreme Court did not reverse a single original ruling or resolution the Uzbek Supreme Court had passed.[42]

In May 1957, the complete reform of industrial administration dwarfed all previous measures directed at reducing Stalinist centralism. This reorganization of economic administration gave the power to run virtually all industry and construction companies to republic authorities—led by the Councils of Ministers. Introducing the territorial principle into economic administration granted more power to the authorities in the non-Russian republics (and, naturally, also in the RSFSR) than ever before.

The CC had already issued several resolutions criticizing the trade principle dominating economic administration because it was impossible for central ministries to manage reasonably and economically 200,000 industrial factories and 100,000 construction sites in all parts of the huge country.[43] The law of May 10, 1957, replaced ministries and central authorities with regional economic councils, which managed all factories and construction sites within an economic district, regardless of what trade they belonged to. In addition to the necessity "of bringing production and management closer together," the Soviets were primarily interested "in expanding the Union Republics' rights for further developing the economy." The Union Republics' Supreme Soviets or their Councils of Ministers created economic regions and corresponding regional economic councils. The law's Article 5 reads, "The Union Republic's Council of Ministers supervises all activities of an economic region's regional economic council." "The USSR's Council of Ministers manages the regional economic councils through the Union

Republics' Councils of Ministers." This gave the Union Republics' Councils of Ministers a key role in managing the economy. The fact that the Soviets officially appointed the Chairmen of the Councils of Ministers to the USSR's Council of Ministers strengthened that key role. Ten all-Union and fifteen Union-Republic ministries disappeared. The Soviets transferred many of their personnel to rural and peripheral areas to work in the newly created regional economic councils.[44]

In addition to the named ministries in Moscow, the Khrushchev government also dissolved all ministries of industry in the Union Republics. A flick of the pen terminated the existence of more than 140 all-Union, Union-Republic, and Republic ministries. Initially, they were replaced by 105 regional economic councils (in 1960, this number was reduced to 101). In 1960, the Soviets also formed economic councils on the republic level in the three largest Union Republics — RSFSR, the Ukraine, and Kazakhstan — to coordinate and supervise local economic councils. From the beginning, the Soviets had organized the other Union Republics, Autonomous Republics, and Autonomous Regions as regional economic districts with only one economic council each. This gave all leadership elites in the non-Russian territories direct access to economic management.[45] Moving economic administration to the Union Republics and their subordinate territorial units not only gave more power to local state bureaucracy but also to local Party leaders because naturally they were responsible for management of the local economic councils.

Only three all-Union ministries — which specialized in production of war materials — remained in economic administration: the Ministry of the Mid-Level Machine Building Industry, the Ministry of Power Plant Construction, and the Ministry for Manufacturing Means of Transportation. In the early 1960s, factories managed by the Union Republics' Councils of Ministers produced 94 percent of the industrial goods.[46] The USSR's state budget also reflected the shift of economic administration from the center to the periphery — although not as drastically. The Union's share of the total budget decreased from its highest level (in peacetime), 79.3 percent in 1952, to its lowest level in the Soviet Union's history, 40.3 percent in 1961. Correspondingly, the Union Republics' share increased from 6.8 percent to 38 percent in the same period, and the share of the subordinate territorial units rose from 13.9 percent to 21.7 percent.[47]

Khrushchev's decentralization policy entailed many unpredictable risks. Nobody — not even Khrushchev — was able to anticipate the consequences this shift of actual power to the non-Russian periphery might bring for the Party's dictatorship. More immediately, however, Khrushchev faced another risk: Stalinists within the CC's Presidium formed a group opposed to Khrushchev's rise to power and determined to act in May 1957 after Khrushchev successfully reorganized economic administration. The

Stalinists were not willing to just sit and watch as Khrushchev and his followers destroyed the central bureaucratic structures that had been the foundation of Stalinist rule since the 1930s. The opposition became more intense, and the Stalinists conspired to overthrow Khrushchev. By the summer of 1957, this group held the majority in the CC's Presidium. Among its most important arguments against Khrushchev's policy was the fear that decentralization of industrial administration would cause chaos and allow local chauvinism (*mestnichestvo*) to prosper. Particularly in the national territories, Stalinists expected trends towards autonomy to arise and strengthen centrifugal forces and "bourgeois nationalism."[48]

The CC's Presidium, which was continuously in session, demanded Khrushchev's resignation. He succeeded, however, in forcing the CC's plenum to convene, and he could reasonably count on a solid majority of its members to support him because of his decentralization measures. Aided by the CC's plenum, Khrushchev surprised the Presidium — a milestone of de-Stalinization — and managed to dispose of some of his opponents. The plenum, which was in session from June 22, 1957 to June 29, 1957, excluded Malenkov, Kaganovich, and Molotov, who allegedly formed an "anti-Party group," from the Presidium and the CC. Shepilov lost his positions as the CC's secretary, candidate for the Presidium, and CC member. Khrushchev's lieutenants developed a long list of this "anti-Party group's" sins and chose a prominent place to accuse its members of having prevented the Party "from amending past distortions of Lenin's nationalities policy." "They [the members of the anti-Party group] were opposed to the expansion of Union Republics' rights in economic and cultural development, legislation, and were even against strengthening the role local soviets played in carrying out these tasks." The "anti-Party group" had "resisted rapid economic and cultural development in the national republics."[49]

The Union Republics heartily applauded Khrushchev for fighting the "anti-Party group." The Ukrainian media were particularly prominent in this effort, and for years, they used this opportunity to articulate Ukrainian interests while settling accounts with the "anti-Party group." On July 12, 1957, *Pravda Ukrainy* wrote, "One of the Party's greatest achievements is in disposing of previous distortions in nationalities policy and in not hesitating to set a course to quickly develop the national republics economically and culturally."[50] Kaganovich in particular became the target of hateful public attacks in the Ukraine. In 1947, Stalin had dispatched him to Kiev for six months to monitor Khrushchev's activities. At the Twenty-second Party Congress, in October 1961, Podgornyi, the head of the Ukrainian Party, called Kaganovich a "real sadist" who, in 1947, "virtually with no cause accused prominent authors and many prominent Party functionaries of nationalism," "simultaneously made himself an idol, and presented himself as the 'leader' of the Ukrainian people."[51]

By eliminating the "anti-Party group," Khrushchev essentially secured his one-man rule. His dependence on the active support of functionaries from the periphery dramatically decreased. All this had an immediate effect on nationalities policy.

However, another aspect of de-Stalinization emphatically documents the new leadership's departure from the mass terror of the Stalin era: rehabilitation of the deported peoples. At the Twentieth Party Congress, in February 1956, Khrushchev said in his "secret speech": "No Marxist-Leninist and no sensible human being, for that matter, can understand how anyone can hold an entire people—including women and children, old people, communists, and Comsomol members—responsible for hostile activities, to inflict mass reprisals on them, and to expose them to hardship and misery for the subversive actions of individuals or small groups."[52] He called these reprisals "abominable." His list of deported peoples, however did not mention the two largest: the Germans and the Crimean Tatars. This was no oversight, and it quickly became apparent that these two peoples did not profit from the rehabilitation as much as the four Caucasian peoples Khrushchev explicitly rehabilitated in his speech: the Karachai, Balkars, Chechens and Ingush, and Kalmyks.

In the summer of 1954, the Soviets began to relax the policy of forced settlement of all deported peoples. In July 1954, the USSR's Council of Ministers issued a resolution "On Repealing Certain Restrictions on the Legal Status of Banished Peoples."[53] The Soviets granted limited mobility to the gainfully employed among the deported people. They removed children under the age of ten (!) from the lists of deported people. On December 13, 1955, a resolution by the Presidium of the USSR's Supreme Soviet made the Germans the first people released from forced settlement.[54] This was probably a gesture of good will towards the Federal Republic of Germany, with which the Soviet Union had just entered into diplomatic relations. The reinstitution of the Germans' freedom to move within the USSR did not include two important restrictions: The Germans were released from their special settlements only if they agreed in writing not to return to their homelands on the Volga, in the Ukraine, or the Caucasus and did not seek return or replacement of property they lost during their deportation.[55]

Four months later, on April 28, 1956, the Presidium of the USSR's Supreme Soviet revoked the policy of forced settlement of the Crimean Tatars, Balkars, Turks, and Khemshil.[56] However, these peoples were not allowed to return to their homelands, nor were their possessions returned that had been confiscated during the deportation.

The Caucasian peoples' movement to return had developed its own dynamics, which the Khrushchev leadership probably could not and did not want to stop during the years when the leadership was making concessions to non-Russian peoples. In the summer of 1954, when the deported peoples perceived the first signs that the Soviets were relaxing their control, at first hundreds, then thousands of families—particularly Chechens and Ingush—set out on their own to return to their homelands. In spite of arrests and compulsory transport back to Central Asia, the number of Chechens and Ingush returning to the Caucasus continued to increase after the Twentieth Party Congress (February 1956) and reached a total of 25,000 to 30,000 by late 1956. On November 24, 1956, the CC resolved to submit to this pressure from below. The resolution said that previous measures had been insufficient and that the rights of the deported peoples had to be reinstituted. Because these peoples were spread over a vast territory, they did not have the prerequisites necessary to develop their economies and cultures fully. As a result, the CC decided to reinstitute the national territories of the Kalmyks, Karachai, Balkars, Chechens and Ingush.[57]

One can assume the Caucasian peoples owed this success to their challenging courage, their indifference to what the Soviets did or did not allow them, and taking advantage of the moment. The Crimean Tatars and Germans, who thought in "more political" terms and were waiting for permission from the authorities, missed this opportune time and, to this very day, have fought in vain to return to their original homelands and to reestablish their national territories.

The Presidium of the RSFSR's Supreme Soviet followed the provisions of the CC resolution and, in January 1957, reestablished the Chechen-Ingush ASSR, formed the Kalmyk Autonomous Region, and converted the Kabardin ASSR into the Kabardino-Balkar ASSR and the Cherkess Autonomous Region into the Karachai and Cherkess Autonomous Region. On February 11, 1957, the USSR's Supreme Soviet passed a law that confirmed this reestablishment of the deported peoples' national autonomy.[58] When the law was presented, A.F. Gorkin, the secretary of the Presidium of the USSR's Supreme Soviet, said the Soviet power "considered the [Balkars', Chechens', Ingush's, Kalmyks', and Karachai's] wish and requests justified and decided to make complete amends for the injustices committed against these peoples."[59] In July 1958, the Soviets upgraded the Kalmyks' Autonomous Region to ASSR and reestablished the status it had before the deportation.[60] Apart from the fact that in 1957, the Soviets had joined the previously separate Autonomous Regions of the Cherkess and Karachai into one Autonomous Region for both peoples, from a constitutional perspective, they had nearly completely reestablished the status quo for these five peoples.[61]

However, the Soviets considerably changed the borders of the most important Chechen and Ingush Autonomous Republic, extending its northern reaches by adding to it a mostly unpopulated strip of steppe north of the Terek. In return, however, the republic had to give up one of its western raions to the North Ossetian ASSR. This raion borders immediately on

Ordzhonikidze, the capital of the North Ossetian ASSR, but it also is one of the most important areas in which Ingush settlement is concentrated. As a result, when they returned from banishment, many Ingush lived outside the borders of their national territory and were not entitled to schools, media, and cultural facilities in their native language. This caused considerable tension, which lasted until the 1970s.

Apparently, the Khrushchev leadership had underestimated the conflicts the peoples' return to the Northern Caucasus would trigger. Hardly anywhere were the authorities able to carry out the plan they had laid out in the CC resolution of December 1956, which called for an orderly, well-organized, and gradual repatriation of the peoples. This plan outlined repatriation of peoples with small populations—Kalmyks, Karachai, and Balkars—over two years, in 1957 and 1958, and of the Chechens and Ingush in four years from, 1957 to 1960.[62]

Although the authorities promised the returning peoples credit, housing, and work, the available means usually did not suffice to facilitate quick integration of the repatriated peoples. In addition, the returnees were not willing to settle in the plains in newly established sovkhozes and kolkhozes but wanted to return to their home towns and villages, demanding that their houses and property be returned to them. The repatriation of Balkars went relatively smoothly. They returned to the thinly populated and, in many cases, fallow mountain villages, from which they had been deported in 1944. By 1959, 36,000 people had returned. By late 1959, 72,700 Kalmyks again lived in their homeland. Many Russians, who had appropriated and lived in Kalmyk houses, hurried to leave Kalmykia.[63]

The return of the Chechens and Ingush caused the gravest and most lasting tensions. On the one hand, their return involved 500,000 people. On the other hand, the Soviets had systematically colonized the depopulated regions after the war. In the repatriation's first year, available housing and employment were not at all sufficient, particularly because many more families returned to their homelands than the plan had envisioned. In the spring of 1957, 77,000 Caucasian settlers—mostly Avars, Dargins, and Ossetians—asked the authorities to relocate them to Daghestan and Ossetia because Chechens and Ingush demanded the return of the houses and homesteads they had previously owned. But even Russians, who lived in the cities, left the Chechen and Ingush ASSR. About 36,000, most of whom were skilled workers, returned to Russia on their own and against the express wishes of Party and state. In a climate of national resentment and personal hate, the return of one group and the displacement of others made public opinion very volatile.

From August 24 to 28, 1958, great disturbances occurred in the capital Groznyi. A comparatively insignificant event—the funeral of a Russian sailor killed in a brawl with Ingush—brought the Russian population to the streets in protest. The demonstrations turned into looting and fist fights between the Russians on the one hand and Chechens and Ingush on the other. People handed out pamphlets asking the Russian population to fight for the "Russian cause" and the Chechens and Ingush to leave the country. After four days, the troops that had arrived reestablished order and peace. However, the Soviets did not try any of the Russian instigators, and the local press continued to complain about the Chechens' and Ingush' nationalist prejudices and "bourgeois nationalism."[64]

Violence also occurred east of Ordzhonikidze, where the Ingush did not accept the fact that this raion was now part of North Ossetia. On February 23, 1973, sixteen years after the Ingush had returned, they demonstrated in Groznyi for several days, protesting discrimination against Ingush in neighboring North Ossetia. The Party leadership in Groznyi received petitions with thousands of signatures. This time, violence was avoided, primarily because high-ranking Ingush Party functionaries and authors supported the demonstrations.[65]

Apparently, deportation and rehabilitation reinforced the peoples' vigor and desire for national self-preservation in spite of great sacrifices. Appendix Table A.1 shows how much the population of the four previously deported North Caucasian peoples increased after 1959. Their birth rates were not only above the Soviet average and far above Slavic and Baltic rates, but the previously deported North Caucasians come out ahead in inner-Soviet comparisons, and only the birth rates of the large Central Asian peoples surpass theirs. The number of Chechens increased from 419,000 in 1959 to 756,000 in 1979. In addition, an unusually high number of these peoples have maintained their national languages. Censuses reveal that 98 percent consider their respective people's language their primary language. In respect to this indicator, they also surpass many nations that have their own Union Republic and nearly all those that have a lower federative status (cf. Appendix Table A.8). The previously deported North Caucasians were among the peoples that most resisted the spread of Russian. After 1959, the percentage of Chechens and Ingush in the Party remained well below the average of other nationalities.[66] Considering all this, we can assume that it is close to impossible to integrate these peoples into Soviet society.

It is possible that the conflicts the Soviet power encountered in repatriating the rehabilitated peoples reinforced the inclination not to allow repatriation of the Germans and Crimean Tatars. For years, the Soviets even delayed their political rehabilitation. They allowed the other peoples to return to their homelands but granted the Germans and Crimean Tatars only a few cultural concessions and some linguistic autonomy. In 1957, the Soviets permitted publication of the Crimean Tatarian newspaper *Lenin bayragy* (*Lenin's Banner*) and the German newspaper *Neues Leben* (*New Life*). Radio Moscow and Radio Alma-Ata began broadcasting weekly programs in German. The Soviets "registered" or legalized a few Lutheran and Catholic congregations.

In 1957, the ministries of education in several Union Republics issued decrees concerning "expanded German lessons" for children of German extraction. This provided the prerequisites for the establishment of primary language German courses for German children attending Russian schools. If enough children were interested, a German teacher was available, and local authorities took the necessary initiative. Actually, only a small minority of German children had the opportunity to participate in primary language German classes. Beginning in the academic year of 1968–1969, similar services began for Crimean Tatarian children. Some schools in Uzbekistan included primary language Crimean Tatarian classes.[67]

Only on August 29, 1964, did the Soviets politically rehabilitate the Soviet Union's Germans. The Presidium of the USSR's Supreme Soviet now declared "accusations" that "the Germans with Soviet citizenship" "had actively helped and supported the German-Fascist aggressors" as "unsubstantiated and a reflection of the tyranny caused by cult of personality around Stalin."[68]

The Crimean Tatars were much more bothersome for Soviet authorities than the Germans. The Crimean Tatars did not wait until the Soviets treated them as equal to the other rehabilitated peoples but, in the late 1950s, began to organize an extensive national movement to return them to the Crimean peninsula. This Crimean-Tatarian movement became evident primarily in thousands of collective and individual letters to every Soviet authority, a permanent people's representation in Moscow, protest gatherings, and an extensive Samizdat. In 1959, the Soviets began to arrest many of the movement's activists (which included practically the whole people), and sentenced them to prison camps. Only on September 5, 1967, did the Presidium of the Supreme Soviet rehabilitate the last of the deported peoples and declare as "unsubstantiated" accusations that "the whole Crimean-Tatarian population" "had actively collaborated."[69] Like the Germans, however, the Crimean Tatars were not permitted to return to their homelands.

Reaction

Until the summer of 1957, Khrushchev pursued a policy of concessions initially intended to look like a return to the nationalities policy of the 1920s. Remarkably, however, he did not revive korenizatsiia although the Soviet behavior in many non-Russian republics seemed as if this policy had again become the Party line. Economic and administrative decentralization were not accompanied by corresponding linguistic and educational measures, which had been the focus of korenizatsiia. In the second half of 1958, Khrushchev's firmly established leadership was already making very clear that they were not interested in continuing the nationalities policy. The dispute was triggered by the language issue, which became even more topical because of the 1958–1959 school reform. In this important area, Khrushchev's leadership was determined not only not to return to the concept of modernization in a hundred languages, but also to make Russian even more dominant in education than before.

In August 1958, an article by former Tadzhik Party head Gafurov, which appeared prominently in the magazine *Kommunist*, signaled a change in course. "Some localities exhibit a tendency to compare the cadres of the local nation to the cadres of other nations. This is an extremely detrimental attitude."[70] A year later, in the same magazine, secretary of the Kazakh CC Dzhandildin criticized even more openly "individual intellectuals," who think "it is necessary to return to the policy of the apparatus' 'korenizatsiia,' which the Soviet state pursued during its first years."[71] Gafurov also lamented the "local chauvinist currents" that had emerged with economic reform and were accompanied "by artificial exaggerations of the national particularities of one or another republic. This made republics think they were entitled to handouts, and they demanded special privileges and large financial contributions to their economies from the all-Union budget."[72] This *Kommunist* article also refers to the final goal of all nations' "continued rapprochement" and "future merging." In previous years, publicity had repressed this goal. The article points out that "learning Russian" was very important because of its status as the "second native tongue of all nations in the land of socialism."[73] This is one of the earliest testimonies to demands to establish Russian as "second native tongue" for all the USSR's peoples. In the early 1960s, propaganda began to repeat this topic over and over.

On November 16, 1958, the CPSU's CC and the USSR's Council of Ministers published "theses" concerning the planned educational reform, under the title, "On Stabilizing the Connections Between School and Life."[74] Thesis 19 included very strange and obscure regulations concerning the language issue, and these seemed particularly democratic at first glance. Parents were to be given a choice between sending their children to schools with instruction either in the child's native language or in Russian. The respective non-Russian language was to be offered as an elective. On the surface, Khrushchev upheld his "Back to Lenin!" principle. Russian classes were not to be obligatory and mandatory. In reality, however, the expectation that Russian classes, which had been mandatory in all national schools since 1938, were open to discussion was not reasonable. This became apparent during the subsequent public discussion of educational reform.

In the public discussions, authors from the Union Republics were surprisingly united in rejecting of Thesis 19's principal premises. No one questioned the necessity of learning Russian, but the Union Republics correctly suspected the intention to push the Union Republics' languages out of Russian schools and opposed this plan. In reality, the "choice" educational reform offered by necessity resulted in Russian schools' abandonment of a Union Republic's language, but did not get Russian classes removed from the curricula of national schools. As a result, Soviet media greatly supported maintaining the language issue's status quo in most republics: Russian as a requirement in national schools and each republic's respective language as a requirement in local Russian schools. In *Pravda,* two prominent Ukrainian writers, M. Rylskyi and M. Bazhan, demanded "obligatory and equal classes in Ukrainian and Russian in all the Ukrainian SSR's schools."[75] Lithuanian Deputy Minister for Lithuanian Education Iu. Kavalauskas wrote, "Most teachers and parents of children attending Russian and Polish schools requested that Lithuanian be a required subject in these schools."[76]

Not everywhere were the voices defending local languages in general education heard equally loudly. The five Asian republics and Moldavia opposed Thesis 19 only weakly; in the Transcaucasian and Baltic Union Republics, however, even educational functionaries and prominent politicians publicly supported maintaining the status quo. In the Ukraine, the press published statements from teachers, writers, and mid-level Party functionaries pleading for Ukrainian to be a requirement in all Ukrainian schools.[77]

The republics' public criticism of Thesis 19 also continued in the USSR's Supreme Soviet on December 23–24, 1958, as it conferred on the education laws. Georgian delegate I.V. Abashidze declared, "Knowledge of the local language is a powerful moral factor in creating brotherly unity among people of different nationalities. . . . We think local languages must be required subjects in all curricula in the republics' schools."[78] The Ukrainian CP's CC secretary S.V. Chervonenko also stated his opposition: "Many years of experience with national education in the republics show that obligatory Russian classes and the local language classes have proven a complete success. . . . Resolving the issue differently seems like a step backwards." Protecting students from too great a work load must not be accomplished by removing the republics' national languages from the curricula.[79] All deputies from the Baltic republics, among them Deputy Chairman of the Latvian Council of Ministers Berklavs and Latvian Second Party Secretary Pelshe, issued similar statements.[80]

In the end, the skeleton education law the Supreme Soviet passed on December 24, 1958, contained no regulations pertaining to the language issue. Moscow, however, pressured the republic governments, with the effect that the Union Republics' implementation statutes that were announced in March and April 1959 contained the regulations of Thesis 19 essentially unrevised. Two Union Republics were notable exceptions. The Azeri education law made Russian compulsory in national schools and Azeri a compulsory subject in Russian schools. The law did not provide for a parents' declaration act. The Latvian education law contained no regulations pertaining to the language issue. However, at the Supreme Soviet's previous session in Riga, Deputy Chairman of the Council of Ministers Berklavs had made it very clear that "our republic's eight-grade school absolutely requires the continuation of traditional classes in three languages — Latvian, Russian, and one foreign language."[81]

Khrushchev's leadership had tolerated public protest against the new language provision. But the leaders perceived that two Union Republics were openly deviating from the official course as a provocation. In July 1959, Khrushchev visited Riga to remove Berklavs from office and to initiate an extensive purge of the Latvian Party and state apparatus. On August 11, the Latvian Supreme Soviet passed an unpublished resolution "Concerning Some Issues in the Latvian SSR's Educational System," which aligned Latvia with official Soviet policy. A joint resolution of the CC and Council of Ministers had already put Azerbaidzhan back on track in June 1959: Parents were to decide whether their children were to learn Russian or Azeri. Extensive purges were the price this republic government paid for its independence and this political demonstration.[82]

The education laws signaled a change in the overall thrust of nationalities policy, and purges quickly spread to nearly all Union Republics. Of course, educational reform and the language issue no longer were the only issues at stake, but the majority of concessions granted since 1953 were in danger. On the whole, however, it seems that in the non-Russian Union Republics, the immediate effects of the education laws on Russian classes or national language classes were minor. Despite the fierce disputes and the ultimate anchoring of Thesis 19 in the education laws of all Union Republics, practically nothing changed: The Union Republics did not implement language regulations.[83] They did not give parents the privilege of deciding whether their children were to learn Russian, nor did they permit Russian parents living outside of Russia to choose whether their children were to attend classes in the local language. At least in the Baltic and Transcaucasian Union Republics, as well as in the Ukraine, both languages remained mandatory because of instructions issued by subordinate educational organs.

Nor did anything change for Russian children — probably with the exception of those in Central Asia and Kazakhstan — who did not become proficient in the local languages although they were required to attend classes in the national languages. The 1970 census, which was the first to produce such data, demonstrated that the Russians are the least proficient in foreign languages of all the USSR's peoples. Only 3 percent of the Russians (= 3.8 million people) claimed to be fluent in another of the USSR's languages, and 2.37 million of them claimed to speak Ukrainian. Competency in one of the USSR's non-Slavic languages was an exception among Russians although they attended mandatory classes in schools outside the RSFSR.

De-Stalinization

Only 3.8 percent of the 1.473 million Russians in Uzbekistan, 7.6 percent of the 0.51 million Russians in Azerbaidzhan, and 17 percent of the 0.7 million Russians in Latvia reported they were fluent in the local language.[84] These data best document the failure of the early Soviet nationalities policy. The Soviets had designed many measures requiring all Russians to become fluent in local languages. During the thaw, some national communists believed the Party would return to this strategy. In 1956, the CC Bureau of the Latvian CP issued a resolution requiring executives of the Party, soviets, and economy to be proficient in Latvian and Russian.[85] The reaction beginning in 1958 left no doubts that the Khrushchev government was not willing to accept these national communists' demands. Secretary of the Kazakh CC Dzhandildin wrote, "A short while ago, our republic's citizens explicitly condemned statements by some intellectuals who said that only people fluent in Kazakh should be eligible to work in positions of responsibility in Kazakhstan...."[86] The language chauvinism of the Russians originates from imperial thinking and, at the same time, reinforces it.

The published versions of the education laws do not mention that the most important innovation in language policy was to repress and, finally, nearly completely do away with teaching in non-Russian languages in general schools within the RSFSR. Relevant regulations were either included in an unpublished section of the RSFSR's education law of April 16, 1959,[87] or — the more probable alternative—in unpublished normative acts by the RSFSR's Ministry of Education and the authorities in the national territories subordinated to it. Numerous public accounts leave no doubt that the transition to teaching in Russian has accelerated in the RSFSR's national schools since the end of the 1950s. At the same time, most native languages have continued to exist as school subjects. "Most of the RSFSR's Autonomous Republics, Autonomous Regions, and National Territories honor parents' wishes and very actively promote national schools teaching in Russian on different grade levels." In the academic year 1962–1963, 27 percent of all the RSFSR's non-Russian elementary school children, 53 percent of children in grades 5–8, and 66 percent of the children in grades 9–10 were taught in Russian.[88]

What Khrushchev's government praised as a promising socialist accomplishment, Stalinist legislation had considered "wrong" and "detrimental." The resolution of the CC and the Council of People's Commissars of March 13, 1938, which introduced mandatory teaching of the Russian language, said that "classes in schools in the national republics and regions are primarily in the native language. Thus the exceptions to this rule in some of the RSFSR's Autonomous Republics can only be temporary, and the tendency to convert Russian from a subject to a medium of teaching and, as a result, to compromise the native language, is detrimental and wrong."[89]

Karelians had already lost all native language schools by 1958; Kabards and Balkars by 1965–1966; and Kalmyks by 1968.[90] Soviet data from 1958 and 1972 lead to a comparison with the way the RSFSR's national schools handled the issue of what language to teach in. However, these data only reveal which grade levels the individual peoples taught in the local language or Russian; they do not show how many students were taught in each respective language. In 1958, ten-grade middle schools taught Tatars and Bashkirs in their native languages; incomplete middle schools (grades 1–7) existed for Buriats, Chuvash, Komi, Komipermiaks, Koreans, Mari, Mordvinians, Tuvinians, Udmurts, and Yakuts. The following peoples could attend elementary classes (grades 1–4) in their native language: Abazins, Altai, Adygei, Balkars, Chechens, Cherkess, Khakass, Ingush, Kabards, Kalmyks, Karachai, Ossetians, and Daghestan's nationalities (Avars, Dargins, Kumyk, Lezgins, Lak, Nogai, and Tabasarans). In addition, the nationalities of the far north received native-language instruction on the preschool level and in first and second grade if their language had a writing system (Nenets, Evenks, Khants, Chukchi, Nanai, Koriaks, Eskimoes, and Evens).

By 1972, most peoples had to accept a considerable reduction in native-language instruction. The native languages of the far northern nationalities completely disappeared from schools as the medium of teaching. Whereas previously, native-language instruction had been provided through fourth grade, now this was only the case through third grade for Altai and Khakass, through second grade for Dargins, Kumyk, Lezgins, Lak, and Tabasarans, only in first grade for Avars, or no longer at all for Adygei, Balkars, Chechens, Cherkess, Ingush, Kabards, Kalmyks, Karachai, and Ossetians. Buriat seven-grade schools started using native language for teaching only the first six grades, Chuvash schools the first four grades, and Komi, Komipermiaks, Mari, Mordvinian, and Udmurt schools the first three grades. Only Tuvinians and Yakuts retained the opportunity to be taught in their native languages for all seven grades. Tatars and Bashkirs preserved their native languages through their ten-grade middle schools.[91]

The data clearly reveal that educational policy gradually moved towards stripping the RSFSR's non-Russian languages of their status as a teaching medium. Most nationalities maintaining four-grade native-language schools lost them in the 1960s; most seven-grade native-language schools shrank to three-grade schools. However, native languages remained a subject in all national schools through eighth or tenth grade. Only in the national schools of the peoples from the far north did local languages disappear as an academic subject above the elementary level. After 1958, the Soviets not only forced the adoption of Russian as the teaching medium in the RSFSR's national schools, but the ubiquitous Russian schools tried to enroll non-Russian students, explaining to the parents that their children had a better chance for advancement if they attended Russian schools. In addition, Russian schools were better equipped. Like the Russian population, Russian schools were located primarily in the cities of the ASSR and AR. As a result, the percentage of non-Russian students attending Russian schools increased in the 1960s. In 1961–1962, only 6 percent of the Tatar children living in the Tatar ASSR's cities attended schools that taught in Tatar.[92]

Party and state efforts to establish Russian in the RSFSR's public life did not remain limited to education. Although the Soviets did not publish any statistical data, Soviet scholarly literature generally explains that the ASSR, AR, and National Territories converted to conducting their correspondences in Russian in the 1960s. This not only affected academia and technology but particularly economics, administration, and the legal system.[93]

The purges that began in the Union Republics in 1958–1959 showed not only that the reaction would affect the new course in language policy, but that the period of concessions was over in general. The wave of removing from office high-ranking Party functionaries in the Union Republics began in Turkmenistan in December 1958 and—with interruptions and changing focuses—continued until 1961. Unlike events during the Stalin era, arrests and convictions were the exception. The Soviets demoted some high-ranking Party functionaries and expelled others from the Party. For most of these functionaries, this meant the end of their careers, but not the end of their lives as it would have before. Despite the relative "leniency" Khrushchev showed in removing high-ranking cadres, this turn-about quickly destroyed the support he had systematically developed in the national republics until 1957. He disappointed expectations and hopes he had created.

Khrushchev's first victim, Turkmenian Party chief S. Babaev, was a particularly impressive example of this political turnabout. In the wake of the new nationalities policy, this Turkman had become first Party secretary in Ashkhabad in 1956. As early as in December 1957, he published an article that proudly reported that 70 percent of Turmenistan's Party functionaries were Turkmen, as opposed to only about 50 percent five years earlier. All first secretaries of the Party's rural raion committees and all chairmen of the raions' executive committees were local nationals. Nevertheless, Babaev complained that korenizatsiia—a term he did not use—was not progressing fast enough. Only 18.8 percent of the students enrolled in the six technical schools for industrial professions were Turkmen. At the state university in Ashkhabad, the number was at least 52.6 percent. The shortage of high-ranking cadres in industry, agriculture, and construction could be relieved only "if more and more local-national specialists were employed in factories and at construction sites."[94] Only a year later, Khrushchev removed from office Babaev and his high-ranking supporters in the Turkmenian Party and state and expelled them from the Party, charging them with nationalism and "mechanical" favoritism towards national cadres.[95]

In March 1959, the Uzbek CC's first secretary, S. Kamalov, was accused of false cadre policy and "favoring nationalist movements," and was removed from office. Also, CC secretary for ideology, Kh. Tursunov, was forced to resign. In Tashkent, the winner was Sh. Rashidov who held the office of Uzbek Party chief from March 1959 until his death on October 31, 1983. This made him one of the longest-lasting republican Party chiefs in the history of the USSR. From 1959 to 1961, he confirmed his reputation of being a reliable tool of Moscow by conducting extensive purges. He replaced dozens of Uzbek ministers and heads of agencies with Russians: ninety-nine of 564 directors of large industrial facilities; many secretaries of the Party committees in the raions, cities, and regions; and 214 secretaries of primary Party organizations lost their positions. Five of the nine first secretaries of the regional Party committees, all of whom were Uzbeks, were forced to resign. Even many Russians who had grown up in Uzbekistan and held prominent positions were replaced by Russians from the RSFSR; this was particularly true for the judicial system and the KGB. In a closed meeting of functionaries on February 4, 1961, Rashidov thanked the Moscow leadership and the KGB organs of the Slavic republics "for eliminating nationalist elements on time and saving the Uzbek people from imperialist attempts to subjugate it once more."

Accusations of nationalism continued to revolve around personnel policy. The reprimanded had assigned local nationals to responsible positions preferentially. The Soviets also accused them of cultural nationalism, conserving or reviving old Muslim traditions, favoring Muslim religious institutions, and propagandizing the superiority of the Uzbek life style and culture over Soviet-Russian ideals. Indeed, during the "thaw" even the Uzbek establishment returned to practicing undisturbed and openly, such traditional customs as circumcision of male infants, religious weddings and funerals, or collection of offerings for mosques. Because these traditions documented Uzbek affiliation with Muslim culture, Stalin had forced them underground.[96]

In July 1959, the wave of purges began to sweep into Azerbaidzhan and Latvia, the two Union Republics that had not conformed with education legislation. The most prominent victims in Baku were the Azeri CC's first secretary, I.D. Mustafaev, and the chairman of the Azeri Supreme Soviet's Presidium, I.A. Ibragimov.[97] In Latvia, the list of removed Nomenklatura functionaries was particularly long. There, the purge also affected apparatuses outside Party and state. The "rotation of cadres" began with the removal of the Deputy Chairman of the Council of Ministers, Berklavs in July 1959. In November, the Chairman of the Council of Ministers, V. Latsis and Party chief I. Kalnberzinsh lost their positions. However, Kalnberzinsh retained some of his positions and took over as Chairman of the Supreme Soviet's Presidium in Riga—in comparison to the position of first secretary of the Latvian CC, this was a second-string office. The new Party chief, A. Pelshe, accused the reprimanded functionaries of "national limitedness and anti-state local patriotism." "In some places, cadres were chosen based on their nationality or whether they spoke the local national language. When cadres were transferred, many non-Latvian functionaries saw their rights violated. There were suggestions to increase investment in consumer goods industries that produced goods consumed primarily within the republic, and to reduce machine building and car building necessary for the whole country." The removed politicians had also resisted "using laborers and specialists from other republics."[98] This was quite true: Mass immigration of Slavs to the Baltic republics ended in 1953. However, the number of immigrants to Latvia unexpectedly jumped to 26,800 in 1956, surpassing the number of immigrants in the previous six years. In the Latvian Party and state apparatus, opposition formed to this development and to quickly increasing investment in heavy industry. Latvian economists from the State Planning Commission (*Gosplan*) and the Latvian Academy of Sciences' Institute for Economy supported prominent functionaries in their opposition. Economic planners thought forcing heavy industry would harm Latvia's balanced economic development. Instead they called for more support for consumer goods industries. At the same time, in the summer of 1957, Latvia's communist press began using threatening terms of warning against the dangers of "national communism," which was in reality nothing but "an ingenious form of bourgeois nationalism." Among the expelled functionaries were the Deputy Chairman of the Latvian Gosplan, E. Mukins; the director of the Institute for Economy P. Dzerve; and his deputy, P. Treiis.

The wave of expulsions lasted through 1960 and also swept through the ranks of labor union functionaries and Komsomol. Russians took over many positions previously held by Latvians. In Riga, not a single Latvian remained to head departments in the CC apparatus. The Soviets expelled a total of several thousand Party members.[99]

In May 1961, the head of the Moldavian Party was also replaced. I.I. Bodiul took the place of Z.T. Serdiuk. As in other Union Republics, the fall of prominent politicians was accompanied by vehement attacks on the cultural intelligentsia, cultural functionaries, individual magazines, or historical accounts. Most accusations revolved around "nationalistic tendencies," "national limitedness," and "idealization of the past."[100] In Kirgizistan in 1959 and 1960, CC first secretary I. Razzakov vehemently attacked local-national intellectuals, who had rehabilitated the Kirgiz poets Moldo Kylych (1860–1917) and Kasy Tynystan (who was shot in 1934) during the "thaw." This was "regression to bourgeois nationalism." However, Razzakov's attack could not save the Party chief. In May 1961, he left his office to "assume different activities." His successor was T. Usubaliev.[101]

The fall of the Tadzhik leadership in April 1961 developed into an extensive scandal, which *Pravda* covered in relative detail. The paper accused first secretary T. Uldzhabaev of "incorrect practices in selecting and deploying cadres, cheating Party and state." "Executive cadres were chosen strictly according to nationality, kinship, and personal devotion." For years and on a grand scale, the republic's leadership falsified statistics on cotton harvests. "First, incorrect reports on plan fulfillment were fabricated with crooked data, direct forgery, and pressure on kolkhoz chairmen and directors of cotton mills. Then an unbelievable fuss was made over these reports: Festive demonstrations and meetings took place, celebratory speeches were made, and a flood of congratulatory telegrams poured in."[102] The Soviets stripped the CC's first secretary, the second secretary, P. Obnosov, and the Chairman of the Council of Ministers, N. Dodkhudoev of all functions and expelled them from the Party. Dozens of "leading functionaries" joined them. D. Rasulov became first secretary in Tadzhikistan and held this office until his death on April 4, 1982.

During the following two decades, the Party's political course was remarkably consistent. Typically, many Party leaders in the Union Republics, who owed their positions to Khrushchev's reaction, remained in office into the 1980s (Bodiul, Rasulov, Rashidov, Usubaliev). In the Ukraine, no "rotation of cadres" occurred from 1959 to 1961. This again documents Khrushchev's special relationship with his native land.

When the "thaw" in the nationalities policy ended, however, two important architects of this policy lost their positions at the center of power: A.I. Kirichenko and N. Mukhitdinov. We have already analyzed Kirichenko's rise and fall in connection with Khrushchev's Ukrainian lobby. From 1955 to 1957, the Uzbek Mukhitdinov had been first secretary in Tashkent; in 1956, he became a candidate to the Presidium of the CPSU's CC. In 1957, Khrushchev brought him to Moscow and promoted him to full member of the Presidium and secretary of the CC. Consequently, Mukhitdinov belonged to the inner circle of power. At the Twenty-second Party Congress in October 1961, he lost these responsibilities and, in 1966, he was expelled from the CPSU's CC.[103]

At the Twenty-second Party Congress, a new Party program was announced which adopted a tone clearly contradictory to Khrushchev's words and actions before 1957. The speech, in which Khrushchev introduced the Party program, was remarkable and had serious consequences even if the rhetoric did not reappear in the text of the Party program: "In the USSR, a new historical community of people of different nationalities and who share common characteristics has arisen — the Soviet people. These nationalities share a common socialist motherland, the USSR; a common economic base, socialist economy; a common class structure; a common philosophy, Marxism-Leninism; a common goal, the development of communism; and many common spiritual and psychological features." Khrushchev applied Stalin's familiar definition of the term "nation" to the Soviet people—of course, without referring to its author. This triggered an ideological revision that developed during the two following decades. Again, since 1964, Soviet leaders have been quiet about who started this revision. Only one characteristic Stalin had attributed to a nation did Khrushchev not apply to the Soviet people—the common language. However, Khrushchev referred to Russian as "the peoples' second native language, the medium of international communication and of every nation's and nationality's access to the cultural accomplishments of all the USSR's peoples and to world culture."

Now, the two "dialectic" processes of "universal development of every nation" and "drawing-together of the socialist nations," were characterized as "interrelated, progressive tendencies." This was fundamentally novel terminology because Soviet ideology had so far always assumed that the nations' "development" or "blossoming" and their "drawing together" would occur in two consecutive periods. Now, the Soviets presented them as simultaneous processes. The logic required to define this terminology more closely demanded some contortions, but in practice, this new ideology was well suited to legitimize assimilatory policy.[104]

On the one hand, the Party program said, "Under socialism, the nations will flourish, their sovereignty will be assured." On the other hand, it said, "The borders among the Union Republics within the USSR are increasingly losing the significance they used to have." The future would "be marked by further drawing-together of the nations and the accomplishment of complete unity...." The Party program avoided the ominous term, "merger of the nations," and unlike Khrushchev in his speech, did not mention Russian as a "second native tongue." The program toned down the phrase: "Russian has practically become the common means of communication for all the USSR's peoples."[105]

Following the Twenty-second Party Congress, historical, legal, and philosophical magazines started a vehement and sometimes polemic discussion about the present condition of the multi-national Soviet society, its prospects for the future, and the socialist nations' "flourishing" and "drawing-together." Some participants in this discussion took positions that probably would not have gotten past the censors in the second half of 1953 because of Great-Russian chauvinism. "National states and the federation in general" had "served their historical function" and "the complete constitutional merger of nations" is "a matter of the foreseeable future."[106] "The intensive and continuously accelerating process of drawing-together of the nations already exhibits ... certain elements of merger."[107]

However, this position met with considerable resistance even from Soviet experts and did not find its way into official Party documents. The Party line and the majority of the scholarly publications continued to maintain that the present period was not witnessing a merger of the USSR's peoples and that, as Lenin had predicted, this would only happen on a worldwide scale after the victorious revolution. Some other arguments by the proponents of assimilation, however, prevailed. Their claim that presently "the process of the peoples' drawing-together was the prominent one" in the "dialectic unity" of "flourishing" and "drawing-together" became the accepted ideological terminology.[108]

Khrushchev began to restrict the decentralization measures of 1954–57 even in the area of economic administration. His intention was to revoke them. He knew from the beginning that opponents of the measures were correct in warning of the peoples' intentions of becoming self-sufficient, in warning of economic local patriotism, and of neglecting the interests of the Union in favor of those of the national republics.[109] But Khrushchev's leadership underestimated the dangers that the transfer of operative economic competencies to the periphery posed to a Party dictatorship conceived to be centralized. These competencies not only strengthened local and national organs of economic administration, but also contributed to the growth of a new self-confidence within the national republics. National and territorial autonomy were about to overcome their status as propaganda slogans and become reality.

At the CC's June plenum in 1959, Khrushchev gave examples: "During the first semi-annual period ending on June 1, the Kazakh SSR met 111 percent of its meat production quota; 28 percent of its delivery quota to the All-Union fund, but 95 percent of the quota for local supplies. In the same period, the Ukrainian SSR met 95 percent of its meat production quota, delivered 47 percent of its delivery quota to the All-Union fund, but 92.1 percent of its own needs. Violations of Party and state discipline and examples of local patriotism (*mestnichestvo*) also occurred in the Kaliningrad region, and in the Latvian, Kirgiz, and Uzbek Republics."[110]

In late 1962, recentralization measures began to affect economic administration. In November, the Economic Council of the USSR was founded as the supreme authority for coordinating the activities of the territorial economic councils.[111] Before 1962, only twelve State Committees existed for industrial administration; by 1963, their number had grown to thirty. They were organized according to trades and served the same function as had the ministries of industry before 1957.[112] Also in November 1962, the Central Asian Economic Council was founded to supervise the economic councils of Uzbekistan, Kirgizistan, Tadzhikistan, and Turkmenistan. Simultaneously, the Party created a CC Bureau for Central Asia and one for the Transcaucasus.[113] These organizational measures climaxed on March

13, 1963, with the creation of the Supreme Economic Council of the USSR as the "supreme state organ controlling industry and construction."[114] This new super organ was not only to supervise all existing economic councils, but also the USSR's State Planning Committee (*Gosplan*), the USSR's State Committee for Construction (*Gosstroi*), and all State Committees for managing trade industries.[115]

This reform of the reform considerably reduced the competencies of the republican Councils of Ministers. Local economic councils that had been under the exclusive supervision of these Councils of Ministers became Union-Republic organs. They were also supervised by the USSR's Economic Council, which in turn was supervised by the USSR's Supreme Economic Council. In practice, this double supervision meant that the real supervising authority rested with the USSR's Economic Council and the USSR's Supreme Economic Council.[116]

The parallel structure of the trade principle and vertical supervision on the one side and of the territorial principle and horizontal supervision on the other created the most intricate economic bureaucracy that had ever existed in the Soviet Union and an inextricable variety of competencies. Khrushchev's reaction was intended to reestablish centralism without stripping the republics of all the competencies they had only won a few years earlier. The resulting opacity and antagonism among the apparatuses made it easier for the new Brezhnev leadership to reverse everything Khrushchev had accomplished in decentralizing economic administration one year after his fall: Brezhnev dissolved all the economic councils and reinstituted the system of economic administration organized vertically by trades and managed by ministers.[117] Essentially, this was the economic administration created in the early 1930s. These structures still survive.

Khrushchev's experiments had failed. Only insignificant economic branches remained under the supervision of pure republic ministries and, as a result, under the Union Republics' Councils of Ministers. In the RSFSR in 1972, the following republic ministries existed: local industries, automobile transport, road construction, civil housing, communal housing, inland navigation, fuel industries, service industries, and social welfare.[118]

After Khrushchev's fall, centralization and recentralization measures began to restrict the national republics' competencies in other areas as well. In January 1960, the Ministry of the Interior lost its status as a Union-Republic organ and became a pure republic ministry, making the administration of public order the responsibility of the Union Republics. In July 1966, this decision was reversed. Until 1968, the ministries were called the Ministry for the Protection of Public Order.[119] In August 1966, for the first time in the Soviet Union's history, the Soviets created a central Ministry for Education in the USSR, among whose responsibilities was the supervision of general education and teacher training. Up to this point, these tasks had been the responsibility of pure republic ministries, which now became Union-Republic ministries.[120]

Finally, with some delay the Soviets reestablished the Ministry of Justice as a Union-Republic organ in August 1970.[121] In his era, Khrushchev had completely dissolved the ministries of justice and had distributed their responsibilities among the Supreme Courts and Legal Commissions. Now, the Soviets restored pre-1956 conditions. On the level of the Union and the republics, they returned the supervision of legal administration, including courts, notaries, lawyers, and lawyer training, to ministries of justice.

Was the reversal of Khrushchev's reforms and decentralization measures a return to Stalinism? Without doubt, the Soviets reinstituted most of the Stalin era's organizational structures in the power bureaucracies. Nevertheless the return to the old tools of power was not a return to totalitarian dictatorship. Two factors essentially prevented such a return: First, in a kind of "election capitulation," the Brezhnev-Kosygin leadership, installed in October 1964, had to promise to maintain the "stability of the cadres." This prevented a policy of "continuous purges" (Brzezinski), like Stalin's, or continuous reorganization of all apparatuses like Khrushchev's. This nullified an important prerequisite for totalitarian dictatorship: unrestricted and arbitrary power of disposal over all institutions of power, including the Politburo. Second, Soviet society was undergoing fundamental changes, which did not make a return to Stalinism impossible but made it considerably more difficult. The next chapter will analyze how these changed social conditions affected nationalities policy. We will see that this policy, which so far had primarily been active and offensive, now was often only a reaction to social changes.

Notes

1. *Chruschtschow erinnert sich,* p. 335.
2. The resolution of June 12, 1953, has never been published. The quote comes from the version in the letter seventeen Latvian Communists wrote to the international Communist movement in the summer of 1971 (AS 1042, in German: Lewytzkyi, *Politische Opposition in der Sowjetunion,* pp. 215–230). Khrushchev's memoirs and the actual Soviet measures in the summer of 1953 confirm the resolution's authenticity.
3. *Chruschtschow erinnert sich,* p. 335.
4. *Pravda,* June 13, 1953.
5. *Pravda,* June 18, 1953.
6. *Pravda,* June 28, 1953.
7. Misiunas/Taagepera, *Baltic States,* p. 271.
8. S. Iakubovskaia, "Obrazovanie i rastsvet sotsialisticheskikh natsii v SSSR," in: *Kommunist,* 9/1953, pp. 29–45; the quotes are on p. 44.

9. *Literaturnaia gazeta,* April 21, 1953.
10. Ch.H. Fairbanks, "National Cadres as a Force in the Soviet System: The Evidence of Beriia's Career. 1949–1953," in: *Soviet Nationality Policies and Practices,* pp. 144, 172.
11. *Izvestiia,* July 12, 1953; Fairbanks, op. cit., p. 174.
12. *Chruschtschow erinnert sich,* p. 342.
13. *Pravda,* December 24, 1953.
14. S. Bialer, "How Russians Rule Russia," in: *Problems of Communism,* XIII, 5/1964, pp. 46f.
15. Sullivant, *Soviet Politics and the Ukraine,* pp. 288f.; V.K. Sulzhenko, *Internatsionalizm na etape razvitogo sotsializma. Osushchestvlenie leninskoi natsionalnoi politiki KPSS na Ukraine* (Lvov, 1981), p. 35.
16. Y. Bilinsky, "Assimilation and Ethnic Assertiveness Among Ukrainians of the Soviet Union," in: *Ethnic Minorities,* p. 152.
17. Ibid., pp. 147–151; Bilinsky, *Second Soviet Republic,* pp. 233–249; Lewytzkyi, *Sowjetukraine,* pp. 154–174.
18. *Pravda,* January 12, 1954; May 22, 1954; May 23, 1954; J.S. Reshetar, "The Significance of the Soviet Tercentenary of the Pereyaslav Treaty," in: *Annals of the Ukrainian Academy of Arts and Sciences in the U.S.,* vol. IV (1955), pp. 981–994.
19. *Pravda,* February 27, 1954.
20. *Istoriia sovetskoi konstitutsii (v dokumentakh),* p. 889.
21. Ibid., pp. 891f.
22. Ibid., p. 913.
23. "Resolution of the CPSU's CC and the USSR's Council of Ministers on the Transfer of Factories from many Different Economic Branches to the Union Republics' Management and on the Execution of Connected Measures of May 30, 1956," in: Ibid., pp. 924–927.
24. Ibid., pp. 930f.
25. Ibid., p. 925.
26. Ibid., p. 927.
27. Article 67 of the 1923–1924 constitution, in: *Istoriia sovetskoi konstitutsii (v dokumentakh),* p. 472.
28. G. Brunner, "Die Reform der sowjetischen Justizverwaltung," in: *Recht in Ost und West,* XV, 1971, p. 152.
29. *XX sezd KPSS. Stenograficheskii otchet,* vol. 2 (Moscow, 1956), p. 422.
30. M.I. Piskotin, *Sovetskoe biudzhetnoe pravo* (Moscow, 1971), pp. 191f.
31. Bilinsky, *Second Soviet Republic,* p. 19.
32. "Resolution of the Council of Ministers of the USSR on Changing the Regulations Concerning State Planning and Financing of the Union Republics' Economy," on May 5, 1955, in: *Direktivy KPSS po khoziaistvennym voprosam,* vol. IV, pp. 400–417.

33. "Law for the USSR's and the Union Republics' Budgetary Rights of October 30, 1959," in: *VVS SSSR 1959*, No. 44, art. 221, article 20.

34. M.I. Piskotin, *Sovetskoe biudzhetnoe pravo* (Moscow, 1971), pp. 111f.; Sh.R. Rashidov, "Leninskaia natsionalnaia politika v deistvii," in: *VI KPSS*, 1/1959, p. 56.

35. "Resolution of the Council of Nationalities of the USSR's Supreme Soviet Concerning the Establishment of an Economic Commission of the Council of Nationalities," on February 11, 1957, in: *Istoriia sovetskoi konstitutsii (v dokumentakh). Prilozhenie*, pp. 6f.

36. "Law of the USSR's Supreme Soviet, Concerning the Transfer of Decisions About the Administrative-Territorial Organization into Regions and Krais to the Union Republics' Competence," on February 11, 1957, in: ibid., pp. 5f.

37. "Law of the USSR's Supreme Soviet, Concerning the Transfer of Legislation on the Structure of the Union Republics' Judiciary, the Passing of Codes of Civil, Criminal, and Procedural Law into the Power of the Union Republics," on February 11, 1957, in: ibid., p. 4.

38. J.N. Hazard, "Statutory Recognition of Nationality Differences in the USSR," in: *Soviet Nationality Problems*, pp. 91–98.

39. "Law of the USSR's Supreme Soviet, Concerning the Confirmation of the Rules on the USSR's Supreme Court and the Changes in and Amendments to Articles 104 and 105 of the USSR's Constitution," on February 12, 1957, in: ibid., p. 10.

40. "Rules About the USSR's Supreme Court," of November 23, 1923, article 6 (Istoriia sovetskoi konstitutsii [v dokumentakh], p. 449) and "Law of the USSR's Supreme Soviet About the Structure of the Judiciary of the USSR, the Union and Autonomous Republics, of August 16, 1938, Article 65 (ibid., p. 801).

41. Cf. note 39.

42. Sh.R. Rashidov, "Leninskaia natsionalnaia politika v deistvii," in: *VI KPSS*, 1/1959, p. 53.

43. Resolution of the CPSU's CC plenum: "Issues Concerning the Improvement of the Management of the USSR's Economy," December 1956, in: *Direktivy KPSS po khoziaistvennym voprosam*, vol. 4, pp. 674–677; "Resolution by the CPSU's CC Plenum About Further Perfecting the Organization of the Management of Industry and Construction," of February 14, 1957, in: ibid., pp. 679–686.

44. "Law by the USSR's Supreme Soviet Concerning the Further Perfecting of the Organization of the Management of Industry and Construction," of May 10, 1957, in: ibid., pp. 732–738.

45. M. Fainsod, *Wie Ruland regiert wird* (Cologne, 1965), pp. 440–442.

46. Sh. B. Batyrov, *Formirovanie i razvitie sotsialisticheskikh natsii v SSSR* (Moscow, 1962), p. 257.

47. Penkaitis, *Der Finanzausgleich in der Sowjetunion,* pp. 110f.
48. S.A. Billon, "Centralization of Authority and Regional Management," in: *Soviet Economy in Regional Perspective,* p. 224.
49. "Resolution of the Plenum of the CPSU's CC Concerning the Anti-Party Group, G.M. Malenkov, L.M. Kaganovich, V.M. Molotov, June, 22–29, 1957," in: *KPSS v rezoliutsiiakh i resheniiakh,* vol. 7, pp. 267–273.
50. Quoted from Lewytzkyj, *Sowjetische Nationalitätenpolitik nach Stalins Tod,* p. 37.
51. *XXII s-ezd KPSS. Stenograficheskii otchet,* vol. 1 (Moscow, 1962), p. 280.
52. *Chruschtschow erinnert sich,* p. 565.
53. As they did with most other normative acts associated with the rehabilitation of banned peoples, the Soviets did not publish this resolution. Most Party and government resolutions are quoted from Nekrich, *Punished Peoples,* pp. 129ff. The author relies on unpublished Soviet dissertations.
54. The text of this legislative act, which the Soviets also have not published in the USSR, is in: *Osteuropa–Recht,* IV, 1958, p. 223.
55. Ibid.
56. Nekrich, *Punished Peoples,* p. 134. The term "Turks" refers to Turkicized and Islamicized Georgians in Meskhetia on the Turkish border, whom the Soviets had deported on November 15, 1944, together with the Turkicized Armenians (=Khemshils) and Kurds living there–a total of 200,000 people–to Central Asia (Conquest, *Nation Killers,* pp. 48f., 64f.).
57. Nekrich, *Punished Peoples,* p. 136.
58. *Pravda,* February 12, 1957.
59. Ibid.
60. *VVS SSSR,* 1958, No. 17, article 912.
61. Cf. the two maps in: Conquest, *Nation Killers,* pp. 45, 159.
62. Nekrich, *Punished Peoples,* p. 136.
63. Ibid., pp. 139–143.
64. Ibid., pp. 144–154. The details of the Groznyi excesses were made public only by Nekrich's book twenty years after the fact. These excesses were among the most violent clashes in the post-Stalin era. An earlier, deviating report by the Samizdat: *Ferment in the Ukraine,* p. 104.
65. Ibid., pp. 158–160.
66. Carrère d'Encausse, *L'Empire éclaté,* p. 139; Appendix, Table 15.
67. Sheehy, *Crimean Tatars, Volga Germans, and Meskhetians,* pp. 12, 15.
68. *VVS SSSR,* 1964, No. 52, article 592; in German: *Jahrbuch für Ostrecht,* VI, 1965, pp. 58f.
69. *VVS SSSR,* 1967, No. 36, article 493; in German: *WGO. Monatshefte für osteuropäisches Recht,* IX, 1967, p. 320.
70. B. Gafurov, "Uspekhi natsionalnoi politiki KPSS i nekotorye voprosy internatsionalnogo vospitaniia," in: *Kommunist,* 11/1958, pp. 10–24; the

quote is on pp. 17f. Gafurov was first party secretary in Tadzhikistan from 1946 to 1956.

71. N. Dzhandildin, "Nekotorye voprosy internatsionalnogo vospitaniia," in: *Kommunist,* 13/1959, pp. 30–43, the quote is on p. 34.

72. Gafurov, op. cit., p. 18.

73. Ibid., pp. 16, 23.

74. *Pravda,* November 16, 1958; German in: O. Anweiler/K. Meyer (eds.), *Die sowjetische Bildungspolitik seit 1917. Dokumente und Texte.* (Heidelberg, 1961), pp. 308–339.

75. *Pravda,* December 11, 1958.

76. *Sovetskaia Litva,* December 23, 1958; quoted from: Y. Bilinsky, "The Soviet Education Laws of 1958–59 and Soviet Nationality Policy," in: *Soviet Studies,* XIV, 1962/63, pp. 138–157. This article also contains an abundance of bibliographical press statements against Thesis 19 from the republics.

77. Bilinsky, ibid.

78. *Zasedaniia Verkhovnogo Soveta SSSR, piatogo sozyva, vtoraia sessiia (22.–25. dekabria 1958 g.). Stenograficheskii otchet* (Moscow, 1959), pp. 346f.

79. Ibid., p. 356.

80. Ibid., pp. 341, 380, 404, 409.

81. *Sovetskaia Latviia,* March 17, 1959. Bilinsky, op. cit., p. 155 contains a bibliography of the publication of all Union Republics' education laws in the Union Republics' major daily newspapers.

82. Bilinsky, op. cit., pp. 146f.

83. Lewytzkyj, *Sovetskii narod—Das Sowjetvolk,* p. 50.

84. *Itogi vsesoiuznoi perepisi naseleniia 1970 goda,* vol. IV.

85. A. Shilde, *Die Sowjetisierung Lettlands,* p. 39.

86. N. Dzhandildin, "Nekotorye voprosy internatsionalnogo vospitaniia," in: *Kommunist,* 13/1959, p. 34.

87. *Sovetskaia Rossiia,* April 17, 1959.

88. "Sblizhenie natsii i russkii iazyk," in: *Russkii iazyk v natsionalnoi shkole,* 6/1963, pp. 4f.

89. The resolution of March 13, 1938, has not yet been published; the quote from this resolution is in: *Natsionalnye shkoly RSFSR za 40 let,* p. 15; for more details on this matter, refer to chapter VI.3 on Soviet Patriotism and Russification.

90. Silver, "The Status of National Minority Languages in Soviet Education," pp. 31f.

91. 1958: *Natsionalnye shkoly RSFSR za 40 let,* p. 23; 1972: A. Danilov, "Mnogonatsionalnaia shkola RSFSR—prakticheskoe voploshchenie leninskoi natsionalnoi politiki," in: *Narodnoe obrazovanie,* 12/1972, p. 23. These data were compared for the first time in: Silver, "The Status of National Minority Languages," pp. 33f.

92. Silver, op. cit., p. 38.

93. Iu.D. Desheriev, *Zakonomernosti razvitiia i vzaimodeistviia iazykov v sovetskom obshchestve* (Moscow, 1966), pp. 76, 89; Iu.D. Desheriev/I.F. Protchenko, *Razvitie iazykov narodov SSSR v sovetskuiu epokhu* (Moscow, 1968), p. 122.

94. S. Babaev, "Vospitanie natsionalnykh kadrov," in: *Partiinaia zhizn*, 23/1957, pp. 9–15; the quote is on p. 13.

95. *Turkmenskaia iskra*, December 16, 1958, January 19, 1959, January 20, 1959.

96. Kh. Levush/B. Kamenetskii, *Rusifikatsiia Uzbekistana i zakulisnye storony borby za vlast v respublike v kontse 50-kh nachalo 60-kh godov* (unpublished manuscript); the quotes are on pp. 7, 12.

97. *Bakinskii rabochii*, July 11, 1959, December 11, 1959 (quoted from Lewytzkyj, *Die sowjetische Nationalitätenpolitik nach Stalins Tod*, pp. 62f.).

98. A. Pelshe, "O nekotorykh voprosakh internatsionalnogo vospitaniia," in: *V pomoshch politicheskomu samoobrazovaniiu*, 1/1960, pp. 28–37; the quotes are on p. 34.

99. Soviet sources covering the purge in Latvia: V. Latsis, "Blagotvornye preobrazovaniia," in: *Partiinaia zhizn*, 16/1959, pp. 14–21; *Sovetskaia Latviia*, October 13, 1959, March 10, 1960; letter by seventeen members of the Latvian CP — 1, in: Lewytzkyj, *Politische Opposition in der Sowjetunion*, pp. 226ff. Western research: A. Shilde, *Die Sowjetisierung Lettlands*, pp. 39–42; M.J. Widmer, "Nationalism and Communism in Latvia: The Latvian Communist Party Under Soviet Rule," Ph.D. dissertation (Harvard University, 1969), pp. 196–217; Misiunas/Taagepera, *Baltic States*, pp. 130–141.

100. *Pravda*, October 3, 1959, May 30, 1961.

101. Lewytzkyj, *Die sowjetische Nationalitätenpolitik nach Stalins Tod*, pp. 66–68; *Pravda*, May 11, 1961.

102. *Pravda*, April 16, 1961; Rakowska-Harmstone, *Russia and Nationalism in Central Asia*, pp. 161f.

103. *Prominent Personalities in the USSR* (Metukhen, 1968), p. 423.

104. Khrushchev's speech about the new Party program at the Twenty-second Party Congress: *XXII sezd KPSS. 17–31 oktiabria 1961 goda. Stenograficheskii otchet*. Vol. I (Moscow, 1962) pp. 148–257; the quotes are on pp. 153, 215, 217; J.W. Stalin, "Marxismus und nationale Frage," in: Stalin, *Werke*, vol. 2, pp. 268–272.

105. B. Meissner, *Das Parteiprogramm der KPdSU, 1903–1961* (Cologne, 1962), pp. 222–225.

106. P.G. Semenov, "Programma KPSS o razvitii sovetskikh natsionalno-gosudarstvennykh otnoshenii," in: *Sovetskoe gosudarstvo i pravo*, 12/1961, pp. 15–25; the quotes are on pp. 23, 25.

107. P.M. Rogachev/M.A. Sverdlin, "O deistvii zakona razvitiia natsionalnykh otnoshenii pri kapitalizme i pri sotsializme," in: *Filosofskie nauki*, 2/1964, pp. 126–135; the quote is on p. 133.

108. P. Rogachev/M. Sverdlin, "Sovetskii narod-novaia istoricheskaia obshchnost liudei," in: *Kommunist,* 9/1963, p. 12. On the Soviet discussion: E. Oberländer, "Der Sowjetische Nationsbegriff," in: *Aus Politik und Zeitgeschichte,* B 12, March 20, 1968, pp. 3–19; G. Hodnett, "What's in a Nation?" in: *Problems of Communism,* XVI, 5/1967, pp. 2–15.

109. *Pravda,* May 8, 1957.

110. *Plenum CK KPSS, 24–29 iiunia 1959 goda. Stenograficheskii otchet* (Moscow, 1959), p. 477.

111. *VVS SSSR 1962,* no. 48, article 495.

112. A. Bilinsky, "Die Zuständigkeit der Union und der Unionsrepubliken auf dem Gebiet der Wirtschaftsverwaltung von 1922 bis 1972," in: *Bundesstaat und Nationalitätenrecht,* p. 147.

113. N.V. Mantsvetov, "Sblizhenie natsii i vozniknovenie internatsionalnoi obshchnosti narodov v SSSR," in: *VI,* 5/1964, p. 47.

114. *VVS SSSR 1963,* no. 11, article 132.

115. *VVS SSSR 1963,* no. 11, articles 133, 134, 135, 136.

116. A. Bilinsky, "Die Entwicklung der sowjetischen Wirtschaftsverfassung," in: *Bilanz der Ära Chruschtschow,* E. Boettcher/H.-J. Lieber/B. Meissner (eds.) (Stuttgart, 1966), pp. 176–181.

117. "Resolution by the CPSU's CC and the USSR's Council of Ministers, Concerning the Perfection of Planning and the Strengthening of Economic Stimulation of the Industry, October 4, 1965," in: *KPSS v rezoliutsiiakh i resheniiakh,* vol. 8, pp. 523–552.

118. Article 55 in the constitution of the RSFSR, in: *Konstitutsiia (osnovnoi zakon) RSFSR* (Moscow, 1972), p. 18.

119. *VVS SSSR 1966,* no. 30, article 594; *1968,* no. 48, article 467.

120. *VVS SSSR 1970,* no. 32, article 692.

121. *VVS SSSR 1970,* no. 36, article 361; G. Brunner, "Die Reform in der sowjetischen Justizverwaltung," in: *Recht in Ost und West,* XV, 1971, pp. 153ff.

IX

A New Nationalism

The New Intelligentsia and the Participation Crisis

In the 1930s, the high-priority policy of disproportionately furthering development of the non-Russian peoples came to a halt. Stalin perceived the new sovietized Russian intelligentsia as a reliable instrument for controlling the empire, particularly the non-Russian territories. He did not want the cohesiveness (and possibly continued existence) of the multinational state to depend on the loyalty of native national elites. Decolonialization, which began to stir in many parts of the world, possibly increased his distrust of the developing local intelligentsia that was to lead independence movements everywhere.

Nevertheless, modernization continued in the Soviet Union's underdeveloped territories, though at a slower pace. In the east, the war made modernization particularly desirable. The decade of Khrushchev's rule further encouraged modernization. The broad spectrum of modernization efforts included construction of railroad lines and roads, establishment of basic public health services, industrialization, and urbanization. This study cannot detail all these processes. In the decades after Stalin's death, they converged and culminated in the development of new groupings of national intellectuals that not only radically changed their respective peoples' social structures but basically created a new basis for Soviet nationalities policy. Ever since, the Soviets have had to recognize that in all large non-Russian nations, more and more prospective leaders in the areas of economics, administration, education, and the Party are available, making Russian leaders superfluous. Overall, the Soviet Union is experiencing an inconspicuous but probably irreversible decolonialization. Although these processes differ from other processes of decolonialization in many ways, they also mark a historical turning point. The integration of the multinational empire increasingly depends on the loyalty of non-Russian elites—Stalin had feared this situation, and his policy had delayed it for several decades.

The prerequisite for developing a modern, non-Russian intelligentsia was extending educational opportunities in the Soviet Union's developing regions. The pace was unprecedented in comparison with other countries.

Soviet accomplishments in this area dwarf the efforts of many southern European countries, let alone those of Third World countries. A quantitative and relative perspective on this explosive development in education and the development of national strata of intellectuals is instructive. Thus, it is important to ask how many non-Russians were involved in education and were skilled workers and what their percentage was relative to the size of their own nation and in comparison to the all-Union scale.

Table 9.1 compares the number of people who had an "incomplete middle school education" or who completed a higher level, for three sample years between 1939 and 1970. After 1939, the number of people graduating from general education schools increased considerably. In addition, the tendency towards balancing the national percentages was obvious. From 1939 to 1959, the number of Russians graduating from an educational facility increased three-and-a-half times; the number of Uzbeks increased thirteenfold. Georgians, however, who had been second only to Jews in the level of education in the USSR since the 1920s — a situation that still prevails — exhibited the lowest growth rate. By 1970, the USSR had achieved a high rate of "incomplete middle school education" and a balance among the nations. Although all nations still exhibited a large difference in educational level between urban and rural areas in 1970 — Table 9.1 does not reflect this situation — the Soviets had created institutional prerequisites that guaranteed to the members of the Union Republics' titular nations a high degree of equal opportunity in elementary education.

But, the number of non-Russians getting a higher education also increased impressively. In the academic year 1927–1928, there were 74,000 non-Russian college students; in 1959–1960, 506,300; and in 1980–1981, 2.219 million. Midlevel facilities for vocational education (*srednie spetsialnye uchebnye zavedeniia*) developed in a similar way. In 1927–1928, 84,300 non-Russian students were enrolled in these facilities; 502,200 in 1959–1960; and in 1980–1981, 2.0 million.[1]

Appendix Table A.12 details the development of the national origins of Soviet students. This table illustrates the sudden increase in the number of students in general and the efforts of post-Stalinist education policy to give the large non-Russian nations with their own Union Republics proportionate access to college. Only after Stalin's death did the number of non-Russian students grow faster than that of Russian students; previously, the number of Russians grew faster than the average. Appendix Table A.12 illustrates only a few aspects of the actual preferential treatment Russian students enjoyed after the 1930s. The unpublished figures would show that the number of Russian students decreased until about 1939 and later increased until the early 1950s. The available data from 1927–1928 and 1960–1961 do not include the extreme figures of the particularly low percentage of Russians in the late 1930s and the highest percentage in the early 1950s.[2]

Table 9.1: Seven-Year Education per 1,000 people[1]

	1939	1959		1970
Russians	82	284	364	494
Ukrainians	81	278	343	458
Belorussians	58	219	282	401
Moldavians	–	151	208	337
Estonians	–	307	358	462
Latvians	–	369	426	490
Lithuanians	–	170	209	356
Georgians	137	375	474	578
Armenians	92	320	451	519
Azeri	52	247	365	437
Kazakhs	22	194	282	403
Kirgiz	10	206	309	407
Tadzhiks	11	201	298	387
Turkmen	14	242	363	433
Uzbeks	16	214	318	420

[1]The first two columns are based on 1,000 people, the last two on 1,000 people over age ten. All figures pertain to the portion of the nationality group residing within its national territory. In the 1960s, the Soviet authorities expanded seven-year schools to eight-year schools.

Source: B. Silver, "Levels of Sociocultural Development Among Soviet Nationalities: A Partial Test of the Equalization Hypothesis," in: *American Political Science Review*, vol. 68, 1974, pp. 1624f.

Nevertheless, we must remember that in 1960–1961, as compared to 1927–1928, the differences between the developed and underdeveloped Soviet nations had decreased and that by 1980–1981, the large Central Asian peoples in particular made up a surprising percentage of students. Relative to their population, Kazakhs and Kirgiz had as many as or more students than the Russians, and the percentage of Uzbek students was equal to that of Ukrainians. The increase in the number of Jewish and Georgian students, however — who had always made up an unusually high percentage of intellectuals — was below average.

Comparing the number of students to the number of seventeen-to-twenty-nine-year-olds in each nation — as far as Soviet data permit — produces different figures, in some cases due to differences in the distribution of age groups in each nation. In 1980–1981, the "older" nations (Estonians, Latvians, Ukrainians) had a stronger presence, and the "younger" nations (particularly the large Central Asian peoples) continued to trail Russians by more than Table A.12 indicates. Using age-group figures, for every 100 Russian students in 1980-1981 for example, there were eighty-six Ukrainian students in the universities, 122 Estonians, sixty-nine Uzbeks, ninety-two Kazakhs, seventy-four Azeri, and eighty-six Kirgiz.[3]

As Appendix Table A.12 suggests, bringing non-Russian students into the institutions of higher education has not been a continuous process since 1960. A closer look at short intervals (1959, 1970, 1980) shows that in 1970, the proportion of Islamic students (seventeen-to-twenty-nine-year-olds) to Russian students was higher than in 1980. In the large Central Asian nations, the wild growth in higher education in the 1960s did not continue into the 1970s for two reasons: In the 1970s, an extraordinarily large number of these "young" peoples reached college age. The expansion of the university system did not keep up with this growth, and the Soviets could not advance the system at the same pace. The economic recession that began in the 1970s—the second factor—added to the slowed growth of the system of institutions of higher education. As a result, in the 1970s, enrollment in the universities became considerably more difficult for the "young" peoples' youth than it had been in the 1960s, increasing the relative distance in the rate of non-Russian participation as compared with the Russians. If 100 Russian youths between the ages of seventeen and twenty-nine participated, the ninety-six Uzbeks in the same age group in 1970, and only sixty-nine in 1980. Corresponding figures for Kazakhs are ninety-nine and ninety-two, for Azeri 118 and seventy-four, and for Kirgiz 114 and eighty-six.

Since the mid-1970s, the Soviets could no longer satisfy the Islamic peoples' expectations, which they themselves had awakened. The youths turned away from the universities constituted a potential for dissatisfaction and conflict, particularly because the mid-level technical schools were not able to enroll these youths either. In these facilities, in the 1970s, the rate of participation of the "young" peoples, which climaxed in 1970, also declined as compared to the Russians.

In contrast, the "old" peoples (Ukrainians, Belorussians, Estonians, Latvians, Lithuanians, Tatars) whose respective age groups were considerably smaller managed to improve their enrollment position relative to the Russians even in the 1970s, experiencing continuous growth since the 1960s.[4]

Although the overall trend towards national balance is obvious, some peoples have to do without equal opportunity (cf. Appendix Table A.12). Particularly noteworthy is the fact that, in the 1920s, these peoples had enjoyed better starting conditions than the Central Asian peoples: This disadvantage affects the smaller ASSR peoples in the area of the Middle Volga, the far north, and the Northern Caucasus (Bashkirs, Chuvash, Mordvinians, Udmurts, Mari, Komi, Karelians, Chechens).[5] The fundamental cause for this disadvantage lies in the fact that native-language secondary education was much less developed among these peoples than among the peoples with their own Union Republics. In the 1960s, native-language education was virtually discontinued among these ASSR's peoples, making them dependent on Russian-language secondary schools and, of course, putting non-Russian students at a disadvantage against their Russian fellow students. Ossetians and Abkhaz, most of whom live in Georgia, are the exceptions to this rule because they are probably integrated into Georgia's very-well developed higher education system. The unusually large number of students from two Mongolian peoples, Buriats and Kalmyks, comes as a surprise. In 1980–1981, their numbers had surpassed Georgian students and, relative to their total population, constituted (probably jointly with Jews) the largest percentage of students.

The numbers of students at technical schools increased along the same lines as at institutions of higher education and the students' national origins followed the same pattern. The percentage of non-Russians increased from 36.3 percent in 1959–1960 to 43.4 percent in the 1980–1981 academic year. During this period, the total number of technical students increased by two-and-a-half times. The peoples of the Middle Volga and the far north produced more technical students than students at institutions of higher education; by contrast, the number of technical students from Islamic peoples with their own Union Republic remained below average.[6] As a result, few members of the Islamic peoples are technicians; the ASSR peoples profited from the rapidly increasing demand for technicians and mid-level technical personnel in the RSFSR.

These data show that after Stalin's death, education gradually and rather quietly resumed its role as an important part of the korenizatsiia policy: equal educational opportunity for the nations. However, integration into the economy of graduates with qualified professional training and their introduction into the leading social groups and into power was considerably slower and triggered friction and conflicts with the old, in many cases Russian, elites in the national territories that remained from the Stalin era. The participation crisis was focused in Central Asia, but also had an impact in the Caucasus, the Ukraine, and Belorussia.

Although the growth in the number of Russian university students has been below average since 1960 (Appendix Table A.12), the number of Russian specialists in the national economy with a college degree has continued to increase faster than the average (Appendix Table A.13). Even in 1975, 58.8 percent of all specialists in the national economy who have a higher education were Russian. This percentage was even slightly above that of 1960; during the same period, the total number of specialists with a higher education increased two-and-a-half times.[7] Appendix Table A.13 illustrates that the number of non-Russian university graduates in the national economy massively increased in comparison to pre-World War II figures and that there was a trend towards balance among nations. On the other hand, it also shows that in 1970, Russians were further from the all-Soviet average than in 1941. Even in 1970, only half as many Uzbeks—relative to their total population—as Russians with a higher education were employed in the national economy. Compared to the situation before World War II, Ukrainians and Belorussians made up considerable ground and reached 89 and 79 percent, respectively, of the Soviet average.

Discrimination clearly continued against most of the peoples of the RSFSR's ASSRs, which had fewer graduates of institutions of higher education than the Central Asian nations with their own Union Republic. Discrimination against these peoples weighs even more gravely because they adopted Russian to a much greater degree than the Central Asian and Caucasian peoples and had lived with the Russian people in a mutually beneficial relationship for many centuries. Most of the peoples of the RSFSR's ASSRs are much more proficient in Russian than the peoples with their own Union Republics (Appendix Table A.8). A people's proficiency in Russian does not automatically mean it rises socially. The reason why these peoples' efforts to develop new national elites met with discrimination is closely related to the fact that the status of an Autonomous Republic is considerably lower than that of a Union Republic. Russians and the use of Russian dominate education and professional life in the ASSRs to such an extent that equal opportunity for natives is virtually nonexistent. Soviet federalism is a political reality in that it clearly grants Union Republics more linguistic autonomy and, as a result, grants natives more participation than natives of national territories of lower status enjoy. Of course, Jews are an exception to this rule because their representation among academics by far surpasses that of all other nations.

Comparing the number of academics with people of working age (twenty-five to fifty-nine) in every nation produces a somewhat different picture than Appendix Table A.13:[8] The Islamic peoples with their own Union Republics had moved closer to the Soviet average by 1970 (Uzbeks, for example, to 85 percent, Kazakhs even to 101 percent). As expected, among the Islamic nations the rate of participation among people of working age was higher among the Islamic nations than in the total national population. By comparison, at 82 percent and 76 percent respectively, Ukrainians and Belorussians lagged further behind the Soviet average for university graduates employed in the economy. Progress continued until 1975 towards proportional participation of people of working age (twenty-five to fifty-nine year-olds) with a higher education in nations with their own Union Republic. Islamic nations caught up with Russians to about 90 percent and clearly surpassed Ukrainians and Belorussians (between 70 percent and 80 percent).

A New Nationalism

The number of specialists with a midlevel education who were employed in the economy increased from 5.2 million in 1960 to 13.3 million in 1975. In 1960, 1.8 million of these were non-Russians; in 1975, 4.9 million (cf. Appendix Table A.14). Nevertheless, the predominance of Russians in this area is more noticeable than among students at institutions of higher education or among academics in the economy. In addition, this supremacy is being broken down more slowly than the percentage of Russians in midlevel technical schools.[9] This means that in the 1960s and 1970s, Russians managed to maintain their dominance among skilled workers, who constitute a privileged class in Soviet society. This was primarily to the disadvantage of Islamic peoples with their own Union Republic. In the mid-1970s, the number of Ukrainians and Belorussians in the professions requiring a technical education was proportionate to their percentage of the total population. In the 1960s, the differential quotient, which illustrates each people's number of specialists with a technical education, even increased slightly.[10]

The available figures substantiate the fact that after Stalin's death, the number of people with qualified vocational training rapidly increased in all nations. The Russian overrepresentation in the individual groups has decreased at different speeds. Nations with their own Union Republic have already achieved almost equal inter-national opportunity in respect to seven-year schools and institutions of higher education since the late 1970s, however, opportunities for peoples with a low average age have decreased. Slavs and in particular Russians remained dominant among professions requiring mid-level technical training.

Due to insufficient Soviet data, a more detailed description of the professional situation of new national elites is not possible. Probably, only Georgians, Armenians, Estonians, Latvians, and Lithuanians have a spectrum of qualified specialists that is broad enough to meet all requirements of a modern society. By contrast, the infra-structures of intellectuals in the RSFSR's ASSR nations are not sufficiently developed to let these nations qualitatively and quantitatively meet their own territories' needs. The new Central Asian intellectual classes are incomplete. Teachers, cultural-artistic intellectuals, social scientists and humanists, and public health professionals dominate. By comparison, locals are represented in the industrial-technological sector at a level far below their percentage among the whole population. From 1956 to 1967, 11,070 engineers (among them, 4,834 — or 44 percent — Asians) graduated from the Tashkent Polytechnical Institute — one of the largest Central Asian institutes of technology. In the late 1960s, probably only about 10 percent of the engineering-technological intellectuals employed in the Central Asian economy were locals.[11]

This imbalance is primarily a product of the language situation in education. Central Asian institutions of higher education offered educational and medical curricula in the languages of the titular nations; however, they teach natural sciences and technological subjects only in Russian. This puts natives at a disadvantage in the entrance examinations and also in the later course of their studies. Until the mid-1970s, only the five Union Republics mentioned above could guarantee a complete range of vocational training in the national primary language.

To a certain degree, Table 9.2 also reflects the development of national strata of intellectuals although the intelligentsia is not identical with any of the "Soviet classes." Intellectuals are primarily included in the "class" of "employees," to a lesser degree, also among "workers"; many of them are graduates of technical schools.[12] The percentage of employees in the total population increased from 20 percent in 1959 to 25 percent in 1979. This means that the number of employees increased twice as fast as in the two preceding decades (Appendix Table A.6). In 1959, only 8 percent of Uzbeks were "employees;" in 1979, this percentage had increased to 18 percent. Among Ukrainians, the respective figures were 13 and 23 percent; among Lithuanians, 14 and 27 percent.[13] From the perspective of inter-national homogenization, the figures in Table 9.2 are ambiguous. On the one hand, in the 1970s, many nations with a Union Republic (particularly, Ukrainians, Belorussians, and Moldavians) with below-average participation managed to catch up a little with the average number of employees. On the other hand, the nations with an above-average number of employees continued to progress and managed to increase their distance from the average. These peoples maintained a fully developed education system in the primary language: Russians, Georgians, Armenians, Estonians, Latvians, and Lithuanians. Kazakhs also increased the number of employees beyond the average; this may be the result of their exceptionally good knowledge of Russian and their privileged position in their own Union Republic.

What effect did the development of new strata of intellectuals have on the nations' participation in the Party and their republics' leaderships? After Stalin's death, the increase in the percentage of non-Russian Party members was considerably slower than that of college students or professionals who were college graduates. In other words, Russian dominance in the Party — a heritage of the Stalin era — decreased much more slowly (Appendix Tables A.12, A.13, A.15). In November 1970, 41.2 percent of professionals with higher education were non-Russians; on January 1, 1972, only 39 percent of Party members were non-Russians.[14] Even on January 1, 1982, 59.8 percent of Party members were Russian, meaning they were still considerably overrepresented because they were only 52.4 percent (in 1979) of the total population.

Considering the nations' different age structures and comparing the number of Party members with the number of citizens over twenty years of age preserves the picture that the participation of non-Russians in the Party was low: The below-average participation of the Ukrainian, Belorussian, and the

Table 9.2: The Nations' Social Structures in 1970 and 1979 (in percent)

	1970							1979						
	Blue-Collar Workers		White-Collar Workers		Kolkhoz Peasants			Blue-Collar Workers		White-Collar Workers		Kolkhoz Peasants		
	%	Index	%	Index	%	Index	%	Index	%	Index	%	Index	%	Index
Total USSR	57	100	23	100	20	100	60	100	25	100	15	100		
Russians	63	111	25	109	12	60	63	105	31	124	6	40		
Ukrainians	47	82	16	70	37	185	56	93	23	92	21	140		
Belorussians	53	93	15	65	32	160	59	98	23	92	18	120		
Estonians	57	100	25	109	18	90	57	95	32	128	11	73		
Latvians	52	91	18	78	30	150	56	93	27	108	17	113		
Lithuanians	54	95	23	100	23	115	58	97	28	112	14	93		
Georgians	41	72	26	113	33	165	49	82	32	128	19	127		
Armenians	60	105	25	109	15	75	62	103	31	124	7	47		
Azeri	50	88	21	91	29	145	58	97	23	92	19	127		
Uzbeks	39	68	16	70	45	225	50	83	18	72	32	213		
Kazakhs	65	114	22	96	13	65	64	107	28	112	8	53		
Turkmen	32	56	17	74	51	255	39	65	16	64	45	300		
Kirgiz	41	72	15	65	44	220	56	93	20	80	24	160		
Tadzhiks	37	65	15	65	48	240	55	92	15	60	30	200		
Moldavians	32	56	7	30	61	305	54	90	15	60	31	207		

Source: Iu.V. Arutiunian, "Korennye izmeneniia v sotsialnom sostave sovetskikh natsii," in: *Sotsiologicheskie issledovaniia*, 4/1982, p. 23.

Baltic nations was even more pronounced in the 1960s and 1970s. This statistical method, however, shows that the Islamic nations, which had a very young average age, were better represented in the Party. In 1976, as many Azeri and Kazakhs over the age of twenty were represented among the Party members as Russians; however, only 77 percent as many Uzbeks and 62 percent as many Lithuanians as the Soviet average were represented.[15]

In the past decades, the Soviets—in contrast to the Stalin era—have let more and more Ukrainians and Belorussians join the Party. As a result, these nations had caught up to the Soviet average by the early 1980s, and for the first time in the history of the Soviet Union, Ukrainians were represented in the Party in proportion to their percentage in the total population. Participation in the three Baltic and four Central Asian nations lagged behind. These nations' respective age groups are better represented among university students and professionals than in the Party.

Most of the Turkic and Finnic peoples of the Volga region are represented in the Party in numbers lower than the Russian average, particularly considering the fact that they—unlike the Baltic peoples—were involved in the Soviet Union from the beginning. These peoples' weak representation corresponds to their educational disadvantages. Nevertheless, the trend towards proportional balance is also unmistakable. Compared with the conditions in the 1920s, even these ASSR peoples were much better integrated in the Party in the 1980s. As compared to the other nations, the participation of the Tatars, by far the largest people without their own Union Republic, progressed the least. Chechens and Ingush are the nations least integrated into the Party. This results from their deportation and the conflicts that surfaced during their return, and must also be seen as a general expression of these peoples' resistance to Sovietization.[16] The people with the strongest representation in the Party and seven times as many members as the Ingush are the Jews, who are still overrepresented as they were in the late 1920s.

Were the new national elites co-opted into the Party leadership? The picture is ambiguous. Since the mid-1950s, on the level of the Union Republics, locals have been represented in surprisingly large numbers in the Party's executive positions and other bureaucratic apparatuses. This fact supports the hypothesis that korenizatsiia was a silent policy after Stalin's death. By contrast, after many non-Russians had advanced into the leadership of the whole Party in the Khrushchev era, a distinct process of re-Russification began under Brezhnev. As a result, in the early 1980s Russians dominated CC and Politburo as much as they did in the Stalin era (Appendix Table A.16). Two Party members achieved particularly high levels of adaptation: From 1974 to 1979, N.I. Ryzhkov, a member of the Politburo since April 1985, metamorphosed from being Ukrainian to being Russian; N.A. Tikhonov, who was the Chairman of the USSR's Council of Ministers until September 1985, paid tribute to the zeitgeist in the same manner and from 1979 to 1984, changed from being Ukrainian to being Russian.[17]

Towards the end of the Stalin era, Slavs made up about three quarters of the political leadership elite (members of the CCs, the Councils of Ministers, and the Presidia of the Supreme Soviets) in the Central Asian Union Republics; by the 1970s, the percentage had dropped to one quarter.[18] In 1969, 52 percent of the 2,635 full-time Party functionaries in the Uzbek CC and Party committees on the regional, municipal, and district level were Uzbek (percentage in the total population in 1970: 64 percent).[19] In 1980, corresponding positions in Tadzhikistan were held by 61 percent Tadzhiks, 18 percent Uzbeks, and 13 percent Russians (percentages in the total population in 1979: 59 percent Tadzhiks, 23 percent Uzbeks, 10 percent Russians). In 1980, among the 2,085 "executives of the Kirgiz ASSR" — apparently, this includes the top functionaries of all important apparatuses — 56 percent were Kirgiz and 29 percent Russian (percentages in the total population in 1979: 48 percent Kirgiz, 26 percent Russian).[20]

In the Baltic republics, "nationalization" of leadership groups was as radical as in Central Asia. In both cases, the number of locals in the leadership groups increased more than those in the Party. The percentage of Lithuanians in the Lithuanian CC (members and candidates) increased from 56 percent in 1952 to 77 percent in 1976. Among the members of the Lithuanian CC's Bureaus and secretariat, 87 percent were locals in 1971 and 93 percent in 1976. The corresponding numbers for members of the Council of Ministers were 55 percent in 1947 and 93 percent in 1975.[21] In 1980, Latvians made up about 66 percent of the Presidium of the Latvian Supreme Soviet and Council of Ministers; they also constituted about 60 percent of the CC, whose members and candidates were elected in Riga in January 1981 (percentage in the total population in 1979: 54 percent).[22]

Khrushchev's purges from 1959 to 1961 and later purges in individual republics temporarily reduced the numbers of locals in leadership groups. On the whole, however, these purges did not change the trend of titular nations participating in leadership groups on the republic level in number at least equal to their number in the total population and often beyond. Only in Moldavia and Belorussia from 1955 to 1972, did locals participate in CC Bureaus in numbers lower than their percentage in the total population. In all other Union Republics, more locals participated in their republics' supreme Party executive body than was proportionate to their number in the total population — in some cases, considerably more. From 1955 to 1972, 93 percent of the Ukrainian Politburo's members were Ukrainian; in Dushanbe, 72 percent of Tadzhik CC Bureau's members were Tadzhik; in Baku, 87 percent were Azeri; and in Riga, 80 percent were Latvian.[23]

However, Union Republics differed considerably in the way they assigned locals to leadership positions and in the positions to which they appointed them. Since the 1950s, some top functions in the apparatuses have been exclusively or primarily the domain of locals; other functions, however, are exclusively or primarily reserved for Russians or Russified Ukrainians sent to the Union Republics. All Union Republics appointed members of the titular nations to the three most visible political positions (first Party secretary, Chairman of the Council of Ministers, Chairman of the Presidium of the Supreme Soviet). From the mid-1950s to the early 1960s, some Party chiefs, such as those in Kazakhstan and Moldavia were non-locals.[24] Second Party secretaries were as likely to be foreigners as first Party secretaries were to be locals. This pattern gradually began to develop in the 1950s and became the norm in all Union Republics in the late 1970s. The second secretary was responsible for personnel policy and was thus Moscow's most important watchdog in the Union Republics. In the Khrushchev era, several Union Republics (particularly, the Ukraine, Belorussia, and the Transcaucasus) had the privilege of appointing a local second secretary. In the 1970s, this privilege was withdrawn. Since the 1960s, the pattern of appointing a local first secretary and a Russian second secretary has also caught on in many ASSRs. Some ASSRs, however, have reversed this combination: These are the strongly Russified Autonomous Republics (Mari, Udmurtia, Mordvinia) and the problem case Checheno-Ingushetia.[25]

In addition to the position of second secretary, non-locals held two other important functions in the republics: head of the KGB and chairman of the CC Department for Organization and Party Work. From 1955 to 1972, only 26 percent of the KGB heads in the Union Republics were locals.[26] In the 1970s, however, the Soviets began to appoint more locals to this position. In 1979, 50 percent of the KGB heads in the Union Republics were locals.[27] Also, executive positions in construction (CC secretary for construction, chairman of the CC Department for Construction) were reserved for Russians in the Union Republics.

However, locals held virtually all top positions in propaganda and culture (CC secretary for propaganda, chairman of the CC department for culture and propaganda, minister for culture and education, chairman of the writers' union). In similar fashion, the first secretary of the Komsomol and the chairman of the workers' unions were natives. Executive positions in agriculture present a diverse picture: From 1955 to 1972, 75 percent of the CC secretaries for agriculture and the ministers for agriculture were natives of the titular nation; only about 50 percent of the Deputy Chairmen of the Council of Ministers in charge of agriculture and the heads of the CC Department for Agriculture, however, were locals.

The levels of self-administration varied greatly among the Union Republics. Hodnett examined forty-nine executive positions in the Union Republics to see whether locals (i.e., members of the titular nation) held them from 1955 to 1972. In the three Transcaucasian Union Republics, 90 to 100 percent of incumbents were locals. In Moldavia and Kazakhstan—at the other end of the scale—less than 50 percent of incumbents were natives of the titular nations; in the Ukraine, Lithuania, Estonia, Latvia, and Uzbekistan, 75 to 89 percent were locals. In Tadzhikistan, Belorussia, Turkmenistan, and Kirgizistan, 50 to 74 percent of the top functionaries were natives of the titular nations. Only in Moldavia and Belorussia, was the percentage of locals among the top functionaries below the percentage in the total population.[28]

In clear contrast to the Union Republics' advanced "self-administration" by locals, non-Russian politicians remained an insignificant minority among Party leaders in Moscow. Appendix Table A.16 shows that Khrushchev made great efforts to co-opt non-Russians into the CC and Politburo (CC Presidium). In the early 1980s, however, Russian dominance among Party leaders had returned to the level of the late Stalin era. Only Ukrainians and Belorussians managed to maintain their representation in the CC on a reduced scale. In addition, a particularly large number of Ukrainians and Belorussians joined the Party in the Brezhnev era (Appendix Table A.15). Was this supposed to lead to a strong Slavic bloc, in which common interest prevailed over what was foreign to all?

The CC's re-Russification primarily put the Islamic peoples at a disadvantage. In the mid-1980s, the number of Uzbeks—the nation with the greatest political, economic, and numerical clout among the Islamic peoples—representing their people in the CC was smaller than in 1939. Among the great Asian peoples, only Kazakhs are represented in the CC in proportion with their percentage in the total population—another indication that, after the genocide in the 1930s, they are among the nations most integrated into Soviet society. Many peoples in the RSFSR (like the Finnic peoples) either had no CC representatives or—like the Tatars—had far less representation than their percentage in the total population would require. This once more confirms the previous observation that in spite of their favorable starting conditions, most RSFSR peoples are at a disadvantage as measured by all indicators of their participation in society and power. The implication is that Soviet society discriminates against them.

In late 1983, nearly 66 percent of the Politburo's members and candidates and CC secretaries were Russian. In addition to letting some Ukrainians and Belorussians represent their nations in the Politburo, the Soviets apparently made it a practice after Khrushchev's fall to co-opt one or two Transcaucasians and one or two Asians (usually one Kazakh and one Uzbek) into the Politburo. After the Khrushchev era, unwillingness to involve non-Russians in the leadership increased. An analysis of the name lists of top functionaries of different apparatuses substantiates this trend. In 1980, only three non-Slavs were among the 150 top functionaries in the CC apparatus (department heads, their deputies, heads of subordinated departments [*sek-*

tor]); only three non-Slavs were among the 97 members of the Council of Ministers and another three non-Slavs among the 150 top military leaders.[29]

Apparently, because the Brezhnev leadership was unable to keep nationals from participating in the governments of the Union Republics, they were determined to keep them from becoming involved with governing the whole state. This backwards step for co-opting non-Russians into the leadership clearly contrasts with Brezhnev's general style of leadership, which was characterized by increasing involvement of bureaucratic apparatuses in political decisions. The Soviets apparently saw increasing the involvement of local nationals as a considerable risk. This discrimination against non-Russians also shows that top politicians were very aware of their Russian heritage and were interested in surrounding themselves primarily with fellow Russians. This situation heightened the participation crisis.

National Consciousness and Its Manifestations

To what extent did the new national intelligentsia become a genuine part of Soviet society and influence its policies? How loyal are they to the whole state and the political power system? How developed is their desire for autonomy, and where does it lead them? Are these new elites a threat to the whole state, or are they smoothly integrated into the "new historical community of men — the Soviet people?"

It is impossible to answer these questions in a satisfactory way although they are central to any description of the state of Soviet society. The way the Soviets describe themselves systematically obscured the issues involved, and as a result, Western researchers have not yet been able to analyze them in a way that is sufficiently differentiated and encompasses geographical considerations. There are many indications that these new "socialist nations" are behaving in the same way as new strata of intellectuals do in any other society: In the Soviet Union, national consciousness is growing among both Russians and non-Russians.

On the sixtieth anniversary of the founding of the USSR, Party Chief Andropov declared, "Life shows that growth in national consciousness accompanies the economic and cultural progress of all nations and nationalities. This is a principled, objective process."[30] "Negative phenomena" influencing the nations' coexistence — such as "national conceit and arrogance" and "disregard for other nations and nationalities" — cannot be "traced back only to historical survival." This marked the first time a Soviet Party chief confirmed that, in the Soviet Union, modernization has the same effect as in other societies and that "modernization stimulates transformation of traditional values into ethnic nationalism"[31] and "creates the framework for a kind of nationalism that articulates itself more strongly than before and, what is more, more consciously."[32]

Although Soviet researchers have never analyzed this phenomenon in detail, they have repeatedly acknowledged that modernization strengthens and expands national self-consciousness.[33] Socialism opens "extensive opportunities for the growth of national consciousness," and the Party's nationalities policy promotes "the development of national pride and the socialist national consciousness of the USSR's peoples."[34] "All ethnocultural regions" exhibit the stabilization of the individual socialist nations' and nationalities' internal unity and monolithic unanimity."[35] The intellectuals carry this new self-consciousness in the cities. "National self-consciousness is becoming more and more determined and motivated because so many people have graduated from secondary schools and institutions of higher education."[36] "Perhaps even more than the villages, the USSR's cities have become the 'carriers of ethnos.'"[37] Arutiunian summarized his ethnosociological field research, saying "[In the process of urbanization,] some traditional ethnic characteristics get 'lost' as national self-consciousness grows. The findings of Soviet sociologists permit the conclusion that the high level of national self-consciousness primarily characterizes large multinational settlement centers with a high level of education. The growth of national self-consciousness is closely related to personal involvement in international culture, to forming attitudes and values in the context of international contacts."[38]

Thus, Soviet researchers confirm the main findings of comparative research on nationalism and simultaneously refute two important ideological postulates and expectations: that the increasing intensity of inter-ethnic contacts would cause independent national self-consciousness to level off and that the new intellectuals, who were socialized by the Soviet education system, would stop identifying with their national traditions, languages, and national characteristics and adopt only all-Soviet values, attitudes, and behaviors. Soviet sociologists find that international collectives and living and working intensively with various ethnic groups do not necessarily promote friendship among the peoples. On the contrary, these situations can create friction and conflict that would not arise as long as the milieu remained nationally homogeneous. Multi-national collectives can be expected to produce positive effects only if "there is already a history of favorable and long-lasting contacts."[39]

Intellectuals have proven particularly susceptible to negative nationalism: to resentments, to favoring people of their own nationality in professional and private life. Social conditions quickly and deeply effect the way people think about and behave towards other nations. People take out their general dissatisfaction with living conditions, with unsatisfactory professional advancement, and with bad housing on other nationalities. People blamed social dissatisfaction on national issues.[40] From a socio-psychological perspective, the economic recession since the late 1970s, which, in many cases, has kept the standard of living from growing, has reinforced resentments of the nationalities.

Of course, individual nations differ from each other greatly in national consciousness make-up, goals, and priorities noticeable to outsiders because the way the Soviets present themselves obscures these differences. National consciousness is always tied to a number of other philosophies and political goals that are often incompatible. This is even truer in the Soviet Union because the nations grew out of different cultures and historical traditions and their ideas of their national future vary widely. Lithuanian national consciousness is closely tied to Catholicism; Armenian national consciousness is influenced by hatred of Turks. A symbiotic relationship exists between national consciousness and liberal-democratic political efforts entertained by the Helsinki committees or between an integral nationalism promoted by the remnants of the Ukrainian nationalist organizations, which date back to World War II, and that created by Russian anti-Semites.

The manifestations of the new nationalism were equally varied and contradictory. They span from a revival of national commercial art and folklore to underground terrorist groups. To evaluate all these manifestations adequately, one must remember that until the mid-1980s they were subject to tight control and censorship or could survive only in the underground. The Soviets considered it necessary to restrict national rhetoric and national actions before they could become a political issue. This also applied to Russian nationalism, although some politicians among the Party leaders favored it. Some folklore traditions — like the song festivals in Estonia and Latvia — were crucial to national identity. "In the late 1970s, interest in folk music increased. In general, You can see increasing interest in all forms of folk art everywhere. Many of these forms are experiencing a kind of rebirth."[41]

National idiosyncracies are particularly apparent in the family. Life styles and norms distinguish European families from Asian families. The relationship between the sexes and among generations or distribution of privileges and duties within the family distinguish the nations even in situations where they live in close proximity. The question, "Do you think parental consent is necessary for marriage?" triggered extremely divergent answers: 92 percent of rural Uzbeks said yes, but only 34 percent rural Russians and 25 percent of rural Estonians considered parental consent necessary. These percentages did not change significantly in respect to urban populations or younger generations. Among urban Uzbeks, 88 percent thought marriage required parental consent; 38 percent of urban Russians and only 22 percent of urban Estonians agreed with them. Among the twenty to twenty-four year-old rural population, respective percentages were 90 percent, 28 percent, and 13 percent.[42]

Under the specific conditions in the Soviet Union, national consciousness often manifested itself in the private sector. Professional life, however, is dominated by all-Soviet standards and behavioral expectations. But even here, nations display considerable differences in such areas as their attitude towards work.

As always, historiography plays a special role in giving a form and means of expression to national consciousness. Although the procrustean bed of ideological bias and Party requirements, which was binding for everyone, affected the non-Russian nations' historiography, it has grown to a surprising degree since Stalin's death and, as a result, developed its own extensive dynamics. Since the late 1950s, all major and many minor peoples—the exceptions being the Germans, Jews, and Poles—have published histories (most of them several volumes long) "from the beginning to the present." The "creation of comprehensive views of history" "contributes to national consolidation." In the national territories, the phalanx of professional historians has grown considerably as evidenced by the number of doctoral degrees awarded and the fact that formal qualifications have increased considerably faster than in Russia.[43]

It was important for the old nations of Georgia, Armenia, and Lithuania to illustrate the independence of their historical traditions. At the same time, they had to fit these traditions into the necessities of the Party's historiography, which still maintained unwaveringly that annexation to Russia was of "objective, progressive importance" from the beginning.[44] Georgian, Armenian, and Lithuanian historians are the only ones to publish their representative comprehensive accounts in their native language instead of Russian. This may be an "evasive strategy" (Martiny) designed to counter the central power's demands and control.

For many Asian peoples, the issue was to create a national history of their own. Because they wanted to display their traditions as old, venerable, and culturally advanced as possible, they did not hesitate to create many legends. Some came about because historians equated the history of a geographical area into the history of the nationality living there at present. Everything that occurred in the present Tadzhik and Uzbek settlement areas—the definition of these areas was very liberal—was considered their national history. As a result, modern Central Asian intellectuals appear as the "worthy heirs and continuers" of the pre-Islamic, primarily Sogdian tradition and of the intellectual life of the Middle Ages, which culminated in the works of poets like Firdousi (943–1025) or the polyhistorians Abu Reikhan al-Biruni (973–1048) and Abu ali ibn Sina (Avicenna) (980–1037).[45]

The momentum national historiography generated shook several dogmas. According to some Tatar historians, for example, the integration of the Khanat Kazan into the state of Moscow in the sixteenth century was Russian imperialism. This harks back to the Soviet-Marxist interpretation in the 1920s. Other historical "laws" from the Stalin era, which were officially still in effect, were slowly eroding. Some Tatar historians deny that Russia was more developed than the non-Russian nations when they were incorporated into the Russian state. Historians not only shook the dogma that incorporation was voluntary but also the one that it was progressive. They contended that at the time it was incorporated into the Russian state, Tatar society was culturally and economically relatively highly developed, and nineteenth century bourgeois Tatar society required far less Russian help to overcome alleged underdevelopment than Soviet historiography has suggested.

The implicit, although not yet openly declared rehabilitation of Jadidism, the nineteenth century Islamic revival movement that had a long-range effect on Sultan Galiev's national communism, also deserves mention in this context. This silent revision of Stalinism, which was not limited to historiography but was also supported by Tatar writers and critics, occurred in the name of Mirasism, the search for one's own roots and reverence for one's heritage. Mirasism, which has been growing noticeably since the 1960s, "is likely to have a lasting effect on Tatar society."[46]

Since the 1960s, belles-lettres has been among the most important manifestations of national consciousness. Literature is accessible to a much larger audience than historiography. "Many writers, who have achieved great things in today's poetry and prose, try extremely hard to advance national tradition. 'Ancestors, help me fight!'—these poetic lines by the Kazakh O. Suleimenov can be interpreted as the metaphoric embodiment of many artists' quest, and not only in Kazakhstan."[47] As Misiunas and Taagepera state, the Baltic nations "have been considerably increasing the historical depth of modern nations" since 1940. They accomplish this "increase in socio-cultural depth" by taking advantage of their "very real cultural autonomy."[48] In respect to the development of national identity, literature has been crucial to this cultural autonomy.[49]

Finally, what are the goals of the new national consciousness? In this context, again no goals are common to all nations and consequently, to no common political movement. Again, the Soviets tried hard to hide political realities behind an obscure "continued drawing together socialist nations." The scope of goals is wide. Jewish and German emigration or nationalist Transcaucasian and Baltic opposition groups demanding secession marked one end of the spectrum. The other end consisted of the Party's efforts to train more Asian specialists or integrate more representatives from the Union Republics' national minorities (for example, Abkhaz in Georgia or Germans in Kazakhstan) into local soviets. Among the national goals, the demand for more investment in the cotton industry in Central Asia exists side by side with the rejection of massive capital investment in Estonia and Latvia, where the continued Russian influx associated with such investment met resistance. Culture and language are the targets of most efforts towards national self-consciousness. All nations join in the desire to preserve their native language in media and education and to perpetuate their specific traditions in literature and fine arts. However, the nations had to articulate their goals under extremely divergent starting conditions. In Georgia, for example, the Georgian constitution determined Georgian as the state language; in Birobidzhan, only a handful of schools teach Yiddish, none teaches in Yiddish.

In general, until the mid-1980s, the political goals the new intelligentsia pursued were primarily for participation, not separation. This self-restriction possibly reflected a realistic assessment of what was feasible under the existing power system. The nations demanded more consideration for their economic, cultural, and personnel interests within their territories and the whole state. This included distribution of economic resources in the face of a dwindling total volume and preservation and expansion of cultural autonomy — primarily the perpetuation of the native language for public functions. Sociological polls of Soviet emigrants confirmed (about Central Asia and Kazakhstan at least) that the influence of the nations in their own territories was growing. The polled German emigrants attribute this development primarily to the fact that more and more locals are moving into leadership positions. "For the Russians, too, it is getting difficult to live in Kazakhstan."[50] Another poll reflected the overall importance of the nationalities issue for Soviet society: Two-thirds of the polled emigrants thought an applicant's nationality had great influence on his/her chances of receiving housing, being accepted at the university, or being hired after training. More than half of those polled believed that in the Soviet Union, "friendship among the peoples" was fiction.[51]

In the following, two very different examples illustrate how the promotion of national interests manifested itself in the post-Stalin era: The first example is Ukrainization of the Ukraine in the 1960s and early 1970s. The second is the revival of the Islamic life style in Central Asia.

Researchers have referred to the years during which Petro Iukhymovych Shelest was Ukrainian Party chief (1963 to 1972) as a period of "revival of controlled Ukrainian autonomism."[52] Reversing the conditions of the Stalin era, Ukrainians took over virtually all political leadership positions in their republic. From 1955 to 1972, 93 percent of all members of the Ukrainian CC's Politburo were Ukrainians.[53] The Party leadership's Ukrainization continued into many areas of society and began to change the ethnosociological stratification of Ukrainian society. The preferential acceptance of Ukrainians into the Party illustrates the intention to involve more Ukrainians in the privileged strata. Within the republic's Party organization, the percentage of Ukrainians increased from 60.3 percent in 1958 to 65.1 percent in 1968. After this point, the percentage virtually stopped increasing and reached 66 percent on January 1, 1981.[54] The percentage of Ukrainians in the Soviet population dropped from 17.8 percent in 1959 to 16.9 percent in 1970; their percentage among professionals with a college education, however, increased to 15 percent in 1970. Although they had not reached proportionate representation among university graduates, they had moved closer to the average (cf. Appendix Table A.13). In 1975, 16.4 percent of specialists with mid-level vocational training were Ukrainian, giving this nation proportionate representation in this group for the first time (Appendix Table A.14).

Modernization was also affecting Ukrainian social structure as shown in the fact that the percentage of white collar workers increased from 16 percent in 1970 to 23 percent in 1979. At the same time, the Ukraine caught up with the Soviet average faster than most other nations, reaching 92 percent of the Soviet average for this indicator in 1979. Even in 1979, however, this trend could not change the fact that the number of Ukrainian kolkhoz peasants was above the average (Table 9.2, see above).

The Shelest leadership slowed down the officially propagated exchange of cadres and pushed for hiring Ukrainians with degrees from Ukrainian institutions of higher education and technical schools in the Ukraine. This put more qualified Ukrainians in higher positions in the economy.[55]

Shelest expressed Ukrainian economic interests relatively openly and publicly and did not prevent Ukrainian economists from criticizing the center's investment policy. As in the 1920s, the issue in the 1960s was whether the Ukraine or Siberia was to have priority in developing an energy base. Pointing out the Ukraine's advantageous location and lower costs, Ukrainian economists demanded priority for the construction of hydroelectric power plants on the Dnieper and investment in the Donbas coal fields. Gosplan supported Siberia's application to develop an energy industry in Siberia. Behind closed doors, some Ukrainian functionaries were quite frank in their contention that the Ukraine was being economically exploited. They claimed the Ukraine would long since have solved its housing problem, for example, if it were not required to contribute such a large sum to the All-Union budget.[56]

At the Twenty-third Party Congress in 1966, Chairman of the Ukrainian Council of Ministers Shcherbitskii demanded increased capital investment in the Ukraine; at the Twenty-fourth Party Congress in 1971, Party Chief Shelest repeated this demand. In his speech at the Ukrainian CP's Party Congress in 1971, Shelest criticized the USSR's Gosplan and the All-Union Ministry for Coal Mining, which had not paid "sufficient attention" to Ukrainian interests. In Moscow, before the delegates at the Twenty-fourth Party Congress, he repeated his demands for increased coal mining production in the Donbass. Neglecting coal mining in favor of mineral oil and natural gas, as "someone" had suggested, was "wrong." This "someone" was the chairman of the USSR's Council of Ministers, Kosygin. In addition, Shelest demanded more and better fodder and more agricultural machinery for the Ukraine.[57]

The "second Ukrainization" manifested itself primarily in the areas of culture and language. Such intellectuals as writers, journalists, philologists, and educators were the most important social foundation. In Kiev, from February 11 to February 15, 1963, the university and the Ukrainian Academy of Sciences' Institute for Linguistics hosted a conference on the culture of the Ukrainian language. By "unanimously condemning the absurd theory that a nation has two languages," the participants contradicted the official policy of bilingualism. The conference resolved to present to the Ukrainian CC and Council of Ministers its demands for language policy: All institutions of higher education and mid-level technical schools were to teach in Ukrainian. All authorities, factories, the railroad, and trades were to conduct business in Ukrainian. Most scholarly papers were to be published in Ukrainian. Finally, outside the Ukraine, Ukrainian schools that had existed until the late 1930s were to be reopened to serve Ukrainian minorities in the diaspora, "just as has been done in the Ukraine for the Russians and other peoples."[58]

These were not the lofty ideas of patriotic but unrealistic intellectuals but a program supported by the Ukrainian Party leadership. This becomes evident in a speech, which Ukrainian Minister for Institutions of Higher Education and Mid-Level Technical Education Iu.M. Dadenkov (1960–1973) delivered to rectors of institutions of higher education in August 1965. He described in detail the unsatisfactory level of Ukrainization at institutions of higher education. Only 55 percent of the 318,000 students (about 25 percent of all college students in the Ukraine) attending his ministry's fifty institutions of higher education were Ukrainians; less than 50 percent of the college teachers were Ukrainian. Textbooks and teaching materials for technical and natural science subjects were printed exclusively in Russian. Only 33 percent of college teachers at the Ukraine's eight universities taught their classes in Ukrainian; at the University of Odessa, only 10 percent. The Kiev Institute for Economy was the only institution of higher education in the Ukraine that trained specialists for the republic's planning organs; 87 percent of its students were Ukrainian, and in the previous five years, 90 percent of its graduates had been employed in the Ukraine. However, only 5 percent of its teachers taught in Ukrainian. In Kharkov, at the Ukraine's only law school, all classes were taught in Russian. Most of the thirty-six technical institutions of higher education also taught in Russian. The minister referred to the Lvov Polytechnical Institute as a positive example because at least 30 percent of its teachers taught in Ukrainian. At the Kiev Polytechnical Institute, on the other hand, none of the lectures were in Ukrainian. The minister outlined a clear picture for the future: Conditions were to be created that allowed "the gradual adoption of Ukrainian as the only teaching language." The institutions of higher education were also to make Ukrainian their official language and conduct all business and correspondence in Ukrainian.[59] Although Dadenkov's proposals were not realized, the fact that they were outlined is proof of a cultural and political climate in which Ukrainian self-consciousness could express itself as never again since the mid-1930s.

At the Fifth Ukrainian Writers' Congress in November 1966, Shelest addressed the writers: "We must treat our beautiful Ukrainian native tongue with great care and reverence.... Your efforts in this direction have and always will have the Communist Party's support."[60] The chairman of the Ukrainian Writers' Union, Oles Honchar, implicitly not only voiced criticism but also expressed explicit expectations for the future when he pointed out that "because of prevailing conditions, the native tongue is worse off in some schools than a foreign language. A nation's language is an extremely valuable treasure, which we must preserve using all means including state authority."[61]

In belles-lettres, the "second Ukrainization" climaxed in the publication of Hochar's novel *The Cathedral* in 1968. In vain, the novel's hero attempts to save an old Cossack cathedral from destruction. The cathedral is a symbol of libertarian Cossack tradition, which fell victim to Russification and modernization. Initially, critics welcomed the novel's content and high literary quality. Later, a press campaign began against Honchar, who nevertheless remained chairman of the Ukrainian Writers' Union until 1971.[62]

Other literary men and writers went further than Honchar and, in a climate of national thaw, were no longer willing to give in to the constraints of censorship and self-censorship. After the mid-1960s, a literary underground developed — similar to the one in Russia. But in contrast to Russia, from the beginning liberation from Stalinism and Stalinist cultural policy in the Ukraine meant returning to Ukrainian national heritage, to Ukrainian history. One of the spokesmen for the "Sixtiers" (the national literary opposition, named for the radical *intelligentsia* of the nineteenth century), Ievhen Sverstiuk, expressed this in a programmatic statement: After the failure of ideology and proletarian internationalism, only the nation can provide the foundation for and justification of morality and moral behavior. It is the source of spiritual and moral values; only returning to national tradition can overcome the kind of amorality, opportunism, and irresponsibility Stalinism created.[63]

For several years the Shelest leadership protected some of the literary opposition. Until the mid-1960s, most of its comrades-in-arms had been part of the cultural establishment, and even later there was no clear line between official literature and literary criticism, on the one hand, and Samizdat, on the other. Initially, the literary opposition was neither anti-communist nor separatist; it sought out contacts to the Shelest leadership. In a voluminous study, *Internationalism or Russification?*, the literary critic and historian Ivan Dziuba addressed the republic's leadership. Assuming a Leninist point-of-view, he heavily criticized Russification of education and culture, chided Moscow for violating the Union Republics' sovereign rights, and stated that dejure equality among nations (which the Soviets had been declaring since the revolution) had never become actual equality. Russian chauvinism had prevented this. Dziuba denied that a society without nations had ever been the objective of scientific communism.[64] Although Dziuba's book (written in 1964) was not published at that time in the Soviet Union, a limited edition was distributed in the Ukraine among high-ranking functionaries. Attacks on the author began only after the book was published in the West in 1968.[65]

In May 1972, Shelest was removed from his position as the Ukrainian CC's first secretary. In April 1973, he had to give up his membership in the CPSU's Politburo.[66]

An editorial in the Ukrainian CC's magazine *Komunist Ukraiiny,* in which Shelest's book *Our Soviet Ukraine* received devastating criticism, summarized public attacks accusing him of Ukrainian nationalism.[67] The fallen Party chief had idealized Cossack traditions, played down the significance of the 1654 "reunification" of the Ukraine with Russia, and concealed Russian influence on the development of Ukrainian literature, art, and music. In addition, Shelest had also leaned toward Ukrainian economic autonomy.

Shelest's fall was the beginning of a purge in which probably about one thousand functionaries, scholars, and publicists lost their positions. The purge focused on ideology, literature, and history. F.P. Shevchenko, the Ukrainian Academy of Sciences' director of the Institute of Archeology and publisher of the leading historical magazine, *Ukraiinskyi istorychnyi zhurnal,* also had to resign. Publication of many series—among them *The Middle Ages in the Ukraine* (*Seredni viky na Ukraiini*) and *Kiev Antiquities* (Kyiivska starovyna)—ceased. The announced multi-volume publication of sources on the *Zaporogian Sich* did not materialize. Cautious attempts to rehabilitate Hrushevskyi, the nestor of Ukrainian historiography, were abandoned.[68]

During the Ukrainian purge from 1971 to 1973, there was a campaign against "nationalist remnants" in the other Union Republics. Again, the activities focused on writers, journalists, and historians. They had to face stereotypical reproaches of "idealizing the past," "lack of topical themes," "national exclusiveness and local chauvinism," "neglect of the class perspective," "glorification and poetization of long-obsolete customs and traditions" (Bodiul). National historians tended to whitewash "their" bourgeois-national ideologists, to "present them as noble patriots who were not dedicated to one class alone but altruistically loved their whole nation and all classes. Concealing their class objectives confuses our adolescent generation" (Snieckus).[69]

The Islamic peoples' national self-consciousness manifested itself as the consolidation of the Islamic way of life. After his atheistic speech about the origin of Islam, a member of the audience asked the lecturer, "Are you a Muslim?" "His answer, 'I do not believe in God. This means I am not a Muslim,' outraged them [the audience]. 'How dare you say something like this. You are a Kirgiz!'"[70] "Non-believing Muslims" determined the social reality of the major Central Asian and many Northern Caucasian peoples. This obvious oxymoron coined in the Soviet Union accurately reflects reality: Although Islam barely survived as an institutional religious congregation, the new elites did not at all stop feeling part of the Islamic cultural complex. They separate their way of life consciously from European, i.e., Russian, lifestyles even if most Uzbek doctors or Tadzhik Party functionaries have never set foot in a mosque for Friday prayers. About 450 registered, i.e., legally active, "great mosques" (*diami*) existed in the early 1980s; 200 of them were in Central Asia and Kazakhstan.[71]

As a way of life, Islam emanates from the family, extending its influence deeply into society. As a result, Islam splits the populations of Central Asia and the Caucasian Islamic territories into a European and non-European sub-society. Circumcision is among the most important characteristics of membership in the Islamic society. Nearly 100 percent of the men in Central Asia, Kazakhstan, and the Caucasus are circumcised. Asians and Europeans funeral ceremonies also differ. Even Party functionaries and other members of the leadership bury their dead in Islamic cemeteries according to Islamic rites. Many people choose an Islamic wedding ceremony. There were 2,000 to 3,000 officially registered Islamic clerics who could not keep up with the demand for their services. In addition to them, thousands of so-called travelling mullahs and dervishes were active.

All over Central Asia, the Islamic New Year's Day (*nauruz*) is a holiday, which the Soviets have given up on fighting, and they also tolerate the tradition of circumcision now. They integrate New Year's festivities into their system and re-label it as a spring and peasant festival. A similar situation is true of the council of *aksakals* (council of elders) that has great moral authority in Central Asia and the Caucasus, which the Party wants to use to its own advantages. The council of *aksakals* "meets at the initiative of Party, soviet, or social organs whenever it is necessary to mobilize public opinion against one or the other anti-social phenomenon, to condemn the behavior of individual fanatic believers."[72]

Although collectivization stripped the extended family of its economic foundations, many elements of the patriarchal family survived. The family head's authority seems unbroken. He manages the income of all the household's family members and is instrumental in choosing the daughters' bridegroom. In contrast, the wife's position is secondary within and without the family; the great number of children occupies the wife for the most part. Apparently, the *kalym* – the groom's payments to his bride's parents – is still a quite common custom. These payments are just as illegal as maintaining a harem—a not-infrequent practice among higher functionary circles.[73] There are almost no mixed marriages to "reconcile" the differences between Asians and Europeans. Aside from very few exceptions, people strictly follow the *sharia*, which prohibits Islamic women from marrying European men.

From 1940 to 1960, Kokchetav, Kustanai, Pavlodor, and Tselinograd, the four northern Kazakh regional capitals whose populations are nationally not at all homogeneous, registered 109,000 marriages. Depending on the city, 34 to 40 percent of all marriages were mixed. This percentage was far above the Soviet average. In a period of nearly thirty years, however, there were only 49 marriages between a Kazakh woman and a Russian man.[74] Other studies show that the Islamic peoples' endogamous tendencies even increased in the 1960s and 1970s. This is particularly true in Dushanbe and such rural raions as those in Northern Kazakhstan, where such a development was the least expected because the environment provides many interethnic contacts.[75]

The consolidation of secularized Islam created a mixed culture of traditional Islamic values and norms and of Soviet modernization and Russian-Western culture. Secularized Islam did not dissolve into a homogeneous Soviet society but took advantage of modernization to increase its impact on society. The Islamic heritage displayed in particular ways of life ties together many peoples in the USSR. This decreased the significance of linguistic and cultural differences among Central Asian peoples in post-Stalin society. The awareness of a common Islamic heritage supersedes people's awareness that they are part of a nation—an attitude that has never been as pronounced in Central Asia as in Europe.[76]

The Asian peoples' modern literature, which only developed in Soviet times, has become one of the most important means of expressing and promoting the new consciousness. The young literatures replaced the motifs of Stalinist realism—cotton-picking and the love of tractors—with the search for cultural roots and the heritage of the past. Literature focuses on sagas and legends and the poetic-patriotic depiction of history's great epochs. In his novel *The Architect*, Uzbek writer Mirmukhsin resurrects the fifteenth-century Timurids and presents their era not only as a period of political greatness but also as the high point of culture and humanist thinking.[77]

In his book *Az i ia*,[78] Kazakh writer Suleimenov even goes a step further and claims most of the *Tale of the Host of Igor*, the most important epic of the Russian Middle Ages, for his own, Turkic tradition. He accuses Russian historians of suppressing the Turkic roots of the *Tale of the Host of Igor* for patriotic reasons and because they suffered from "inferiority complexes." Igor was "no hawk but a despicable bird feeding on carcasses." Suleimenov triggered a storm of outrage in the Russian press. In February 1976, a conference hosted by the Academy of Sciences of the USSR's Bureau of the

Department of History and the Bureau of the Department for Literature and Language condemned the book and accused its author of Turkic chauvinism.[79] In March 1977, Suleimenov published a partial recantation. However, according to a prominent Soviet scholar and department head at the CPSU's Institute for Marxism-Leninism, this disclaimer did "not factually condemn the damage the book had caused." The book's "tone and its meaning even more" are "unprecedented in Soviet literature, particularly in the literature dedicated to the mutual relationship among the sister nations." In December 1983, the author of "blatant preaching of national exclusiveness"[80] was elected chairman of the Writers' Union of Kazakhstan in the presence and, consequently, with the consent of the Kazakh Party leadership.[81]

One of the novels by the Kirgiz Chingiz Aitmatov revolves around preserving the memory of the past. People without memory become slaves. It is necessary to preserve the old Islamic cemetery threatened by space technology as well as the memory of the terror the Stalin era caused. Only a living collective memory (i.e., history) can protect man from the total manipulation threatening him.[82]

In 1981, the leading Uzbek literary magazine *Star of the East* (*Zhark iulduzi*), which has a circulation of over 200,000, published the novel *Immortal cliffs* (*Olmas gaialar*) by the young Uzbek writer, Mamadali Makhmudov. This novel openly expresses nationalist and anti-Russian emotions. The story takes place in the mid-nineteenth century and focuses on the Russian conquest of Central Asia. Contrary to Party doctrine, which says that all Tsarist conquests "objectively" served historical progress, Makhmudov's protagonists bitterly complain that Turkestan's people have no desire to resist. The novel paints a gloomy picture of the Russian conquest and rule. The novel's hero organizes local resistance, and the antagonist collaborates with the intruders. The resistance quickly collapses because the tribes fight individually and do not coordinate their efforts. For the future, the main protagonist Boranbek demands the cooperation of Central Asia's five major peoples and compares them to the five fingers of a hand. Although in early 1982, a resolution by the Writers' Union of Uzbekistan and the Uzbek press heavily criticized the novel for "ideological errors," it nevertheless passed censorship and was officially published.[83] Of course, not all the literature the Islamic writers produced serves to consolidate a new, decidedly non-Russian, non-European culture. Typically however, the most creative writers see their task in reviving their peoples' old traditions.

Ethno-Social and Economic Imbalance

Collectivization and the "revolution from above" rocked the foundations of the peoples' traditional societies. The violent, revolutionary changes everybody was exposed to, however, diminished the differences among the peoples. Although Estonian and Uzbek kolkhozniks did not become interchangeable, revolutionizing the village brought their social positions closer together. This is even more true for the new Soviet intelligentsia, whom the mostly conforming educational system socialized. Ukrainian and Buriat doctors are more similar to each other than Ukrainian Orthodox priests and Buriat Buddhist monks. These examples suggest that post-Stalinist society is experiencing a great deal of ethno-social rapprochement.

On the other hand, Soviet modernization created new ethno-social differences among the nations, that had not existed before and had developed against the planners' desires and expectations. This is *inter alia* due to the peoples' birth rate differences and the nations' different population growth. Before World War II, the peoples' birth rates were quite balanced. In 1926, Russian women between the ages of 20 to 49 had 1.23 children aged 0–9 on the average; Uzbek women in the same age group only had a slightly below the Soviet average 1.13 children aged 0–9.[84] In 1940, the birth rate in the USSR was 31.2 per thousand, in the RSFSR 33 per thousand, in the Ukraine 27.3 per thousand, and in Uzbekistan 33.8 per thousand; only Kazakhstan and Armenia had birth rates considerably above the average, Latvia and Estonia had clearly below average birth rates.[85]

After 1950, the peoples' birth rates and population growth progressed at dramatically different paces. The birth rates of the Slavic and Baltic peoples declined; at the same time, the birth rates of the Islamic peoples increased. There, they climaxed in about 1960 and then also began declining. However, the difference that had developed between peoples with high birth rates and those with low birth rates not only persisted but even increased. The population growth among those peoples that had a slow growth rate to begin with declined faster than among Islamic peoples that started out with a high growth rate. In 1970, Russian women of child bearing age (20–49 years) had an average of 0.73 children aged 0–9; Uzbek women in the same age group, however, had 2.40 children. Among the other Slavic peoples, Estonians, and Latvians, the mother-child ratio was about the same as among Russians; among all Asian peoples with a Union Republic of their own and several Northern Caucasian peoples (Daghestani peoples, Chechens, Ingush), however, this ratio ranged from 2.21 to 2.44.[86] In 1980, the population in the RSFSR grew naturally by 4.9 per thousand, in the Ukraine by 3.4 per thousand, in Uzbekistan, however, by 26.4 per thousand.[87] This means that the population in the four Central Asian republics was growing five times as fast as in the Russian Federation (cf. Table A.1 in the Appendix).[88]

In the next decades, the population balance will continue to tip in favor of Islamic peoples because extremely strong age groups are entering child bearing age. In 1970, 48 to 51 percent of the population of the six Islamic peoples with a Union Republic of their own were between 0 and 14 years old; this age group made up 26 percent of the Russian population, 24 percent of the Ukrainian population, and 21 percent of the Estonian population. Islamic peoples as a whole will increase their percentage in the Soviet Union's population from 11 percent in 1959 to more than 20 percent in 2000. Uzbeks, the largest Islamic people, will grow to about 25 million, surpassing Belorussians at a ratio of 2.5 to one. As to their demographic potential, i.e., concerning the number of children born, it is possible for Uzbeks to surpass Ukrainians by the year 2000 and they will be about to become the Soviet Union's second largest people.[89]

Already today, these demographic shifts have considerable effects in many different areas and will be even more noticeable in the future. From 1971 to 1985, the USSR's working age population increased by thirty million people; from 1986 to 2000 the working age population will only grow by another six million people. Nearly 100 percent of this increase in work force potential originates in the country's southern regions; at the same time, work force potentials in the Baltic and Slavic republics will experience a net decline.[90] Because the growth of the Soviet economy essentially depends on extensive factors like the increase of work force potential, changed demographic conditions have an immediate effect on the economy's efficiency.

The nations' different birth rates also have direct impact on the national make-up of the Soviet armed forces. Already in 1980, 23.5 percent of the Soviet Union's eighteen year-old males were Turkic men; by 1990, the percentage of Turkic recruits will climb to nearly 30 percent.[91] Because of this, the Soviet armed forces have to deal with more and more integration problems including many recruits' insufficient knowledge of Russian, their divergent eating habits (pork!), and national resentments and conflicts that surface in brawls and mutiny. Top military personnel even publicly talk about the "unfavorable demographic situation," which was not to "influence fighting power."[92]

The fact that the nations' population growth developed in different directions halted or reversed trends that had provided specific conditions for nationalities policy for decades. In the 1950s, the percentage of Russians in the total population began to decrease; by 1979, it had dropped to 52.4 percent. This halted a development that had begun at least in the late nineteenth century and caused the Russian percentage in the USSR's total population (within the USSR's contemporary borders) to increase continuously from 44.4 percent in 1897 to 54.6 in 1959.[93] The dramatic decline of Russian population growth from an annual 2.15 percent in the 1930s to 0.72 percent in the 1970s (Appendix Table A.1) had two kinds of effects in the national territories: For the most part, the Russian eastward migration has come to a halt and some territories even saw more Russians leave than arrive. In addition, the percentage of the native population began to increase in all Asian and Transcaucasian Union Republics and the Northern Caucasian Autonomous Republics in the 1950s (Appendix Table A.2). Just like the development of national classes of intellectuals, demographic development suggests that there is a trend towards national autonomization.

In the 1960s, smaller numbers of Russians continued migrating to Kazakhstan (from 1959 to 1970, the net migration of Russians numbered about one million because of the virgin-land campaign in northern Kazakhstan) and Central Asia.[94] In Georgia at this time, not only the percentage of Russians was declining but also their absolute numbers (Appendix Table A.2). Russians were leaving Georgia. In the 1970s, more Russians definitely left Georgia and Azerbaidzhan and probably also Armenia, Kazakhstan, and Kirgizistan than moved there.[95] In contrast, Russian migration westward, which started only after World War II (with the exception of the Ukraine), continued even in the time when the number of Russians in the overall population declined. In the 1950s, the number of Russians in the populations clearly began to grow in the Ukraine, Belorussia, Moldavia, Latvia, and Estonia. In Estonia and Latvia, Russian immigrants caused the most lasting changes in the population mixture. Lithuania was the only western republic not to become an immigration territory. This had several causes: the fact that industrialization only began in the late 1960s, the relatively high Lithuanian birth rate (for European standards), and the Lithuanian Party leadership's clever anti-immigration policy.

In the 1930s, peoples had exhibited extremely varied migratory behavior. This fact did not change in post-Stalin times. After 1959, the concentration of nationals of a Union Republic increased in their own territories or remained at the same level for all nations but Russians and Belorussians (Table A.3 in the Appendix). Armenians and members of the Baltic peoples began to move back to their own Union Republics. Non-Slavic peoples with a Union Republic of their own continued their tendencies of not migrating to other republics.

As a rule, a considerably larger share of the ASSR peoples lived outside their own territories. Nevertheless, concentration in their own territories, the degree of compact settlement, also increased in many of these peoples. Several peoples—like Tatars and Bashkirs—migrated less after 1959 than they had in the previous decades. Only few peoples—like Udmurts and Mari—tended to emigrate from their Autonomous Republics at a higher rate in the post-Stalin period. This is tied to the fact that the Finnic peoples in the Volga area tend to assimilate Russian culture—a tendency other indicators also suggest.

However, other factors besides the migration behavior also influenced the degree of compact settlement. For example, the increasing percentages of Karelians, Mordvinians, and Komi living in their own territory is due to the assimilation of nationals living outside national territories to Russian culture. Also, the number of Ukrainians emigrating from the Ukraine must be assumed to be greater than the figures in Table A.3 in the Appendix indicate because a certain number of Ukrainians living outside the Ukraine absorb Russian tradition.[96]

In comparison to the Stalin era, the last three decades, on the whole, have witnessed less intermixing of the peoples through migration. This development is *inter alia* due to the declining Russian birth rate and the increasing worker shortage in Siberian industrial areas and Russian villages. Both factors discourage Russian from emigration to national territories where they also have to compete with locals for qualified employment and frequently are the subject of discrimination.

That migration no longer intermixes the peoples as much is also a consequence of the fact that the rapidly growing Asian peoples are extremely disinterested in migrating. In 1979, 99.3 percent of Uzbeks, 98.5 percent of Kirgiz, Tadzhiks, and Turkmen, and 91.8 percent of Kazakhs lived in the five Asian Union Republics. So far, many organized recruiting measures and corresponding propaganda efforts to entice members of the Asian peoples to relocate to Russian or Siberian industrial centers have failed. Also, the recruitment of young people by offering them training and education in Russia has only been moderately successful. Members of the Islamic peoples are tied to their homelands by their extended families, cultural integration, and language. It is very difficult to get them to move into the cities in their own republics let alone to move away from home altogether. The Russian look of the cities is like a barrier. A poll conducted by the Academy of Sciences' Institute for Ethnography revealed that only 8 percent of young rural Uzbeks were interested in moving to the cities (within Uzbekistan!); 34 percent of young rural Russians were interested in such a move.[97] As a result, the number of under- or unemployed Asian workers, many of whom are skilled professionals, has been increasing rapidly since the 1960s; other parts of the country are experiencing worker shortages. Soviet estimates suggest that, in the 1970s, 20 to 25 percent of the Uzbek work force were not involved in the socialized sector of the economy. Many of these uninvolved were the victims of hidden unemployment.[98]

For a long time, Asian Party leaders have been demanding higher capital investment, which they consider the only means to remedy the social and political problems caused by Asia's structural unemployment. However, Moscow has not responded to these demands. The percentage of capital investment in the Asian Union Republics has not increased since the mid-1960s, in Kazakhstan, it even dropped slightly.[99] In 1984, the Politburo decided to build a 2,000 kilometer long canal from the Ob to Lake Aral to increase the amount of farmland in Asia. This decision seemed to indicate that the Asian lobby had scored a partial victory. The leadership, however, made new decisions in the second half of 1985 that put the completion of the "structure of the century" off into the far future.[100] Later, the Gorbachev leadership scrapped the plan of *Sibaral* altogether. The Party leaders do not think it opportune to follow the advice expressed in Soviet literature and entice Asian peoples to migrate by exerting more economic and administrative pressure on them.[101] To date, the Asian lobby has even prevented measures that were considerably milder than any administrative pressure to stimulate worker migration: The Soviets have not yet been able to establish birth control or planned-parenthood programs in the Asian republics. There is no differentiated population policy in the USSR deserving of this name although Soviet experts have been demanding such a policy for a long time and Brezhnev promised it at the Twenty-sixth Party Congress in February 1981.[102]

Urbanization was another area in which Soviet modernization was unable to meet its own standards of homogenizing peoples and areas. With the exception of Jews, Russians have been the by far most urbanized people (Table A.5 in the Appendix). For many peoples, the urbanization gap, relative to the Soviet average, is wider today than in 1926 (Georgians, Azeri, Uzbeks, Tadzhiks), some have come a little closer to the average (Ukrainians, Belorussians, Kazakhs, Turkmen, Kirgiz). Although the growth rate of Russians in city populations remained below the Soviet average after 1959 — in the Stalin era it had been clearly above the average — other factors have prevented the other nationalities from gaining ground (Table A.4 in the Appendix). The most important reason for this was that the developments of European and Asian rural populations were at opposite end of the growth scale. From 1959 to 1979, the rural populations in the three Slavic and three Baltic Union Republics declined by 22 percent — primarily because of migration to the cities. In the same twenty-year period, the natural growth of rural populations in the four Central Asian Union Republics increased by 70 percent.[103] Although the USSR is considerably more urbanized (62 percent in 1979 as compared to 48 percent in 1959) and urban populations in the Asian nations have grown above average, developmental distances among the nations have barely changed in the post-Stalin era. In 1979, Azeri and Turkmen were even less urbanized, relative to the average, than in 1959 (Table A.5 in the Appendix). In the same time period, the European peoples — Ukrainians, Belorussians, and Lithuanians — managed to become considerably more urbanized without reaching the Soviet average, much less getting near the Russians.

With the exception of Jews and Armenians, the majority of non-Russians continued to live in rural environments. In 1979, 75 percent of the Russians, between 50 and 60 percent of the Slavic and Baltic peoples, and only 30 percent of the Asian peoples lived in cities. About 40 percent of the ASSR peoples in the Volga area and the European north were urbanites in 1979. At 63 percent, only Tatars were more urbanized; 75 percent of this people lived outside its own republic and many Tatars migrated from rural environments to cities.[104] Considerably more than half of the non-Russians lived in villages, a relatively nationally homogeneous environment with limited interethnic contacts. As a result, the new classes of national intellectuals coexist with a social "back-country" that is still largely determined by traditional values, behaviors, and rhythms of life.

Some aspects of the Islamic peoples' urbanization occur along lines that distinguish this process from urbanization in the country's European part and from corresponding social changes in the Third World. Beginning in the 1950s, local urban populations in the Soviet east essentially grew because of natural reproduction; migration to the cities contributed only marginally. In the RSFSR and western republics, migration to the cities was the major contributor to the cities' growth. Moving into the cities changed the Slavic and Baltic peoples' demographic behavior and also lowered their birth rates. Islamic peoples did not undergo such changes. Birth rates among urbanites were only slightly below rural birth rates. At the height of births in about 1960, even more Turkmen were born in the cities than in the rural areas.[105] Unlike in Third World countries, improved opportunities to get an education, higher standards of living, and partial emancipation of women did not lower the number of births considerably. However, most Third World governments have adopted birth control measures. Apparently, the multi-people state of the USSR is unable to introduce such measures for political reasons because they would only target Asian peoples.

The elevated position of Russians in the Union Republics' social structure is among the most visible ethno-social imbalances. There, "most of them have considerable advantages" and are overrepresented "in the more influential, better paid or socially more prestigious professions."[106] The visibility of this imbalance increases its political significance, creates resentment, and challenges locals to counter actions. A comparison of the level of education of Russians living outside the RSFSR with that of Russians living in the RSFSR and with that of the titular nation reveals that — with the single exception of Georgia — most Russians living outside the RSFSR are much more educated than locals and Russians living in the RSFSR. In 1970, for example, 4.3 percent of Russians in the RSFSR over the age of ten graduated from an institution of higher education; in Belorussia, however, 9.7 percent graduated; in Uzbekistan, 6.8 percent; and in Lithuania, 5.6 percent; the corresponding figures for the respective titular nation in its own republic are 2.4 percent, 2.6 percent, and 3.3 percent. Even more serious is the fact that, in respect to the indicator mentioned, the Russian lead in education has increased everywhere but in Estonia from 1959 to 1970. Even in a period when education grew quickly in the non-Russian Union Republics, there was no rapprochement between locals and the Russians living there. The split became even bigger.

The degree of urbanization also reflects the privileged position Russians enjoyed outside Russia. In 1959, 55 percent of Russians living within the RSFSR were urbanites; in the other Union Republics, however, 74 percent of Russians lived in cities. Corresponding 1970 figures were 66 percent and 80 percent. In 1970, at 66 percent and 69 percent respectively, Russians were least urbanized in Kirgizistan and Kazakhstan, which were the only republics a significant number of Russian peasants had migrated to. Most Russian urbanites lived in Turkmenistan and Tadzhikistan. In 1970, 96 percent and 94 percent of the Russians lived in cities in these areas. The distance from locals remained significant everywhere although, in respect to this indicator, the European republics showed a trend towards drawing together.[107]

The Soviet Union has published virtually no data pertaining to the peoples' economic equality or inequality. Western researchers are limited to regional data, which are revealing, however. In spite of noisy propaganda assurances to the contrary, Soviet economic policy has never — not in the Stalin era or after — made overcoming the rift between economically underdeveloped national territories a high-priority issue. Wherever economic equalization occurred, it was only a side effect of other planning priorities, such as development of new resources, increasing regional economic specialization, and primarily military-strategic conceptions. In economic planning, such geopolitical factors had priority over criteria of economic efficiency, such as maximum production increase at minimal costs.[108] The economic planning and administrative system, which was once again organized according to specific trades after Khrushchev's failed experiments, is also proof of the fact that the objective of regional equalization was subordinated to more important priorities of economic policy. There are no effective instruments of regional planning and development, and, even at the level of the Union Republics, the influence of territorial organs is limited to the functions of consultants and lobbyists.

Ideological language also acknowledged the demotion of the goal of balanced development in the national territories because in the Brezhnev era, functionaries consistently emphasized that the Party assessed economic issues "primarily from the perspective of the interests of the whole state."[109] In addition, propaganda fell back on its proven strategy of sweeping problems under the carpet: The "task of balancing the levels of economic development among the Soviet republics" is "essentially solved."[110]

Actually, neglecting this task in the post-Stalin era has aggravated the problems. After 1960, the developmental rift between the relatively advanced republics (Estonia, Latvia, Lithuania, RSFSR) and the economically underdeveloped (Central Asia) even began to increase; this holds true for industrial production and productivity and for the standard of living. However, what makes the process of the republics' growing apart somewhat less dramatic is the fact that it was accompanied by considerable economic growth. According to Western calculations, actual per capita spending increased Union-wide by 3.4 percent per annum from 1950 to the early 1980s and nearly tripled the standard of living. In the 1970s, growth rates clearly declined, dropping below 2 percent by 1981 and below 1 percent by 1982.[111]

The country's regions and nations have been part of the overall economic growth to varying degrees. Outside Russia, efforts to stimulate economic development focused on Siberia preserving Stalin's priorities, and on the western republics of Belorussia, Lithuania, and Moldavia creating new centers of development after 1960. The three Siberian economic regions (Western Siberia, Eastern Siberia, Far East) received 16.6 percent of the country's capital investment in 1960 and 18 percent in 1980. Supporting the three heavily underdeveloped western Union Republics, which are the bridge to the COMECON countries, reduced the developmental differences among the European republics but indirectly contributed to increasing the differences between the developed northwest and the underdeveloped southeast. The planners did not acknowledge the Asian population's different growth rate and its greater demand for capital and jobs, let alone recover lost ground in industrialization. The six Islamic Union Republics had 13.2 percent of all capital investment available in 1960 and 14 percent in 1980. This was considerably less capital than Siberia received (Table 9.3).

As a result, industry's per capita gross republican products developed at different rates after 1960. In 1974, the combined per capita gross products of Turkmenistan, Tadzhikistan, and Uzbekistan, which were the three economically least developed republics, amounted only to a quarter of that of the three industrially most advanced republics (Estonia, Latvia, RSFSR). After this point, the relationships did not change significantly. From 1960 to 1974, Belorussia, Lithuania, and Moldavia had the highest growth rates, the least industrialized republics of Uzbekistan, Tadzhikistan, and Turkmenistan had the lowest.

From 1960 to the mid-1970s, agriculture developed along the same lines because the more industrialized Union Republics also showed higher agricultural production. However, the agricultural per capita gross republican products did not develop at as different a rate as they did in industry. Some underdeveloped republics (Turkmenistan, Tadzhikistan) had above-average growth rates. From 1960 to 1974, Moldavia and Georgia achieved the highest growth rates in agriculture—they were, nevertheless, only half as high as the Unionwide industrial growth rates.[112]

Industrial and agricultural productivity also show considerable regional differences. After 1960, there was no trend towards equalization. Productivity varies more in agriculture than industry. In the 1970s, industrial productivity deviated up to 30 percent above or below the average in some Union Republics. Agricultural productivity in the Baltic republics was three

Table 9.3: Distribution of Capital Investment According to Union Republics (in comparable prices)

	1950	1960	1970	1980
USSR (in millions of Rubles)	12,768	42,017	82,053	133,700
Percentages				
RSFSR	63.00	62.20	59.40	62.40
Ukraine	17.90	17.10	16.10	14.20
Belorussia	2.12	2.28	3.28	3.22
Moldavia	0.59	0.89	1.16	1.12
Estonia	0.67	0.64	0.71	0.62
Latvia	0.72	0.87	1.09	0.96
Lithuania	0.53	0.84	1.39	1.18
Georgia	2.08	1.29	1.35	1.38
Armenia	0.79	0.69	1.01	0.85
Azerbaijan	2.70	1.52	1.46	1.50
Kazakhstan	4.10	6.72	6.57	5.98
Uzbekistan	2.33	2.71	3.80	4.10
Kirgizistan	0.66	0.71	0.88	0.75
Tadzhikistan	0.60	0.69	0.78	0.73
Turkmenistan	0.93	0.82	0.96	0.92

Sources: *Narodnoe khoziaistvo SSSR v 1970 g.* (Moscow, 1971), p. 488; *v 1982*, p. 345.

to four times as high as it was in the Transcaucasian and Central Asian Republics.[113]

In many cases, growth rates were counterproductive in respect to equalization. Productivity grew faster in republics with high agricultural productivity and slower in those with low productivity. From 1966 to 1974, agricultural productivity grew Union-wide at a rate of 5.3 percent annually. However, productivity increased by 9.5 percent in Lithuania, 8.1 percent in Latvia, 7.8 percent in Estonia, 7.9 percent in Belorussia, and by 5.6 percent in the RSFSR. In contrast, productivity grew only by 2.8 percent in Kirgizistan and by 2.2 percent in Uzbekistan. In these republics, the fact that an above-average and in some cases unnecessarily high number of workers went into agriculture lowers productivity and its growth rate. In addition, Central Asian peasants had considerably fewer machines and less fixed capital than peasants anywhere else. In 1972, the average basic fund accounted for 4,400 Rubles per farm worker; Uzbekistan provided only 2,300 Rubles.[114]

In the 1970s, a regional comparison of industrial productivity showed less diversity than corresponding figures for agricultural productivity. Starting with 1940 figures, however, industrial productivity also grew at very different rates until the early 1980s. Estonian, Latvian, and Belorussian industry grew the fastest, with Estonia reaching nearly twice the Union average. Industrial productivity increased most slowly in Tadzhikistan, Uzbekistan, Turkmenistan, and Moldavia. These republics' growth rates were only marginally above half of the Union average.[115] As a result, a Central Asian industrial worker produced only half as much production value as did workers in other parts of the country.[116]

Table 9.4 illustrates the absolute and relative post-1960 development of the standard of living. The figures document the fact that income has increased considerably on the whole and that the hierarchies between poor and rich republics have not changed, while the differences in per capita income have increased. In respect to the all-Union average, the Asian Union Republics lost ground from 1960 to the late 1970s, the Baltic Republics managed to preserve their lead, and only Belorussia and Moldavia succeeded in gaining considerable ground. Their improving standards of living show that these two republics received considerable investment and increased their productivity at above-average rates.

Regional differences in income are comparable to those in Italy and Yugoslavia; they are greater than in the Federal Republic of Germany; however, they are considerably smaller than in some developing countries, such as Brazil.[117]

What standard of living is possible with the income documented in Table 9.4? In the mid-1960s, Soviet economists calculated that the poverty level was 50 Rubles a month. In 1974, the Soviets accepted this figure officially by basing the calculation of the allowance for children on it. Families making less than 50 Rubles per member per month were considered poor (*maloobespechennye*); this entitled them to collect an allowance for children.[118] In 1960, only Estonia and Latvia barely reached this poverty level; in Central Asia, Azerbaidzhan, Moldavia, and Belorussia, per capita monthly income was below 30 Rubles. Even ten years later, average income in the four Central Asian Republics and Azerbaidzhan was around or below the official Soviet poverty level. This means that the majority of the republics' population had to live on an income below the poverty level.[119] In the late 1970s, average income was above the poverty level in all republics. Of course, these figures are only approximations because they cannot account for inflation. Fifty Rubles must be considered the cut-off value for 1960 and is too low for 1978.

Even after Stalin's death, most non-Russians continued to live in rural areas; there are many more kolkhozniks among them than among Russians (cf. chapter IX, section 1). As a result, the regionally differentiated income

A New Nationalism

Table 9.4: Nominal Per Capita Income

	1960	1970	1978
USSR (in Rubles)	446	799	1259
Index (USSR = 100)	100	100	100
RSFSR	108	108	111
Ukraine	94	97	96
Belorussia	81	94	98
Moldavia	70	86	90
Estonia	129	133	127
Latvia	125	125	114
Lithuania	108	118	115
Georgia	94	89	94
Armenia	85	87	87
Azerbaijan	73	66	63
Kazakhstan	95	87	88
Uzbekistan	77	74	72
Kirgizistan	72	72	70
Tadzhikistan	66	63	60
Turkmenistan	74	79	75

Sources: A. McAuley, *Economic Welfare in the Soviet Union* (Madison, Wisc., 1979), p. 109; G. Schroeder, "Regional Living Standards," in: I.S. Koropeckij/G.E. Schroeder (eds.), *Economics of Soviet Regions* (New York, 1981), p. 120. The term "nominal per capita income" includes the wages of blue- and white-collar workers and kolkhoz peasants, the income from money and value of the products produced on private plots, productions-in-kind of the kolkhozes, social security payments, public subsidies (*posobie*), stipends and interest from savings. It does not include government expenditures for child care, education, and public health. The source did not subtract direct taxes from the "nominal income" and did not consider inflation and income from the second economy (McAuley, op. cit., pp. 9ff.).

of kolkhoz peasants reveals the standard of living of a large cross section of non-Russian peoples (Table 9.5). As was to be expected, the income of kolkhozniks was considerably below that of the total population. Also, their income in the individual Union Republics deviated more from the Union average; from 1960 to 1970, the deviation increased slightly. Table 9.5 compares Western and Soviet calculations, which were conducted independently from one another. Using 1970 figures, they largely agreed in respect to most

Table 9.5: Nominal Per Capita Income of Kolkhoz Peasants

	1960	1965	1970		Income per Family in 1970
USSR (in Rubles)	329	460	659	–	–
Index (USSR = 100)	100	100	100	100	100
RSFSR	104	103	109	108	99
Ukraine	99	105	103	109	91
Belorussia	99	99	104	107	98
Moldavia	76	94	92	98	97
Estonia	167	203	202	182	127
Latvia	196	178	170	151	119
Lithuania	153	172	162	143	136
Georgia	111	94	106	106	127
Armenia	69	77	78	77	122
Azerbaijan	72	55	64	65	106
Kazakhstan	98	90	95	77	119
Uzbekistan	100	81	76	68	120
Kirgizistan	77	85	72	71	107
Tadzhikistan	59	69	60	58	105
Turkmenistan	73	95	98	78	140

Sources: A. McAuley, *Economic Welfare in the Soviet Union* (Madison, Wisc., 1979), p. 128 (columns 1-3; see Table 9.4 for an explanation of the term "nominal income"); A. Teriaeva, "Neobkhodimyi trud i ego oplata v selskom khoziaistve," in: *Voprosy ekonomiki*, 5/1972, p. 71 (columns 4-5; the author does not provide any absolute figures pertaining to income).

Union Republics. Although McAuley's figures pertaining to the Baltic states are higher than Teriaeva's, they show the same trend. McAuley's high figures for 1970 Kazakhstan, and particularly for 1965 and 1970 Turkmenistan, are difficult to explain and improbable. Teriaeva's considerably lower figures are preferable because they fit the pattern of the Asian territory and time; McAuley's figures conflict with both. In addition, McAuley himself explicitly pointed out the tentativeness of his figures for 1970.[120] Teriaeva's figures indicate that in the 1960s, the kolkhozniks' per capita income lagged progressively behind the Union average in all Asian Union Republics – with the exception of Turkmenistan. The peasants' income lagged particularly in Uzbekistan, which is the main Asian republic. In 1970, Latvian and Lithuanian kolkhozniks had to cut back on some of their far-above-average income; only Estonian peasants managed to increase their lead over the average. As a group, Baltic kolkhozniks — led by Estonian peasants — were among the USSR's top money earners. Only in the Baltic states did kolkhozniks have a higher standard of living than workers and employees after the 1960s; in all other republics, conditions are reversed. Baltic peasants owe this advantage to a combination of their above-average kolkhoz wages and high income as private producers — with the second factor being the crucial one in the 1960s.[121]

From the perspective of inter-republican equalization, only Moldavia exhibited a tendency to homogenize kolkhoznik income in the 1960s because its per capita income increased at an above-average rate. Although an overall inter-republican equalization never materialized, the kolkhozniks' standard of living increased noticeably all over the country. Of course, this increase varied from republic to republic and from people to people, but no one missed out altogether.

If we compare the income of kolkhozniks in different parts of the country on the basis of what the average kolkhoz family makes, the picture changes dramatically, and it seems as if homogenization had progressed considerably (Table 9.5, column 5). However, this is a fallacy. If a Latvian peasant family consisting of 3.1 members and an Uzbek family consisting of 6.0 members have the same nominal income, their standards of living nevertheless differ greatly from one another.[122] Of course, per capita calculations of income also measure the standard of living in a distorted manner because they do not account for demographic differences and do not consider that children need less to live on than adults or a larger family's economics of scale. However, such inaccuracies are closer to the truth than calculations based on the family.[123]

Table 9.6 measures economic imbalance among regions based on per capita retail sales. It illustrates that differences among individual regions, as well as their development after 1960, show similar tendencies for retail sales as per capita income: Retail sales increased, but differences among the Union Republics also increased. For more than two decades, the depth chart ranking the republics according to the volume of their retail sales essentially did not change. Only Belorussia, Moldavia, and Lithuania managed to move up considerably in the depth chart because they became industrialized and urbanized faster than the USSR as a whole. However, all the six Islamic Union Republics moved down in the depth chart. Estonia achieved about 150 percent of the average retail sales, Azerbaidzhan and Tadzhikistan had only a little over 50 percent of the average in 1982.

The differences among the RSFSR's economic regions were less distinct than among the Union Republics. Also — at least in the 1960s — there was a trend towards their equalization. Contrary to appearances, the above-average retail sales figures for Eastern Siberia and the Far East do not indicate an above-average standard of living. They are only a consequence of

Table 9.6: Per Capita Retail Sales in State and Cooperative Trade (in current prices)

	1960	1970	1982
USSR (in Rubles)	367	639	1095
Index (USSR = 100)	100	100	100
RSFSR	111	110	110
Economic Regions:			
North-West	143	135	
Center	141	132	
Volga-Viatka	85	89	
Central Chernozem	72	80	
Volga	92	90	
Northern Caucasus	91	90	
Ural	98	100	
Western Siberia	97	100	
Eastern Siberia	113	107	
Far East	157	145	
Ukraine	85	91	91
Belorussia	73	91	99
Moldavia	61	76	86
Estonia	142	150	147
Latvia	139	148	139
Lithuania	87	110	115
Georgia	81	77	84
Armenia	76	79	80
Azerbaijan	69	62	58
Kazakhstan	93	87	85
Uzbekistan	74	65	66
Kirgizistan	74	73	70
Tadzhikistan	66	62	56
Turkmenistan	84	73	69

Sources: Narodnoe khoziaistvo SSSR v 1960 g. (Moscow, 1961), p. 685; *v 1970 g.,* p. 579; *v 1982 g.,* p. 430; *Narodnoe khoziaistvo RSFSR v 1960 g.* (Moscow, 1961), pp. 34-37, 433-434; *v 1970 g.,* pp. 12-15, 368-369. The RSFSR's statistical yearbook for 1982 does not provide any data pertaining to retail sales in the administrative-territorial units.

A New Nationalism

these regions' considerably higher grocery prices and the higher costs of living overall. In 1968, per capita costs of living were 21 percent higher in Eastern Siberia and 30 percent higher in the Far East than in central Russia; higher wages compensated for this, though.[124] In the north-western and central regions, which are dominated by the Leningrad and Moscow metropolitan areas, retail sales were at a Baltic level, thus clearly surpassing all other regions in the RSFSR. This reflects the "capital's" higher standard of living.

One may object that per capita retail sales are not the appropriate tool to measure differences in the standards of living because they do not account for the fact that most rural populations supply themselves with home-grown food. This exaggerates the differences between urban and rural territories. After all, in 1960, 55 percent of Soviet per capita retail sales were groceries. In 1982, this figure was still at 50 percent. Another objection is that the USSR's different regions had different retail prices, which means that even given the same number of sales, the quantity of goods sold is different.

In principle, both objections are justified. Practically, however, they are less consequential than they appear on first sight, and they do not alter the results presented. With the exception of the extreme regions of the Far East, Eastern Siberia and the European north, regional price differences are surprisingly small. In comparison to central Russian prices, price differences for a four-member family's shopping basket ranged from 10 percent higher in the Ural region to 4 percent lower in the Ukraine.[125] An analysis of retail sales of non-groceries downgrades the objection that retail sales do not account for rural populations' grocery self-supply. Regional differences and their development over time do not essentially deviate from the figures in Table 9.6.[126]

Expenditures for education, public health, and retirement funds, that is payments from social consumption funds, show a picture quite different than the previous data on production, income, and consumption. Table 9.7 illustrates that the Union's average growth rate in this area was also high after 1960. Contrary to the other areas, however, these growth rates served to reduce regional inequalities. In 1970, differences among Union Republics were smaller than they had been ten years earlier. With the exception of Georgia and Azerbaidzhan, all Union Republics profited from the tendency to balance per capita expenditure for education, public health and social services. This trend also involved the Asian republics, which had lost ground in respect to all per capita indicators from the areas of production and distribution because of their high birth rates. From the perspective of budget expenditures, Table 9.7 documents (as section 1 mentioned) that the non-Russian republics made great efforts to develop their education systems.

Table 9.7: Per Capita Payments and Expenditures from Social Consumption Funds

	1960	1965	1970
USSR (in Rubles)	127	182	263
Index (USSR = 100)	100	100	100
RSFSR	113	111	111
Ukraine	87	89	95
Belorussia	75	82	84
Moldavia	58	65	73
Estonia	126	130	129
Latvia	116	118	121
Lithuania	74	81	86
Georgia	84	81	77
Armenia	--	84	86
Azerbaijan	74	73	69
Kazakhstan	--	88	87
Uzbekistan	65	67	70
Kirgizistan	--	73	76
Tadzhikistan	64	65	70
Turkmenistan	--	79	85

Sources: G.E. Schroeder, "Regional Differences in Incomes and Levels of Living in the USSR," in: V.N. Bandera/Z.L. Melnyk (eds.), *The Soviet Economy in Regional Perspective* (New York, 1973), p. 171. Payments and expenditures from the consumption funds include government expenditures for "free" medical care, education, social security, and subsidies for public housing; they include transfer payments for social security and subsidies and scholarships for high school and college students.

Analyzing expenditures for education and public health independent of the total figures for the consumption funds makes the trend towards relative balance even more apparent. In 1965, public budget per capita expenditures for public health stayed within fairly narrow margins: Estonia spent 127 percent of the Union average, Uzbekistan and Tadzhikistan 81 percent. Interregional equality of per student expenditures in general schools was also quite advanced. In 1965, Kazakhstan spent 91 percent of the Union average (minimum), Latvia 132 percent (maximum).[127]

In summary: With the exception of expenditures from consumption funds, economic differences among the Union Republics increased after 1960. Asia is a territory in which more and more national elites were educated in regions that are continuously becoming poorer in comparison to the Union average. Ethno-social and economic inequalities are essential aspects of the participation crisis.

Ideological Revision

Motivated by Khrushchev's reactionary policy, after 1961, Soviet scholars and journalists began to intensively address the "Party's nationalities policy," the "nationalities issue," "national relations," and the "Soviet people's internationalism." The numbers of publications went through the roof.[128] This was even more remarkable because there were relatively few publications on this topic after the mid-1930s. This new abundance of publications subscribed to the Party's prescribed credo: The Soviet Union has "solved . . . the nationalities issue;" the "socialist nations" are becoming progressively assimilated; their union is "indestructible;" the nations jointly constitute the "Soviet people;" it is on course toward "complete unity;" at the end of the road in the unspecified future the nations will "merge." The nations' "blossoming" accompanies "advancing rapprochement." In the 1960s, ideological literature focused on the "dialectics" of "rapprochement" and "blossoming" and on defining the term "nation."[129] In the 1970s, its ideological catchword was the "Soviet people." It served to determine the status quo and outline future perspectives.

"The Soviet people is a new historical socio-political and international community. It is an inseparable unity of classes and social groups, of nations and nationalities, which is founded on mature socialism, Marxism-Leninism, and the internationalism characteristic of it and on common interests and goals, the unity of economic, socio-political, and cultural life, common traits of character, morals, lifestyle, and the traditions of the creators of communism."[130] Soviet literature repeated this definition in many variations. As demonstrated earlier, it originated from a remark in Khrushchev's speech on the new Party program at the Twenty-second Party Congress in October 1961. One ethno-sociological study lists the characteristics of the Soviet people: "a common economic life;" "a common social and class structure;" "a common political life;" "a common intellectual life;" "the international unity of all nations, nationalities, national and ethnic groups;" "common Soviet lifestyle (*obraz zhizni*);" "a single international language for the whole community."[131]

When Khrushchev coined the formula that "the Soviet people is a new historical community of people," he only revised his predecessor's famous definition: Stalin had said that a nation was a stable community of people that has grown over the course of history as a result of a common language, territory, economic life, and psychological characteristics, which become apparent in the common culture.[132] In the Soviet Union, this application of

Stalin's definition of a nation to the Soviet people was not openly addressed." Most Western researchers have also remained unaware of this connection.

However, this ideological revision was along the lines the dead dictator had envisioned because his policy had been directed at forming a "Soviet people" ever since the 1930s. Probably the doctrine was never revised while Stalin was still alive because it would have contradicted previous statements of the "leader of the peoples" too strongly, and he would have had to dump his own definition of the term nation on the "garbage pile of history," so to speak. In 1961, this was very convenient for Khrushchev, it fit the political course of the Twenty-Second Party Congress.

In the late 1960s, the ideological theorem of the "Soviet people" as a "new historical community of people" began to become the central term of nationalities theory. In 1969, the term appeared in the CC's theses on the occasion of Lenin's 100th birthday. At the Twenty-fourth Party Congress in March/April 1971 and in his speech on the occasion of the fiftieth anniversary of the foundation of the USSR in December 1972, Brezhnev canonized the concept for good. Finally, the Soviets included it into the preamble to the new 1977 constitution.[133]

Of course, it was difficult to adapt Stalin's concept of "common language" to the Soviet people. On the other hand, this concept was particularly suited to adding additional ideological emphasis to the political demand for bilingualism for non-Russians. This is where Soviet ideology clearly deviated from Stalin's idea that, sometime in the future, after the revolution's victory on a worldwide scale, languages would "melt" into a uniform world language. On occasion, Stalin was confronted with claims that this mirage had obstructed the spread of Russian. "He (Stalin) ignored the objective and progressive process of developing and spreading Russian as the language of international communication. This slowed down the learning and spreading of this process."[134] However, the fact that another writer declared the "unification of languages" a fantasy of Sovietologists is even more bizarre than this outgrowth of Khrushchevist excitement.[135]

The Soviet people doctrine cannot be reconciled with the idea that the processes of the nations' "rapprochement" and "development" or "blossoming" occur at the same time or are even equally important. In principle, the 1961 Party program maintained this equality and simultaneity, which in itself was a drastic revision of 1920s and 1930s Soviet ideology. Into the 1930s, functionaries continuously emphasized that the Soviet Union was in the phase of the "nations' blossoming;" they reserved the phases of "rapprochement" and "merging" for the distant future. Adopting the Soviet people doctrine, Soviet ideologists were consistent in declaring "rapprochement" to be the "dominant tendency" in this "dialectic process." Their logic was that, until the late 1930s, underdeveloped nations had focused their energies on "blossoming." In the phase of developed socialism, however, the "tendency towards rapprochement" had "priority."[136]

Within the framework of the Soviet people doctrine, most ideologists described the "dialectics" of these two processes, saying that "blossoming" was part of "rapprochement." Not only were these two processes not mutually exclusive, but the nations' "development" strived towards their "rapprochement." "... the nations' blossoming, which strives towards rapprochement, strengthens rapprochement."[137] Wording like this more or less openly illustrated that ideological revision demoted the nations' "development" to second place and subordinated it to "rapprochement." "The primary law governing the Soviet people's development is the continuous stabilization of its unity on the basis of the society's social homogeneity and the movement of all nations and nationalities towards complete unity."[138]

Some writers described the nations' "continuous rapprochement" as "the disappearance of national differences, the removal ... of the remnants of detrimental and obsolete national customs and behaviors ... "[139] At the same time, "internationalization" expands "common characteristics among the peoples' lifestyles in all areas."[140] Some Soviet writers described the situation in less harmonizing words: "In some way or other," rapprochement "invades the sanctum of intellectual national values, collides with the conservativism of national consciousness, and does not take place painlessly, without resistance and without zigzagging."[141] However, this position, which questions the assumption that the interests of "national issues" and "international issues" are immaculately identical, has been attacked. This position implied an antagonistic contradiction — something socialism did not permit.[142]

Some ideologists did not even respect the decade-old sanctity of the term "friendship of the peoples." They declared that this term was no longer appropriate to describe "national relations" within the Soviet people, which were increasingly characterized by commonalities and similarities and had to be replaced by the term "international unity of Soviet society."[143]

Because the Soviet people doctrine transferred the essential characteristics of a nation to the Soviet people, one question arises: What effect did the ideological revision have on the characteristics of the "socialist nation?" Is it only the homogeneous part of a homogeneous larger whole? "The features characteristic of the whole Soviet people become extremely significant for the intellectual make-up of every socialist nation." This was not only true for culture but also for economy, social structure, and (Marxist-Leninist) philosophy.[144] What are the differences among socialist nations and between them and the Soviet people? Surprisingly, the prestigious term "nation" is one of the differences between the parts and the whole. The Party's official statements and the overwhelming majority of ideologists and scholarly experts—apart from a few agitators—declined to speak of a "Soviet nation." This title was reserved for the individual peoples. In this respect, ideologists distinguished between "Soviet people" and "nations." In addition, they had problems describing the specific differences among socialist nations and were content to illustrate the "essential" differences between "bourgeois" and "socialist" nations. Without naming him as the source, they emulate Stalin's ideas.[145]

Contrary to societies under the yoke of capitalism, socialist nations are "free of class antagonisms," and "monolithic in respect to their economic foundation and moral-political make-up." The "progressive features" of "national character" from the pre-revolutionary period have survived, enriched by "new features developed in the socialist period." However, "those features of national character reflecting the antiquated living conditions of the nation in its historical past" disappeared.[146] Soviet theory said that in "essence," socialist nations developed during the period from the revolution to the late 1930s. Some of them changed from bourgeois nations into socialist ones (among these are the three Eastern Slavic, the three Baltic nations, and Armenians and Georgians); others skipped the capitalist stage and became socialist right away (among these are all Central Asian peoples). From this perspective, the development of socialist nations also retains its positive significance within the framework of the theory of the Soviet people. Dialectics even makes it possible to say that "the process of developing communism will strengthen the internal unity of the Ukrainian socialist nation."[147]

On the one hand, the concept of Soviet people obscures the contours of socialist nations, which are part of the Soviet people; on the other hand, the Soviet people cannot exist without socialist nations. "Softening national differences" is a process progressing at different rates in different areas; in some, it is unnoticeable. In mature socialism, "national factors . . . have shifted . . . to a large degree . . . from the political and economic sphere to the socio-psychological, to the area of intellectual life." Today, socialist nations embody the national aspect in their "national consciousness; national psychology; language; national culture; lifestyle, traditions, and customs; national statehood; and economy." (The order in which these aspects are listed reflects a progression from the important to the less important).[148]

The Soviet people did not develop spontaneously on its own as a result of socio-economic conditions. Soviet ideology emphatically stressed the "subjective factor:" the "Party's leading role." " . . . the formation and development of the Soviet people are not ungovernable, spontaneous phenomena, dependent on the desires of individual groups, but a scientifically controlled process . . . " This control is the Party's task.[149] Some Soviet studies presented the Party's role with disarming openness, leaving no doubts that the Soviets mostly "produced" socialist nations and the Soviet people. A representative collection titles the chapter on Lithuania, "The Communist Party's Policy—the Foundation of the Formation of the Lithuanian Socialist Nation."[150] Assuming an anti-Marxist perspective, this study correctly explains that the Party created the two essential conditions responsible for the beginning of the Lithuanian socialist nation: 1. "Elimination of private property as a means of production, elimination of the class of exploiters, creation of socialist economy, and the formation of new classes of socialist society." 2. "Overcoming bourgeois ideology and the formation of socialist philosophy. In other words, one concerns more the foundation; the other the superstructure."[151] In another paragraph, the author is not afraid of mentioning that in February 1941—six months *after* the Red Army's occupation and including the emigrants and Russians it brought along—the Lithuanian Party had only 3,133 members and candidates.[152]

Under the conditions created by "mature socialism" and the "building of a communist society" the Party's leadership task does not decrease but continues to grow. Post-Stalin ideology emphasized the validity of this general postulate, particularly for the area of national relations. Due to the "extraordinary complexity" the Party's leadership task may be referred to as the "most political of political activities."[153] The Party regulates the speed of "rapprochement" and "development." It determines the political tools, deploys them, and develops new ones if necessary.

The "Party's management of national relations" is the most advanced form of and most general expression possible for scientifically based and insured management.[154] The Party's management function is particularly effective and needed in situations when it is necessary to check individual interests and enforce the interests of the whole state.[155]

The Soviet people is not a nation but has the characteristics of a nation. It owes its existence to the revolutionary elimination of capitalism but increasingly requires the Party's leadership to prevent its breakup. The question arises whether there are historical models or historical analogies in other multi-national empires. Soviet ideologists found a relatively simple solution to this problem: "The Soviet people has no analogy in history. It represents a new form of human community, which is the highest form known . . ." The Soviet people is not only the "first new historical community of people," but also "the highest form of social and international union of people."[156] "Of course, there were many multi-national and multi-ethnic states in the past, but their tribes and nations did not form uniform peoples. Tsarist Russia is a particularly good example because dozens of nations, nationalities, and ethnic groups lived next to one another in a territory but did not form a community."[157]

However, this historically inaccurate position has not remained unchallenged. Kim, for example, demanded that more attention be paid to the Soviet people's "pre-history." "The cultural-ideological line of succession ties the spirit of Russia's pre-revolutionary people to that of the Soviet people, which initiated and continued the struggle for the ideals of communism."[158] However, so far there are no serious Soviet scholarly attempts to compare, for example, the nationalities policies of Tsarist Russia and the Soviet Union. Soviet ideology persisted on its point of view that the Soviet people is unique and also claimed that the Soviet people serve as a model for the future. This claim was not restricted to the more-or-less abstract projection that all nations had to pass through the stage of the Soviet people on their way towards a communist society but said that such social and national communities were actually in the process of developing in some socialist states (e.g., CSSR, Vietnam, Yugoslavia).[159]

It is not surprising that Soviet scholars cannot agree on how to define the developmental periods of an artifact such as the Soviet people. Most of them said that the "foundations" for the "new community" were laid before World War II and "the final stage in the development of the Soviet people" took place from 1945 to 1965.[160] Some scholars, however, did not at all agree with this division. Some claimed that the "construction of socialism" and the evolution of the Soviet people are simultaneous processes. According to this opinion, the development of the "new community" began with the October Revolution and had essentially come to an end by the late 1930s.[161] Other scholars claimed the Soviet people developed "during the late 1960s."[162]

After Stalin, the Party was afraid of mentioning in official documents that the final goal of its nationalities policy was the "merger of nations." Soviet scholars, however, began to make a habit of pointing out this objective in the early 1960s. The spectrum of their positions ranged from the claim that the USSR was already in the process of "merging" to the soothing statement that the nations would only merge after communism's worldwide victory.[163]

In December 1982, on the occasion of the sixtieth anniversary of the foundation of the USSR, Secretary General Andropov broke this rule in his speech and—hidden in a Lenin quote—mentioned the "merger of nations" as the goal.[164] However, Soviet journalists were very hesitant to adopt this ominous term; even the Union Republics' Party chiefs avoided it. It has nevertheless since become part of the official Party line, and prominent scholars use the term explicitly.[165] Only communism could bring a "full merger," but "on the basis of the nations' blossoming and rapprochement, it begins in the socialist stage." Kaltakhchian distinguishes different areas. At the socialist stage, mergers occur in the economy, politics, and ideology; however, the nations' cultures, lifestyles, traditions, and idiosyncracies in nataional character only become more similar.[166]

The idea of merger became somewhat less threatening because Soviet ideologists usually said nations only merge after class differences have disappeared. In other words, they expected nations to have a higher historical life expectancy than classes. In the early 1960s, some Soviet scholars proclaimed that the end of Soviet federalism was near; today, virtually no Soviet publication refers to this. The 1977 constitution did not touch the basic structures of the Union Republics' and Autonomous Republics' "national statehood," and in his speech about the constitution, Brezhnev explicitly refuted all such demands.[167] As a result, Soviet scholars still argued that "the national form of statehood" was "necessary until statehood had died altogether."[168]

The Soviet people doctrine did not revise the 1940s ideology of the "great Russian people," the "older brother," and "first among equals." Apparently, Soviet ideologists did not see any logical problems in simultaneously emphasizing the "equality of all nations" and referring to the Russian people as the "leading" one. "The language of the Union's most developed nation, which has guided the country through its revolutionary transformation," is Russian.[169] Batyrev writes "the Russian socialist nation ... is the primary force in our country's family of socialist nations." In the process "of the Soviet socialist nations' mutual enrichment in art and in other spheres of life, the art of the Russian people plays the leading role."[170]

Because Russian has been declared the "second native tongue" of non-Russians and as such to be a characteristic feature of the Soviet people, journalists and scholars began to paint the "more equal than equal" status of the Russian language in glowing colors in the early 1960s. They even did justice to panegyric: The "Russian socialist nation" had "reached the heights of human science and culture." "Because of its richness and diversity," the Russian language is "quite an extraordinary treasure chest of the accomplishments of civilization." Russian is "an exceptionally rich and beautiful language." "And finally, Russian is the language of Vladimir Ilich Lenin."[171] Another typical text claims that Russian is "more advanced" than the USSR's other languages "in the areas of politics, economy, and science." However, this is not true for the areas of culture and every day life.[172]

In combination with the Russian people's "dominant" role, the Soviet people doctrine, which is directed at the progressive repression of national idiosyncracies and differences, is, of course, suited to awaken fear of denationalization and Russification. Several writers tried to counteract this fear and the passive resistance it might trigger by emphasizing the positive role the nationality factor plays now and will play in the foreseeable future even within the "new community of people." "The inventions of the anti-communists" that claim "Marxist-Leninists are of the opinion" that "the national aspect in peoples' lives" contradicts "socialism" are "unfounded." The "new community" is nothing "super-national." Of course, "national cultures" would continue to exist and progress in their development; they are by no means restricted to the "national idiosyncracies" of a "uniform human culture." "As a result, the international aspect does not and will not — either in part or completely — 'repress' the national aspect." Even in the future "stage of the nations' complete unity, ethnic differences among the peoples—language, traditional characteristics of national culture and customs—will survive."[173] Ethno-sociologists drew crucial conclusions that went beyond this position and called the whole Soviet people ideology in question. "Technological progress," which "undoubtedly" has an effect on "peoples' development" does not level "national differences." "To a certain degree, the acceleration of economic and cultural development lays the foundation for peoples' growing variety of ways of expressing themselves and their national values."[174]

What was the political function of the ideological revision? To see the Soviet people doctrine only as a result of scholarly theorizing contradicts the self-concept of scientific communism. Of course, the Soviet people doctrine was suited to justifying assimilation policy, and it was also used for this purpose. It was no accident that the Soviet people ideology was developed during Khrushchev's attempt to subdue autonomization desires and expectations and to mark the limits of de-Stalinization.

The Soviet people doctrine one-sidedly emphasizes the assimilation and rapprochement processes, which undeniably exist in Soviet society, and represses or completely suppresses differentiation processes. Propaganda and agitation suggest the picture of a mostly uniform society in which linguistic, cultural, and historical differences are without political relevance, do not provoke conflicts, and will become progressively less significant in the future. The surfacing "nationalist remnants" appear either as a consequence of "diversion" from the outside or as a blemish on the building of "developed socialism," which cannot destroy the overall impression of harmony. Although, or because, this picture that ideology developed and propaganda has reproduced thousands of times is incorrect, it was extremely politically useful. The picture of a nearly conflict-free Soviet society served to sweep existing conflicts under the carpet or at least to diminish them. Scholars and journalists described as few conflicts as possible or repressed them altogether if this was opportune. This reduction or tabooization is an instrument to manage conflicts.

From this perspective, the Soviet people ideology more served the purpose of hiding existing conflicts to make them more easily manageable than to create new ones as a result of an aggressive policy. This doctrine was the product of a defensive stance. It was designed to counteract the new national self-consciousness. It was to subdue economic egotisms and to strive for cultural independence. The Soviet people doctrine is an integrative instrument that provided the Party with a justification for fighting objective conflicts with subjective policy. The doctrine does not express a policy that actively changes or even revolutionarily restructures society. It resulted from the necessity of reacting to preceding social changes and of fighting autonomization.

National Assimilation, Language, and Language Policy

At the same time as many peoples' national self-consciousness was growing, national assimilation was occurring and still is occurring in many ways — some of which can be described as "merging." After Stalin, Soviet scholars distinguished two basic ethno-sociological processes: national or ethnic "consolidation" — this study has termed this process nation-building — and national or ethnic "assimilation." Ethnic consolidation is "the amalgamation of more or less independent ethnic communities whose languages and cultures are very similar in one large community."[175] Assimilation primarily means the national adaptation of nationals living dispersed in the surrounding nation, which may have a very different language and culture. National assimilation requires an individual, conscious change of ethnic identity. As a rule, linguistic assimilation precedes this change in ethnic identity.[176]

Consolidation and assimilation took place even before 1917: After the Revolution, however, these processes accelerated. In the 1980s, the Soviet Union considered both ethno-social processes as progressive and desirable. Even in the 1930s, national assimilation had carried the epithets "reactionary" and "chauvinist," and, for example, the Ukraine, Belorussia, and Bashkiria actively fought against it. Soviet scholars assume national assimilation continued even after Stalin and has grown to considerable, if often difficult-to-measure proportions. Their opinions on national consolidation disagree. Kozlov often emphasized that nation-building had come to an end before 1959.[177] In contrast, most Soviet experts seem to think that, in the present-day USSR, "there is no foundation to warrant the assumption that the process of national consolidation has come to an end."[178]

Chapter II dealt in detail with the political instruments, successes, and failures of nation-building. In addition, here are a few more examples of national consolidation, which accelerated after 1917 but probably has not yet come to an end in many cases. In the Middle Volga region, the two ethnic-linguistic groups of Erzia and Moksha became the Mordvinian nation. Among Mari, the differences between "highland," "lowland," and "eastern" Mari moved into the background. Tatars have integrated the ethnic groups of Mishars, Nagaibak, Kryashen, Kasimov-Tatars, and Astrakhan Tatars, all of which are closely related to them. This explains why the Tatar population increased by 48 percent (this is twice the growth rate of their neighboring peoples in the Volga region) between the 1926 census and the 1939 census. In the same period, the Avar population in Daghestan increased by 59 percent. In Daghestan, however, more than a dozen smaller nationalities disappeared from the 1939 census lists.

In the twentieth century, Georgians integrated a number of local ethnic groups living in relative isolation from one another in the mountainous regions of the western Caucasus, including Mingrelians, Laz, Svanetians, and the Islamicized Georgian ethnic groups of Adzhars and Ingiloi. The Turkmen absorbed the Teke, Ersari, Yomud, Saryk, and Göklen tribes. Uzbeks also assimilated related ethnic groups, including Sarts in Bukhara and Khorezm, Kypchak in Bukhara and Fergana, Turks in Fergana and Samarkand, and Lokais east of Bukhara.

National consolidation not only enlarged already existing peoples or merged tribal loyalties in favor of nations but also produced completely new ethnic groups. This included Altai, Shors, and Khakass, peoples that did not exist at the beginning of the twentieth century and that developed from the Turkic groups in the mountains of southern Siberia.[179]

Many of the tribes and smaller ethnic groups mentioned were still listed in the 1926 census. The number of official ethnonyms decreased by nearly 50 percent, from 196 in the 1926 census to 105 in the 1939 census. This is not explained by the fact that the 1926 census asked about "ethnic community," and the 1939 and all following censuses were interested in "nationality." Because the Soviets wanted to show off their political success, they exaggerated the level of national consolidation. Probably, many of the processes of national merging, which statistics declared complete as early as 1939, have not yet come to an end. According to Kulichenko "the development of a linguistic community and national consciousness among the socialist nations of Mordvinians and Mari reached its final stage" only in the 1980s.[180]

Although the tribal loyalties of the former Central Asian nomads have become less pronounced, they have not disappeared. In many cases, the tribes' and clans' feelings of solidarity have joined in a close and "fruitful" symbiosis with the career patterns of Soviet apparatuses. The Islamic peoples' cultural traditions, which make caring for one's relatives and tribal members a duty, reinforce and legitimize the widely prevalent practice of "rope parties," "patron," and "clientele." As a result, members of the Great Hord (*Ulu Iuz*) hold many prominent positions in the Kazakh Party and state apparatus. In Turkmenistan, members of the Teke tribe dominate political and cultural management functions.[181]

The appearance of new regional ties among the nations and the evolution of a supra-national regionalism, which the Party supported on the one hand and observed with distrust on the other, has more impact on the society as a whole than the merging of smaller ethnic groups in the Caucasus or Siberia. After Stalin, the three Baltic republics and Central Asia in particular have developed such consciousness of regional solidarity from below; the authorities promoted consciousness of solidarity from above for the three Eastern Slavic peoples, which are supposed to see themselves —

under the leadership of their "elder brother" — as the nucleus of the multinational Soviet state. The facts that the Baltic republics share the common fate of having experienced independence between the two world wars, of the Soviet Union eliminating this independence by force, and of considering themselves, unlike Russia, as part of Central European, and consequently, of "Western" history, contributed to the development of a consciousness of regional solidarity. Massive industrialization, which began in Estonia and Latvia in the 1940s and in Lithuania in the 1960s, has created similar structural problems in the three republics. Even the center considered the Baltic republics a unit because they have constituted a common economic administrative region (which is not to be confused with the — separate — economic councils under Khrushchev!) and a common military district.

As in the Baltic states, regionalism is growing in Central Asia. This is, in part, because Central Asian republics share a common historical and cultural heritage, which the relative similarity of the different Turkic languages emphasizes. Soviet modernization is another reason for this development because it produced similar social problems everywhere and created national intelligentsias that sometimes function as the proponents of common cultural and political interests in Central Asia.

These regionalisms are in their early developmental stages; they are new phenomena in post-Stalin society. Although there are points of contact, Central Asian regionalism is not identical with pre-1917 Panislamic efforts in Russia. Baltic regionalism, as defined as interests shared by Estonia, Latvia, and Lithuania, did not exist in the nineteenth century.

Aside from national consolidation and the development of new regionalisms, national assimilation into the Russian nation is quantitatively the most significant and politically the most important adaptive process. It dates back to pre-revolutionary times, but it began accelerating in the 1930s. Lewis, Rowland, and Clem calculated that from 1926 to 1970, at least four to six million people abandoned their national identity and adopted a Russian identity. Bruk and Kabuzan estimated that, in the same period, 17.1 million people were assimilated into the Russian nation, 9.9 million from 1926 to 1939, 4.7 million from 1939 to 1959, and 2.5 million from 1959 to 1970. From 1970 to 1979, assimilation increased the size of the Russian nation by 1.4 million. According to this Soviet calculation, assimilation was a major factor in the Russian growth rate. It suggests that 45 percent of the growth from 1926 to 1939 was due to assimilation (55 percent was due to high birth rates). Assimilation accounted for 34 percent of the Russian nation's total growth from 1939 to 1959, for 17 percent from 1959 to 1970, and for 16 percent from 1970 to 1979. Probably, this Soviet calculation sets the assimilation rate for the 1930s too high because it interprets the decline of the

Ukrainian nation, for example, exclusively as gains in assimilation for the Russian nation, without considering the several million famine victims.

Contrary to expectations derived from modernization- and urbanization-processes in other countries, most people assimilated before 1959 came from rural regions. Ukrainians living outside the Ukraine—a primarily rural population—were the largest group. The 1926 census counted 3.1 million Ukrainians in the region of the Northern Caucasus. In 1959, only about 170,000 people declared themselves to be Ukrainian in the Northern Caucasian economic administrative region, which was nearly identical with that region. In 1926, 1.63 million people declared themselves to be Ukrainian in the provinces of Voronezh and Kursk; in 1959, this was true only for 260,000 people in the regions of Belgorod, Voronezh, and Kursk, which were nearly identical with those provinces. Although many Ukrainians starved to death in the Northern Caucasus during the 1932–1934 famine, the decrease in people of Ukrainian heritage here and in the Central Chernozem territory was also the result of assimilation into the Russian environment—a process that began long before the Revolution (cf. Chapter II, Section 6). After 1959, Ukrainian assimilation focused on Siberia and the Far East. Again, it affected primarily rural Ukrainians, most of whom had migrated eastward around the turn of the century.[182]

Like the Ukrainian settlers, many Belorussians within the RSFSR changed their nationality. Lewis, Rowland, and Clem estimated that, between 1926 and 1970, this applied to at least 100,000 Belorussians, most of whom lived in Western Siberia.[183] Assimilation into Russian culture and Ukrainian and Belorussian national consciousness among those living outside their national republics continued after 1970. The natural growth rates of these two Eastern Slavic peoples, which are considerably lower than the Russian growth rates, clearly demonstrate this (Appendix Table A.1). Because there are no indications of significant differences between the birth and death rates of the three Eastern Slavic people, the different population growth rates essentially must be the result of assimilation.

In addition to Ukrainians and Belorussians living outside their republics, national assimilation into the Russian nation had other primary subjects: Many among the Finnic peoples of the Middle Volga region and the European north and the peoples without their own territory, primarily Jews and Germans, changed their nationality in favor of becoming Russian. Again, the fact that these peoples lived dispersed demographically in a Russian environment was an essential prerequisite for assimilation. (The dispersion was either the result of migration [Jews] or deportation [Germans and some Poles] or of large numbers of Russians migrating to the nations' traditional settlement territories [Mordvinians, Karelians, Komi, Mari, Udmurts]. Most of the Russians had already immigrated there during Tsarist times.) Assimilation is most effective where several prerequisites are met:

geographic dispersion; settlement outside the group's own national territories; settlement in Russian environments over generations; and elimination of educational, cultural, and administrative facilities using the national language since the late 1930s. In 1932, all these conditions applied to the 170,000 Karelians living around Moscow. In 1970, only 38,000 of them still considered themselves Karelian.[184]

Kozlov estimated that, from 1926 to 1979, assimilation losses for the small Mordvinian people numbered at least 400,000 people; this is about one-third of the total population in 1979.[185] Like the Karelians, Mordvinians are among the few peoples in the USSR whose numbers have continuously decreased since 1939. The growth rates of Komi, Udmurts, Mari, and Chuvash, which have been relatively low since 1970, are also the result of assimilation (Appendix Table A.1). The Chuvash are the only Turkic people that have exhibited some assimilation into Russian culture during the last decades. However, they have assimilated considerably less than the Mordvinians and Karelians. Assimilation is due to the fact that the Chuvash live widely dispersed in the Volga region outside their territory (Appendix Table A.3). In addition, the Chuvash are not Muslims. The Christianization of the Chuvash and most of the Finnic peoples in the Tsar's empire is an important prerequisite for their assimilation into Russia.

In contrast, ethnic Russification was apparently very limited among Tatars and Bashkirs — the Islamic peoples living in the Volga regions. This is even more remarkable because the Tatars are among the most widely dispersed peoples in the USSR. They have already exhibited unusually great geographic and social mobility under the Tsars and again since the 1930s, and they are highly urbanized. In 1959, 47 percent of Tatars lived in urban communities; in 1979, 63 percent.[186] Nevertheless, they preserved most of their national identity after they migrated to the cities in central Russia, the Urals, western Siberia, or Central Asia.

After Stalin (however, not before 1939), migration, urbanization, and upward social mobility brought about the ethnic Russification of many Jews. From 1970 to 1979, the number of Jews decreased by 340,000. Only about half this number of Jews emigrated from the Soviet Union during this period. Also, the total number of Poles decreased during the period from 1926 to 1939 and again after 1959 (Appendix Table A.1). In addition to the few Poles being assimilated into Russia in the former deportation territories in Siberia and Kazakhstan, some Poles in Belorussia and the Ukraine were assimilated into Belorussia or the Ukraine, respectively. Since the late 1950s, the growth rates of the German minority — traditionally an ethnic group with a very high birth rate — have increasingly begun to drop below the Soviet average although the total number of Germans — unlike the number of Jews and Poles — continues to increase. German emigration is not a factor sufficient to explain the decreases in their growth rate. After the Soviets abolished compulsory settlement, many Germans migrated to the cities (in 1979, their urbanization rate was 50 percent), and the younger generations again had the opportunity to undergo qualified professional training. Germans as an ethnic group were able to improve their social status, and many new German intellectuals were assimilated into the Russian lifestyle or even changed their national identity.

Until the 1950s, national assimilation into Russia was mostly a rural phenomenon and particularly affected large groups of non-Russian peasants who had been living in a Russian environment for generations; only later did assimilation become primarily a process of the city. Many non-Russian urbanites from the nations mentioned, which are exposed to Russian urban culture and have no or only very limited access to their native culture and education in their national language, adopt Russian nationality. The Soviets welcomed this assimilation. It is not the result of all-out administrative force but mostly the indirect consequence of the elimination of educational and cultural native-language facilities, which began in the late 1930s among Ukrainian, Belorussian, Karelian, and German minorities outside their national territories. Later, this development included all Germans and Jews, and since the late 1950s, it has affected the peoples in the Middle Volga region as well.

National assimilation almost exclusively benefits the Russian nation. Among the few exceptions are Poles being assimilated into the Ukrainian or Belorussian nation and several Siberian nationalities converting to become Yakuts. Except for some individual cases, Russians do not adopt other nationalities in the USSR. Also, the three Baltic nations, Georgians, Armenians, and the Islamic peoples (including the ASSR's peoples) within their own territories do not adopt Russian ways.

It is one of the inconsistencies of Soviet nationalities policy that the Soviets have taken no administrative action to document changes of national identity, which have happened a million times since the 1930s and which they welcome. In principle, holders of inland passports cannot have their nationality altered once it has been entered in their passport. Only census results permit rough estimates of national assimilation because everyone is allowed subjectively—and regardless of what their passports say—to proclaim their nationality.

Changing one's primary language is a crucial preliminary stage in the process of changing one's national identity. As a rule, there is no national assimilation without linguistic assimilation. However, linguistic assimilation does not automatically necessitate national assimilation. The fact that certain groups in the population change their primary language reveals that assimilation is taking place and suggests that some members in these groups also change their national identity. In 1926, 8.1 million (or 5.5 percent of the total population) spoke a primary language different from that of their nationality; by 1959, this number had increased to 11.7 million (or 5.6 percent) and by 1979, to 17.9 million (or 6.8 percent). In 1926, 81 percent of those who had changed their primary language had switched to Russian; in 1979, this percentage increased to 91 percent (Appendix Table A.10). Linguistic Russification affects essentially the same peoples and groups as national assimilation: Ukrainians and Belorussians, members of the Finno-Ugrian peoples (excluding Estonians), Jews, Germans, and Poles. Among them are also Armenians and Tatars living outside their republics, although linguistic Russification of Tatars outside their republics has been relatively limited. In 1979, linguistic Russification affected only 17 percent of those Tatars (Appendix Table A.11). Of course, linguistic Russification primarily affects peoples outside their own territories. The tendency towards linguistic Russification usually also increases as the geographic distance from the original settlement areas and the severity of the diaspora situation increases. The longer peoples live in a Russian environment the more likely they are to undergo linguistic assimilation. Linguistic Russification is more widespread among urban populations than rural populations. Already in 1926, more of the peoples' urbanites were linguistically Russified than peasants; in 1959 this tendency was even stronger.[187]

After Stalin, only few peoples submitted themselves to linguistic Russification within their own republics: Belorussians, Ukrainians, Karelians, Komi, Udmurts, and Chuvash (however, Mordvinians are an exception as they are very Russified outside of their republic). As in many other respects, the Ukraine does not offer a uniform picture. In 1979, the percentages of Ukrainians speaking Russian as their primary language varied from 0.3 percent in the Ternopol region and 0.5 percent in the Ivano-Frankovsk region to 37.6 percent in the Donetsk region and 47.3 percent in the Crimean region.[188] In comparison, Russification affected the primary language of Belorussians evenly across their republic. They only exhibit dramatic differences between urbanites and peasants. In 1979, only 75.5 percent Belorussian urbanites in their republic declared Belorussian as their primary language; in the country, the percentage was 98.8 percent.[189] Virtually all Belorussian urbanites who have preserved their national language declared that they were also proficient in Russian (cf. Appendix Table A.9). As a result, Russian has become the language of public and cultural life, middle and higher education, economy, administration, jurisprudence, and naturally of the Party in Belorussia's cities. Linguistic Russification of non-Russian urbanites in national territories was as extensive only in the industrial cities of the Donets; in the southern Ukraine; and in the cities of Karelia, the Komi ASSR, Udmurtia, and Chuvashia.

Jews are linguistically the most Russified people; Greeks, Koreans, and Germans follow at a great distance (Appendix Table A.11). Even outside Russia, Jews adopted Russian as their primary language. For all practical purposes, they do not adopt Ukrainian. On the contrary, the Jews' linguistic adoption of Russian reached the same level in the RSFSR and in the Ukraine. In comparison, more Germans preserved German as their primary language in Kazakhstan than in the RSFSR. In 1979, 64.5 percent of the Germans living in Kazakhstan declared German as their primary language; in the RSFSR, this percentage was 47.5 percent.[190] In Kazakhstan's international environment, where Russian does not exclusively dominate public life, German has managed to survive better. In addition, Germans live in relatively large groups in Kazakhstan. They are also less urbanized.

Although national assimilation and the abandonment of the national languages in favor of Russian were pushed, this was never a priority in the Party's nationalities policy. National assimilation is not a unilateral process, and its success also depends on whether the "host" nation is willing to integrate groups of different national heritage. After Stalin, the assimilation of Jews, who are the best prepared, have increasingly encountered difficulties because the Russians have rejected them. Presently, most Russians will probably not accept the integration of national groups that clearly look different from them.

National assimilation was not a political priority. The Soviets rather focused on establishing Russian in as many areas of the non-Russian nations' public lives as possible and converting Russian "from the language of international communication into the second native language of the USSR's peoples."[191] By focusing on this goal, in the 1970s, language policy became the focus of nationalities policy. The 1970 census asked non-Russians for the first time if they were "proficient in Russian" (*svobodno vladeiut russkim iazykom*). People were also offered the alternative of indicating another of the USSR's languages. Of course, although answers to such questions are subject to many subjective and unverifiable imponderabilities, there seems to be no other way, within the framework of a census, to collect data about language proficiency. In the census, 41.8 million non-Russians (or 37.1 percent of non-Russians) declared they were proficient in Russian. Another 13 million non-Russians declared Russian was their native language. This means that, in 1970, 48.7 percent of the non-Russian population could communicate fluently in Russian. It also means that half a century after the revolution and more than thirty years after the introduction of obligatory Russian classes in all general schools, still more than half of the non-Russian population or 24 percent of the total population was not very proficient or not at all proficient in the "language of international communication" (Appendix Tables A.8 and A.9). Less than 20 percent of the population of the large Islamic peoples with their own Union Republic (excluding Kazakhs) were able to communicate in Russian. From Moscow's perspective, the Soviets had more or less solved the language issue only in Belorussia. In the census, 67.9 percent of Belorussians declared that Russian was their primary or secondary language; but only 50.6 percent of Ukrainians made the same declaration.

In the RSFSR, the situation was very different; 50 to 80 percent of the members of peoples with Autonomous Republics declared they were proficient in Russian (exceptions are the Yakuts, the nationalities in Daghestan, and Tuvinians). In 1970, peoples without a national territory of their own had adopted Russian even more: 94.5 percent of Jews, 92.3 percent of Germans, 81.6 percent of Koreans, 83.2 percent of Bulgarians, and 84.9 percent of Greeks declared Russian as their first or second language.[192]

The demographic and ethno-social changes described earlier in this chapter and the information about the unsatisfactory spread of Russian provided by the 1970 census must have convinced the Brezhnev leadership that new initiatives were necessary in language policy. If the Russian percentage of the population decreased in spite of considerable adoption of Russian and if national elites increasingly forced their way into social and political leadership positions, in the future, the Russian language had to take over the leavening role the Russians had played. The ethno-social changes progressed towards de-Russification and linguistic disintegration, which could easily turn into political disintegration. The Brezhnev leadership was determined to counteract these social processes. If they could not prevent non-Russians from participating—we must assume that this was the Party leadership's calculation—at least the non-Russians would pay the price, namely of their "proficiency in Russian" so that at least some participation would take place in Russian. This was based on the conviction that non-Russian elites that were educated and trained in Russian and spent a large part of their professional lives using Russian could be politically more easily controlled and directed. The future showed that the Party leadership's assumptions did not come true.

This assumption resulted from the observation of conditions within the RSFSR, which are very different from those in most Union Republics, though. Nevertheless, there is no question that the conditions prevailing in the RSFSR around 1970 were the model on which the formulation of language policy's goals and practical measures was based: Language policy in the RSFSR had already eliminated non-Russian languages from most spheres of public life and restricted their use to the family, literature, and political propaganda.

Thus, the ideological slogan proclaiming Russian the "second native tongue" advanced to become the practical nucleus of the policy that was to make the Soviet people a reality. The role of Russian went far beyond that of a *lingua franca*, it "was to be the chief forger of a common supra-national identity, one of the essential hallmarks of the 'Soviet people.'"[193] The Russian language became a pivotal part of the Soviet people doctrine. The Uzbek Party chief Rashidov, who was one of the primary supporters and designers of this policy, said that Russian was to be a "language ... of unity" and serve as an "effective accelerator of the nations' approximation."[194]

Of course, the demands and expectations for complete bilingualism in the non-Russian nations, frequently expressed in the agitation, were an illusion and at the same time a feint, masking the policy's true goals. In reality, the policy of Russian as a "second native language" aimed at assigning different functions to the languages. Even many Soviet scholars saw the situation this way. All the USSR's languages are equal, "but their social functions are different."[195]

The Soviet linguist Desheriev who is an expert in this domain could not be clearer in his assessment: "Of the 130 languages in the USSR, about 115 are unable to express on their own the national and international, which comprises all aspects of the material and intellectual culture of the developed socialist society ... "[196] But also the remaining fifteen Union Republics' languages could not claim equal functions and were not capable of equal social development in the future. The Union Republics' languages "carry a rather extensive amount of information in the different areas of science, technology, art, and literature, but in respect to the total amount of information about the accomplishments of mankind, they lagged considerably behind the Russian language. The Autonomous Republics', regions' and territories' young written languages reflect this body of accomplishments even less."[197] In a different study, Desheriev summarized his chauvinistic linguistic theory: Of all the USSR's languages, only Russian reflects the full extent of present material and intellectual culture, only Russian was used in all areas of science and technology.[198] From this perspective, it seems consistent that the author sees Russian as the "fundamental language" or "main language," coming very close to using hitherto the despised term "state language."[199]

In the 1970s, ideologists and linguists developed a hierarchy of languages, which granted an unrestricted range of functions and developmental capabilities in all aspects of life only to Russian and as a result more or less limited the functions of all other languages. According to the pattern of Soviet federalism, which again proved its political relevance, they assigned a higher status to the Union Republics' languages than to all others. In most cases, they did not consider the number of native speakers or the ages of written languages. For example, Soviet power granted Estonian, which was spoken by one million people in 1979, more functions than Tatar, which about six million people spoke.

Practical measures to establish the "second native language" affected primarily education in non-Russian Union Republics. Mid-range goals included improvement and intensification of Russian classes on all levels of education by increasing the number of lessons assigned to Russian and employing extracurricular measures, introduction of Russian classes to na-

A New Nationalism

tional kindergartens, enforcing Russian as the only language of instruction at all institutions of higher education and technical middle schools. National schools of general education in the Union Republics—except for Ukraine and Belorussia—were not affected and continued to teach classes in the pupils' native language. Because of this, the Russification of education did not yet reach the level of the RSFSR, where Russian had replaced non-Russian languages in most general middle schools in the 1960s and early 1970s (cf. chapter VIII, section 3).

The CPSU's CC among others convened many All Union congresses to prepare and discuss educational measures to improve Russian classes in national republics: in Baku in 1969, Frunze in 1971, Kishinev in 1972, Alma-Ata in 1973, Erevan in 1974, and Tashkent in 1975 and 1979.[200] The "recommendations" of the first Tashkent Congress in 1975 focused on improving Russian classes on the national schools' elementary level and introducing Russian classes into national kindergartens, and establishing of preschools for six-year-olds.[201]

Some Union Republics had made such measures law before. From 1973 to 1975, the Georgian, Kirgiz, Armenian, and Uzbek CCs and Councils of Ministers passed resolutions to improve Russian classes in general schools. The introduction of Russian classes to kindergarten and the establishment of preschool classes focusing on Russian were the most significant innovations. Now, Russian classes started in first grade, not in second or third as previously. The quality of Russian classes in rural national schools and the qualifications of teachers were to be improved.[202] Other Union Republics followed suit and also started Russian classes in first grade. By 1979, all Union Republics except Ukraine, Belorussia, and Lithuania had adopted this approach.[203]

At the same time, the Soviets introduced measures at the top of the educational hierarchy. On December 29, 1975, the USSR's Council of Ministers approved "Regulations Concerning the Conferment of Academic Degrees and the Award of Academic Titles." It stated that all dissertations, synopses, and all documents required by the Supreme Certification Commission had to be written in Russian. Previously, the commission had only required a Russian synopsis.[204]

In 1978 and 1979, several legislative acts summarized and intensified previous individual measures and made them legally binding for all Union Republics. On October 13, 1978, the USSR's Council of Ministers passed a—so far unpublished—resolution "On Measures to Continue the Improvement of the Learning and Teaching of Russian in the Union Republics." On the basis of this resolution, the USSR's Minister for Institutions of Higher Education and Technical Middle School Education signed a decree with the same title on December 6, 1978. "Excerpts" of this decree were published.[205] According to these excerpts and reports in Soviet media concerning the resolution of October 13, 1978[206] the following innovations were introduced: General national schools increased the number of Russian lessons and offered two to three hours per week more for all grade levels. This made "Russian Language and Literature" the most frequently taught subject in national schools. This subject had dominated curricula even before. In 1975, for example, national schools taught "Russian Language and Literature" in the ten grades (eleven grades in the Baltic republics) for 51.5 hours per week per year in Kirgizistan, 48 hours in Latvia, 46.5 hours in Belorussia, 43 hours in Estonia, 42 hours in Lithuania, 41 hours in Moldavia, and 40.5 hours in Ukraine. On the whole, in 1975, national schools taught from 1260 to 1715 Russian classes in the course of 10 (or eleven) academic years. In the mid-1930s, students of non-Russian ten-grade schools received from 400 to 550 hours of Russian.[207]

Further measures were deployed to increase the effectiveness of Russian classes: For Russian classes, classes with more than twenty-five students were divided. The number of schools and classes offering "intensified Russian" were increased to the disadvantage of other subjects. "Intensified Russian" meant an additional three to five hours of Russian per week. Teacher competence was improved by creating a new program for teachers of "Russian Language and Literature at National Schools" at institutions of higher education and teachers colleges.

New regulations for institutions of higher education and technical schools were passed. Their objective was to conduct "technical classes in Russian" and to continuously increase the number of classes and subjects taught in Russian.[208] This entailed a fundamental step beyond the introduction of compulsory Russian classes for all non-Russian students at institutions of higher education and technical schools in 1964.[209] Now, heads of institutions of higher education and technical school principals were required to establish annual lists of the subjects in which all classes were taught in Russian. In addition, more and more students and technical students were expected to write their annual studies and theses in Russian. The Soviets ordered non-Russian Union Republics to publish more institution of higher education and technical school level textbooks in Russian.

These measures challenged the function of national languages as teaching languages at institutions of higher education and technical schools although not all institutions of higher education and technical schools were expected to teach exclusively in Russian in a few years. In some Union Republics massive resistance has developed. Russification affected particularly those republics, which had taught college classes primarily in their national language, i.e., the three Baltic and the three Transcaucasian Union Republics. But in 1968–1969, about 70 percent of Uzbek college students at the institutions of higher education of the Ministry for Institutions of Higher Education and Middle Technical School Education studied in Uzbek.[210]

An unpublished resolution by the USSR's Council of Ministers of late June 1979 decreed the compulsory introduction of Russian classes in all non-Russian kindergartens and preschools. On July 18, 1979, the USSR's Ministry of Education supported this resolution with an implementation statute.[211] Beginning in 1980, it mandated the introduction of Russian classes in all non-Russian kindergartens and in all national schools' preschool classes beginning in the academic year 1979–1980.

Reissuing legislative measures after a short period of time while barely changing their content is not indicative of their effectiveness. Another new joint resolution by the CPSU's CC and the USSR's Council of Ministers of May 26, 1983 "Concerning Additional Measures to Improve the Study of Russian in General Schools and Other Educational Facilities in the Union Republics" seems to support this interpretation. Although this resolution is also unpublished, the decision by the board of the Ukrainian SSR's Ministry of Education of June 29, 1983, which spread in the Samizdat, revealed some of its contents.[212] This decision refers to fluency in Russian as a "citizen's duty" for every young person and every secondary school graduate. The board also decreed that the network of Ukrainian secondary schools teaching in Russian be expanded. In addition, more schools teaching in both Russian and Ukrainian were to be established. On the whole, however, it seems that language policy did not compromise considerably the position of native languages as the language of instruction in the Union Republics' general schools. In the 1970s, the percentage of children who received instruction in their respective national language was about equal to the titular nations' percentage in the Union Republic's total population; in most Islamic republics (except in Kazakhstan) the percentage was considerably higher. The Ukraine and Belorussia were the exceptions to the rule. This does not mean that no children of the titular nations attended Russian schools; particularly Kazakh and Azeri children attended Russian schools. On the other hand, many children of the non-Slavic minorities attended schools of the respective titular nations.

Since Stalin's death, only Ukraine and Belorussia have clearly Russified their general schools by adopting Russian as the language of instruction. In Ukraine, the percentage of children taught in Ukrainian decreased from 72.2 percent in 1955 to about 60 percent in 1974 and 50.5 percent in 1987; in the same period, the percentage of children taught in Russian increased from 25.9 percent to about 40 percent and to 48.7 percent. In Belorussia in 1972–1973, 51.4 percent of all children were taught in Russian, in the cities this percentage was 97.6 percent. In Minsk, no secondary school taught in Belorussian any more.

Educational conditions in Belorussian cities were the same as in the RSFSR. In 1974–1975, 96 percent of all the RSFSR's children were taught in Russian; in 1955–1956, this percentage had been only 94 percent. In 1974–1975, 64.3 percent of the Union's students attending general schools were taught in Russian, 35.7 percent or 15.4 million children were taught in other languages.[213]

After 1970, the pressure on the Union Republics to adopt the "second native tongue" was not limited to education. It was felt in many public sectors. However, there is hardly any detailed information about this phenomenon. The judicial system and state administration restricted the use of indigenous languages—particularly in their correspondence. The constitutions of six Union Republics (Ukraine, Belorussia, Estonia, Latvia, Lithuania, and Georgia), which dated back to the Stalin era, had stipulated that the official language used in court be the language of the respective titular nation. In contrast, the new 1978 constitutions of all republics agreed that the official language used in court either be the language of the respective titular nation or "the language of the majority of the population of a given locality." The Belorussian, Moldavian, and Kazakh constitutions explicitly mentioned Russian as a national language of the respective republic.[214] In reality, this undermining of constitutional regulations was an indication of the continuous advance of Russian in courtrooms and particularly in the courts' correspondence.[215]

In many Union Republics, even most regional authorities adopted Russian as the official language. Valdo Randpere, an executive of the Estonian Ministry of Justice who had defected to Sweden in 1984, declared that all correspondence addressed to the authorities of the Estonian SSR's Council of Ministers had to be in Russian. Letters in Estonian were returned to the sender.

Publication statistics of books, magazines, and newspapers illustrate the pressure exerted on non-Russian languages.

Table 9.8 shows that in respect to the number of titles and printed copies, the percentage of books in Russian increased continuously in the documented period. In 1982, only 13 percent of all books and pamphlets printed were published in the languages of the non-Russian peoples. Among magazines, the number of Russian titles also increased continuously. Until 1975, however, the number of copies printed in Russian decreased and has begun to increase ever since. There is a relatively large number of non-Russian newspapers (by titles). Concerning the available number of copies, however, the percentage of newspapers in Russian clearly increased from 1958 to 1982.

After 1975, the Russian percentages increased for all indicators documented in Table 9.8. The new measures in language policy had direct consequences for publications. Even the number of newspaper titles in Russian increased.[216]

Table 9.8: Publications in Russian

	1958		1970			1975			1982	
	Number of Titles	Million Copies	Number of Titles	Million Copies		Number of Titles	Million Copies		Number of Titles	Million Copies
Books and Brochures in the Languages of the USSR's Peoples in Russian (percent)	61,940 73.2	1,073.9 82.5	75,731 79.5	1,260.4 82.0		79,961 80.9	1,596.0 84.2		80,671 80.9	1,925.1 87.0
	Number of Titles	Annual Circulation (million copies)	Number of Titles	Annual Circulation (million copies)		Number of Titles	Annual Circulation (million copies)		Number of Titles	Annual Circulation (million copies)
Magazines in Russian (percent)	830 69.9	452.6 88.4	1,131 72.7	1,979.7 85.1		1,243 74.7	2,273.7 83.2		1,342 75.3	2,341.1 84.2
Newspapers in Russian (percent)	7,662 67.1	57,468[1] 78.6	7,231 68.5	31,091.7 81.0		7,964 62.1	37,887.5 80.9		8,264 64.6	39,772.8 81.9

[1] Daily circulation in thousands of copies. No data on the 1958 circulation were available.

Sources: *Pechat SSSR v 1958 g., 1970 g., 1975 g., 1982 g.* (Moscow, 1959, 1971, 1976, 1983).

According to the objectives of education policy, particularly the number of scholarly and technical books and magazines published in languages other than Russian declined. Literature and political propaganda were not as much subject to this decline. In 1970, in Ukraine 472 scholarly books were published in Ukrainian, by 1980, this number had decreased to only 298. In the same period, the number of scholarly books and brochures (by title) published in Ukraine increased from 947 to 1906. In 1969, the Academy of Sciences of the Ukrainian SSR published fourteen journals in Ukrainian and eleven in Russian, in 1980, it only published eight in Ukrainian and thirty-two in Russian.[217]

Publications in the native languages are not at all evenly distributed among the non-Russian peoples. Generally, the Union Republics' languages are published considerably more often than the other languages. However, there are considerable differences between individual Union Republics. In 1982, 1.8 percent of all books and brochures were published in Estonian (1414 titles) although in 1979, only 0.39 percent of the total population was Estonian. In contrast, only 2064 titles (= 2.7 percent) were published in Ukrainian although in 1979, 16.2 percent of the total population was Ukrainian. In 1982, statistical data document only 171 book titles in Tatar with a total of 2.2 million copies printed. The significance of this figure becomes apparent only if one considers that in 1911, 375 book titles were published in Tatar in Kazan with a total of 2.2 million copies printed.[218]

A number of factors determine how many books and magazines are published in the individual languages. Probably, the most important factor is whether education and training are conducted in the native languages. Also, a language's position in the hierarchy of Soviet federalism determines the number of publications it is used in. However, this number is not only determined from above by the planning mechanism. Claims and demands from below, the emphasis with which peoples stress their national interests and traditions have an influence. As a result, damages remained within limits in the three Baltic republics and in Georgia but also in Uzbekistan and Kazakhstan. In this group, Estonians are an exception because they were able to increase the percentage of books and brochures published in Estonian (by titles and copies) from 1958 to 1982. The percentage of printed products in Ukrainian, Belorussian, and the languages of the RSFSR decreased the most.[219]

The policy of promoting the "second native language" had ambiguous results. On the one hand, the number of people proficient in Russian increased. On the other hand, the pressure exerted on the native languages triggered resistance from authors, teachers, and even Party elites of many Union Republics. The 1979 census recorded that 49 percent of non-Russians were proficient in Russian; considering that an additional 13.1 percent of non-Russians spoke Russian as their native language, in 1979, 62.1

A New Nationalism

percent of all non-Russians were proficient in Russian (cf. Table A.9 in the Appendix). Some figures, however, are suspicious. Even the prominent Soviet ethnographer, Kozlov, thinks that it is "strange" that the relative percentages of Uzbeks and Ukrainians proficient in Russian are the same.[220] The far away Karakalpaks probably set a record that is difficult to beat by increasing the number of people among them proficient in Russian by 459 percent from 1970 to 1979. In 1983 and 1984, the Rashidov leadership in Tashkent had to face accusations of massively falsifying Uzbekistan's economic statistics. This increases the doubts in the correctness of the census language statistics. However, the language statistics seem to be correct insofar as the number of people proficient in Russian did increase in the 1970s.

However, the resistance against the policy of administrative Russification has also increased. This resistance materialized in different forms. It was particularly apparent and public in Georgia, Lithuania, and Estonia. At the Eighth Georgian Writers' Congress in April 1976, author Revaz Dzhaparidze caused a scandal in the presence of the Georgian Party elite and First Secretary Shevardnadze by heavily attacking plans forcing professors at the University of Tbilisi to lecture in Russian. He shouted, "This idea, friends, the creation of a non-Georgian university in Tbilisi is not new!" Dzhaparidze also protested against the new regulation that all dissertations had to be written in Russian "even if they are about a Georgian verb." The audience's thundering applause lasted for minutes and drowned Shevardnadze's heckling.[221]

The protests against the functional constraints imposed on Georgian climaxed two years later. Moscow's Party leadership was determined to use the occasion of the revisions of republic constitutions and do away with the anomaly that existed only in the constitutions of the three Transcaucasian republics and guaranteed the respective national language as "official language." The drafts of the three Transcaucasian republics' constitutions published in March 1978 no longer contained the article about the "state language." The outrage in Georgia climaxed on April 14, 1978 when Tbilisi's main street was the stage for demonstrations that lasted for hours. University professors and students had initiated them. Shevardnadze addressed the thousands of demonstrators twice in front of the building housing the Supreme Soviet. It is admirable how he managed to express his solidarity with the demonstrators' issues without losing face with Moscow. Before the Supreme Soviet in Tbilisi he declared that "we conducted a study of public opinion" and analysis had revealed that "it is advisable to leave in force the known formulation of the existing constitution. . . . " Moscow gave in and the constitutions of the three republics retained the regulations concerning the "state language."[222]

Of course, these considerable gains in prestige did not mean that Georgia and the other Transcaucasian republics were exempted from the central power's concrete measures of language policy. However, this resistance documented the Georgian intelligentsia's unbroken self-confidence and even feeling of superiority and limited the implementation of Moscow's measures. In June 1980, 365 prominent scholars, authors, and artists, including several members of the Georgian Academy of Sciences, signed a letter addressed to Brezhnev and Shevardnadze. The letter protested against the regulation decreed by the Minister for Institutions of Higher Education and Technical School Education on December 6, 1978 and the reduction of classes in the native language and the repression of Georgian history in middle schools in favor of the additional expansion of Russian classes. The letter claimed that these measures were in contradiction to "Lenin's nationalities policy" and constituted a "violation of the Georgian people's constitutional status."[223]

On March 23 and 30, 1981, again student demonstrations took place in Tbilisi against the Russification of institutions of higher education and schools, the discrimination against Georgians in the Abkhaz ASSR, and the dismissal of the popular literature professor A. Bakhradze. Afterwards, he was able to resume his lectures about Georgian literature at the university.[224]

The Party leaderships of Georgia and other Union Republics also initiated measures of their own to keep the protests from reaching dangerous dimensions and—if possible—to deflate them. In April 1979, the Georgian CC and Council of Ministers passed a resolution "Concerning the Status of Education in the Georgian Language and Literature at the Republic's Educational Facilities and Measures of Improving It." They complained vigorously about the fact that students were insufficiently able to express themselves in their native tongue orally and in writing and that the mass media mutilated Georgian. One consequence of this resolution was among other innovations the introduction of new textbooks in the native language on all grade levels. Armenia had made a similar resolution already in November 1978. At the same time, for example, Georgian, Armenian, Ukrainian, and Estonian media published articles that demanded more native language literature, demanded of Russians living in Union Republics to learn the respective republic's national language, and warned against letting the native languages degenerate. "A good knowledge of his native language is proof of a person's spiritual culture."[225]

Insofar as republican Party congresses in 1981 dealt with the nationalities issues, language policy was their main topic. This indicated that the Party leaderships faced considerable resistance—even in Central Asia—and attempted to compensate for it at Party congresses with propaganda efforts. At the Party congress in Tallinn, Estonian Party chief Karl Vaino expressed the indignation which was widespread in the Party and was primarily directed against himself, and lamented that schools did not pay enough attention to education in the vernacular.[226]

The Russian linguistic arrogance, which is such a blatant contradiction to the bilingualism demanded of the non-Russians, triggered particularly strong resentment. High-ranking Party functionaries expressed this resentment and demanded that Russians living in the republics "be proficient in the vernacular of the native nationality."[227] Also scholars consider this a prerequisite necessary for the integration of non-natives.[228]

The Lithuanian Samizdat magazines articulated the protest against the new language policy particularly vehemently. In February 1981, *Aushra (Dawn)* published an article titled "Enough Russification in Lithuania" and encouraged all Lithuanians to boycott Russian and to speak only Lithuanian with authorities and in public. In the fall of 1979, more than 5,000 Lithuanians signed a letter of protest addressed to the CPSU's CC and the Lithuanian Party leadership and government to defend Lithuanian in kindergartens, schools, and universities.[229]

In October 1980, for the first time in forty years, Estonia witnessed open anti-Soviet and anti-Russian demonstrations. High school and college students walked the streets in Tallinn (Reval), later also in Tartu (Dorpat) and Pärnu (Pernau), sang patriotic songs, and chanted "Russians, get out of Estonia!" Forty representatives of the artistic, literary, and scholarly establishment risked their privileges and positions and, on October 28, 1980, in a letter to *Pravda* and Estonian newspapers expressed their solidarity with the manifestants. The letter lamented the "perilous split" in Estonian society, which was caused particularly by "the fear that the national identity is in danger." The authors of the letter, thirteen of which are listed in the Estonian Soviet Encyclopedia,[230] blame the massive immigration of Slavs to Estonia and the increasingly more limited opportunities to use Estonian in the economy, science, and everyday life for the "insecurity" and "aggressiveness" prevailing in Estonia. They complain about the increasing lack of publications in Estonian and consider wrong and detrimental the campaign to push Russian in schools and kindergartens and also the propagation of unilateral bilingualism. Leadership positions in the area of cultural policy were held by people who were neither sufficiently proficient in Estonian nor had sufficient interest in the nation's language and culture. The open letter demanded that the status of Estonian in Estonia be concretely and in detail safeguarded by a law.[231]

National Opposition

In the period since Stalin, opposition against the Party's nationalities policy has taken many forms. The existence of this opposition is among the most significant symptoms indicating the processes of change that have been transforming Soviet society since 1953. Although the Soviets suppressed and persecuted oppositional efforts in many ways, they no longer subscribed to Stalin's strategy and exterminated them by means of mass terror. In the 1960s and 1970s, police and justice smashed individual manifestations of national opposition. However, protest and resistance would continue to crop up in other locations and in different forms. This would continue to be the case also in the future — even more so — because this resistance was founded on objective prerequisites: The Party's antidote to the increasing national self-confidence in a rapidly changing society determined by processes of modernization was a more aggressive nationalities policy whose effects must feel like an attempt to Russify essential aspects of public life.

In the 1950s, opposition began to develop forms that had nothing to do with the individuals, institutions, and social prerequisites that determined opposition in the 1920s and 1930s. It was a new phenomenon — result and consequence of the past half century of changes. "National opposition" does not imply that there was a political organization — particularly not beyond the boundaries of individual peoples — or a well-defined alternative political concept. What happened was that smaller or larger groups, who rejected the Party's nationalities policy either in part or completely, developed within individual peoples. These groups made concrete demands.

As has been characteristic for any form of nationalism, national opposition associated with many different intellectual and political trends. In Lithuania and to a lesser degree in Georgia, Armenia, and the Western Ukraine, oppositional efforts were in close symbiosis with the respective national churches. In several Islamic regions, particularly in the Northern Caucasus, Sufi brotherhoods represented a specific form of anti-Soviet resistance. In other areas, demands for national self-determination were tied into the liberal civil rights movement (Helsinki Committees). As has been demonstrated already, however, in some republics, dissatisfaction with and resistance against specific measures and tendencies of nationalities policy involved the establishment of Party and government bureaucracy (Baltic republics, Ukraine, Transcaucasus). Due to the different make-ups of these "coalitions" they represented very different demands ranging from the reinstitution of Lenin's nationalities policy to secession from the Union.

Remigration and emigration movements constitute a particular form of opposition. In the late 1950s, the deported peoples who were not allowed to return to their homelands began to initiate political campaigns promoting that they be allowed to return home (Crimean Tatars, Meskhets, Germans). In the late 1960s, a mass movement developed among Jews and Germans that was directed at winning them the right to emigrate to their respective "historical homelands." Even about 20,000 Armenians took advantage of the less restrictive emigration opportunities in the 1970s.

The Crimean Tatars, a small people, accomplished what must be the most amazing political mass movement in the history of the Soviet Union. Nearly every adult among the 500,000 Crimean Tatars, most of whom the Soviets had forced to settle in Uzbekistan, participated in the campaign to return to the Crimean peninsula and reinstitute the Crimean ASSR. From July 1957 to March 1961, they addressed five major petitions, each one signed by from 6,000 to 18,000 Crimean Tatars, to Party and government. In October 1961, 25,000 Crimean Tatars signed a petition to the Twenty-Second Party Congress. In March/April 1966, they submitted a petition with 120,000 signatures to the Twenty-Third Party Congress. Tatars supported their efforts with tens of thousands of individual letters, telegrams, and personal visits on all levels of the administrative hierarchy. From 1964 to the late 1970s, the Crimean Tatars periodically maintained permanent representatives in Moscow, who were identified as elected representatives by the written mandates from the Crimean Tatars of a village or town and were to put through their people's demands before the capital's supreme authorities. At times, there were several hundred representatives in Moscow. They were repeatedly arrested and forcibly returned to Uzbekistan (1966, 1970, 1979).

Crimean Tatars have always viewed their movement for their political rehabilitation and the reinstitution of their territorial autonomy on the Crimean peninsula as legal and in agreement with the Soviet system. Many of their spokesmen called themselves Leninists and communists who demanded restitutions for Stalin's crimes — as much as this is possible — from the Party leadership. After 1968, they entertained connections with the Russian civil rights movement, which primarily the writer A. Kosterin and General P. Grigorenko had arranged. The national movement of the Crimean Tatars accomplished little: political rehabilitation on September 5, 1967, minor cultural-linguistic concessions like the publication of a few Crimean Tatarian books and the establishment of a Crimean Tatarian department within Uzbekistan's Writers' Union. They fell short of their actual goals. The Soviets did not reinstitute the Crimean ASSR and have permitted up to the mid-1980s only about 5,000 Crimean Tatars to return to the Crimean peninsula since 1968. An additional few thousand Crimean Tatars returned to their homeland without permission. The Soviets deported hundreds of them back to Uzbekistan one more time.

Crimean Tatar data document that Soviet courts sentenced more than 200 national movement activists from 1959 to 1968. The 1970s witnessed additional trials. For all practical purposes, the 1979 sentencing of seventeen Crimean Tatar spokesmen (including E. Shabanov, M. Chobanov, Mustafa Dzhemilev, Reshat Dzhemilev) to serve terms in prison camps or internal exile seemed to have suppressed the movement. In the spring of 1982, only four Crimean Tatar political prisoners whose names were known in the West remained imprisoned in camps. The Crimean Tatar movement reemerged under perestroika after 1985.[232]

In the aftermath of the Twentieth Party Congress in February 1956, Meskhetians also started a surprisingly concerted national campaign to win permission to return to their homelands and sustained it for two decades. They adopted the same objectives, used the same methods and failed in the same way as did the Crimean Tatars. The Soviets had deported Meskhetians from southwestern Georgia, along the Turkish border on November 15, 1944. Probably, Stalin had thought them unreliable people of the border zone in connection with the Turks. Meskhetian settlements were located in the Adzhar ASSR, Georgia proper, and expanded to the Georgian-Armenian border. The Meskhetians are an ethnically heterogeneous group and consist primarily of Georgians who adopted Islam and speak Turkic. In addition to the Meskhetians, the Soviets also deported Karapalpaks, Turkish Kurds, and Turkicised Armenians (Khemshil) from the regions along the border to Central Asia and Kazakhstan. About 200,000 people lost home, property and many even their lives because the dictator was under the impression that deportations served the reason of state.

In the 1960s, the Meskhetians created a great solidarity movement. In February 1964, they founded the "Turkish Society for the Defense of the Exiled Turkish People's National Rights," which headed the movement and included a "Provisional Organizational Committee for the People's Return to the Homeland." Enver Odabashev chaired this organizational committee until a Soviet court tried and sentenced him in 1971. The organizational committee convened regular "people's assemblies," which drew up to 6,000 delegates and sent more than thirty delegations to the Moscow Party and government leadership. After all efforts had failed and the Soviets had again deported several hundreds of families, who had returned to their homeland without official permission, to Central Asia, the organizational committee approached Turkey in 1970 and asked if Turkey would support Meskhetian immigration to Turkey. The Soviets neither permitted the Meskhetian Turks to emigrate nor to return to their homeland. They did not even permit them to settle in other locations in Georgia, outside the confines of their immediate homeland.[233]

German and Jewish emigration movements, which appealed to foreign states and were supported by them, were more successful. In the 1970s, the Soviet Union wanted to demonstrate its interest in detente and therefore issued a considerable number of emigration visas. At the same time, the Soviets hoped to get rid of troublemakers.

After the political rehabilitation of the German minority on August 29, 1964, German initiative groups developed that demanded reestablishment of the ASSR of Volga Germans, return to their old homeland, comprehensive cultural and linguistic autonomy. These activities climaxed on June 7,

1965, when A.I. Mikoian, the Chairman of the Supreme Soviet's Presidium, received a German delegation which presented a corresponding petition with 4,500 signatures to him. However, the primary demands of the German minority were refused and the small linguistic and cultural concessions (for example the printing of more books in German, publication of a third German newspaper *Freundschaft (Friendship)* in Tselinograd after 1967, establishment of German sections in several writers' unions) did not satisfy the Germans. As a result of this—and probably in analogy to the Jewish movement that occurred at the same time—the late 1960s witnessed a rapidly growing movement to emigrate to the Federal Republic of Germany. Around 1970, Soviet authorities were faced with tens of thousands of individual and collective applications for emigration, some of which were even published in samizdat.

In 1971, the Soviet Union began to permit some of the applicants to emigrate. The number of emigration visas for Germans increased from 340 in 1970 to 1,145 in 1971. In 1976, this number climaxed at 9,704. From 1971 to 1983, a total of 70,500 Germans emigrated to the Federal Republic of Germany. In 1981, the Soviets began to reduce the number of emigration visas issued considerably; in 1983, the number had dropped to 1,447. Apparently, the Soviet government was determined to suppress people's desire to emigrate. Contrary to the Soviet government's assumption its strategy to grant emigration visas to only a few stirred up the desire to emigrate in many and the wave of people willing to emigrate rose more and more in the 1970s. In the early 1980s, the German Red Cross officially listed the names of about 100,000 people who were willing to emigrate.

Most people claim that they want to emigrate primarily to preserve their national, cultural, and linguistic identity. Many Germans are faced with the alternative of either assimilating Russian language and culture or emigrating. The restrictions the Soviet Union places on the freedom of religion is another reason why people want to emigrate. Unusually many emigrants are Baptist, Mennonite, Lutheran, Pentecostal, and Adventist believers and preachers. The Soviet Power adopted an unusual strategy to prevent Germans who were members of a church from emigrating: In the late 1970s and the early 1980s, nearly 200 Lutheran congregations were registered in the areas of exile and so granted the legal basis to operate. In Kazakhstan and neighboring southern Siberia, also several Mennonite and Baptist congregations (the latter are all nationally mixed) were legalized.

The emigration movement's success is unimaginable without the pressure from below. Most emigrants fought for their emigration visas for years. Ninety percent of them had to go through the visa application process more than once; they risked their jobs and reputations. In 1972, they founded an "Association of Germans in the USSR Willing to Emigrate." Rejected applicants demonstrated in public squares in Moscow and in front of the German Embassy. However, the emigration movement was never as united and organized as were the Crimean Tatars because the ethnic Germans are not united on this issue but hold extremely diverse opinions. The Soviets have permitted many Germans to emigrate and have rejected even more applications. At the same time, police and courts attempted to keep the movement within limits by persecuting its spokesmen. From 1974 to 1977, more than forty activists were arrested and sentenced, most of them to one–three year terms in prison camps. In March 1982, Western sources had the names of fourteen Germans who were in prisons or camps (one of them underwent forced psychiatric treatment) because of their involvement with the emigration movement.[234]

In the late 1960s, the Jewish emigration movement became the by far most successful effort in respect to the number of emigration permits. From 1971 to 1981, 236,217 Jews were able to leave the Soviet Union legally. This emigration wave climaxed in 1973 (34,733 Jewish emigrants) and again in 1979 (51,320 Jewish emigrants). In 1980, Soviet authorities began to cut the number of emigration permits more than in half each year. In 1983, they granted only 1,315 emigration permits.

The fact that Jewish national consciousness began to experience a renaissance in the USSR in the 1960s and the resulting determination of hundreds of thousands of Soviet Jews to leave the USSR was primarily a consequence of the official and traditional anti-Semitism, which makes it impossible for Soviet Jews to give up their Jewish identity in Soviet society. Official anti-Semitism, which was camouflaged in the term anti-Zionism, reached proportions from 1967 to 1971 that were reminiscent of Stalin's last years. When Soviet foreign policy increased its support for the Arabs' cause after the Six Day War in June 1967 and began a propaganda campaign against Israel, Zionism, and World Jewry, it was only logical that these actions had repercussions on Jews in the Soviet Union. Any kind of support for Israel or American Jews was considered anti-Soviet. In addition to this official anti-Semitism, traditional anti-Semitism existed, which ignited as usual because so many Jews were among the different elites (science, art, Party) and because of the protectionist bonds among Jews. Emigration permits for hundreds of thousands of Jews fueled anti-Semitism even more. One of its products was the "Soviet Anti-Zionist Committee," which was founded in April 1983.

After 1965, Jewish emigration demands turned into a Zionist movement. Initially, many of the emigrants were Oriental Jews, and the comparatively few assimilated Jews from Lithuania and Latvia. From 1971 to 1973, 30 percent of the Jewish emigrants were Georgian Jews, who made up only 3 percent of Soviet Jews. Later, the focus of the exodus shifted to the Ukrainian and Russian metropolises. As a result, the percentage of Jewish emigrants who did not leave Vienna to immigrate into Israel, soared from 4 percent in 1973 to approximately 60 percent in 1978.

As was characteristic for other migration movements, police and courts had the task to keep this exodus and protests against its obstruction within limits. In the fall of 1977, at least twenty-one Jewish activists were in prisons, camps, or internal exile; by May 1, 1982 this figure had not changed.

The fact that Jewish, German, and Armenian emigration was interrupted in the early 1980s was not because there was less pressure from below, but because the leaders in the Kremlin made a political decision, which was equally influenced by factors of foreign and domestic policy. Foreign policy no longer required the Soviets to issue tens of thousands of emigration visas every year for the sake of détente. From a domestic perspective, the idea to get rid of restless elements by opening the borders to a certain degree had proven wrong. To the contrary, issuing emigration permits for only a few had mobilized many others among the respective nationality and had demonstrated to the Party leadership to what unpredictable extent nations could be mobilized. This demonstration was even more impressive and unexpected because Jews and Germans were among the nationalities that were most assimilated and previously had given no indication that their national issues were not "resolved."[235]

Just like the Russian civil rights movement, national opposition arose from disappointed expectations of the period of the "thaw." After 1959, the reaction (and later the nationalities policy of the Brezhnev leadership) provoked resistance because they contradicted the expectations the liberalization from above had evoked. Contrary to the Russian civil rights movement, large strata within society potentially supported national opposition. In several republics, this latent support from the masses turned into an open crisis of loyalty that large groups within the respective nations carried (in Lithuania since the early 1970s, in Georgia and Estonia since the late 1970s). The Lithuanian masses not only supported the rejection of Soviet power and Russian foreign rule more explicitly than any other republic but also expressed it more openly. In 1968, Lithuanian Catholics began a protest movement against restrictions of their freedom of religion and the discrimination of Church and believers. A movement for national self-determination, which gained public attention by staging demonstrations in the streets of Kaunas in May 1972, closely collaborated with the religious dissidents. On May 14, 1972, nineteen-year-old Romas Kalanta burned himself in Kaunas' downtown, "I am dying for Lithuania's freedom." Four days later, his funeral triggered demonstrations that lasted for two days. Special units of the Ministry of the Interior subdued these demonstrations and arrested 500 people. Later, Lithuanian authorities tried and sentenced eight of them. In May and June 1972, several other people burned themselves for political reasons.[236]

Simultaneously, unrest in the Catholic Church climbed to heights previously unknown. Thousands of Lithuanians signed petitions, open letters, and letters of protest addressed to Lithuanian authorities, courts, and the Party leadership in Moscow. In February 1972, within two months, 17,000 Lithuanians signed a petition addressed to the UN and Secretary General Brezhnev. Catholics demanded that their civil rights be respected and that they be accepted as "equal citizens of the Soviet Union."[237] In 1979, 148,149 Lithuanians signed a petition addressed to Brezhnev, which demanded that their church, which was built in Klaipeda in 1960 and confiscated upon completion, be returned to the congregation.[238] In 1979 and 1982, about 75 percent of the priests signed several letters to the USSR's prosecutor general and Brezhnev explaining their determination to civil disobedience. The priests protested against the new religious law, which the Lithuanian Supreme Soviet passed on July 28, 1976, and spoke of "the Soviet government's illegitimate demands." The priests of the Telshiai Diocese wrote, "We priests think that we are absolutely right in ignoring regulations that contradict the constitution, canons, and our immediate duties."[239]

Religious and national resistance manifested itself primarily in a network of underground magazines, which became increasingly tighter in the 1970s. In 1976, several publications with a national-Lithuanian perspective joined the *Chronicle of the Lithuanian Catholic Church*, which was founded in 1972.[240] *Aushra* (*Dawn*) followed the tradition of the late nineteenth century movement of national awakening, the primary publication of which had the same title. Since 1976, also *Dievas ir tevyne* (*God and Homeland*), since 1977, *Varpas* (*The Bell*), since 1978, *Aushrele* (*Little Dawn*) and *Perspectyvos* (*Perspectives*), and since 1979, *Alma mater,* a magazine addressing the students of the University of Vilnius, which celebrated the 400th anniversary of its foundation in 1979, have been in existence. In 1979, *Vytis* (*The Knight*) and in 1980, *Tautos kelias* (*The Nation's Path*) were founded. Both magazines have a perspective of radical nationalism. Since 1982, the teen magazine *Lietuvos ateitis (Lithuania's Future*) appeared. Of course, it is impossible to publish all of these magazines and others I did not mention in the underground on a regular basis. The KGB dispersed the publishing teams of *Alma mater* and *Aushrele*. But in spite of a number of trials, the primary magazines have been published surprisingly consistently: In April 1984, *Aushra*, vol. 42 was published, in late 1985, the sixth-seventh volume of the *Chronicle*.[241]

The different groupings of national opposition share two principles: the demand for the reinstitution of Lithuania's independence and the opposition's concept of itself as a democratic movement founded on basic and civil rights. Sakharov became an often mentioned example and the Lithuanian opposition maintained close contacts with the liberal-democratic branch of the Russian civil rights movement. National opposition strived to enlist as much support from within the nation as possible. A programmatic editorial in *Aushra,* no. 1/1976, addressed "all those who sincerely love Lithuania regardless of their convictions, Party affiliation, or status. Today, many important officials do not cease loving their motherland and as much as possible are concerned with its welfare."[242] However, this magazine also published chauvinistic articles. One author argued that to make Lithuania a free country, all Russians unwilling to become Lithuanians ought to be asked to leave the country.[243] However, the Lithuanian opposition does not support integral nationalism as a developed philosophical system.

Before 1985, Estonian and Latvian masses did not support national opposition to a comparable extent particularly because Estonia and Latvia could not fall back on national Churches that were deeply rooted in society. In 1972, the "Estonian National Front" and the "Estonian Democratic Movement" went public and sent a memorandum to the United Nations on October 24, 1972. In the name of national self-determination, these organizations demanded the withdrawal of Soviet troops from Estonia, free elections that were to involve all democratic parties, and the reinstitution of Estonian independence and Estonia's membership in the United Nations. In Tallinn in October 1975, a trial against the "Estonian Democratic Movement" resulted in sentences of five and six years of camp imprisonment for four men.[244]

Many Estonian samizdat materials meet high intellectual standards and a certain number of the national and civil rights movement's activists whose names are known are university professors. Since 1978, the magazine *Lisandusi motete ia uudiste vabale levikule Eestis* (*Some Supplements to the Free Exchange of Ideas and News in Estonia*) has been in existence and fought for Estonia's independence from a moderate liberal-national point of view.[245] The Polish revival and the development of "Solidarity" in the summer of 1980 had a great impact on Estonia. Estonia received the Polish revival without the historical and psychological barriers, which still exist in Lithuania. *Some Supplements* dedicated several of its issues to "Solidarity." On September 11, 1980, ten Estonians and ten Lithuanians signed a declaration promising Lech Walesa their sympathy and support. In early October, 1,000 workers in the tractor factory in Tartu went on strike—the first major strike to hit Estonia's industry since 1940. In November 1981, pamphlets surfaced in Tallinn calling for a thirty-minute strike on December 1, 1981—apparently, the success of this effort was very limited. Even publicly, the Estonian CP chief Vaino termed this action a result of the "Solidarity" movement. The high school and university student demonstration in October 1980 (cf. section 5) were not triggered by the events in Poland that went on at the same time but probably were psychologically influenced by them.[246]

In Latvia, oppositional national groups have operated less publicly than in its neighboring republics. In April 1962, eight young Latvians received prison terms of six to fifteen years because they had formed the group "Baltic Federation," a political circle whose members discussed measures against Russification and dreamed of a federation of Baltic states independent of the USSR.

In the summer of 1971, seventeen anonymous members of the Latvian CP wrote a long letter to the "international communist movement" and harshly criticized Stalin's and Brezhnev's nationalities policies from a national-communist perspective by presenting many concrete details. The fact that the letter could present so much detailed information indicates that at least some of its authors belonged to the Latvian nomenklatura. They represented a national-communist tradition, which has always been particularly prevalent in Latvia.

In contrast, groups and actions that gained notoriety afterwards saw themselves as part of a democratic civil rights movement and perceived national self-determination and the resulting independence as an inalienable civil right. After 1975, the groups "Independence Movement of Latvia," "Democratic Youth Committee of Latvia," and "Christian-Democratic Association of Latvia" became known by sending petitions to international organizations. In 1981, the KGB disbanded a social-democratic group that maintained contacts with the Latvian Social-Democratic Labor Party in Sweden. I. Bumeisters and D. Lismanis received prison terms of fifteen and ten years respectively for "espionage."[247]

The joint actions of the oppositional groups reflected the development of a Baltic regional consciousness. Although the KGB prevented the foundation of a joint "Committee of the National Movements of Estonia, Latvia, Lithuania" in 1977, the number of actions reaching beyond national borders increased. In September 1975, six groups (Estonian National Front, Estonian Democratic Movement, Independence Movement of Latvia, Democratic Youth Committee of Latvia, Latvian Christian Democrats, Lithuanian National-Democratic Movement) produced a joint declaration in which they asked the West to be more firm with the Soviet Union and declared their program was directed at implementing basic rights and reinstituting national self-determination in the Baltic republics under the supervision of the United Nations.

On August 23, 1979 – the fortieth anniversary of the Ribbentrop-Molotov treaty – prominent representatives of the Baltic opposition sent petitions to the Soviet, East German, and West German governments and the United Nations. From a perspective of international law, they demanded the three governments approached declare that treaty "null and void from the very beginning" because it contradicted the principle of self-determination guaranteed by international law. They asked these governments "to rescind the consequences of this treaty" and to create the prerequisites for the Baltic nations to "determine their own fates." Forty-five people signed these petitions: thirty-seven Lithuanians, four Estonians, and four Latvians.

Other joint actions of the Baltic opposition included a declaration of January 17, 1980 protesting the invasion of Afghanistan (seventeen Lithuanian, one Latvian, three Estonian signers), and a letter to the Soviet, Islandic, and the four Scandinavian governments demanding the inclusion of the Baltic republics in a nuclear-free zone in northern Europe (fifteen Latvian, thirteen Estonian, and ten Lithuanian signers).[248]

The organized cooperation of opposition groups across national borders — most of which was conducted in Russian — was particularly alarming to the KGB. On May 1, 1982, Western sources were aware of the names of forty-one Lithuanian, 34 Estonian, and sixteen Latvian prisoners who were arrested or sentenced because they had worked in national opposition groups.[249]

The range of national opposition was particularly wide in Ukraine. It spanned from the remnants of organizations dating back to the guerrilla war in the 1940s to national-communist efforts within the Party apparatus. Since the 1960s, opposition — similar to the Baltic republics — has revolved around liberal-democratic groups. However, unlike in the Baltic republics, primarily the literary and artistic intelligentsia kept opposition alive.

From the late 1950s to the late 1960s, several conspiring underground groups — Farmer mentions ten groups — existed in the Ukraine. These groups either followed in the tradition of the OUN or were oriented towards national communism.[250] From 1964 to 1967, the "Ukrainian National Front" operated in the Ivano-Frankovsk region. It perceived itself as an organization continuing the OUN's political ideas and, for a short time, published a samizdat magazine *Volia i batkyvshchyna* (*Liberty and Fatherland*). In 1967, five members of the Ukrainian National Front received prison terms from five to six years and had to go into internal exile after their release from prison.[251]

For the future, national-communist groups became more important because they appealed more to the Ukrainian elites and did not have to defend themselves against accusations that they had collaborated with the Nazis. The most important organization was the "Alliance of Ukrainian Workers and Peasants," which existed in Lvov until late 1960. This alliance was headed by two lawyers, L.H. Lukianenko (born in 1927) and I.A. Kandyba (born in 1930); part of its members were functionaries in Lvov's Party and state apparatus. Referring to the constitution, the group demanded Ukraine's legal and non-violent secession from the Soviet Union. It claimed that within the Union, Ukraine was deprived of determining its own culture, economy, and foreign policy. The "Alliance of Ukrainian Workers and Peasants" advocated the maintenance of the Soviet socialist order of society in a sovereign Ukrainian republic that was to be part of a system of a socialist union of peoples. In May 1961, this Marxist-Leninist group became subject to draconic punishment in Lvov. Initially, Lukianenko received the death penalty. Later, this sentence was commuted to a fifteen-year prison term. Three other accused received prison terms from ten to fifteen years although the group's activities never progressed beyond discussions and plans.[252]

In contrast to the conspiring groups, a literary-publicist opposition formed in the mid-1960s — at the same time as the civil rights movement in Russia. Its strategy was to appeal to the public, send petitions and complaints to the Ukrainian Party leadership, and begin a lively samizdat activity. A wave of arrests in August 1965, which involved at least twenty-five intellectuals — professors, teachers, scientists, students — triggered the formation of this opposition. Most of these intellectuals faced trial in Lvov, Ivano-Frankovsk, Kiev, Lutsk, and Ternopol between January and April 1966 and received sentences. They were accused of conducting propaganda for Ukraine's secession, owning foreign books, openly criticizing the Party's nationalities policy, and writing articles for the Ukrainian press in the West. V. Moroz, one of the intellectuals sentenced in 1966, later became a figure head of the Ukrainian opposition. Apparently, the KGB conducted these trials to destroy opposition in its beginning stages. Like the trial against the writers A. Siniavskii and Iu. Daniel in Moscow in February 1966, however, these trials triggered a wave of solidarity that included well-known authors, critics, and also politicians.

Kiev journalist V. Chornovil systematically collected information about these trials, most of which took place behind closed doors, castigated the abundance of violations of the law, and the untenability of the accusations. In 1966, he followed I. Dziuba's example (Chapter IX, section 2) and presented his records to the Ukrainian Party and government leadership.[253] From 1970–1974, the literary-national opposition's primary publication was the samizdat magazine *Ukraiinskyi visnyk* (*Ukrainian Herald*, eight issues).[254] The spokesmen of this opposition originated from among the anti-Stalinist, so-called Young Writers; they referred to themselves as "Sixtiers." These writers and publicists, most of whom had previously been part of the Ukrainian establishment, were not willing to abandon their hopes for a cultural and political new beginning, which Khrushchev had fostered. For them, a better, anti-Stalinist future was associated with the remembrance of their own national culture and language and, consequently, was equivalent to the fight against the Russian foreignization of the Ukrainian culture and language. The historian V. Moroz represented the most extreme nationalist platform within the opposition, "The nation is the synthesis of everything spiritual. The Christian Shevchenko places the nation above God (the formal, dogmatic God. The true, living God — is the nation)." In a 1970 samizdat essay, he wrote, "A nation can only live if there are people who are willing to die for it."[255]

Although some people in the Party leadership, Writers' Union, Academy of Sciences, and at several institutions of higher education sympathized with the opposition, the number of its supporters among the masses remained low. In January 1972, the KGB started the greatest single action against political dissidents since Stalin's death and succeeded in virtually destroying the literary national opposition: In 1972–1973, at least seventy Ukrainian dissidents were arrested or sentenced. The Ukrainian courts passed sentences that were considerably harsher than in other republics. For example, they sentenced the literary critics I. Svitlichnyi and Ie. Sverstiuk to seven years in camp and five years of exile. The journalist V. Chornovil received six years in camp and five years of exile, the historian I. Dziuba five years in camp and five years of exile, the poet V. Stus five years in camp and three years of exile, and the Orthodox priest V. Romaniuk seven years in camp and three years of exile. In November 1973, Dziuba publicly repented and was released from camp. Stus died in September 1985 in camp after he had been handed another sentence.

The removal of a number of prominent scholars — including several directors of institutes — from their positions accompanied the persecution of at least seventy Ukrainian intellectuals. In February 1973, at least twenty professors of the University of Lvov were removed from their chairs, twenty-three students were suspended. The removal of the Shelest leadership (cf. chapter IX, section 2) paralleled the destruction of the opposition. The attempt to establish a dialogue between an anti-Stalinist, Ukrainian-national intelligentsia and a Party leadership open to national ideas had failed. Moscow had prevented both parties from talking to one another on the basis of their common national-communist learnings.[256]

Massive police measures resulted in making the opposition more radical and incarcerated dissidents from the camps as well as those replacing them in the communities became more extreme. Previously, the *Ukrainian Herald* had been restrained in making programmatic statements. In its last issue 7–8 in the spring of 1974, the magazine supported the "clearly defined political platform" of "uncompromising anti-colonialism," "struggle for national liberation and democracy."[257] After the 1972–1973 pogrom, the voices promoting Leninist and national-communist ideas became weaker.

On November 9, 1976 — in cooperation with the already existing Moscow Committee — the Ukrainian Helsinki Committee came into being in Kiev. On November 25, 1976 the Lithuanian Helsinki Committee was founded, in January 1977, the Georgian, and on April 1, 1977, the Armenian. This was the first time that a rudimentary organization came into being going beyond nations and regions. Although it did not challenge the Soviet system as such, it demanded implicitly fundamental changes in the system in the name of basic rights and the right to national self-determination. The author M. Rudenko, who had been secretary of the Ukrainian Writers' Union from 1947 to 1950, became the chairman of the Ukrainian Committee. The foundation members included the well-known science fiction writer O. Berdnyk, General P. Grigorenko (Hryhorenko), and the lawyers L. Lukianenko and I. Kandyba, who had been released from camp after serving their terms.

The Kiev Helsinki Committee published memoranda explaining that the sovereignty of Union Republics, which the Soviet constitution guaranteed, was fiction. "The national rights guaranteed to Ukraine as a member of the Union are no longer a social reality." But: "Relationships within the Union are not eternal, they change over time." "Why is it necessary to define and plan Ukraine's cultural, scholarly, agricultural, and international problems and their solution in the neighboring state's capital, even if it is an ally? We are not that naive. We understand that this . . . is the spirit of imperialism and chauvinism in action. . . . " In its memorandum no. 2 of January 20, 1977, the Committee says that one day "the Eastern European nations will achieve complete independence." As memorandum no. 5 explains, however, the Committee does not see this as "secession" of Ukraine but as "evolution" of the USSR into a "brotherhood of the world's free peoples."[258]

The Helsinki Committees were very successful domestically and abroad. From all over the Union, they received hundreds of letters telling of incidents where the civil rights of individuals and groups were violated. The fact that these committees maintained supra-regional contacts and the possibility that they might become the centers of massive national movements, motivated the KGB from the very beginning to employ the harshest police actions. As a result, the national committees were forced to heavily limit their activities already in 1980. On September 8, 1982, the Moscow Committee declared its formal dissolution. In the summer of 1983, of the thirty-three members of the Kiev Committee twenty-one were under arrest, four in internal exile, and five exiled abroad. The other committees, all of which counted fewer members, experienced similar reprisals. For example, the Moscow Committee had twenty-one members, the Lithuanian eleven, the Georgian seven, and the Armenian six.[259]

Like the Kiev Committee, the Armenian Helsinki Committee revived the ideas of oppositional groups from the 1960s (also some of its personnel was the same). From the beginning, it combined the struggle for civil rights in general with Armenian national demands. The "Armenian question" has essentially two aspects: demands for "reunification" with Turkish western Armenia within the borders of Sevres (1920) and integration of Mountainous Karabakh and Nakhichevan in the Armenian SSR. Although Mountainous Karabakh and Nakhichevan are part of Azerbaidzhan, historically they have been Armenian territories. Eighty percent of the population of Mountainous Karabakh are Armenian, but only 2–3 percent of the population in Nakhichevan are Armenian.

In both irredenta cases, the dissidents could assume that the vast majority of the Armenian population and many from among the cultural and political establishment agreed with them. Ever since the 1960s, the Armenian samizdat has frequently demanded the integration of Mountainous Karabakh in particular, where the Armenian population is suffering from massive discrimination. In this case, official Armenian media had to rely on the Aesopian language. In contrast, anti-Turkism has been able to articulate itself officially relatively unimpeded since 1965.[260]

The foundation declaration of the Helsinki Committee in Erevan listed among the committee's objectives the reunification of Mountainous Karabkh and Nakhichevan with the Armenian SSR and solidarity with the eighteen political prisoners, who had received prison terms ranging from six months to ten years in 1973–1974.[261]

These political prisoners were members of the "National United Party" ("Natsionalno-obedinennaia partiia," NOP), which was founded in 1966 and was the most important national underground group in Armenia. On the occasion of its tenth anniversary, the group listed as its objectives "the reinstitution of national statehood on the territory comprising historical Armenia, the reunification of all Armenians, dispersed all over the world, in a homeland whose territory and statehood is reinstituted, and national renaissance." A referendum was to determine whether Armenia was to secede from the USSR. A future "independent Armenia does not imply an anti-Soviet Armenia."[262]

Up to the mid-1980s, no national or democratic civil rights groups have developed in the Islamic territories. As far as Western sources know, there were no conspiratory national groups, no political or nationalist samizdat. The Islamic samizdat circulates only religious texts. The only known exceptions are the previously described Crimean Tatar and Meskhetian movements. But after World War II, an old Islamic institution experienced a renaissance and is considered a center of religious and national resistance: the Sufi brotherhoods. Today, the Sufi brotherhoods (Tariqa) have more members than before the revolution. Probably nowhere in the Islamic world is the Sufi's popular, mystical-ecstatic tradition more alive than in the Soviet Union. The brotherhoods are tightly organized groups with a rigid hierarchy. These groups are headed by a sheikh or myrshid or ishan, who leads the Tariqa, which is organized over several hierarchical levels. The members are called myrids; many Tariqas recruit their members only from a specific clan (not the Qadiriya). Because of this, the brotherhoods play a major role in the preservation of traditional social orders.

Today, the Northern Caucasus is the center of Sufism. The Tariqas (meaning "Path" or "Path towards God") arrived there fairly recently in the late eighteenth century as Naqshbandiya brotherhoods, which Baha ud-Din Naqsheband had founded in Bukhara in the fourteenth century. In the Northern Caucasus, they lead active military and passive civilian resistance against the Russian conquest in the nineteenth century. In the 1850s, another order, the Qadiriya brotherhood, which Abd al-Qadir Gilani founded in Baghdad in the twelfth century, began to thrive in the Northern Caucasus. Kunta Haji, the founder and preacher of Qadiriya in the Northern Caucasus, died in a Siberian prison camp in 1867. The Qadiriya practice the aloud zikr, the Naqshbandiya the silent zikr. The zikr, whose prayers are like a litany, promote believers' concentration and mystical meditation; specific breathing exercises and dance-like movements accompany these prayers.

After the revolution and civil war, and after the Red Army, in 1921, had defeated the Imamat of Daghestan and Chechenia, where the Naqshbandi sheikhs Najmuddin of Gotso and Uzun Hadji led the development of a theocratic Islamic state, the Sufi seemed to have lost their religious and social importance. The deportation of Chechens and Ingush to Central Asia opened unexpected new realms of action to the brotherhoods: First, the Tariqas gave Chechens and Ingush a tremendously strong feeling of solidarity and desire to resist during their banishment, when they returned to their homeland, and in the decades following. Second, the deportation spread and revived Sufism in Central Asia.

To date, Soviet society has been unable to integrate Chechens and Ingush (cf. chapter VIII, section 2). This is due to the fact that the deportation made brotherhoods and clans the dominant principle of social order. According to data of Soviet experts, practically all Chechen and Ingush Islamic clergymen are members of a brotherhood.[263] In addition, more than half of the believers in Checheno-Ingushetia were myrids in a brotherhood in the 1970s. Soviet polls indicate that in this ASSR 50 to 60 percent of the adult Muslims are believers. This means that in Checheno-Ingushetia about 150,000 to 200,000 people are members in the Sufi brotherhoods. Western experts estimate the number of myrids in the Northern Caucasus—in addition to Checheno-Ingushetia, Daghestan is another center—from 250,000 to 500,000.[264]

The Naqshbandiya predominate in Daghestan, the Qadiriya in Chechenia. The Vis Haji group, which Vis Haji Zagiev founded during the deportation in Kazakhstan in the early 1950s and follows the tradition of the Qadiriya, is particularly lively and is gaining members fast. Vis Haji introduced many innovations to the zikr, for example the use of violins and drums during funerals. Soviet literature refers to the Vis Haji group also as "White Hats" (in Russian: "beloshapochniki") because its members wear white fur hats during the zikr. Innovations that made the Tariqas particularly successful under Soviet living conditions included the admission of women to the brotherhoods. The Qadiriyas maintain special women's groups that are led by female sheikhs.

The Sufi could evolve into a determining force in Islamic society—at least in the Northern Caucasus—because they address this society's central needs. Soviet power prevents the satisfaction of these needs or at least does not meet them adequately—practicing religious cult and religious and national identification with Islamic culture in an emotional and aesthetic form. Sufi brotherhoods not only represent conservative Islam but are also anti-Russian and anti-European. Their basic values include the rejection of everything foreign. Of course, this fundamentalist, anti-modernist Islam is not oriented towards the nation in the sense that it associates exclusively with the Chechen, Kirgiz, or any other nation. Rather, it sees Russians and all "infidels" as a threat to Islam, which can only be defended if the Sufi are totally dedicated to it.

By destroying nearly all Islamic religious institutions (mosques, medreses) Soviet power left the Sufi an unlimited field of action particularly in the Northern Caucasus. The tombstones of the nineteenth and twentieth century heroes, who fought the Russians, replaced the closed mosques. Led by the members of brotherhoods, this is where believers meet to pray. This is also where believers meet for zikr, teach the Koran, the prayers and Arabic, and conduct religious rituals, particularly funerals because the saints' graves are often in cemeteries. Because there are only very few mullahs, the Sufi conduct religious rites at the major family celebrations like circumcisions and weddings. In 1970, 300 inofficial mosques existed in Azerbaidzhan alone, only sixteen were registered.[265] The Sufi probably controlled many of them. Thus, the Sufi appear as preservers and defenders of traditions, old values, and historical origin.

With the exception of the Qadiriya's Batal Haji group, which is a group derived from the brotherhood of Kunta Haji, the Tariqas are not secret societies. From the perspective of Soviet law, however, nearly all of their activities—from the conduction of zikr to the organization of Koran schools and pilgrimages to the holy graves—were illegal. For the most part the Sufi are nevertheless left alone because apparently they have advocates and sympathizers in the Soviet Islamic establishment. Several militant sheiks and myrids of the Batal Haji group and the Naqshbandiya, however, turned to violence and launched armed attacks against Soviet institutions. Several trials that ended with death sentences, for example in Makhachkala in 1964 and Groznyi in 1970, are known.[266]

In Central Asia, the Sufi play a less significant role than in the Northern Caucasus. But even there, the Vis Haji Tariqa, which deported Chechens founded, is expanding. The Sufi have a stronghold among the previously nomadic Turkmen and Kirgiz. These peoples maintained much of their traditional tribal structure and yielded the least to modernization. Paradoxically, nomadic peoples were the least religious before the revolution.

The Sufi fascinate the new Central Asian national intelligentsia because they are the ties to the cultural roots of a rediscovered tradition. Since the twelfth century, nearly all poets in Turkestan — particularly those who developed a Turkic writing system, like Ahmed Yasawi and ali-Shir Navoi — were Sufi members and Islamic mysticism had great influence on their poetry. The Naqshbandiya brotherhood, the most significant order in Central Asia, played a dominant role during Central Asia's heyday under the rule of the Timurids and also later, in the defense of the crumbling empire against the infidels. As a result, the rediscovery and the reestablishment of Central Asia's great culture (mirasism) are unimaginable without Sufi involvement.[267]

In summary, oppositional efforts manifested themselves in many different forms. Their effect on individual national societies was different. They seem to have had the greatest impact in the Baltic states, Armenia, Georgia, and the Northern Caucasus. Opposition against the Party's nationalities policy manifested itself most coherently among the deported peoples and Jews. Until the mid-1980s, the KGB prevented the development of large organizations.

Also, oppositional groups maintained varying distances to the respective national nomenklatura. In Georgia and Ukraine, contacts probably were the closest. Those groups that can combine the old cultural and moral traditions with the new needs of the socialist intelligentsia have the best chances to change the Soviet system.

Notes

1. *Narodnoe khoziaistvo SSSR v 1959 godu* (Moscow, 1960), p. 752; *Narodnoe khoziaistvo SSSR 1922–1982. Iubileinyi sbornik* (Moscow, 1982), p. 517. The 1960–1961 student figures do not include correspondence students; however, they are included in the 1980–1981 figures.

2. Cf. above chapter II, section 5.

3. E. Jones/F.W. Grupp, "Modernization and Ethnic Equalization in the USSR," in: *Soviet Studies*, XXXVI, 1984, pp. 163f.; idem, "Measuring Nationality Trends in the Soviet Union: A Research Note," in: *Slavic Review*, 41, 1982, p. 119.

4. Jones/Grupp, "Modernization and Ethnic Equalization," pp 163f. Cf. R. Karklins, "Ethnic Politics and Access to Higher Education," in: *Comparative Politics*, XVI, 1984, pp. 277–294. Karklins is right in pointing out the deficiencies of the statistical methods, which I also adopted, to deter-

mine the level of equality and discrimination. As no other Soviet data are available, she is also forced to rely on these figures.

5. Cf. Pennar/Bakalo/Bereday, *Modernization and Diversity in Soviet Education*, pp. 202–209.

6. See notes 1 and 3.

7. *Narodnoe obrazovanie, nauka i kultura v SSSR* (Moscow, 1975), p. 296; Appendix Table A.13).

8. Jones/Grupp, "Measuring Nationality Trends," (note 3), p. 117; idem., "Modernization and Ethnic Equalization," pp. 171f.

9. In 1959–1960, 63.7 percent of mid-level technical students were Russian; in 1974–1975, 60.7 percent. By comparison, in 1960, 65.6 percent of specialists with a mid-level technical education were Russian; in 1975, 63.4 percent. (*Narodnoe khoziaistvo SSSR v 1959 godu* (Moscow, 1960), p. 752; *Narodnoe obrazovanie, nauka i kultura v SSSR* (Moscow, 1977), p. 208; Appendix Table A.14).

10. Silver, "Levels of Sociocultural Development," p. 1627.

11. Valiev, *Sovetskaia natsionalnaia intelligentsiia*, pp. 48–58.

12. W. Teckenberg, *Die soziale Struktur der sowjetischen Arbeiterklasse im internationalen Vergleich* (Munich/Vienna, 1977), pp. 66–68, 115ff.

13. Appendix Table A.6. However, these figures are only approximations because Appendix Table A.6 includes only the members of one nation within its own republic; Table 9.2 in the text includes the members of one nation in the USSR. Appendix Table A.6 refers to individuals employed in the economy; Table 9.2 in the text refers to the total population, including unemployed family members.

14. Appendix Table A.13; *Kommunist vooruzhennykh sil 24/1972*, p. 12.

15. Jones/Grupp, "Measuring Nationality Trends," note 3, p. 116.

16. See chapter VIII, section 2 above.

17. *Deputaty Verkhovnogo Soveta. Deviatyi sozyv* (Moscow, 1974), p. 379; *Desiatyi sozyv* (Moscow, 1979), pp. 385, 436; *Odinnadtsatyi sozyv* (Moscow, 1984), p. 430. I owe these references to Prof. Yaroslav Bilinsky and Dr. Eberhard Schneider.

18. *Deputaty Verkhovnogo Soveta. Deviatyi sozyv* (Moscow, 1974), p. 379; *Desiatyi sozyv* (Moscow, 1979), pp. 385, 436; *Odinnadtsatyi sozyv* (Moscow, 1984), p. 430. I owe these references to Prof. Yaroslav Bilinsky and Dr. Eberhard Schneider.

19. D. Carlisle, "Uzbekistan and the Uzbeks," in: *Handbook of Major Soviet Nationalities*, p. 290.

20. Z.S. Chertina, *Protiv burzhuaznykh falsifikatsii natsionalnykh otnoshenii v SSSR* (Moscow, 1983), p. 25.

21. Th. Remeikis, "Political Developments in Lithuania During the Brezhnev Era," in: *Nationalism in the USSR and Eastern Europe*, p. 166. As

far as they are the result of Western research, all data pertaining to the national make-up of leadership groups on the level of republics and below are based on analyzing name lists and determining nationalities based on names. As a result, these figures can only be approximations. However, in the case of the Baltic and Central Asian nations, names are mostly indicative of nationality, and the contrast with Slavic names is clear. By comparison, differentiation between Ukrainians and Russians on the basis of names is very prone to error. Results of Western analyses illustrate a trend identical with Soviet data—as far as they are available.

22. Th. Remeikis, "Political Developments in Lithuania During the Brezhnev Era," in: *Nationalism in the USSR and Eastern Europe*, p. 166. As far as they are the result of Western research, all data pertaining to the national make-up of leadership groups on the level of republics and below are based on analyzing name lists and determining nationalities based on names. As a result, these figures can only be approximations. However, in the case of the Baltic and Central Asian nations, names are mostly indicative of nationality, and the contrast with Slavic names is clear. By comparison, differentiation between Ukrainians and Russians on the basis of names is very prone to error. Results of Western analyses illustrate a trend identical with Soviet data—as far as they are available.

23. Corresponding figures for all Union Republics and pertaining to every year from 1955 to 1972 cf.: Hodnett, *Leadership in the Soviet National Republics*, pp. 377f.

24. Ibid., pp. 89–94.

25. J.H. Miller, "Cadres Policy in Nationality Areas," in: *Soviet Studies*, XXIX, 1977, pp. 3–36; Carrère d'Encausse, *L'Empire éclaté*, pp. 144–158.

26. Hodnett, *Leadership in the Soviet National Republics*, p. 93.

27. Jones/Grupp, "Modernization and Ethnic Equalization," p. 174.

28. Hodnett, *Leadership in the Soviet National Republics*, pp. 104f.

29. S. Bialer, *Stalin's Successors. Leadership, Stability, and Change in the Soviet Union* (Cambridge, Mass., 1980), pp. 219f.

30. *Pravda*, December 22, 1982.

31. Rakowska-Harmstone, "The Study of Ethnic Politics in the USSR," in: *Nationalism in the USSR and Eastern Europe*, p. 23.

32. Carrère d'Encausse, *L'Empire éclaté*, p. 272.

33. Cf. among others Kim, *The Soviet People—A New Historical Community* (Moscow, 1974), p. 181; I.S. Gurvich, "Osobennosti sovremennogo etapa etnokulturnogo razvitiia narodov SSSR," in: *Sovetskaia etnografiia*, 6/1982, p. 24; Iu. Bromlei, "Etnicheskie protsessy v SSSR," in: *Kommunist*, 5/1983, pp. 56–64.

34. O.S. Redzhepova, "Natsionalizm — orudie ideologicheskikh diversii imperializma," in: *Izvestiia A.N. Turkmenskoi SSR. Seriia obshchestvennykh nauk,* 4/1981, p. 14.

35. Gurvich, "Osobennosti sovremennogo etapa" (cf. note 33), p. 26.

36. Ibid., p. 24.

37. V.V. Pokhshishevskii, "Urbanization and Ethnographic Processes," in: *Soviet Geography,* XIII, 2/1972, p. 116.

38. Iu. V. Arutiunian, "Natsionalno-regionalnoe mnogoobrazie sovetskoi derevni," in: *Sotsiologicheskie issledovaniia,* 3/1980, p. 81. Cf. idem, "Konkretno-sotsiologicheskoe issledovanie natsionalnykh otnoshenii," in: *Voprosy filosofii,* 12/1969, pp. 129–140.

39. Iu. V. Bromlei, "Etnograficheskoe izuchenie sovremennykh natsionalnykh protsessov v SSSR," in: *Sovetskaia etnografiia,* 2/1983, p. 13.

40. Drobizheva, *Dukhovnaia obshchnost narodov SSSR,* particularly pp. 204f.

41. Bromlei, "Etnograficheskoe izuchenie" (cf. note 39), p. 12.

42. Arutiunian, "Natsionalno-regionalnoe mnogoobrazie sovetskoi derevni," p. 79.

43. A. Martiny, "Das Verhältnis von Politik und Geschichtsschreibung in der Historiographie der sowjetischen Nationalitäten seit den sechziger Jahren," in: *Jahrbücher für Geschichte Osteuropas,* XXVII, 1979, pp. 237–272. The quote is on p. 258.

44. L.R. Tillett, "Nationalism and History," in: *Problems of Communism,* XVI, 5/1967, pp. 36–45.

45. Valiev, *Formirovanie i razvitie,* pp. 56–61.

46. E.J. Lazzerini, "Tatarovedenie and the 'New Historiography' in the Soviet Union: Revising the Interpretation of the Tatar-Russian Relationship," in: *Slavic Review,* 40, 1981, pp. 625–635. The quote is on p. 635. Idem, "Ethnicity and the Uses of History: The Case of the Volga Tatars and Jadidism," in: *Central Asian Survey,* I, 2–3/1982/83, pp. 61–69; Kappeler, *Die Geschichte der Völker der Mittleren Volga,* pp. 229ff.

47. "Sovetskaia mnogonatsionalnaia," in: *Literaturnoe obozrenie,* 11/1982, p. 24.

48. Misiunas/Taagepera, *Baltic States,* p. 261.

49. Ekmanis, *Latvian Literature,* pp. 342ff.; *Discordant Voices. The Non-Russian Soviet Literatures. 1953–1973.*

50. R. Karklins, "Nationality Power in Soviet Republics," pp. 70–93. The quote on p. 77 reflects the opinion of one of the people polled.

51. Z. Gitelman, "Are Nations Merging in the USSR?," in: *Problems of Communism,* XXXII, 5/1983, pp. 41–42.

52. J. Pelenski, "Shelest and His Period in Soviet Ukraine (1963–1972): A Revival of Controlled Ukrainian Autonomism," in: *Ukraine in the Seventies*, pp. 283–305.
53. Hodnett, *Leadership in the Soviet National Republics*, p. 378.
54. Bilinsky, "Mykola Skrypnyk and Petro Shelest: An Essay on the Persistence and Limits of Ukrainian National Communism," in: *Soviet Nationality Policies and Practices*, p. 120; Z.S. Chertina, *Protiv burzhuaznykh falsifikatsii natsionalnykh otnoshenii v SSSR* (Moscow, 1983), p. 25.
55. Carrère d'Encausse, *L'Empire éclaté*, p. 220.
56. Bilinsky, "Mykola Skrypnyk" (note 54), p. 123; V. Holubnychy, "Some Economic Aspects of Relations Among the Soviet Republics," in: *Ethnic Minorities*, pp. 87f., 117f.
57. *Pravda*, April 1, 1971; Bilinsky, "The Communist Party of Ukraine after 1966," in: *Ukraine in the Seventies*, p. 249.
58. *Nasha kultura*, 3/1963, p. 5–6. Only this Ukrainian magazine, published in Warsaw, extensively covered this conference. The quote from this report is from Bilinsky, *Second Soviet Republic*, pp. 32–34f., cf. p. 322.
59. Only the Samizdat publicized Dadenkov's speech: V. Chornovil, "Iak i shcho obstoiuie Bohdan Stenchuk?" in: *Ukraiinskyi visnyk*, 6 (Paris/Baltimore, 1972), pp. 24–30; in German in: *Osteuropa*, XXIII, 1973, pp. A 190–A 194.
60. *Radianska Ukraiina*, November 17, 1966.
61. *Literaturna Ukraiina*, November 17, 1966.
62. O. Honchar, *Sobor* (Kiev, 1968); Farmer, *Ukrainian Nationalism in the Post-Stalin Era*, pp. 106–108.
63. Ievhen Sverstiuk, "A Cathedral in Scaffolding," in: idem, *Clandestine Essays* (Cambridge, Mass., 1976), pp. 17–68.
64. I. Dziuba, *Internatsionalizm chy rusifikatsiia?* (Munich, 1968); in English: (New York, 1974), 3rd edition.
65. Farmer, *Ukrainian Nationalism in the Post-Stalin Era*, pp. 170–172, 195–197.
66. G. Hodnett, "The Views of Petro Shelest," in: *Annals of the Ukrainian Academy of Arts and Sciences in the United States*, XIV, 1978–80, pp. 209–243.
67. P.Iu. Shelest, *Ukraiino nasha radianska* (Kiev, 1970); "Pro seriozni nedoliky ta pomylky odniieii knyhy," in: *Komunist Ukraiiny*, 4/1973, pp. 77–82.
68. J. Pelenski, "Shelest and His Period in Soviet Ukraine," in: *Ukraine in the Seventies*, pp. 283–305; R. Solchanyk, "Politics and the National Question in the Post-Shelest Period," in: *Ukraine After Shelest*, pp. 1–15.
69. Groshev, *Borba partii protiv natsionalizma*, pp. 118–120; Revecz, *Volk aus 100 Nationalitäten*, pp. 333–337. The quote by Party chief Bodiulis in: *XXIV s-ezd KPSS. Stenograficheskii otchet*, vol I, (Moscow, 1971), p. 374.

The quote by Lithuanian Party Chief Snieckus is in: *Sovetskaia Litva*, March 4, 1971, p. 7.

70. S. Dorzhenov, "Musulmanin li ia?" in: *Nauka i religiia*, 4/1967, p. 50.
71. Bennigsen/Lemercier-Quelquejay, *Les musulmans oublis*, pp. 193–200.
72. I.A. Makatov, *Ateisty v nastuplenii: preodolenie perezhitkov islama v natsionalnom soznanii* (Moscow, 1978), p. 114.
73. B. Kamenetskii/A. Aleksandrova, "Ispoved zhenshchiny," in: *Kontinent*, no. 38, 1983, pp. 209–220.
74. Iu. A. Evstigneev, "Mezhetnicheskie braki v nekotorykh gorodakh severnogo Kazakhstana," in: *Vestnik Moskovskogo universiteta. Seriia istoriia*, 6/1972, pp. 73–82.
75. A. Kozenko/L. Monogarova, "Statisticheskoe izuchenie pokazatelei odnonatsionalnoi i smeshannoi brachnosti v Dushanbe," in: *Sovetskaia etnografiia*, 3/1971, pp. 112–118; A.B. Kalyshev, "Mezhnatsionalnye braki v selskikh raionakh Kazakhstana," in: *Sovetskaia etnografiia*, 2/1984, pp. 71–77.
76. On the topic of secularized Islam see: Carrère d'Encausse, *L'Empire éclaté*, pp. 233ff.; Bennigsen/Broxup, *The Islamic Threat to the Soviet State*; Bennigsen/Lemercier-Quelquejay, *Les musulmans oublis*; R. Karklins, "Islam: How Strong Is It in the Soviet Union?" in: *Cahier du Monde russe et sovitique*, XXI, 1980, pp. 65–81.
77. Mirmukhsin, *Zodchii* (Moscow, 1978). For general information about literature, see: W. Fierman, "Uzbek Feelings of Ethnicity. A Study of Attitudes Expressed in Recent Uzbek Literature," in: *Cahiers du Monde russe et sovitique*, XXII, 1981, pp. 187–229; D.C. Matuszewski, "The Turkic Past in the Russian Future," in: *Problems of Communism*, XXXI, 4/1982, pp. 76–82.
78. *Az i ia* (Alma-Ata, 1975). The title is a word play involving the Old-Slavic (az) and the Russian (ia) words for "I." However, the title can also be read as Aziia (= Asia). The following quotes are on pp. 187, 106.
79. *Voprosy istorii*, 9/1976, pp. 147–154.
80. Kulichenko, *Rastsvet i sblizhenie natsii v SSSR*, pp. 400f.; *Kazakhstanskaia pravda*, March 19, 1977.
81. A. Sheehy, "Olzhas Suleimenov Elected First Secretary of Writers' Union of Kazakhstan," in: *RL*, 114/84, March 20, 1984.
82. Chingiz Aitmatov, *I dolshe veka dlitsia den* (Frunze, 1981).
83. A. Sheehy, "Uzbek Novel Found Ideologically Unsound," in: *RL*, 337/82, August 20, 1982.
84. Lewis/Rowland/Clem, *Nationality and Population Change*, p. 290.
85. Kozlov, *Natsionalnosti SSSR*, 2nd edition, pp. 174f.
86. Lewis/Rowland/Clem, *Nationality and Population Change*, p. 290.
87. Kozlov, *Natsionalnosti SSSR*, 2nd edition, pp. 174f.

88. Many Soviet and Western researchers have extensively analyzed the different developments of the nations' birth rates. Consequently, I will only outline the issue. Examples of Soviet literature are: B.Ts. Urlanis, *Problemy dinamiki naseleniia SSSR* (Moscow, 1974); G.A. Bondarskaia, *Rozhdaemost v SSSR. Etnograficheskii aspekt* (Moscow, 1977); V.I. Kozlov, "Dinamika natsionalnogo sostava naseleniia SSSR i problemy demograficheskoi politiki," in: *Istoriia SSSR*, 4/1983, pp. 20–30. Examples of Western literature are: B. Knabe, *Bevölkerungsentwicklung und Binnenwanderung in der UdSSR* (Berlin, 1978); J.F. Besemeres, *Socialist Population Politics: The Political Implications of Demographic Trends in the USSR and Eastern Europe* (White Plains, N.Y., 1980); *Soviet Population Policy: Conflicts and Constraints* H. Desfosses (ed.), (New York, 1981); S. Rapaway/G. Baldwin, "Demographic Trends in the Soviet Union: 1950–2000," in: *Soviet Economy in the 1980s: Problems and Prospects* vol. II, (Washington, D.C., 1983), pp. 265–296.

89. Kozlov, *Natsionalnosti SSSR*, 2nd edition, pp. 199, 293f.

90. M. Feshbach, "Social Maintenance in the USSR: Demographic Morass," in: *Washington Quarterly*, V, 1982, p. 93.

91. Wimbush/Alexiev, *Ethnic Factor in the Soviet Armed Forces*, p. 2.

92. A.I. Sorokin, "Vooruzhennye sily razvitogo sotsializma," in: *Voprosy filosofii*, 2/1983, p. 11. The author was the First Deputy Head of the Main Political Administration of the Army and Navy.

93. Lewis/Rowland/Clem, *Nationality and Population Change*, p. 278.

94. S. Bruk, "Natsionalnost i iazyk v perepisi naseleniia v 1970 godu," in: *Vestnik statistiki*, 5/1972, pp. 48f.

95. A. Sheehy, "The National Composition of the Population of the USSR According to the Census of 1979," in: *RL*, 123/80, March 27, 1980, p. 16.

96. V.I. Kozlov, "Izmeneniia v rasselenii i urbanizatsiia narodov SSSR kak usloviia i faktory etnicheskikh protsessov," in: *Sovremennye etnicheskie protsessy v SSSR*, pp. 141–143. The Soviet Union has published virtually no direct statistical data pertaining to the nations' migrations. As a result, this analysis depends on figures illustrating the nations' compact settlement.

97. Arutiunian, "Natsionalno-regionalnoe mnogoobrazie sovetskoi derevni," p. 80.

98. N. Lubin, *Labor and Nationality in Soviet Central Asia. An Uneasy Compromise*, Foreword M. Feshbach, (London/Basingstoke, 1984), pp. 62f., cf. pp. 59, 69–71.

99. J.W. Gillula, "The Growth and Structure of Fixed Capital," in: *Economics of Soviet Regions*, p. 162.

100. "Plan 'povorota rek': Popytki dogovoritsia s nesoglasnymi?" in: *RL*, 178/84, August 16, 1984; B. Brown, "Whatever happened to 'Sibaral'?" in: *RL*, 420/85, December 13, 1985.

101. G.I. Litvinova, "Vozdeistvie gosudarstva i prava na demograficheskie protsessy," in: *Sovetskoe gosudarstvo i pravo*, 1/1978, pp. 134f.; R. Galetskaia, "Demograficheskaia politika i ee napravleniia," in: *Voprosy ekonomiki*, 8/1975, pp.149–152. In the USSR and the West, the discussion whether the Asian peoples will migrate and how else the abundance of workers in Asia can be reduced is controversial. It is summarized in: Rywkin, *Moscow's Muslim Challenge*, pp. 72ff.

102. V.I. Kozlov, "Dinamika natsionalnogo sostava naseleniia SSSR i problemy demograficheskoi politiki," in: *Istoriia SSSR*, 4/1983, pp. 20–30. Brezhnev's remarks at the Twenty-sixth Party Congress are in: *Pravda*, February 24, 1981. The weak beginnings to establish a differentiated population policy directed at stimulating more births among the peoples with low birth rates and a reduction in the number of births in Asia are presented in: "Maternity Benefits for Soviet Women are Expanded," in: *RL*, 158/81, April 10, 1981.

103. S.I. Brook (= Bruk), "Demographical and Ethnographical Changes in the USSR According to Post-War Data up to 1979," in: *Geo Journal*, Supplementary Issue I, 1980, pp. 14f.

104. Kozlov, *Natsionalnosti SSSR*, 2nd edition, p. 100; D. Bahry/C. Nechemias, "Half Full or Half Empty? The Debate Over Soviet Regional Equality," in: *Slavic Review*, 40, 1981, p. 373. These two authors are correct in pointing out that the individual Union Republics define the terms "city" and "urban settlement" along different criteria. Probably, this raises the figures of non-Russian urbanization and lowers those of Russian urbanization in the statistics. Consequently, the differences between the two groups would be even greater, if their level of urbanization were assessed according to the same criteria.

105. Kozlov, *Natsionalnosti SSSR*, 2nd edition, p. 191; Carrère d'Encausse, *L'Empire éclaté*, pp. 83–85.

106. Martiny, "Sozialstruktur und nationale Beziehungen," pp. 57f.

107. Ibid., pp. 49–56; Kozlov, *Natsionalnosti SSSR*, 2nd edition, pp. 89, 100.

108. I.S. Koropetskii, "Growth and Productivity," in: *Economics of Soviet Regions*, pp. 101, 104; A. Woroniak, "Regional Aspects of Soviet Planning and Industrial Organization," in: *Soviet Economy in Regional Perspective*, pp. 295ff.

109. E. Bagramov, "Kommunisticheskoe stroitelstvo i internatsionalizatsiia obshchestvennoi zhizni," in: *Pravda*, August 3, 1973.

110. Resolution of the CPSU's CC "On the Sixtieth Anniversary of the USSR's Foundation" on February 19, 1982, in: *Kommunist*, 4/1982, p. 5. On the occasion of the fiftieth anniversary of the USSR's foundation on Decem-

ber 21, 1972, Brezhnev expressed the same idea in his speech (*Partiinaia zhizn*, 1/1973, p. 11).

111. G.E. Schroeder, "Soviet Living Standards: Achievements and Prospects," in: *Soviet Economy in the 1980s: Problems and Prospects*, vol. II, Selected Papers Submitted to the Joint Economic Committee, Congress of the U.S. (Washington, D.C., 1983), pp. 367f.

112. Penkaitis, *Finanzausgleich*, pp. 167–173.

113. *Aktualnye problemy natsionalnykh otnoshenii v svete konstitutsii SSSR* (Moscow, 1981), pp. 110–126; Iu.V. Bromlei, et al. (eds.), *Razvitie natsionalnykh otnoshenii v SSSR* (Moscow, 1982), p. 132.

114. *Natsionalnye otnosheniia v SSSR na sovremennom etape* (Moscow, 1979), p. 98.

115. *Narodnoe khoziaistvo SSSR v 1982 g.* (Moscow, 1983), pp. 128, 283.

116. A. McAuley, "Labour Supply and Living Standards in Soviet Central Asia. Paper Prepared for a Seminar on Soviet Central Asia, held at the Foreign and Commonwealth Office" (London, April 9/10, 1981), p. 6.

117. Wagener, *Wirtschaftswachstum*, p. 92.

118. G.S. Sarkisian/N.P. Kuznetsova, *Potrebnosti i dokhod semi* (Moscow, 1967), p. 67; *Pravda*, September 27, 1974.

119. McAuley, *Economic Welfare in the Soviet Union*, pp. 109f.

120. Ibid., p. 127.

121. Ibid., pp. 135–138; K.-E. Wädekin, "Income Distribution in Soviet Agriculture," in: *Soviet Studies*, XXVII, 1975, pp. 12–19.

122. *Itogi vsesoiuznoi perepisi naseleniia 1970 goda*, vol. VII (Moscow, 1974), pp. 286f., 296f. (1970 figures).

123. Cf. the exact calculations in: McAuley, *Economic Welfare in the Soviet Union*, pp. 112–114.

124. Ibid., p. 118.

125. Ibid. Cf. Wagener, *Wirtschaftswachstum*, pp. 150f.

126. G.E. Schroeder, "Regional Living Standards," in: *Economics of Soviet Regions*, pp. 131–136.

127. G.E. Schroeder, "Regional Differences in Incomes and Levels of Living in the USSR," in: *Soviet Economy in Regional Perspective*, p. 170; cf. Penkaitis, *Finanzausgleich*, pp. 178f.

128. R.M. Iudina/E.I. Burkhanova (eds.), *Natsionalnyi vopros i natsionalnye otnosheniia v SSSR. Bibliograficheskii ukazatel literatury 1963–1973 gg.* (Dushanbe, 1976): This bibliography lists 2,500 Russian and 186 Tadzhik titles. V.P. Sherstobitov (ed.), *Internatsionalizm Sovetskogo naroda* (Moscow, 1982): This collection contains a bibliography of 1,650 Soviet books from the 1970s alone. It does not include the extensive Soviet magazine literature. E. Allworth's 1971 estimate that the USSR published "seventy-five books, pamphlets, and magazine articles annually" on the nationalities issue in Russian was much too conservative (*Soviet Nationality Problems*, p.

242; ibid., pp. 261-272 a bibliography of Soviet publications from 1967 to 1969).

129. E. Oberländer, "Der sowjetische Nationsbegriff," in: *Aus Politik und Zeitgeschichte*, B 12, 20, March 1968, pp. 3-19; idem, "Der sowjetische Nationsbegriff heute," in: *Osteuropa*, XXI, 1971, pp. 273-279; G. Hodnett, "What's in a Nation?" in: *Problems of Communism*, 5/1967, XVI, pp. 2-15; Y. Bilinsky, "The Concept of the Soviet People and its Implications for Soviet Nationality Policy," in: *The Annals of the Ukrainian Academy of Arts and Sciences in the United States*, XIV, 1978-1980, pp. 112-118.

130. M.I. Kulichenko, in: *Osnovnye napravleniia izucheniia natsionalnykh otnoshenii v SSSR*, p. 76.

131. Iu. Arutiunian/Iu. Kakhk, *Sotsiologicheskie ocherki v Sovetskoi Estonii* (Tallinn, 1979), p. 72.

132. Stalin, "Marxismus und nationale Frage (1913)," in: idem, *Werke*, vol. 2, p. 272.

133. *Pravda*, December 23, 1969; March 31, 1971; December 22, 1972; October 8, 1977. A detailed analysis of how the term "Soviet people" is used in official Party documents is in: Y. Bilinsky, The Concept of the Soviet People and its Implications for Soviet Nationality Policy," in: *The Annals of the Ukrainian Academy of Arts and Sciences in the United States*, XIV, 1978-1980, pp. 91ff.

134. N.V. Mantsvetov, "Sblizhenie natsii i vozniknovenie internatsionalnoi obshchnosti narodov v SSSR," in: *VI*, 5/1964, p. 50.

135. Khanazarov, *Reshenie natsionalno-iazykovoi problemy*, p. 214.

136. Tsamerian, *Teoreticheskie problemy*, pp. 233f.; *Sovetskii narod-stroitel kommunizma*, p. 326.

137. M.I. Kulichenko, "Aktualnye problemy razvitiia natsii natsionalnykh otnoshenii v svete novoi konstitutsii SSSR," in: *Nauchnyi kommunizm*, 6/1977, p. 13.

138. M.I. Kulichenko, "Osnovnye zakonomernosti formirovaniia i razvitiia novoi istoricheskoi obshchnosti — sovetskogo naroda," in: *Istoriia SSSR*, 6/1980, p. 41.

139. Malanchuk, *Istoricheskii opyt KPSS*, p. 258.

140. E.V. Tadevosian/V.A. Shpiliuk, *Internatsionalizatsiia zhizni narodov SSSR v usloviiakh razvitogo sotsializma* (Moscow, 1980), p. 22.

141. B.A. Martynov, "Metodologichicheskie voprosy dialektiki natsionalnogo i internatsionalnogo," in: *Natsionalnoe i internatsionalnoe v zhizni naroda. Materialy mezhrespublikanskoi nauchnoi konferentsii*, vol. I (Kiev, 1970), p. 127.

142. *Sovetskii narod-stroitel kommunizma*, p. 303.

143. *Sovetskii narod-stroitel kommunizma*, pp. 335f.

144. Groshev, *Istoricheskii opyt KPSS*, pp. 292f., 329f.

145. Cf. chapter VI, section 1.

146. Tsamerian, *Teoreticheskie problemy,* pp. 130f., 138f. Similar phrases can be found, for example, in: S.B. Batyrev, *Formirovanie i razvitie sotsialisticheskikh natsii v SSSR* (Moscow, 1962, pp. 177f.; *Stanovlenie sovetskogo naroda,* pp. 25–29.
147. *Formirovanie sotsialisticheskikh natsii v SSSR,* p. 119.
148. Kulichenko, *Rastsvet i sblizhenie natsii,* p. 17.
149. *Stanovlenie sovetskogo naroda,* p. 31.
150. G.O. Zimanas, in: *Formirovanie sotsialisticheskikh natsii v SSSR,* pp. 404ff.
151. Ibid., p. 404.
152. Ibid., pp. 387f.
153. Kulichenko, *Rastsvet i sblizhenie natsii,* p. 136.
154. A.I. Kholmogorov, in: E.M. Tiazhelnikov (ed.), *Partiinyi komitet-organizator patrioticheskogo i internatsionalnogo vospitaniia trudiashchikhsia* (Moscow, 1982). The quote is taken from: *Referativnyi zhurnal. Problemy nauchnogo kommunizma,* 4/1983, pp. 146f.
155. *Sovetskii narod-stroitel kommunizma,* p. 15.
156. Ibid., pp. 3, 310, 382.
157. Ibid., p. 8.
158. M.P. Kim, in: "Stanovlenie i razvitie novoi istoricheskoi obshchnosti sovetskogo naroda. Kruglyi stol 'Istorii SSSR,'" in: *Istoriia SSSR,* 6/1980, p. 48.
159. Iu.V. Bromlei, in: ibid., p. 49.
160. For example, F.Ia. Gorovskii, *Sovetskii narod kak internatsionalnaia obshchnost* (Kiev, 1982), pp. 36, 39.
161. Kim, in: "Stanovlenie i razvitie novoi istoricheskoi obshchnosti" (note 158), p. 46.
162. V.S. Semenov, in: ibid., p. 75.
163. Cf. For example, E. Bagramov, "Kommunisticheskoe stroitelstvo i internatsionalizatsiia obshchestvennoi zhizni," in: *Pravda,* August 3, 1973; E. Tadevosian, "Voprosy teorii sovetskogo mnogonatsionalnogo gosudarstva," in: *Politicheskoe samoobrazovanie,* 8/1974, p. 137; E.M. Babosov (ed.), *Internatsionalizatsiia: sushchnost, tendentsii, perspektivy* (Minsk, 1977), p. 19; Kulichenko, *Rastsvet i sblizhenie natsii,* pp. 427ff. This publication offers more bibliographical data.
164. *Pravda,* December 22, 1982.
165. Iu. Bromlei, "Etnicheskie protsessy v SSSR," in: *Kommunist,* 5/1983, pp. 56–64. Excerpts of this study are published in German in: *Osteuropa,* XXXIV, 1984, pp. A 144–A 150.
166. S.T. Kaltakhchian, *Marksistsko-leninskaia teoriia natsii i sovremennost* (Moscow, 1983), p. 356.
167. *Pravda,* October 5, 1977.

168. S.Z. Zimanov/I.K. Reitor, *Sovetskaia natsionalnaia gosudarstvennost i sblizhenie natsii* (Alma-Ata, 1983), p. 149. Similar arguments are presented in: Tsamerian, *Teoreticheskie problemy*, pp. 258f.

169. Isayev, *National Languages in the USSR*, pp. 299, 351.

170. Batyrev, *Formirovanie i razvitie sotsialisticheskikh natsii v SSSR*, pp. 104, 333.

171. V. Kuznetsov, "Iazyk mezhnatsionalnogo obshcheniia," in: *Pravda Ukrainy*, September 12, 1972.

172. V.A. Shpiliuk, *Internatsionalizm sotsialisticheskogo obraza zhizni* (Lvov, 1979), p. 63. Many bibliographical references pertaining to the ideological substantiation of the "second native language" is in: Kreindler, "The Changing Status of Russian in the Soviet Union," pp. 17–21.

173. M.I. Kulichenko, "Dialektika natsionalnogo i internatsionalnogo v zrelom sotsialisticheskom obshchestve," in: *Obshchestvennye nauki*, 2/1980, pp. 55–68; the quotes are on pp. 58, 60, 61, 68.

174. Drobizheva, *Dukhovnaia obshchnost narodov*, p. 238.

175. V.I. Kozlov, "Ethnic Processes and Trends in the Ethnic Composition of the Population in the USSR," in: *Geo Journal, Supplementary Issue*, 1, 1980, p. 24.

176. Ibid., pp. 25f.

177. Ibid., p. 25; idem, *Natsionalnosti SSSR*, 1st edition, p. 254.

178. Iu.V. Bromlei, *Sovremennye problemy etnografii* (Moscow, 1981), p. 330. The same opinion is expressed in: I.P. Tsamerian, in: *Sovetskii narod-stroitel kommunizma*, p. 299.

179. Kozlov, *Natsionalnosti SSSR*, 1st edition, pp. 196–201; V.K. Gardanov/V.O. Dolgikh/T.A. Zhdanko, "Osnovnye napravleniia etnicheskikh protsessov u narodov SSSR," in: *Sovetskaia etnografiia*, 4/1961, pp. 11–18; table 1 in the Appendix.

180. M.I. Kulichenko, in: M.I. Kulichenko (ed.), *Aktualnye problemy natsionalnykh otnoshenii v svete konstitutsii SSSR* (Moscow, 1981), p. 45. Using other examples, incomplete national consolidation is also the topic in: I.S. Gurvich, "Osobennosti sovremennogo etapa etnokulturnogo razvitiia narodov SSSR," in: *Sovetskaia etnografiia*, 6/1982, p. 25.

181. A. Bennigsen, "Les Musulmans de l'URSS et la crise afghane," in: *Politique trangre*, 1/1980, p. 19.

182. Lewis/Rowland/Clem, *Nationality and Population Change in Russia and the USSR*, pp. 219–220, 282–286; S.I. Bruk/V.M. Kabuzan, "Dinamika chislennosti i rasseleniia russkikh posle Velikoi Oktiabrskoi sotsialisticheskoi revoliutsii," in: *Sovetskaia etnografiia*, 5/1982, p. 13; Kozlov, *Natsionalnosti SSSR*, 1st edition, pp. 251f.

183. Lewis/Rowland/Clem, *Nationality and Population Change in Russia and the USSR*, pp. 286f.

184. Today the Karelian settlement territory is part of the Kalinin region. In 1932, four Karelian raions and forty-four Karelian village soviets existed in this area. M. Sabirziakov, "Natsmenrabota profsoiuzov Moskvy," in: *RN,* 9/1932, p. 69; *Itogi vsesoiuznoi perepisi naseleniia 1970 goda,* vol. IV, p. 89.

185. V.I. Kozlov, "Ethnic Processes and Trends in the Ethnic Composition of the Population in the USSR," in: *Geo Journal,* Supplementary Issue, 1/1980, p. 28; Kreindler, "The Mordvinians — a Doomed Soviet Nationality?"

186. Kozlov, *Natsionalnosti SSSR,* 2nd edition, pp. 89, 100.

187. Ibid., pp. 240–260.

188. *Vestnik statistiki,* 8/1980, pp. 64–68.

189. Kozlov, *Natsionalnosti SSSR,* 2nd edition, p. 255.

190. *Vestnik statistiki,* 7/1980, p. 43; 9/1980, p. 65.

191. Khanazarov, *Reshenie natsionalno-iazykovoi problemy,* p. 195.

192. *Itogi vsesoiuznoi perepisi naseleniia 1970 goda,* vol. IV.

193. Kreindler, *The Changing Status of Russian,* p. 27.

194. *Pravda,* May 23, 1980.

195. V. Shatalov, *Migratsiia naseleniia i internatsionalnoe vospitanie* (Alma-Ata, 1977); quoted in: *Referativnyi zhurnal. Seriia 1. Problemy nauchnogo kommunizma,* 4/1978, p. 115.

196. Iu. D. Desheriev, "Bytovaia kultura i ee otrazhenie v iazyke," in: *Natsionalnyi iazyk i natsionalnaia kultura,* p. 125.

197. Iu.D. Desheriev/A.N. Baskakov (eds.), *Iazyk v razvitom sotsialisticheskom obshchestve. Iazykovye problemy razvitiia sistemy massovoi kommunikatsii v SSSR* (Moscow, 1982), p. 70.

198. Iu.D. Desheriev, in: Iu.V. Bromlei (ed.), *Mezhnatsionalnye sviazi i vzaimodeistvie kultur narodov SSSR* (Tallinn, 1978), quoted in: *Referativnyi zhurnal. Seriia 1. Problemy nauchnogo kommunizma,* 3/1979, p. 121. Cf. also Desheriev, *Razvitie obshchestvennykh funktsii literaturnykh iazykov,* p. 421.

199. Desheriev, *Bytovaia kultura* (cf. note 196), p. 119.

200. Solchanyk, "Russian Language and Soviet Politics," p. 25.

201. "Recommendations of the Scholarly-Practical All Union Congress on the Perfection of Russian Classes in National Schools, Technical Middle Schools, and Institutions of Higher Education (Tashkent, October 1975)," in: *Russkii iazyk v natsionalnoi shkole,* 1/1976, pp. 79–82.

202. K.Kh. Khanazarov, "Vazhnoe napravlenie politiki KPSS v oblasti resheniia natsionalnogo voprosa i razvitiia natsionalnykh otnoshenii," *VI KPSS,* 1/1978, p. 53.

203. Solchanyk, "Russian Language and Soviet Politics," p. 27.

204. "On the Regulations Concerning the Conferment of Academic Degrees and the Award of Academic Titles," in: *Biulleten Ministerstva vysshego i srednego spetsialnogo obrazovaniia SSSR,* 4/1976, pp. 12–26, cf. item 83, p. 23.

205. "'On Measures to Continue the Improvement of the Learning and Teaching of Russian in the Union Republics.' Excerpts from the Decree of the USSR's Ministry for Institutions of Higher Education and Technical Middle School Education of December 6, 1978," in: *Biulleten Ministerstva vysshego i srednego spetsialnogo obrazovaniia SSSR*, 2/1979, pp. 20–22.

206. Particularly "Sovershenstvovat izuchenie i prepodavanie russkogo iazyka," in: *Russkii iazyk v natsionalnoi shkole*, 1/1979, p. 2.

207. Khanazarov, *Reshenie natsionalno-iazykovoi problemy*, p. 176; Solchanyk, "Russian Language and Soviet Politics," pp. 30f.

208. Excerpts from the decree of December 6, 1978, point 1.6 (cf. note 205).

209. Decree by the minister for the USSR's Institutions of Higher Education and Technical Middle School Education of May 19, 1964 "Concerning the Perfectioning of Russian Classes at Institutions of Higher Education and Technical Schools in Union Republics and Autonomous Republics," in: *Biulleten Ministerstva vysshego i srednego spetsialnogo obrazovaniia SSSR*, 7/1964, p. 5–8; German excerpts in: *Die Sowjetische Bildungspolitik von 1958 bis 1973*, pp. 91–93.

210. Desheriev, *Razvitie obshchestvennykh funktsii literaturnykh iazykov*, pp. 121 (Uzbekistan), 176 (Georgia), 198 (Azerbaidzhan), 218 (Lithuania), 340 (Armenia).

211. "V Ministerstve prosveshcheniia SSSR," in: *Russkii iazyk v natsionalnoi shkole*, 5/1979, p. 92.

212. *Soviet Nationality Survey*, vol. I, 2/1984, pp. 7–8.

213. Khanazarov, *Reshenie natsionalno-iazykovoi problemy*, pp. 173–178; *Sovremennye etnicheskie protsessy v SSSR*, pp. 268–270; Bilinsky, "Mykola Skrypnyk and Petro Shelest: An Essay on the Persistence and Limits of Ukrainian National Communism," in: *Soviet Nationality Policies and Practices*, p. 124; Silver, *The Status of National Minority Languages*, p. 38.

214. "A Preliminary Evaluation of the New Republican Constitutions," in: *RL*, 82/78, April 18, 1978.

215. *Vospityvat ubezhdennykh patriotov-internatsionalistov*, p. 157.

216. R. Szporluk, "Recent Trends in Soviet Policy Towards Printed Media in the non-Russian Languages," in: *RL*, Supplement, 2/84, November 7, 1984.

217. *Presa Ukraiinskoii RSR. 1918–1980. Statychnyi dovidnyk* (Kharkov, 1981), pp. 82f.; R. Solchanyk, "The Non-Russian Languages in the USSR – Only for Poetry and Memoirs?," in: *RL*, 376/84, October 3, 1984.

218. *Pechat SSSR v 1982 g.* (Moscow, 1983), pp. 24f.; Cypin, "Respublika ordena Lenina," in: *RN*, 5/1934, p. 90.

219. *Pechat SSSR v 1958 g., 1970 g., 1975 g., 1982 g.* (Moscow, 1959, 1971, 1976, 1983).

220. V.I. Kozlov, "Ethnic Processes and Trends in the Ethnic Composition of the Population of the USSR," in: *Geo Journal*, Supplemental Issue, 1/1980, p. 29.

221. *Zaria vostoka*, April 24, 1976, August 25, 1976. Dzhaparidze's speech is published in: "AS No. 2583. Georgian Writer Speaks Out Against Russification," in: *RL*, 406/76, September 8, 1976; "Expressions of Official and Unofficial Concern Over the Future of the Georgian Language," in: *RL*, 149/81, April 7, 1981.

222. A detailed analysis of this issue is in: A. Sheehy, "The National Languages and the New Constitutions of the Transcaucasian Republics," in: *RL*, 97/78, May 3, 1978; G. Simon, "Die nichtrussischen Völker in Gesellschaft und Innenpolitik der UdSSR," in: *Berichte des BIOst*, 10/1979, February 1979, pp. 23–26. The quote from Shevardnadze's speech is in: *Zaria vostoka*, April 15, 1978; the articles of the respective constitutions about "state language" are in: *Kommunist (Erevan)*, April 15, 1978, article 72; *Zaria vostoka*, April 16, 1978, article 75; *Bakinskii rabochii*, April 23, 1978, article 73.

223. *AS*, no. 4167 and *Russkaia mysl*, December 4, 1980; in German in: Lewytzkyj, *Sovetskii narod—Das Sowjetvolk*, pp. 134–136.

224. "Volneniia v Gruzii (Samizdat)," in: *Forum*, 1/1982, pp. 86–88; "Expressions of Official and Unofficial Concern Over the Future of the Georgian Language," in: *RL*, 149/81, April 7, 1981.

225. *Radianska osvita*, December 12, 1981, quoted from: R. Solchanyk, "Soviet Language Policy: Two Steps Forward, One Step back?" in: *RL*, 47/82, January, 28, 1982. Other references to the Union Republican press are in: "Expression of Official and Unofficial Concern Over the Future of the Georgian Language," in: *RL*, 149/81, April 7, 1981; "Armenian Writer Deplores Preference Shown for Russian Language in Republican Education," in: *RL*, 230/82, June 8, 1982; A. Sheehy, "Why Shouldn't Russians Learn the Vernacular?" in: *RL*, 18/82, January 14, 1982.

226. B. Lewytzkyj, *Die Parteitage in den Unionsrepubliken 1981*. Special publication by BIOst, July 1981, pp. 17–21.

227. Latvian Party chief A.E. Voss expressed these sentiments at an All Union congress in Riga in June 1982 dedicated to national relations (*Sovetskaia Latviia*, June 29, 1982). G.O. Zimanas, the leading Lithuanian ideologist and editor of the Lithuanian CC's journal (*Kommunist*, Vilna), expressed similar feelings at the same congress ("Sotsialnaia politika i natsionalnye otnosheniia" quoted from: *Referativnyi zhurnal. Seriia 1, Problemy nauchnogo kommunizma*, 3/1983, p. 178).

228. Iu.V. Arutiunian/L.M. Drobizheva, "Sotsialnaia struktura sovetskikh natsii na sovremennom etape," in: *VI*, 7/1982, p. 14.

229. I. Papertis, "Unofficial Lithuanian Journal Cites Peril to the Native Language," in: *RL*, 223/81, June 2, 1981. Letter of protest to the CPSU's

CC: *AS*, no. 3937, German in: Lewytzkyj, *Sovetskii narod – Das Sowjetvolk*, p. 137.
230. *Eesti Noukogude Entsüklopeedia*, 8 vol. and 1 *index volume (Tallinn, 1968–1978)*.
231. An English translation of this letter is in: J. Estam/J. Pennar, "Estonian Intellectuals Express Their Views on the Causes of Recent Demonstrations in Open Letter," in: *RL*, 477/80, December 15, 1980.
232. The samizdat magazine *A Chronicle of Current Events* reported about the movement extensively and in detail. The first eleven volumes of the magazine (April 1968 to December 1969) were translated into English under the title *Uncensored Russia*. Amnesty International Publications (London) have published volume 12 and all following volumes of *A Chronicle of Current Events*. Khronika Press (New York) began publishing the original text of *Khronika tekushchikh sobytii* in December 1972 (volume 28). Earlier volumes are published in Russian in *AS*. The Moscow "Group Supporting the Implementation of the Helsinki Agreements in the USSR" (Moscow Helsinki Committee) published documents pertaining to the situation of the Crimean Tatars on several occasions: "Document No. 10" of November 10, 1976 (=*AS*, no. 2830, 2831); "Document No. 24" of November 4, 1977 (=*AS*, no. 4096); "Document No. 43" of April 6, 1978 (=*AS*, no. 3327). The Alexander Herzen Foundation Amsterdam published files and notes concerning the Tashkent trial of ten Crimean Tatar spokesmen in July and August 1969: *Tashkentskii protsess. Sud nad desiatiu predstaviteliami krymskotatarskogo naroda* (1 iiulia–5 avgusta 1969 g.) (Amsterdam, 1976). Western literature: P.J. Potichnyj, "The Struggle of the Crimean Tatars," in: *Canadian Slavonic Papers*, XVII, 1975, pp. 302–319; G. Simon, "Die nationale Bewegung der Krimtataren," in: *Berichte des BIOst*, 30/1975 (part 1), 31/1975 (part 2); A.W. Fisher, *The Crimean Tatars* (Stanford CA, 1978), pp. 165–201; Sheehy/Nahaylo, *Crimean Tatars*, pp. 6–17.
233. *Uncensored Russia*, pp. 270–279; *Chronicle of Current Events*, no. 45, May 25, 1977 (cf. note 231); S.E. Wimbush/R. Wixman, "Meskhetian Turks: A New Voice in Soviet Central Asia," in: *Canadian Slavonic Papers*, XVII, 1975, pp. 320–340; Sheehy/Nahaylo, *Crimean Tatars*, pp. 24–27.
234. German samizdat: "Re Patria Nr. 1. Sbornik materialov, posviashchennykh nemtsam Sovetskogo Soiuza," in: *Volnoe slovo*, no. 16 (Frankfurt/Main, 1975); "Auszüge aus Petitionen und offenen Briefen," in: CDU/CSU-Fraktion des Deutschen Bundestages (ed.), *Weißbuch über die menschenrechtliche Lage in Deutschland und der Deutschen in Osteuropa* (Bonn, 1977), pp. 55–74; Dortleff, K. (ed.), *Laßt sie selber sprechen. Berichte rußlanddeutscher Aussiedler* (Hannover, 1978). The Internationale Gesellschaft für Menschenrechte (International Society for Human Rights) in Frankfurt/Main has an extensive collection of German samizdat. Western literature: Karklins, R., "Interviews mit deutschen Spätaussiedlern aus der

Sowjetunion, in: *Berichte des BIOst,* no. 42/1978; Schnurr, J., "Die Aussiedler aus dem sowjetischen Bereich," in: Arnold, W. (ed.), *Die Aussiedler in der Bundesrepublik Deutschland* (Vienna, 1980), pp. 57–101; Heitman, S. "The Soviet Germans in the USSR Today," in: *Berichte des BIOst,* no. 35/1980; Kussmann, Th./Schäfer, B., "Nationale Identität: Selbstbild und Fremdbild von deutschen Aussiedlern aus der Sowjetunion," in: *Berichte des BIOst,* no. 46/1982; Internationale Gesellschaft für Menschenrechte (ed.), *Deutsche in der UdSSR. Dokumentation. Bestandsaufnahme, März 1982* (Frankfurt/Main, 1982); Oschlies, W. "Die Deutschen in der Sowjetunion," in: *Berichte des BIOst,* no. 13/1983; Pinkus, B., "The Emigration of National Minorities from the USSR in the Post-Stalin Era," in: *Soviet Jewish Affairs,* XIII, 1/1983, pp. 3–36; Ständiges Sekretariat für die Koordinierung der bundesgeförderten Osteuropaforschung beim BIOst (ed.), *Deutsche in der Sowjetunion, Berichte über die 1. bzw. 2. bzw. 3. Arbeitskonferenz am 9. Februar 1982, bzw. 5. Oktober 1982, bzw., 10. April 1984 in Köln.*

235. Jewish samizdat: Rozhanskii, A. (ed.), *Antievreiskie protsessy v Sovetskom Soiuze. 1969–1971 gg.* 2 volumes (Jerusalem, 1979); Redlikh, Sh. (ed.), *Evrei i evreiskii narod. Petitsii, pisma i obrashcheniia evreev SSSR. 1968–1970.* 2 volumes (Jerusalem, 1973); Ben-Arie, A. (ed.), *Evreiskii samizdat.* 22 volumes (Jerusalem, 1974–1980). Western Literature: Sawyer, T.E., *The Jewish Minority in the Soviet Union* (New York, 1979); Bland-Spitz, D. *Die Lage der Juden und der Jüdischen Opposition in der Sowjetunion 1967–1977* (Diessenhofen, 1980); Florsheim, Y., "The Demographic Significance of Jewish *Emigration from the USSR,"* in: *Soviet Jewish Affairs,* X, 1/1980, pp. 5–22; "The Soviet Anti-Zionist Committee," in: *Soviet Jewish Affairs,* XIII, 3/1983, pp. 55–72; Pinkus, B., "The Emigration of National Minorities from the USSR in the Post-Stalin Era," in: *Soviet Jewish Affairs,* XIII, 1/1983, pp. 3–36; Zaslavsky V./Brym, R.J., *Soviet-Jewish Emigration and Soviet Nationality Policy* (London, 1983); Friedgut, T.H., "Soviet Anti-Zionism and Anti-Semitism: Another Cycle," in: *The Hebrew University of Jerusalem. Soviet and East European Research Center,* Research Paper no. 54, January 1984.

236. The most important books on the Lithuanian opposition are: Vardys, *Catholic Church, Dissent and Nationality in Soviet Lithuania* (cf. pp.173–181 about the events in Kaunas in May 1972); Remeikis, *Opposition to Soviet Rule in Lithuania;* Bourdeaux, *Land of Crosses.* All books contain *extensive samizdat materials in English.*

237. German in: *Acta Baltica,* vol. XII, 1972, pp. 76–79 (= *Chronik der Litauischen Katholischen Kirche,* no., 2, 1972); English in: Remeikis, *Opposition,* pp. 531–534.

238. *Chronik der Litauischen Katholischen Kirche,* no. 41, 1980, in: *Chronik der Litauischen Katholischen Kirche,* no. 39–46, (Königstein in Ts., 1983), 160–165.

239. "Chronik der Litauischen Katholischen Kirche, no. 55, 1982," in: *Informationsdienst Glaube in der 2. Welt,* 4/1983, pp. 26–28 (first quote); "Chronik der Litauischen Katholischen Kirche, no. 38, 1979," in: *Chronik der Litauischen Katholischen Kirche,* no. 32–38 (Königstein i. Ts., 1981), p. 288 (second quote).

240. *Acta Baltica,* vol. XIII, 1973 contains the first of a series of German translations of the *Chronicle.* After 1977, these translations have been published in special volumes of this yearbook. This series is published by the Institutum Balticum in Königstein i. Ts.

241. Vardys, *Lithuania's Catholic Movement Reappraised,* pp. 66ff. RL reported regularly about new volumes of Lithuanian samizdat magazines.

242. An English version of this programmatic editorial is in: Remeikis, *Opposition,* pp. 373–375.

243. *Aushra,* no. 14/1978, quoted in: V.S. Vardys, "The Nature and Philosophy of Baltic Dissent: A Comparative Perspective," in: *Nationalities Papers,* X, 2/1982, p. 132.

244. English translations of the most important Estonian samizdat documents from 1972 to 1976 (including the memorandum of October 24, 1972 and records and files of the trial in October 1975) are in: Estonian Information Center (ed.), *Documents from Estonia on the Violation of Human Rights* (Stockholm, 1977). Western presentations: A. Zarins, "Dissent in the Baltic Republics: A Survey of Grievances and Hopes," in: *RL,* 496/76, December 14, 1976, pp. 6–12; A. Küng, *A Dream of Freedom. Four Decades of National Survival Versus Russian Imperialism in Estonia, Latvia, and Lithuania. 1940–1980* (Cardiff, 1981).

245. J. Pennar, "Third and Sixth Issues of Estonian Samizdat Periodical," in: *RL,* 373/82, September 15, 1982; idem, "Fourth, Seventh, and Thirteenth Issues of Estonian Samizdat Publication," in: *RL,* 57/83, January 31, 1983.

246. *Declaration of Twenty Estonian and Lithuanian Dissidents for Walesa of September 11, 1980: AS 4452;* K. Vaino, "S tochnym znaniem obstanovki," in: *Kommunist,* 4/1983, p. 52; Vardys, *Polish Echoes in the Baltic,* pp. 25–27.

247. Zarins, *Dissent in the Baltic Republics,* pp. 12–21; Alexiev, *Dissent and Nationalism in the Soviet Baltic,* pp. 35ff.; "Letter of the Seventeen Latvian Communists," German in: Lewytzkyj, *Politische Opposition,* pp. 215–230.

248. Declaration of six groups of September 1975: *AS 2435;* petition of August 23, 1980 in English: Remeikis, *Opposition,* pp. 659–663; *Afghanistan declaration of January 1980: AS 3857;* letter concerning the nuclear-free zone: *AS 4570.* S. Girnius, "The Arrest of Enn Tarto and the Crackdown on Baltic Dissent," in: *RL,* 364/83, September 29, 1983.

249. Liubarskii, *O strukture politicheskikh repressii,* p. 46.

250. Farmer, *Ukrainian Nationalism,* pp. 154–160.

251. Lewytzkyj, *Politische Opposition,* p. 114; *Ukrainian Review,* XVI, 2/1969, pp. 9–12; XXI, 2/1974, pp. 83–85.

252. Extensive collections of documents: *Ukraiinski iurysty pid sudom KGB* (Munich, 1968); S. Sadovskyi (ed.), *Zupynit kryvosuddia! Sprava Levka Lukianenka* (1980) (= *Zoshyty ukrainskogo samvydavu*, vol. 3); English translations of the prisoners' documents from the prison camps: M. Brown (ed.), *Ferment in the Ukraine* (London, 1971), pp. 31-93.

253. *The Chornovil Papers* (New York, 1968); V. Chornovil, *Lycho z rozumu. Portrety dvadtsiiaty 'zlochyntsiv'* (Paris, 1967); *Ukraiinska inteligentsiia pid sudom KGB. Materialy z protsesiv V. Chornovola, M. Masiutka, M. Ozernogo ta in.* (1970). Western accounts of the persecution of 1965-1966 and their consequences are in: M. Brown (ed.), *Ferment in the Ukraine* (London, 1971), pp. 1-28.

254. Issues 1, 2, 3, 4, 6, 7-8 were published as single copies in Paris and Baltimore, 1970-1975. English translations are in: *Ukrainian Herald*, 4 (Munich, 1972); *Dissent in Ukraine, The Ukrainian Herald*, 6 (Baltimore, 1977); *Ethnocide of Ukrainians in the USSR*, in: *The Ukrainian Herald*, 7-8 (Baltimore, 1976).

255. V. Moroz, "'Moisei i Datan.' Biloruskii poetesi Ievdokiii Los z pryvodu iiii statti 'Bessylnaia iarost osleplenyia. Otvet radyovraliam yz Miunkhena' (Literaturnaia hazeta, chyslo 36 za 1969 r.)," in: *SDS*, vol. XVIII, no. 980. After serving prison terms for years (1966-1969; 1970-1979), Moroz was released to the U.S.A. in April 1979 in the course of an exchange of political prisoners.

256. Extensive collections of Ukrainian samizdat materials and documents of the persecution are in: *SDS*, vol. XVIII (Munich, 1973); R. Kupchynskyi (ed.), *Pogrom v Ukraiini. 1972-1979* (1980) (= *Zoshyty ukraiinskogo samvydavu*, vol. I). An extensive bibliography lists materials of the Ukrainian opposition: G. Liber/A. Mostovykh (eds.), *Nonconformity and Dissent in the Ukrainian SSR. 1955-1975. An Annotated Bibliography* (Cambridge, Mass., 1978). A German translation of texts and poems by Ukrainian dissidents also exists: *Ein Dichter im Widerstand. Aus dem Tagebuch des Wassyl Stus*. Translated from Ukrainian by Anna-Halja and Marina Horbatsch (Hamburg, 1984); I. Swietlytschnyj/Je. Swerstjuk/W. Stus, *Angst — ich bin dich losgeworden! Ukrainische Gedichte aus der Verbannung*. Translated from Ukrainian by Anna-Halja Horbatsch (Hamburg, 1984). Western accounts of the 1972-1973 reprisals are in: B. Nahaylo, "Ukrainian Dissent and Opposition After Shelest," in: *Ukraine After Shelest*, pp. 30-54.

257. *The Ukrainian Herald, issue 7-8. Ethnocide of Ukrainians in the USSR* (Baltimore, 1976), p. 15.

258. *Human Rights Movement in Ukraine. Documents of the Ukrainian Helsinki-Group*, pp. 36, 64, 74-76. Additional materials by the Kiev Helsinki Committee are: O. Zinkevych (ed.), *Ukraiinskyi pravozakhysnyi rukh. Dokumenty i materialy kyiivskoii Ukrainskoii Hromadskoii Hrupy Spryiannia Vykonanniu Helsinkskykh Uhod* (Toronto/Baltimore, 1978); O. Zinkevych

(ed.), *Ukraiinska Helsinkska Hrupa. 1978–1982. Dokumenty i materialy* (Toronto/Baltimore, 1983). Materials by the Ukrainian, Lithuanian, Georgian, and Armenian Helsinki Committees from 1976 and 1977 are in: *SDS*, vol. XXX, 1978, pp. 39–94. Western studies include: Y. Bilinsky/T. Parming, "Helsinki Watch Committees in the Soviet Republics. Implications for Soviet Nationality Policy," in: *Nationalities Papers*, IX, 1981, pp. 1–25; Nahaylo, "Ukrainian dissent and Opposition After Shelest," in: *Ukraine After Shelest*, pp. 30–54.

259. "The Members of the Public Groups for Furthering the Implementation of the Helsinki Agreements in the USSR," in: *RL*, 4/84, December 29, 1983; S. Girnius, "The Demise of the Lithuanian Helsinki Group," in: *RL*, 20/84, January, 11, 1984.

260. Mouradian, *L'Armnie sovitique depuis la mort de Staline*, pp. 203–255.

261. The Russian text is in: *SDS*, vol. XXX, pp. 78–81; a French translation is in: Mouradian, op. cit., pp. 276f.

262. The Russian text is in: *AS*, no. 3119; a French translation is in: Mouradian, op. cit., pp. 270–272.

263. L.I. Klimovich, "Borba ortodoksov i modernistov v islame," in: *Voprosy nauchnogo ateizma*, vol. II, 1966, p. 67.

264. V.G. Pivovarov, "Sotsiologicheskie issledovaniia problem byta, kultury, natsionalnykh traditsii i verovanii v Checheno-Ingushskoi ASSR," in: *Voprosy nauchnogo ateizma*, vol. XVII, 1975, p. 316; Lermercier-Quelquejay, *Sufi Brotherhoods in the USSR*, p. 18.

265. Lemercier-Quelquejay, op. cit., p. 21.

266. A. Bennigsen/Ch. Lemercier-Quelquejay, "Muslim Religious Conservatism and Dissent in the USSR," in: *Religion in Communist Lands*, IV, 1978, p. 160f.

267. An extensive bibliography of Soviet literature about the Sufi published since the 1960s: A. Bennigsen, "Sufism in the USSR: A Bibliography of Soviet Sources," in: *Central Asian Survey*, II, 4/1983, pp. 81–107. In addition to the references mentioned in notes 263–265, there are other Western studies: A. Bennigsen, "Muslim Conservative Opposition to the Soviet Regime: The Sufi Brotherhoods in the North Caucasus," in: *Soviet Nationality Policies and Practices*, pp. 334–348; Bennigsen/Lemercier-Quelquejay, *Les musulmans oublis*, pp. 231–250.

Statistical Appendix

Table A.1: Ethnic Composition of the USSR's Population (Within the Respective Borders)

	Total Number (in thousands)					Increase (in percent)		
	1926	1939	1959	1970	1979	1926-1939	1939-1959	1959-1970	1970-1979
Total Population	147,027.9	170,557.1	208,826.7	241,720.1	262,084.7	15.7	9.5[1]	15.8	8.4
Russians	77,791.1	99,591.5	114,113.6	129,015.1	137,397.1	28.0	13.7[1]	13.0	6.5
Ukrainians	31,195.0	28,111.0	37,252.9	40,753.2	42,347.4	-9.9	4.6[1]	9.4	3.9
Belorussians	4,738.9	5,275.4	7,913.5	9,051.8	9,462.7	11.3	-4.4[1]	14.4	4.5
Lithuanians	41.5	32.6	2,326.1	2,664.9	2,850.9	-21.4	14.4[1]	14.6	7.0
Latvians	141.6	128.0	1,399.5	1,429.8	1,439.0	-9.6	-14.1[1]	2.2	0.6
Estonians	154.7	143.0	988.6	1,007.4	1,019.9	-7.2	-13.6[1]	1.9	1.2
Moldavians	278.9	260.4	2,214.1	2,698.0	2,968.2	-6.6	7.5[1]	21.8	10.0
Georgians	1,821.2	2,249.6	2,692.0	3,245.3	3,570.5	23.5	19.7	20.5	10.0
Armenians	1,567.6	2,152.9	2,786.9	3,559.2	4,151.2	37.3	29.4	27.7	16.6
Azeri	1,706.6	2,275.7	2,939.7	4,379.9	5,477.3	33.3	29.2	49.0	25.1
Uzbeks	3,904.6	4,845.1	6,015.4	9,195.1	12,456.0	24.1	24.2	52.8	35.5
Kazakhs	3,968.3	3,100.9	3,621.6	5,298.8	6,556.4	-21.9	16.8	46.3	23.7
Turkmen	763.9	812.4	1,001.6	1,525.3	2,027.9	6.3	23.3	52.2	33.0
Tadzhiks	978.7	1,229.2	1,396.9	2,135.9	2,897.7	25.6	13.6	52.9	35.7
Kirgiz	762.7	884.6	968.7	1,452.2	1,906.3	16.0	9.5	49.9	31.3
Tatars	2,916.3	4,315.5	4,967.7	5,930.7	6,317.5	47.9	15.2	19.4	6.5
Chuvash	1,117.4	1,369.6	1,469.8	1,694.4	1,751.4	22.6	7.3	15.2	3.4
Mordvinians	1,340.4	1,456.3	1,285.1	1,262.7	1,191.8	8.4	-11.8	-1.7	-5.6
Mari	428.2	481.6	504.2	598.6	622.0	12.5	4.7	18.8	3.9

(continued)

Table A.1 (continued)

	Total Number (in thousands)					Increase (in percent)			
	1926	1939	1959	1970	1979	1926-1939	1939-1959	1959-1970	1970-1979
Udmurts	504.2	606.3	624.8	704.3	713.7	20.2	3.1	12.7	1.3
Komi and Komi-Permiaks	375.9	422.3	430.9	475.3	477.5	12.0	2.0	10.2	0.5
Karelians	248.1	252.7	167.3	146.1	138.4	1.8	-33.8	-12.7	-5.3
Kalmyks	132.0	134.4	106.1	137.2	146.6	1.8	-21.1	29.1	6.9
Chechens	318.5	408.0	418.8	612.7	755.8	28.1	2.6	46.3	23.4
Bashkirs	713.7	843.6	989.0	1,239.7	1,371.5	18.2	17.2	25.4	10.6
Kabardins	139.9	164.2	203.6	279.9	321.7	17.4	24.0	37.3	15.0
Balkars	33.3	42.7	42.4	59.5	66.3	28.2	-0.7	40.3	11.4
Ossetians	272.2	354.8	412.6	488.0	541.9	30.3	16.3	18.3	11.0
Ingush	74.1	92.1	106.0	157.6	186.2	24.3	15.1	48.7	18.1
Karachai	55.1	75.8	81.4	112.7	131.1	37.6	7.4	38.4	16.3
Cherkess	65.3	–	30.5	39.8	46.5	–	–	30.5	16.8
Avars	158.8	252.8	270.4	396.3	482.9	59.2	7.0	46.6	21.9
Lezgians	134.5	221.0	223.1	323.8	382.6	64.3	1.0	45.1	18.2
Dargins	109.0	153.8	158.1	230.9	287.3	41.1	2.8	46.1	24.4
Kumyk	94.6	112.6	135.0	188.8	228.4	19.0	19.9	39.8	20.8
Lak	40.4	56.1	63.5	85.8	100.1	38.9	13.2	35.1	16.7
Nogai	36.3	36.6	38.6	51.8	59.5	0.8	5.5	34.2	14.9
Tabasarans	32.0	33.6	34.7	55.1	75.2	5.0	3.3	58.8	36.5
Tats	28.7	–	11.5	17.1	22.4	–	–	48.7	31.0

(continued)

Table A.1 (continued)

	Total Number (in thousands)					Increase (in percent)			
	1926	1939	1959	1970	1979	1926-1939	1939-1959	1959-1970	1970-1979
Adygei	65.3	88.1	79.6	99.9	108.7	39.8	-9.6	25.5	8.8
Abaza	13.8	15.3	19.6	25.4	29.5	10.9	28.1	29.6	16.1
Abkhaz	57.0	59.0	65.4	83.2	90.9	3.5	10.8	27.2	9.3
Karakalpaks	146.3	185.8	172.6	236.0	303.3	27.0	-7.1	36.8	28.5
Buriats	237.5	224.7	253.0	314.7	352.6	-5.4	12.6	24.4	12.0
Yakuts	240.7	242.1	236.7	296.2	328.0	0.6	-2.2	25.1	10.74
Tuvinians	—	0.8	100.1	139.4	166.1	—	—	39.3	19.2
Altai	37.6	47.9	45.3	55.8	60.0	27.4	-5.4	23.2	7.5
Khakass	45.6	52.8	56.8	66.7	70.8	15.8	7.6	17.4	6.1
Shors	12.6	16.3	15.3	16.5	16.0	29.4	-6.1	7.8	-3.0
Evenk	32.8	29.7	24.7	25.1	27.5	-9.5	-16.8	1.6	9.6
Nenets	18.8	24.8	23.0	28.7	29.9	31.9	-7.3	24.5	4.2
Khant	19.7	18.5	19.4	21.1	20.9	4.3	4.9	8.8	-0.9
Chukchi	13.1	13.9	11.7	13.6	14.0	6.1	-15.8	16.2	2.9
Even	—	9.7	9.1	12.0	12.3	—	-16.2	31.9	2.5
Jews	2,600.9	3,028.5	2,267.8	2,150.7	1,810.9	16.4	-25.1	-5.2	-15.8
Germans	1,238.5	1,427.2	1,619.7	1,846.3	1,936.2	15.2	13.5	14.0	4.9
Poles	782.3	630.1	1,380.3	1,167.5	1,151.0	-19.5	119.1	-15.5	-1.4
Bulgarians	111.2	113.5	324.2	351.2	361.1	2.1	185.6	8.3	2.8
Greeks	213.8	286.4	309.3	336.9	343.8	34.0	8.0	9.0	2.0

(continued)

Table A.1 (continued)

	Total Number (in thousands)				Increase (in percent)			
	1926	1939	1959	1970	1979	1926-1939	1939-1959	1959-1970	1970-1979
Hungarians	5.5	—	154.7	166.5	170.6	—	—	7.6	2.5
Romanians	4.6	—	106.4	119.3	128.8	—	—	12.2	8.0
Gypsies	61.2	88.2	132.0	175.3	209.2	44.1	49.6	32.8	19.3
Uigurs	42.6	—	95.2	173.3	210.6	—	—	82.0	21.5
Gagauz	0.8	—	123.8	156.6	173.2	—	—	26.5	10.6
Koreans	87.0	182.3	313.7	357.5	388.9	109.5	72.1	14.0	8.8
Kurds	54.6	45.9	58.8	88.9	115.9	-15.9	28.1	51.4	30.4
Finns	134.7	143.1	92.7	84.8	77.1	6.2	-35.2	-8.5	-9.1
Turks	8.6	—	35.3	79.0	92.7	—	—	123.8	17.3
Dungans	14.6	—	22.0	38.6	51.7	—	—	75.5	33.9

Sources: Itogi Vsesoiuznoi perepisi naseleniia 1959 goda, 16 vol. (Moscow, 1962-1963); *Itogi Vsesoiuznoi perepisi naseleniia 1970 goda*, vol. 4 (Moscow, 1973); *Naselenie SSSR, Po dannym Vsesoiuznoi perepisi naseleniia 1979 goda* (Moscow, 1980); *Chislennost i sostav naseleniia SSSR, Po dannym Vsesoiuznoi perepisi naseleniia 1979 goda* (Moscow, 1984); V.I. Kozlov, *Natsionalnosti SSSR* (Moscow, 1975), pp. 249-250.

[1]These figures are calculated on the basis of the population after the occupation of the western territories in 1939/40. In late 1940, 100,392,000 Russians, 35,611,000 Ukrainians, 8,275,000 Belorussians, 2,033,000 Lithuanians, 1,628,000 Latvians, 1,144,000 Estonians, 2,060,000 Moldavians lived in the USSR (*Narody SSSR. Kratkii spravochnik* [Moscow]).

Table A.2: National Composition of the Union Republics and Autonomous Republics (Within the Respective Borders)

Union Republics and Autonomous Republics	Years	Total Population (thousands)	Percent		
			Titular Nation	Russians	Others
RSFSR	1926[1]	100,981	73.4	73.4	
	1939	108,264	83.4	83.4	
	1959	117,534	83.3	83.3	
	1970	130,079	82.8	82.8	
	1979	137,410	82.6	82.6	
Bashkir ASSR	1926	2,666	23.5	39.9	Tatars - 17.3
	1939	3,159	21.2	40.6	Tatars - 24.6
	1959	3,342	22.1	42.4	Tatars - 23.0
	1970	3,818	23.4	40.5	Tatars - 24.7
	1979	3,844	24.3	40.3	Tatars - 24.5
Tatar ASSR	1926	2,594	44.9	43.1	
	1939	2,915	48.8	42.9	
	1959	2,850	47.2	43.9	
	1970	3,131	49.1	42.4	
	1979	3,445	47.6	44.0	

(continued)

Table A.2 (continued)

Union Republics and Autonomous Republics	Years	Total Population (thousands)	Percent		
			Titular Nation	Russians	Others
Daghestan ASSR	1926	788	64.5	12.5	
	1939	930	76.3	14.3	
	1959	1,062	69.3	20.1	
	1970	1,429	74.3	14.7	
	1979	1,628	77.8	11.6	
Udmurt ASSR	1926	756	52.3	43.3	
	1939	1,219	39.4	55.7	
	1959	1,337	35.6	56.8	
	1970	1,418	34.2	57.1	
	1979	1,492	32.1	58.3	
Chuvash ASSR	1926	894	74.6	20.0	
	1939	1,077	72.2	22.4	
	1959	1,098	70.2	24.0	
	1970	1,224	70.0	24.5	
	1979	1,299	68.4	26.0	

(continued)

Table A.2 (continued)

Union Republics and Autonomous Republics	Years	Total Population (thousands)	Percent		
			Titular Nation	Russians	Others
Chechen-Ingush ASSR	1926	385	93.8	2.6	
	1939	697	64.8	28.8	
	1959	710	41.1	49.0	
	1970	1,064	58.5	34.5	
	1979	1,156	64.5	29.07	
Komi ASSR	1926	207	92.2	6.6	
	1939	319	72.5	22.0	
	1959	806	30.4	48.4	
	1970	965	28.6	53.1	
	1979	1,110	25.3	56.7	
Mordvinian ASSR	1939[2]	1,188	34.1	60.5	
	1959	1,000	35.8	59.0	
	1970	1,029	35.4	58.9	
	1979	989	34.2	59.7	

(continued)

Table A.2 (continued)

Union Republics and Autonomous Republics	Years	Total Population (thousands)	Percent		
			Titular Nation	Russians	Others
Buriat ASSR	1926	491	43.8	52.7	
	1939	546	21.3	72.0	
	1959	673	20.2	74.6	
	1970	812	22.0	73.5	
	1979	899	23.0	72.0	
Yakut ASSR	1926	289	81.6	10.4	
	1939	413	56.6	35.5	
	1959	487	46.4	44.2	
	1970	664	43.0	47.3	
	1979	852	36.8	50.4	
Karelian ASSR	1926	270	37.4	57.1	
	1939	469	23.2	63.2	
	1959	651	13.1	63.4	
	1970	713	11.8	68.1	
	1979	732	11.1	71.3	

(continued)

Table A.2 (continued)

Union Republics and Autonomous Republics	Years	Total Population (thousands)	Percent		
			Titular Nation	Russians	Others
Mari ASSR	1926	482	51.4	43.6	
	1939	580	47.2	46.1	
	1959	648	43.1	47.8	
	1970	685	43.7	46.9	
	1979	704	43.5	47.5	
Kabardino-Balkar ASSR	1926	204	76.3	7.5	
	1939	359	53.7	35.9	
	1959	420	53.4	38.7	
	1970	588	53.7	37.2	
	1979	666	54.5	35.1	
North Ossetian ASSR	1926	152	84.2	6.6	
	1939	329	50.3	37.2	
	1959	451	47.8	39.6	
	1970	553	48.7	36.6	
	1979	592	50.5	33.9	

(continued)

Table A.2 (continued)

Union Republics and Autonomous Republics	Years	Total Population (thousands)	Percent	
			Titular Nation	Russians
Kalmyk ASSR	1926	141	75.6	10.7
	1939	221	48.6	45.7
	1959	185	35.1	55.9
	1970	268	41.1	45.8
	1979	294	41.5	42.6
Tuvinian ASSR	1959[3]	172	57.0	40.1
	1970	231	58.6	38.3
	1979	267	60.5	36.2
Ukrainian SSR	1926	29,018	80.0	9.2
	1939	31,785	73.5	12.9
	1959	41,869	76.8	16.9
	1970	47,126	74.9	19.4
	1979	49,609	73.6	21.1

(continued)

Table A.2 (continued)

Union Republics and Autonomous Republics	Years	Total Population (thousands)	Percent Titular Nation	Percent Russians	Others	
Belorussian SSR	1926	4,983	80.6	7.7		
	1939	5,569	82.9	6.5		
	1959	8,055	81.1	8.2		
	1970	9,002	81.0	10.4		
	1979	9,532	79.4	11.9		
Uzbek SSR	1926[7]	5,273	65.9	4.7	Tadzhiks -	18.4
	1939	6,271	64.4	11.5		
	1959	8,106	62.2	13.5	Tadzhiks -	3.8
	1970	11,799	65.5	12.5	Tadzhiks -	3.8
	1979	15,389	68.7	10.8	Tadzhiks -	3.9
Karakalpak ASSR	1939[4]	470	33.8	5.3	Uzbeks -	24.9
	1959	510	30.6	4.5	Uzbeks - 28.8; Kazakhs -	26.3
	1970	702	31.1	3.6	Uzbeks - 30.3; Kazakhs -	26.5
	1979	905	31.2	2.4	Uzbeks - 31.5; Kazakhs -	27.0

(continued)

Table A.2 (continued)

Union Republics and Autonomous Republics	Years	Total Population (thousands)	Percent		
			Titular Nation	Russians	Others
Kazakh SSR	1926	6,503	57.1	19.7	Ukrainians - 13.2
	1939	6,094	38.2	40.3	Ukrainians - 10.8
	1959	9,310	30.0	42.7	Ukrainians - 8.2; Germans - 7.1
	1970	13,008	32.6	42.4	Ukrainians - 7.2; Germans - 6.6
	1979	14,684	36.0	40.8	Ukrainians - 6.1; Germans - 6.1
Georgian SSR	1926	2,666	67.1	3.6	Armenians - 11.5
	1939	3,540	61.4	8.7	Armenians - 11.7
	1959	4,044	64.3	10.1	Armenians - 11.0
	1970	4,686	66.8	8.5	Armenians - 9.7
	1979	4,993	68.8	7.4	Armenians - 9.0
Abkhaz ASSR	1926	201	27.8	6.2	Georgians - 33.5
	1939	312	18.0	19.3	Georgians - 29.5
	1959	405	15.1	21.4	Georgians - 39.1
	1970	487	15.9	19.1	Georgians - 41.0
	1979	486	17.1	16.5	Georgians - 43.8

(continued)

Table A.2 (continued)

Union Republics and Autonomous Republics	Years	Total Population (thousands)	Percent		
			Titular Nation	Russians	Others
Adzhar ASSR (Adzhars and Georgians)	1926	132	57.9	7.7	
	1939	200	63.7	15.2	
	1959	245	72.8	13.4	
	1970	310	76.5	11.5	
	1979	354	80.2	10.0	
Azeri SSR	1926	2,315	62.1	9.5	Armenians - 12.2
	1939	3,205	58.4	16.5	
	1959	3,698	67.5	13.6	Armenians - 12.0
	1970	5,117	73.8	10.0	Armenians - 9.4
	1979	6,027	78.1	7.9	Armenians - 7.9
ASSR Nakhichevan (Azeri)	1926	105	84.3	1.8	
	1939	127	85.6	2.0	
	1959	141	90.2	2.2	
	1970	202	93.8	1.9	
	1979	240	95.8	1.6	

(continued)

Table A.2 (continued)

Union Republics and Autonomous Republics	Years	Total Population (thousands)	Percent		Others	
			Titular Nation	Russians		
Lithuanian SSR[5]	1959	2,711	79.3	8.5		
	1970	3,128	80.1	8.6	Poles -	8.5
	1979	3,392	80.0	8.9	Poles -	7.7
Moldavian SSR[6]	1926	572	30.1	8.5	Ukrainians -	48.5
	1939	599	28.5	10.2	Ukrainians -	51.0
	1959	2,884	65.4	10.2	Ukrainians -	14.6
	1970	3,569	64.6	11.6	Ukrainians -	14.2
	1979	3,950	63.9	12.8	Ukrainians -	14.2
Latvian SSR[5]	1959	2,093	62.0	26.6		
	1970	2,364	56.8	29.8		
	1979	2,503	53.7	32.8		
Kirgiz SSR	1926	993	66.6	11.7	Uzbeks -	11.0
	1939	1,458	51.7	20.8	Uzbeks -	10.3
	1959	2,066	40.5	30.2	Uzbeks -	10.6
	1970	2,933	43.8	29.2	Uzbeks -	11.3
	1979	3,523	47.9	25.9	Uzbeks -	12.1

(continued)

Table A.2 (continued)

Union Republics and Autonomous Republics	Years	Total Population (thousands)	Percent			
			Titular Nation	Russians	Others	
Tadzhik SSR[7]	1926	827	74.6	0.7	Uzbeks -	21.2
	1939	1,484	59.6	9.1	Uzbeks -	23.8
	1959	1,980	53.1	13.3	Uzbeks -	23.0
	1970	2,900	56.2	11.9	Uzbeks -	23.0
	1979	3,806	58.8	10.4	Uzbeks -	22.9
Armenian	1926	880	84.0	2.2	Azeri -	8.7
	1939	1,282	82.8	4.0		
	1959	1,763	88.0	3.2	Azeri -	6.1
	1970	2,492	88.6	2.7	Azeri -	5.9
	1979	3,037	89.7	2.3	Azeri -	5.3
Turkmen SSR	1926	1,001	71.9	7.5	Uzbeks -	10.5
	1939	1,252	59.2	18.6	Uzbeks -	8.5
	1959	1,516	60.9	17.3	Uzbeks -	8.3
	1970	2,159	65.6	14.5	Uzbeks -	8.3
	1979	2,765	68.4	12.6	Uzbeks -	8.5

(continued)

Table A.2 (continued)

Union Republics and Autonomous Republics	Years	Total Population (thousands)	Percent		
			Titular Nation	Russians	Others
Estonian SSR[5]	1959	1,197	74.6	20.1	
	1970	1,356	68.2	24.7	
	1979	1,465	64.7	27.9	

Sources: Censuses results; for 1939: V.I. Kozlov, *Natsionalnosti SSSR* (Moscow, 1975), pp. 108-112.

[1] The Kazakh ASSR, Kirgiz ASSR, and Crimean ASSR are part of the RSFSR as it existed in 1926. Without these territories (Kazakhstan and Kirgizistan seceded from the RSFSR in 1936, the Crimean ASSR in 1954), the RSFSR's total population numbered 92,681,000 in 1926. 78.1 percent of this population was Russian.
[2] In 1930, this ASSR was created as an Autonomous Region; it acquired its status as an ASSR in 1934.
[3] This ASSR became a part of the USSR in 1944.
[4] Since 1925, the Karakalpaks had their own Autonomous Region. In 1932, it acquired the status of ASSR and, in 1936, became a part of the Uzbek SSR. Up to 1936 Karakalpakija was part of the RSFSR.
[5] Under the provisions of the pact between Hitler and Stalin, the USSR annexed Lithuania, Latvia, and Estonia in 1940.
[6] From 1924 to 1940, a Moldavian ASSR was a part of the Ukrainian SSR. When the USSR annexed Bessarabia and Northern Bukovina in 1940, Moldavia's territory and the national composition of its population changed completely.
[7] Since 1924, the Tadzhik ASSR was a part of the Uzbek SSR. In 1929, it became the independent Tadzhik SSR and included a larger territory.

Table A.3: Titular Nations and the Percentage Living in Their Own Republics

Union Republics and Autonomous Republics in the RSFSR	1926			1959			1979	
	Total Number of Titular Nationals in the USSR (thousands)	Percentage in Their Own Republic		Total Number of Titular Nationals in the USSR (thousands)	Percentage in Their Own Republic		Total Number of Titular Nationals in the USSR (thousands)	Percentage in Their Own Republic
RSFSR	77,791	95.2		114,114	85.8		137,182	82.7
Ukrainian SSR	31,194	74.4		37,253	86.3		42,347	86.2
Belorussian SSR	4,739	84.8		7,913	82.5		9,463	80.0
Uzbek SSR	3,905	89.0		6,015	83.8		12,456	84.9
Kazakh SSR	3,968	93.6		3,622	77.2		6,556	80.7
Georgian SSR	1,821	98.1		2,692	96.6		3,571	96.1
Azeri SSR	1,707	84.2		2,940	84.9		5,477	86.0
Lithuanian SSR	—	—		2,326	92.5		2,851	95.1
Moldavian	—	—		2,214	85.2		2,968	85.1
Latvian SSR	—	—		1,400	92.7		1,439	93.4
Kirgiz SSR	763	86.7		969	86.4		1,906	88.5
Tadzhik SSR	979	63.0		1,397	75.2		2,898	77.2
Armenian	1,568	47.4		2,787	55.7		4,151	65.6
Turkmen SSR	764	94.2		1,002	92.2		2,028	93.3
Estonian SSR	—	—		989	90.3		1,020	92.9
Bashkir ASSR	714	87.6		989	74.6		1,371	68.3
Tatar ASSR	2,917	39.9		4,968	27.1		6,317	26.0
Daghestan ASSR[1]	575	88.0		944	78.0		1,657	76.0

(continued)

Table A.3 (continued)

Union Republics and Autonomous Republics in the RSFSR	1926		1959		1979	
	Total Number of Titular Nationals in the USSR (thousands)	Percentage in Their Own Republic	Total Number of Titular Nationals in the USSR (thousands)	Percentage in Their Own Republic	Total Number of Titular Nationals in the USSR (thousands)	Percentage in Their Own Republic
Udmurt ASSR	504	78.5	625	76.2	714	69.7
Chuvash ASSR	1,117	59.8	1,470	52.4	1,751	50.7
Chechen-Ingush ASSR	393	89.3	525	55.7	932	80.1
Komi ASSR	226	84.6	287	85.4	327	85.9
Mordvinian ASSR[2]	1,340	–	1,285	27.9	1,192	28.4
Buriat ASSR	238	90.3	253	53.7	353	58.6
Yakut ASSR	241	97.9	237	95.5	328	95.7
Karelian ASSR	248	40.6	167	51.1	138	58.9
Mari ASSR	428	57.9	504	55.4	622	49.3
Kabardino-Balkar ASSR	173	89.9	204	91.2	389	93.4
North Ossetian ASSR[3]	272	47.1	413	52.2	542	55.1
Kalmyk ASSR	129	83.0	106	61.2	147	83.1
Tuvinian ASSR[4]	–	–	100	97.9	166	97.5

Source: Censuses results

[1] This table combines the Daghestan peoples (most of whom speak Yaphetic) into one titular nation.
[2] This ASSR was created as an Autonomous Region in 1930. In 1934, it acquired its present status as an ASSR.
[3] Ossets have two National Territories named after them. The South Ossetian Autonomous Region is part of the Georgian SSR. In 1926, 69.3 percent of all Ossetians lived in both regions combined; in 1959, 67.7 percent, and in 1979, 67.2 percent.
[4] In 1944 this ASSR became a part of the USSR.

Table A.4: Urbanization

	Percentage of Urban Population in the Total Population				Increase of the Urban Population (percent)		
	1926	1939[1]	1959	1979	1926-1939	1939-1959	1959-1979
I. Union Republics							
RSFSR	18	33	52	69	121	70	55
Ukrainian SSR	19	34	46	61	139	41	59
Belorussian SSR	17	21	31	55	62	119	112
Lithuanian SSR	–	23	39	61	–	59	97
Estonian SSR	–	34	56	70	–	90	51
Latvian SSR	–	35	56	68	–	77	47
Moldavian SSR	–	13	22	39	–	95	79
Georgian SSR	22	30	42	52	79	61	52
Armenian SSR	19	29	50	66	119	140	126
Azeri ASSR	28	36	48	53	78	53	81
Kazakh SSR	9	28	44	54	226	141	95
Uzbek SSR	22	23	34	41	45	86	133
Turkmen SSR	14	33	46	48	204	68	89
Kirgiz SSR	12	19	34	39	121	158	96
Tadzhik SSR	10	17	33	35	135	159	105
Total USSR	18	32	48	62	130	65	64

(continued)

Table A.4 (continued)

	Percentage of Urban Population in the Total Population				Increase of the Urban Population (percent)		
	1926	1939[1]	1959	1979	1926-1939	1939-1959	1959-1979
		II. Nations					
Russians	21.3	38	58	74	127	75	54
Ukrainians	10.4	29	39	56	153	78	62
Belorussians	10.3	21	32	55	125	143	104
Lithuanians	–	–	35	57	–	–	101
Latvians	–	–	47	58	–	–	27
Estonians	–	–	47	59	–	–	30
Moldavians	–	–	13	27	–	–	176
Georgians	16.9	25	36	49	83	72	81
Armenians	35.6	41	57	70	58	79	82
Azeri	15.7	21	35	44	75	118	137
Kazakhs	2.2	16	24	32	468	76	138
Uzbeks	18.6	15	22	29	-2	83	175
Turkmen	1.5	10	25	32	638	200	162
Kirgiz	1.4	4	11	20	212	213	250
Tadzhiks	15.3	12	21	28	-2	94	178
Jews	82.4	–	94.8	99	–	–	-17

Sources: Iu. V. Arutiunian, "Izmenenie sotsialnoi struktury sovetskyh natsii," in: *Istoriia SSSR*, 4/1972, p. 18; censuses results; V.I. Kozlov, *Natsionalnosti SSSR* (Moscow, 1982, 2nd edition, p. 100.

[1]This includes the annexations of 1939/40.

Table A.5: Differences in the Degree of Urbanization (USSR Average = 100)

	1926	1939	1959	1979
Russians	118	118	120	119
Ukrainians	58	91	82	90
Belorussians	57	65	68	89
Lithuanians	--	--	73	92
Latvians	--	--	99	93
Estonians	--	--	98	95
Moldavians	--	--	27	43
Georgians	94	79	75	79
Armenians	198	128	118	113
Azeri	87	65	73	71
Kazakhs	12	50	50	52
Uzbeks	103	46	45	47
Turkmen	8	33	53	52
Kirgiz	8	12	23	32
Tadzhiks	85	38	43	45
Jews	458	--	197.5	160

Sources: Iu. V. Arutiunian, "Izmenenie sotsialnoi struktury sovetskikh natsii," in: *Istoriia SSSR*, 4/1972, p. 18; results of the censuses; V.I. Kozlov, *Natsionalnosti SSSR* (Moscow, 1982), 2nd edition, p. 100.

Table A.6: The Union Republics' Social Structure (Percent of People Working in the Economy)

	Blue-Collar Workers				White-Collar Workers				Kolkhoz Peasants			
	1939		1959		1939		1959		1939		1959[2]	
	Total Population	Titular Nationals	Total Population	Titular Nationals	Total Population	Titular Nationals	Total Population	Titular Nationals	Total Population	Titular Nationals	Total Population	Titular Nationals
USSR	32.5	--	48	--	17.7	--	20	--	47.2	--	32	--
RSFSR	35.0	38.2	54	54/23[1]	18.6	18.7	22	22	43.9	38.5	24	24
Ukraine	32.6	29.3	41	34/15	17.2	13.1	17	13	48.7	54.6	42	53
Belorussia	21.9	20.7	35	31/11	14.5	10.8	16	12	57.2	60.4	49	57
Moldavia	--	--	21	13/4	--	--	11	4	--	--	68	83
Estonia	--	--	55	51/19	--	--	24	22	--	--	21	27
Latvia	--	--	52	46/19	--	--	21	18	--	--	27	36
Lithuania	--	--	40	34/12	--	--	16	14	--	--	44	52
Georgia	19.5	12.4	32	23/10	17.2	17.0	24	23	52.7	58.2	44	54
Armenia	17.6	21.5	40	40/17	14.6	19.7	22	20	64.1	52.5	38	40
Azerbaijan	25.1	12.2	35	24/8	16.6	9.5	23	15	54.2	70.1	42	61
Kazakhstan	33.8	25.6	58	44/6	17.4	8.0	21	16	47.5	60.8	21	40
Kirgizstan	21.3	7.5	40	22/4	12.4	4.6	18	8	62.2	83.8	42	70
Tadzhikistan	12.9	8.7	30	18/4	10.2	5.7	16	8	72.5	79.2	54	74
Turkmenistan	25.2	11.7	37	22/5	15.4	6.1	20	9	56.3	77.2	43	69
Uzbekistan	19.3	11.1	40	27/4	12.9	5.4	17	8	64.9	79.6	43	65

Source: Iu. V. Arutiunian, "Izmenenie sotsialnoi struktury sovetskikh natsii," in: *Istoriia SSSR*, 4/1972, pp. 6, 13.

[1] The first figure includes agricultural workers (on the sovkhozes), the second reflects the number of industrial workers. For 1939, only data reflecting the total number of workers were available.

[2] These figures include people working out of their own homes and individual peasants. This group makes up about 1 percent of the total number.

Table A.7: Structure of the Intelligentsia[1] 1939, 1959 (per 10,000 People)

	Total Number of Intelligentsia		Increase (in percent)	Administration		Employed in: Production		Academia		Art		Education, Medicine, Law, Cultural Work with the Masses	
	1939	1959		1939	1959	1939	1959	1939	1959	1939	1959	1939	1959
Russians	1,091	1,513	139	261	212	493	747	10	33	23	28	304	493
Ukrainians	800	1,022	128	182	157	335	437	7	15	15	15	261	398
Belorussians	910	904	99	181	144	268	360	5	12	8	10	248	378
Georgians	1,170	1,726	147	286	270	405	597	20	50	33	43	426	766
Armenians	1,304	1,560	120	338	279	467	585	20	36	65	57	414	603
Azeri	692	1,078	156	223	195	159	315	9	31	31	29	270	508
Turkmen	508	769	151	175	188	68	193	2	15	16	22	247	351
Uzbeks	447	636	142	173	146	63	170	2	12	20	17	189	291
Tadzhiks	525	637	121	190	160	55	129	2	11	15	17	263	320
Kazakhs	605	1,040	172	213	223	117	362	2	14	15	20	258	421
Kirgiz	453	688	152	158	141	45	179	1	13	16	23	233	332
Estonians	--	1,531	--	--	263	--	694	--	36	--	57	--	481
Latvians	--	1,340	--	--	22	--	613	--	28	--	47	--	430
Lithuanians	--	974	--	--	188	--	384	--	21	--	30	--	351
Moldavians	--	361	--	--	47	--	78	--	4	--	15	--	217

Source: Iu. V. Arutiunian, "Izmenenie sotsialnoi struktury sovetskikh natsii," in: *Istoriia SSSR*, 4/1972, pp. 9, 16.

[1] According to the Soviet definition adopted in this table, intelligentsia includes people with technical school or college education and individuals holding jobs that require mid-level or higher special training (the so-called practitioners). Consequently, the intelligentsia includes primarily brain-workers.

Table A.8: Nations and Languages

Titular Nations in the Union Republics	Language of the Titular Nation as Native Language (percent)			Russian as Second Language (percent)	
	1926	1959	1979	1970	1979
Ukrainians	87.1	87.7	82.8	36.3	49.8
Belorussians	71.9	84.2	74.2	49.0	57.0
Uzbeks	99.1	98.4	98.5	14.5	49.3
Kazakhs	99.6	98.4	97.5	41.8	52.3
Georgians	96.5	98.6	98.3	21.3	26.7
Azeri	93.8	97.6	97.9	16.6	29.5
Lithuanians	46.9[1]	97.8	97.9	35.9	52.1
Moldavians	92.3[1]	95.2	93.2	36.1	47.4
Latvians	78.3[1]	95.1	95.0	45.2	56.7
Kirgiz	99.0	98.7	97.9	19.1	29.4
Tadzhiks	98.3	98.1	97.8	15.4	29.6
Armenians	92.4	89.9	90.7	30.1	38.6
Turkmen	97.3	98.9	98.7	15.4	25.4
Estonians	88.4[1]	95.2	95.3	29.0	24.2
Titular Nations in the RSFSR's Autonomous Republics					
Bashkirs	53.8	61.9	67.0	53.3	64.9
Tatars	98.9	92.1	85.9	62.5	68.9
Daghestan Peoples	99.3	96.2	95.9	41.7	60.3
Udmurts	98.9	89.1	76.5	63.3	64.4
Chuvash	98.7	90.8	81.7	58.4	64.8
Chechens and Ingush	99.7	98.7	98.4	67.6	76.7
Komi	96.5	89.3	76.2	63.1	64.5
Mordvinians	94.0	78.1	72.6	65.7	65.5
Buriats	98.1	94.9	90.2	66.7	71.9
Yakuts	99.7	97.6	95.3	41.7	55.6
Karelians	95.5	71.3	55.6	59.1	51.3
Mari	99.3	95.1	86.7	62.4	69.9
Kabardins and Balkars	99.4	97.7	97.7	71.5	77.1
Ossetians	97.9	89.1	88.2	58.6	64.9
Kalmyks	99.3	91.0	91.3	81.1	84.1
Tuvinians	--	99.1	98.8	38.9	59.2

(continued)

Table A.8 (continued)

Titular Nations in the Union Republics	Language of the Titular Nation as Native Language (percent)			Russian as Second Language (percent)	
	1926	1959	1979	1970	1979
Nations Without Their Own Territories[2]					
Germans	94.9	75.0	57.0	59.6	51.7
Jews[3]	71.9	21.5	14.2	16.3	13.7
Poles	42.9	45.2	29.1	37.0	44.7
Koreans	98.9	79.3	55.4	50.3	47.7
Bulgarians	92.4	79.4	68.0	58.8	58.2
Greeks	72.7	41.5	38.0	35.4	34.1
Karakalpaks[4]	87.5	95.0	95.9	10.4	45.1
Uigurs	52.7	85.0	86.1	35.6	52.1
Gypsies	64.2	59.3	74.1	53.0	59.1
Gagauz	--	94.0	89.3	63.3	68.0
Hungarians	--	97.2	95.4	25.8	34.2
Peoples of the North[5]	--	75.7	61.8	52.3	54.0

Source: Censuses results.

[1] Before 1939/40, the number of Lithuanians, Latvians, Estonians, and Moldavians was only a fraction of what it was after the USSR occupied the western territories.
[2] This table includes only peoples that numbered more than 150,000 persons in 1979.
[3] Officially, the Jewish Autonomous Region (Birobidzhan) exists for Jews.
[4] An ASSR for Karakalpaks exists within the Uzbek Union Republic.
[5] Since 1930, ten Autonomous Territories have been in existence for the peoples of the North within the RSFSR.

Table A.9: Non-Russians Speaking Russian as a Second Language

	Total Number (in thousands)		Number Living				Percentage of a Nation Speaking Russian as a Second Language					
			Within Their Own Republic		Outside		Total		Within Its Own Republic		Outside	
	1970	1979	1970	1979	1970	1979	1970	1979	1970	1979	1970	1979
Titular Nations in the Union Republics												
Ukrainians	14,780.8	21,087.3	12,637.1	18,881.2	2,152.7	2,206.1	36.3	49.8	35.82	51.75	39.36	37.66
Belorussians	4,431.6	5,396.3	3,809.1	4,759.4	622.5	636.9	49.0	57.0	52.25	62.89	35.32	33.61
Uzbeks	1,330.9	6,136.4	1,010.4	5,591.6	320.5	554.8	14.5	49.3	13.08	52.91	21.80	29.40
Kazakhs	2,215.9	3,430.4	1,762.5	2,676.6	453.4	753.8	41.8	52.3	41.63	50.60	42.57	59.49
Georgians	690.8	954.8	628.7	876.5	62.1	78.3	21.3	26.7	20.08	25.53	54.47	56.74
Azeri	725.0	1,613.8	564.0	1,312.3	161.0	301.5	16.6	29.5	14.93	27.87	26.69	39.26
Lithuanians	956.3	1,486.2	873.1	1,415.6	83.2	70.6	35.9	52.1	34.83	52.19	52.65	50.79
Moldavians	974.7	1,405.8	780.5	1,165.6	194.2	240.2	36.1	47.4	33.88	46.15	49.28	54.34
Latvians	646.0	816.0	608.5	783.6	37.5	32.4	45.2	56.7	45.35	58.30	42.61	34.11
Kirgiz	277.1	559.4	253.9	480.5	23.2	78.9	19.1	29.4	19.76	28.48	13.89	36.03
Tadzhiks	328.8	857.2	270.0	662.0	58.8	195.2	15.4	29.6	16.57	29.59	11.62	29.53
Armenians	1,071.8	1,603.9	514.6	932.0	557.2	671.9	30.1	38.6	23.30	34.20	41.24	47.12
Turkmen	234.7	514.9	210.1	456.9	24.6	58.0	15.4	25.4	14.83	24.15	22.77	42.65
Estonians	292.0	247.3	254.9	218.6	37.1	28.7	29.0	24.2	27.55	23.06	45.24	39.86

(continued)

Table A.9 (continued)

	Total Number (in thousands)		Number Living				Percentage of a Nation Speaking Russian as a Second Language					
			Within Their Own Republic		Outside		Total		Within Its Own Republic		Outside	
	1970	1979	1970	1979	1970	1979	1970	1979	1970	1979	1970	1979
Titular Nations in the RSFSR's Autonomous Republics												
Bashkirs	661.0	890.4	427.7	584.7	233.3	305.7	53.3	64.9	47.94	62.47	67.04	70.28
Tatars	3,709.0	4,353.5	840.7	1,083.4	2,868.3	3,270.1	62.5	68.9	54.72	66.00	65.26	69.95
Daghestan Peoples	569.5	998.9	463.1	827.9	106.4	171.0	41.7	60.3	43.66	65.34	35.00	43.85
Udmurts	445.7	459.5	330.7	338.7	115.0	120.8	63.3	64.4	68.30	70.61	52.27	51.62
Chuvash	988.8	1,133.8	499.2	604.9	489.6	528.9	58.4	64.8	58.30	68.14	58.42	61.29
Chechens and Ingush	521.0	722.7	423.0	578.0	98.0	144.7	67.6	76.7	67.94	77.47	66.21	73.83
Komi	203.1	210.8	178.6	187.9	24.5	22.9	63.1	64.5	64.66	66.92	53.26	49.78
Mordvinians	829.4	781.0	275.8	274.5	553.6	506.5	65.7	65.5	75.62	81.00	61.64	59.38
Buriats	209.8	253.5	116.1	150.5	93.7	103.0	66.7	71.9	64.97	72.74	68.89	70.55
Yakuts	123.5	182.4	116.7	173.1	6.8	9.3	41.7	55.6	40.85	55.14	68.00	66.43
Karelians	86.3	71.1	56.6	46.8	29.7	24.3	59.1	51.3	67.22	57.56	47.90	42.63
Mari	373.8	434.5	198.7	238.4	175.1	196.1	62.4	69.9	66.41	77.76	58.36	62.25

(continued)

Table A.9 (continued)

	Total Number (in thousands)		Number Living				Percentage of a Nation Speaking Russian as a Second Language					
			Within Their Own Republic		Outside		Total		Within Its Own Republic		Outside	
	1970	1979	1970	1979	1970	1979	1970	1979	1970	1979	1970	1979
Kabardins and Balkars	242.5	299.1	227.4	280.8	15.1	18.3	71.5	77.1	71.96	77.29	65.65	73.20
Ossetians[1]	285.9	351.8	229.3	281.9	56.6	69.9	58.6	64.9	68.44	77.44	37.00	39.26
Kalmyks	111.3	123.3	92.0	108.1	19.3	15.2	81.1	84.1	83.41	88.46	71.48	60.80
Tuvinians	54.2	98.4	51.4	95.3	2.8	3.1	38.9	59.2	37.99	58.86	70.00	77.50
Nations Without Their Own Territories[2]												
Germans	1,100.4	1,001.3					59.6	51.71				
Jews[3]	350.2	248.8					16.3	13.74				
Poles	432.6	514.6					37.0	44.71				
Koreans	179.8	185.4					50.3	47.66				
Bulgarians	206.4	210.0					58.8	58.15				
Greeks	119.4	117.2					35.4	34.10				
Karakalpaks[4]	24.5	136.8	20.2	125.7	4.3	11.1	10.4	45.10	9.29	44.60	23.88	52.85
Uigurs	61.7	109.7					35.6	52.10				
Gypsies	92.9	123.6					53.0	59.10				
Gagauz	99.1	117.8					63.3	68.00				

(continued)

Table A.9 (continued)

	Total Number (in thousands)		Number Living				Percentage of a Nation Speaking Russian as a Second Language					
			Within Their Own Republic		Outside		Total		Within Its Own Republic		Outside	
	1970	1979	1970	1979	1970	1979	1970	1979	1970	1979	1970	1979
Hungarians	43.0	58.2					25.8	34.20				
Peoples of the North[5]	79.1	85.5					52.3	54.00				

Source: Censuses results.

[1]This table considers both the Ossetians' National Regions: the Northern Ossetian ASSR within the RSFSR and the Southern Ossetian Autonomous Region in Georgia.
[2]This table does not consider peoples whose population was below 150,000 in 1979.
[3]Formally, there is a Jewish Autonomous Region (Birobidzhan) for Jews. In 1979, however, only 10,166 Jews (i.e., 0.56 percent of the USSR's Jewish population), lived there. Consequently, this table does not include Birobidzhan.
[4]The Karakalpaks have an ASSR within the Uzbek Union Republic.
[5]Within the RSFSR, ten Autonomous Territories exist for the peoples of the North.

Table A.10: Non-Russians and Their Native Languages

	Total Number of People (in thousands)			Percentage		
	1926	1959	1979	1926	1959	1979
Total Non-Russian Population	68,846	94,713	124,688	100	100	100
People Considering Their Nation's Language as Their Native Language	60,706	82,972	106,800	88.2	87.6	85.6
People Considering Russian as Their Native Language	6,593	10,183	16,300	9.6	10.8	13.1
People Considering Other Languages as Their Native Language	1,547	1,558	1,600	2.2	1.6	1.3

Source: Censuses Results

Table A.11: Non-Russians Speaking Russian as Their Native Language

	Total Number		Number Living				Percentage of a Nation that was Linguistically Russified					
			Within Their Own Republic		Outside		Total		Within Its Own Republic		Outside	
	(in thousands)											
	1959	1979	1959	1979	1959	1979	1959	1979	1959	1979	1959	1979

Titular Nations in the Union Republics

Ukrainians	4,541.1	7,253.6	2,075.5	3,986.7	2,465.6	3,266.9	12.19	17.13	6.45	10.92	48.38	55.76
Belorussians	1,212.3	2,400.0	441.9	1,247.7	770.4	1,152.3	15.32	25.36	6.76	16.48	55.75	60.80
Uzbeks	30.1	78.2	17.6	43.5	12.5	34.7	0.50	0.63	0.34	0.41	1.28	1.83
Kazakhs	44.2	131.3	21.4	72.3	22.8	59.0	1.22	2.00	0.76	1.36	2.78	4.65
Georgians	34.7	59.2	11.6	16.2	23.1	43.0	1.29	1.66	0.44	0.47	25.27	31.15
Azeri	36.3	97.8	19.8	49.0	16.5	48.8	1.23	1.79	0.79	1.04	3.58	6.35
Lithuanians	28.8	47.1	2.5	5.7	26.3	41.4	1.24	1.65	0.11	0.21	14.85	29.78
Moldavians	79.3	177.1	24.3	82.5	55.0	94.6	3.58	5.97	1.28	3.26	16.81	21.40
Latvians	64.2	69.3	19.0	28.9	45.2	40.4	4.59	4.82	1.46	2.15	44.11	42.52
Kirgiz	2.9	9.3	1.6	6.0	1.1	3.3	0.30	0.49	0.21	0.35	0.75	1.50
Tadzhiks	7.7	22.7	4.4	12.2	3.3	10.5	0.55	0.78	0.41	0.54	0.86	1.58
Armenians	232.7	350.1	11.1	15.3	221.6	334.8	8.35	8.43	0.71	0.56	17.97	23.47
Turkmen	6.5	19.4	4.7	14.0	1.8	5.4	0.65	0.96	0.50	0.74	2.56	3.97
Estonians	46.1	46.3	5.9	9.4	40.2	36.9	4.66	4.54	0.66	0.99	41.66	51.25

(continued)

Table A.11 (continued)

	Total Number (in thousands)		Number Living				Percentage of a Nation that was Linguistically Russified					
			Within Their Own Republic		Outside		Total		Within Its Own Republic		Outside	
	1959	1979	1959	1979	1959	1979	1959	1979	1959	1979	1959	1979
Titular Nations in the RSFSR's Autonomous Republics												
Bashkirs	26.2	97.5	7.6	25.2	18.6	72.3	2.65	7.11	1.03	2.69	7.56	16.62
Tatars	349.2	832.7	15.1	37.8	334.1	794.9	7.03	13.18	1.12	2.30	9.21	17.00
Daghestan Peoples	15.3	38.6	4.6	9.6	10.7	29.0	1.62	2.33	0.62	0.75	5.26	7.43
Udmurts	66.7	166.7	32.5	84.6	34.2	82.1	10.68	23.36	6.82	17.63	22.81	35.08
Chuvash	132.4	317.5	19.1	90.2	113.3	227.3	9.01	18.13	2.47	10.16	16.14	26.33
Chechens and Ingush	6.3	14.4	0.9	2.5	5.4	11.9	1.20	1.53	0.30	0.33	2.13	6.07
Komi	30.1	77.4	15.3	56.1	14.8	21.3	10.49	23.69	6.24	19.97	35.71	46.30
Mordvinians	280.0	326.1	9.7	19.4	270.3	306.7	21.79	27.36	2.70	5.72	33.11	35.95
Buriats	12.9	34.6	4.4	14.3	8.5	20.3	5.11	9.81	3.24	6.91	6.83	13.90
Yakuts	5.7	15.3	4.0	11.3	1.7	4.0	2.41	4.66	1.76	3.59	24.29	28.57
Karelians	47.7	61.1	16.2	31.0	31.5	30.1	28.51	44.15	18.94	38.13	39.02	52.80
Mari	23.2	80.9	6.2	19.2	17.0	61.7	4.60	13.01	2.21	6.26	7.55	19.58
Kabardins and Balkars	4.8	8.2	1.7	3.4	3.1	4.8	1.95	2.11	0.75	0.93	13.63	19.20

(continued)

Table A.11 (continued)

	Total Number (in thousands)		Number Living				Percentage of a Nation that was Linguistically Russified					
			Within Their Own Republic		Outside		Total		Within Its Own Republic		Outside	
	1959	1979	1959	1979	1959	1979	1959	1979	1959	1979	1959	1979
Ossetians	20.3	35.5	4.5	5.3	15.0	30.2	4.92	6.55	1.61	1.45	11.24	16.96
Kalmyks	7.6	8.7	1.1	3.5	6.5	5.2	7.16	5.93	1.69	2.86	18.05	20.80
Tuvinians	0.8	2.0	0.7	1.5	0.1	0.5	0.80	1.20	0.71	0.92	5.00	12.50
Nations Without Their Own Territories[2]												
Germans	392.7	824.6					24.25	42.59				
Jews[3]	1,733.2	1,508.2					76.43	83.28				
Poles	203.3	301.4					14.73	26.19				
Koreans	64.4	172.7					20.53	44.41				
Bulgarians	58.9	105.1					18.16	29.11				
Greeks	142.5	195.3					46.07	56.81				
Karakalpaks[4]	0.5	1.5	0.2	0.7	0.3	0.8	0.29	0.49	0.12	0.02	1.76	3.80
Uigurs	2.2	7.5					2.31	3.56				
Gypsies	31.0	31.1					23.48	14.87				
Gagauz	4.9	15.0					3.96	8.66				

(continued)

Table A.11 (continued)

	Total Number (in thousands)		Number Living				Percentage of a Nation that was Linguistically Russified					
			Within Their Own Republic		Outside		Total		Within Its Own Republic		Outside	
	1959	1979	1959	1979	1959	1979	1959	1979	1959	1979	1959	1979
Hungarians	2.7	4.4					1.75	2.58				
Peoples of the North[5]	18.8	45.4					14.78	28.68				

Source: Censuses results.

[1] This table considers both Ossetian National Territories: the Northern Ossetian ASSR within the RSFSR and the Southern Ossetian Autonomous Region in the Georgian SSR.
[2] This table does not consider peoples whose population was below 150,000 in 1979.
[3] Formally there is a Jewish Autonomous Region (Birohidzhan) for Jews. In 1979, however, only 10,166 Jews (i.e., 0.56 percent of the USSR's Jewish population) lived there. Consequently, this table does not include Birobidzhan.
[4] The Karakalpaks have an ASSR within the Uzbek Union Republic.
[5] Within the RSFSR, ten Autonomous Territories exist for the peoples of the North. This table does not include them.

Table A.12: National Composition of College Students

1	2	3	4	5	6	7	8	9
	1927/28	1960/61	1980/81	Increase from 1927/28 to 1960/61 (percent)	Increase from 1960/61 to 1980/81 (percent)	Number of Students per 10,000 People		
						1927/28	1960/61	1980/81
Total No. of Students in the USSR	162,928	2,395,545	5,235,200	1,370	119	11.08	114.7	199.7
Percentage of								
Russians	58.30	61.8	57.6	1,457	104	12.20	129.6	219.5
Ukrainians	10.10	14.3	13.4	1,995	104	5.30	92.2	165.7
Belorussians	3.10	2.7	3.2	1,174	164	10.50	80.5	177.4
Lithuanians	—	1.1	1.2	—	151	—	110.0	226.9
Latvians	—	0.7	0.5	—	55	—	117.7	177.9
Estonians	—	0.5	0.4	—	58	—	130.6	200.0
Azeri	0.92	1.2	1.9	1,800	258	8.80	96.9	186.2
Armenians	2.90	1.5	1.7	681	144	30.00	131.8	215.6
Georgians	4.90	2.0	1.7	514	86	43.40	180.0	252.1
Moldavians	—	0.5	0.7	—	219	—	54.1	129.0
Uzbeks	0.11	2.2	3.8	28,992	273	0.50	89.0	160.2
Kazakhs	0.08	1.7	3.0	30,566	281	0.30	112.6	237.2
Tadzhiks	0.01	0.5	0.8	170,300	253	0.10	85.4	144.9

(continued)

Table A.12 (continued)

1	1927/28	1960/61	1980/81	Increase from 1927/28 to 1960/61 (percent)	Increase from 1960/61 to 1980/81 (percent)	Number of Students per 10,000 People		
	2	3	4	5	6	1927/28	1960/61	1980/81
						7	8	9
Percentage of								
Turkmen	0.01	0.4	0.6	72,823	213	0.20	94.6	146.5
Kirgiz	0.06	0.4	0.8	10,111	302	1.30	102.25	208.8
Germans	0.60	—	—	—	—	8.00	—	—
Jews	14.40	3.2	—	230	—	90.00	340.3	—
Poles	0.60	—	—	—	—	13.20	—	—
Tatars	0.70	1.7	2.3	3,625	300	3.70	80.3	190.3
Chuvash	0.40	0.3	0.5	1,216	185	5.50	55.3	136.5
Bashkirs	0.05	0.3	0.4	7,207	252	1.20	63.5	161.9
Mordvinians	0.24	0.2	0.3	993	256	2.90	33.4	128.4
Udmurts	0.10	0.1	0.2	1,821	206	3.30	51.7	137.3
Mari	0.07	0.1	0.1	1,926	239	2.70	46.2	125.4
Komi and Komipermiaks	0.15	0.1	0.1	1,109	107	6.40	67.3	125.7
Karelians	0.04	0.03	0.03	1,213	121	2.50	48.7	130.1
Daghestan Peoples	—	0.3	0.6	—	314	—	77.9	184.7
Chechens	—	0.1	0.2	—	533	—	35.1	125.7

(continued)

Table A.12 (continued)

1	1927/28	1960/61	1980/81	Increase from 1927/28 to 1960/61 (percent)	Increase from 1960/61 to 1980/81 (percent)	Number of Students per 10,000 People		
						1927/28	1960/61	1980/81
	2	3	4	5	6	7	8	9
Percentage of								
Ossetians	0.40	0.2	0.3	813	171	22.10	133.2	275.0
Kabardins	–	0.1	0.1	–	200	–	101.4	295.8
Ingush	–	0.03	0.1	–	322	–	71.6	171.9
Abkhaz	0.03	0.04	0.04	2,296	136	8.10	168.5	286.0
Balkars	–	0.02	0.03	–	187	–	164.4	301.7
Buriats	0.04	0.2	0.3	6,514	248	2.90	180.4	453.8
Yakuts	0.03	0.1	0.2	6,778	229	1.70	119.1	280.5
Karakalpaks	–	0.1	0.1	–	239	–	104.9	201.1
Tuvinians	–	–	0.05	–	–	–	–	174.6
Kalmyks	0.02	0.03	0.1	2,728	464	2.40	85.3	347.9
Others	–	1.2	2.65	–	–	–	–	–

Sources: *Natsionalnaia politika VKP (b) v tsifrakh* (Moscow, 1930), pp. 288f.; *Vysshee obrazovanie v SSSR, Statisticheskii sbornik* (Moscow, 1961), p. 185; *Narodnoe khoziaistvo SSSR 1922-1982. Iubileinyi statisticheskii sbornik* (Moscow, 1982), p. 517. The calculation of the number of students per 10,000 people is based on the censuses results of 1926, 1959, and 1979 (cf. Table 1).

Table A.13: College-Graduate Specialists Working in the Economy

1	1-1-1941	1-12-1960	16-11-1970	Increase from 1941 to 1960 (percent)	Increase from 1960 to 1970 (percent)	Number of Specialists per 10,000 People		
						1941	1960	1970
	2	3	4	5	6	7	8	9
Total No. of Specialists in the USSR	909,000	3,545,200	6,852,600	290	93.3	47.7	169.8	283.5
Percentage of								
Russians	54.4	58.4	58.8	319	94.8	49.2	181.4	312.6
Ukrainians	14.2	14.6	15.0	300	99.2	36.2	139.0	253.0
Belorussians	2.3	2.7	3.0	350	114.6	25.6	120.2	225.5
Lithuanians	0.6	0.8	1.0	370	122.7	31.5	129.0	250.7
Latvians	0.76	0.7	0.6	240	73.5	44.8	178.0	302.1
Estonians	0.5	0.5	0.5	370	85.0	35.8	195.2	354.4
Azeri	0.9	1.4	1.4	500	105.0	35.2	162.9	224.2
Armenians	2.2	2.1	1.9	280	73.0	91.0	265.9	359.9
Georgians	2.5	2.5	2.2	280	68.5	103.6	329.1	460.0
Moldavians	0.1	0.3	0.5	1,520	189.4	3.4	51.0	121.2
Uzbeks	0.3	1.3	2.0	1,500	200.2	6.0	77.3	151.8
Kazakhs	0.2	1.0	1.4	1,830	178.2	5.8	96.1	182.7

(continued)

Table A.13 (continued)

				Increase from 1941 to 1960 (percent)	Increase from 1960 to 1970 (percent)	Number of Specialists per 10,000 People		
	1-1-1941	1-12-1960	16-11-1970			1941	1960	1970
1	2	3	4	5	6	7	8	9
Percentage of								
Tadzhiks	0.02	0.3	0.4	3,520	171.6	2.4	78.0	138.6
Turkmen	0.02	0.3	0.4	5,080	150.0	2.5	103.8	170.5
Kirgiz	0.01	0.3	0.4	9,350	155.3	1.1	97.0	165.3
Germans	–	–	–	–	–	–	–	–
Jews	–	–	5.2	–	–	–	–	1,659.0
Poles	–	–	–	–	–	–	–	–
Tatars	–	–	1.6	–	–	–	–	184.1
Chuvash	–	–	0.4	–	–	–	–	152.3
Bashkirs	–	–	0.2	–	–	–	–	118.6
Mordvinians	–	–	0.2	–	–	–	–	108.5
Udmurts	–	–	0.1	–	–	–	–	119.3
Mari	–	–	0.1	–	–	–	–	93.6
Komi and Komipermiaks	–	–	0.1	–	–	–	–	176.7
Karelians	–	–	0.03	–	–	–	–	164.3
Daghestan Peoples	–	–	0.3	–	–	–	–	37.7
Chechens	–	–	0.04	–	–	–	–	50.6

(continued)

Table A.13 (continued)

	1-1-1941	1-12-1960	16-11-1970	Increase from 1941 to 1960 (percent)	Increase from 1960 to 1970 (percent)	Number of Specialists per 10,000 People		
						1941	1960	1970
1	2	3	4	5	6	7	8	9
Percentage of								
Ossetians	--	--	0.3	--	--	--	--	368.9
Kabardins	--	--	0.1	--	--	--	--	182.2
Ingush	--	--	0.01	--	--	--	--	82.5
Karachai	--	--	0.04	--	--	--	--	283.9
Adygei	--	--	0.04	--	--	--	--	290.3
Abkhaz	--	--	0.03	--	--	--	--	288.5
Balkars	--	--	0.01	--	--	--	--	218.5
Cherkess	--	--	0.01	--	--	--	--	301.5
Buriats	--	--	0.2	--	--	--	--	394.0
Yakuts	--	--	0.1	--	--	--	--	273.5
Karakalpaks	--	--	0.1	--	--	--	--	228.8
Tuvinians	--	--	0.03	--	--	--	--	172.2
Kalmyks	--	--	0.03	--	--	--	--	153.1

(continued)

Table A.13 (continued)

				Increase from 1941 to 1960 (percent)	Increase from 1960 to 1970 (percent)	Number of Specialists per 10,000 People		
	1-1-1941	1-12-1960	16-11-1970			1941	1960	1970
1	2	3	4	5	6	7	8	9
Percentage of								
Khakass	--	--	0.02	--	--	--	--	209.9
Altai	--	--	0.03	--	--	--	--	465.9

Sources: Vysshee obrazovanie v SSSR (Moscow, 1961), p. 69; *Narodnoe obrazovanie, nauka i kultura v SSSR* (Moscow, 1971), p. 240. The calculation of the number of specialists per 10,000 people is based on the censuses results of 1939, 1959, and 1970. In the following cases, however, the figures for 1939 are based on data reflecting conditions existing *after* September 17, 1939: total population 190,678,000; Russians 100,392,000; Ukrainians 35,611,000; Belorussians 8,275,000; Lithuanians 2,033,000; Latvians 1,628,000; Estonians 1,144,000; Moldavians 2,060,000 (V.I. Kozlov, *Natsionalnosti SSSR.* Moscow, 1975, p. 250).

Table A.14: Specialists with Mid-Level Technical School Training Who Work in the Economy

	December 1, 1960	November 14, 1975	Increase (percent)
Total Number of Specialists in the USSR	5,238,500	13,319,300	154
Percentage of			
Russians	65.6	63.4	146
Ukrainians	15.7	16.4	165
Belorussians	3.1	3.5	189
Lithuanians	0.8	1.1	226
Latvians	0.7	0.6	93
Estonians	0.6	0.5	110
Azeri	0.9	1.0	178
Armenians	1.1	1.0	148
Georgians	1.3	1.1	114
Moldavians	0.4	0.6	262
Uzbeks	0.9	1.6	327
Kazakhs	0.8	1.2	188
Tadzhiks	0.2	0.3	202
Turkmen	0.2	0.2	213
Kirgiz	0.2	0.3	248
Germans	--	--	--
Jews	2.6	1.4	32
Poles	--	--	--
Tatars	1.6	1.9	204
Chuvash	0.4	0.5	182
Bashkirs	0.2	0.3	268
Mordvinians	0.2	0.3	205
Udmurts	0.2	0.2	178
Mari	0.1	0.1	181
Komi and Komipermiaks	0.2	0.2	128
Karelians	0.1	0.1	116
Daghestan Peoples	0.2	0.3	265
Chechens	0.01	0.07	840
Ossetians	0.2	0.2	180
Kabardins	0.05	0.06	225
Ingush	0.007	0.02	600
Karachai	--	0.02	--
Adygei	--	0.03	--
Abkhaz	0.02	0.02	122

(continued)

Table A.14 (continued)

	December 1, 1960	November 14, 1975	Increase (percent)
Percentage of			
Balkars	0.01	0.01	257
Cherkess	--	0.01	--
Buriats	0.1	0.1	178
Yakuts	0.11	0.11	164
Karakalpaks	0.03	0.06	332
Tuvinians	--	0.04	--
Kalmyks	0.02	0.04	331
Khakass	--	0.01	--
Altai	--	0.02	--

Sources: *Vysshee obrazovanie v SSSR* (Moscow, 1961), p. 49; *Narodnoe obrazovanie, nauka i kultura v SSR* (Moscow, 1977), p. 296.

Table A.15: National Composition of the Party (Members and Candidates)

1	1927		1946		July 1, 1961		January 1, 1982	
		Per 10,000 People		Per 10,000 People		Per 10,000 People		Per 10,000 People
	2	3	4	5	6	7	8	
Total Number of Party Members	1,061,860	72	5,513,649		9,626,700	461	17,769,668	678
Percentage of								
Russians	64.9	88	67.8	63.5	536	59.8	774	
Ukrainians	11.6	39	12.1	14.7	379	16.0	672	
Belorussians	3.1	69	2.1	3.0	363	3.8	706	
Lithuanians	—	—	0.1	0.4	184	0.7	459	
Latvians	—	—	0.1	0.3	242	0.4	508	
Estonians	—	—	0.1	0.2	247	0.3	561	
Azeri	1.0	64	1.0	1.1	361	1.6	534	
Armenians	1.7	116	1.8	1.8	578	1.5	645	
Georgians	1.5	88	2.0	1.8	633	1.7	826	
Moldavians	—	—	0.1	0.3	121	0.5	316	
Uzbeks	1.2	34	1.1	1.5	237	2.3	330	
Kazakhs	1.1	30	1.7	1.5	412	1.9	525	
Tadzhiks	0.1	14	0.2	0.3	234	0.4	268	
Turkmen	0.3	38	0.2	0.3	273	0.4	320	
Kirgiz	0.2	35	0.3	0.3	282	0.4	348	

(continued)

Table A.15 (continued)

1	1927 Per 10,000 People		1946	July 1, 1961 Per 10,000 People		January 1, 1982 Per 10,000 People	
	2	3	4	5	6	7	8
Percentage of							
Germans	0.5	42				—	—
Jews	4.3	155				1.4	1,423
Poles	1.0	143				—	—
Tatars	1.4	51				2.0	557
Chuvash	0.3	32				0.5	544
Bashkirs	0.2	33				0.4	489
Mordvinians	0.3	27				0.5	678
Udmurts	0.08	16				0.2	512
Mari	0.1	25				0.1	406
Komi	0.1	71				0.2	839
Karelians	0.07	29				0.1	762
Daghestan Peoples[1]	0.2	47				0.5	602
Chechens	0.04	13				0.1	243
Ossetians	0.4	163				0.2	738
Kabardins	0.1	81				0.1	566
Ingush	0.04	61				0.02	200
Karachai	0.02	35				0.04	478

(continued)

Table A.15 (continued)

1	1927		1946		July 1, 1961		January 1, 1982	
		Per 10,000 People		Per 10,000 People		Per 10,000 People		Per 10,000 People
	2	3	4	5	6	7	8	
Percentage of								
Adygei	–	–				0.04	677	
Abkhaz	0.03	61				0.04	714	
Balkars	0.02	79				0.03	698	
Cherkess	0.03	42				0.02	724	
Buriats	0.1	46				0.1	695	
Yakuts	0.03	14				0.1	521	
Karakalpaks	0.04	33				0.1	373	
Uigurs	0.08	197				–	–	
Tuvinians	–	–				0.05	505	
Kalmyks	0.08	66				0.05	561	
Khakass	–	–				0.02	415	
Altai	0.01	40				0.02	674	

[1] Among the Peoples of Daghestan, this table only reflects the Party membership of the Avars, Dargins, Kumyks, Lak, and Lezgins. They make up about 90 percent of the Peoples of Daghestan.

Sources: Natsionalnaia politika VKP (b) v tsifrakh (Moscow, 1930), p. 137; "KPSS v tsifrakh," in: *Partiinaia zhizn*, 1/1962, p. 49; in: *Partiinaia zhizn*, 15/1983, p. 23; *Die Völker der UdSSR, Zahlen und Fakten, 1922-1982* (Moscow, 1982), pp. 30f. The calculation of the number of Party members per 10,000 people is based on the censuses results of 1926, 1959, and 1979.

Table A.16: National Composition of the Party's Leading Bodies (in percent)

	CC (Members and Candidates)					Politburo (Members and Candidates) and Secretariat		
	1939	1952	1961	1966	1981[1]	1939-1952 Total Number: 37	1961 Total Number: 21	December 1, 1983 Total Number: 22
1	2	3	4	5	6	7	8	9
Russians	66.2	71.5	55.2	55.0	68.3	81	61.9	72.7
Ukrainians	7.9	6.8	17.9	15.8	14.1	5	14.3	9.1
Belorussians	0.7	1.3	3.3	3.3	2.2	0	4.8	4.5
Lithuanians	0	1.3	0.9	0.8	0.3	0	0	0
Latvians	0	0.8	0.9	1.1	1.3	0	0	0
Estonians	0	0.8	0.9	0.8	0.6	0	0	0
Azeri	0.7	0.8	0.6	0.6	0.6	0	0	4.5
Armenians	3.6	2.6	1.5	1.4	0.9	3	4.8	0
Georgians	5.0	3.0	0.6	0.8	0.3	5	4.8	4.5
Moldavians	0	0	0.6	0.6	0.6	0	0	0
Uzbeks	1.4	1.3	2.1	1.4	1.3	0	4.8	0
Kazakhs	0	0.8	0.9	1.4	2.2	0	0	4.5
Tadzhiks	0	0.4	0.6	0.6	0.3	0	0	0
Turkmen	0	0.4	0.6	0.6	0.3	0	0	0

(continued)

Table A.16 (continued)

	CC (Members and Candidates)					Politburo (Members and Candidates) and Secretariat		
	1939	1952	1961	1966	1981[1]	1939-1952	1961	December 1, 1983
						Total Number: 37	Total Number: 21	Total Number: 22
1	2	3	4	5	6	7	8	9
Kirgiz	0	0.4	0.6	0.6	0.3	0	0	0
Others and of Unknown Nationality	14.3	7.6	12.7[2]	15.3[3]	6.3[4]	6	4.8[5]	0

[1]Members only.
[2]These forty-two people included one Finn (= 0.3 percent), one Jew, one Pole, one Bashkir, one Buriat, one Kabardin, one Ossetian, one Tatar, one Tuvinian, one Chuvash, one Yakut, one Avar, and one Uigur.
[3]These fifty-five people included one Jew (= 0.3 percent), one Pole, one Bashkir, one Buriat, one Kabardin, one Kalmyk, one Ossetian, two Tatars (= 0.6 percent), one Tuvinian, one Chuvash, one Yakut, and one Avar.
[4]These twenty people included two Jews (= 0.6 percent), two Tatars, two Bashkirs, one Buriat (= 0.3 percent), one Komi, one Chuvash, one Karelian, one Dargin, and one Yakut.
[5]One candidate of the CC's Presidium was a Finn (= 4.8 percent).

Sources: S. Bialer, "Soviet Political Elite" (Ph.D., Columbia University, 1966), pp. 188, 217; Y. Bilinsky, "The Rulers and the Ruled," in: *Problems of Communism*, XVI, 5/1967, p. 23; S. Voronitsyn, "The Social Structure of the Newly Elected CC's Voting Membership," in: *RL*, 159/81, April 13, 1981; E. Schneider, "Die sowjetische Elite," in: *Berichte des BIOst*, 21/1981, p. 31; H. Kraus, "The Composition of the CPSU CC Politburo and Secretariat," in: *RL*, 448/83, December 1, 1983.

Abbreviations

AoS	Academy of Sciences
AR	Autonomous Region
AS	Arkhiv Samizdata, Radio Liberty, Munich
ASSR	Autonomous Socialist Soviet Republic
ACEC RSFSR	All-Russian Central Executive Committee of the Russian Socialist Federative Soviet Republic
BIOst	Bundesinstitut für ostwissenschaftliche und internationale Studien, Cologne
BSE	Bolshaia Sovetskaia Entsiklopediia
GPU	Gosudarstvennoe Politicheskoe Upravlenie
HZ	Historische Zeitschrift
JGO	Jahrbücher für Geschichte Osteuropas
NKVD	Narodnyi Komissariat Vnutrennikh Del
OGPU	Obshchee Gosudarstvennoe Politicheskoe Upravlenie
PC	Problems of Communism
RL	Radio Liberty Research Bulletin
RN	Revoliutsiia i natsionalnosti
SDS	Sobranie dokumentov samizdata
SZ SSSR	Sobranie zakonov i rasporiazhenii raboche-krestianskogo pravitelstva Soiuza Sovetskikh Sotsialisticheskikh Respublik
VI	Voprosy istorii
VI KPSS	Voprosy istorii Kommunisticheskoi Partii Sovetskogo Soiuza
VVS RSFSR	Vedomosti Verkhovnogo Soveta RSFSR
CEC USSR	Central Executive Committee of the USSR

Selected Bibliography

This bibliography primarily contains recent Western and Soviet publications. I have included older sources and secondary literature when these were crucial for the completion of this book. Due to the size of the topic, I did not attempt to provide a complete bibliography. Additional resources and literature are listed in the notes.

Abdulatipov, R. G./Burmistrova, T. Ju. *Konstitutsiia SSSR i natsionalnye otnosheniia na sovremennom etape.* Moscow, 1978.

_____. *Leniniskaia politika internatsionalizma v SSSR. Itoriia i sovremnost.* Moscow, 1982.

Abdusattarov, G. S. *Iz istorii stroitelstva mestnukh organizatsii Kompartii Turkestana.* Tashkent, 1984.

Abdushukurov, T. R. "Problemy sotsialnogo razvitiia rabochego klassa respublik Srednei Azii v usloviiakh razvitogo sotsializma," in: *Voprosy filisofii,* 10/1984, pp. 53–61.

Agaev, A. G. *Patriotizm i internatsionalizm sovetskogo cheloveka.* 2nd edition, Moscow, 1975.

Agurskii, M. *Ideologiia natsional-bolshevizma.* Paris, 1980.

Akiner, S. *Islamic Peoples of the Soviet Union.* London, 1983.

_____. *Aktualnye problemy istorii sotsialisticheskogo stroitelstva v Moldavii.* L. E. Repida, et al. eds., Kishinev, 1982.

_____. *Aktualnye problemy natsionalnykh otnoshenii v svete novoi konstitutsii SSSR.* Ju. V. Bromlei et al. eds., Moscow, 1979.

_____. *Aktualnye problemy natsionalnykh otnoshenii v svete novoi konstitutsii SSSR.* M. I. Kulichenko ed., Moscow, 1981.

_____. *Aktualnye problemy razvitiia natsionalnykh otnoshenii v SSSR.* A. K. Alaiev ed., Kakhachkala, 1973.

Alekseeva, L. *Istoriia inakomysliia v SSSR. Noveisii period.* Benson, 1984.

Alexiev, A. R. *Dissent and Nationalism in the Soviet Baltic.* Rand Corporation: Santa Monica, 1983.

_____. *Soviet Nationalities in German Wartime Strategy 1941–1941.* Rand Corporation: Santa Monica, 1982; also in: *Conflict IV,* 1983, pp. 181–237.

Aliev, G. A. "Sovetskii Azerbaidzhan – natsionalnaia politika KPSS v deistvii," in: *Voprosy filisofii,* 5/1980, pp. 3–21.

Allworth, E. "Mainstay or Mirror of Identity. The Printed Word in Central Asia and Other Soviet Regions Today," in: *Canadian Slavonic papers*, XVIII, 1975, pp. 436–461.

_____. *Soviet Asia. Bibliography . . . With an Essay on the Soviet-Asian Controversy*. New York, 1975.

Altmyshbaev, A. A. *Oktiabr i razvitie obshchestvennogo soznaniia kirgizkogo naroda*. Frunze, 1980.

Aminova, R. Kh. *Pobeda kolkhoznogo stroia v Uzbekistane 1935–1941 gg.* Tashkent, 1981.

Anweiler, O./Kuebart, F. "'Internatsionalnoe vospitanie' und 'multicultural education.' Aspekte eines vergleichs zweier politischer Konzepte," in: Mitter, W./Swift, J. eds., *Education and the Diversity of Cultures*. Cologne, 1985, pp. 219–24.

Aranchyn, Ju. *Istoricheskii put tuvinskogo naroda k sotsializmu*. Novosibirsk, 1982.

Arifkhanova, Z. Kh./Chebotareva, V. G. *Reshenie natsionalnogo voprosa v Uzbekistane*. Tashkent, 1979.

Armstrong, J. A. *The Soviet Bureaucratic. A Case Study of the Ukrainian Apparatus*. New York, 1959.

_____. *Ukrainian Nationalism*. 2nd edition, Littleton, 1980.

Arnold, J. *Die nationalen Gebietseinheiten der Sowjetunion*. Cologne, 1973.

Artemev, A.P. *Bratskii boevoi soiuz narodov SSSR v Velik. Otech. voine*. Moscow, 1975.

_____. "Iz istorii boevogo sodruzhestva narodov SSSR v Velik. Otech. voine," in: *Bratskoe sotrudnichestvo sovetskikh respublik*, pp. 57–90.

Arutiunian, Ju. V. "Izmenenie sotsialnoi struktury sovetskikh natsii," in: *Istoriia SSSR*, 4/1972, pp. 3–20.

_____. "Konkretno-sotsiologicheskoe issledovanie natsionalnykh otnoshenii," in: *Voprosy filosofii*, 12/1969, pp. 129–139.

_____. "Korennye izmeneniia v sotsialnom sostave sovestkikh natsii," in: *Sotsiologocheskie issledovaniia*, 3/1980, pp. 73–81.

_____. "Natsionalnye osobennosti sotsialnogo razvitiia," in: *Sotsiologocheskie issledovaniia*, 3/1985, pp. 28–35.

_____. "Oboshchee i natsionalno-osobennoe v sotsialno-kulturnom oblike selskogo naseleniia SSSR," in: *Istoriia SSSR*, 6/1985, pp. 24–31.

Arutiunian, Ju. V./Drobizheva, L. M. "Etnosotsiologicheskie issledovaniia v SSSR," in: *Sotsiologicheskie issledovaniia*, 1/1981, pp. 64–70.

_____. "Sotsionalnaia structura sovetskikh natsii na sovremennom etape," in: *VI*, 7/1982, pp. 3–14.

Arutiunian, Ju. V./Kakhk, Ju. *Sotsiologicheskie ocherki o Sovetskoi Estonii*. Tallinn, 1979.

Ashirov, N. *Evoliutsiia islama v SSSR*. Moscow, 1972.

Aspaturian, V. "The Non-Russian Nationalities," in: Kassof, A., ed., *Prospects for Soviet Society.* New York, 1968, pp. 143–198.

Aster, H./Potichnyj, P. J. *Jewish-Ukrainian Relations. Two Solitudes.* Oakville, 1983.

Avksentev, A. V. *Islam na Severnom Kavkaze.* Stavropol, 1973.

Badzo, Ju. "An Open Letter to the Presidium of the Supreme Soviet of the USSR and the CC of the CPSU," in: *Journal of Ukrainian Studies IX,* 1/1984, pp. 74–94; 2/1984, pp. 47–70.

Bagramov, E. A. *Leninskaia natsionalnaia politika. Dostizheniia i perspektivy.* Moscow, 1977.

———. *Natsionalnyi vopros v borbe idei.* Moscow, 1982.

Bahry, D./Nechemias, C. "Half Full or Half Empty? The Debate Over Soviet Regional Equality," in: *Slavic Review,* XL, 1981, pp. 366–383.

Baktygulov, D. S. *Sotsialisticheskoe preobrazovanie kirgizskogo aula 1928–1940.* Frunze, 1978.

Baranova, T.I./Rosyeva, N. Z. "Iz istorii prepodavaniia russkogo iazyka v nerusskikh shkolakh SSSR 1938–1966," in: *Sovetskaia pedagogika,* 12/1977, pp. 115–123.

Barghoorn, F. C. *Soviet Natsionalism.* New York, 1956.

Barsukov, N. A./Saidullin, A. R./Judin, I. N. "KPSS — partiia internationalnaia," in: *VI KPSS,* 7/1966, pp. 3–15.

———. *Basmachestvo. Sotsialno-politicheskaia sushchnost.* B. Lunin et al. eds., Tashkent, 1984.

Batyrev, S. B. *Formirovanie i razvitie sotsialisticheskikh natsii v SSSR.* Moscow, 1962.

Belkov, O. A. "Boevoe sodruzhestvo narodov SSSR v gody Velikoi Otechestvennoi voiny," in: *Istoriia SSSR,* 4/1985, pp. 64–72.

Beloded, I. K. *Leninskaia teoriia natsionalno-iazykovogo stroitelstva v sotsialisticheskom obshchestve.* Moscow, 1972.

Benet, S. *Abkhasians, the Long Living People of the Caucasus.* New York, 1974.

Bennigsen, A. A. "The Crisis of the Turkic National Epics 1951–52. Local Nationalism or Proletarian Internationalism?" in: *Canadian Slavonic Papers,* XVII, 1975, pp. 463–474.

———. "Mullahs, Mujahidin, and Soviet Muslims," in: *PC XXXIII,* 6/1984, pp. 28–44.

———. "Panturkism and Panislamism in History and today," in: *Central Asian Survey III,* 3/1984, pp. 39–50.

———. "Soviet Muslims and the World of Islam," in: *PC XXIX,* 2/1980, pp. 38–51.

———. "The Soviet Union and Muslim Guerilla Wars. 1920–1981. Lessons for Afghanistan," in: *Conflict,* IV 1983, pp. 301–324.

Bennigsen, A./Broxup, M. *The Islamic Threat to the Soviet Union.* London, 1983.

Bennigsen, A./Lemercier-Quelquejay, Ch. *Islam in the Soviet Union.* New York, 1967.

———. *Les movements nationaux chez les musulmans de Russie. Le sultangalievisme au Tartarstan.* Paris, 1960.

———. "Der 'Sultangalievismus' und die nationalistischen Abweichungen in der Tatarischen Autonomen Sowjetrepublik," in: *Forschungen zur osteuropäischen Geschichte,* VII, 1959, pp. 323–396.

———. *Les musulmans oubliés. L'islam en URSS aujourd'hui.* Paris, 1981.

Bennigsen, A. A./Wimbush, S. E. *Muslim National Communism in the Soviet Union.* Chicago, 1979.

Besemeres, J. F. *Socialist Population Politics. The Political Implications of Demographic Trends in the USSR and Eastern Europe.* White Plains, 1980.

Bialer, S. *Soviet Political Elite. Concept, Sample, Case Study.* Ph.D., Colombia University, 1966.

———. *Bibliographie zum Nationalismus.* H. A. Winkler/Th. Schnabel (eds.), Göttingen, 1979.

———. *Bibliography of Regional Handbooks in the USSR.* J. W. Gillula (ed.), 2nd edition, Washington, 1980.

Bilinsky, Y. "The Concept of Soviet People and its Implications for Soviet Nationality Policy," in: *The Annals of the Ukrainian Academy of Arts and Sciences in the U.S.,* XIV, 1978–80, pp. 87–133.

———. "Education of the Non-Russian Peoples in the USSR 1917–1967," in: *Slavic Review,* XXVII, 1968, pp. 411–437.

———. "Expending the Use of Russian or Russification?" in: *Russian Review,* XL, 1981, pp. 317–332.

———. "The Rulers and the Ruled," in: *PC,* XVI, 5/1967, pp. 16–26.

———. *The Second Soviet Republic. The Ukraine After World War II.* New Brunswick, 1964.

———. "The Soviet Education Laws of 1958–59 and Soviet Nationality Policy," in: *Soviet Studies,* XIV, 1962/1963, pp. 138–157.

Bilinsky, Y./Parming, T. "Helsinki Watch Committees in the Soviet Republics. Implications for Soviet Nationality Policy," in: *Nationalities Papers,* IX, 1981. pp. 1–25.

Birch, J. *The Ukrainian Nationalist Movement in the USSR Since 1956.* London, 1971.

Bland-Spitz, D. *Die Lage der Juden und die jüdische Opposition in der Sowjetunion.* Diessenhofen, 1980.

Bociurkiw, B. "The Catacomb Church. Ukrainian Greek Catholics in the USSR," in: *Religion in Communist Lands,* V, 1/1977, pp. 4–12.

———. "The Uniate Church in the Soviet Union. A Case Study in Soviet Church Policy," in: *Canadian Slavonic Papers,* VII, 1965, pp. 89–113.

Bohmann, A. *Menschen und Grenzen.* vol. III. *Strukturwandel der deutschen Bevölkerung im sowjetischen Staats- und Verwaltungsbereich.* Cologne, 1970.

Bondarskaia, G. A. *Rozhdaemost v SSSR. Etnodemograficheskii.* Moscow, 1977.

Borzykh, N. P. "Mezhnatsionalnye braki v SSSR v seredine 1930-kh godov," in: *Sovetskaia etnografiia,* 3/1984, pp. 101–112.

Bourdeaux, M. *Land of Crosses. The Struggle for Religious Freedom in Lithuania 1939–1978.* Devon, 1979.

Bräker, H. *Kommunismus und Weltreligionen Asiens. Zur Religions- und Asienpolitik der Sovietunion.* 2 volumes, Tübingen, 1969.

———. "Sowjetunion und Volksrepublik China," in: Ende, W./Steinboch, U. (eds.), *Der Islam in der Gegenwart.* Munich, 1984, pp. 248–273.

———. *Bratskii soiuz – osnova rastsveta sovetskikh respublik.* M. P. Kim et al. (eds.), Kishinev, 1982.)

———. *Bratskoe sodruzhestvo narodov SSSR 1922–1936 gg. Sbornik dokumentov i materialov.* I. I. Groshev (ed.), Moscow, 1964.

———. *Bratskoe sodruzhestvo soiuznykh respublic v razvitii narodnogo khoziaistva SSSR 1917–1971.* M. P. Kim et al. (eds.), Moscow, 1973.

———. *Bratskoe sotrudnichestvo sovetskikh respublic v khoziaistvennom i kulturnom stroitelstve.* M. P. Kim et al. (eds.), Moscow, 1971.

Bromlei, Ju. V. "Etnograficheskoe izuchenie sovremennykh natsionalnykh protsessov v SSSR," in: *Sovetskaia etnografiia,* 2/1983, pp. 4–14.

———. "K izucheniiu natsionalnykh protsessov sotsialisticheskogo obshchestva v kontekste etnicheskoi istorii," in: *Istoriia SSSR,* 6/1984, pp. 40–56.

———. "K izucheniiu osnovnykh etapov i napravlenii natsionalnykh otnoshenii v SSSR," in: *Istoriia SSSR,* 2/1979, pp. 58–67.

———. "O nekotorikh aktualnykh zadachakh etnograficheskogo izucheniia sovremennosti," in: *Sovetskaia etnografiia,* 6/1983, pp. 10–23.

———. *Ocherki teorii etnosa.* Moscow, 1983.

———. "Sovremennye etnosotsialnye protsessy u vostochnoslavianskikh narodov SSSR," in: *Soviet Studies,* XXVI, 1984, pp. 108–126.

———. *Nations-Nationalities-People. A Study of the Nationalities Policy of the Communist Party in Soviet Moldavia.* New York, 1984.

———. *One Step Back, Two Steps Forward. On the Language Policy of The Communist Party of the Soviet Union in the National Republics. Moldavia: A Look Back, a Survey, and Perspectives 1924–1980.* Boulder, 1982.

Brook [= Bruk], S. I. "Demographical and Ethnographical Changes in the USSR According to Post-War Data up to 1979," in: *Geo Journal,* special issue 1, 1980, pp. 7–21.

Bruk, S. I./Guboglo, M. N. "Faktory rasprostraneniia dvuiazuchiia u narodov SSSR," in: *Sovetskaia etnografiia,* 5/1975, pp. 17–30.

Bruk, S. I./Kabuzan, V. M. "Dinamika chislennosti i rasseleniia russkikh posle Vel. Oktiab. sots. revoliutsii," in: *Sovetskaia etnografiia*, 5/1982, pp. 3–20.

Brunner, G. "Der Schutz der ethnischen Minderheiten in Osteuropa," in: *Jahrbuch für Ostrecht*, XXV, 1984, pp. 9–41.

Buchsweiler, M. *Ethnic Germans in the Ukraine Towards the Second World War. A Case of Double Loyalty?* Tel Aviv, 1980.

_____. "Deutsche Landkreise (Rayons) und deutsche Kreiszeitungen in der UdSSR," in: *Osteuropa*, XXXII, 1982, pp. 671–682.

_____. *Bundesstaat und Nationalitätenrecht in der Sowjetunion*. Schröder, F.-Ch./Meissner, B. (eds.), Berlin, 1974.

Burg, S. L. "Russians, Natives, and Jews in the Soviet Scientific Elites. Cadre Competition in Central Asia," in: *Cahiers du Monde russe et soviétique*, XX, 1979, pp. 43–60.

_____. "Soviet Policy and the Central Asian Problem," in: *Survey*, XXIV, 3/1979, pp. 65–82.

_____. *Sovetskoe mnogonatsionalnoe gosudarstvo, ego osobennosti i puti razvitiia*. Moscow, 1958.

_____. *Teoreticheskie problemy obrazovaniia i razvitiia sovetskogo mnogonatsionalnogo gosudarstva*. Moscow, 1973.

Carlisle, D. S. "Modernization, Generations, and the Uzbek Soviet Intelligentsia," in: Cocks, P./Daniels, R. V./Herr, N. W. (eds.), *The Dynamics of Soviet Politics*. Cambridge, 1976. pp. 239–264.

Caron, Y. "Les allemands de Russia," in: *Est et Ouest*, XXX, July 1, 1978, pp. 14–20.

Carrére d'Encausse, H. *L'Empire éclaté. La révolte des nations en URSS*. Paris, 1978.

_____. "A Case Study of a Soviet Republic. The Estonian SSR," in: T. Parming/E. Järvesoo (eds.), Boulder, 1978.

_____. *Central Asia. A Century of Russian Rule*. E. Allworth (ed.), New York, 1967.

Chertina, Z. S. *Protiv burzhuaznykh falsifikatsii natsionaknykh otnoshenii v SSSR*. Moscow, 1983.

Cherot, R. A. "Nativization of Government and Party Structure in Kazakhstan. 1920–1930," in: *American Slavic and East European Review*, XIV, 1955, pp. 42–58.

Clem, R. S. "The Ethnic Dimension of the Soviet Union," in: Pankhurst, J. G./ Sacks, M. P. (eds.), *Contemporary Soviet Society*. New York, 1980, pp. 11–62.

Connor, W. *The National Question in Marxist-Leninist Theory and Strategy*. Princeton, 1984.

_____. "Nation-Building or Nation-Destroying?" in: *World Politics*, XXIV, 3/1972, pp. 319–355.

Conolly, V. *Sibiria Today and Tomorrow. A Study of Economic Resources, Problems, and Achievements.* London, 1975.
Conquest, R. *The Great Terror. Stalin's Purge of the Thirties.* London, 1968.
_____. *The Nation Killers. The Soviet Deportation of Nationalities.* London, 1970.
_____. *Soviet Nationalities Policy in Practice.* New York, 1967.
_____. *The Constitutions of the USSR and the Union Republics. Analyses, Texts, Reports.* F. J. M. Feldbrugge (ed.), Alphen, 1979.
Crosnier, M.-A./Kahn, M. "Développement et dépendance économique de l'Asie centrale soviétique. I. Le dualisme du développement," in: *Le courrier des pays de l'est,* no. 276, September 1983, pp. 3–51.
Curran, S. L./Ponomareff, D. *Managing the Ethnic Factor in the Russian and Soviet Armed Forces. A Historical Overview.* Rand Corporation, Santa Monica, 1982; also in: *Conflict,* IV, 1983, pp. 239–300.
Dallin, A. *Deutsche Herrschaft in Rußland 1941–1945.* Düsseldorf, 1958.
Dalrymple, D. G. "The Soviet Famine of 1932–1934," in: *Soviet Studies,* XV, 1963/64, pp. 250–284.
Danilov, A. "Mnogonatsionalnaia shkola RSFSR – prakticheskoe voploshchenie leninskoi natsionalnoi politiki," in: *Narodnoe obrazovanie,* 12/1972, pp. 21–25.
Davies, R. W. *The Industrialization of Soviet Russia. vol I. The Socialist Offensive. The Collectivization of Soviet Agriculture 1929–1930. vol. II. The Soviet Collective Farm 1929–1930.* London, 1980.
Dellenbrant, J. A. *Soviet Regional Policy.* Stockholm, 1980.
_____. *Demographic Developments in Eastern Europe.* L. A. Kosinski (ed.), New York, 1977.
Desheriev, Ju., D. *Razvitie obshchestvennykh funktsii literaturnykh iazykov.* Moscow, 1976.
_____. *Zakonomernosti razvitiia i vzaimodeistviia iazykov v sovetskom obshchestve.* Moscow, 1966.
Deutsch, K. W. *Nationalism and Social Communication. An Inquiry into the Foundations of Nationality.* 2nd edition, Cambridge, 1966.
_____. *Dialektika internatsionalnogo i natsionalnogo v sotsialisticheskom obshchestve.* F. T. Konstantinov (ed.), Moscow, 1981.
Diat, F. "Olzhas Suleimenov 'Az i ia'," in: *Central Asian Survey,* III, 1/1984, pp. 101–121.
Dima, N. *Bessarabia and Bukovina. The Soviet-Romanian Territorial Dispute.* Boulder, 1982.
_____. *Direktivy KPSS i Sovetskogo pravitelstva po khoziaistvennym voprosam 1917–1957 gg.* 4 vol., Moscow, 1957–1958.
_____. *Discordant Voices. The Non-Russian Soviet Literatures 1953–73.* G. S. N. Luckyj (ed.), Oakville, 1975.

Dolot, M. *Who Killed Them and Why? In Remembrance of Those Killed in the Famine of 1932-1933 in the Ukraine.* Cambridge, 1984.

_____. *Dostizheniia sovetskoi vlasti za 40 let v tsifrakh. Statisticheskii sbornik.* Moscow, 1957.

Dreifelds, J. "Demographic Trends in Latvia," in: *Nationalities Papers,* XII, 1984, pp. 49-84.

Drobizheva, L. M. *Dukhnovnaia obshchnost norodov SSSR.* Moscow, 1981.

_____. "Natsionalnoe samosoznanie: baza formirovaniia i sotsialno-kulturnye stimuly razvitiia," in: *Sovetskaia etnografiia,* 5/1985, pp. 3-15.

_____. *Druzhba i bratstvo russkogo i ukrainskogo narodov.* 2 volumes, Ju. Ju. Kondufor (ed.), Kiev, 1982.

Dunlop, J. P. *The Faces of Contemporary Russian Nationalism.* Princeton, 1983.

Dunn, D. J. *The Catholic Church and the Soviet Government 1939-1949.* Boulder, 1977.

Dushnych, W. *50 Years Ago. The Famine Holocaust in Ukraine.* New York, 1983.

Dyadkin, J. G. *Unnatural Deaths in the USSR 1928-1954.* New Brunswick 1983.

Dzhunusov, M. S. *Dve tendentsii sotsializma v natsionalnykh otnosheniiakh.* Tashkent, 1975.

_____. "Sblizhenie natsii v usloviiakh razvitogo sotsializma," in: *Sotsiologicheskie issledovaniia,* 4/1976, pp. 42-51.

Dzyuba, I. *Internationalism or Russification? A Study in the Soviet Nationalities Problem.* 2nd edition, London, 1970.

_____. *Economics of Soviet Regions.* I. S. Koropechyj/G. E. Schroeder (eds.), New York, 1981.

Eisenstadt, S. N. "Varieties of Political Development. The Theoretical Challenge," in: *Eisenstadt, S. N./Rokkan, S. (eds.), Building States and Nations. Models and Data Resources.* vol. 1, Beverly Hills, 1973, pp. 41-72.

Eisfeld, A. "Deutsche in der Sowjetunion – zwei Jahrzehnte nach der Rehabilitierung," in: *Osteuropa,* XXXV, 1985, pp. 653-669.

_____. *Die Deutschen in Rußland und in der Sowjetunion.* Vienna, 1986. (= *Eckartschriften,* vol. 97.)

Ekmanis, R. *Latvian Literature Under the Soviets 1940-1975.* Belmont, 1978.

Engel, A. "Russisches und Deutsches bei den Sovetdeutschen," in: *Korrespondenzen. Festschrift D. Gerhardt.* Giessen, 1977, pp. 139-166.

Eremei, G. I. *Internatsionalizatsiia dukhovnoi zhizni v usloviiakh razvitogo sotsializma. Na materialakh Mold. SSR.* Moscow, 1981.

Erzhanov, A. *Uspekhi natsionalnoi politiki KPSS v Kazakhstane 1946-1958 gg.* Alma-Ata, 1969.

_____. *Ethnic Minorities in the Soviet Union.* E. Goldhagen (ed.), New York, 1968.

_____. *Ethnic Russia in the USSR. The Dilemma of Dominance.* E. Allworth (ed.), New York, 1980.

_____. *Etnicheskie protsessy i obraz zhizni. Na materialakh issledovaniia naseleniia gorodov BSSR.* V. K. Bondarchik (ed.), Minsk, 1980.

_____. *Etnosotsiologiia: tseli, metody i nekotorye rezultaty issledovaniia.* Iu. V. Arutiunian/I. D. Kovalkhenko (eds.), Moscow, 1984.

_____. *Evrei v SSSR. Materialy i issledovaniia.* vol. IV, Moscow, 1929; reprinted: Tel Aviv, 1970.

Faensen, J. *Sprachen in der UdSSR.* Osnabrück, 1983.

Farmer, K. C. *Ukrainian Nationalism in the Post-Stalin Era.* The Hague, 1980.

Fedko, Z. A./Petrovskaia, N. B. *Intelligentsiia Moldavskoi SSR 1940-1975.* Kishinev, 1979.

_____. *Ferment in the Ukraine. Documents by V. Chornovil, K. Kandyba, L. Lukyanenko, V. Moroz and others.* M. Brown (ed.), London, 1971.

Feshbach, M. "The Age Structure of Soviet Population. Preliminary Analysis of Unpublished Data," in: *Soviet Economy,* I, 1985, pp. 177-193.

_____. "Trends in the Soviet Muslim Population — Demographic Aspects," in: *Problems and Prospects,* vol. II, Washington, 1983, 297-322.

Fierman, W. "Cultural Nationalism in Soviet Uzbekistan. A Case Study of 'The Immortal Cliffs'," in: *Soviet Union/Union Soviétique,* XII, 1/1985, pp. 1-41.

_____. *Nationalism, Language Planning, and Development in Soviet Uzbekistan 1917-1941.* Ph.D., Harvard University, 1979.

_____. "Uzbek Feelings of Ethnicity. A Study of Attitudes Expressed in Recent Uzbek Literature," in: *Cahiers du Monde russe et soviétique,* XXII, 1981, pp. 187-229.

Fisher, A. *The Crimean Tatars.* Stanford, 1978.

Fisher, W. A. "Ethnic Consciousness and and Intermarriage. Correlates of Endogamy Among Major Soviet Nationalities," in: *Soviet Studies,* XXIX, 1977, pp. 395-408.

Fleischhauer, I. *Das Dritte Reich und die Deutschen in der Sowjetunion.* Stuttgart, 1983.

_____. "'Unternehmenr Barbarossa' und die Zwandgsumsiedlung der Deutschen in der UdSSR," in: *Vierteljahreshefte für Zeitgeschichte,* XXX, 1982, pp. 299-321.

Formirovanie i razvitie mnogonatsionalnogo rabochego klassa SSSR v period stroitesltva sotsializma 1921-1937 gg. L. S. Bogachevskaia et al. (eds.), Tbilisi, 1980.

_____. *Formirovanie sotsialisticheskikh natsii v SSSR.* Moscow, 1962.

Fragner, B. "Die Revolution von Buchara," in: Haarmann, U./Bachmann P. (eds.), *Die islamische Welt zwischen Mittelalter und Neuzeit. Festschrift H. R. Roemer.* Beirut, 1979, pp. 146-166.

Freedman, Th., ed. *Antisemitism in the Soviet Union. Its Roots and Consequences.* New York, 1984.

Gapurov, M. G. "V bratskoe seme narodov po puti sotsialnogo progressa," in: *Voprosy filosofii,* 10/1984, pp. 20–33.

Gardanov, V. K./Dolgikh, V. O./Zhdanko, T. A. "Osnovnye napravleniia etnicheskikh protsessov u narodoc SSSR," in: *Sovetskaia etnografiia,* 4/1961, pp. 9–29.

———. *The German Russians. A Bibliography of Russian Materials.* J. Long (ed.), Santa Barbara, 1978.

Gicquiau, H. "Développement et dépendance économique de l'Asie centrale soviétique. II. Complémentarités et dépendances à l'égard de l'URSS," in: *Le courrier des pays de l'est,* no. 277, October 1983, pp. 3–34.

Giesinger, A. *From Catherine to Khrushchev. The Story of Russia's Germans.* Battleford, 1974.

Gilboa, Y. A. *The Black Years of Soviet Jewry 1939–1953.* Boston, 1971.

Gitelman, Z. "Are Nations Merging in the USSR?" in: *PC,* XXXII, 5/1983, pp. 35–47.

———. *Jewish Nationality and Soviet Politics. The Jewish Sections of the CPSU 1917–1930.* Princeton, 1972.

Gleserman, G. E. *Klassy i natsii.* 2nd edition, Moscow, 1977.

Golotvin, Zh. G. "Bankrotstvo burshuaznykh falsifikatsii natsionalnoi politiki KPSS i natsionalnykh otnoshenii v SSSR," in: *VI KPSS,* 8/1984, pp. 50–63.

Golovnev, A. I./Melnikov, A. P. *Sblizhenie natsionalnykh kultur v protsesse kommunisticheskogo stroitelstva.* Minsk, 1979.

Gorovskii, F. Ia. *Sovetskii narod kak internationalnaia sushchnost.* Kiev, 1982.

Grant, N. "Sprache und Bildungspolitik in der UdSSR," in: Anweiler, O. (ed.), *Bildung und Erziehung in Osteuropa im 20. Jahrhundert.* Berlin, 1982, pp. 140–163.

Grdzelidze, R. K. *Mezhnatsionalnoe obshchenie v razvitom sotsialisticheskom obshchestve.* Tbilisi, 1980.

———. *The Great Famine in Ukraine. The Unknown Holocaust.* Jersey City, 1983.

Grishkiavichus, P. P. *Sovetskaia Litva.* Moscow, 1978.

Groshev, I. I. *Borba partii protiv natsionalizma.* Moscow, 1974.

———. *Istoricheskii opyt KPSS po osushchestvlenniiu leninskoi natsionalnoi politiki.* Moscow, 1967.

———. *Sushchnost natsionalnoi politiki KPSS.* Moscow, 1982.

Groshev, I. I./Chechenkina, O. N. *Kritika burzhuaznoi falsifikatsii natsionalnoi politiki KPSS.* Moscow, 1974.

Guboglo, M. N. "Leninskaia natsionalno-iazykovaia politika KPss—internatsionalizm v deistvii," in: *Sovetskaia etnografiia*, 1/1984, pp. 3–15.

―――――. "Ukreplenie edinstva natsionalnogo i internatsionalnogo v obraze zhizni sovetskogo naroda," in: *Istoriia SSSR*, 6/1983, pp. 3–21.

―――――. *Guide to the Study of the Soviet Nationalities. Non-Russian Peoples of the USSR*. S. M. Horak (ed.), Littleton, 1982.

Gumpel, W. "Entwicklungspolitik in Sowjet-Mittelasien," in: *Crossroads*, 8/1982, pp. 189–212.

Gurevitz, B. *National Communism in the Soviet Union 1918–1928*. Ph.D. University of Rochester, 1973.

Gurvich, I. S. "K voprosu o vliianii Vel. Otech. voiny 1941–1945 gg. na khod e tnicheskikh protsessov v SSSR," in: *Sovetskaia etnografiia*, 1/1976, pp. 39–49.

―――――. "Osobennosti sovremennogo etapa etnokulturnogo razvitiia narodov Sovetskogo Soiuza," in: *Sovetskaia etnografiia*, 6/1982, pp. 15–27.

―――――. "Polveka avtonomii narodnostei Severa SSSR," in: *Sovetskaia etnografiia*, 6/1980, pp. 3–17.

Gurvich, I. S./Taksami, Ch. M. "Sotsialnye funktsii iazykov narodnostei Severa i Dalnego Vostoka SSSR v sovetskii period," in: *Sovetskaia etnografiia*, 2/1985, pp. 54–63.

Guthier, S. L. "The Belorussians. National Identification and Assimilation 1897–1970," in: *Soviet Studies*, XXIX, 1977, pp. 37–61, 270–283.

Haarmann, H. *Multilinguale Kommunikationsstrukturen. Spracherhaltung und Sprachwechsel bei den romanischen Siedlungsgruppen in der Ukrainischen SSR und anderen Sowjetrepubliken*. Tübingen, 1979.

―――――. *Quantitative Aspekte des Multilingualismus. Studien zur Gruppenmehrsprachigkeit ethnischer Minderheiten in der Sowjetunion*. Hamburg, 1979.

Halevy, Z. *Jewish Schools Under Czarism and Communism. A Struggle for Cultural Identity*. New York, 1976.

―――――. *Handbook of Major Soviet Nationalities*. Z. Katz/R. Rogers/F. Harned (eds.), 1975.

Hanusiak, M. *Ukrainischer nationalismus. Theorie und Praxis*. Vienna, 1979.

Hayit, B. *Sowjetrussische Orientpolitik am Beispiel Turkistan*. Berlin, 1962.

―――――. *Turkestan im Herzen Eurasiens*. Cologne, 1980.

―――――. *Turkestan im XX. Jahrhundert*. Darmstadt, 1956.

―――――. *Turkestan zwischen Rußland und China*. Amsterdam, 1971.

Hehn, J. v. *Die Umsiedlung der baltischen Deutschen — das letzte Kapitel baltischdeutscher Geschichte*. Marburg, 1982.

Heitman, S. *The Soviet Germans in the USSR Today. Berichte des BIOst*. 35/1980.

Hillgruber, A. "Der Hitler-Stalin-Pakt und die Entfesselung des zweiten Weltkriegs — Situationsanalyse und Machtkalkül der beiden Pakt-Partner," in: *HZ*, 230/1980, pp. 349–361.

Hodnett, G. *Leadership in the Soviet National Republics. A Quantitative Study of Recruitment Policy*. Oakville, Ontario, 1978.

———. "Technology and Social Change in Soviet Central Asia. The Politics of Cotton Growing," in: Morton, H. W./Tökés, R. L. (eds.), *Soviet Politics and Society in the 1970s*. New York, 1974, pp. 60–117.

Hodnett, G./Ogareff, V. *Leaders of the Soviet Republics 1955–1972. A Guide to Posts and Occupants*. Canberra, 1973.

Hoffmann, J. *Deutsche und Kalmycken 1942–1945*. 2nd edition, Freiburg, 1974.

———. *Die Geschichte der Wlassow-Armee*. Freiburg, 1984.

———. *Die Ostlegionen 1941-1943*. Freiburg, 1976.

Horn, H. "Wirtschaftliche Niveauangleichung der Nationalitäten zwischen Anspruch und Wirklichkeit," in: *Sozialismus in Theorie und Praxis. Festschrift R. Löwenthal*, Berlin, 1978, pp. 141–176.

Hovannasian, R. *The Republic of Armenia*. Vol. I, Berkeley, 1971; Vol. II, Berkeley, 1982.

Hryshko, W. *The Ukrainian Holocaust of 1933*. Toronto, 1983.

———. *The Human Rights Movement in Ukraine. Documents of the Ukrainian Helsinki Group 1976–1980*. Verba, L./Yasen, B. (eds.), Baltimore, 1980.

Humphry, C. *Karl Marx Collective. Economy, Society, and Religion in a Siberian Collective Farm*. Cambridge, 1983.

Iakubovskaia, S. I. *Razvitie SSSR kak zoiuznogo gosudarstva 1922–1936 gg*. Moscow, 1972.

Iakutov, V. D. *N. M. Goloded. Stranitsy biografii*. Minsk, 1981.

———. *Iazyk v razvitom sotsialisticheskom obshchestve. Iazykovye problemy razvitiia sistemy massovoi kommuniatsii v SSSR*. Desheriev, Ju. D./Baskakov, A. N. et al. (eds.), Moscow, 1982.

———. *The Jews in Soviet Russia Since 1917*. Kochan, L. (ed.), 3rd edition, Oxford, 1978.

Igritskii, Iu. I. "Kritika falsifikatsii natsionalnoi politiki KPSS na sovremennom etape," in: *VI KPSS*, 1/1984, pp. 62–75.

Imart, G./Dor, R. *Le chardon déchiqueté. Etre Kirgiz au XX siecle*. Aix-en-Provence, 1982.

———. *The Influence of East Europe and the Soviet West on the USSR*. Szporluk, R. (ed.), New York, 1975.

Inoiatov, Kh. Sh. *Narody Srednei Azzi v Borbe protiv interventov i vnutrennei kontrrevoliutsii*. Moscow, 1984.

———. *Internatsionalizm i patriotizm. Istoriia i sovremennost*. Khromov, S. S. et al. (eds.), Moscow, 1977.

_____. *Internatsionalizm mnogonatsionalnogo kollektiva*. Aksenev, M. S. et al. (eds.), Alma-Ata, 1984.
_____. *Internatsionalizm sovetskogo naroda. Istoriia i sovremennost*. Sherstobitov, V. p. (ed.), Moscow, 1982.
_____. *Internatsionalnoe i natsionalnoe v sotsialistecheskom obshchestve*. Evdokimenko, V. E. (ed.), Kiev, 1976.
Isaev, M. I. *Iazykovoe stroitelstvo v SSSR. Protsessy sozdaniia pismennostei narodov SSSR*. Moscow, 1979.
_____. *O iazykakh narodov SSSR*. Moscow, 1978.
_____. *National Languages in the USSR. Problems and Solutions*. Moscow, 1977.
_____. *Islam v SSR*. Abdusamedov, A. I./Filimonov, E. G., et al. (eds.), Moscow, 1983.
_____. *Istoriia natsionalno-gosudarstvennogo stroitelstva v SSSR*. Sherstobitov, V. P. et. al. (eds.), 2 volumes, 3rd edition, Moscow, 1979.
_____. *Istoriia sovetskoi konstitutsii (v dokumentakh) 1917–1956*. Studenikina, S. s. (ed.), Moscow, 1957.
_____. *Itogi razresheniia natsionalnogo voprosa v SSSR*. Dimanshtein, S. M. (ed.), Moscow, 1936.
_____. *Itogi Vsesoiuznoi perepisi naseleniia 1959 goda*. 16 volumes, Moscow, 1962–1963.
_____. *Itogi Vsesoiuznoi perepisi naseleniia 1970 goda*. 7 volumes, Moscow, 1972–1974.
_____. *Izmenenie sotsialnoi struktury narodov SSSR*. Selunskaia, V. M. (ed.), Moscow, 1982.
Jachomovski, D. *Die Umsiedlung der Bessarabien-, Bukowina-, und Dobrudschadeutschen. Von der Volksgruppe in Rumänien zur 'Siedlungsbrücke' an der Reichsgrenze*. Munich, 1984.
Jones, E. "Minorities in the Soviet Armed Forces," in: *Comparative Strategy*, III, 4/1982, pp. 285–318.
Jones, E./Grupp, F. W. "Modernization and Traditionality in a Multiethnic Society: The Soviet Case," in: *American Political Science Review*, 79, 1985, pp. 474–490.
_____. "Modernization and Ethnic Equalization in the USSR," in: *Soviet Studies*, XXXVI, 1984, pp. 159–184.
Joukovsky, A. "L'ukrainisation, aspect de la question nationale en Ukraine soviétique dans les années 1920," in: *Nationalities Papers*, IX, 1981, pp. 63–79.
Iuldashbaev, V. Kh. *Sotsialisticheskaia natsiia Bashkir. Politicheskie i ekonomicheskie aspekty problemy*. Ufa, 1981.
Jurmalnieks, J. "Die Einverleibung Lettlands in die Sowjetunion—deren Vor- und Nachspiel," in: *Acta Baltica*, XVII, 1977, pp. 118–181.
Kalmyrzaev, A. S. *Natsiia i obshchestvennoe soznanie*. Alma-Ata, 1984.

Kaltakhchian, S. I. *Leninizm o sushchnosti natsii i puti obrazovaniia internatsionalnoi obshchnosti liudei*. 2nd edition, Moscow, 1976.

_____. *Marksistsko-leninskaia teoriia natsii i sovremennost*. Moscow, 1983.

Kanimetov, A. I. "Rol Sovetskoi Rossii v podgotovke natsionalnykh kadrov Kirgizii 1924–1954 gg.," in: *Istoriia SSR*, 5/1982, pp. 32–38.

Kappeler, A. "Die Geschichte der Völker der Mittleren Wolga (vom 10. Jh. bis in die zweiten Hälfte des 19. Jh.) in der sowjetischen Forschung," in: *JGO N. F.*, XXVI, 1978, pp. 70–104, 222–257.

_____. *Rußlands erste Nationalitäten. Das Zarenreich und die Völker der Mittleren Wolga vom 16. bis 19. Jahrhundert*. Cologne, 1982.

_____. "Zur Nationalitätenfrage in der Sowjetunion," in: *Neue politische Literatur*, XXV, 1980, pp. 327–340.

Karchava, V. I. *Abkhazskaia ASSR na etape stroitelstva razvitogo sotsializma 1945–1965 gg*. Tbilisi, 1981.

Karklins, R. "Ethnic Interaction in the Baltic Republics. Interviews With Recent Emigrants," in: *Journal of Baltic Studies*, XII, 1/1981, pp. 16–34.

_____. "Ethnic Politics and Access to Higher Education. The Soviet Case," in: *Comparative Politics*, XVI, 1984, pp. 277–294.

_____. *Ethnic Relations in the USSR. The Perspective From Below*. London, 1985.

_____. "Islam. How Strong is It in the Soviet Union? Inquiry Based on Oral Interviews With Soviet Germans Repatriated From Central Asia in 1979," in: *Cahiers du Monde russe et soviétique*, XXI, 1980, pp. 65–81.

_____. "Nationality Power in Soviet Republics. Attitudes and Perspectives," in: *Studies in comparative Communism*, XIV, 1981, pp. 70–93.

_____. "The Uighurs Between China and the USSR," in: *Canadian Slavonic Papers*, XVII, 1975, pp. 341–365.

Kasbarian-Bricout, B. *Les Arméniens au xxe siècle*. Paris, 1984.

Kaslas, B. J. *La Lithuanie et la Second Guerre mondiale. Recueil des documents*. Paris, 1981.

Khanazarov, K. Ts. "Rastsvet i sblinizhenie natsionalnykh kultur v usloviiakh razvitogo sotsializma," in: *Voprosy filisofii*, 9/1984, pp. 42–52.

_____. *Reshenie natsionalno-iazykovoi problemy v SSSR*. 2nd edition, Moscow, 1982.

_____. *Sblizhenie natsii i natsionalnye iazyki v SSSR*. Tashkent, 1963.

Kholmogorov, A. I. *Internatsionalnye cherty sovetskikh natsii. Na materialakh konkretno-sotsiologicheskikh issledovanii v Pribaltike*. Moscow, 1970.

_____. *Natsionalnye otnosheniia v sotsialisticheskom obshchestve. Problemy nauchnogo upravleniia*. Kiev, 1982.

_____. *The Chornovil Papers*, V. Chornovil (ed.), New York, 1968.

_____. "Chronik der litauischen katholischen Kirche. Nr. 7–9," in: *Acta Baltica*, XIV, 1974, no. 10–12; *Acta Baltica*, XV, 1975, no. 13–14; *Acta Baltica*, XVI, 1976, no. 15 ff. in special issues of the *Acta Baltica*.

———. *Chruschtschow erinnert sich.* S. Talbott (ed.), Reinbek, 1971.
———. *Krushchev Remembers. The Last Testament.* S. Talbott (ed.), Boston, 1974.
Khudoiberdiev, O. *Boevaia druzhba, rozhdennaia Oktiabrem. Iz Istorii voennogo stroitelstva i likvidatsii kontrrevoliutsii v Srednei Azzii.* Moscow, 1984.
———. *Chislennost i sostav naseleniia SSSR. Po dannym Vsesoiuznoi perepisi naseleniia 1979 goda.* Moscow, 1984.
Kim, M. P. *Sovetskii narod—novaia istoricheskaia obshchnost.* Moscow, 1972.
Kipnis, M. "The Georgian National Movement. Problems and Trends," in: *Crossroads,* 2, 1978, pp. 193–215.
Kleiner, I. "Contemporary Ukrainian National Movement in the USSR," in: *Crossroads,* 4, 1979, pp. 205–253.
———. "Contemporary Russian Nationalism and the Nationality Problem in the USSR," in: *Crossroads,* 3, 1979, pp. 321–346.
———. *Natsionalni problemy ostannoii imperiii.* Paris, 1978.
Knabe, B. *Bevölkerungsentwicklung und Binnenwanderung in der UdSSR 1967–1974.* Berlin, 1978.
Koch, F. C. *The Volga Germans in Russia and the Americas from 1763 to the Present.* University Park, 1977.
Kolarz, W. *Die Nationalitätenpolitik der Sowjetunion.* Frankfurt/M., 1956.
Kolasky, J. *Two Years in the Soviet Ukraine. A Canadian's Personal Account of Russian Oppression and the Growing Opposition.* Toronto, 1970.
Koliak, T. N. *Vlas Iakovlevich Chubar. Zhizn i deiatelnost.* Kiev, 1981.
———. *Kommunisticheskaia partiia Gruzii v tsifrakh 1921–1970 gg.* E. G. Kurtsikidze, et al. (eds.), Tbilisi, 1971.
———. *Kommunisticheskaia partiia Kazakhstana v dokumentakh i tsifrakh.* S. B. Beisembaev/P. M. Pakhmurnyi (eds.), Alma-Ata, 1960.
———. *Kommunisticheskaia partiia Kirgizii 1918–1973 gg. Rost i regulirovanie sostava.* Frunze, 1973.
———. *Kommunisticheskaia partiia Latvii v tsifrakh 1904–1971 gg.* Riga, 1972.
———. *Kommunisticheskaia partiia Sovetskogo Soiusa v rezoliutsiiakh i resheniiakh sezdov, konferentsii i plenumov TK.* 14 volumes, Moscow, 1970–1982.
———. *Kommunisticheskaia partiia Tadzhikistana v dokumentakh i tsifrakh 1924–1963 gg.* Dushanbe, 1965.
———. *Kommunisticheskaia partiia Turkestana i Uzbekistana v tsifrakh.* Tashkent, 1968.
———. *Kommunisticheskaia partiia Uzbekistana v tsifrakh 1924–1977.* N. T. Bezrukova (ed.), Tashkent, 1979.
Koropeckyj, I. S. *Location Problems in Soviet Industry Before World War II. The Case of the Ukraine.* Chapel Hill, 1971.

Korzh, D. "Rodnoi i russkii iazyki v natsionalnykh shkolakh," in: *Narodnoe obrazovanie*, 7/1974, pp. 42–45.

Koshelivets, I. *Mykola Skrypnyk*. Munich, 1972.

Kossior, S./Postyschew, P. *Der bolschewistische Sieg in der Ukraine*. Moscow, 1934.

Kossko, N. "Die Letzten unter den 'Gleichen.' Die Deutschen in der UdSSR," in: *Wege und Wandlungen. Die Deutschen in der Welt heute*. Vol. I, Berlin, 1981, pp. 218–243.

Kostiuk, H. *Stalinist Rule in the Ukraine. A Study of the Decade of Mass Terror 1929–1939*. Munich, 1960.

Kosyk, W. "Der Hunger-Genozid in der Ukraine 1932–1933," in: *Jahrbuch der Ukrainekunde*, 1983, pp. 89–126.

Kozlov, v. I. "Dinamika natsionalnogo sostava nasileniia SSSR i problemy demograficheskoi politiki," in: *Istoriia SSSR*, 4/1983, pp. 20–30.

_____. "Ethnic Processes and Trends in the Ethnic Composition of the Population in the USSR," in: *GEO Journal*, Special Issue, 1/1980, pp. 23–30.

_____. *Natsionalnosti SSSR. Etnograficheskii obzor*. Moscow, 1975, 2nd edition, 1982.

Krag, H. L. "Die Sowjetunion – Staat, Nationalitätenfrage und Sprachenpolitik," in: *Sprache und Herrschaft. Zeitschrift für eine Sprachwissenschaft als Gesellschaftswissenschaft*, no. 13, 1983, pp. 4–108.

Kravchenko, T. F. "Istochniki i formy popolneniia rabochego klassa Kirgizskoi SSR v gody dovoennykh piatiletok," in: *VI*, 3/1982, pp. 3–16.

Krawchenko, B. "The Impact of Industrialization on the Social Structure of Ukraine," in: *Canadian Slavonic Papers*, XXII, 1980, pp. 338–357.

_____. *Social Change and National Consciousness in the 20th-Century Ukraine*. Basingstoke/London, 1985.

Kreindler, I. "The Changing Status of Russian in the Soviet Union," in: *International Journal of the Sociology of Language*, XXXIII, 1982, pp. 7–39.

_____. "The Mordvinians – A Doomed Soviet Nationality?" in: *Cahiers du Monde russe et soviétique*, XXVI, 1/1985, pp. 43–62.

_____. "The Soviet Deported Nationalities. A Summary and an Update," in: *Soviet Studies*, XXXVIII, 1986, pp. 387–405.

_____. *Kritika falsifikatsii natsionalnykh otnoshenii v SSSR*. Moscow, 1984.

Kulichenko, M. I. *Natsiia i sotsialnyi progress*. Moscow, 1983.

_____. *Natsionalnye otnosheniia v SSSR i tendentsii ikh razvitiia*. Moscow, 1972.

_____. "Obrazovanie i razvitie sovetskogo naroda kak novoi istoricheskoi obshchnosti," in: *VI*, 4/1979, pp. 3–23.

_____. *Rastsvet i sblizhenie natsii v SSSR. Problemy teorii i metodologii*. Moscow, 1981.

_____. *Kulturne budivnytstvo v Ukraiinskii RSR. Zbirnyk dokumentiv.* 2 volumes, Kiev, 1960–1961.
_____. *Kulturnoe stroitelstvo SSSR.* Leningrad, 1927.
_____. *Kulturnoe stroitelstvo SSSR. Statisticheskii sbornik.* Moscow, 1940.
_____. *Kulturnoe stroitelstvo SSSR. Statisticheskii sbornik.* Moscow, 1956.
_____. *Kulturpolitik der Sowjetunion.* O. Anweiler/K.-H. Ruffmann (eds.), Stutt-gart, 1973.
Kunaev, D. A. *Leninskaia natsionalnaia politika KPSS v deistvii.* Moscow, 1981.
Küng, A. *Dream of Freedom. Four Decades of National Survival Versus Russian imperialism in Estonia, latvia, and Lithuania 1940–1980.* Cardiff, 1981.
_____. *Estland zum Beispiel. Nationale Minderheit und Supermacht.* Stuttgart, 1973.
Kurbanov, A. A./Kuzmin. O. D. *Osushchestvlenie leninskoi natsionalnoi politiki v oblasti narodnogo obrazovaniia v Sovetskom Turkmenistane.* Ashkhabad, 1976.
Kuts, A. M. *Vzaimosviaz klassovykh i natsionalnykh otnoshenii v razvitom sotsialisticheskom obshchestve.* Kharkov, 1982.
Kuzuev, P. G./Babenko, V. Ia, "Malye etnicheskie gruppy. Osnovnye etapy etnokulturnogo razvitiia (pomaterialam SSSR)," in: *Sovetskaia etnografiia,* 4/1985, pp. 13–22.
Lane, D. "Ethnic and Class Stratification in soviet kazakhstan 1917–1939," in: *Comparative Studies in Society and History,* XVII, 1975, pp. 165–189.
Lang, M. A. *A Modern History of Soviet Georgia.* London, 1962.
_____. "Language Policy and Language Behavior in Soviet Central Asia. Symposium," in: *Slavic Review,* XXXV, 1976, pp. 405–462.
Lapidus, G. W. "Ethnonationalism and Political Stability. The Soviet Case," in: *World Politics,* XXXVI, 1984, pp. 553–580.
Lazarev, A. M. *Vossoedinenie moldavskogo naroda v sovetskoe gosudarstvo.* Kishinev, 1965.
Lazzerini, E. J. "Tatarovedenie and the 'New Historiography' in the Soviet Union. Revising the Interpretation of Tatar-Russian Relationship," in: *Slavic Review,* XL, 1981, pp. 625–635.
Lemercier-Quelquejay, Ch. "From Tribe to Umma," in: *Central Asian Survey,* III, 3/1984, pp. 15–26.
_____. "Sufi Brotherhoods in the USSR. A Historical Survey," in: *Central Asian Survey,* II, 4/1983, pp. 1–36.
Lenin, W. I. *Werke.* 40 volumes, East-Berlin, 1955–1972.
_____. *Leninizm i natsionalnyi vopros v sovremennykh usloviiakh.* P. N. Fedoseev (ed.), Moscow, 1972, 2nd edition, 1974.
_____. *Leninskaia natsionalnaia politika i borba protiv ee falsifiktorov.* M. B. Mitin (ed.), Ashkhabad, 1975.

Levits, E. "Die demographische Situation in der UdSSR und in den baltischen Staaten unter besonderer Berücksichtigung von nationalen und sprachsoziologischen Aspekten," *Acta Baltica*, XXI, 19181, pp. 18–142.
Lewin, M. *Russian Peasants and Soviet Power. A Study of Collectivization*. London, 1968.
Lewis, G. *Multilingualism in the Soviet Union. Aspects of Language Policy and Its Implementation*. The Hague, 1972.
Lewis, R./Rowland, R. H./Clem, R. S. *Nationality and Population Change in Russia and the USSR. An Evolution of Census Data 1897–1970*. New York, 1976.
Lewytzkyj, B. *Politics and Society in Soviet Ukraine 1953–1980*. Edmonton, 1984.
_____. *Politische Opposition in der Sowjetunion 1960–1972*. Munich, 1972.
_____. *"Sovetskii narod" – "Das Sowjetvolk." Nationalitätenpolitik als Instrument des Sowjetimperialismus*. Hamburg, 1983.
_____. *Die sowjetische Nationalitätenpolitik nach Stalins Tod 1953–1970*. Munich, 1970.
_____. *Die Sowjetukraine 1944–1963*. Cologne, 1964.
Liber, G. "Language, Literacy, and Book Publishing in the Ukrainian SSR 1923–1928," in: *Slavic Review*, XLI, 1982, pp. 673–685.
Likholat, A. V. *Sodruzhestvo narodov v borbe za postroenie sotsializma 19171–1937*. Moscow, 1976.
Likholat, A. V./Panibudlaska, V. F. *V edinoi semie narodov. Druzhba i sotrudnichestvo narodov SSSR v usloviiakh razvitogo sotsializma*. Moscow, 1979.
Lipkin, S. *Dekada*. New York, 1983.
_____. *Litauen 1939–1940. Die Wende zum Sozialismus*. V. Kantsevichius (ed.), Vilnius, 1976.
_____. *Lithuania Under the Soviets. Portrait of a Nation 1940–1965*. V. S. Vardys (ed.), New York, 1965.
_____. *Litopys Ukraiinskoii Povstanskoii Armiii*. Vol. 1–9, Toronto, 1978–1982.
Liubarskii, K. "O strukture politicheskikh repressii v SSSR," in: *Forum*, 1, 1982, pp. 45–53.
Lorenz, R. *Sozialgeschichte der Sowjetunion. Vol. I, 1917–1945*. Frankfurt/M., 1976.
Lorimer, F. *The Population of the Soviet Union. History and Prospects*. Geneva, 1946.
Lubachko, I. S. *Belorussia Under Soviet Rule 1917–1957*. Lexington, 1972.
Lubin, N. *Labour and Nationality in Soviet Central Asia*. London, 1984.
_____. "Women in Soviet Central Asia. Progress and Contradictions," in: *Soviet Studies*, XXXIII, 1981, pp. 182–203.

Lüdemann, E. "Zur patriotischen Tendenz in der sowjetukrainischen Geschichtsschreibung," in: *Osteuropa*, XXIX, 1979, pp. 311–322.

———. *L'vovskii tserkovnyi sobor. Dokumenty i materialy. 1946–1981*. Moscow, 1982.

Mace,, J. E. *Communism and the Dilemma of National Liberation. National Communism in Soviet Ukraine 1918–1933*. Cambridge, 1983.

———. "Famine and Nationalism in Soviet Ukraine," in: *PC*, XXXIII, 3/1984, pp. 37–50.

Magocsi, P. R. *The Shaping of National Identity. Subcarpathian Rus 1848–1948*. Cambridge, 1978.

Maistrenko, I. *Istoriia komunistycgnoii partii Ukraiiny*. 1979.

———. *Natsionalnaia politika KPSS v ee istoricheskom razvitii*. Munich, 1978.

Makarov, N. "Stroitelstvo mnogonatsionalnykh Vooruzhennykh Sil SSSR v 1920–1930 gg.," in: *Voenno-istoricheskii zhurnal*, 10/1982, pp. 39–43.

Maksudov [sic], "Pertes subies par la population de l'URSS 1918–1958," in: *Cahiers du Monde russe et soviétique*, XVIII, 1977, pp. 223–265.

Malanchuk, V. E. *Istoricheskii opyt Kpss po resheniiu natsionalnogo voprosa i razvitiia natsionalnykh otnoshenii v SSSR*. Munich, 1972.

Mandelstam-Balzer, M. "Ethnicity without Power. The Siberian Khanty in Soviet Society," in: *Slavic Review*, XLII, 1983, pp. 633–648.

Markish, D. *Priskazka*. Tel Aviv, 1978.

Markstein, E. "Die Russischnationalen," in: *Osteuropa*, XXXIV, 1984. pp. 159–167.

Markus, v. *L'incorporation de l'Ukraine Subcarpathique a l'Ukraine soviétique 1944–1945*. Louvain, 1956.

Marples, D. R. "The Soviet Collectivization of Western Ukraine 1948–1949," in: *Nationalities Papers*, XII, 1/1985, pp. 24–44.

Martin, N. A. *Krushchev and the Non-Russians. A Study of Soviet Nationality Policy Since the Death of Stalin*. Ph.D. Georgetown University, Washington, 1968.

Martiny, A. "Sozialstruktur und nationale Beziehungen in der UdSSR. Zur These der 'odnorodnost' der Sozialstruktur der sowjetischen Nationen," in: *Nationalities Papers*, IX, 1981, pp. 45–62.

———. "Das Verhältnis von Politik und Geschichtsschreibung in der Historiographie der sowjetischen Nationalitäten seit den 60er Jahren," in: *JGO N. F.*, XXVII, 1979, pp. 237–273.

Martovych, O. "The Ukrainian Insurgent Army," in: *Ukrainian Review*, XXX, 2/1982, pp. 3–26; 3/1982. pp. 3–28.

———. *Martyrologiia ukraiinskykh tserkov. Vol. 2. Ukraiinska katolytska tserkva. Dokumenty, materiialy, khrystyianskyi samvydav Ukraiiny*. O. Zinkevich/T. P. Lonchyna (eds.), Toronto/Baltimore, 1985.

Massell, G. "Modernization and national Policy in Soviet Central Asia," in: Cocks, P./Daniels, R. V./Heer, N. W. (eds.), *The Dynamics of Soviet Politics*. Cambridge, 1976, pp. 265-290.

―――――. *The Surrogate Proletariat. Moslem Women and Revolutionary Strategies in Soviet Central Asia 1919-1929*. Princeton, 1974.

Matiuskin, N. I. *Armiia druzhby narodov i proletarskogo internatsionalizma*. Moscow, 1982.

Matossian, M. K. *The Impact of Soviet Policies in Armenia*. Leiden, 1962.

McAuley, A. *Economic Welfare in the Soviet Union. Poverty, Living Standards, and Inequality*. Madison, 1979.

McAuley, M. "Party Recruitment and the Nationalities in the USSR. A Study in Centre-Republican Relationships," in: *British Journal of Political Science*, X, 1980, pp. 461-487.

Medlin, W. K./Cave, W. M./Carpenter, F. *Education and Devlopment in Central Asia. A Case Study on Social Change in Uzbekistan*. Leiden, 1971.

Medwedew, R. A. *Die Wahrheit ist unsere Stärke. Geschichte und Folgen des Stalinismus*. Frankfurt/M., 1973.

Meissner, B. *Partei, Staat und Nation in der Sowjetunion. Ausgewählte Beiträge*. Berlin, 1985.

―――――. *Das Parteiprogramm der KPdSu 1903-1961*. Cologne, 1962.

―――――. *Die Sowjetunion, die baltischen Staaten und das Völkerrecht*. Cologne, 1956.

―――――. "Mezhnatsionalnye konflikty v Zakavkaze. Iz materialov gruzinskogo samizdata," in: *Forum*, 9, 1984, pp. 134-153.

―――――. *Mezhnatsionalnye sviazi i vzaimodeistvie kultur narodov SSSR*. Iu. V. Bromlei (ed.), Tallinn, 1978.

Miller, J. H. "Cadres Policy in Nationality Areas. Recruitment of CPSU First and Second Secretaries in Non-Russian Republics of the USSR, " in: *Soviet Studies*, XXIX, 1977, pp. 3-36.

Misiunas, R. J./Taagepera, R. *The Baltic States. The Years of Dependence 1940-1980*. London, 1983.

―――――. *Mnogonatsionalnoe sovetskoe gosudarstvo*. M. I. Kulichenko et al. (eds.), Moscow, 1972.

Montgomery, D. "The Uzbeks in Two States. Soviet and Afghan Politics Towards an Ethnic Minority," in: McCagg Jr., W. O./Silver, B. D. (eds.), *Soviet Asian Ethnic Frontiers*. New York, 1979.

―――――. *Morva. Istoriko-etnograficheskie ocherki*. V. I. Kozlov et al. (eds.), Saransk, 1981.

Motyl, A. J. *The Turn to the Right. The Ideological Origins and the Development of Ukrainian Nationalism 1919-1929*. New York, 1980.

Mouradian, C. *L'Arménie soviétique depuis la mort de Staline*. Diss. Ecole des Hautes Etudes en Sciences Sociales, Paris, 1982.

_____. "L'immigration des Arméniens de la diaspora vers la RSS d'Arménie 1946–1962," in: *Cahiers du Monde russe et soviétique*, XX, 1979, pp. 79–110.
_____. *Sowjetarmenien nach dem Tode Stalins*. Berichte des BIOst, 11/1985.
Muggeridge, M. *Like It Was*. New York, 1982.
Mühlen, P. v.z. *Zwischen Hakenkreuz und Sowjetstern. Der nationalismus der sowjetischen Orientvölker im zweiten Weltkrieg*. Düsseldorf, 1971.
Myhul, I. "L'historiographie et la politique a la lumière du 'renouveau national' soviétique ukrainien," in: *Revue du Monde russe et soviétique*, XXV, 1984, pp. 463–480.
Myllyniemi, S. *Der baltische Krieg 1938–1941*. Stuttgart, 1979.
_____. *Die Neuordnung der baltischen Länder 1941–1944. Zum nationalsozialistischen Inhalt der deutschen Besatzungspolitik*. Helsinki, 1973.
_____. *Natsionalnaia politika KPSS. Ocherk istoriografii*. T. Iu. Burmistrova et al. (eds.), Moscow, 1981.
_____. *Natsionalnaia politika VKP (b) v tsifrakh*. Moscow, 1930.
_____. *Natsionalnoe i internatsionalnoe v sovremennom mire*. Iu. V. Bromlei et al. (eds.), Kishinev, 1981.
_____. *Natsionalnyi iazyk i natsionalnaia kultura*. Iu. D. Desheriev (ed.), Moscow, 1978.
_____. *Natsionalnyi vopros i natsionalnye otnosheniia v SSSR. Bibliograficheskii ukazatel literatury 1963–1973 gg.* R. M. Iudina/E. I. Burkhanova (eds.), Dushanbe, 1976.
_____. *Natsionalnyi vopros v SSSR. Sbornik dokumentov*. R. Kupchinskii (ed.), New York, 1975.
_____. *Natsionalnye otnosheniia v razvitom sotsialisticheskom obshchestve*. M. I. Kulichenko et al. (eds.), Moscow, 1977.
_____. *Natsionalnye otnosheniia v SSSR na sovremennom etappe. Na materialakh respublik Srednei Azii i Kazakhstana*. V. P. Sherstobitov et al. (eds.), Moscow, 1979.
_____. *Natsionalnye sholy RSFSR za 40 let*. F. F. Sovetkin (ed.), Moscow, 1958.
_____. *Narodnoe obrazovanie, nauka i kultura v SSSR. Statisticheskii sbornik*. Moscow, 1971.
_____. *Narodnoe obrazovanie, nauka i kultura v SSSR. Statisticheskii sbornik*. Moscow, 1977.
_____. *Nationalism. The Nature and Evolution of an Idea*. E. Kamenka (ed.), London, 1976.
_____. *Nationalism and Human Rights. Processes of Modernization in the USSR*. I. Kamenetsky (ed.), Littleton, 1977.
_____. *Nationalism in the USSR and Eastern Europe in the Era of Brezhnev and Kosygin*. G. W. Simmonds (ed.), Detroit, 1977.
_____. *Nationalismus*. H. A. Winkler (ed.), Königstein/Ts., 1978.

_____. *Nationalismus und sozialer Wandel.* O. Dann (ed.), Hamburg, 1978.
_____. *Nationalitätenprobleme in der Sowjetunion und Osteuropa.* G. Brunner/B. Meissner (eds.), Cologne, 1982.
_____. "Nationalities and Nationalism in the USSR. Special Issue," in: *PC,* XVI, 5/1967
_____. *Nationality Group Survival in Multi-ethnic States. Shifting Support Patterns in the Soviet Baltic Region.* E. Allworth (ed.), New York, 1977.
_____. *The Nationality Question in Soviet Central Asia.* E. Allworth (ed.), New York 1973.
_____. *Nations and Peoples. The Soviet Experience.* M. Bechtel/D. Rosenberg (eds.), New York, 1984.
Nekrich, A. N. *The Punished Peoples.* New York, 1978.
Nemec, F./ Mondry, V. *The Soviet Seizure of Subcarpathian Ruthenia.* 1955, reprinted Westport, CT, 1981.
_____. *Nonconformity and Dissent in the Ukrainian SSR 1955–1975. An Annotated Bibliography.* G. Liber/ A. Mostovych (eds.). Cambridge, 1978.
_____. *The Non-Slavic Peoples of the Soviet Union. A Brief Ethnographical Survey.* K. Symmons-Symonolewicz. Meadville, PA, 1972.
_____. *Novaia istoricheskaia obshchnost liudei. Sushchnost, formirovanie, razvitie.* L. S. Ganonenko, et al. (eds.). Moscow, 1976.
Nove, A./Newth, J. A. *The Soviet Middle East.* London, 1967.
Novikov, N. "Nationalitäten der UdSSR im Lichte des Parteikongresses und der Volkszühlungsergebnisse," in: *Osteuropa,* XXXI, 1981, pp. 812–824.
Oberländer, E. *Sowjetpatriotismus und Geschichte.* Cologne, 1967.
_____. *Der sowjetische Nationsbegriff. Zur Diskussion in "Voprosy istorii."* Berichte des BIOst 40/1967.
_____. *Obrazovanie i razvitie SSSR – triumf idei leninizma.* V. P. Shevchuk et al. (eds.). Kiev, 1982.
_____. *Ocherki istorii kollektivizatsii selskogo khoziaistva v soiuznykh respublikakh.* V.P. Danilov (ed.). Moscow, 1963.
Oganesian, E. "Ia – natsionalist!" in: *Kontinent* 13, 1977, pp. 235–252.
Ogareff, V. *Leaders of the Soviet Republics 1971–1980. A Guide to Posts and Occupants.* Canberra, 1980.
Olcott, M. B. "The Basmachi or Freemen's Revolt in Turkestan 1918–1924," in: *Soviet Studies* XXXIII, 1981, pp. 352–369.
_____. "The Collectivization Drive in Kazakhstan," in: *Russian Review,* XL 1981, pp. 122–142.
_____. "Pastoralism, Nationalism, and Communism in Kazakhstan," in: *Canadian-American Slavic Studies,* XVII, 1983, pp. 528–544.
_____. "Yuri Andropov and the 'National Question'," in: *Soviet Studies,* XXXVII, 1985, pp. 103–117.
Oliver, K. *Ukranian Nationalism in the 1970s.* Ph.D., Indiana University, Bloomington, 1981.

———. *Osnovnye napravleniia izucheniia natsionalnikh otnoshenii v SSSR.* M. I. Kulichenko, et al. (eds.). Moscow, 1979.

———. *Osushchestvlenie leninskoi natsionalnoi politiki u narodov Krainego Severa.* I. S. Gurvich (ed.). Moscow, 1971.

———. *Osushchestvlenie printsipov internatsionalizma v natsionalnoi politike KPSS.* I. I. Groshev (ed.). Moscow, 1975.

Pajaujis-Javis, J. *Soviet Genocide in Lithuania.* New York, 1980.

Palij, M. "The First Experiment of National Communism in Ukraine in the 1920s and 1930s," in: *National Papers,* XII, 1984, pp. 85–106.

Parsons, J. W. R. "National Integration in Soviet Georgia," in: *Soviet Studies,* XXXIV, 1982, pp. 547–569.

Penkaitis, N. *Der Finanzausgleich in der Sowjetunion und seine Bedeutung für die Wirtschaftsentwicklung der Unionsrepubliken.* Berlin, 1977.

Pennar, J./Bakalo, I. I./ Bereday, G. Z. F. *Modernization and Diversity in Soviet Education. With Special Reference to Nationality Groups.* New York, 1977.

Petrov, V. T. *Tvorcheskoe sotrudnichestvo narodov SSSR.* Moscow, 1971.

Pietsch, A.-J/ Uffhausen, R. *Arbeitskräftepotenzial und Migrationsverhalten in den zentralasiatischen Republiken und Kazachstan.* Arbeiten aus dem Osteuropa-Institut München, no. 38, 1981.

Pinchuk, B.-C. "Elimination as the 'Highest Stage' of Sovietization," in: *Ukranian Quarterly,* XXXIII, 3/1977, pp. 279–293.

Pinkus, B. "Die Deutschen in der Sowjetunion beim Ausbruch des Zweiten Weltkrieges," in: *Heimatbuch der Deutschen aus Rußland 1973–1981.* Pp. 9–19.

———. "The Emigration of National Minorities from the USSR in the Post-Stalin Era," in: *Soviet Jewish Affairs,* XIII, 1/1983. Pp. 3–36.

———. "National Identity and Emigration Patterns Among Soviet Jewry," in: *Soviet Jewish Affairs,* XV, 3/1985. Pp. 3–28.

———. *The Soviet Government and the Jews 1948–1967.* Cambridge, 1984.

Pipes, R. *The Formation of the Soviet Union. Communism and Nationalism 1917–1923.* 2nd edition, Cambridge, MA, 1957.

———. "'Solving' the Nationality Problem," in: *PC,* XVI, 5/1967. Pp. 125–131.

———. *Pohromv Ukraiini 1972–1979.* R. Kupchynskyi, 1980.

———. *Politische Kultur, Nationalitäten und Dissidenten in der Sowjetunion.* Brunner/ H. Herlemann (eds.). Berlin, 1982.

Poliakov, Iu. A./Chugunov, A. I. *Borba s basmachestvom v sredneaziatskikh respublikakh SSSR.* Moscow, 1983.

———. *Konets basmachestva.* Moscow, 1976.

Ponomarev, A. P. *Mezhnatsionalnye braki v USSR i protsess internatsionalizatsii.* Kiev, 1983.

Pospielovsky, D. "Einige Aspekte nationaler Spannungen in der UdSSR," in: *Osteuropa*, XXVII, 1977. Pp. 210-225.

_____. *Postroenie sotsializma v sovetskoi Pribaltike. Istoricheskii opyt kompartii Litvy, Latvii, Estonii*. A. D. Pedosov, et al. (eds.). Riga, 1982.

_____. *Presa Ukraiinkoii RSR 1918-1980. Statystychnyi dovidnyk*. Kharkov, 1981.

_____. *Problems of Mininations. Baltic Perspectives*. A. Ziednois, Jr., et al. (eds.). San Jose, CA, 1973.

Prokop, M. "Porushennia politychnykh i natsionalnykh prad v Ukraiini 1975-1980," in: *Suchasnist*, XX, 9/1980, pp. 90-106.

_____. "Ukraiinski samostiinytski politychni syly v drugii svitovii viini," in: *Suchasnist*, XXV, 10/1985, pp. 70-80.

Rabinovich, M. G./Shmelov, M. N. "Gorod i etnicheskie porotsessy," in: *Sovetskaia etnografiia*, 2/1984, pp. 3-14.

Radziejowski, J. *Kommunistyczna partia Zachodniej Ukrainy. 1919-1929*. Krakow, 1976. English: *The Communist Party of Western Ukraine. 1919-1929*. Edmonton, 1983.

Rakhmanny, R. *In Defense of the Ukrainian Cause*. North Quincy, MA, 1979.

Rakowska-Harmstone, T. "Die aktuelle Problematik sowjetischer Nationalitätenpolitik," in: *Osteuropa*, XXXV, 1985, pp. 488-505.

_____. "The Dialectics of Nationalism in the USSR," in: *PC*, XXIII, 3/1974, pp. 1-32.

_____. "The Dilemma of Nationalism in the Soviet Union," in: Strong, J. W. (ed.) *The Soviet Union Under Brezhnev and Kosygin*. New York, 1971, pp. 115-134.

_____. "Islam and Nationalism. Central Asia and Kazakhstan Under Soviet Rule," in: *Central Asian Survey*, II, 2/1983, pp. 7-88.

_____. "The Nationalities Question," in: Wesson, R. (ed.), *The Soviet Union. Looking to the 1980s*. Stanford, 1980, pp. 129-153.

_____. *Russia and Nationalism in Central Asia. The Case of Tadzhikistan*. Baltimore, 1970.

Rapaway, S./Baldwin, G. "Demographic Trends in the Soviet Union 1950-2000," in: *Soviet Economy in the 1980s. Problems and Prospects*. Vol. 2, Washington, D. C., 1983, pp. 265-296.

Rashidov, Sh. R "Leniniskaia natsionalnaia politika v deistvii," in: *VI KPSS*, 1/1959, pp. 41-60.

_____. *Sovetskii uzbekistan*. Moscow, 1978.

Rauch, G. v. *Geschichte der baltischen Staaten*. Stuttgart, 1970.

_____. *Razvitie natsionalnykh iazykov v sviazi s ikh funktsionirovaniem v svere vysshego obrazovaniia*. A. N. Baskakov, et al. (eds.), Moscow, 1982.

_____. *Rasvitie natsionalnykh otnoshenii v SSSR v svet reshenii XXVI sezda KPSS*. Iu. V. Bromlei, et al., Moscow, 1982.

Redzhepov, P. P./Chirkov, N. P. *V edinom stroiu narodov-bratev. rastsvet i sblizhenie natsii v usloviiakh razvitogo sotsialisticheskogo obshchestva.* Moscow, 1980.

_____. *Regional Development in the USSR. Trends and Prospects.* Newtonville, MA, 1979.

_____. *Religion and Nationalism in Soviet and East European Politics.* P. Ramet (ed.), Durham, 1984.

Remeikis, T. *Opposition to Soviet Rule in Lithuania 1945-1980.* Chicago, 1980.

_____. *Respubliki Srednei Azii v period razvitogo sotsializma.* A. N. Mikhailov (ed.), Moscow, 1980.

Révész, L. *Volk aus 100 Nationalitäten. Die sowjetische Minderheitenfrage.* Bern, 1979.

_____. *Revoliutsiia i natsionalnosti 1930-1937.*

Rigby, T. H. *Communist Party membership in the USSR 1917-1967.* Princeton, 1968.

Ritter, W. S. "The Final Phase in the Liquidation of Anti-Soviet Resistance in Tadzhikistan. Ibrahim Bek and the Basmachi. 1924-1931," in: *Soviet Studies,* XXXVII, 1985, pp. 484-493.

Rockett, R. L. *Ethnic Nationalities in the Soviet Union.* New York, 1981.

Rogachev, P./Sverdlin, M. "Sovetskii narod-novaia istoricheskaia obshchnost liudei," in: *Kommunist,* 9/1963, pp. 11-20.

Rohrbacher, H. *Materialien zur georgischen Bibliographie. Deutsches Schrifttum.* Bonn, 1981.

Rokkan, S. "Die vergleichende Analyse der Staaten- und Nationenbildung. Modelle und Methoden," in: Zapf, W. (ed.), *Theorien des sozialen Wandels.* Cologne, 1969, pp. 228-252.

Rothenberg, J. *The Jewish Religion in the Soviet Union.* New York, 1971.

Rowland, R. H. "Regional Migration and Ethnic Russian Population change in the USSR 1959-1979," in: *Soviet Ukraine,* XXIII, 1982, pp. 557-583.

Rudnytsky, I. L. "The Soviet Ukraine in Historical Perspective," in: *Canadian Slavonic Papers,* XIV, 2/1972, pp. 235-250.

_____. *Russkii iazyk. Ego rol v razvitii i ukreplenii sovetskogo obshchestva i mezhdunarodnogo sotrudnichestva. Referativnyi sbornik.* F. M. Berezin, et al. (eds.), Moscow, 1977.

_____. *Russkii iazyk-iazyk druzhby i sotrudnichestva narodov SSSR. Materialy Vsesoiuz. nauch.-teoret.-konferentsii 22-24 maia 1979 g.* F. G. Panachin, et al. (eds.), Moscow, 1981.

_____. *Russkii iazyk-iazyk mezhnatsionalnogo obshcheniia narodov SSSR. Materialy Vsesoiuz. nauch.-prakticheskoi konferentsii po sovershenstvovaniiu prepodavaniia russk. iazyka v nats. shkolakh 21-23 okt. 1975 g.* Tashkent, Moscow, 1976.

_____. *Russkii iazyk–iazyk mezhnatsionalnogo obshcheniia i edineniia narodov SSSR*. I. K. Beloded, et al. (eds.), Kiev, 1976.
_____. *Russkii iazyk kak sredstvo mezhnatsionalnogo obshcheniia*. F. B. Filin, et al. (eds.), Moscow, 1977.
_____. *Russkii iazyk v natsionalnykh respublikakh Sov. Soiuza*. V. V. Ivanov, et al. (eds.), Moscow, 1980.
Rutkevich, M. N. "Sblizhenie natsionalnykh respublik i natsii SSSR po sotsialno-klassovoi strukture," in: *Sotsilogicheskie issledovaniia*, 2/1981, pp. 14–24.
Ruziev, M. R. *Vozrozhdennyi uigurskii narod*. 2nd edition, Alma-Ata, 1982.
Rywkin, M. "The Impact of Socio-Economic Change and Demographic Growth on National Identity and Socialization," in: *Central Asian Survey*, III, 3/1984, pp. 79–98.
_____. *Moscow's Muslim Challenge. Soviet Central Asia*. London, 1982.
_____. "Power and Ethnicity. Regional and District Party Staffing in Uzbekistan (1983/84)," in: *Central Asian Survey*, IV, 1/1985, pp. 3–40.
_____. "Power and Ethnicity. Party Staffing in Uzbekistan (1941/46, 1957/58)," in: *Central Asian Survey*, IV, 1/1985, pp. 41–74.
Sabaliunas, L. *Lithuania in Crisis. Nationalism to Communism 1939–1940*. Bloomington, 1972.
Sadykov, M. B. *Edinstvo internatsionalnykh i natsionalnykh interesov v sovetskom mnogonatsionalnom gosudarstve*. Kazan, 1975.
Saidbaev, T. S. *Islam i obshchestvo. Opyt istoriko-sotsiologicheskogo issledovaniia*. Moscow, 1978.
Sanzhiev, G. L. *Perekhod narodov Sibiri k sotsializmu, minuia kapitalizm*. Novosibirsk, 1980.
Saran, S. M. *The Truth About Ukraine*. 1963.
Savchenko, V. I. *Latyshskie formirovaniia Sovetskoi Armii na frontakh Velikoi Otechestvennoi voiny*. Riga, 1975.
Sawyer, Th. E. *The Jewish Minority in the Soviet Union*. New York, 1979.
_____. *Sblizhenie sotsialno-klassovoi struktury sovetskikh natsii i narodnostei*. M. S. Dzhunusov, et al. (eds.), Moscow, 1977.
Schäfer, M. *Nationaltätenpolitik der KPdSU in Geschichte und Gegenwart*. East-Berlin, 1982.
Scharff, R. "60 Jahre Sowjetunion–60 Jahre Nationalitätenpolitik. Der Vielvölkerstaat in Spiegel ethnosoziologischer Studien," in: *Aktuelle Ostinformationen*, XV, 1983, volume 1/2, pp. 44–62.
Schnurr, J. "Aussiedler aus dem Sowjetischen Bereich," in: Arnold, W., (ed.), *Die Aussiedler in der Bundesrepublik Deutschland*. Vienna, 1980, pp. 57–102.
Seton-Watson, H. *Nationalism and Communism*. New York, 1964.
_____. *Nations and States. An Inquiring into the Origins of Nations and the Politics of Nationalism*. London, 1977.

Shafer, B. C. *Faces of Nationalism.* New York, 1972.
Shams-ud-din, *Secularization in the USSR. A Study of Soviet Cultural Policy in Uzbekistan.* New Delhi, 1982.
Shamsutdinov, R. T. "K voprosu ob osobennostiakh stanvleniia i razvitiia Sovetov Srednei Azii i Kazakhstana. 1917–1925," in: *Istoriia SSSR,* 5/1985, pp. 73–80.
Sharipov, I. *Zakonomernosti formirovaniia sotsialisticheskikh obshchestvennykh otnoshenii v Tadzhikistane.* Dushanbe, 1983.
Shcherbitskii, V. V. "Internationalnoe edinstvo i druzhba narodov SSSR– voploshchenie idei Vel. Oktiabria," in: *VI KPSS,* 11/1977, pp. 3–20.
Shelest, P. *Ukraiina Nasha Radianska.* Kiev, 1970.
Shermukhamedov, S. *Rastsveti sblizhenie natsionalnykh kultur narodov SSSR.* Moscow, 1974.
Sherstobitov, V. P. *Razvitie natsii i natsionalnykh otnoshenii v SSSR.* Frunze, 1984.
_____. *Shestdesiat let Sovetskoi Latvii.* P. M. Bondarev, et al. (eds.), Riga, 1979.
Sheehy, A. *The Crimean Tatars, Volga Germans, and Meskhetians. Soviet Treatment of Some National Minorities.* London, 2nd edition, 1973.
_____. "The National Languages and the New Constitutions of the Transcaucasian Republics," in: *RL,* 97/78, May 3, 1978.
_____. "Some Aspects of Regional Development in Soviet Central Asia," in: *Slavic Review,* XXXI, 1972, pp. 535–563.
Sheehy, a./Hahaylo, B. *The Crimean Tatars, Volga Germans, and Meskhetians. Soviet Treatment of Some National Minorities.* London, 3rd edition, 1980.
Shilde, A. *Die Sowjetisierung Lettlands.* Berichte des BIOst, 1/1967.
Shiriiazdanov, Sh. Kh. *Rabochii klass Kirgizstana v usloviiakh razvitogo sotsializma.* Frunze, 1979.
Shister, G. A. "Istochniki popolneniia rabochego klassa Uzbekistana na etape razvitogo sotsializma," in: *Istoriia SSSR,* 6/1981, pp. 26–40.
Shtromas, A. "Soviet Occupation of the Baltic States and Their Incorporation Into the USSR," in: *East European Quarterly,* XIX, 1985, pp. 289–304, 459–467.
Silnitskii, F. *Natsionalnaia politika KPSS v period s 1917 po 1922 god.* Munich, 1978, 2nd edition, 1981.
Silver, B. "Ethnic Intermarriage and Ethnic Consciousness Among Soviet Nationalities," in: *Soviet Studies,* XXX, 1978, pp. 107–116.
_____. "Levels of Sociocultural Development Among Soviet Nationalities. A Partial Test of the Equalization Hypothesis," in: *American Political Science Review,* 68, 1974, pp. 1618–1637.
_____. "Social Mobilization and the Russification of Soviet Nationalities," in: *American Political Science Review,* 68, 1974 pp. 45–66.

_____. "The Status of National Minority Languages in Soviet Education. An Assessment of Recent changes," in: *Soviet Studies*, XXVI, 1974, pp. 28–40.
Skrypnyk, M. *Statti i promovy z natsionalnogo pytannia*. Munich, 1974.
Slider, D. "A Note on the Class Structure of Soviet Nationalities," in: *Soviet Studies*, XXXVII, 1985, pp. 535–540.
Slobodian, M. I. *Proletarskii internatsionalizm–faktor sotsialnogo razvitiia. Na materialakh zapadnykh oblastei*. Kiev, 1981.
Smith, A. P. *Theories of Nationalism*. New York, 1971.
Snyder, L. L. *Varieties of Nationalism. A Comparative Study*. Hinsdale, 1976.
_____. *Sobranie dokumentov samizdata*. 30 volumes, Radio Liberty Committee, Munich,–1978.
_____. *Sobranie zakonov i rasporiazhenii raboche-krestianskogo pravitelstva*. Moscow, 1924–1937, 1938–1949, 1957–1958.
_____. *Sotsialisticheskie revoliutsii 1940 g. v Litve, Latvii i Estonii,Vosstanovlenie sovetskoi vlasti*. I. I. Mints, et al. (eds.), Moscow, 1978.
_____. *Sotsialisticheskoe stroitelstvo v Tadzhikistane*. K. P. Marsakov, et al. (eds.), Dushanbe, 1979.
_____. *Sotsialnaia politika i natsionalnye otnosheniia. Po materialam Vsesoiuz. nauch.-prak. konferentsii Razvitie nats. otnoshenii v usloviiakh zrelogo sotsializma. Riga 28–30 iunia 1982 g.* P. I. Kosolapov, et al. (eds.), Moscow, 1982.
_____. *Sotsialnoe i natsionalnoe. Opyt etnosotsiologicheskikh issledovanii po materialam Tatarskoi ASSR*. Iu. V. Arutiunian, et al. (eds.), Moscow, 1973.
_____. *Sociolinguistic Perspectives on Soviet National Languages. Their Past, Present, and Future*. I. T. Kreindler (ed.), Berlin, 1985.
Soktoev, Iu. *Formirovanie i razvitie sovetskoi intelligentsii Kirgizstana*. Frunze, 1981.
Soldatov, S. "Estonskii uzel. Razmyshleniia o natsionalnoi sudbe i mezhnatsionalnykh othosheniiakh," in: *Kontinent*, 32, 1982, pp. 223–239.
_____. *Zarnitsy vozrozhdeniia*. London, 1984.
_____. *Sotrudnichestvo narodov SSSR v kulturnom stroitesltve*. A. N. Vinogradov, et al. (eds.), Moscow, 1973.
_____. *Sovetskii narod–novaia istoricheskaia obshchnost liudei. Stanovlenie i razvitie*. V. P. Sherstobitov, et al. (eds.), Moscow, 1975.
_____. *Sovetskii narod–stroitel kommunizma*. C. A. Stepanian (ed.), Moscow, 1981.
_____. *Soviet Asian Ethnic Frontiers*. W. O. McCagg Jr./B. D. Silver (eds.), New York, 1979.
_____. *The Soviet Economy in Regional Perspective*. V. N. Bandera/Z. L. Melnyk (eds.), New York, 1973.

Bibliography

———. *Soviet Jewry in the Decisive Decade, 1971–1980.* R. O. Freedman (ed.), Durham, 1984.

———. *Soviet Nationalities in Strategic Perspective.* S. E. Wimbush (ed.), London, 1985.

———. *Soviet Nationality Policies and Practices.* J. R. Azrael (ed.), New York, 1978.

———. *Soviet Nationality Problems.* E. Allworth (ed.), New York, 1971.

———. *Soviet Population Policy. Conflicts and Constraints.* H. Desfosses (ed.), New York, 1981.

———. *The Soviet State. The Domestic Roots of Soviet Foreign Policy.* C. Keeble (ed.), London, 1985.

———. *The Soviet West. Interplay Between Nationality and Social Organization.* R. C. Clem (ed.), New York, 1975.

———. *Sovremennye etnicheskie protsessy v SSSR.* Iu. V. Bromlei, et al. (eds.), 2nd edition, Moscow, 1977.

———. *Sovremennyi byt i etnokulturnye protsessy v Buriatii.* P. T. Khaptaev (ed.), Novosibirsk, 1984.

———. *Die sowjetische Bildungspolitik seit 1917. Dokumente und Texte.* O. Anweiler/K. Meyer (eds.), Heidelberg, 1961.

———. *Die sowjetische Bildungspolitik von 1958–1973. Dokumente und Texte.* O. Anweiler/I. Kuebart/K. Meyer (eds.), Heidelberg, 1976.

Solkhanyk, R. "The Comintern and the Communist Party of Western Ukraine 1919–1928," in: *Canadian Slavonic Papers,* XXIII, 1981, pp. 181–197.

———. "Russian Language and Soviet Politics," in: *Soviet Studies,* XXXIV, 1982, pp. 23–42.

Spechler, M. C. *Regional Trends in the USSR 1958–1978.* Research Paper No. 33, Hebrew University of Jerusalem. Soviet and East European Research Center, April 1979.

Spiliuk, V. A. *Mezhrespublikanskaia migrtsiia i sblizhenie natsii v SSSR.* Lvov, 1975.

Stalin, J. W. *Werke.* 13 volumes, East-Berlin, 1950–1955.

———. *Sochineniia.* 2 volumes, Stanford, 1967.

———. *Stalinism. Essays in Historical Interpretation.* R. C. Tucker (ed.), New York, 1977.

———. "Stanovlenie i razvitie novoi istoricheskoi obshchnosti–sovetskogo naroda. Kruglyi stol 'Istoriia SSSR'," in: *Istoriia SSSR,* 6/1980, pp. 23–83.

———. *Stanovlenie sovetskogo naroda i razvitie sotsialisticheskikh natsii.* V .E. Evdokimov, et al. (eds.), Kiev, 1978.

Steiman, I. A. *Politicheskaia aktivnost mass. Revoliutsionnye preobrazovaniia v Latvii letom 1940 g.* Riga, 1979.

Stökl, G. "Die Entstehung der Sowjetunion und die nationale Frage," in: Schieder, Th./Alter, P., *Staatsgründungen und Nationalitätenprinzip*. Munich, 1974, pp. 73–83.
Strobel, G. W. "Ethnie-Nationalität und der Führungsanspruch der Sowjetunion," in: *Deutsche Studien*, 65, 1979, pp. 21–37.
Stumpp, K. *Das Schrifttum über das Deutschtum in Rußland. Eine Bibliographie*. 5th edition, Tübingen, 1980.
Sullivant, R. S. *Soviet Politics and the Ukraine 1917–1957*. New York, 1962.
Sulzhenko, V. K. *Internatsionalizm na etape razvitogo sotsializma. Osushchestvlenie leninskoi natsionalnoi politiki KPSS na Ukraine*. Lvov, 1981.
Suny, R. G. *Armenia in the 20th Century*. Chico, 1983.
_____. *Soviet Georgia in the Seventies*. Kennan Institute, Occasional Paper No. 64, Washington, 1979.
Sverdlov, F. D. "Boevoi put Litovskoi divisii v gody Velikoi Otechestvennoi voiny," in: *Istoriia SSSR*, 6/1984, pp. 30–39.
Sverstiuk, I. *Clandestine Essays*. Cambridge, 1976.
Swietlytschnyj, I./Swerstjuk, J./Stus, W. *Angst–ich bin Dich losgeworden! Ukrainische Gedichte aus der Verbannung*. Translated by A.-H. Horbatsch, Hamburg, 1983.
Szporluk, R. "History and Russian Nationalism," in: *Survey*, XXIV, 3/1979, pp. 1–17.
_____. "Nationalities and the Russian Problem in the USSR. A Historical Outline," in: *Journal of International Affairs*, XXVII, 1973, pp. 22–40.
_____. "West Ukraine and West Belorussia. Historical Tradition, Social Communication, and Linguistic Assimilation," in: *Soviet Studies*, XXXII, 1980, pp. 379–397.
Tadesvosian, E. V. *Sovetskaia natsionalnaia gosudarstvennost*. Moscow, 1972.
Tastanov, Sh. Iu. *Kazakhskaia sovetskaia intelligentsiia*. Alma-Ata, 1982.
Tavadov, G. T. "K kharakteristike sovremennogo etapa natsionalnykh otnoshenii v SSSR," in: *Nauchnyi kommunizm*, 5/1984, pp. 33–46.
Telepko, L. N. *Urovni ekonomicheskogo razvitiia raionov SSSR*. Moscow, 1971.
Ten, V. *Rukovodstvo KPSS protsessom sblizheniia natsii v usloviiakh razvitogo sotsializma 1959–1975 gg. Na materialakh respublik Srednei Azii*. Tashkent, 1981.
_____. *Teoriia i praktika razvitiia sotsialisticheskikh natsii*. T. Iu. Burmistrova (ed.), Leningrad, 1984.
Terenteva, L. "Opredelenie svoei natsionalnoi prinadlezhnosti podrostkami v natsionalno-smeshannykh semiakh," in: *Sovetskaia etnografiia*, 3/1969, pp. 20–30.
Tillett, L. *The Great Friendship. Soviet Historians and the Non-Russian Nationalities*. Chapel Hill, 1969.

Timofeev, P. T. *Formirovanie natsionalnykh kadrov rabochego klassa SSSR.* Moscow, 1982.

Titov, A. G. *Borba partii za leninskuiu chistotu natsionalnoi politiki v period stroitelstva sotsializma v SSSR.* Moscow, 1978.

―――. *Torzhestvo leninskikh idei proletarskogo internatsionalizma. Na materialakh Srednei Azii i Kazakhstana 1917-1972 gg.* M. P. Kim (ed.), Moscow, 1974.

―――. *Torzhestvo leninskoi natsionalnoi politiki KPSS.* A. N. Nusupbekov (ed.), Alma-Ata, 1973.

―――. *Transcaucasia. Nationalism and Social Change. Essays in the History of Armenia, Azerbajdjan, and Georgia.* R. G. Suny (ed.). Ann Arbor, MI, 1983.

Trapeznikov, G. E. *Rastsvet i vzaimovliianie natsionalnykh kultur respublik Srednei Azii 1959-1972 gg.* Frunze, 1975.

Tsamerian, I. P. *Natsii i natsionalnye otnosheniia v razvitom sotsialisticheskom obshchestve.* Moscow, 1979.

Tucker, R. C. *Stalin as Revolutionary 1879-1929. A Study in History and Personality.* New York, 1973.

Tulebaev, B. A. *Sotsialisticheskie agramye preobrazovaniia v Srednei Azii i Kazakhstane.* Moscow, 1984.

Tys-Krokhmaliuk, Y. *UPA Warfare in Ukraine.* New York, 1972.

Ubushaev, V. B. "Izuchenie deiatelnosti sovetov natsionalnykh raionov Povolzhia v period postroeniia sotsializma," in: *VI,* 10/1985, pp. 116–125.

Uibopuu, H. J. "Die Verfassungen der Unionsrepubliken der UdSSR." in: *Osteuropa,* XXIX, 1979, pp. 789–810.

―――. *Die Völkerrechtssubjektivität der Unionsrepubliken der UdSSR.* Vienna, 1975.

―――. *Ukraine After Shelest.* B. Krawchenko (ed.). Edmonton, Alberta, 1983.

―――. *Ukraine in the Seventies.* P. Potichnyj (ed.). Oakville, Ont., 1975.

―――. *The Ukraine Within the USSR. An Economic Balance Sheet.* I. S. Koropeckyj (ed.). New York, 1977.

―――. *Ukrainians in World War II. Views and Points. Symposium.* in: *Nationalities Papers,* X, 1982, pp. 1–39.

―――. *Ukraiinska Helsikska Hrupa 1978-1982. Dokumenty i materialy.* O. Zinkevich (ed.), Toronto, 1983.

―――. *Ukraiinskyi pravozakhysnyi rukh. Dokumenty i materialy Kyiivskoii Ukraiinskoii Hrupy.* O. Zinkevich (ed.), Toronto, 1978.

Ulam, A. B. *Stalin. The Man and His Era.* New York, 1973.

―――. *Uncensored Russia. The Human Rights Movement in the Soviet Union. The Annotated Text of the Unofficial Moscow Journal: A Chronicle of Current Events.* (No. 1–11). P. Reddaway (ed.). London, 1972.

_____. "U piatdesiattylittia smerty M. Hrushevskoho," in: *Ukraiinskyi istorik,* XXI, 1984.
Upton, A. F. *Finland 1939–1940.* London, 1974.
Urlanis, B. C. *Problemy dinamiki naseleniia SSSR.* Moscow, 1974.
Usmankhodzhaev, I. b. "Leninskaia natsionalnaia politika KPSS i dalneishee razvitie natsionalnykh otnoshenii v usloviiakh zrelogo sotsializma," in: *Voprosy filosofii,* 9/1984, pp. 3–15.
_____. *The USSR and the Muslim World.* Y. Ro'i (ed.). London, 1984.
Usubaliev, T. V. *Leninizm–velikii istochnik druzhby i bratstva narodov.* 2nd edition, Moscow, 1974.
_____. *V druzhnoi seme ravnopravnykh narodov. Dokumenty, materialy.* N. M. Kulagina, et al. (eds.), Petrozavodsk, 1982.
Vagabov, M. V. *Leninskaia natsionalnaia politika KPSS v mnogonatsionalnom Dagestane.* Moscow, 1982.
Vakar, N. P. *Belorussia. The Making of a Nation.* Cambridge, MA, 1956.
Vakhabov, M. G. *Formirovanie uzbekskoi sotsialisticheskoi natsii.* Tashkent, 1961.
Valiev, A. K. *Formirovanie i razvitie sovetskoi natsionalnoi intelligentsii v Srednei Azii.* Tashkent, 1966.
_____. *Sovetskaia natsionalnaia intelligentsiia i ee sotsialnaia rol.* Tashkent, 1969.
Vardys, V. S. *The Catholic Church, Dissent and Nationality in Soviet Lithuania.* New York, 1978.
_____. "Lithuania's Catholic Movement Reappraised." in: *Survey,* XXV, 3/1980, pp. 49–73.
_____. "The Nature and Philosophy of Baltic Dissent. A Comparative Perspective." in: *Nationalities Papers,* X, 1982, pp. 121–136.
_____. "Polish Echoes in the Baltic." in *PC,* XXXII, 4/1983, pp. 21–34.
Veliev, T. S. *Vyravnivanie urovnei ekonomicheskogo razvitiia sovetskikh respublik.* Moscow, 1973.
_____. *Velikaia sila internatsionalnogo edinstva. Deiatelnost KPSS po dalneishemu ukrepleniiu internatsionalnogo edinstva i razvitiiu sotrudnichestva narodov SSSR.* L. A. Nagornaia, et al. (ed.), Kiev, 1979.
_____. *Velikii sovetskii narod.* A. I. Shinkaruk/A. G. Shevelev (eds.), Kiev, 1976.
_____. *Velikoe sodruzhestvo narodov-bratev. K 60-letiiu obrazovaniia SSSR.* Iu. Iu. Kondufor, et al. (ed.), Kiev, 1982.
Volkova, Iu. E./Romanovskii, N. V. "Bankrotstvo kontseptsii burzhuaznoi istoriografii o natsionalnykh otnosheniiakh v SSSR," in: *VI,* 12/1982, pp. 34–48.
Vorobev, Iu. V. *Vyravnivanie urovnei ekonomicheskogo razvitiia soiuznykh respublikh.* Moscow, 1965.

Bibliography

_____. *Vospityvat ubezhdennykh patriotov-internatsionalistov. Po materialam Vsesoiuz. nauts.-prakt. konferentsii Razvitie nats. otnoshenii v usloviiakh zrelogo sotsializma. Riga 28-30 iiunia 1982 g.* E. M. Tiazhelnikov (ed.), Moscow, 1982.

_____. *Vsesoiuznaia perepis naseleniia 17 dekabria 1926 g., Vol. IV, Narodnost i rodnoi iazyk naseleniia SSSR.* Moscow, 1928.

_____. *Vysshee obrazovanie v SSSR. Statisticheskii sbornik.* Moscow, 1961.

Wagener, H. -J. *Wirtschaftswachstum in unterentwickelten Gebeiten. Ansätze zu einer Regionalanalyse der Sowjetunion.* Berlin, 1972.

Waskowycz, H. "Das Bildungswesen in der Ukraine im ersten Jahrzehnt unter bolschewistischer Herrschaft." in: *Jahrbuch der Ukrainekunde,* 1983, pp. 178–188.

Werth, A. *Rußland im Krieg 1941-1945.* Munich, 1965.

Wexler, P. N. *Purism and Language. A Study in Modern Ukrainian and Belorussian Nationalism.* Bloomington, Indiana, 1974.

Wheeler, G. *The Modern History of Soviet Central Asia.* London, 1964.

Widmer, M. J. "Nationalism and Communism in Latvia. The Latvian Communist Party Under Soviet Rule." Ph.D. Harvard University, 1969.

Wimbush, S. E. "The Politics of Identity Change in Soviet Central Asia." in: *Central Asian Survey,* III, 3/1984, pp. 69–78.

Wimbush, S. E./Alexiev, A. *The Ethnic Factor in the Soviet Armed Forces.* Rand Corporation. Santa Monica, CA, 1982.

_____. "Soviet Central Asian Soldiers in Afghanistan." in: *Conflict,* IV, 1983, pp. 325–338.

Wixman, R. "Ethnic Nationalism in the Caucasus." in: *Nationalities Papers,* X, 1982, pp. 137–156.

_____. "Ethno-linguistic Data in Soviet Censuses." in: *Canadian-American Slavic Studies,* XVII, 1983, pp. 545–558.

_____. *The Peoples of the USSR. An Ethnographic Handbook.* London, 1984.

Yanov, A. *The Russian New Right.* Berkeley, CA, 1978.

_____. *Zakonomernosti formirovaniia sovetskogo naroda kak novoi istoricheskoi obshchnosti liudei. Materialy Vsesoiuz. nautsnoi konferentsii posviashch. 50-letiiu obrazovaniia SSSR 12-14 dekbr. 1972 g.* 2 volumes, Moscow, 1975.

_____. *Zakonomernosti internatsionalizatsii obshchestvennoi zhizni.* M. M. Suzhikov (ed.), Alma-Ata, 1981.

Zarins, A. "Dissent in the Baltic Republics. A Survey of Grievances and Hopes." in: *RL,* 496/76, December 14, 1976.

Zaslavsky, V. *The Neo-Stalinist State. Class, Ethnicity, and Consensus in Soviet Society.* New York, 1982.

Zaslavsky, V./Brym, R. J. *Soviet-Jewish Emigration and Soviet Nationality Policy.* London, 1983.

Zemtsov, I. "Andropov and the Non-Russian Nationalities." in: *Nationalities Papers,* XIII, 1/1985, pp. 5–23.
Zevelev, A. I./Poliakov, Iu. A./Chugunov, A. I. *Basmachestvo. Vozniknovenie, sushchnost, krakh.* Moscow, 1981.
Zezina, M. R. *Sovetskaia intelligentsiia v usloviiakh razvitogo sotsializma.* Moscow, 1982.
Zibaev, V. A. "Leninskaia natsionalnaia politika KPSS i malye narody Severa," in: *Istoriia SSSR,* 3/1981, pp. 44–59.
Zimanov, S. Z./Reitor, I. K. *Sovetskaia natsionalnaia gosudarstvennost i sblizhenie natsii.* Alma-Ata, 1983.
_____. *Zupynit kryvosuddia! Sprava Levka Lukianenka.* S. Sadovskyi (ed.), 1980.

Index

Abashidze, I.V.: quote of, 247
Abyzbaev, Commissar, 161
Academics, number of, 270, 409–412
Afghanistan, protest over, 343
Agriculture, mechanization of, 115, 119
Ainikeit (Jewish Antifascist Committee), founding of, 208
Aitmatov, Chingiz: novel by, 290
Alash-orda (autonomy movement), 81
  purge of, 87
al-Biruni, Abu Reikhan, 281
Alliance of Ukrainian Workers and Peasants, work of, 343–344
All-Ukrainian Conference of Tatar Union Functionaries, 122
All-Union Central Committee for the New Alphabet of the CEC of the USSR, 44
All-Union Central Trade Union Council, 178
All-Union Committee for Advanced Technical Training, establishment of, 146
All-Union Committee for Institutions of Higher Learning, work of, 146
All-Union Ministry for Coal Mining, Ukraine and, 284
All-Union Ministry for Inland Navigation, dissolution of, 234
All-Union Ministry of Coal Mining, dissolution of, 233
Alma mater (magazine), 340
Alpamysh (Uzbek epic), criticism of, 206
Alphabets
  Arabic, 44
  changing, 154, 178
  Cyrillic, 45, 153–154, 178
  Latin, 44–45, 153–154, 170(n81), 178
Andropov, Yuri
  merger of nations and, 312
  quote of, 7, 278
Annexation, 174–177, 180, 216
  chronology of, 219(n12)
  Stalin and, 173–174
Anti-Party group, eliminating, 240–241
Anti-Semitism, 34, 122, 225(n138), 280
  Soviet, 207–209, 338
  traditional, 338
  See also Jews; Zionism
Architect, The (Mirmukhsin), 289
Armed forces. *See* Red Army
Armenia, 2, 27, 147
  birth rate in, 291
  collectivization of, 95
  history of, 205–206, 281
  intelligentsia, 130
  Karabakh and, 346–347
  korenizatsiia in, 36
  migration to, 293
  nationalization in, 229

protest in, 332, 334, 346–347
purge in, 160
Armenian Academy of Sciences, criticism of, 206
Armenian question, aspects of, 346–347
Armenians, 5
  collaboration by, 197–198
  communist, 30, 34, 36
  education for, 56, 58
  migration of, 334, 339
  recruiting, 189
  skilled, 126
  social structure of, 128, 129
  Turks and, 280
  urbanization of, 125, 295
Armenian Union of Writers, criticism of, 206
Artels, 98
Artemev, A.P., 186
Arutiunian, Iu.V.: quote of, 279
Assimilation, 3, 44, 61, 122, 130, 215, 255, 293–294, 307, 314, 317, 337, 338
  birth rates and, 317–318
  growth rates and, 319
  language policy and, 315–333
  national, 138, 315, 317, 320, 321, 322
  prerequisites for, 318–319
  Stalin and, 150
  See also Consolidation; Nation-building; Russification
Association of Germans in the USSR Willing to Emigrate, 337
Aushra (Dawn), 333, 340, 341
Aushrele (Little Dawn), 340
Autonomous Regions (*oblasti*), 14, 38, 147
  Council of Nationalities and, 237
  purge in, 159
  Russian language in, 40–41
Autonomous Republics, xiii, 4, 14, 147
  Council of Nationalities and, 237
  decentralization and, 236
  migration and, 120
  national composition of, 376–387, 388–389
  national military units from, 185
  occupation of, 173
  purge in, 160
  Russians in, 120, 124–125, 165
  schools in, 51, 52
Autonomous Territories (*okrugi*), 14
Autonomy, 3–4, 13
  cultural, xv, 5, 8, 43, 282, 283
  demands for, 80
  growth of, 131
  linguistic, 43
  opposition to, 85, 117
  reestablishment of, 242
Avars, relocation of, 243
Azerbaidzhan, 147, 349
  Armenian question and, 346–347
  collectivization of, 95
  income in, 303
  migration to, 293
  purges in, 252
  social structure of, 129
  spending for, 305
  standard of living in, 300
Azeri, 25
  collaboration by, 198
  education for, 268
  urbanization of, 295
Az i ia (Suleimenov), criticism of, 289–290

Babaev, S., 251–252
"Back to Lenin!" principle, 246
Bagirov, A.A., 206
Bahazii, Mayor, 193
Bakhradze, A., 332
Balickii, A.: purge of, 83

Index

Balkars
  collaboration by, 197
  deportation of, 201, 202
  forced settlement of, 241
  rehabilitation of, 241, 242, 243
Baltic Federation, 342
Baltic states. *See* Estonia; Latvia; Lithuania
Bandera (partisan), collaboration by, 192
Bashkir language, 43–44, 73
Bashkir Regional Committee, 73
Bashkirs, 20, 115, 123
  assimilation of, 44, 319
  education for, 268
  migration of, 293
Basmachi. *See* Islamic guerrillas
Batal Haji group, 349
Batyrev, quote of, 313
Bazhan, M., 247
Bednyi, Demian, 149
Bek, Ibragim, 106
Belorussia, 20, 25, 27
  collaboration in, 195–196
  development in, 116, 298
  education in, 49, 171, 268, 296, 325
  income in, 303
  korenizatsiia in, 36
  leadership cadres in, 210
  migration to, 293
  partisans in, 186
  productivity in, 299, 300
  Russification of, 120, 321, 327–328
  skilled workers in, 127
  Sovietization of, 176, 181
  standard of living in, 300
  See also Western Belorussia
Belorussian Independence Party, 196
Belorussian language
  education in, 49, 325
  introduction of, 43
Belorussian People's Front, 196
Belorussians, 2, 59, 175, 131
  assimilation of, 318
  communist, 30, 34
  deportation of, 179
  migration of, 211
  recruiting, 189
  social structure of, 129–130
  urbanization of, 295
Beloruthenian Central Council (BCR), 196
Beloruthenian Defensive Corps (BKA), 196
Berdnyk, O., 346
Bergelson, David, 208
Beriia, L., 159, 160, 165, 228
  quote of, 158
  fall of, 229–231
Berklavs, Chairman, 247, 248, 252
Bessarabia, 219(n17)
  illiteracy in, 179
  land reform in, 178
  reintegration of, 174–175
  Sovietization of, 177–178, 181
Bilingualism, 324, 333
  demand for, 308
Birobidzhan (Jewish Autonomous Region)
  establishment of, 61, 147
  purge in, 159
  See also Jews
Birobidzhaner Shtern, 208
Birth control, 295, 296
Birth rates, 305
  assimilation and, 317–318
  changes in, 291, 292, 356(n88), 357(n102)
  rural and urban, 296
  Russian, 294
Blossoming, 307, 308–309, 312
Blue-collar workers, 273
  number of, 236, 393

Bodiul, I.I, 253, 254
Books, 45–46
  native-language, 330, 335
  Russian-language, 329
  Ukrainian-language, 47, 330
Borders, marking, 211
Boriev, Commissar, 81
Bourgeois nationalism, 2, 84, 136, 205, 206, 214, 244, 253, 287, 310, 311
  condemnation of, 87–88, 104, 204, 230
  See also Nationalism
Brezhnev, Leonid, 163, 295, 308, 313, 332, 357(n102), 358(n110)
  centralization and, 258
  economic councils and, 257
  Lithuania and, 340
  nationalities policy and, 342
  non-Russians and, 278
  re-Russification and, 274
  Ukraine and, 232
Building socialism, 161, 162
Bukharin, 24, 155
  trial of, 164
Bulashov, Chairman, 160
Bumeisters, I., 342
Buriat language, 40
Burun-ogli, Garaia: self-criticism by, 88
Buryat-Mongolia
  collectivization of, 98
  purge in, 160
  Sovietization of, 104
Buryats, 206
  forced settlement of, 107
Bykin, Secretary, 161

Cadres, 210
  local, 229–230
  rotation of, 254
  Russian, 2, 6, 181
Candidate members, non-Russian, 231
Capital investment, 116, 284, 298, 299
Capitalism, competing with, 114
Carpathian Ukraine
  reunification with, 174, 210
  See also Ukraine
Carrère d'Encausse, Henri, 11
Cathedral, The (Hochar), 286
Catholic Church, protest by, 339–340
Catholicism, 11, 280
Central Asia, 23, 40
  birth rate in, 291
  collectivization of, 98
  unemployment in, 294
Central Asian Bureau, 143
Central Asian Combine for Irrigation Engineers and Technicians, 84
Central Asian Economic Council, 143, 256
Central Asian State University, non-Russians at, 55–56
Central Committee
  national composition of, 418–419
  Russians on, 230–231
  Ukrainians on, 231, 232
Centralization, 71, 138–148, 256, 257
  direction of, 115
  self-determination and, 20
  See also Decentralization
Chauvinism, xvii, 24, 27, 84–85, 153, 315
  denunciation of, 73, 75–77
  Great Russian, 72–75, 84, 118, 137, 158, 207, 230, 255
  linguistic, 248–249, 324–325, 333
  local, 240
  national, 12
  Stalin and, 84, 207
  Turkic, 290

Index

Checheno-Ingushetia, rebellion in, 96
Chechens, 10, 349
  collaboration by, 203
  deportation of, 201, 202, 203
  education for, 268
  rehabilitation of, 241–244
  resistance by, 348
Chervonenko, S.V., 247
Chobanov, M., 335
Chornovil, V., 344, 345
Christian-Democratic Association of Latvia, 342
Chronicle of the Lithuanian Catholic Church, 340
Chuvash, 27
  assimilation of, 319
  education for, 268
Chuvash Communist Party, 40
Chuvash language, 40, 75
Civil rights movement, 339–342, 344, 346, 347
Clan loyalty, relaxation of, 98
Collaboration, 190–203, 214
  deportation for, 201–203
  extent of, 191, 222(n68)
  rehabilitation and, 245
  retaliation for, 173
Collectivization, 9, 10, 31, 131, 149, 176, 216–217, 288
  clan-affiliated, 98
  famine and, 99
  impact of, 3, 97–99, 109, 118–119, 290
  nation-building and, 97, 109
  nationalities policy and, 93–99, 103–104
  productivity and, 105
  resistance to, 85, 95–96, 99, 161
  Stalin and, 3, 93, 109(n1)
Colleges
  native languages at, 57
  non-Russians at, 54–56, 58
  quotas for, 55
  See also Universities
College students
  national composition of, 406–408, 409–412
  non-Russian, 266, 269–270
  Russian, 269–270
  Ukrainian, 231, 270, 283–284
Colonialization
  fear of, 77
  Stalin and, 1–2
  See also Decolonialization
Commissariats, creation of, 144
Commission for Working Among National Minorities, 61
Committee for Rural Settlement of Working Jews, 61
Committee for the Liberation of Russia's Peoples, 194
Committee of the National Movements of Estonia, Latvia, Lithuania, 342
Communist Party
  Jews in, 34–35
  korenizatsiia of, 32–33
  leadership of, xv, 311
  lost legitimacy of, xvi
  nation-building and, 71–72
  nationalities policy and, 11, 141
  non-Russians in, 30, 31, 34–36, 275
  Russians in, 30, 34, 272
  See also various ethnic communist parties
Communist society, building, 311–312
Compulsory settlement. *See* Forced settlement
Concerning Additional Measures to Improve the Study of Russian in General Schools and Other Educational Facilities in the Union Republics, 327

Concerning Some Issues in the Latvian SSR's Educational System, 248
Concerning the Status of Education in the Georgian Language and Literature at the Republic's Educational Facilities and Measures of Improving It, 332
Consolidation, 23, 315–317
 See also Assimilation; Nation-building
Cossacks, collaboration by, 197
Cotton, forced production of, 104–106
Council of *aksakals,* 288
Council of Deputies, national makeup of, 36
Council of Ministers, 275, 325, 327, 332
 decentralization and, 234, 236
 economic councils and, 238–239, 257
 State Plan and, 235–236
 theses of, 246
Council of Nationalities, 59, 141, 147
 delegates to, 140
 non-Russians in, 36
 Presidium of, 148
 role of, 148, 237
Council of People's Commissars, 144, 146, 153
 nationalities policy and, 74
 Ukrainian, 163, 169(n68)
Council of the People's Commissariat for Education, resolution of, 50
Crimean Tatarian language, teaching in, 245
Crimean Tatars, 40, 121, 335, 347, 365(n232)
 deportation of, 241
 execution of, 79
 rehabilitation of, 242, 244–245, 335–336
 See also Tatars
Criminal law, decentralization of, 237
Culture, xv, 5, 8, 43
 defense of, 182
 destruction of, 205–208, 344
 national consciousness and, 252, 282–283
 Russian, 205, 207–208
 Ukrainian, 30, 285
Curzon Line, 211, 212

Dadenkov, Iu.M.: proposals of, 285–286
Daghestanis, 21
 collaboration by, 197
Dampilov, Chairman, 160
Daniel, Iu., 344
Dargins, relocation of, 243
Dashnaks, purge of, 87
Decentralization, 6, 234–235, 238
 Council of Ministers and, 236
 Khrushchev and, 235–237, 239–240, 245, 256, 258
 promotion of, 233–234
 See also Centralization
Decolonialization, 1, 265
 process of, 5
 See also Colonialization
Dede-Korkut (Azeri epic), criticism of, 206
Dekulakization, 95, 155
 See also Kulaks
Democracy-building, xvii
Democratic Youth Committee of Latvia, 342
Department for Organization and Party Work, 276

Index

Deportation, 31, 176, 179–180, 190–203, 208–209, 212, 216, 217, 318, 334, 336, 348
  rehabilitation and, 241–242, 244–245
  resisting, 202
De-Russification, 6, 30, 51, 78, 85, 323
  See also Russification
Desheriev, Iu.D.: quote of, 324
De-Stalinization, 9–10, 16, 233–245
  Khrushchev and, 240–241
  See also Stalinism
Deutsch, Karl: on nationalism, 7
Dictionaries, compilation of, 44
Dievas ir tevyne (*God and Homeland*), 340
Dimanshtein, Ia.V., 117
Dimanshtein, S.M., 118, 138
Discrimination, 84–85, 270, 278, 294
  determining, 351(n4)
  fighting, 76–77
Disintegration, 1
  causes of, xiv, xvi–xvii
  linguistic, 323
  preventing, 2
Dissidents, Ukrainian, 345
"Dizzy with Success" (Stalin), impact of, 96, 98
Dnipro (*Dnieper*), criticism of, 204
Doctors' plot, Jews and, 209
Doctors
  nationality of, 127–128
  relocation of, 126
Dodkhudoev, N., 254
Drawing-together, 255–256
  description of, 137–138
Dzerve, P., 253
Dzerzhinskii, F., 72
Dzhandildin, Secretary, 246
  quote of, 249
Dzhaparidze, Revaz, 331
Dzhemilev, Mustafa, 335

Dzhemilev, Reshat, 335
Dzhidigian (Great Bear), 80
Dziuba, Ivan, 286–287, 344, 345
  attacks on, 287

Economic administration, decentralization of, 234–235, 238–240, 256
Economic Council of the USSR, 256
Economic councils
  dissolution of, 257
  establishing, 143–144
  supervision of, 256
Economic development
  balancing, 297–298
  factors in, 114–115, 297
Education, 4–5, 8, 296
  compulsory, 57
  higher, 266, 268–271, 284
  korenizatsiia and, 269
  language issue and, 269, 271–272
  middle school, 51–52, 266, 271
  non-Russian, 68(n122), 265–266, 305
  quota system of, 54–55
  reform in, 246–248
  Russification of, 325–329
  school policy and, 48–58
  self-consciousness and, 279
  spending for, 305, 306
  Stalin and, 146, 151, 152
  supervision of, 257
  vocational, 56–57, 127–128, 266, 272
Education law, 247–249
Eiche, Secretary: purge of, 159
Eighteenth Party Congress, Stalin and, 165
Eizenshtein, Sergei, 204
Elementary schools
  development of, 57
  korenizatsiia of, 67(n100)
  language in, 50, 53–54

See also Schools
Elites, elimination of, 3
Emigration, 294, 334, 336–339
  See also Migration

Emigration permits, issuing, 339
Empire
  dismantling of, xvi–xvii, 1
  preservation of, 9
"Enough Russification in Lithuania," 333
Epics. *See* Islamic epics
Erbanov, M.N., 160
Erenburg, Ilia, 208
  quote of, 182
Estonia, xiii, 317
  annexation of, 175
  birth rate in, 291
  education in, 267, 268, 296
  income in, 302, 303
  industrialization of, 217–218
  intelligentsia of, 130
  migration to, 218, 293
  nationalization in, 229
  occupation of, 194–195
  population shift in, 292
  productivity in, 299, 300
  reintegration of, 174
  resistance in, 331–333, 339, 341
  Sovietization of, 176, 179, 181, 215–218
  spending in, 306
  standard of living in, 300
Estonian Democratic Movement, 341, 342
Estonian National Front, 341, 342
Estonians
  collectivization of, 217
  deportation of, 216, 217
  social structure of, 129
Ethnological issues, xvii, 10
Ethnonyms, official, 316
Evacuation treaties, 211–212

Ezhov, N.I., 156, 163, 165
Ezhovshchina, 156

Factory combines, establishment of, 144
Famine, 94–95, 99–104, 107, 131, 149, 155, 205, 318
  collectivization and, 99
  deaths from, 100
  Stalin and, 101
Federalism, 78
  development of, 146–147
  Soviet, xiv, 4, 22, 139, 190, 233, 270, 313, 330
Feffer, Itsik, 208
Fifteenth Party Congress, 114, 117
Fifth Comintern Congress, 175
Finland, 1
  relations with, 175, 176
  resistance from, 174
Finnish language, 59–60
Finns, 59
  collectivization of, 60
  deportation of, 199
Firdousi, 281
First Congress of the People's Committees of the Carpathian Ukraine, 210
First Five-Year Plan, 114, 115, 128, 137, 144, 157, 161
  Kazakhstan and, 107
  nationalities policy and, 93
  Tadzhikistan and, 106
  See also Second Five-Year Plan
Five-Year Plans, 9, 31
Flourishing, 137, 255–256
Forced settlement, 101, 104–105, 107–109, 120, 123, 199, 320
  revocation of, 241
  Stalin and, 108
Foreign affairs, Union Republics and, 189–190
Forest Brothers, 216, 217

Friendship among the peoples,
    182, 183, 197, 200, 206, 233, 309
  concept of, 150
  fiction of, 283

Gafurov, B., 246, 262(n70)
Galicia, 1, 181, 192
  reintegration of, 174
Geller, Chairman: purge of, 159
Georgia, xiii, 2, 27, 147
  collectivization of, 95
  education in, 56, 58, 266, 267, 269, 296
  growth rates in, 298
  historical traditions of, 281
  intelligentsia of, 130
  korenizatsiia in, 36
  kulaks in, 103
  migration to, 293
  nationalization in, 229
  purge in, 160
  resistance in, 331, 332, 334, 339
  Russians in, 124
  spending in, 305
  state language and, 283
Georgian Academy of Sciences, 332
Georgians, 5
  collaboration by, 197, 198
  communist, 30, 34, 36
  integration of, 316
  recruiting, 189
  skilled, 126
  social structure of, 128, 129
  urbanization of, 295
Georgian Writers' Congress, Russification at, 331
Geradymenko, V.P., 190
German language, teaching in, 245
Germans, 10, 323
  assimilation of, 318
  deportation of, 198–200, 241
  emigration of, 319–320, 334, 336–338

  migration of, 179, 320, 339
  occupation by, 191
  rehabilitation of, 241, 242, 244–245
  Russification of, 321–322
  See also Volga Germans
German-Soviet Frontier and Friendship Treaty, 173–174
Gilani, Abd al-Qadir, 348
Glasnost, impact of, xvi
Glavkhlopkom, 106
Godlevskii (Hadlevskii) (priest): collaboration by, 196
Goldman (supervisor), conviction of, 76
Goloshchekin, F.I., 107
Gorbachev, Mikhail, xv, 165, 295
Gorkin, A.F., 242
Gosplan. *See* State Planning Committee
Grain, production of, 100
Great-Russian people, doctrine of, 313
Great purge, 9, 10
  description of, 155–166
  nationalities policy and, 163–164
  Stalin and, 155–158, 160–165
  victims of, 159–160
  See also Purges; Show trials
Grechko, A.A., 231
Greek Catholic Church, 193, 213
Grigorenko (Hryhorenko), P., 346
Grigorian, Secretary: criticism of, 206
Group of Initiators for the Unification of the Greek Catholic Church and the Russian Orthodox Church, 214
Growth rates, 298–299
  assimilation and, 319

Hadji, Uzun, 348
Haji, Kunta, 348

brotherhood of, 349
Haji, Uzun, 21
Helsinki Committees, 334, 345, 346, 347
Hero in the Leopard's Skin, The, 206
Historical homelands, emigration to, 334
Historiography, national consciousness and, 281, 282
History, teaching, 88
History of the Ukraine, criticism of, 204
Hochar, 286
Honchar, Oles, 286
Hrushevskyi, M.
  criticism of, 83, 204, 205
  rehabilitation of, 287

Iakovlev, I.D., 232
Iavorskyi, M.: purge of, 83
ibn Sina, Abu ali (Avicenna), 281
Ibragimov, I.A., 252
Ibragimov, Veli, 79
Ideology
  political function of, 314
  revision of, 307–314
Ignatovskii, V.: purge of, 83
Ikramov, Akmal, 106
  trial of, 161
Immortal cliffs (Olmas gaialar) (Makhmudov), 290
Income, per capita, 301–303
Independence Movement of Latvia, 342
Indirect rule, establishing, 3
Industrialization, 25, 30, 214–215, 265, 317
  Baltic state, 217–218
  consequences of, 118–119
  forced, 76, 93, 114–118
  Jews and, 121
  migration and, 126
  nationalities policy and, 119
  Stalin and, 115, 118
Ingush, 10
  collaboration by, 203
  deportation of, 201, 203
  rehabilitation of, 241–244
  resistance by, 348
Institute for Ethnography (Academy of Sciences), poll by, 294
Institute for the Northern Peoples, function of, 143
Institute for Ukrainian Scientific Terminology, purge of, 83
Integration, 13, 41
  non-Russian, 74
Intelligentsia, 78, 272, 278, 291
  definition of, 5, 14, 281
  non-Russian, 193, 228, 265–266, 285–286
  political goals of, 283
  purge of, 155
  self-consciousness and, 279
  social structure of, 130, 394
  Stalin and, 265
Internationalism, 153
  Marxist-Leninist, xv
Internationalism or Russification? (Dzuiba), 286
Irredentism, 179
  Soviet, 174–175
Islamic epics, 289–290
  denunciation of, 206–207, 224(n121)
Islamic guerrillas (Basmachi), 22, 78, 104, 106, 108
Islamic peoples, 2
  brotherhoods of, 347–349
  birth rate of, 291
  communist, 30
  integration of, 38
  leadership from, 40
  modernization and, 289
  opposition from, 334, 348–350

Index

population shift of, 291, 292
rootedness of, 294
self-consciousness of, 287-290
urbanization of, 296
See also Pan-Islamic movements
Israilov, Khasan, 202-203
Izvestiia, translation of, 47

Jadidism, 3, 78, 80
  influence of, 88
  rehabilitation of, 282
Jewish Antifascist Committee, 208
Jewish State Theater, 208
Jews, 5, 11, 25, 69(n133), 141, 179, 215, 323, 350
  assimilation of, 122, 318, 320, 322, 338
  campaign against, 122, 207-209, 225(n138), 322
  communist, 30, 34-36
  deportation of, 180, 199, 208-209
  education of, 56, 58, 60-61, 266, 267
  emigration of, 334, 336-339
  intelligentsia of, 130
  national consciousness of, 338
  Russification of, 319, 321
  settlement of, 121-122
  skilled, 126
  social mobility of, 122, 128
  Stalin and, 208-209, 338
  urbanization of, 118, 125, 295
  See also Anti-Semitism; Birobidzhan; Zionism
Judiciary
  decentralization of, 41, 234-235, 237-238
  recentralization of, 258

Kabardins, 96, 242
  collaboration by, 197
  deportation of, 202
Kaganovich, L.M., 86, 107, 127, 240

Kalanta, Romas: protest of, 339
Kalinin, M.N.: quote of, 103
Kalmyks, 40, 242
  collaboration by, 197
  collectivization of, 98
  deportation of, 201
  forced settlement of, 107
  rehabilitation of, 241, 242, 243
Kalnberzinsh, I., 253
Kamalov, S., 252
Kandyba, I.A., 343, 346
Karachai
  collaboration of, 197
  deportation of, 201
  rehabilitation of, 241, 242, 243
Karakalpaks, forced settlement of, 107
Karelians, 175, 176, 362(n184)
  assimilation of, 319
  education for, 268
Kasymov, Chairman: trial of, 80
Kasymov, Sultan Kenesary, 183
Kattel, Chairman: purge of, 159
Kavalauskas, Iu., 247
Kazakhs, 129
  communist, 30, 34, 165
  education for, 267, 268
  forced settlement of, 107-109
  intelligentsia of, 130
  migration of, 294
  skilled, 126, 127, 128
  urbanization of, 295
Kazakhstan, 20, 23, 25, 27, 79, 183
  birth rate in, 291
  collectivization of, 98, 109
  famine in, 94, 99, 100
  income in, 302
  industrialization of, 34, 115, 119
  migration to, 293
  purge in, 81, 160
  Sovietization of, 104
  spending in, 116-117, 306
  tribal loyalties in, 316

Kerbabai-ogli, Berdi: self-criticism by, 88
KGB, 252, 340, 342–346, 350
   non-locals in, 276
Khanat Kazan, integration of, 281
Khandzhian, Secretary: murder of, 158
Khataevich, M.M., 99
Khatskevich, Secretary, 45
Khemshil, forced settlement of, 241
Khmelnytski, Bohdan, 183
Khodzhaev, Faizulla, 79, 162
   execution of, 147
   trial of, 105–106, 161
Khodzhanov, S., 81
Khodzhibaev, Abdurakhim: removal of, 87
Khrushchev, Nikita S., 4, 152, 162, 179, 180, 204, 209, 308, 314, 344
   decentralization and, 235–237, 239–240, 245, 256, 258
   economic administration and, 239–240, 297
   fall of, 257, 258
   famine and, 205
   language issue and, 249, 251–252, 255
   modernization and, 265
   nationalities policy and, 15, 241, 245–246, 254–255
   non-Russians and, 228, 230, 232, 245, 277
   opposition to, 239–240
   purges and, 163, 251–253, 275
   reform of, 10, 233–234, 245–246
   rehabilitation and, 241–242
   rise of, 232–233
   secret speech of, 224(n106), 241, 307
   Ukrainians and, 211–213, 230–233
   Union Republics and, 235–237
Khvylovyi, M.: purge of, 82–83

Kiev Antiquities (*Kyiivska starovyna*), 287
Kiev Institute for Economy, 285
Kiev Rus, 205, 207
Kirgiz, 120
   forced settlement of, 107
   migration of, 294
   skilled, 126, 128
   urbanization of, 295
Kirgizistan, 79
   education in, 52, 54, 267, 268
   Communist Party members from, 165
   productivity in, 299
   Russians in, 124
Kirichenko, A.I., 229, 254
   fall of, 232
Kirilenko, A.P., 163, 231
Koch, Erich, 198
Kohn, Hans: on nationalism, 6–7
Kolkhozes, 102, 103, 217
   clan, 98
   development of, 124, 178
   national, 97–98
   resistance to, 95–96, 101
Kolkhozniks, 130, 273, 291, 300–301
   income of, 301, 302, 303
   non-Russian, 128–129, 284
   number of, 393
Kommunist (magazine), 246
Komsomol, nationalization of, 41, 276
Komunist Ukraiiny, 287
Konstantinov, T.A., 178
Korenizatsiia, 9, 13, 15, 20–25, 31–33, 36–38, 40, 41, 56, 65(n58), 67(n100), 71, 80, 85, 93, 135, 139, 140, 141, 177, 251, 274
   defamation of, 152
   education and, 269
   end of, 27, 34
   enforcement of, 5
   goal of, 51

Index

return to, 246
Stalin and, 137
success of, 57–58
Korkut-Ata (Turkmenian epic), criticism of, 206
Korneichuk, A.E., 229
Kosior, S.V., 96, 162
  purge of, 163
Kosygin, 284
Kovpak (partisan), 183
Kozlov, V.I, 315, 331
Kremlinology, 11
Kubiiovych, 193
Kuibyshev, V.V., 118
Kulaks
  deportation of, 176, 202
  purge of, 94, 101–103
  taxes on, 217
  See also Dekulakization
Kulichenko, M.I., 316
Kunta Haji, brotherhood of, 349
Kurdzhiev, Chairman, 161
Kvitko, Leib, 208
Kylych, Moldo, 253

Laboka, Chairman: poisoning of, 159
Labor army (*trudarmiia*), serving in, 200, 201
Language
  changing, 320–321
  clinging to, 8
  common, 308
  constructing, 44–46
  national consciousness and, 3–5, 48, 282–283
  nationalities policy and, 322
  non-Russian, 185, 248–250, 401
  official, 40–44, 328
  state, 283, 331
  unification of, 308
  written, 47
  social function of, 324–325
  See also Native language; various ethnic languages
Language issue, 245–248, 322
  education and, 271–272
  Khrushchev and, 255
  nationalities issue and, 248, 249
  vocational training and, 272
Language policy, xiv, xv, 251
  achievements of, 46–47
  assimilation and, 315–333
  press and, 42–48
  resistance to, 331–333
Latsis, V., 252–253
Latvia, xiii, 317
  annexation of, 175
  birth rate in, 291
  economic development of, 253
  income in, 302, 303
  industrialization of, 217–218
  migration to, 218, 293
  nationalization in, 229
  occupation of, 194–195
  productivity in, 299, 300
  protest in, 341–343
  purges in, 252
  reintegration of, 174
  Sovietization of, 176, 179, 181, 215–218
  spending in, 306
  standard of living in, 300
Latvian Christian Democrats, 342
Latvian Communist Party, purge of, 248
Latvians
  collectivization of, 217
  communist, 30, 253
  deportation of, 216, 217
  education for, 248, 267–268
Latvian Social-Democratic Labor Party, 342
Law school, non-Russians at, 41
Leadership
  non-local, 276

non-Russian, 275–278, 352(n21), 352(n22)
re-Russification of, 277–278
Ukrainian, 231–232, 275–276
Lenin, Vladimir Ilich, 15, 84, 131(n1), 150, 313
  nationalities policy and, 21–23, 62(n12), 72, 74, 138, 164, 334
  on self-determination, 20–21, 63(n27)
Lenin bayragy (*Lenin's Banner*), 244
Leningrad (magazine), quote from, 184
Liberberg, Chairman: purge of, 159
Lietuvos ateitis (*Lithuania's Future*), 340
Lisandusi motete ia uudiste vabale levikule Eestis (*Some Supplements to the Free Exchange of Ideas and News in Estonia*), 341
Lismanis, D., 342
Literacy, 48–49, 154 179
  Jewish, 122
Literaturnaia gazeta, 230
Lithuania, xiii, 8, 11, 121, 317
  annexation of, 175
  anti-migration policy of, 293
  collectivization of, 217
  development in, 298
  education in, 268, 296
  historical traditions of, 281
  immigration to, 218
  income in, 302, 303
  independence for, 340–341
  industrialization of, 218
  occupation of, 194–195
  productivity in, 299
  protest in, 339–341, 343, 366(n236)
  reintegration of, 174
  resistance in, 331, 333, 334
  Sovietization of, 176, 179, 181, 215–218
Lithuanian Activist Front (LAF), 194
Lithuanian National-Democratic Movement, 342
Lithuanians, 10
  collectivization of, 217
  deportation of, 216, 217
  migration of, 211
  urbanization of, 295
Litvin, K., 205
  criticism by, 204
Liubchenko, P.: purge of, 163
Lukianenko, L.H., 343–344, 346
Lvov Polytechnical Institute, 285

Machine-tractor stations (MTS), 102, 127
  growth of, 115
Magazines
  native-language, 330
  Russian-language, 329
Makarenko, quote of, 148
Makhmudov, Mamadali, 290
Maksum, Nusratula: removal of, 87
Malenkov, G.M, 160, 240
Malinovskii, R.K., 231
Management, concentration of, 145–146
Manas (Kirgiz epic), criticism of, 206
Mansurov, Chairman: purge of, 79
Mari, 27
  education for, 268
Markish, Perets, 208
Marxism-Leninism, nationalism and, xv
Mdivani, Budu, 24
  purge of, 164
Medvedev, Roi: quote of, 7
Melnikov, L.G., 229

Index

Melnyk (partisan), 193
  collaboration by, 192
Meskhetians, 347
  deportation of, 336
Methodological problems, discussing, 9–16
Middle Ages in the Ukraine, The (*Seredni viky na Ukraiini*), 287
Middle schools, 51–52
  language in, 53–54
  non-Russian, 54, 59
  See also Schools
Migration, xiv–xv, 127, 178–179, 296, 318–320, 333, 334, 339, 356(n96), 357(n101)
  assimilation and, 3
  effects of, 120
  forced, 101, 104–105, 107–109, 120, 123, 199, 320
  industrialization and, 126
  patterns of, 292–295
  Russian, 1–2, 125, 189
  urbanization and, 118–125
  wartime, 189
  See also Emigration
Mikoian, A.I., 160, 337
Military. *See* Red Army
Milli-isitiklal (National Independence), 80
Milli-ittikhad (National Association), 80
Ministries, decentralization of, 234
Ministry for Higher Learning, 146
Ministry for Institutions of Higher Education and Technical School Education, 325, 326, 332
Ministry for Manufacturing Means of Transportation, 239
Ministry for the Protection of Public Order, 257
Ministry of Defense, Ukrainians at, 231
Ministry of Education, 257, 327
  language issue and, 249
Ministry of Foreign Affairs, Union Republic, 190
Ministry of Justice
  dissolution of, 234
  reestablishment of, 258
Ministry of Power Plant Construction, 239
Ministry of the Interior, 257
Ministry of the Mid-Level Machine Building Industry, 239
Mirasism, 282
Mirmukhsin (author), 289
Mirzoian, L.I., 108
Modernization, 6–7, 126, 127, 130–131, 246, 286, 318
  consequences of, 118–119, 291
  Islam and, 289, 350
  Khrushchev and, 265
  nationalism and, 12, 278, 279
  purges and, 157
  Soviet, 4–5, 317
  Ukrainians and, 284
  urbanization and, 295–296
Moldavia, xiii, 175
  development in, 298
  income in, 303
  migration to, 293
  productivity in, 300
  Sovietization of, 176–179, 181
  standard of living in, 300
Moldavian language, 178–179, 220(n20)
Molotov, V.M., 161, 163, 240
  quote of, 150, 174
Mordvina, 37, 40
Mordvinian language, 37
Mordvinians
  assimilation of, 319
  education for, 268
Moroz, V., 344–345, 368(n255)
Moscow Patriarchate, Uniate Church and, 214

Moskalenko, K.S., 231
MTS. *See* Machine-tractor stations
Mukhitdinov, N., 254
Mukins, E., 253
Muslims. *See* Islamic peoples
Mussavatists, purge of, 87
Mustafaev, I.D., 252
MVD, 213, 216, 217
Mzhavanadze, V.P., 232

Najmuddin of Gotso, 348
Naqshbandiya brotherhood, 348, 349, 350
Naqsheband, Baha ud-Din, 348
Narkomnats, 138, 139
Nation
  definition of, 14
  Soviet, 309–310
National commission (*natskomissiia*), 142
National communism, 72, 77–79, 253, 282, 343, 345
National consciousness, 140
  counteracting, 204, 314
  goals of, 282–283
  historiography and, 281–282
  Islamic, 287–290
  manifestations of, 278–290
  modernization and, 279
  Ukrainian, 285–286
  upsurge in, xiii, 315
  See also Self-determination
National identity, 8, 280
  changing, 320
  cultural autonomy and, 282
National idiosyncracies
  dealing with, 313–314
  impact of, 280
National institutions, abandonment of, 138–148
National interests, promotion of, 283
Nationalism, xvii, 12–13, 96, 228, 334
  comparative research on, xvi, 279
  definition of, 12
  development of, 5–7, 10
  fighting, 7, 14, 77, 82–84, 117, 252
  integral, 12, 280, 341
  local, 84, 230
  manifestations of, 8, 280
  Marxism-Leninism and, xv
  modernization and, 12, 278
  nation-building and, 23
  negative, 279–280
  non-Russian, 204
  patriotism and, 149, 158
  Russian, 73, 149, 150, 158, 183, 204, 230, 280
  self-consciousness and, 284–287
  socialism and, 135
  Stalin on, 204
  strength of, xvi
  Ukrainian, 186, 213, 280, 284–287
  See also Bourgeois nationalism
Nationalist deviations, Stalin and, 2
Nationalist remnants, 314
Nationalists, Ukrainian, 191–192, 194, 210–213
Nationalities (*narodnosti*), 14
  concessions to, 21–22
  conflicts among, 75–76
  determining, 352(n21), 352(n22)
Nationalities issue
  importance of, 135, 141
  journalists and, 307
  language issue and, 248, 249
  principles of, 135
  publications on, 358–359(n128)
  socialism and, 6
  social structure and, 125–131
  Stalin and, 21–22, 136, 147
Nationalities policy, xiii, xv, 1–5, 10, 60, 166(n5), 308, 316, 320
  Brezhnev and, 342

Index

collectivization and, 93–99, 103–104
Communist Party and, 11
comparing, 312
end of, 109
forced industrialization and, 119
goals of, 22–23
journalists and, 307
Khrushchev and, 15, 241, 245–246, 254–255
language and, 322
Lenin and, 21–23, 62(n12), 72, 74, 138, 164, 334
opposition to, 81, 333–334, 344, 350
People's Commissariats and, 74
purge and, 157–158, 163–164
reform of, 137–138, 228–229
socialism and, 6
Soviet constitution and, 166(n1)
Stalin and, 15, 16, 21–24, 62(n12), 72, 80, 88, 138, 143, 152, 163–164, 166, 228, 255, 342
Nationalities Soviet, 139, 140
Nationalization, 51, 176, 275
  opposition to, 85
  Stalin and, 38
  weakening of, 86
National language. *See* Native language
National military units, 190
  collaboration by, 195, 222(n68)
  elimination of, 153
  language of, 185–186
  mobilization of, 185
  non-Russian, 186
  reintroduction of, 184–185
National minorities
  assimilation of, 61
  resistance by, 74
  rights of, 58–62
  school laws and, 151
  sections for, 142

National opposition, manifestations of, 334
National Territories, 143, 147
  Communist Party locals in, 31
  Council of Nationalities and, 237
  industrial workers in, 25–26
  purge in, 155
National United Party (NOP), 347
National work brigades
  conditions for, 123–124
  discrimination against, 76–77
Nation-building, xvii, 5, 6, 13, 15, 63(n17), 81, 82, 122, 137, 162, 315
  artificial, 43
  collectivization and, 97, 109
  consequences of, 138
  end of, 9, 158
  limits of, 71, 73
  nationalism and, 23
  policy of, 23–24
  Stalin and, 80, 136
  Ukrainian Communist Party and, 30
  See also Assimilation; Consolidation
Nations
  emerging, 307
  merger of, 136, 255–256, 312–313
Native language, 42–43
  abandonment of, 151–152, 322
  instruction in, 51–52, 57–58, 152, 250
  merging, 136
  number using, 395–396
  preserving, 250, 283
  pressure on, 328
  requiring, 247, 249
  resisting, 75, 332
  Russian as, 328
  See also Language
Navoi, ali-Shir, 350
NEP, 9, 155
Neues Leben (*New Life*), 244

Newspapers
  Jewish, 208
  non-Russian, 46
  Russian-language, 328, 329
  Ukrainian-language, 47
"Nightingale," 192, 193
Nineteenth Party Congress, 230
  Russians at, 165
NKVD, 179, 192, 212
  arrests by, 199
  collaborators and, 200–201, 203, 214
  deportation by, 176, 180, 199, 200, 202
NKWD, 80, 161
Nomads, forced settlement of, 101, 104–105, 107–108, 120
Non-Russian language. *See* Native language
Non-Russians
  assimilation of, 41, 320
  Brezhnev and, 278
  collaboration by, 191, 197–198
  discrimination against, 76, 278
  education of, 269, 272, 296
  Khrushchev and, 228, 230, 232, 245, 277
  mobilization of, 189
  See also various ethnic groups
Nonaggression pact. *See* German-Soviet Frontier and Friendship Treaty
Northern Bukovina, Sovietization of, 174, 177
Northern Caucasus, 38, 40, 59, 119
  birth rate in, 291
  collaboration in, 197, 198
  deportations from, 243–244
  famine in, 99
  occupation of, 196
  rehabilitation in, 243
  resistance in, 96
  Sufis in, 349

Northern Caucasus Area Executive Committee, 42

Obnosov, P., 254
Occupation, 173, 176, 186, 191, 194–196, 198, 210
Ögädäi, Khan, 183
OGPU, 81
  purges by, 83–84
Oirot Autonomous Region, purge in, 159
On Measures to Continue the Improvement of the Learning and Teaching of Russian in the Union Republics, 325–326
On Repealing Certain Restrictions on the Legal Status of Banished Peoples, 241
"On Rural Work" (Stalin), 101
On Stabilizing the Connections Between School and Life, 246
On the Political Errors and Deficiencies in the Work of the Institute of History at the Academy of Sciences of the Ukrainian SSR, 205
On the Procedure for Reestablishing the Civil Rights of Former Kulaks (CEC), 103
Orazov, Commissar, 81
Ordzhonikidze, 72, 164
Organization of Instruction and Internal Order, contents of, 146
Organization of Ukrainian Nationalists (OUN), 191–193, 205, 211, 212, 343
Organization of Ukrainian Nationalists (OUN-B), 192, 193, 212–214
Organization of Ukrainian Nationalists (OUN-M), 192, 193
Ossetians, relocation of, 242, 243, 244

Index

Our Soviet Ukraine (Shelest),
 criticism of, 287

Pan-Islamic movements, 78, 80
 preventing, 43
 See also Islamic peoples
Pan-Turkish movements, 78–81, 88
 preventing, 43
Parliamentarism, Bolshevik, 139
Partisans, 197, 199, 217
 deportation of, 201
 fighting, 195, 213
 nationality of, 186, 216
 Stalin and, 203
 Ukrainian, 193, 203, 212
Party apparatus
 nationalization of, 30–42, 165, 229
 See also State apparatus
Party members, national composition of, 272, 274, 275, 276, 415–417
Patriotism, 12
 local, 253, 256
 nationalism and, 6, 149, 158
 non-Russian, 183–184, 204
 role of, 148–155
 Russian, 149, 181, 182
 Soviet, 149, 150, 158, 181, 183, 189, 206, 262(n89)
 Stalin and, 149
Pelshe, A., 247, 253
People, definition of, 14
People's Commissariats, 138, 145–146, 189–190
 creation of, 145, 148
 dissolution of, 139, 141
 nationalities policy and, 74
 non-Russians in, 140
 Stalin and, 140–141
Perspectyvos (*Perspectives*), 340
Petrovskii, G.I., 162
 purge of, 163

Plenipotentaries, work of, 142
Pluralism, xvii, 8–9
 linguistic, 150–151
Podgornyi, N.V., 231, 232, 240
Poland, 1
 invasion of, 174, 175
Poles
 assimilation of, 319
 communist, 30
 deportation of, 180, 199
 migration of, 211
 Sovietization of, 179–180
Polianskii, D.S., 231
Polish Committee for National Liberation, 211
Polit-sections, 103
 description of, 102
Politburo
 arrest of, 155, 163
 non-Russians in, 36, 277, 418–419
 Russians in, 36, 277, 418–419
 Ukrainian, 163
Population
 ethnic composition of, 372–375
 growth of, 292
 shift in, 291–292
Postyshev, P.P., 85, 86, 162
Pravda, 247
 translation of, 47
Pravda Ukrainy, quote from, 240
Presidium, non-Russians in, 36
Prices
 comparative retail, 305
 See also Retail sales
Prishchepov, Z.: purge of, 83
Productivity
 agricultural, 298–299
 growth of, 299
 imbalances in, 297
 increasing, 123
 industrial, 300
 raising, 236

Provisional Organizational Committee for the People's Return to the Homeland, 336
Publications
  native-language, 330, 335
  Russian-language, 328, 329
  substandard, 133(n46)
Public health, spending for, 305, 306
Purges, 31, 81–87, 209
  Khrushchev and, 163, 251–253, 275
  nationalities policy and, 157–158
  pattern of, 162
  Stalin and, 102–103
  in Ukraine, 87, 287
  See also Great purge; Show trials

Qadiriya brotherhood, 348, 349

Racism, xvii
Radianskyi Lviv (Soviet Lvov), criticism of, 204
Raions, 68(n126)
  dissolution of, 61
Rakovskii, Ch.G., 164
Ramzi, Commissar, 80
Randpere, Valdo, 328
Rapprochement, 308, 311, 312
  advancing, 307
  continuous, 309
Rashidov, Sh., 252, 254, 323, 331
Rasulov, D., 254
Razzakov, I., 253–254
Red Army, 177, 180, 182
  collaborators and, 193–194
  demographic shifts and, 280
  language of, 151, 153, 185
  national units in, 185–189
  nation-building and, 71–72
  occupation by, 176
  officers of, 186, 188–189

purge of, 155
Reform
  administrative, 233–234
  school, 245–246
Regional Economics Council, 74
Regionalism, evolution of, 316–317
Regulations Concerning the Conferment of Academic Degrees and the Award of Academic Titles, 325
Rehabilitation, 243, 261(n53), 335–337
  deportation and, 241–242, 244–245
  Khrushchev and, 241–242
Reich Commissariat of the Ukraine, 198
Reich Commissariat Ukraine, 193, 194
Repatriation. *See* Rehabilitation
Republic of Turan, Sultan-Galiev and, 78
Retail sales
  per capita, 304, 305
  See also Prices
Reunification, national, 174–176
Revoliutsiia i natsionalnosti (Revolution and Nationalities), 15
Revolution, definition of, 12
Revolution from above, 3, 13, 131, 138, 157, 158, 202, 290
Rodnichev, B., 74
"Roland," 192
Romania, relations with, 174, 180
Romaniuk, V., 345
Rudenko, M., 346
Russian Empire, disintegration of, 20
Russian language, 6
  adoption of, 308, 323
  dominance of, xiv, 40–41
  native use of, 328, 402–405

non-Russian use of, 397–400, 402–405
proficiency in, 322–323, 327, 330–331
publications in, 328, 329
requiring, 150–152, 189, 247, 249
as second native tongue, 246, 255, 313, 384, 395–400
teaching in, 150–153, 246–247, 250–251, 324–327, 332
Russian Orthodox Church, 214
Russians
leadership and, 313, 352(n21), 352(n22)
migration of, 127, 253, 292–293
skilled, 126
urbanization of, 125, 297
Russification, 3, 31, 60, 120, 138, 148–155, 262(n89), 274, 286–287, 313, 318, 321–322, 326–328
ethnic, 319
linguistic, 321
resistance to, 331–334, 342
Stalin and, 5, 150
See also Assimilation; De-Russification
Russo-Japanese war of 1904–1905, 181
Rylskyi, M., 204, 247
Ryskulov, Turar, 72, 79
purge of, 164
Ryzhkov, N.I., 274

Sabirov, Secretary: purge of, 79
Sadvokasov, S., 81
Sakharov, Andrei, 340
Samizdat, 14, 261(n64), 327, 345, 365(n232)
Armenian, 347
Estonian, 341, 367(n244)
German, 337, 365(n234)
Islamic, 347
Jewish, 366(n235)
linguistic, 333
Lithuanian, 340, 367(n242)
nationalist, 347
Ukrainian, 343, 344, 368(n256)
School laws, consequences of, 151
Schools
Belorussian-language, 49
military, 153
native-language, 50, 249–250
non-Russian, 51–52, 153
Stalin and, 151
types of, 146
Ukrainian-language, 49, 51, 285
Yiddish, 208, 283
See also Elementary schools; Middle schools; Technical schools; Vocational schools
Secession, xiv, 21, 23, 25, 63(n27)
Second Belorussian Congress, meeting of, 196
Second Five-Year Plan, 117, 157, 165
expectations of, 118, 140
industrialization and, 115, 116
See also First Five-Year Plan
Second native language, 246, 255, 313, 322–325, 328, 361(n172)
promoting, 330–331
Secretariat, national composition of, 418–419
Section for the nationalities (*otdel natsionalostei*), 142
Sector for National Minorities, 61
Self-consciousness. See National consciousness
Self-determination, xvii, 3, 4, 8, 10, 20–25, 72, 194, 277, 341
Bolsheviks and, 20–21, 23
disintegration of, 25
industrial workers and, 25–30
Lenin and, 20–21
national, 334, 342, 346

See also National consciousness
Semichastnyi, V.E., 231
Separatism, 71, 78–79, 139
   decline of, 135
Serdiuk, Z.T., 232, 253
Seventeenth Party Congress, 117, 155
   Stalin and, 84
Shabanov, E., 335
Shamil, Imam, 202
Sharia, 21, 22
   following, 289
Shaumian, S.G., 20
Shelekhes (Politburo member), arrest of, 162
Shelest, P.E., 4, 231, 232, 345
Shelest, Petro Iukhymovych, 283, 284, 286
   removal of, 287
Shepilov, Secretary, 240
Sheptytskyi, Andrei, 192, 213–214
Shevardnadze, Eduard, 332
   address by, 331, 364(n222)
Shevchenko, F.P., 344
   resignation of, 287
Show trials, 83, 84, 86, 156, 161, 164, 171(n113)
   See also Great purge; Purges
Shukhevich, death of, 213
Shukhevych, Roman, 193
Shumskyi, A., 82
Shur, Chairman, 105
Siberia, development in, 284, 298
Siniavskii, A., 344
Sixteenth Party Congress
   chauvinism and, 73
   Stalin and, 84, 137
"Sixtiers." *See* Young Writers
Skeleton laws (*osnovy*), 237
Skilled workers, relocation of, 126, 127, 128
Skrypnyk, M., 4
   purge of, 82–83, 85–86, 162

Slipyi, Metropolitan: arrest of, 214
Socialist nation, 313
   clarification on, 136–137
   development of, 310–312
Socialist realism, 87, 123
Socialization, internationalist, 153
Social mobility, 130–131, 319
   controlled, 128
   Russian language and, 152
Social services, spending for, 305–307
Social structure, 273, 284, 393
   nationalities issue and, 125–131
Society for Rural Settlement of Working Jews, 61
Solidarity, Estonia and, 341
Sovereignty, xiii–xiv, 4
   declarations of, xiii–xiv
Soviet Anti-Zionist Committee, formation of, 338
Soviet constitution
   description of, 148
   nationalities policy and, 166(n1)
Sovietization, 104, 107, 131, 143, 177–181, 184, 209–218, 274
   resisting, 180, 202
   steps for, 176–177, 213
Soviet people, 311, 313, 314, 323
   concept of, 309, 310, 359(n133)
   development of, 307–308, 312
Sovkhozes, 102, 127, 129
   development of, 178
   resistance to, 101
Specialists, nationality of, 127–128, 271, 409–412, 413–414
Spivak, Eliagu, 208
Stalin, Josef, 77, 78, 181, 184, 252, 258, 307, 334
   chauvinism and, 84, 207
   collaborators and, 191, 199, 200–201
   collectivization and, 3, 93, 109(n1)

colonialization and, 1–2
Crimean Tatars and, 336
education and, 146, 151, 152
famine and, 101
great purge and, 102–103, 155–158, 160–165
industrialization and, 115, 118
intelligentsia and, 265
Jews and, 208–209, 338
language policy and, 308
nationalities policy and, 15, 16, 21–24, 38, 62(n12), 72, 80, 88, 136, 138, 143, 152, 163–164, 166, 204, 228, 255, 342
partisans and, 203
patriotism and, 149
People's Commissariats and, 140–141
on Russification, 5, 150
on secession, 21
Ukraine and, 82, 85, 194, 230
Stalinism, xvi, 10, 27, 239–240
return to, 258
See also De-Stalinization
Standard of living
development of, 298, 300
imbalances in, 297
kolkhoznik, 303
non-Russian, 300–301
per capita, 303, 305
Star of the East (Zhark iulduzi), 290
State apparatus
nationalization of, 30–42, 38, 229
See also Party apparatus
State Bank, loans from, 144
State Committee for Construction, 257
State Defense Committee, national units and, 184, 185
State Plan, Councils of Ministers and, 235–236
State Planning Committee (Gosplan), 257

non-Russians on, 140
purge of, 81
Uzbek, 106
Stetsko, Iaroslav, 192
Struev, A.I., 232
Students
Jewish, 269
non-Russian, 266–269
Russian, 351(n9)
technical, 269
Stus, V., 345
Sufi brotherhoods, 8, 11, 21, 202, 334, 347–350
Suleimenov, O., 282
criticism of, 289–290
Sultan-Galiev, 4, 80
accusations against, 78–79
national communism of, 282
purge of, 77, 87
Sultanbekov, Zh.: purge of, 81
Supreme Certification Commission, 325
Supreme Court (Union Republic), 238
Supreme Court (USSR), 238
Supreme Economic Council of the USSR, 146
creation of, 257
elimination of, 144–145
non-Russians in, 140
Supreme Soviet
role of, 148
Ukrainians on, 231
Supreme Ukrainian Council for Liberation (UHVR), creation of, 212–213
Survey of the History of Ukrainian Literature, criticism of, 204
Sverstiuk, Ie., 345
Svitlichnyi, I., 345

Tadshik-Gold Company, 84
Tadzhikistan, 25, 79

collectivization of, 98
Communist Party members from, 165
growth rates in, 298
income in, 303
productivity in, 300
purges in, 87
spending in, 298, 306
unrest in, 106
Tadzhiks
    migration of, 294
    skilled, 127–128
    urbanization of, 295
Tagirov, Chairman, 160
Tale of the Host of Igor, 206
    Turkic roots of, 289
Tariqas, 347–349
Tashkent Industrial Institute, 55
Tashkent Polytechnical Institute, 271
Tatars, 5, 11, 25, 121–124, 207
    assimilation of, 315, 319
    collaboration by, 196–197, 198
    communist, 30
    deportation of, 201–202
    education for, 52, 56, 268
    history of, 183–184, 281–282
    Kazan, 121
    migration of, 293
    skilled, 127
    urbanization of, 118, 295–296
    See also Crimean Tatars
Tautos kelias (The Nation's Path), 340
Teacher-training schools, native languages at, 56–57
Teachers
    relocation of, 126
    training of, 50–51
Technical schools, 204
    midlevel, 271, 284
    native languages at, 57
    non-Russians at, 54–56, 284, 412–414
    quotas for, 55
    Russians at, 271
    See also Schools
Tenth Party Congress, 30
    nationalities question and, 24
    Stalin and, 114
Thesis 19, 248
    rejecting, 246–247
Tikhonov, N.A., 274
Titov, V.N., 231
TOZ (*Tovarishchestvo sovmestnoi obrabotki zemli*), 98, 107
Transcaucasian Socialist Federative Soviet Republic, dissolution of, 147
Transcaucasus, 3
    social structure of, 129
    Stalin and, 127
Transnistra, 198
    Germans in, 199
Treiis, P., 253
Tribal loyalty, relaxation of, 98
Trotskyites, 159, 161
Turkestan, 20, 22, 25
    purge in, 161
    separatism in, 79
Turkestan Area Committee, 72
Turkestanis, collaboration by, 197, 198
Turkic languages, 45
Turkish Society for the Defense of the Exiled Turkish People's National Rights, 336
Turkmen, migration of, 294
Turkmenistan, 25, 79
    capital investment in, 298
    Communist Party members from, 165
    famine in, 94
    growth rates in, 298
    income in, 302
    kulaks in, 103

Index

nationalism in, 81
productivity in, 300
purge in, 160, 251
skilled workers in, 127, 128
tribal loyalties in, 316
unrest in, 106
urbanization of, 294
Turks, forced settlement of, 241
Tursunov, Kh., 252
Twelfth Party Congress, 164
  chauvinism and, 72–73
  nationalities question and, 24
Twentieth Party Congress, 15–16, 242, 336
  decentralization and, 235
  Khrushchev at, 224(n106), 241
Twenty-fourth Party Congress, 284, 308
  Brezhnev and, 166
Twenty-second Party Congress, 16, 22, 255
  Crimean Tatars at, 335
  Khrushchev at, 307, 308
  Mukhitdinov at, 254
  Podgornyi at, 240
Twenty-sixth Party Congress, Brezhnev and, 295, 357(n102)
Twenty-third Party Congress, 284
  Crimean Tatars at, 335
Tynystan, Kasy, 253

Udmurt language, 41
Udmurts, 27
  education for, 268
UHVR. *See* Supreme Ukrainian Council for Liberation
Ukraine, xiii, 25, 27
  capital investment in, 116, 284
  collectivization in, 3, 105
  culture of, 204–205
  decentralization in, 235
  dekulakization of, 95
  education in, 285

famine in, 94, 99, 100, 205
  history of, 205
industrialization of, 117
industrial workers in, 30
Jews in, 121
korenizatsiia in, 30, 36, 85
migration to, 293
nationalization of, 38
occupation of, 186, 198, 210
population shift in, 292
purge in, 87, 162–163, 204–205, 287
resistance in, 332, 343–344
Russification of, 120, 327–328
skilled workers in, 127
Sovietization of, 176, 181
special role of, 231–233
Stalin and, 186, 209
See also Carpathian Ukraine; Western Ukraine
Ukrainian Academy of Sciences, 285, 330, 345
  purge of, 83
Ukrainian Autocephalus Orthodox Church (UAPT), 193–194
Ukrainian Communist Party
  Khrushchev and, 230–233
  purge of, 85
Ukrainian Herald, 344, 345
Ukrainian Insurgent Army (UPA), 183, 211, 212, 213
  denunciation of, 209
  members of, 193
Ukrainian language, 30, 38, 42–43, 56
  books in, 46, 47
  conference on, 285
  foreignization of, 344
  newspapers in, 47
  publications in, 330
  requiring, 247, 248
  teaching in, 49, 285, 325
Ukrainian language law (1927), 151

Ukrainian National Front, 343
Ukrainians, 131, 175
  assimilation of, 318
  collaboration by, 191–194, 198
  communist, 30, 34, 36
  deportatio of, 179
  education for, 268, 271
  leadership and, 352(n21), 352(n22)
  migration of, 2, 211, 318
  protecting, 59
  recruiting, 189
  Russification of, 120, 276
  social structure of, 128–130
  urbanization of, 125, 295
Ukrainian Union of Writers, criticism of, 204
Ukrainian Writers' Congress, Shelest at, 286
Ukrainian Writers' Union, 286, 345
  purge of, 83
Ukrainization, 30, 42–43, 56, 86, 125, 177, 215, 230, 232, 283
  campaign against, 213–214
  second, 285, 286–287
  Stalin and, 82, 85
Ulam, Adam, 156
Uldzhabaev, T., 254
Uluots, Prime Minister: collaboration by, 195
Unemployment, structural, 294
Uniate Metropolitan Church, campaign against, 213–214
Union Republics, 14, 16, 147
  Council of Nationalities and, 237
  decentralization and, 144, 234–238
  foreign relations and, 141, 189–190
  industrial workers in, 28–29
  Khrushchev and, 235–237
  korenizatsiia of, 36–37
  language issue and, 248
  leadership in, 275–276
  national composition of, 376–387, 388–389
  occupation of, 173
  Russians in, 124–125
  secession of, 25
  social structure of, 393
  Stalin and, 190
United Democratic Resistance Movement (BDPS), 216
United Nations, 211
  Estonia and, 341
  Union Republics and, 190
Universities
  languages at, 127–128
  See also Colleges
University of Lvov, purge at, 345
University of Odessa, teachers at, 285
UPA. See Ukrainian Insurgent Army
Ural-Kuznetsk Combine, 114
  building, 117
Urbanization, 265, 279, 318, 319
  assessing, 357(n104)
  migration and, 118–125
  modernization and, 295–296
  privilege and, 297
  rate of, 320, 390–392
Use of force, description of, 2–3
Usubaliev, T., 254
Uzbekistan, 25, 27, 79, 115
  collectivization in, 105
  Communist Party members from, 165
  Crimean Tatars in, 335
  dekulakization of, 95
  economic growth in, 162
  famine in, 94
  growth rates in, 298
  income in, 302, 303
  industrialization of, 118
  korenizatsiia in, 37–38

nationalism in, 80
population shift in, 292
productivity in, 299, 300
purge in, 161, 252
resistance in, 96
Russians in, 124
Sovietization of, 104
spending in, 298, 306
Uzbekistan Writers' Union,
    Crimean Tatars in, 335
Uzbekization, 37–38
Uzbek language, 37–38
Uzbeks, 108
    assimilation of, 316
    discrimination against, 76
    education for, 266, 268, 270, 296
    forced settlement of, 120
    migration of, 294
    skilled, 127–128
    social structure of, 129
    urbanization of, 295

Vaino, Karl, 332, 341
Validov (social revolutionary), 78
Varpas (*The Bell*), 340
Virgin land campaign, 117, 293
    Brezhnev and, 232
Vis Haji Tariqa, 348–349
Vitchyzna (*Homeland*), criticism of, 204
Vlasov movement, 194
Vocational schools
    languages at, 127–128, 272
    nationalization of, 56–57
    See also Schools
Volga Germans, 25, 100
    elimination of, 200–201
    rehabilitation for, 336–337
    See also Germans

Volia i batkyvshchyna (*Liberty and Fatherland*), 343
Volobuev, M.: purge of, 82–83
von der Schulenburg, Ambassador, 174
Vydvizhentsy, description of, 128
Vytis (*The Knight*), 340

Walesa, Lech, 341
Western Belorussia
    reintegration of, 174
    Sovietization of, 176, 209–218
    See also Belorussia
Western Ukraine, 179
    annexation of, 174, 214–215
    collaboration in, 192
    industrialization of, 214–215, 218
    migration to, 215
    occupation of, 186
    resistance in, 334
    Sovietization of, 176, 177, 209–218
    See also Ukraine
White-collar workers, 273
    number of, 236, 393
    Ukrainian, 284
Workers, shortage of, 294
Works (Stalin), 137

Yalta Conference, 190
Yawsawi, Ahmed, 350
Young Writers, opposition from, 344

Zagiev, Vis Haji, 348
Zhdanov, A.A.: pogrom by, 204
Zhdanovshchina, 207–208
    description of, 205
Zionism, 209, 338–339
    campaign against, 208
    See also Anti-Semitism; Jews